ID0848862

ROBIN S. HARRIS is a professor of Higher Education at the
University of Toronto.

This book traces the development of higher education in Canada,
through a detailed description and analysis of what was being
taught and of the research opportunities available to professors
in the years from 1860 to 1960. Background is provided in the
opening chapters of Part I, which outline the origins of post-
secondary education in both French and English Canada from 1635
to 1860, and in the parallel chapters of Parts II to V which
describe the establishment of new and the growth of existing
institutions during the periods 1861-90, 1891-1920, 1921-40,
and 1941-60. The remaining chapters of each of the book's main
divisions present an examination of the curricula in arts and
science, professional education, and graduate studies in 1860,
1890, 1920, 1940, and 1960, as well as the conditions pertaining
to scholarship and research in these years. The concluding
chapter identifies the characteristics which differentiate Canadian
higher education from that of other countries. The book includes
a full bibliography, an extensive index, and statistical appendices providing data on enrolment and degrees granted. *A History
of Higher Education in Canada 1663-1960* will be the definitive
work in its field, valuable both for the wealth of information
and the historical insights it contains.

Etudes sur l'Histoire d'Enseignement Supérieur au Canada
Studies in the History of Higher Education in Canada
Sponsored by the Association of Universities and
Colleges of Canada, with financial support from
the Carnegie Corporation of New York

1. Robin S. Harris and Arthur Tremblay
    A bibliography of higher education in Canada

2. W.P. Thompson
    Graduate education in the sciences in Canadian universities

3. Robin S. Harris
    A bibliography of higher education in Canada: supplement 1965

4. D.C. Masters
    Protestant church colleges in Canada: a history

5. Robin S. Harris
    A bibliography of higher education in Canada: supplement 1971

6. Laurence K. Shook
    Catholic post-secondary education in English-speaking Canada
    A History

7. Robin S. Harris
    A history of higher education in Canada 1663-1960

ROBIN S. HARRIS

A History of Higher Education in Canada 1663-1960

UNIVERSITY OF TORONTO PRESS

Toronto   Buffalo   London

© University of Toronto Press 1976

Toronto   Buffalo   London

Printed in Canada

Reprinted 1977, 1978

ISBN 0-8020-3336-9

LC 76-15892

For Patricia

With apologies for time otherwise spent

Contents

Foreword

Much of the writing thus far produced on Canadian universities
has taken the form of institutional histories. Professor Robin
Harris has pulled together from a mass of partial (in both senses
of the word) sources the first history of Canadian universities
as a whole. Not only is *A History of Higher Education in Canada*
a pioneering work; it is also, and more important, a work that
pioneers in the right place and in the right way. There are
other first histories of higher education that might have been
written. Valuable, lively books could have been written about
the shifting composition and concerns of the student body, the
relations between universities and the community or government,
or the development of post-secondary education as a whole.
Professor Harris has wisely chosen to describe the evolution of
the university teaching curriculum and of research and scholarship. This choice permits him to focus his study on the very
heart of the university, its teaching and research, and to base
his work on the hardest data that exist on university offerings,
the calendars. Future historians of Canadian universities can
explore the many other facets of higher education that Professor
Harris leaves largely untouched, confident that the core book
has been written.

Professor Harris sets out to test the hypothesis that Canadian
higher education has characteristics that distinguish it from
higher education in such countries as the United States, Great
Britain, Australia, and France. He concludes that one can fairly
answer 'yes' to the question, 'Is the Canadian university *sui
generis*?' This is a remarkable proposition, when one considers
that few approaches to higher education could have contrasted
more sharply than those of English- and French-speaking Canada.
Examining Professor Harris's evidence that a fundamental com-
monality has evolved among Canadian universities, after just
over a century of co-existence, makes fascinating reading. So
does following him in his arguments that what Canadian universities

have become is distinguishable (in non-trivial ways) from what universities have become in other lands.

The Association of Universities and Colleges of Canada has every right to be gratified as a sponsor of this book, especially because the role that AUCC and its predecessors the National Conference of Canadian Universities and the National Conference of Canadian Universities and Colleges played in the development of higher education receives such extensive and careful treatment. Reflection on the importance of AUCC's role in the 1940s, 1950s, and early 1960s, compared with its much more modest place in the Canadian university scene of the mid-1970s, tells a great deal about the direction that higher education has taken in Canada since the period covered by Professor Harris. For the moment, we will have to do this reflecting on our own, but we can look forward to more perceptive help from Professor Harris when he gives us his promised second volume covering the period 1961 to 1980.

Professor Harris has served us well in giving the history of Canadian universities a shape and form, thereby rescuing it from the inchoateness of the local, the speculative, and often the anecdotal. We owe him much for the painstaking work that has produced a book of great value.

M.K. Oliver   *President*
5 February 1976   *Association of Universities and*
                                                Colleges of Canada

Preface

When in the late 1950s I began the research upon which this study
is based, my intention was a comparatively simple one: to discover whether the Canadian university was an identifiable type of
institution, one which whatever its size, age, or location had
common characteristics that distinguished it from comparable universities in other countries, particularly in the English-speaking
world. Much of the literature of higher education which I had
read and many of the comments of my colleagues in common rooms
and committee meetings suggested that the university in Canada
was a rather pale carbon copy of the American or the British university. This struck me as nonsense. My own experience as a
student and teacher at two universities of comparable size,
Michigan and Toronto, indicated that the resemblances between an
American and a Canadian institution were superficial, the differences fundamental; and my visits to and my reading of the histories of such pairs of institutions as Acadia and Amherst,
Chicago and McGill, Michigan State and Manitoba supported my
belief that the differences between Toronto and Michigan were
typical rather than the exception to the rule. I recalled, too,
that my visits to twelve English and Scottish universities in the
summer of 1955 had left me with the impression that none bore
striking resemblance to any of the thirty Canadian universities
I had visited during the academic year 1951-52. Obviously, however, my experience was limited; the only way to resolve the issue
was to make a detailed study of the Canadian universities and of
the American, English, and Scottish as well. Subsequently I
added the Australian universities to my list because, since higher
education in Australia began at about the same time as in Canada
and under similar influences, the opportunities for comparison and
contrast seemed particularly inviting. Finally, since Canada is
a bilingual nation and the influence of France on the French-
Canadian institutions has been important, I felt I must also examine the universities of France. By this time I was contemplating

a clearly impossible task - the analysis of at least 1000 universities in half a dozen countries. Obviously, a more restricted plan had to be conceived.

Although more modest in scope, the resulting study has still required fifteen years to complete. It encompasses a reasonably detailed description and analysis of what has been taught in Canadian universities since the first charter was granted in the early nineteenth century and of the opportunities available to the professors in these institutions to undertake scholarship and research. In consequence, it is both narrower and wider than the title may suggest. It is not a history of the Canadian universities; nor is it a history of post-secondary education in Canada. It includes no reference to the governance of universities, to questions of academic freedom or tenure, to the daily life of students and professors, to the extracurriculum (athletics, fraternities, student publications, etc.) or, except as these impinge directly on curriculum and research, to the financing of universities or to the relation of universities to government. It includes only incidental reference to the development of non-degree-granting post-secondary institutions, and no reference at all is made to the programs of study offered in such institutions. On the other hand, since it is concerned with the conditions that have encouraged or inhibited the undertaking of scholarship and research, considerable attention is paid to a substantial number of institutions, organizations, and government agencies which, though not directly related to any degree-granting university, have provided opportunities for professors to undertake research and scholarship which were not available in the universities themselves; examples are the Geological Survey of Canada, the Royal Canadian Institute, the Institut Canadien de Montréal, the Royal Society of Canada, the Dominion Experimental Farms, the Carnegie Corporation of New York, the Association Canadienne-Française pour l'avancement des sciences, the National Research Council, the Public Archives of Canada, the National Museum of Canada. The regulations of federal and provincial professional bodies such as the Law Society of Manitoba, the Canadian Medical Association, and the Chemical Institute of Canada have often affected the curriculum in the professional faculties of our universities; consequently there is considerable reference to them. This restriction, but equally this extension, of the range of institutional reference suggests that a more accurate title would be, 'A History of Higher Learning in Canada,' but I find 'higher learning' an awkward phrase, and I suspect that this title would prove more misleading than the one I have adopted. Furthermore, I am convinced that higher education is the proper term to use to refer to the essential functions which all universities are expected to perform.

In a paper entitled 'A Matter of Balance,' presented at the 1967 Conference of the Association of Universities and Colleges of Canada, I argued that universities have but two functions: the provision of instruction and the undertaking of research. The

classic definition of the university is that it is an institution
dedicated to the preservation, dissemination, and advancement of
knowledge; but the first of these, the preservation of knowledge,
is, in my view, simply the necessary prerequisite to the carrying
out of the other two. It is the function of libraries, museums,
and art galleries to preserve knowledge, and, while it is a convenience for universities to have such collections as part of
their physical plant and essential that students and professors
have ready access to them in order that the dissemination (instruction) and the advancement (research) of knowledge can be effectively
pursued, it is not essential, particularly in an age of interlibrary
loan and photocopying, that the institutions themselves act as
repositories. The fact that recently the Royal Ontario Museum
ceased to be an integral part of the University of Toronto has
not in any fundamental way affected the instructional and research
programs that are the university's raison d'être.

Two other functions are frequently ascribed to universities:
service to the community, and criticism of society itself. I
would be the last to deny that universities not only *should* but
always *have* made direct contributions to the welfare of the communities which support them, or to suggest that they have not
frequently acted as a voice of conscience with respect to society's
cultural, economic, political, and social development. But these
are services (for criticism of society is a service) which the
university performs by way of instruction and/or research. The
incalculable benefits of the development of insulin are, in part,
the consequence of a desire to serve society, but above all they
are the result of research by identifiable individuals. The
criticisms of contemporary society offered by Marshall McLuhan,
George Grant, and Gérard Dion are grounded in their activities as
teachers.

It is possible, of course, for the functions of instruction and
research to be carried on separately. The National Research
Council of Canada is, among other things, a research institute,
but as an organization it is not concerned with teaching. All
elementary and secondary schools and many non-degree-granting
educational institutions at the post-secondary level are concerned
with teaching, but as organizations they are not expected to undertake research; this is not to say that a particular teacher in
a high school or a community college may not on his own produce
a work of significant research or scholarship. What distinguishes
universities from public and elementary schools and from non-
degree-granting post-secondary institutions is their commitment
to undertake both functions and to regard them as interlocking
and of equal importance.

It will be noted that in the above paragraph the term *teaching*
has been introduced as a synonym for *instruction*, and that *scholarship* has been equated with *research*. The latter equation poses
no particular problem since it is common parlance in the academic
world to describe scholarly work in the sciences as research,
and comparable work in the humanities and social sciences as

scholarship. What I am referring to in both cases is the disin-
terested pursuit of further knowledge – its advancement as distinct from its dissemination. The terms *instruction* and *teaching*
do, however, pose a problem, not because they cannot be easily
regarded as synonyms but because they tend to place undue emphasis
on the role of the teacher or instructor as distinct from the role
of the student. Ideally, the university teacher's commitment to
the advancement of knowledge is not confined to his activities
as scholar or researcher; it is reflected equally in the spirit
with which he offers his instruction to his students whether at
the undergraduate or graduate level. Similarly, a student,
whether undergraduate or graduate, is regarded as a junior colleague of the professor, and, within the limits of his experience,
he too is expected to discover as well as to absorb. This ideal
has characterized the Canadian university scene from the outset,
and in my view it and only it is the proper criterion by which
the history of higher education in Canada must be judged.

This book, then, is an examination of the development of teaching
and research in the Canadian universities from the time of their
origins in the seventeenth and eighteenth centuries until 1960.
So far as teaching is concerned, the basic data are the courses
of study offered at any time by degree-granting institutions, but
there are two important exceptions to this general rule. The
first university charter was not granted until 1802 and the first
degree was not awarded until 1807; however, as chapter 2 makes
clear, university-level instruction was provided in French Canada
during the late seventeenth and throughout the eighteenth century;
the fact that degrees were not actually awarded has had to be
disregarded at this stage. For essentially the same reason, the
courses of study offered by professional schools in the years
prior to their becoming associated with degree-granting institutions have been included if they were of university standard, as
was the case, for example, at the Montreal Medical Institute for
the six years prior to its transformation into the faculty of
medicine of McGill University in 1829. My procedure has been to
include all programs which in 1975 would have qualified the student for a degree. Thus, in the 1890 and 1920 divisions of the
book there is reference to programs in physical and health education despite the fact that no Canadian university authorized a
degree in this field until 1940. On the other hand, no reference
is made at any point to chiropractic since no Canadian university
has ever offered a degree in this field, even though there is a
Canadian institution that for many years has offered a four-year
program for which the admission requirement is the equivalent of
university matriculation.

The core of the book is a detailed description and analysis of
the situation with respect to teaching and research in the
Canadian universities at five points in time: 1860, 1890, 1920,
1940, 1960; for each of these years separate chapters are devoted
to the programs in arts and science, professional education, and

graduate studies (except for part I, 1860), and to scholarship and research. The conclusions drawn in the final chapter are based on the evidence presented in all the preceding chapters and are essentially an attempt to answer the question that prompted me to undertake this study in 1958: are there characteristics which, as a result of their development over time, distinguish higher education in Canada from higher education in such countries as the United States, Great Britain, Australia, and France? Is the Canadian university *sui generis*?

The dates established as the focal points of the study have been selected not arbitrarily or in the interests of symmetry but for very specific reasons. The year 1860 was chosen as the starting-point because it was not until approximately this date that one could conscientiously describe the Canadian university as having characteristics which clearly differentiated it from institutions in the several countries that provided the models for its first half-dozen degree-granting institutions. Prior to 1850, the Canadian universities were simply transplants from England, Scotland, the United States, and France - the latter in the form of the classical colleges which in the 1860s would constitute the faculté des arts of Université Laval. But in the 1850s a number of significant developments occurred, notably the secularization of the universities of Toronto (1850) and New Brunswick (1859), the chartering of the first French-language university (Laval, 1852), and the assumption of the principalship of McGill University by J.W. Dawson (1855); the result was the emergence by 1860 of distinctively Canadian curricula. The Canadianization of the curricula was somewhat more pronounced by 1865, but with respect to both teaching and research the position in 1860 was not essentially different from that of 1870; it was, however, very different from that of 1850.

The 1880s were marked by a general improvement in Canada's economic position and a consequent increase in the financial support of higher education, and this in part explains the choice of 1890 as the second focal point. The change was particularly evident at Dalhousie, McGill, and Queen's, where during the decade substantial private donations provided for the establishment of endowed chairs at all three institutions and at the latter two for the construction of several new buildings. There were other important developments of the 1880s. At Toronto, where a legislative act of 1853 had restricted the university's powers to the conducting of examinations and the granting of degrees (following the University of London model), a new act of 1887 authorized the university to become once again a teaching institution, and by 1890 it possessed fully operative faculties of arts, law, and medicine, and had affiliation arrangements with schools of agriculture, dentistry, and engineering. By 1890, the first of the provincial universities of the West, the University of Manitoba, had been established for thirteen years, and a branch of Université Laval had been operating in Montreal for fourteen years. The 1880s also saw for the first time the provision in certain institutions of adequate science laboratories, the emergence at Dalhousie of a distinguished law school, at McGill of a distinguished medical school, and at Toronto of a fully developed honours-course system. The founding of the Royal Society of Canada in 1882 provided for the first time a national organization designed to promote scholarship and research in all fields.

An economic depression slackened progress in the 1890s, but the period 1900-14 was a reasonably buoyant one, largely because of heavy immigration, which not only transformed Montreal and Toronto from large towns into sizable cities but opened up the prairie provinces to settlement. Almost the first actions of the legislatures of the provinces of Alberta and Saskatchewan, which were created in 1905, were the establishment of provincial universities and, more important, the provision of adequate financial support for their construction and operation. However, development of all Canadian universities was checked by the outbreak of World War I, and it was not until 1920 that it could be said that any of them had settled back into a normal routine. The year 1920, then, is a third natural focal point. By this time, in Quebec, the branch of Laval at Montreal had become the completely independent Université de Montréal and for the first time the two large French-language institutions began to take serious steps to provide adequate instruction in the sciences.

The fourth focal point, 1940, marks the effective entry of Canada into World War II, an experience with remarkable consequences for the nation's economy, but, more significant (and not unrelated), it marked the end of the Depression which throughout the 1930s had slowed development of the universities almost to a standstill. There had been progress during the 1920s, especially in the initiation of degree programs in a number of new professional fields - library science, nursing, and social work, for example; within the social sciences, the subjects of economics, history, and political science emerged as important disciplines, and, on a small scale, anthropology, geography, sociology, and psychology as well. In 1940, however, the general position with respect to both teaching and research was very similar to that of 1930, though substantially different from that of 1920.

The 1940s were abnormal years for the Canadian universities, with enrolments much reduced during the war years and greatly inflated between 1945 and 1950 by the influx of veterans. The early 1950s represented a return to normalcy, but by 1955 it had become abundantly clear that demands for admission to higher studies across Canada would be enormously increased in the 1960s. The year 1960 has been selected as the final focal point because it represents the position of higher education in Canada immediately prior to the extraordinary expansion of the 1960s which, among other things, was characterized by the growing involvement of provincial governments in university affairs.

The basic chapters in each of the five major divisons of the study are those devoted to a description of the curricula and to the

conditions that facilitated or inhibited scholarly work. There
is in each case a single chapter on scholarship and research but,
in the treatment of the curricula, separate chapters are allocated
to arts and science, professional education, and - except in 1860
when they were non-existent - graduate studies. Each division is
introduced first by a chapter which sets the stage and second by
one (or two in the case of 1860) which identifies the institutional
characters.

The stage-setting chapters centre on events symbolizing the
state of higher education in Canada on or close to the dates
chosen as focal points. In the case of 1860, the occasion is the
visit of the Prince of Wales to the Canadian colonies, which provided an opportunity for the degree-granting institutions to
state their current hopes and concerns through the briefs or memorials presented to the prince. For 1890 it is the annual meeting
of the Royal Society of Canada, an occasion which, as had been the
case since its formation eight years earlier, brought together
presidents and professors from various institutions. For 1920,
the event is the annual meeting of the National Conference of
Canadian Universities, an organization whose membership included
almost all degree-granting institutions from coast to coast.
This body had first been convened in 1911, and in 1915 was formally established for the express purpose of discussing the problems of Canadian higher education. (It continues to hold annual
meetings and is now known as the Association of Universities and
Colleges of Canada.) The symbolic occasion for 1940 is the 1939
Conference on Canadian-American Relations held at St Lawrence
University in Canton, New York. It was attended by equal numbers
of Canadian and American economists, historians, political scientists, journalists, and civil servants, and it indicated the
growing importance of the social sciences and the increasing interaction between universities and government which had characterized
Canadian higher education during the previous two decades. For
1960 two events have been selected: the special meetings of the
National Conference of Canadian Universities and Colleges convened
in 1956 and 1961 for the purpose of alerting the federal and provincial governments and the Canadian public to the grave financial
crisis confronting the universities in their efforts to fulfil
their responsibilities.

Following the stage-setting chapter for each division is one
which provides a description of the establishment and development
of the individual institutions. There are two such chapters for
the 1860 section, one devoted to the progress of higher education
in French Canada, and the other describing the situation in English
Canada. The comparable chapters in the subsequent divisions deal
with developments since the previous focal point; for example
between 1861 and 1890. In these 'institutional development'
chapters, some reference is made to non-degree-granting post-
secondary institutions and to the activities of the federal government in the field of higher education.

Throughout this study, the description of the curricula offered is based on the calendars of the institutions concerned. These have been examined closely not only for the five focal years but also for the two or three years immediately preceding and immediately following each focal year and at selected points in between. If, for example, a program in engineering appears in the 1890-91 calendar of University X but not in its calendar for 1860-61, the calendars have been checked back from 1890 to the year when the program was introduced. Similarly, when the program in engineering has undergone substantial change between focal years, the intervening calendars have been checked to record the sequence of changes.

Calendars are legal documents and, in my view, they qualify as primary source material. However, they are statements of intent rather than of realization. The inclusion of a particular course in the 1940-41 calendar is no guarantee that the course was actually offered in that year, that it was taught by the professor listed, that the text or texts prescribed were actually studied, or that it met for precisely the number of weekly lectures, tutorials, or laboratory hours specified. Nor is the title or description of the course a clear indication of its content; in both cases brevity rather than accuracy is the prime consideration.

Nonetheless, the listing of a course in a given calendar is *prima facie* evidence that the course was offered, that its content was in general terms that suggested by the title and description, and that it did bring together students and professors for the number of hours a week indicated. And if the same course was listed in precisely the same way for the previous and successive years, it is almost certain that it was in fact offered in the year in question. Calendars are particularly reliable in indicating what was *not* offered. The fact that the calendar of no Canadian university for the 1940-41 session included any course in Russian language and literature is evidence that this subject was not available for credit anywhere in Canada at that time.

The study relies heavily on secondary source material with respect to the significance of current changes in particular subjects or fields. I am neither an anthropologist, a dentist, nor a physicist, and in these areas I have had to rely on what persons knowledgeable in these fields have written on this subject. What I have made a point of doing is to identify systematically and then to read what such experts have written. The evidence to support this last statement is provided in the approximately 12,000 entries which appear under such headings as anthropology, dentistry, and physics in the 1960 edition of *A Bibliography of Higher Education in Canada*, and in its 1965 and 1971 supplements, as well as in the first six issues of *Stoa: The Canadian Journal of Higher Education* which appeared between 1971 and 1974. I have not read every word of all these books, articles, and theses, but I have at least scanned 90 per cent of them.

A History of Higher Education in Canada is a synthesis of the many strands that constitute the programs of instruction and research offered by Canadian universities as these have been initiated, developed, or discarded over more than three centuries. Although numerous studies of individual facets of the system have been published, none before has attempted to describe the total picture or to analyse the interrelationships among institutions throughout the various widely scattered and disparate regions of Canada. It is hoped that this publication, despite its unavoidable omissions and obvious limitations, will serve to close that gap and will provide researchers of higher education both in Canada and elsewhere with a pragmatic panoramic view of Canadian higher education as it took root and struggled to survive the hostile climate of the very early colonial period, gradually developing into the sophisticated system that exists today.

I wish to express my thanks to the two organizations which enabled me to devote full time to the study for two academic years, the Canada Council, which awarded me a senior research fellowship in 1959-60, and the University of Toronto, which permitted me to take sabbatical leaves in 1959-60 and 1968-69.

I also wish to acknowledge the assistance rendered to me since 1959 by the registrars, librarians, and archivists of all the Canadian universities who have been providing me with answers to specific questions on a variety of matters; to the students in my graduate classes since 1967, particularly Marni De Pencier and D. McCormack Smyth, who have been reacting critically to the drafts of the chapters as they have been successively produced; and to the following persons who have read and commented critically on specific sections of the manuscript dealing with areas about which they were particularly knowledgeable: Murray Barr, Faculty of Medicine, University of Western Ontario; Maxwell Cohen, Faculty of Law, McGill University; Marcel de Grandpré, Faculté des sciences de l'éducation, Université de Montréal; E.J. Fisher, School of Optometry, University of Waterloo; Claude Galarneau, Faculté des lettres, Université Laval; Jeffrey Holmes, Association of Atlantic Universities; Leopold Lanctôt, University of Ottawa Press; the late Abbé Arthur Maheux, archiviste, Université Laval; Honoré Provost, Faculté de théologie, Université Laval; George Richardson, Faculty of Applied Science, Queen's University; Alexander Ross, University of Guelph; Murray G. Ross, York University; Stephen Stackpole, Carnegie Corporation of New York; Zoltan Zsigmund, Education, Science and Culture Division, Statistics Canada; and 28 of my colleagues at the University of Toronto: Margaret Allemang (nursing), A.D. Allen (chemistry), Iva Armstrong (food science), Carl Berger (history), V.W. Bladen (political economy), Adrian Brook (chemistry), Blanch Duncanson (nursing), Roy G. Ellis (dentistry), the late Donald Gullett (dentistry), Thomas Howarth (architecture), Donald Ivey (physics), A.T. Jousse (rehabilitation medicine), Kathleen King (nursing), Martha Leitch (food science), E.W. Nuffield (geology), G.W. Paterson (pharmacy), Isobel Robinson (nursing), G. de B. Robinson (mathematics), Robert Rosevear (music), Albert Rose (social work), L.K. Shook (medieval studies), Edward Sheffield (higher education), J.W.B. Sisam (forestry), Ernest W.

Stieb (pharmacy), G.S. Vickers (fine art), Harry L. Welsh (physics), John Wilkinson (library science), Kirk Wipper (physical and health education). I am also indebted to Joan Bulger, Ian Montagnes, Gertrude Stevenson, and Ronald Schoeffel of the University of Toronto Press.

My greatest debts are to Claude Bissell, Beverley Carter, Sheila Dutton, Patricia Harris, Muriel Kinney, and Gwendoline Pilkington. Miss Carter and Miss Kinney laboured for three years each in typing successive drafts of the manuscript and the latter made many other contributions as the manuscript approached completion. Mrs Dutton was responsible for checking sources and for organizing a manuscript suitable for presentation to the Press. Claude Bissell and Patricia Harris have been giving me encouragement and counsel for sixteen years and the latter has been heavily involved in the preparation of the bibliography and the index. Dr Pilkington has read in their entirety the final two drafts of the manuscript, and her detailed criticisms and suggested revisions have had the effect of reducing the work by at least 100 pages. So far as form as distinct from content is concerned, a strong case can be made for identifying her as co-author.

This work is the seventh in the series, Studies in the History and Philosophy of Canadian Higher Education, initiated by the Association of Universities and Colleges of Canada (then the National Conference of Canadian Universities) in 1957 and financed by a $25,000 grant from the Carnegie Corporation of New York. Its publication has been made possible by an additional substantial grant from the Carnegie Corporation and by a grant from the Social Science Research Council of Canada, using funds provided by the Canada Council.

R.S.H.

1860

Our beginning is but humble, our hopes are in the future.

L'Université Laval

1
The Royal Visit of
1860

In 1860 an eighteen-year old undergraduate interrupted his studies
at Oxford University to make a four month tour of British North
America, in the course of which he either visited or received briefs
from a dozen universities or colleges. He was not, it must be admitted, a typical undergraduate - he was Albert Edward, Prince of
Wales, heir apparent to the British throne; and there is little evidence to suggest that the future Edward VII had any great interest
in the state of higher education in Canada or anywhere else in the
year 1860. The immediate purpose of his visit was to open a
newly constructed railway bridge crossing the St Lawrence River
at Montreal, which was to be named the Victoria Bridge after his
mother, and this he did on 29 August. But the occasion was seized
upon by the authorities in England as an opportunity for the
people of the British colonies in North America to see their
future king; consequently a tour was arranged which took the
prince to the main centres in what are now the provinces of
Newfoundland, Prince Edward Island, Nova Scotia, New Brunswick,
Quebec, and Ontario. At the conclusion of the Canadian tour, he
proceeded to the United States, where he visited Detroit, Chicago,
St Louis, Cincinnati, Washington, Philadelphia, Boston, and New
York. The official account indicates that he was received with
enthusiasm on both sides of the border.[1]
   In Canada the tour was an occasion for the expression of loyalty
to the British crown; this was its real purpose and the arrangements were designed with this objective in mind. At each centre
there was a levée at which suitable addresses could be presented
and a great variety of organizations availed themselves of this
opportunity, among them the synod of the Presbyterian Church of
Canada, the Raftsmen of the Upper Ottawa, the Royal Canadian
Yacht Club, and the Temperance Reformation Society of Toronto.
Also presenting addresses were a surprising number of universities and colleges, each of which in its address commented upon
its present position and future prospects. For this reason the

prince's tour provides a convenient point of departure for a survey of the state of higher education in Canada in the year 1860.

Fittingly enough, the prince's introduction to Canadian higher education took place at Windsor, Nova Scotia, the seat of the University of King's College, the first institution outside the British Isles in what was to become the British Commonwealth to be granted a university charter. The address of the loyal inhabitants of the township of Windsor reminded the prince that Windsor was the oldest university town in Her Majesty's widely extended colonial possessions and the claim was made that King's College had

> educated in religion, in literature and science a great number of the clergy, many of the most distinguished members of the bench and bar in this and the neighbouring colonies, many military men, whose achievements having been widely celebrated, and several others, including members of the different religious denominations, especially conspicuous in the various walks of life, all of whom have ever mani fested the firmest allegiance to the British Throne and Government.[2]

The statement is embalmed in the imperialistic rhetoric characteristic of most of the addresses presented to the prince during the next several months, but it was nonetheless an accurate reflection of the King's College tradition as it had developed since the establishment of the college in 1790. King's College, Windsor, had been founded by United Empire Loyalists, men who had left the United States at the conclusion of the War of Independence in order to live out their lives as British subjects, and whose idea of a university was that of an Oxford or Cambridge college which like its models would be under the firm direction of the Church of England. In this latter respect, if in no other, the founders were successful; despite protestations to the contrary, King's had from the outset discouraged the enrolment of non-Anglicans, with the result that the other denominations, both Protestant and Catholic, had found it necessary to establish colleges of their own. Hence the enrolment at King's remained small and the curriculum was limited to offerings in arts and theology. A reorganization in 1853 had strengthened the college but at the time of the prince's visit it remained a rather pathetic colonial educational outpost.

The next institution visited by the prince was one of the more recent establishments, Université Laval at Quebec, which had obtained its charter in 1852. In addressing the prince, the faculty were duly modest: 'It is true that unlike the Alma Mater, Oxford, where Your Highness has been pleased to matriculate, our existence cannot be counted by centuries – our alumni are but few, our libraries, our museums, our collections, offer nothing to excite the curiosity of Your Royal Highness, accustomed to visit the great and antique Institutions of Europe; our beginning is but humble – our hopes are in the future.'[3] In comparison with

4

King's, however, there was nothing at all humble about Laval in
1860. Its charter provided for four faculties, arts, law, medicine, and theology, and two of these had been organized almost
immediately - medicine in 1853, law in 1854. Though technically
not established until 1866, the faculty of theology was already
in operation as the Séminaire de Québec, which had been providing
instruction in theology since 1663. The faculty of arts was
conceived of in the European tradition; it would offer instruction exclusively at the graduate level, preparation for the
bachelor's degree being provided in affiliated collèges classiques, of which there were eight in operation in Lower Canada at
the time the charter was granted. In the 1850s, there was not
much demand in Lower Canada, or anywhere else in North America,
for advanced work in arts and science. Nonetheless a start had
been made towards developing an arts and science program: by
1860 professors had been appointed and courses offered in Canadian
and American history (1856), chemistry (1857), physics (1859),
and philosophy (1860). Nor were the physical facilities at Laval
quite so humble as the address suggested. During the 1850s three
buildings were constructed, a main building five stories high
and 300 feet in length, a residence, and a building for the
faculty of medicine, and it is worthy of note that there were no
further buildings at Laval until 1912. A medical professor had
been sent to Europe with $8000 to purchase books and apparatus.
In 1860 the library of the Séminaire de Québec was in all probability the best in Canada.

The prince also visited one of the collèges classiques, le
Petit Séminaire de St Hyacinthe, founded in 1811. Here he was
reminded that 'respect for authority, ... love of liberty ...
and that public spirit which prompts men to devote themselves to
the glory and prosperity of their country' are based on religious
faith, which 'by sanctifying elevates all.' St Hyacinthe spoke
for all colleges of the time, whether French or English, in
asserting that 'by teaching our pupils to fear and honor God,
we instruct them in the respect due to authority.'[4] On the same
day that he visited St Hyacinthe, the prince received an address
from the University of Bishop's College, a Church of England
foundation at nearby Lennoxville, whose objectives were the same
as those of King's College, Windsor: 'As far as our limited
means and opportunities will enable us, in these days of the
infancy of our University, it will be our endeavour to promote
sound learning and true religion amongst the inhabitants of this
province, and to train up the rising generation in feelings of
affection for the mother country and loyalty to their Sovereign.'[5]
Opened in 1845 and chartered in 1853, Bishop's had struggled
along with a tiny enrolment and a small and sometimes unpaid
staff, offering instruction in arts and theology. A statement
of 1857 reported that 'some of the subjects contained in this
course are not yet sufficiently provided for, though they are
not wholly neglected, such as History and Moral Philosophy, and
Chemistry.'[6] In 1860 four students were registered in theology
and sixteen in arts.

One phrase in the Bishop's College address may have sounded familiar to the prince since it echoed a sentiment he had heard at McGill College in Montreal two days earlier. McGill's royal charter, he had been told, 'gives authority to its public acts for the advancement of sound learning and science.'7 But there was a difference; it was sound learning and *science* which McGill was dedicated to advance and not, as at Bishop's, sound learning and *true religion*. The McGill charter of 1821 had been granted to a non-denominational institution, but Anglican and Presbyterian influences were dominant until 1852 when the charter was amended, a new board of governors constituted, and divinity removed from the list of subjects taught. A medical faculty had been instituted in 1829, but no instruction in arts was offered until 1843. Nor, according to McGill's first historian, did the addition of arts (or of law a few years later) signal any significant improvement. 'The nine years between 1846 and 1855 were years of continuous financial perplexity during which the governors had great difficulty in keeping the college in operation. There is little to record other than a discouraging battle with poverty and want.'8 But with the appointment of J.W. Dawson as principal in 1855 McGill was suddenly brought to life. When Dawson arrived in Montreal there were 57 students registered in medicine, 15 in law, and 38 in arts, but none of them had any particular reason to visit the McGill campus; in 1851 the faculty of medicine had moved from McGill College to a downtown building paid for by three members of its staff, and since 1852 the work in arts and law had been carried on in the top floor of the Montreal High School. By 1860 the enrolment had almost exactly doubled - 109 in medicine, 31 in law, 60 in arts - and the arts and law students were back on the campus. In addition, the McGill Normal School had been opened in 1857, a two-year diploma course in civil engineering was being offered in the faculty of arts, and a commercial course for young bankers and accountants was being provided in the late afternoons and evenings. There was an endowed chair of English Language and Literature (established in 1858), and by 1860 St Francis College at Richmond, an early and not long-surviving junior college, had entered into affiliation. In its address to the prince, McGill had insisted that as a university it was still in its infancy and 'could not bear comparison with the venerable institutions of a like nature in the mother country.' Nonetheless, there was a justifiable note of confidence in the address.

From Montreal the prince and his retinue moved westward into Upper Canada or Ontario as it would be called with the formation of the Dominion of Canada in 1867. (Legally the area known as Upper Canada from 1791 became Canada West in 1841, but Upper Canada continued to be the popular designation.) Here he had contact with six institutions. The first was the University of Queen's College at Kingston. It presented to him not an address but a University Ode. Queen's was a Presbyterian foundation which had obtained its charter in 1841 and had begun to offer instruction in March 1842. In 1844 it lost about two-thirds of its students and supporters

when, as a result of the duplication in Canada of the 1843 seces-
sion of the Free Church of Scotland from the Old Kirk, the Canadian
Free Church Presbyterians established a college of their own at
Toronto named after John Knox. Nevertheless, in 1850, despite its
weak financial position, Queen's had made an important decision.
Offered the opportunity to move to Toronto, where it would have
been absorbed into the provincial university, it had decided to
remain independent. In 1858 an Alma Mater Society was founded and
in 1860 the government grant was increased from $3000 to $5000.
These were surely auguries of better days to come. By this time
there were faculties of arts, theology, and medicine, although the
latter was independently financed. The total enrolment was 145
and there were hopes for future growth. However, the position of
Queen's would remain precarious for many years.

The prince's next stop was at Cobourg, a town midway between
Kingston and Toronto, a strong centre of Methodism and the seat
of the principal Methodist institution in Ontario, the University
of Victoria College. Victoria had been established by the
Methodists in 1832 as an academy or secondary school. In 1841 it
attained degree-granting powers, and in 1845 it graduated the first
student from Ontario to obtain a degree 'in course.'[9] Both as an
academy and as a liberal arts college Victoria advocated an academic course that gave due attention to the modern subjects, in
contrast to the traditional emphasis elsewhere on the classics.
A medical faculty was set up in 1854 but it was located in Toronto
and its relationship to Victoria, like that of the medical faculty
at Queen's, was nominal. There was no theology until the 1870s,
and the faculty of law set up in 1862 was short-lived. Although
in 1857 it was proposed that the college be moved to Hamilton, a
town west of Toronto where the population growth was more promising,
this plan was not acted upon and Victoria remained in Cobourg.
But in 1889 it decided to join forces with the provincial University
of Toronto, setting aside its degree-granting powers except in
theology. The move took place in 1892.

After Cobourg the prince next moved to Toronto where he visited
two universities, a theological college, and a normal school. His
first stop was at the University of Trinity College, a Church of
England institution founded by Bishop John Strachan in 1852. On
the occasion of his visit to Trinity he was assured that 'in dis-
charging our duty we can propose to ourselves no better model than
that of the ancient Universities of England.'[10] Presumably, the
special needs of Trinity were also put to the prince by Bishop
Strachan in private conversation, for on this occasion the prince's
usual stereotyped reply to all such addresses included the statement, 'I know the difficulties under which you have laboured, and
I sincerely hope that you may successfully surmount them.'[11] The
difficulties remained. In 1860 there were only 12 students in
divinity and 20 in arts. Nor were the difficulties to be sur-
mounted effectively until Trinity entered into federation with the
University of Toronto in 1904.

Trinity was actually the second university that Bishop Strachan had founded in Toronto, the first being King's College for which he had obtained a royal charter in 1827 but at which no instruction was offered until 1843. In theory a provincial university, King's College was in fact controlled by the Church of England, and dissatisfaction with that arrangement, which it was claimed discriminated against Presbyterians, Methodists, Roman Catholics, and Baptists, led to its abolition by the legislature as of 31 December 1849 and to the creation in its place on 1 January 1850 of a non-denominational University of Toronto. It had been in answer to this move that Strachan had gone to England in 1851 to obtain additional funds and a charter to set up a second Anglican institution, Trinity College, which in his words, 'fed by the heavenly stream of pure religion, may communicate fuel to the lamp of genius and enable it to burn with a brighter and purer flame.'[12]

The newly established University of Toronto which replaced King's College was a teaching institution with professorships in law, medicine, and arts. Divinity was specifically excluded. A new university act of 1853 reduced Toronto to a degree-granting university, but at the same time provided for a non-denominational arts college, University College. To it were transferred the professors of arts subjects at Toronto; thus there were now a council and members (undergraduates) of University College, but a senate and graduates of the University of Toronto. In a joint address before the prince it was explained that although 'framed as our system is upon the model of Institutions of our Mother country.' it is 'adapted in its details to the special wants of this portion of the Empire.'[13]

The 'system,' which already included the rough outline of the honour courses that in time would prove to be one of the great strengths of Canadian higher education, was indeed an adaptation of many models - London, Oxford, Cambridge, Edinburgh, Trinity College Dublin - and it was fitting that the institution should be housed in a building that continues to reflect most of the architectural possibilities known to man. But there was method in the mixing of the compound, and the method was grounded in an awareness that new conditions make necessary new solutions. At the time of the prince's visit, the University of Toronto was under attack (a select committee of the legislature was investigating its affairs), and there would be continual attack for many years to come. But, housed more adequately than it would be for at least a century to come, in possession of ample scholarship funds, and staffed by what was for the time a distinguished faculty, the University of Toronto in 1860 was firmly and permanently established.

The prince visited only one of the three theological colleges located in Toronto at this time - Knox College, established in 1844 by the Free Presbyterian Church of Canada as an offshoot of the University of Queen's College, Kingston. Knox had begun by offering an arts course as well as theology, and by 1850 it was seriously considering applying to the legislature for a degree-granting charter; but the availability of an arts course at the provincial University of Toronto created in 1850 enabled Knox to abandon its ambitions in arts and to concentrate upon theology.

The theological colleges which the prince did not visit were the Congregational College of British North America and St Michael's College. The former was established in 1841 and by 1860 had become residual legatee of collapsed congregational colleges opened at Montreal in 1843 and at Liverpool, Nova Scotia, in 1857; in 1864 it would be moved to Montreal and in 1865 would become an affiliate of McGill University. St Michael's College, primarily a Roman Catholic secondary school and only incidentally a seminary, had been founded in 1852 by Bishop Charbonnel and was under the direction of the Basilian fathers. It would eventually come under the degree-granting wing of the University of Toronto.

From Toronto the prince's party proceeded through the western part of Upper Canada on its way to Detroit and the American portion of the tour. This included visits to Harvard, West Point, Girard College at Philadelphia, the Cooper Union, and the University of New York. Before crossing the border, the prince received at Woodstock an address from the Canadian Literary Institute, a Baptist foundation of 1860 which would evolve in 1890 into McMaster University, originally located in Toronto but after 1930 in Hamilton. He was informed that 'the institution which we represent is designed to impart a higher academic education both to male and female.'[14] This was one of two Canadian institutions in 1860 sufficiently forward-looking to offer education to young women. The other was Mount Allison College at Sackville, New Brunswick.

The Prince of Wales may well have been impressed by the number of universities and colleges his Canadian tour revealed. Certainly he would not have encountered eight chartered institutions in a tour of England in 1860; but the surprising thing is that he could have visited five more degree-granting institutions and seven additional colleges which would become degree-granting in the course of time. Still another college, Assumption (Windsor), destined to become a university, had temporarily closed in 1859, and if the prince had returned in 1866 he would have been able to visit three more institutions which today are universities. By 1868, one year after Confederation, 18 Canadian colleges were authorized to grant degrees, and nine others which now enjoy that privilege were corporate entities.

Two of the chartered institutions not visited by the prince were Roman Catholic institutions, Regiopolis College at Kingston and St Mary's College at Halifax. Though among the earliest Canadian colleges to obtain degree-granting powers (1837 and 1841 respectively), they had little or no opportunity to exercise these powers during the nineteenth century. St Mary's is believed to have granted some degrees in 1843 and in some subsequent years until 1881 when, with the withdrawal of annual government grants to the denominational colleges of Nova Scotia, its activities were suspended for 22 years. Regiopolis was also receiving grants from the Upper Canada legislature from 1847 to 1868. It did not grant any degrees during these years, though two of its students are known to have received B.A.s from Université Laval in 1858.[15]

At the time of the prince's visit, Regiopolis and St Mary's could be described either as small classical colleges offering some theological training or as small seminaries offering some parts of the classical course. Seven other Roman Catholic colleges which have since attained degree-granting powers could similarly be described; the Collège de Sherbrooke, which in 1954 provided a base for the Université de Sherbrooke; St Boniface College at St Boniface, in what is now the Province of Manitoba, a classical college opened in 1855, which in 1877 was one of the founding colleges of the University of Manitoba; St Francis Xavier College, founded in 1853 at Arichat, Nova Scotia, transferred to Antigonish in 1855, chartered in 1866; St Dunstan's College, founded at Charlottetown, Prince Edward Island, in 1855, chartered in 1917 (though not granting degrees until 1941), absorbed within the University of Prince Edward Island in 1969; St Joseph's College at Memramcook, New Brunswick, founded in 1864, chartered in 1868, absorbed within the Université de Moncton in 1963; Assumption College at Windsor, Upper Canada, established by the Jesuits in 1857, closed in 1859, reopened by the Basilians in 1870, chartered as Assumption University in 1953, federated with the University of Windsor in 1963; and the College of Bytown, founded as Collège Saint-Joseph in 1848 and chartered as the University of Ottawa in 1866.

Two of the six institutions still to be mentioned were inactive in 1860. Huron College at London, Upper Canada, from which the University of Western Ontario would evolve in due, if fitful, course, was not founded until 1863. Dalhousie University at Halifax had been chartered since 1818 and had offered an arts course briefly from 1838 to 1843 and even more briefly in the session 1857-58; it would reopen permanently with a highly qualified faculty of six in 1863. Of the institutions active in 1860 three were chartered and one was not. The latter was the Belleville Seminary at Belleville, Upper Canada, founded by the Methodist Episcopal Church in 1857 and chartered in 1866 as Albert College. Albert is the only instance in the history of Canadian higher education of a teaching institution which, having gained university status, subsequently surrendered those powers willingly and irrevocably.[16] After granting degrees in arts, law, music, and theology from 1867 to 1883, it reverted to the status of a secondary school in accordance with the terms of the 1884 union of the several Methodist churches.

The three chartered institutions the prince did not visit were in what are now the Maritime provinces - the University of New Brunswick at Fredericton, Mount Allison Wesleyan College at Sackville, N.B., and Acadia College at Wolfville, Nova Scotia. The charter under which the University of New Brunswick was operating in 1860 was the third granted to the institution at Fredericton. The first was granted by the Province of New Brunswick to the College of New Brunswick in 1800, but no instruction was offered beyond the secondary level until the 1820s. In 1828 a royal charter was granted to what was then called King's College, New Brunswick. Despite the presence on the staff of some of the ablest professors of the day, the college had a difficult history until its reorganization in 1859, at which time, following the recommendations of a royal commission in 1854, it was rechartered by the province as the non-denominational state-supported University of New Brunswick. Theology was no longer to be taught, and a clergyman could no longer occupy the position of president. With the assumption of the presidency by William Brydone Jack, professor of mathematics and philosophy since 1840, the University of New Brunswick was in a position to move steadily if unspectacularly forward.

Acadia and Mount Allison were established by the Baptists and the Methodists respectively because the existing colleges in the Maritime colonies did not meet the needs of the denominations. Acadia's establishment was the consequence of dissatisfaction first with King's College, Windsor, and then with Dalhousie. The decision to found it was made in 1838 when a well-qualified Baptist candidate was *not* appointed to one of the chairs of the about to be opened Dalhousie. Starting in 1839, its survival to 1860 is a remarkable story of triumph over adversity to which we shall have occasion to refer in chapter 3. It faced a serious financial crisis in 1858, but in 1860, largely through the stabilizing influence of its president, the Rev. J.M. Cramp, its principal difficulties appeared to have been overcome. Mount Allison's prospects seemed even more promising. Founded on the basis of the offer by Charles Allison of a building and £100 annually for ten years to support 'a school in which not only the elementary but the higher branches of education may be taught,' Mount Allison had begun as an academy or secondary school for young men in 1843. To this was added in 1848 a Female Academy, also through the generosity of Charles Allison. A charter for Mount Allison Wesleyan College was obtained in 1858. The instruction provided in 1860 was a strange mixture of work in primary, intermediate, classical, and collegiate departments and included (for the ladies) music and fine arts. A Token of Merit granted to the lady graduates since 1857 was replaced in 1863 by the diploma, Mistress of Liberal Arts. In 1875 Grace Lockhart, M.L.A. 1874, received the first bachelor's degree granted to a woman by a university in what was then known as the British Empire.

In summary, the position of higher education in Canada in 1860 can be thus described. In the Maritimes, four chartered institutions were in full operation (King's College; Windsor; the University of New Brunswick; Acadia College; and Mount Allison Wesleyan College), a fifth (Dalhousie) was about to establish itself permanently, and a sixth (St Mary's) existed at least on paper. Two other colleges (St Francis Xavier and St Dunstan's) were in operation and a third (St Joseph's) would be added to the list in 1864. There was also a Presbyterian theological college (Pine Hill) at Halifax,[17] and a Church of England Theological College (Queen's) at St John's, Newfoundland.[18] In Lower Canada (Quebec) there were three chartered institutions, Bishop's and McGill for English-speaking students, and Laval for French-speaking students, the baccalaureate program for the latter being provided by nine collèges classiques. In Upper Canada (Ontario) four institutions were chartered (Queen's, Toronto, Trinity, Victoria); five others which had offered, were offering, or would offer undergraduate instruction had corporate existence (Albert, McMaster, Ottawa, Regiopolis, St Michael's); one (Assumption) had temporarily suspended activities; and one (Western Ontario) would be established shortly. Knox College and the Congregational College of British North America confined themselves to theology. In the West, one of the constituent colleges of the future University of Manitoba (St Boniface) operated as a classical college.

This was the picture in 1860. Before turning to a consideration of what was being studied in these colleges and universities, we shall in the following two chapters review in more detail the history of their establishment and the course of their development to the year 1860.

NOTES TO CHAPTER 1

1 The official account of the prince's tour is *The Tour of H.R.H. The Prince of Wales through British North America and the United States* (1860). An account, which restricts itself to matters related to the visits to educational institutions and includes some addresses not published in the official report, appeared in the *Journal of Education for Upper Canada*, 13 (1860), 131-42, and a parallel account in French in *J. de l'Instruction Publique*, 4 (1860), 148-54, 165-70, 185-91, 203-6; 5 (1861), 9-12, 36-9, 56-9, 70-2, 86-8, 102-3, 118-22.

2 *Tour*, 211-12

3 *Ibid*., 85

4 *J. Education*, 13 (1860), 136

5 *Tour*, 85

6 Quoted by D.C. Masters, *Bishop's University: The First Hundred Years* (1950), 49

7 *Tour*, 224

8 C. MacMillan, *McGill and its Story, 1821-1921* (1921), 186

9 First degrees granted by each Canadian university for each year up to and including 1920 are listed in appendix 1.

10 *Tour*, 251

11 *Ibid*., 252

12 John Strachan, 'To the Clergy and Laity of the Diocese of Toronto,' February 1850, quoted in H. Melville, *The Rise and Progress of Trinity College, Toronto* (1852), 93

13 *Tour*, 178

14 *J. Education*, 13 (1860), 141

15 J.G. Hodgins, ed., *Documentary History of Education in Upper Canada (Ontario)*, XII, 288. For a clear account of the tangled histories of Regiopolis and St Mary's, see L.K. Shook, *Catholic Post-Secondary Education in English-Speaking Canada* (1971).

16 The closest parallel is the University of Halifax which existed
    from 1876 to 1880 and which granted 10 degrees during this
    period; but it provided no instruction. See below, chapter 7.
    King's College, Toronto, could not be said to have surrendered
    its powers - they were abolished. There are a number of
    instances of universities voluntarily placing some or all of
    their degree-granting powers in abeyance, but in such cases
    the decision can be revoked.
17 J.W. Falconer and W.G. Watson, *A Brief History of Pinehill
    Divinity Hall*... (1946), 1-15
18 D.C. Masters, *Protestant Church Colleges in Canada* (1966),
    84-7. References to the development of higher education in
    Newfoundland in the nineteenth and early twentieth centuries
    are included in this study despite the fact that Newfoundland
    was a British colony quite separate from Canada until 1949.

2
The Development of Higher Education in French Canada 1635-1860

Traditionally, higher education in Canada is dated from 1635, the year when the Jesuits established at Quebec a college which eventually offered the complete cours classique or classical college course that until the 1950s constituted the required course of study for the B.A. degree in the Canadian French-language universities. In its early years, however, the Jesuit college was essentially an elementary school (petite école) where the children of the colonists (who in 1635 numbered fewer than 500) and of native Indians could learn the three Rs.[1] It is true that Latin was taught in 1636 and possibly in 1635, and that it continued to be taught without apparent interruption and presumably at an increasingly higher level for the next 15 years. In 1651 the 22 students at the college, including those at the elementary level, were taught by two professors, one of Latin and one of mathematics. Gosselin has reported that four years later there were four professors, one for the petite école, one for 'grammaire,' one for 'humanités' and 'rhétorique,' and one for 'philosophie',[2] thus suggesting that by this time both of the major divisions of the classical college course, *lettres* (embracing grammaire, belles lettres, rhétorique) and *philosophie* (embracing philosophie, sciences, mathématique) were being offered, though in contrast to the contemporary situation in France on a somewhat reduced basis. But it is possible, as Audet argues, that the professor of philosophy of 1655 was the professor of mathematics of 1651, and that the program offered in 1655 extended only so far as *lettres*. It is clear, however, that philosophy as prescribed in the Ratio Studiorum was taught at the Jesuit college in 1659; this was the year when Mgr François de Laval arrived to assume his duties as the first bishop of New France. He was sufficiently impressed with the work being done at the college to request that the Jesuits also offer instruction in theology, for which the work in philosophy would be prerequisite.[3] Theology was introduced at the college in 1661 but two years later Laval established le Grand Séminaire de Québec, which gradually assumed responsibility for this professional work. Nonetheless, the relation between the college and the seminary remained close throughout the French régime and on frequent occasions Jesuit professors offered instruction in theology at the latter.[4] In addition, Bishop Laval established a Petit Séminaire in association with the Grand Séminaire in 1668 as a residence for potential seminarians while they were taking the classical college course at the Jesuit college. A century later the Petit Séminaire took over responsibility for the full classical college course when the Jesuit college was forced to close down by the British authorities following the conquest. But during the French Régime the instruction it offered was confined to preparing students for admission to the Jesuit college.

The availability by the 1660s of the full classical college course at the Jesuit college and of professional instruction in theology at the Grand Séminaire is evidence that higher education in Canada has a history of at least 300 years. By 1700 Greek had been introduced into the classical college course and the course itself expanded to a seven year syllabus with five years for the cours de lettres (three years of grammaire, one each of humanités and rhétorique) and two for philosophie. This syllabus remained in effect for the balance of the French régime. Periodically during the century before 1760, écoles latines were established in various other centres, including Montreal, but only the Jesuit college at Quebec offered the complete classical course, and this was not always possible. In 1728 a petition to found a second Jesuit college in Montreal was rejected by the authorities at Quebec and Paris, Intendant Dupuy arguing that since the course at Quebec was incomplete this was hardly the time to organize a second college.[5]

In addition to the theological training provided at the seminary, there were other efforts to provide specialized training during the French régime, and some of these contained at least the elements of higher education.

By around 1670, Bishop Laval's awareness that the classical college course was not suitable to all the intelligent youth of the colony led him to establish at St Joachim near Quebec a trade school (l'école d'arts et métiers) where attention was given to agriculture, painting, sculpture, stone-masonry, and carpentry. A similar program was offered for the first two decades of the eighteenth century at a school in Montreal.[6] The inclusion of mathematics in the final two years of the classical college course led to the establishment at Quebec of a school for the training of pilots and surveyors - l'école d'hydrographie.[7] This work was carried on with the aid of a government grant, initially by a series of laymen who were attached to the Jesuit college with the title of professeur d'hydrographie, but from 1709 until the outbreak of the Seven Years' War by the Jesuits themselves. The same kind of training was offered for a time at Montreal. In a letter of 20 September 1694 Père Chauchetière, a Jesuit teaching at an école latine, declared: 'J'ai des écholiers qui sont bons cinquiésmes, mais j'en ay d'autres qui ont la barbe au menton aux quelles j'apprends la marine et les fortifications et autre choses de mathématiques.'[8] But as Gosselin has noted, neither les écoles d'arts et de métiers nor les écoles d'hydrographie can be described as 'l'instruction supérieure.' The aim was to produce not engineers or agriculturists but efficient mariners, skilled farmers, and 'de bons et honnêtes artisans.'[9]

Groulx has pointed out that, the church excepted, the professions were effectively closed to the native-born and that such opportunities as were available to the young Canadien required little advanced training.[10] Gosselin, whose *L'Instruction au Canada sous le régime français* is a detailed and wide-ranging study, records no effort to provide professional education in medicine and law. It is known, however, that lectures on jurisprudence and on Roman, civil, and criminal law were given once or twice a week at Quebec by M.-B. Collet and L.G. Verrier, who occupied the position of procureur général of New France for the periods 1712-27 and 1727-58 respectively.[11] There were also attempts to provide formal training for school teachers, most notably by the Frères Hospitaliers de la Croix et de Saint-Joseph (Frères Charon) during the first two decades of the eighteenth century, but such ventures failed to attain permanence owing to inadequate official support.[12] It should be remembered that even at the time of the conquest the population of French Canada was under 60,000.

During the first 20 years of the British régime, from 1763 to the beginning of Dorchester's second term as governor in 1786, the situation deteriorated. The Jesuit college at Quebec suspended its activities between 1759 and 1761 and ceased operating in 1768. In 1758 the Séminaire de Québec closed its doors but reopened in 1763; and in 1768, with the closing of the Jesuit college, the Petit Séminaire took on the responsibility for providing the full classical course. A second classical course was offered by the Sulpicians at Montreal in 1773 - Collège St Raphaël, renamed Collège de Montréal in 1806 but often referred to, both before and since, as the Petit Séminaire de Montréal; but until 1790 it offered only the cours de lettres, the student going to the Petit Séminaire at Quebec for the cours de philosophie.

During this depressed period the idea for a university for French Canada was first proposed. In 1770 a petition claiming to speak for the citizens of Quebec, Montreal, and Trois-Rivières was presented to the governor, asking that a Royal George College be established at which languages, philosophy, mathematics, engineering, navigation, and civil law would be taught, as well as 'tous les arts et toutes les sciences humaines qui rendent l'homme utile à la société et qui font l'honneur d'une nation.'[13] Though it was suggested that such an institution would be of benefit to other British colonies and even to the mother country itself (the French language, it was pointed out, could be learned in a 'friendly' country), the question was not seriously considered by the authorities in London and permission was not granted to obtain in France the services of the six professors required.

The incident reflects the atmosphere of the time - the brave
hopes of the French Canadians, the grave doubts of the British
authorities. The Roman Catholic church was officially recognized
by the Quebec Act of 1774, but for the previous decade it had been
British policy to discourage the Roman religion by encouraging the
Protestant. An obvious way to implement such a policy was to
establish Protestant schools, and the instructions issued to
Governor Murray in 1763 directed him to give all possible encouragement to the construction of Protestant schools and all possible
assistance to the maintenance of Protestant schoolmasters. There
was active discouragement of Roman Catholicism particularly in the
1760s. The Jesuits and Récollets were forbidden to recruit additional members, all teaching orders were viewed with suspicion,
and a steady decline in the number of active priests meant that
fewer and fewer were available for teaching duties. Since the
Roman Catholic church had been the motivating force behind all
teaching efforts in French-speaking Canada for over a century, it
is not surprising that in this antagonistic atmosphere education
made virtually no progress.

By the mid-1780s a new attitude prevailed. Shortly after the
reappointment of Sir Guy Carleton (later Lord Dorchester) as
governor-in-chief of British North America, a special committee
of the legislative council under the chairmanship of Chief Justice
William Smith, was appointed to report on the Means for Promoting
Education. Its recommendations, published in 1790, called for
free parish or village schools for the teaching of the three Rs,
free schools at each county town for the teaching of arithmetic,
languages, grammar, bookkeeping, navigation, surveying, and the
practical branches of mathematics, and 'a collegiate institution,
for cultivating the liberal arts and sciences usually taught in
the European Universities - the Theology of Christians excepted.'[14]
It is a scheme remarkably similar to Jefferson's famous proposal
for the State of Virginia in 1779. According to L.-P. Audet,[15]
the exclusion of theology was the governor's idea and was based
less on adherence to any principle than on the practical consideration that the inclusion of theology would require provision
for at least two faculties of theology since the institution was
to be equally available to Roman Catholics and Protestants. However, the phrasing of the committee's report suggests recognition
of the principle that a university ought to be free of any external
pressures: 'It is essential to the *origin* and *success* of such an
institution, that a society be incorporated for the purpose; and
that the charter wisely provide against the perversion of the
instruction to any sectarian peculiarities; leaving free scope
for cultivating the *general circle* of the sciences.'[16]

On the other hand, a letter of the governor of 10 November 1790
makes it clear that the whole educational system, of which the
university, as with Jefferson's scheme, would be the capstone,
was to be controlled by the state itself: 'It will be very material
so to organize and endow this institution that the inferior
schools ... may be subordinate to its government, and in some
measure dependent upon it for support, so that the whole system

may be animated by one common principle, under the eye and control of the crown.'[17]

Initially, the proposal to establish a state-supported university in the old French colony seemed likely to be implemented. It received enthusiastic support from the coadjutor bishop of Quebec, Mgr Bailly de Messein, who at an earlier period in his career had been tutor to the governor's children. It also appeared to receive more tangible support from a prominent Montreal lawyer, Simon Sanguinet, whose will, drawn up a few days before his death on 16 March 1790, assigned two-thirds of an estate valued roughly at $15,000 for the founding of such a university. A copy of the Smith Committee Report was on his bed at the time the will was being prepared. The announcement of Sanguinet's bequest inspired a petition supporting the committee's recommendation that a Université de la Province de Québec be established. The document was submitted to the governor on 31 October 1790 by 115 prominent citizens of both French and English extraction and of both Roman Catholic and Protestant persuasion. Despite this strong affirmation, the scheme aborted.

Audet suspects that it was temporarily shelved pending the announcement of the terms of what proved to be the Constitutional Act of 1791 which created the provinces of Upper and Lower Canada, and that having been thus set aside, it was never seriously reconsidered. A simpler explanation put forth by Audet is that the bishop of Quebec, Mgr Hubert, supported the idea in principle but strongly objected to it in practice. This is borne out in a letter dated 18 November 1789 from the bishop in response to the Smith Committee's request for factual information about the school situation in the colony. His surface objections to the proposal were that he did not believe that the habitant population were ready for such an institution, and, indeed, would not be prepared to send their sons to it. His rationale was:

Il est fort douteux que la Province puisse fournir présentement un nombre suffisant d'Ecoliers pour occuper les Maîtres et Professeurs que l'on mettroit dans une Université. D'abord tant qu'il y aura beaucoup de terres à défricher en Canada, on ne doit pas attendre que les habitants des campagnes soient curieux des arts libéraux. Un cultivateur aisé qui désirera laisser un bon héritage à ses enfants, aimera mieux communément les appliquer à l'Agriculture et employer son argent à leur acheter des fonds, qu'à leur procurer des connoissances dont il ne connoît pas, et dont il n'est guère possible qu'il connoisse le prix. Tous les pays du monde ont successivement donné des preuves de ce que j'avance, les sciences n'y avant fleuri que quand il s'y est trouvé plus d'habitants qu'il n'en falloit pour la culture des terres. Or ceci n'a pas encore lieu en Canada, pays immense dont les terres peu avancées offrent de toutes parts de quoi exercer l'industrie et piquer l'intérêt de ses Colons. Les villes seroient donc les seules qui puissent fournir des sujets à l'Université. Il y a quatre villes dans la Province: une

William Henri, qui est encore déserte; une autre, les Trois Rivières, qui mériteroit à peine le nom de bourg. Restent Québec et Montréal, dont le peuple comme l'on sait, n'est pas fort nombreux. En outre, est-il probable, attendu la rareté actuelle de l'argent et la pauvreté des citoyens, que Montréal puisse envoyer un grand nombre de sujets à l'Université? Tous les deux ans une dizaine ou douzaine d'écoliers de Montréal sont envoyés ici pour étudier la Philosophie. Il n'en faut pas davantage pour faire murmurer toute leur ville. Plusieurs, faute de moyens suffisants, sont contraints de borner à la Rhétorique finie le cours de leurs études. Néanmoins le Séminaire de Québec donne gratuitement ses instructions sur la Philosophie comme sur les autres sciences, et la plus forte pension alimentaire qu'il exige d'un Ecolier ne monte jamais à 12 liv. sterling par an. Je concluerois de tout cela que le moment n'est pas encore venu de fonder une Université à Québec.[18]

The bishop's more fundamental objection, however, rested on the grounds that there was no guarantee that the church would have any control over the institution, and for this stance he was to receive the full support of Rome: 'vous avez très bien fait d'avoir resisté à la fondation de cette université dans laquelle la tolerance des sectes hétérodoxes aurait servi de base.'[19] By 1790, the British authorities were not likely to proceed in opposition to the wishes of the unofficial leader of His Majesty's French-Canadian subjects, and it is therefore not surprising that a Université de la Province de Québec was not established at that time.

Bishop Hubert, however, strongly favoured increased support for the institutions that were already in existence and were, of course, under his control. Generally speaking, he claimed, the young scholars were capable at the time they finished their studies of embracing with success 'any kind of science taught at a university, whether Jurisprudence, Physics, Surgery, Navigation or Fortification.' If a third institution were to be established, it should confine itself to classics, civil law, navigation, and the mathematics currently taught at the Petit Séminaire. This view was essentially in harmony with a proposal put forward by the Sulpicians in 1790 - that they establish at Montreal a Collège Dorchester (Collège Clarence was also suggested in honour of one of George III's sons) at which would be offered English, French, Latin, belles lettres, philosophy, mathematics in their special branches, especially navigation, surveying, and engineering, and, when circumstances permit, civil law, and the other sciences which would prove most useful to the needs of the province.[20] Such an institution would doubtless have meant an expansion of the existing Sulpician college at Montreal rather than the addition of a third institution. The possibility that a university might thus be provided without substantial cost to the government provides a further explanation for the collapse of the movement to found a French-language university in the eighteenth century.

Unfortunately, the Sulpicians lacked the financial resources to establish such a university; their petition had been based on the assumption that they would have access to the revenues of their estates which, along with those of the Jesuits, had been confiscated by the terms of the Treaty of Paris of 1763. The petition was tabled pending settlement of this very question, which was not resolved until 1889. Consequently, nothing was done, and for the next half-century, i.e., until the 1840s, there is little to record in the development of higher education in French Canada except the gradual strengthening of the two existing classical colleges - those at Quebec and Montreal - and the founding of five other classical colleges which were solidly established by 1860: Nicolet (1803), St-Hyacinthe (1811), Ste-Thérèse-de-Blainville (1825), Ste-Anne-de-la-Pocatière (1827) and L'Assomption (1832).[21] Three other colleges were founded during this period but did not survive - Collège St-Denis-sur-Richelieu (1805-11), Collège de St Roch (1818-30), and Collège de Chambly (1825-57). In all cases the new colleges were established through the initiative of a parish priest, but also - and particularly in the case of those that were successful - with the enthusiastic and tangible support of one or other of the bishops. The latter, individually and collectively, saw in the establishment of the Royal Institution for the Advancement of Learning (1801) and in the subsequent efforts to establish McGill University and a network of Protestant high schools a threat to the language, religion, and culture of French Canada. They therefore urged their clergy to organize écoles paroissiales and they devoted time and money to strengthening the collèges. The latter were quite independent of one another, but they developed academically and administratively on similar lines; this was to be expected since the classical course had long been clearly defined, the faculty were all clerics, and the great majority of the faculty either had been trained or were still in the process of being trained at the Séminaire de Québec. Until well past 1860, the majority of teachers in the classical colleges were seminarians - young men who interrupted their studies for a year or two to teach at one of the colleges and who in their spare time carried on their theological studies under the direction of the priests in charge of their college.

The beginnings of a new order became apparent in the 1830s. It was at this time that the Abbé John Holmes introduced Greek at the Petit Séminaire de Québec and gave increased and enlivened attention in the classical course to geography, history, natural history, and the physical sciences, innovations which would be accepted in all the colleges in due course. During the 1830s, too, an elementary school system was beginning to take form, the consequence of the authorization of écoles de fabrique in 1824 and of the 1829 Act for the Encouragement of Elementary Education. Increased enrolments called attention to the need for teacher training, and, partly through John Holmes's efforts, a normal school was established in 1837. But at this point the troubles attendant on the Rebellion of 1837 postponed further progress. Indeed, there was retrogression, for the normal school, which was almost immediately in difficulties, was closed in 1842.

The very different atmosphere of the 1840s was in considerable measure the result of the Act of Union of 1840, which reunited the provinces of Upper and Lower Canada. In the field of education, the uniting of the provinces was a great advantage to those who sought improvement in French Canada; in a number of respects Upper Canada was more advanced, and it was now possible to insist upon measures that would produce parity. Thus, the Common School Bill of 1846 establishing free schools in Upper Canada was matched by an act of the same year giving Lower Canada a system of state-supported confessional schools. Since a solution to the problem of elementary schooling which French Canadians had been seeking since 1791 had now apparently been achieved, it was possible to turn attention to the expansion of the system at the secondary and tertiary levels. As we shall see, a considerable number of new colleges were founded between 1846 and 1860, and in 1852 the charter for Laval University was obtained.

There was one additional factor which explains the changed atmosphere of the 1840s and 1850s - the arrival in Canada of a number of religious orders: the Christian Brothers in 1837, the Oblate fathers in 1841, the Jesuits in 1842, the Clerics of St Viator and the Congregation of the Holy Cross in 1847, the Basilians in 1852. Of these the Clerics of St Viator were particularly active in Lower Canada; soon they were providing the teaching staff for newly established colleges at Joliette (1846), Rigaud (1850), Verchères (1854), and Longueuil (1855). The educational efforts of the Jesuits were initially concentrated at Montreal where they founded Collège Ste Marie in 1849. By 1852 this college was offering lectures in law in addition to the classical course.

Collège Ste-Marie followed the usual pattern of beginning with the class in elements and adding an additional year of the classical course each September until the full program was available. It was recognized as a classical college from the outset. In contrast, all four of the colleges with which the Clerics of St Viator became associated were known officialy as 'collèges industriels.' The term 'classical college' was restricted to those institutions whose chief concern was the offering of the traditional classical college course.[22] The fact that such a college also offered a 'commercial' course of shorter duration and with more practical aims did not disqualify it from being so classified and therefore of being eligible for the government grant which colleges of this type were authorized to receive by virtue of a law passed in 1846. The same law provided for grants to the collèges industriels, but the amount was approximately half that assigned to the classical colleges. According to P.-J.-O. Chauveau, who became superintendent of public instruction for Lower Canada in 1855, a few of the collèges industriels listed in 1860 had been established with the intention of becoming classical colleges, but the majority were designed to fill a gap in the educational system of the province by providing an alternative form of education for young men to prepare them directly for business and industry rather than for the traditional liberal professions of law, medicine, and theology.[23] Unfortunately, though supported by public funds, these institutions were not under direct government control, and they tended to adopt the same program as that of the classical colleges, partly because the latter would entitle them to receive the larger government grant. By the 1870s there was little to distinguish the two types of college.

But for our purposes the expansion of what in the final analysis was largely secondary education was of lesser importance than the movement, begun in the late 1840s, to establish a French-speaking university. This dream had haunted French Canada since 1770: Groulx has cited evidence of such a proposal in 1830, 1831, 1836, 1837, 1845, and 1848.[24] This time the proposal resulted in attention. The initial stimulus derived from certain members of Séminaire de Québec, notably John Holmes, Jerôme Demers, and L.J. Casault, the supérieur. The interest of Archbishop Turgeon of Quebec and of Bishop Bourget of Montreal was demonstrated between 1850 and 1852. In March 1852, Casault reported that the staff of the séminaire was prepared to proceed if the bishops judged this to be in the interests of religion. It was so judged, and Casault proceeded, with the support of the governor general, to obtain a civil charter on 9 August. In March 1853 Rome granted 'les pouvoirs ordinaires d'une université catholique' the power to confer degrees in theology being vested not in the university but in the archbishop of Quebec. All the Roman Catholic bishops of Canada immediately issued pastoral letters supporting 'cette ôeuvre nationale et religieuse.'

The original idea was to establish a single university for the province in which all or nearly all the colleges would play a part, the séminaire at the head but the others full members. Holmes, for one, was doubtful; quite aside from the likelihood of legitimate differences of opinion about the curricula and the practical problems of arranging regular meetings of a council drawn from many centres at a time when mechanized transportation was still in its infancy, the difficulties currently being experienced in Upper Canada by the University of Toronto in its relations with Queen's, Victoria, and Regiopolis raised questions about the effectiveness of a federation scheme.[25] In consequence, the university was founded and financed by the séminaire alone, the name carefully selected to imply neither provincial jurisdiction nor identification with any particular diocese or district. Proposed terms for affiliation were soon forwarded to all the bishops for transmission to the colleges of their dioceses. The replies were by no means unanimously favourable and nearly ten years of debate ensued before any colleges were affiliated.. But in 1855 Laval announced that it would recognize the graduates of L'Assomption, Nicolet, Ste-Thérèse, St-Hyacinthe, Collège Ste-Marie, and Collège de Montréal, as well as of its own Petit Séminaire as eligible for being granted the B.A. degree.

The University was to consist of the traditional four faculties - arts, law, medicine, theology. Law and medicine were the new departures: 'It is with feelings of deep pain,' admitted Archbishop Turgeon in his pastoral letter of 1852, 'that we have seen our Catholic youth obliged to pass into foreign countries, either to procure academical honours or to follow up the study of medicine or jurisprudence.' But there was no reference to agriculture, to engineering, or to the training of teachers: a university training was not thought to be needed for technological, industrial, or pedagogical pursuits. Nor in contrast to the project of 1790, was there any desire to assume the posture of a state university. Laval would not be all things to all men: its emphasis would be on unity, not on diversity. True, the unity was not that of the collège, where all studied a single course in common:

Il est facile de voir combien le rôle d'une université proprement dite est distinct du rôle d'un collège. Il ne s'agit plus d'un enseignement commun à toute la classe des hommes instruits mais d'un ensemble d'enseignements spéciaux, différents les uns des autres, bien que se touchant par un grand nombre de points de contact, et se prêtant un mutuel appui.[26]

Rather, the unity would derive from the oneness of truth itself, and it was felt to be of the utmost importance that the secular faculties recognize that the principles guiding their work must be philosophic and religious:

Le Droit et la Médecine ... demandent à la Théologie ou à la Philosophie des principes qui les guident, et les Lettres sont comme les liens délicats de ces diverses branches de la science. Que toutes ces parties remontent à la grande Unité, qui est la Vérité incréée, que jamais les enseignements humains ne soient contraires aux enseignements de la foi, et vous aurez une idée de la force d'une université qui se développe et grandit sous les auspices de la religion catholique.[27]

Finally, it must be noted that the unity was to be organized from Quebec, with prime authority over higher education in Lower Canada resting with its archbishop. This view was not enthusiastically embraced by the bishop of Montreal, Mgr Bourget, whose efforts to obtain an independent university for Montreal occupied much of his attention for the next twenty years. As early as 1858 he summoned the heads of a number of the classical colleges to discuss university questions without informing the archbishop of Quebec.[28] In 1862 he made the first of many trips to Rome for the express purpose of founding a second university at Montreal. Thus was begun the academic civil war between Montreal and Quebec, which would not be concluded until the establishment of the Université de Montréal in 1919, and which contributed in no small measure to the failure of Université Laval to achieve the desires of its founders for the best part of a century.

Though it was situated outside the boundaries of Lower Canada, it is appropriate to deal here with the establishment of the University of Ottawa. The decision to establish a classical college for the young men of Bytown had apparently been taken by Bishop Guigues even before his consecration on 30 July 1848. In August the first sod was turned, and in September the Collège de St-Joseph opened in a building that had cost $250. The first prospectus announced a policy of bilingualism and reflected the influence of the Collège Joliette:

> The regular course of instruction will embrace what is generally taught in other Colleges. Besides Latin and other classical studies, bookkeeping will form an essential part of the course. The study of English and French Languages, which are indispensably necessary in all localities where these two languages are spoken, will likewise be peculiarly insisted upon.

The college was renamed the College of Bytown in 1849. Ten years later, the teaching of theology was introduced, and in 1861, coincident with the renaming of the city, it became the College of Ottawa. In 1866 it would receive a charter as the University of Ottawa. From the outset, control of the institution was vested in the Oblate fathers.

In summary, of the many purposes which at one time or another have been advanced as reasons for establishing and maintaining universities and colleges, only two are pertinent to Quebec during the French régime - the training of clergy and the general education of the future leaders of society. Of these, the first was paramount; like the New England Puritans, the French Canadians dreaded 'to leave an illiterate ministry to the churches when our present ministers shall lie in the Dust.' But there was also from the start the desire to provide an education of a certain type for the more gifted laymen; hence the acceptance by the Jesuit college and by the Petit Séminaire de Québec of young boys who had no intention of becoming priests. These two purposes continued to be the motivating forces behind the efforts to provide higher education in Quebec throughout the century following the conquest; indeed, they remained the dominant purposes until the twentieth century.

By 1850 the training of doctors and lawyers was recognized as an additional reason for having a university in French Canada and there were some suggestions of the advantages to be gained by making provision for advanced work in the sciences. Hence the establishment of faculties of law, medicine, and arts by Université Laval within a year or two of the granting of its charter in 1852. Nonetheless, in 1860 higher education in French Canada consisted largely of the work being carried on in the séminaires and in the collèges classiques. There had been no fundamental change in the role played by the former since the establishment of the Grand Séminaire at Quebec in the seventeenth century, though two centuries had brought improvement in facilities and technique. But there had been a significant change, almost a reinterpretation, in the attitude adopted towards the cours classique. Increasingly from 1790 to 1860 it was seen as an instrument for the preservation of the French Canadian tradition; its integrated emphasis upon the French language, the Roman Catholic religion, and a culture based firmly upon the study of the humanities was seen as a bulwark against the threat represented by a Protestant, English-speaking materialism. Etienne Parent's phrase for the classical colleges was 'nos citadelles nationales.'

NOTES TO CHAPTER 2

1   L.-P. Audet, *Historie de l'enseignement au Québec, 1608-1971* (1971), I, 172
2   A.-E. Gosselin, *L'Instruction au Canada sous le régime français (1635-1760)* (1911), 251
3   Audet, *Histoire,* I, 173-4
4   Ibid., I, 174-5
5   Gosselin, *L'Instruction,* 376
6   Audet, *Histoire,* I, 160-9
7   Ibid., I, 193-202
8   P. Desjardins, *Le Collège Ste-Marie de Montréal: la fondation, le fondateur* (1948), 8
9   Gosselin, *L'Instruction,* 450
10 L. Groulx, *L'Enseignement français au Canada I: Dans le Québec* (1931), 25. For the status of the notary, see A. Vachon, *Histoire du notariat canadien, 1621-1960* (1962), 3-50
11 Groulx, *L'Enseignement,* I, 26; Audet, *Histoire,* I, 202-3
12 Audet, *Histoire,* I, 146-50
13 Groulx, *L'Enseignement,* I, 25. For Royal George College see also O. Maurault, 'L'Université de Montréal, *Cahiers des Dix,* 17 (1952), 11-12; and L. Pouliot, 'L'Enseignement universitaire catholique au Canada français de 1760 à 1860, *Rev. d'Histoire de l'Amérique Française,* 12 (1958), 156
14 Quebec, Committee of the Council on the Subject of Promoting the Means of Education / Comité du Conseil sur l'objet d'augmenter les moiens d'education, *Report / Rapport* (1790), 26. The French version is reprinted in 'Lettre de Monseigneur Hubert en reponse au Président de Comité nommé pour l'exécution d'une université mixte en Canada, 18 novembre, 1789' in H. Têtu and C.-O. Gagnon, eds., *Mandements, Lettres pastorales et circulaires des Evêques de Québec* (1888), II.
15 L.-P. Audet, *Le Système scolaire de la Province de Québec,* II (1951), 185. The project for a university in 1790 is treated thoroughly by Audet in *Système,* II, 143-219. See also F.-J. Audet, 'Simon Sanguinet et le projet d'université de 1790,' *Trans. Royal Society Canada 1936,* Section 1, 53-61; and H. Neatby, *Quebec: the Revolutionary Age 1760-1791* (1966), 242-8
16 *Report / Rapport,* 26

17 Dorchester to Lord Grenville, 10 November 1790, quoted by
    Audet, *Système* II, 207
18 Ibid., 7-8
19 Cardinal Antonelli to Mgr Hubert, 6 April 1791, quoted by
    Audet, *Système,* II, 170
20 Groulx, *L'Enseignement,* I, 119. For Dorchester College, see
    Pouliot, 'L'Enseignement universitaire,' 157-9
21 For the founding and early development of the five surviving
    colleges, see their centennial histories; these are listed
    under 'classical colleges in the bibliography. J.B. Meilleur,
    Mémorial de l'education du Bas-Canada 1615-1855 (1860) contains
    brief descriptions of all colleges mentioned in this chapter
    except St-Denis-sur-Richelieu, for which see H. Morisseau, 'Un
    Collège classique à Saint-Denis-sur-Richelieu dès 1805,' *Rev.
    Univ. Ottawa,* 18 (1948), 356-66.
22 Also classified as collèges classiques were three English-
    language institutions; St Francis College at Richmond, and
    the McGill High Schools at Montreal and Quebec.
23 P.-J.-O. Chauveau, *L'Instruction publique au Canada* (1876), 57
24 Groulx, *L'Enseignement,* I, 269-70
25 For the situation in Upper Canada, see, R.S. Harris, 'The
    Evolution of a Provincial University in Ontario' in D.F. Dadson,
    On Higher Education ... (1966), 13-17. For the influence of
    developments in other Roman Catholic jurisdictions, see P.
    Sylvain, 'Les Difficiles Débuts de l'Université Laval,' *Cahiers
    des Dix,* 36 (1971), 211-34.
26 Université Laval, *Mémoire ... avec pièces justicatives* (1862),
    ix
27 Ibid.
28 H. Provost, *Historique de la Faculté des Arts de l'Université
    Laval, 1852-1952* (1952), 11

3

The Development of Higher Education in English Canada 1787-1860

As in French Canada, the same two purposes - the training of
clergy and the general education of the future leaders of society -
underlay the establishment of the first colleges and universities
in English-speaking Canada. These are, of course, related purposes. As John Stuart Mill long ago reminded us, men are men
before they are lawyers, doctors, business men, or priests.
There had to be a petit séminaire as well as a grand séminaire
if the professional training of priests in French Canada was to
be based on a broad general culture; similarly in English Canada
a theological college was hardly practical unless there were an
arts college to which the students could first proceed. Sometimes, as at Queen's and Acadia, the 'literary institution' came
first, the theological school or faculty later. Sometimes, as
at St Michael's and at St Francis Xavier, the order was reversed.
Sometimes, as at Knox College and the Congregational College of
British North America, the theological seminary relied on a nearby university to provide the literary course. But one way or
another, theology invariably presupposed arts.

The education of clergymen was not, however, the primary reason
for the establishment of the earliest colleges in the British
colonies - the King's Colleges at Windsor, Fredericton, and
Toronto - or, theoretically, of the non-denominational universities of McGill and Dalhousie. The founders of these institutions
were impelled by precisely the same motive as inspired their
French Canadian contemporaries who were at this time busily engaged in founding collèges classiques; the preservation of a
tradition, in this case, the British tradition. These colleges
too, in their own way, were to be 'citadelles nationales,' the
enemy being a republican United States rather than a Protestant
English-speaking materialism.

The King's College at Windsor, Nova Scotia, and Fredericton,
New Brunswick, were founded by United Empire Loyalists, some of
whom had expressed their belief that the threat of republicanism

necessitated the establishment of Canadian colleges even before they had arrived on Canadian soil. Five clergymen, including Charles Inglis, who would be appointed the first Bishop of Nova Scotia in 1787, addressed a letter to the governor-in-chief of British North America, Sir Guy Carleton, from New York on 8 March 1783, in which they pointed out the dire consequences of failure to provide immediately for the education of the sons of British emigrants:

> The founding of a College or Seminary of learning on a liberal plan in that province where youth may receive a virtuous education and can be qualified for the learned professions, is, we humbly conceive, a measure of the greatest consequence, as it would diffuse religious literature, loyalty and good morals among His Majesty's subjects there. If such a seminary is not established the inhabitants will have no means of educating their sons at home, but will be under the necessity of sending them, for that purpose either to Great Britain or Ireland, which will be attended with an expense that few can bear, or else to some of the states of this continent, where they will soon imbibe principles that are unfavourable to the British tradition.[1]

The end result was not one college but two. In 1784 the portion of Nova Scotia north of the Bay of Fundy became the colony of New Brunswick; thus a college or seminary of learning was established there at Fredericton in 1787 and another at Windsor, Nova Scotia, in 1789, both of which were originally secondary schools. King's College at Windsor obtained degree-granting powers in 1802 and began to exercise them in 1807. At Fredericton the institution was chartered as the College of New Brunswick in 1800 but did not offer instruction beyond the secondary level until the 1820s; in 1829 it was rechristened King's College, Fredericton.

The basis for a third King's College, at York (Toronto from 1834) in Upper Canada, had also been laid in the late eighteenth century and under the same Anglican and United Empire Loyalist auspices. Upper Canada was created by the Constitutional Act of 1791, and its first lieutenant governor, John Graves Simcoe, a veteran of the Revolutionary War, was active in stimulating migration of the Loyalists to the area. He, too, before coming to Canada, felt strongly the need for a college. As it happened, he failed in his mission, but he was indirectly responsible for obtaining the land grant that ultimately provided the endowment for King's College, Toronto, which became the University of Toronto in 1850. What is significant, here, however, is the attitude of Simcoe towards higher education. On 30 April 1795 he wrote to Jacob Mountain, the Anglican bishop of Quebec, arguing that liberal education was indispensable for those who were to govern themselves. The people already enjoyed the forms and the privileges of the British Constitution and consequently had the requisites for governing themselves. They 'must ever remain a part of the British Empire, provided they shall become sufficiently capable and enlightened to understand their relative position and to manage their own power to the public interest.'[2] Simcoe felt that the establishment of the university in the capital, 'the residence of the Governor and the Council, the Bishop, the heads of Law, and of the general quality of the inhabitants ... would be most useful to inculcate just principles, habits and manners into the rising generation.'

Four years later, Bishop Mountain, subsequently a paramount figure in the founding of McGill, was to write to the lieutenant governor of Quebec in a similar vein:

Let me be permitted, then, to suggest the danger which may result to the political principles and to the future character as subjects of such of our young men among the higher ranks as the exigency of the case obliges their parents to send for classical education to the colleges of the United States. In these Seminaries, most assuredly, they are not likely to imbibe that attachment to our constitution in Church and State, that veneration for the Government of their country, and that loyalty to their King, to which it is so particularly necessary in the present time to give all the advantages of early predilection in order to fix them deeply both in the understanding and the heart.[3]

This distrust of the United States continued for half a century.

The type of institution envisaged by the Loyalists and in fact realized at the King's colleges, as well as at Bishop's and until the 1850s at McGill, is suggested by a resolution of the Nova Scotia Legislature in 1787 to provide two staff members for a projected college. It called for a professor of mathematics and natural philosophy and, as principal, 'an exemplary clergyman of the established church well-skilled in classical learning, divinity, and moral philosophy.[4] The King's College, Windsor Statutes of 1802 were more specific: 'No professor directly or indirectly shall teach or maintain any atheistical, deistical or democratical principles, or any doctrine contrary to the Christian faith, or to good morals, or subversive of the British constitution, as by law established.'[5] Nor were the restrictions limited to the classroom. 'No member of the University shall frequent the Romish mass, or the meeting Houses of Presbyterians, Baptists, or Methodists, or the Conventicles, or places of Worship of any other dissenters from the Church of England ... or shall be present at any seditious or rebellious meetings.'[6]

So far as the academic program was concerned, the model for the King's colleges was what historians now refer to as 'Unreformed Oxford.' T.B. Akins thus described the earliest known course of study, that of King's College, Windsor in 1814:

FIRST CLASS

Works read under the President
Greek Testament
Grotius
Hebrew Bible
Euclid, Algebra
Xenophon
Cicero, Orations, de Amicitia
  and de Senectute
Horace
Virgil, Georgics
Sophocles

Books read under Dr. Cochran
Sophocles
Longinus
Horace, Ars Poetica
Virgil, Georgics
Logic
Cicero, de Officiis and de
  Oratore
Burlemaque, Natural Law

SECOND CLASS

Greek Testament
Grotius
Homer
Horace
Xenophon, Memorabilia
Demosthenes
Cicero, Orations, de Amicitia,
  etc.

Logic
Cicero, de Oratore and de
  Officiis
Xenophon, Cyr
Juvenal

THIRD CLASS

Euclid, Wood's Algebra

Logic
Cicero, de Oratore and de
  Officiis

FOURTH CLASS

Sophocles

Homer
Horace
Logic
Cicero, de Oratore[7]

The emphasis here was almost entirely on the classics, both Greek
and Latin, and the related subjects of logic and rhetoric. Mathematics and natural philosophy, which were receiving significant
attention at contemporary Cambridge, were slighted. The professors
were tutors under whom the books (or works) were read. The same
situation obtained at the College of New Brunswick when it began
to offer instruction at the university level in 1824. All instruction was provided by the principal, Dr Somerville, and it 'encom-
passed the Greek and Roman classics, mathematics, logic, the
principles of universal grammar and the elements of moral science.'[8]

By the 1840s, the course of study in a Church of England college
had become broader through increased attention to mathematics
and the introduction of some natural philosophy (i.e., physics)
and natural history (i.e., botany and zoology), but, in harmony
with the contemporary outlook of the French Canadian authorities,
instruction continued to be based on principles of the Christian
religion. This is how Bishop Strachan concluded his remarks at
the opening of King's College, Toronto, in 1843:

It only remains to make a very few remarks on the way it proposes to meet the requirements of the Royal Charter, which
establishes a College for the education of youth in the principles of the Christian Religion, and for their instruction in
the various branches of Science and Literature, which are taught
in the Universities of Great Britain and Ireland. Such requirements embrace all useful knowledge - Classical Literature,
Mathematical and Physical Science, Mental Philosophy, Law and
the Healing Art, in all their various departments; and they
are all, as the charter provides, to be based on our Holy
Religion, which ought indeed to be the beginning and end of
education in a Christian country.[9]

One of the problems facing colleges like King's in seeking to
establish themselves as institutions deserving public support was
the dissatisfaction caused by the tendency of the authorities to
interpret 'our Holy Religion' as Anglican doctrine. Most Baptists,
Congregationalists, Methodists, Presbyterians, and Roman Catholics
agreed that religion should be taught in a university, but they
were not prepared to equate religion with the beliefs of the
Church of England.

There was, however, a further sound objection to the kind of
curriculum offered by the King's colleges, one raised by non-
Anglicans and Anglicans alike. Was a course of study concentrated
largely on the classics the most appropriate one for the future
leaders of Canada? Despite strong affirmative cases put by individuals such as the provost of Trinity College at his installation
in 1852,[10] or the president of King's College, Fredericton, in a
convocation address in 1851,[11] the claims of science from the
1830s on had become increasingly difficult to deny. In 1853 Sir
Edmund Head, governor of New Brunswick, provided funds from his
own pocket for lectures and practical instruction in civil engineering,[12] and in 1854 the New Brunswick legislature voted to
establish a royal commission to investigate the state of King's
College, Fredericton. The commission reported:

In considering the System of Collegiate Education best adapted
to the circumstances of New Brunswick, we were unanimously of
the opinion that it ought to be at once comprehensive, special,
and practical; that it ought to embrace those Branches of
Learning which are usually taught in colleges both in Great
Britain and the United States, - and Special Courses of Instruction
adapted to the Agricultural, Mechanical, Manufacturing, and
Commercial pursuits and interests of New Brunswick; and that the
subjects and modes of Instruction in the Sciences and Modern
Languages (including English, French, and German) should have
a practical reference to those pursuits and interests.[13]

The report recommended that a special two-year course be established in civil engineering and land-surveying (including the
principles of architecture), in agriculture (including history
and diseases of farm animals), and in commerce and navigation

(with some options 'according as he may intend to be a Merchant, or Navigator'). Five years passed before the legislature acted upon the recommendations of the royal commission and, needless to say, they did not adopt all of the recommendations. However, in 1859 King's College, Fredericton, became the University of New Brunswick with a layman as president and with no chair of theology.

Times had in fact changed, and no one saw this more clearly than Sir Edmund Head. 'It must be recollected,' he wrote,

> that a large portion of the settlers in New Brunswick at the end of the last century were American Loyalists who brought from an older and more advanced Country a feeling for British Institutions and they desired to promote knowledge of a higher kind. These persons and many of their sons could feel a pride in the notion of possessing a University of their own, which has ceased to animate the next generation not imbued with precisely the same feeling and more sensible of the immediate necessity for gaining their own livelihood and supplying their material wants.[14]

But it was not only the loss of a first fine careless rapture and an increasing concern with the economic facts of North American life which explain the changed emphasis so forcibly demonstrated at Fredericton in the 1850s. To be reckoned with also was the infusion of the Scottish tradition formally introduced by Lord Dalhousie in 1820 when he laid the cornerstone of the University that was to bear his name:

> Before I proceed in this ceremony, I think it is necessary to state to you gentlemen, the object and intention of this important work ... This College of Halifax is founded for the instruction of youth in the higher Classics and in all Philosophical studies; it is formed in imitation of the University of Edinburgh; its doors will be open to all who profess the Christian religion; to the youth of His Majesty's North American Colonies, to strangers residing here, to gentlemen of the military as well as the learned professions, to all, in short, who may be disposed to devote a small part of their time to study.[15]

This was not the first occasion on which the relevance of the Scottish university system to the Canadian scene had been noted. The Scottish universities relied on the lecture as the chief means of instruction. That this method had practical advantages was recognized as early as 1815 by John Strachan, an Aberdeen graduate. Strachan was deeply involved in the discussions of the establishment of McGill University and in a letter to three members of the legislature of Lower Canada he strongly urged the acceptance of the Scottish model. His argument was entirely practical. Oxford and Cambridge were well adapted to a rich, populated, and learned country like England, but they were not an appropriate model for Canada, a colony which could afford neither professors who lectured once a week nor the fellowships which allowed tutorial instruction.[16]

Furthermore, the Scottish curriculum already had been introduced to Canada, and by 1850 its effectiveness had been demonstrated. Thomas McCulloch, a presbyterian minister who as early as 1805 contemplated an institution 'to train the youth of the province for better things, and perhaps for the Ministry,' began in 1808 to conduct a grammar school in his own house at Pictou, Nova Scotia and in 1815 he established the Pictou Academy.[17] The curriculum followed the pattern of the Scottish universites: Latin, Greek, logic, moral philosophy, mathematics, political economy, and rhetoric (i.e., exercises in analysis and composition). In 1838, after 30 years' experience in educating Canadian youth, McCulloch, on the point of assuming the presidency of Dalhousie, rejected the proposal that the classics receive special attention:

That he who teaches these languages in Dalhousie College should know his business well, its respectability requires. But that boys should in Halifax or elsewhere spend six or seven years upon Latin and Greek and then four more in college partly occupied with the same languages is a waste of human life adapted neither to the circumstances or the prosperity of Nova Scotia. In the present state of this province all that is requisite is a professor who can give his pupils specimens of just translation and instil into them ideas of accuracy and interpretation. Afterwards if they choose to devote themselves to the study of languages, their collegiate instruction will contribute to their success, but should they direct attention to the real business of life they will not have just cause to complain that they have spent their youth upon studies foreign to their success. If Dalhousie College acquire usefulness and eminence it will be not by an imitation of Oxford, but as an institution of science and practical intelligence.[18]

McCulloch concluded by stating the absolute necessity of establishing a chair of natural history so that adequate instruction in geology, mineralogy, botany, and zoology could be provided. 'This is requisite to render the College a scientific institution. To give it splendour and to give its students general intelligence it ought to contain every kind of natural production to be found in the province and also as much as possible from other quarters.' This was the basic Scottish point of view, a view held both by emigrants like Strachan and native born Canadians like J.W. Dawson and G.M. Grant who went to Scotland for their university education. Such men were particularly influential in the nineteenth-century development of Dalhousie, McGill, Queen's, and Toronto, the four institutions which above all others set the pattern for Canadian higher education in the first 50 years of the twentieth century.

To this point in our review of the early development of higher education in English Canada, we have stressed theory and first principle. But there is more to education than theory. Beneath the rhetoric of convocation addresses and commission reports, and at times ignored in the enthusiastic exposition of what should be done, lie a grammar and a logic. The logic is that of existing circumstances, particularly the financial; the grammar, quite literally, is that of the entering students - the standard of academic achievement the institution can assume as a point of departure. What Anglican divines, colonial governors, college presidents, and royal commissioners might regard as fit and proper for a Canadian college was one thing. What was actually practicable, given the professors, students, and resources at hand, might well be quite another.

It must be remembered that until the 1850s there was no such thing as public secondary education in Canada - or for that matter in any other part of the English-speaking world. Without exception every Canadian university and college that traces its development back as far as 1860 has at some stage in its history been directly involved in the secondary field - Laval is no exception if we regard the collèges classiques as an integral part of its faculty of arts. In some instances (Acadia, Victoria, all three King's colleges) the institution began as a secondary school. In other cases (McGill, St Michael's, Queen's, Trinity) a feeder school soon became desirable - or even necessary. For many years a secondary school was all that Dalhousie could provide. The situation improved as soon as the first steps were taken to establish free school systems (Upper and Lower Canada, 1846; Prince Edward Island, 1852; Nova Scotia, 1854; New Brunswick, 1871), but the first demand in developing such systems was not for secondary but for elementary schools. It was many years before competent secondary schools were organized in the various provinces. These facts must be recalled when assessing the admission requirements and undergraduate offerings of the Canadian colleges, not only in 1860 but in 1890 as well. Indeed, they must be borne in mind in considering the period from 1908 to 1920 when the newly created provinces of Alberta and Saskatchewan were launching their infant universities in a brave but sparsely populated new world.

It must be remembered too that the resources available to early Canadian colleges were limited. Until the 1840s Canada was a frontier community. The first building of King's College, Windsor, had to be completed with wood because a competent mason could not be obtained anywhere in the Maritimes. The history of any one of the early colleges would provide ample illustration of the extraordinary difficulties which were faced and somehow overcome. The situation at Acadia was typical.

Acadia College opened on 21 January 1839 in rooms provided in the Horton Collegiate Academy, a secondary school established by the Baptists in 1829. There were about twenty students, and two professors, both clergymen: John Pryor (classics, natural philosophy), who had been teaching at the Academy since 1830 and Edward Crawley (rhetoric, logic, moral philosophy, mathematics), a disappointed candidate for one of the chairs at the recently opened

Dalhousie University. In January 1840, Isaac Chipman (mathematics, natural philosophy) joined the staff. When the first four graduates received their degrees in 1843, the college still had no building of its own, but the following year an impressive three-storey edifice was built literally without money. From the winter of 1842 to the spring of 1844, Chipman in his spare moments canvassed the Baptist constituency of the Maritimes, appealing not for money (earlier attempts to raise funds had been dismally unsuccessful) but for materials and labour. His success was extraordinary. By the spring of 1844, 22,000 feet of lumber had been assembled. Chipman, 'besides attending faithfully to his class duties,' then proceeded to supervise the construction of the building:

The citizens of Wolfville carried the materials from the wharf to the hill. Boards and laths were sent from Liverpool, Truro, and Onslow; nails, paint, glass, oil, putty, and sheet lead came from Saint John and Halifax; doors and bricks were made at Annapolis and Bridgetown; other gifts came from Amherst and Yarmouth. So general was the interest and enthusiasm that donations of food, clothing and other articles were sent to the resourceful Chipman, who exchanged them for building materials or gave them as wages to the workmen.[19]

A different if related kind of crisis arose in 1850. Since there was no money available to pay the professors' modest salaries, Pryor and Chipman resigned (Crawley had assumed a pastorate in 1846 and his successor had already resigned). But Chipman was persuaded to withdraw his resignation (he also 'forgave' £400 due to him), and for the remainder of the session he carried on with the aid of a teacher from the academy. The Rev. J.M. Cramp was installed as president in time for the session 1851-52, but in the following session he too was required to carry on with the aid of an academy teacher and a senior student when Chipman and four students were drowned on a geological expedition. The return of Pryor and the other resigned professor restored the situation to 'normal' in 1853, but by this time a theological institute had been added to the responsibilities assigned to the teaching staff. It is not surprising that men like Cramp and Chipman contributed few articles to learned journals. Nor is it surprising that on occasion they were called upon to offer instruction in half-a-dozen different subjects.

The history of Acadia in this early period is essentially the story of the triumph of the individual. It was Chipman who held Acadia together in the 1840s, and it was Cramp who placed the institution on a firm and continuing basis in the 1850s and 1860s. It was Cramp too, one suspects, who gave Acadia the character which it has maintained ever since. The history of higher education in Canada throughout the nineteenth century continually reveals the importance of the right individual appearing at the right time - Ryerson at Victoria, Dawson at McGill, Brydone Jack at New Brunswick, Grant at Queen's, and there are others. Not every institution had its great man; the failure of Bishop's and King's College, Windsor, to fulfil their expected promise is perhaps as much as anything due to the fact that a Cramp or a Dawson never appeared. Toronto provides an interesting exception. Apart from Strachan, whose views were out of harmony with the character of the institution as it actually developed, there is no single great man in Toronto's history, no one whose influence is comparable to that of Dawson or Grant. But Toronto's position as a state-supported university in the country's richest province made its survival and expansion inevitable.

NOTES TO CHAPTER 3

1 Quoted by F.W. Vroom, *A Chronicle of King's College* (1941), 10
2 J.G. Hodgins, ed., *Documentary History of Education in Upper Canada* (1894), I, 12
3 Quoted by C. Macmillan, *McGill and its Story, 1821-1921* (1921), 19-20
4 Vroom, *King's College*, 12
5 Ibid., 40
6 Ibid., 41
7 T.B. Akins, *A Brief Account of the Origins, Endowment and Progress of the University of King's College, Windsor, Nova Scotia* (1865), 73
8 W.D. Pacey, 'The Humanist Tradition' in A.G. Bailey, ed., *The University of New Brunswick Memorial Volume* (1950), 57
9 Hodgins, *Doc. Hist.*, (1897) IV, 285
10 H. Melville, *The Rise and Progress of Trinity College, Toronto* (1852), 151-2
11 E. Jacob, *The Experience, Prospects, and Purposes of King's College, Fredericton* (1851), 15
12 D.G. Kerr, *Sir Edmund Head, a Scholarly Governor* (1954), 104-5
13 Hodgins, *Doc. Hist.*, (1906) XVI, 3
14 F.A. Firth, 'King's College, New Brunswick, 1828-1859' in Bailey, *UNB Memorial Volume*, 29-30
15 D.C. Harvey, *An Introduction to Dalhousie University* (1938), 19
16 Macmillan, *McGill and its Story*, 45-8
17 W. McCulloch, et al., *Life of Thomas McCulloch, D.D. Pictou* (1920), 37-50
18 Harvey, *Dalhousie University*, 49-50
19 R.S. Longley, *Acadia University 1838-1938* (1938), 46. Longley's history is also the source for the statements in the following paragraph.

4
Arts and Science

The choice of 1860 as the first of the five points in time which
have been selected for detailed analysis in this study of the
development of higher education in Canada has been dictated by
matters of more significance than the largely accidental fact that
a nineteen-year old British prince happened in this year to pay a
visit to a number of Canadian universities. During the 1850s a
number of developments occurred which, taken together, gave
Canadian higher education an identity and a cohesion not possessed
ten or even five years earlier. There was nothing notably Canadian
about any of the institutions with degree-granting powers in 1849.
What was being done at Acadia, Bishop's, McGill, Queen's, Victoria,
and the three King's colleges was an imitation of what was being
done at Oxford or at Edinburgh or at a New England college, and
the instruction offered was confined to the liberal arts and to
the traditional professional fields - theology, law, and medicine.
By 1860, however, a French-Canadian university had been established,
the King's colleges at Fredericton and Toronto had been reorganized
as provincial universities, agriculture, engineering and commerce
had been added to the curriculum, and there had begun to emerge
an arts and science curriculum that could be described as distinctively Canadian. The arts curricula of 1850 were purely deriva-
tive - the model whether English, Scottish, Irish, or American is
readily seen. However, in the 1850s the several influences began
to merge, and in the English-speaking institutions a new pattern,
different from any of the models, began to come into focus in response to the conditions of Canadian life.
    The classical course taught in the Roman Catholic colleges, in
Quebec and elsewhere, was also a transplantation to Canadian soil
and as yet revealed no distinctively Canadian characteristics other
than, in French-speaking Canada, an increased concern for the study
of English. But 1860 is nonetheless a significant date for the
cours classique. Though none of the classical colleges of Quebec
had yet affiliated with Laval - this would begin in 1862 - they

were already under its directing influence and the systematization of the classical course was almost complete. Henceforth even minor variations in the program would be more difficult to introduce or maintain.

THE THREE B.A. PROGRAMS

In 1860 three distinguishable arts curricula were being offered for the B.A. degree in Canada.[1] One was an eight (sometimes a seven) year course offered in the Roman Catholic colleges. A second was a three year course imitating either the Oxford or the Edinburgh model. The third, a four year course, while resembling the program offered in the New England liberal arts college, was the first draft of a distinctively Canadian pattern. We shall begin by examining the older patterns.

In 1857 there appeared in the *Journal of Education for Lower Canada* an outline of the course of study offered at the Petit Séminaire de Québec. Prepared by P.-J.-O. Chauveau, the superintendent of education for Lower Canada, it is a detailed account of the studies pursued in each of ten classes. The first eight classes (preparatory, seventh up to third, belles lettres, and rhetoric) were said to constitute the classical course, with the remaining two years (junior philosophy, senior philosophy) being devoted to moral and intellectual philosophy, mathematics, and physical sciences; but as commonly understood the classical course began at either the sixth or fifth class and included the two years of philosophy. The work in the preparatory, seventh and sixth classes, as outlined below, was at the elementary rather than the secondary level - French, Latin, and English Grammar, the elements of arithmetic, 'preliminary notions of geography,' and 'sacred history.'

The fifth class go over again Lhomond's latin syntax, begin the *method* by the same author, continue Chapsal's french syntax, translate *Cornelius Nepos, Commentaria Caesaris, Ovidi Metamorphoses* and *Virgil's Eglogues*; they learn ancient history, the geography of Asia, the last part of arithmetic and commence book keeping. They also translate Cornelius from latin into english.

In the fourth class the latin grammar is again reviewed and completed. The latin authors are Caesar, Quintus Curtius, Sallustus and Virgil's Eneid. Burnouf's greek grammar is begun, Esop's greek fables are translated. They also learn Roman history, the geography of Africa and of Oceania, a modern history in english and they translate Caesar into english. They write french, latin, english and greek composition. They practice arithmetic and book keeping. They also learn latin prosody and begin to compose latin verses.

In the third class they review latin prosody and review and continue greek grammar. The Latin authors are Virgil and Cicero: the greek, the Acts of the Apostles and the dialogues of Lucian.

They learn the geography of America; they begin mensuration, the elements of geometry, and french composition.

The next class is called indifferently the second class or *Belles-Lettres*. A course of literature is gone through with numerous examples from the best authors; french, latin and english composition are specially attended to. The latin authors are Virgil, Cicero, and Horace, the greek, Xenophon and Homer.

Rhetoric is the name of the next class. The principles of eloquence are expounded and illustrated by numerous examples. Elocution is attended to; french, latin, english and greek composition are the subject of much attention. Latin verses in this as in the three preceding classes are composed by the pupils. As in the preceding classes some of the latin and greek authors are translated into english. Algebra is introduced. The latin authors are Cicero, Horace and *Conciones latinae*; the greek: Homer and Demosthenes ...

The junior class of philosophy is taught logic, and metaphysics, from the *Institutiones Philosophicae*, written by Mr. Demers ... They review and continue algebra and geometry, they learn rectilinear and spherical trigonometry, the application of algebra to geometry, conical sections, curves in general, the elements of differential and integral calculus and the application of all these to land surveying, drawing, astronomy and navigation. They review book keeping and are taught some notions of military architecture and engineering.

The senior class of Philosophy learns ethics, natural philosophy, natural history, astronomy, chemistry and its application to agriculture and the arts, and the elements of civil architecture and civil engineering.[2]

Chauveau's only criticism of this course, which was essentially what he himself had taken at the Petit Séminaire in the 1830s was the failure to introduce the geography and history of Canada at an earlier stage than the Third Class. His general conclusion was that 'the curriculum as above expounded is one of the most complete and rational that can be found.'

One hundred years later it is difficult not to agree with this judgment. The main emphasis was clearly linguistic, with primary emphasis on the classics – six years of Latin and three of Greek. French and English were also stressed and, although mathematics (other than elementary arithmetic and introductory algebra) was postponed until the final two years, considerable attention was then given both to theory, including the calculus, and its practical applications. Science was reserved for the final year but it included chemistry, physics, biology, and astronomy.

In terms of degrees awarded, success in the classical college course was based on performance at two sets of examinations supervised by Université Laval. The first, called *Lettres*, was taken at the conclusion of the sixth year of the eight year course (Chauveau's Rhétorique); the second (*Science*) was taken at the

conclusion of the eighth year (Chauveau's Senior Philosophy).
The B.A. degree was granted to those who obtained an average of
66% or better at *each* set of examinations. The student who obtained
66% at lettres and at least 33% at science received a B. ès Lettres,
while the B. ès Sciences was awarded to those who obtained 66% at
science and at least 33% at lettres. There were, of course,
examinations set by the individual college each year and tests
almost every week in most subjects; but the passing of the two
major sets of examinations was crucial.

A similar emphasis on major examinations characterized the
Oxford-Cambridge tradition, the model for the three year degree
programs offered in the English-speaking colleges of Canada at
this time. Here success was measured in terms of the passing of
specific examinations rather than on the completion of specific
courses. Thus at the University of Trinity College in 1860 the
degree was granted on successful completion of three sets of examinations: the Matriculation (on entry), the Previous (at the end
of the fifth term - there were three terms each year), and the
B.A. Degree Examination (after nine terms). At Queen's College,
Kingston the Previous Examination was placed at the end of the
second year and a Primary Examination introduced at the close of
the first. In the Anglican colleges, where additional texts were
prescribed for honours, there was also the tendency to use the
terminology of the Oxford Schools. Thus at King's College,
Windsor there were final degree examinations *in Literis Humanioribus,
in Disciplinis Mathematicis et Physicis,* and *in Scientia Naturali*;
in 1861 *in Linguis Recentioribus* would be added.

The content of the Oxford-type course can be deduced from the
subjects set for the Previous and Degree Examinations by Trinity
in 1860:

Previous Examination
One of the Historical Books of the New Testament
Paley's Evidences of Christianity
The Church Catechism
One Greek author ⎱   to be fixed at the beginning
One Latin author ⎰   of the Lent Term
Latin Prose Composition
Euclid, I-IV, VI
Algebra to the end of the Binomial Theorem
Trigonometry to the end of the solution of triangles

B.A. Degree Examination
Old and New Testament History
One of the Historical Books of the New Testament
The Articles of the Church of England
Two Greek authors ⎱   to be fixed at the end of
Two Latin authors ⎰   Easter Term, 2nd year
Greek and Roman History
Latin Prose Composition
Euclid

Algebra to the end of the Binomial Theorem
Trigonometry to the end of the solution of triangles
Mechanics
Hydrostatics

Students at Trinity were also required to attend lectures in physics for four terms and in fortifications, surveying, and physiology in its relation to natural theology for one term each. Trinity, it should be added, was unusual in its ignoring of formal philosophy. Normally, as at King's, Windsor, and Bishop's, logic, rhetoric, and intellectual and moral philosophy received specific attention, and where the Scottish tradition was followed moral philosophy constituted the capstone of the course. At Queen's the degree program was as follows:

First Year
Junior Latin: Cicero, *De Amicitiae*; Virgil, *Aeneid* VI; Horace, *Odes I*; Prosody; Prose Composition; Roman Antiquities
Junior Greek: Homer, *Iliad VI*; Lucian, *Vita et Charon*; Prose Composition
Junior Mathematics: Geometry, Euclid 1-6; Algebra; Plane Trigonometry; Logarithms
Junior Natural History: Preliminary Course (2 lectures per week)
Additional Set Texts for Primary Examination: The Four Gospels & The Acts (in English); Bullion's *English Grammar*; Spalding's *History of English Literature*, Part 1; White *Eighteen Christian Centuries* (1-5)
Second Year
Senior Latin: Cicero, *Pro Milone*; Horace, *Epodes*; Virgil, *Georgics*, Prose Composition
Senior Greek: Demosthenes, *Philippics*; Euripides, *Alcestis*; Prosody; Prose Composition; Greek Antiquities
Senior Mathematics: Euclid 11 and 12 (in part), Plane and Spherical Trigonometry; Conic Sections; Differential and Integral Calculus
Natural Philosophy: Mechanics; Natural Philosophy [Physics]
Senior Natural History: Histology, Botany, Zoology, Geology, Mineralogy
Additional Set Texts for Previous Examination: St. Luke's Gospel (in Greek); Spalding's *History of English Literature*, Part II; White's *Eighteen Christian Centuries* (6-13); Paley's *Natural Theology*
Third Year
Third Latin: Tacitus, *Annals* Bk. I; Livy, Bk. 21; Terence, *Phormio*; Composition
Third Greek: Plato, *Apology* and *Crito*; Sophocles, *Oedipus at Colonnus*; Composition, Greek and Roman Antiquities
Third Math., Natural Philosophy, Newton, *Principia* 1-3; Hydrostatics; Astronomy
Philosophy: Rhetoric (Whately, Part I); Spalding's *History of*

English Literature, Part III; Logic (Whately, Bk. II); Metaphysics (Hamilton's Lectures, 11-20); Moral Science (Alexander)
Additional Set Texts for Degree Examination: Epistle to the
Ephesians (in Greek); White's *Eighteen Christian Centuries*
(14-18); Paley, *Evidences*, Part I.

When we turn to the four-year course of study for the B.A. degree
at McGill, we find ourselves in a different world:
First Year
Classics, French or German, English Literature, Mathematics,
History, Elementary Chemistry
Second Year
Classics, French or German, Logic, Mathematics, Botany, History,
Elocution
Third Year
Classics, French or German, Moral Philosophy and Mental Science,
Mathematics, Natural Philosophy and Astronomy, Zoology or
Chemistry
Fourth Year
Classics, French or German, Rhetoric, Natural Philosophy,
Mineralogy and Geology

A number of things are noteworthy here: the prescription of a
modern foreign language in all four years, the inclusion of science
in a developing sequence throughout the course, the appearance of
English literature as distinct from rhetoric, the absence of
theology. The classics are retained throughout the four-year
course but their proportional weight in any given year has been
reduced.
    It was also possible at McGill for a student to obtain a B.A.
with honours in one of classics, mathematics and natural philosophy,
or natural history by writing additional examinations on additional
texts set by the department concerned. But candidates for honours
were not exempt from any portion of the ordinary course.
    Essentially the same course was being offered at Toronto but,
as will be noted, with one significant difference:

First Year
Greek and Latin; English; French; History; Natural Theology and
Evidences of Christianity; Mathematics, Elementary Chemistry;
Elementary Natural History
Second Year
Greek and Latin; English; French and German; History; Logic;
Ethics and Metaphysics; Mathematics and Natural Philosophy;
Chemistry and Chemical Physics; Elementary Mineralogy, Geology,
and Physical Geography
Third Year
Greek and Latin; French, German and Italian; History and Ethno-
logy; Ethics, Metaphysics and Civil Polity; Mathematics and
Natural Philosophy; Applied Chemistry; Natural History

Fourth Year
Greek and Latin; English; French, German, Italian and Spanish;
Ethics, Metaphysics, and Logic; Mathematics and Natural Philo-
sophy; Organic and Qualitative Analytical Chemistry; Mineralogy,
Geology, and Physical Geography; Meteorology

Here again there are the modern languages, the science sequence,
the provision for English literature and the absence of divinity.
However, in contrast to McGill, Toronto would permit a candidate
for honours to disregard portions of the ordinary course: 'A
Candidate for honors in any department, who has obtained First
Class Honors in the University, in his first year, either in Greek
and Latin or in Mathematics, or in both Modern Languages and in
Natural Sciences, is not required in any other departments to pass
an examination in any branch in which he has already been examined
in his first year.' Similar regulations applied to the work of
the third and fourth years. Five departments offered honours
work; classical literature, logic, and rhetoric; metaphysics and
ethics; history and English literature; mathematics and natural
philosophy; modern languages.
  To provide such a range of subjects and particularly to offer
the specialized instruction involved in an honour course required
a large staff, and it was here that McGill and Toronto, located
in growing industrial and commercial centres, enjoyed a clear
advantage over institutions like King's, Bishop's, New Brunswick,
Queen's, and Victoria which were situated either in villages or
in small towns. In 1860 when Bishop's, King's, and Victoria had
five professors, McGill and Toronto had eleven. The difference
was particularly noticeable in the sciences. In addition to a
professor of mathematics and natural philosophy, both Toronto and
McGill had professors of chemistry and of natural history; Toronto
had a professor of mineralogy and geology as well. Bishop's had
only a professor of mathematics and natural philosophy. Victoria
had three professors in the mathematics-science area but one was
also responsible for modern languages.
  Nevertheless, within the limits necessarily imposed by a small
staff, two of the smaller institutions, Victoria and New Brunswick,
were pursuing the same path as Toronto and McGill. Victoria's
course had been four years from the outset; in 1860 it was arranged
as follows:

First Year
Classics, English Composition, Geometry, Chemistry, Scripture
History
Optional Study: French
Second Year
Classics, English Composition, Mathematics, Geology, and
Mineralogy
Optional Study: French

Third Year
Classics, English Composition, Natural Philosophy, Philosophy
Optional Study: German
Fourth Year
Classics, Mathematics and Astronomy, Political Economy, Evidences
of Christianity, Hebrew
Optional Study: German

At New Brunswick the same effect was attempted in a three year
course (a four year course was not introduced until 1887):

First Year
Classics, Mathematics, Chemistry, French, English, History
Second Year
Classics, Mathematics, Geology and Mineralogy, French, English,
History
Third Year
Classics, Mathematical Physics, Natural History, French,
English, History

One or two additional texts each year were set in classics, mathematics, science, French, and English, and honour certificates were
awarded to students who passed examinations on these texts.

The Victoria Course of Studies outlined above was essentially
the curriculum adopted when the college opened in 1841, and the
address delivered by Egerton Ryerson on his installation as the
first principal outlined the philosophy underlying the course.[3]
The aim was a broad general education. There were five branches
to the collegiate course (classics, mathematics, moral philosophy,
rhetoric and belles lettres, theology) and *together* they provided
the perspective and self-knowledge required of the clergyman,
the lawyer, and the doctor: 'Nor can I imagine any good reason
why the *Merchant* ... the Farmer, ... the Mechanic should be dis-
qualified, by want of a liberal education, from advancing the
literature, the science, the arts, the civilization of this
country.'[4] Ryerson was entirely convinced that a Canadian college
must pursue its own path:

As to the *general* character of the Education imparted in this
College, it is to be *British* and *Canadian*. Education is
designed specially to fit the student for activity and usefulness in the country of his birth or adoption; an object which
it is not likely to accomplish, if it be not adapted to, as
well as include an acquaintance with, the civil and social institutions, and society, and essential interests of his country.
Youth should be educated for their country as well as for themselves.[5]

But a college education was to be pre-professional, not professional: 'It is intended to maintain such a proportion between
the different branches of Literature and Science as to form a

44

proper *symmetry* and balance of character ... The object of the
Collegiate Course is not to teach what is *peculiar* to any one of
the professions; but to lay the foundation which is *common to them
all.*[6] Twenty years later Ryerson (and Victoria) held precisely
the same view.

By 1860, however, there were other views about the degree of
generality that was appropriate for the Canadian student. In that
year a select committee of the House of Assembly of Upper Canada
was appointed to investigate the 'University Question' and specifically to inquire into two charges: first, that there was extra-
vagance and deliberate waste in the administration of the University
of Toronto endowment, second that the Senate of the University of
Toronto had lowered the standard of higher education. The public
hearings before this committee provided an opportunity to debate
the question of honour courses, which as developed by this time
at Toronto permitted a considerable degree of specialization at
the undergraduate level. Ryerson speaking on behalf of Victoria
opposed the Toronto system:

> The individuals connected with myself, - the party unconnected
> with what may be called the National University of the Country,
> stand as the conservators of a high standard of education, and
> appear before you as the advocates of a thorough course of
> training that will discipline, in the most effectual manner,
> the powers of the mind and prepare the youth of our Country for
> those pursuits and those engagements which demand their atten-
> tion as men, Christians, and patriots, while the very Persons
> to whom has been allotted this great interest, this important
> trust, stand before you as the advocates of a reduction, of a
> puerile system which has never invigorated the mind, or raised
> up great men in any Country; which can never lay deep and broad
> the foundations of intellectual grandeur and power anywhere,
> but which is characterized by that superficiality which marks
> the proceedings of the educational Institutions in the new and
> Western States of the neighbouring Republic.[7]

But it could also be argued that the good of the country could be
advanced more effectively by the provision of some specialization
at the undergraduate level. This was the view of Daniel Wilson,
professor of history and English literature at the University
of Toronto, speaking on behalf of his colleagues:

> With regard to Options, our aim has been in like manner to
> devise such a Course of Study as would prove an effective
> source, not only of intellectual culture, but would prepare
> the youth of Canada for the practical duties of life. The old
> Classical Course of Oxford is not fitted to accomplish that
> object. Notwithstanding the distinguished names to be found
> among the Graduates of that University, to which the sons of
> England's Nobles almost exclusively resort, - the majority of
> Oxford-trained Students, whom I have seen do not strike me as

men whose University training seems to have had practical business and duties in view. Not a few of them rather seem like men who have just emerged from the cloister, and are far from being at home in the ordinary business of life. We, therefore, adopted a plan which the Commissioners of Oxford University have recommended for the improvement of that very Institution; and some credit may be claimed for the men of your own Canadian University, that they have carried into practice what the wisest men connected with Oxford University are only yet recommending. They recommend that the young men attending Oxford shall, at a certain point, take Options, under the advice of their Tutors. That is precisely what our young men do. A youth enters our College and goes through the first two years of the Course. He then comes to the President, or one of the Professors, for advice as to what Options he shall take. The matter is very simply dealt with. He is asked what is your object in life? If you intended to be a Medical man drop your Greek and Latin and go on with the Natural Sciences and Modern Languages, for every educated man in this Country, and especially every Medical man, ought to know at least French - which here is a spoken Language, - and German also. If the young man intends to become a Theological Student, to qualify himself for entering the Ministry of any of our Churches, then we say go on with your Classics, your Moral Science, your Mental Philosophy. If he proposes to become a Grammar School Teacher, we say - go on with your Classics and Mathematics. If a Land Surveyor, - devote your chief attention to your Mathematics, Geology, and Mineralogy. If a Farmer, - and I hope that is a class of Students which will be found to multiply every year, for I trust we are to educate not merely professional men, but the youth of Canada generally; and men will make all the better Farmers and Merchants and Tradesmen for having highly cultivated minds, - if a Farmer, we say, go on with Modern Languages, and still more with Natural Sciences, which will be of practical use to you in all the future duties of life. Is there not common sense in that? Is not that the most rational system for Canada, whatever may be the proper system for Oxford and Cambridge, - a system which the Chief Superintendent of Education seems disposed to dictate to us and to you?[8]

As has happened so often with special parliamentary committees on educational subjects, no decision was rendered in consequence of the month-long hearings of the Select Committee. The status quo prevailed, and Toronto had the opportunity to develop its honour courses further. In the course of the next three decades it proceeded to do so. By 1890 Victoria had entered into federation with the University of Toronto, a clear indication that, in the interim, the place of the honour course had become generally recognized and that the views of Ryerson and Wilson had been reconciled.[9]

It must by now have become obvious that the classics occupied a
dominant position in the undergraduate curriculum of 1860. Except
at Toronto, where the undertaking of honours work in mathematics,
science, or modern languages permitted the dropping of classics
after the first year, Greek and Latin were compulsory subjects in
all years of *all* courses in the English-speaking institutions; in
the French system they were the principal ingredient of the classical course until the final two years, at which point their mastery
was assumed for the work in philosophy. Both Greek and Latin were
required for matriculation. The classics were, indeed, the basis
for admission to university, the additional requirements being,
normally, elementary mathematics and some knowledge of English
grammar. Toronto's requirements were more extensive than most:
Xenophon's *Anabasis* Book I; *Aeneid* Book II; Sallust, *Cataline*;
Translation from English into Latin prose; Ordinary Rules of
Arithmetic, Vulgar and Decimal Fractions, Extraction of a Square
Root; first four Rules of Algebra; Euclid Book I; English Grammar;
English, Roman and Greek History; Ancient and Modern Geography.
Nor was the end in sight. The University of New Brunswick *Calendar*
of 1862 announced that 'more classics and mathematics will be
required as soon as the state of the grammar and superior schools
in the Province may appear to warrant the raising of the standard
of admission to the University.'

Under the guise of functionalism, the modern foreign languages
had made their way by 1860 into some though not all arts programs.
Dalhousie had appointed a professor of modern languages in 1842
with a view to the practical advantages of a knowledge of French
and Spanish in the world of commerce.[10] Without exception the professors (or lecturers) of modern languages appointed up to 1860
were Europeans who were well qualified to teach the languages but
who seldom had the necessary background for the teaching of literature. Furthermore, their status as professors was suspect; their
remuneration normally consisted of the fees paid by students who
attended their classes. Their uneasy position is witnessed on one
hand by the lecturer at McGill who in 1847 was granted the use of
half an acre of land by the governors to pasture a cow and to make
a garden, and on another by the fact that the professor of modern
languages at King's College, Fredericton, was able to take on the
duties of superintendent of education in New Brunswick from 1854
to 1858 without interfering with his duties at the College.[11]
The prevailing attitude was expressed to the select committee of
1860 by Dr Cook, the principal of Queen's:

> I do not think that a University is intended to teach all sorts
> of things to all sorts of people. I think its purpose is to
> give a Classical and Scientific education and, in particular,
> to fit young men for entering advantageously on what are called
> the learned professions; ... With respect to modern languages, I

must not be understood to undervalue the acquisition of them.
But I think the ... proper subjects of a University Course, both
are, and ought to be engrossing; that modern languages should be
acquired before, or after, such a Course; and that where there
is a taste, or necessity, for such Languages, private tutors can
generally be found at a College seat to give the required instruction quite as effectually as should be done in a College class.[12]

The Provost of Trinity, Dr. Whittaker, told the same committee that
the study of modern languages, 'belongs rather to the Education of
Schools, than to that of the Universities.'[13] The irony of this
was that at this stage the schools were not teaching the modern
languages to any great extent; nor, it could be argued, were they
likely to do so until these subjects were recognized at matriculation. Consequently, such French, German, Italian, and Spanish as
was being taught in the universities was of an elementary nature.
The Christmas report of the professor of modern languages at King's
College, Windsor, in 1860 indicates the general approach:[14]

FIRST YEAR
Ollendorff's Grammar
Ollendorff's Grammar, combined with a systematic course of the
pronunciation and the regular and irregular verbs. In this year
the scholars *read* the reading-pieces in *Pinney's First Book of
French*, because I find them excellent to practice the pronunciation.

SECOND YEAR
A continuation of Ollendorff's Grammar. The students begin to
read and *learn by heart* the Causeries Parisiennes, by Peschier,
a book which I find better adapted for my purpose than any I ever
met with. They are supposed to finish Ollendorff's Grammar in
two years, at latest. If it is finished sooner, I begin my course
of Syntax, etc., which is generally reserved for the third year,
in the second.

THIRD YEAR
In this year, I go through a regular course of Syntax, partly as
a repetition, and partly to supply the wants of Ollendorff's system.
The scholars are then supposed to be familiar with all the leading
rules of Syntax from Ollendorff's Grammar, and, in going through
them, I call their attention to the niceties, *dictate rules* on them,
and cause the class to practise them, by writing and exercises after
my own dictation, principally consisting of *letters* and *conversa-
tions* on *topics of general interest*, etc. In this year I have,
moreover, constant *verbal* exercises in conversation and the scholars
are obliged to speak French as much as possible. They read
Christomathie Française, par Boniface, an excellent book, containing
all the varieties of style to be found in French authors.

At Toronto, with its honours courses in modern languages, a different
situation obtained. James Forneri's lectures on French, German,
Italian, and Spanish included serious attention to literature.

Third-year French, for example, included grammatical analysis of a scene from Racine's *Phèdre*, Racine's *Athalie* and Bossuet's *Orasions Funèbres*; history of French literature in the seventeenth century, and composition. For honours, Rotrou's *Venceslas*, Boileau's *l'Art Poétique*, and conversation were added. Literature also received solid attention at New Brunswick, where the first professor of modern languages in a Canadian institution had been appointed in 1837.

English was a required subject for all undergraduates in 1860 despite the fact that it was not listed in all the courses of study, for example at Trinity. As academic subjects both English composition and English literature are developments from rhetoric, composition directly and literature by way of belles lettres, which evolved from the detailed examination of the literary works drawn upon to illustrate the various devices of rhetoric. Since a knowledge of the literature of Greece and Rome was the ultimate object of classical studies, and since the devices of rhetoric were a key to that knowledge, the study of rhetoric was inevitably associated with the study of Latin and Greek. The easy transition from regarding rhetoric as a means to an end to regarding it as a worthy end in itself is illustrated in the remarks of the Rev. John McCaul at the opening of King's College, Toronto, in 1843:

> I would here glance ... at the kindred pursuits of logic, rhetoric, and belles lettres, for the advantages to be derived from their cultivation, must commend themselves to a judgement of every one, who desires to reason with correctness and precision – to express their sentiments or communicate his knowledge with perspicuity and grace – or to wield that magic influence, whereby the orator lulls or rouses the passions of his audience.[15]

Though elocution was sometimes assigned separate identity (as at McGill and Victoria), the study of oral and written communication was normally combined under English composition. All colleges in 1860 were concerned that undergraduates should be able to 'communicate their knowledge with perspicuity and grace'; written assignments were numerous in all subjects, and there was a great deal of recitation in class. The only difference between the institutions which prescribed English and those which did not was that the former approached rhetoric directly through the example of English authors while the latter continued to deal with it indirectly through the study of Latin and Greek.

In 1860, English literature was only beginning to establish itself as a subject for academic study; the main concern of teachers of English was with English language. This is reflected in the course of instruction offered over three years by the Molson Professor of English Language and Literature at McGill:

> I. Affinity of Languages – History of the Origin and Successive Improvements of the English Languages – Its Constituent Elements – Text-book, Latham's Handbook.

II.   Grammar of the English Language - Text-book, Crombie and
Latham.

III.   History of English Literature and Criticism of Literary
Works - Early English Literature before the time of Queen
Elizabeth - English Literature in the age of Spenser, Shakespeare,
Milton, &c., - in the age of the Restoration and Revolution, -
in the Eighteenth and Nineteenth Centuries - Text-books, Shaw's
Outlines and Spalding's History of English Literature.

The Lectures on the above subjects will be accompanied with
frequent exercises in the practice of composition.

Literature, it will be noted, was primarily the *history* of English
literature; Spalding's *History of English Literature* was also the
principal text at Acadia, New Brunswick, Queen's and Toronto.
Even at Toronto, where there was an honour course, the study of
texts was limited in 1860 to a single Shakespeare play.
    That three of the authors prescribed in English at Toronto were
the historians Clarendon, Gibbon, and Macaulay is explained in
part by the fact that the instruction was offered by the professor
of history and English literature. Daniel Wilson, whose chair was
established in 1853, was one of three professors of history in
Canada in 1860; the others were J.-B.-A. Ferland, professeur
d'histoire du Canada et de l'Amérique en générale at Laval, whose
activities we shall discuss under the heading Adult Education at
the end of this chapter, and the Rev. J.M. Cramp, whose chair at
Acadia was entitled History and Moral Science. The problem of
history as an academic subject at this time was described in a
letter written by Daniel Wilson to his wife on 21 September 1853:
'I suspect I shall have a battle to fight about my chair. He
[the Rev. John McCaul] wants to make it a Chair of Ancient History,
being imbued with all the old scholastic exclusive preference for
everything classical. But I have not the slightest intention of
being dictated to by anyone as to what or how I shall teach.'[16]
    Wilson, one of Canada's cannier Scots, was successful in main-
taining his chair. That his fears were justified is indicated
by the fate of the chair of ancient and modern history established
at McGill in 1855; ancient history was soon transferred to classics,
and modern history to a new chair of English language and literature. These incidents remind us that the history, the geography,
and (under the title "Antiquities") the archaeology of the ancient
world had long been regarded as subjects naturally associated with
the study of the classics. Medieval and modern history, however,
were receiving little attention in 1860 at any university in the
English-speaking world. Wilson's lectures, which provided for all
students a general survey from early Athens to 'Britain and her
colonies from the era of the Revolution' and for honour students
an introduction to ancient and modern ethnology, were at least a
beginning.
    The problem that periodically faces us today of deciding whether
history should be assigned to the humanities or to the social

sciences did not arise in 1860. The social sciences as we now know them did not exist. Economics, political science, and psychology were subsumed under philosophy, while history and geography were appendages to classics. Anthropology was dimly visible in Wilson's ethnology. Sociology was an affair of the future.

The professors of philosophy bore a great variety of titles in 1860: metaphysics and ethics (Toronto); metaphysics and belles lettres (Acadia); logic and mental and moral philosophy (Queen's); logic, intellectual and moral philosophy (McGill); and – the most all-embracing – mental philosophy, logic, ethics and the evidences of Christianity (Victoria). At King's, Windsor, philosophy was taught by the professor of theology. Nor were the possibilities exhausted; when Dalhousie reopened in 1863, there were professors of logic, ethics, and political economy and of metaphysics, ethics and belles lettres, the latter chair becoming psychology and metaphysics in 1866. In refreshing contrast, the professor in charge of the final year of the classical college course in French Canada was, quite simply, professeur de philosophie.

The various titles reflected minor changes of emphasis rather than difference in basic approach. There were three subjects embraced by philosophy in the first half of the nineteenth century; rhetoric (including aesthetics and belles lettres), logic (which at times included the beginnings of psychology), and philosophy proper – a coordinated view of man and nature in a universe presided over by a deity. Fundamentally, logic and rhetoric were tool subjects, the mastery of which was a necessary step if the goal of philosophic study was to be realized. We have already seen that rhetoric was gravitating towards literature – either classical or modern. Logic remained under the professor of philosophy and served as his introductory course. Normally offered in the second year, it consisted of a series of lectures emphasizing the points developed in the prescribed textbook – in most cases Whately's *Logic*.

But the main purpose of philosophy was to develop in the young undergraduate what can best be described quite literally as a philosophy of life. This is most easily recognized in the case of the French-speaking colleges where, 'ayant fait sa Rhétorique,' the student devoted the final two years to philosophie, during which the relations between the various compartments in the world of knowledge were established and the responsibilities of the individual in a social and natural world were defined. The philosophy of life cultivated by the classical course naturally enough was that of the Roman Catholic Church. Paquet, who has traced the development of philosophic studies in Quebec from the time of their introduction at the Jesuit college in the seventeenth century, shows that the tradition has always been the scholastic.[17] He notes a renewed interest in St Thomas in the 1850s, no doubt stimulated by the return of the Jesuits in 1842. Twenty-five years before the encyclical *Aeterni Patris* of 1879, students at the Collège de St-Hyacinthe petitioned the superior that St Thomas

Aquinas replace St Catherine as their *premier patron*.

Because in the Protestant world philosophy did not enjoy as intimate a relation with religion as it did in the Roman Catholic, its position in the English-speaking colleges was more tenuous and its program less easy to define. But the aim of the professors of philosophy was precisely the same. Without exception they were ordained clergymen, and since many of them were the presidents of their colleges, they were in a position of influence. The Rev. John McCaul's remarks to the students at the opening of King's College, Toronto, are again apposite:

> I would next direct your attention to that elevated philosophy, which will render you conversant with the powers and operations of the mind, and enable you to prosecute your search into the hidden springs of intellectual energy and activity - which analyses and unfolds the machinery, which is put into motion, in a process of mental exertion. Let me unite with this, that allied branch, which will lead you not to the springs of thought but of action - which developes the principles, on which your conduct to God, your fellow-creatures, and yourselves should be based, and establishes those rights and obligations, which belong not merely to individuals, but to nations - the origin of the social system and the elements of civil government - and ascends to the investigation of those evidences, which reason furnishes for the existence, the perfection, and superintending care of the Supreme Being, the immortality of the soul, and a future state of retribution.[18]

It is easy to see within McCaul's terms of reference the elements which, during the next thirty years, would separate themselves out as economics, political science, and psychology. It is also possible to find in the texts read in philosophy examples of early works in these newer fields; for example, Wayland's *Political Economy* and Reid's *Intellectual Powers*. But in 1860 these subjects remained within the province of philosophy, and philosophy retained its position as the great synthesizing force.

The philosophic system propounded in the English-speaking Canadian colleges a century ago was that which had been developed by the Scottish common sense school; the texts prescribed everywhere were by such authors as Reid, Stewart, McIntosh, and Sir William Hamilton. But also prescribed universally were the works of Paley and Butler, for it was agreed that God was in his heaven and that his evidences were everywhere apparent in the natural world. In 1860, Paley still provided a solution for the problem posed by experimental science. But copies of *The Origin of Species* were already in print and the old synthesis was about to be subjected to stronger and more sustained attacks.

The three basic professorships in the first half of the nineteenth century were classics, philosophy, and mathematics and natural philosophy. Natural philosophy had originally embraced all aspects of the natural world in contradistinction to mental and moral philosophy, which embraced all aspects of man as an individual and as a member of society. But by 1860 natural philosophy had been pared down to physics. Earlier in the century, chemistry and natural history had attained their independence, initially through their relevance to the study of medicine. Later the practical applications of geology, particularly pertinent in a new country, had led to its separation from natural history. By 1860 these developments had led at Toronto to the establishment of four separate chairs: mathematics and natural philosophy, chemistry, natural history, and mineralogy and geology. The normal pattern in 1860, however, was a chair of mathematics and natural philosophy and a chair of chemistry and natural history. The association of natural philosophy or physics with mathematics gave to physics a mathematical rather than an experimental bias.

The title of the chair mattered little, however, since the scientist of 1860 had been generally rather than specifically trained. During his three-and-a-half postgraduate years at Berlin, H.H. Croft, the professor of chemistry at Toronto, had studied chemistry, mineralogy, geology, botany, zoology, physics, physiology, entomology, and metaphysics.[19] Such a man was capable of offering an elementary if not an advanced course in any one of these fields - not excluding metaphysics, for at that time all professors had received a solid general education in their arts courses. William Brydone Jack, the president and professor of mathematics and natural philosophy at New Brunswick, was sufficiently well versed in the classics to take over the lectures of the professor of classics when the latter died in the middle of the academic year 1870-71.[20] The well-trained scientist - and Croft and Brydone Jack were both very well trained - was capable of turning his hand in many directions.[21] But their very capacity to teach any of the science courses offered in the B.A. program is evidence that most courses were, by twentieth century standards, at an elementary level. The elementary nature of the instruction is also indicated by the fact that it was often offered by professors who had received very little training in science. Nathaniel Burwash, later the distinguished principal of Victoria, was appointed professor of science in the late 1860s, with the understanding that he would be transferred to theology as soon as arrangements could be made. After attending the Sheffield Scientific School at Yale for a few months of review, Burwash taught science at Victoria for seven years, 'meanwhile giving what assistance he could to students in divinity.'[22] 'I can remember,' wrote the Rev. S.S. Nelles, a colleague of Burwash, who had been appointed to the Victoria staff in 1850, 'when a Canadian University could venture to issue its calendar with an announcement of a single professor for all the natural sciences, and with a laboratory something similar to an ordinary black-smith's shop, where the professor was his own assistant, and compelled to blow not only his own bellows, but his own trumpet as well.'[23] A more detailed reference to the teaching of the sciences at this time is provided by the biographer of Sir William Mulock, a student at the University of Toronto in 1860:

> Prior to 1876 [when a physics laboratory was established at Toronto], the subjects of Natural History and Zoology were taught in the lecture room upon a blackboard. Students knew nothing about the structure of living things except through occasional glances at dead specimens ... Names of animals, living, dead, and pre-historic, great and small, and infinitesimal, were memorized ... In the subject of Natural Philosophy, the modern Physics, a few pieces of ancient mechanical apparatus did duty for a laboratory. The theory of light and all its fundamental principles were daily taught by old professors who had never seen a lens ... Astronomy was propounded with the aid of drawing on a blackened globe, some spheres of brass that represented the sun and moon and stars, and endless formulas that filled the board ... Botany and Zoology were studied with the aid of books, filled with long and tedious lists. One large binocular microscope ... was the only sign of modern progress.[24]

There can be little doubt of the inadequacies of such facilities in terms of twentieth-century standards. But there is no doubt at all that a great deal can be done by a gifted and enthusiastic professor despite inadequate facilities; and this was as true in 1860 as it is today.

Elementary as the instruction may well have been, it is still a fact that the undergraduate of 1860 was at least introduced to the main compartments of the world of science. To take two examples, the B.A. of New Brunswick during his three year course had taken mathematics (including astronomy), physics, chemistry, geology and mineralogy, and (under natural history) botany and zoology, while to qualify for the B.A. at Laval, the student had had to pass a four hour examination in physics and chemistry, a four hour examination in mathematics and astronomy, and a two hour examination in natural history. Furthermore, the relations of the individual sciences to each other and of science to religion and literature were called directly to the attention of the undergraduate of 1860 through the medium of philosophy. In its treatment of science, quite as much as in its treatment of the other subjects of the course of study, the curriculum of 1860 emphasized the unity of the world of knowledge. It is this emphasis on unity which so sharply distinguishes the curriculum of 1860 from that of today.

EXTENSION

Very early in their history a few Canadian colleges made efforts
to place their services at the disposal of the community at large
by offering free public lectures, inspired no doubt by the desire
to encourage public interest in the infant college. But these
first tentative steps in the field of adult education were also a
recognition of the responsibilities of the university in a new and
sparsely populated country. Some of these early lectures were
designed to be of practical benefit to farmers and engineers, and
hence are more appropriate to the following chapter, which deals
with professional education. However, the instruction was usually
provided by professors in the faculty of arts and consequently can
properly be dealt with here. Departments of extension are, of
course, a twentieth-century development.

The earliest developments appear to have taken place in the
Maritimes. In 1841, Thomas McCulloch, the president of Dalhousie,
held evening classes for special students in logic and composition
and offered as well a series of illustrated lectures on mathematics
and natural philosophy.[25] 'General lectures' were contemplated at
Acadia from the outset. In 1851-52 Dr Cramp and Isaac Chipman
offered a joint course of lectures on subjects of general interest:
'Dr. Cramp began the series with a discussion of methods "for the
successful prosecution of studies." Later he gave talks on the
history and culture of Ancient Egypt and the Greek city states.
At the end of each month Chipman reviewed current events and kept
his students informed concerning the latest publications in the
fields of biography, literature and science.'[26] In 1855 J.W.
Dawson, who had relinquished the post of superintendent of education in Nova Scotia to become principal of McGill, offered a
course of public lectures on zoology, natural philosophy, chemical
engineering, paleontology and the chemistry of life.[27] At Queen's,
in 1859, George Lawson sought and obtained permission from the
trustees to give a course of lectures to workingmen on the application of chemistry 'to the useful arts of life.'[28]

As we shall see in chapter 5, Dawson's 1855 lectures developed
into regular courses for undergraduates, but the lectures at
Dalhousie, Acadia, and Queen's were affairs of the moment. At
Laval, on the other hand, a sustained program of adult education
was introduced in 1859. Since undergraduate instruction was
intended to be provided by the classical colleges, the faculty of
arts at Laval was designed from the outset to provide instruction
at a graduate level, and the first three professors, J.-B.-A.
Ferland, Canadian and American history (1856), T.S. Hunt, chemistry
(1857), and T.-H. Hamel, physics (1859), were appointed with this
in mind. But in 1860 there were few candidates for advanced work
in arts and science. Hunt and Hamel could obviously provide
courses that would be functional for students in medicine, and all
three could offer courses that would contribute to the general

education of students in law, in medicine, and in theology. These general lectures were made available to the public and scheduled at 7:45 p.m. First offered in 1859, they were continued for many years.[29]

NOTES TO CHAPTER 4

1 Unless otherwise noted, the course of study reported in this chapter is that outlined in the calendar or equivalent publication of the institution in question for the session 1860-1.
2 P.-J.-O. Chauveau, 'The Colleges of Canada - the Laval University,' *J. Education Lower Canada,* 1 (1857), 110-1
3 *Inaugural Address on the Nature and Advantages of an English and Liberal Education. Delivered by the Rev. Egerton Ryerson* (1842). Much of the address is reprinted in N. Burwash, *A History of Victoria College* (1927), 495-507.
4 Ryerson, *Inaugural,* 25
5 Ibid., 27
6 Ibid., 27
7 J.G. Hodgins, ed., *Documentary History of Education in Upper Canada* (1906), XV, 264
8 Ibid., 214-15
9 Victoria students were notably successful at the first examinations they sat as University of Toronto students in 1893. See C.B. Sissons, *A History of Victoria University* (1952), 211.
10 D.C. Harvey, *An Introduction to the History of Dalhousie University* (1938), 61. The appointment was influenced by the fact that St Mary's College had from its establishment in 1841 'made ample provision for instruction in these languages' and in consequence was 'attracting most of the Halifax students to its classrooms.'
11 Marshall d'Avray, Professor of Modern Languages at New Brunswick from 1852 until his death in 1871, was an exception to the rule in being well trained in both language and literature. See W.B. Hamilton 'Marshall d'Avray, Precursor of Modern Education' in Robert S. Patterson, et al., eds., *Profiles of Canadian Educators* (1974), 338-41.
12 Hodgins, *Doc. Hist.,* XV, 107-8
13 Ibid., 202
14 A report of the instruction in all departments is included in the King's College *Calendar* for 1860-1.
15 King's College, Toronto, *Proceedings at the Ceremony of Laying the Foundation Stone, April 23, 1842: and at the Opening of the University, June 8, 1843* (1843), 57
16 H.H. Langton, *Sir Daniel Wilson: a Memoir* (1929), 59
17 L.-A. Paquet, 'Histoire de l'enseignement de la philosophie,' *Trans. Royal Society Canada 1917,* section 1, 37-60. See also H. Bastien, *L'Enseignement de la philosophie au Canada français* (1931); and Marc Lebel, 'L'Enseignment de la philosophie' in *Aspects de l'enseignement au Petit Séminaire de Quebec* (1968), 11-71.

18 King's College, *Proceedings*, 59–60
19 J. King, 'Henry Holmes Croft' in *McCaul, Croft, Forneri: Personalities of Early University Days* (1914), 103–58
20 W.D. Pacey, 'The Humanist Tradition' in A.G. Bailey, ed., *University of New Brunswick Memorial Volume* (1950), 64
21 Another example is Sir William Dawson who, as E.A. Collard has noted, was a geologist, specializing in palaeontology but also a mineralogist, botanist, zoologist, ethnologist, agronomist, archaeologist, linguist (especially in Hebrew), and theologian. 'In all these fields he wrote books and scholarly papers and in several of them textbooks': 'Sir William Dawson's Principalship' in H. MacLennan, ed., *McGill: The Story of a University* (1960), 56.
22 N. Burwash, *The History of Victoria College* (1927), 237–8
23 Burwash, *Victoria College*, 526
24 W.J. Loudon, *Sir William Mulock: A Short Biography* (1932), 69–70
25 Harvey, *Dalhousie University*, 61
26 R.S. Longley, *Acadia University 1838–1928* (1938), 68
27 C. Macmillan, *McGill and its Story, 1821–1921* (1921), 230–1
28 D.D. Calvin, *Queen's University at Kingston, 1841–1941* (1941), 204–5
29 H. Provost, *Historique de la Faculté des Arts de l'Université Laval, 1852–1952* (1952), 8–9, 25

5
Professional Education

It was noted in the Preface that this is a history of higher education in Canada, not a history of the Canadian universities. Were our attention confined strictly to the work of degree-granting universities there would be little to record in this chapter, for, despite charters which in almost all cases authorized degrees in law, medicine, and theology, the efforts of the Canadian universities in 1860 were concentrated almost entirely on undergraduate programs in arts. There were, it is true, a number of faculties of theology, law, and medicine, and, within the framework of the faculty of arts, engineering and agriculture had made an appearance. But Principal Dawson's comment of 1863 was an accurate summary of the situation: 'If we have any provision for educational qualifications in the civil and military services of this country, it is a dead letter.'[1]

This concentration on an arts course which, as we have seen, was designed to provide a liberal education along classic and classical lines is somewhat surprising in a country faced by a multitude of practical problems requiring for their solution a multitude of skilled professionals – administrators, engineers, teachers, doctors, lawyers, and clergymen. The needs of the times had been well expressed by the royal commissioners who had examined the affairs of King's College, Fredericton, in 1854: their recommendations included the provision of special courses 'adapted to the Agricultural, Mechanical, Manufacturing and Commercial pursuits and interests of New Brunswick.'[2] But five years elapsed before these recommendations were acted upon by the legislature, and many more years were to elapse before the University of New Brunswick would be granted the funds to provide the professional courses advocated by the commission.[3] The year 1860 was in fact a moment of transition. The need for a greatly expanded curriculum was generally recognized, but the steps actually being undertaken to meet the situation were tentative, hesitant, and ill-financed. Money was one problem. A scarcity of well-trained professors to organize and to teach professional subjects was a second. A third, and in many respects the most difficult to resolve, was the long arm of tradition.

The organization adopted by Université Laval at the time of its establishment in 1852 reminds us that the four traditional faculties were arts, law, medicine, and theology. Since the last three of these are clearly in the field of professional education, it may be asked why the Canadian institutions were not biased towards professionalism from the start, particularly as the need for an educated clergy was the prime force which lay behind the founding of the earliest colleges. The answer lies partly in the fact that the early Canadian colleges were established at a time when in the English-speaking world the university was chiefly concerned with the education of undergraduates. In 1800 at Oxford and Cambridge it was the colleges which were dominant - as teaching institutions the universities could hardly be said to exist and the colleges enrolled only undergraduates. There were no other universities in England. The position of professional education was somewhat better in Scotland where the university rather than the college was dominant and where, through Dutch influence, medicine was well established as a degree program. But even in Scotland the main emphasis was on the general or liberal education of young men, most of whom came to the universities from small and poorly equipped country schools. Throughout Great Britain, apprenticeship rather than attendance at a university was the normal method of entry to the professions of law and medicine, and this tradition had been carried across the ocean to the Canadian colonies. In 1860 apprenticeship arrange-ments organized by the provincial law society continued to be the means of preparing for the practice of law. The need for clinical instruction in the hospital setting had rendered apprenticeship obsolete in the field of medicine, and the instruction of doctors was now carried on by institutions rather than by individuals. Such institutions, however, had only a nominal relationship with a university.

Since the need for an educated clergy was pressing in both the French and English colonies, theology might have been expected to have strengthened the position of professional education in the Canadian university. But here force of circumstance intervened. So urgent was the need for trained clergy that the Churches could not afford to wait for the development of universities; hence, for example, the establishment of the Séminaire de Québec nearly two hundred years before the founding of Université Laval. In the British colonies, theology was given attention at the time of the founding of the first institutions, but the theology concerned was Church of England theo-logy, and this led to the establishment of rival colleges by the other denominations, who soon found - as did the King's colleges - their limited resources inadequate for the support of both theology and arts. The consequence was either tiny departments of theology at such institutions as Acadia, Queen's, and St Francis Xavier, or small colleges concerned only with theology, such as Knox College and the Congregational College of British North America.

For a variety of reasons, then, none of the traditional professions occupied in 1860 a position of great significance in the
Canadian universities. Nor at this time had any of the newer professional fields - agriculture, engineering, dentistry, veterinary
medicine, teaching - truly established itself as a profession, let
alone one requiring that its practitioners be university graduates.
Nonetheless, provision was being made in 1860 by Canadian universities for professional training in theology, medicine, law, engineering (including architecture), agriculture (including veterinary medicine), and commerce. One degree in music had been granted.
Teachers and nurses were being trained. We shall review these
fields in turn.

THEOLOGY

Few specific details about theological education in French Canada
prior to 1860 have been recorded. The subject is not referred to
in Gosselin's *L'Instruction au Canada sous le régime français* and
none of the documents reproduced in Provost's *Le Séminaire de
Québec* outlines a course of study in theology. It is not even
possible to determine the exact length of the theological course
since students at Le Grand Séminaire often interrupted their studies
to teach at the Petit Séminaire or at one of the new classical
colleges which were established elsewhere in the province in the
nineteenth century. Much has been written about the Grand Séminaire
but the emphasis has been on its internal organization, its relations to the parishes, and its role in the administration of the
church in New France.
    All professional education involves a combination of instruction
in theoretical and practical matters (medical students are taught
surgery as well as anatomy and physiology, law students are taught
procedure as well as jurisprudence), and it is normal for the
practical to receive more attention than the theoretical in the
early stages of the development of a profession in any country.
The practical emphasis was apparent in the portion of the Act of
Foundation of Le Séminaire de Québec dealing with the training of
young priests: 'On enseignera la manière de bien administrer les
sacrements, la méthode de catéchiser et de prêcher ... la théologie
morale, les ceremonies, le plain chant grégorien et autres choses
appartenant aux devoir d'un bon ecclésiastique.'[4] The main object
was to produce not a learned priest but one who could function
effectively in the relatively primitive society in which he would
serve his God. At the same time it should be noted that theory
was included in the program from the outset - moral theology was
specifically mentioned - and that candidates were not admitted to
theological studies at the Grand Séminaire until they had completed
the classical college course, which included two years of philosophy.
The connection between philosophy and theology was close throughout
the French régime and it remained an intimate one for the next 200
years.

The Grand Séminaire at Québec continued to be the only institution in French Canada offering formal theological training until the 1820s when the Sulpicians began activities which led to the formal establishment of le Grand Séminaire de Montréal in 1840.[5] By 1860 the course of study offered at the grand séminaires at Québec and Montréal was of four years duration, the basic subjects being dogmatic theology, moral theology, holy scriptures, preaching and ceremonies. The element of theory in the compound had been increased, but practical matters remained important. Université Laval did not establish its faculty of theology until 1866. Then, however, the personnel were drawn entirely from the Grand Séminaire; the creation of the university had little if any immediate effect on the theological program. By 1860 there was a third Roman Catholic program available at the College of Bytown, which would become the University of Ottawa in 1866; a theological course had been instituted in 1851 and 39 priests completed their theological studies at Ottawa during the ensuing nine years.[6]

The mixture of practical and theoretical was also evident in the arrangements at the Diocesan Theological Institution, a Church of England College established at Cobourg, Upper Canada, in the 1840s. In 1841 John Strachan, named the first Bishop at Toronto in 1839, nominated the Rev. Alexander Bethune as professor of theology in the diocese of Toronto and announced that henceforth all candidates for ordination would take a prescribed course of study under Dr Bethune, who was the rector of the Anglican church at Cobourg. Years later one of the candidates described the daily routine:

We had our lectures in Classics in the morning at the Rectory in the Archdeacon's study, where we read Plato and some of the Greek dramatists, as well as some of the Roman poets. Later on in the day we attended lectures in Divinity in the Parochial Schoolhouse near the sounding shore of the lake. We had to compose sermons on set texts, some of which were read every Saturday by the writers. Previous to our reading the sermons in the presence of Dr. Bethune and our fellow students, they were taken in charge by the Principal, criticized, corrected, and given back to us.[7]

The candidates also lived in Dr Bethune's immediate presence for the best part of three years, some of them in the rectory itself, and the preparation of effective priests was higher on Bethune's list of priorities than the preparation of learned ones. This joint emphasis on theory and practice was continued when the Diocesan Theological Institution was transferred to Toronto in 1852 as the faculty of divinity of the University of Trinity College.

All the leading Protestant denominations, except the Methodists, had established institutions for theological training by 1860 – the Congregationalists and the Free Church Presbyterians in separate institutions, the Anglicans, the Baptists, and the Kirk Presbyterians in association with universities. The Methodists relied on a

prescribed course of reading during the four years of probationary
service, the texts being prescribed by the Annual Conference, which
also appointed an examination committee. As outlined by J.G.
Hodgins in 1864 the course of study was as follows:[8]

First Year
The Bible
Horner, *Introduction to the Bible*
Wesley, *Sermons* (first series)
Wesley, *Christian Perfection*
Wesley, *Notes on the New Testament*
Watson, *Theological Institutes* (Part I)

Second Year
Watson, *Theological Institutes* (Part II)
Mosheim, *Ecclesiastical History*
Smith, *History of Methodism*
Bangs's *History of the Methodist-Episcopal Church*

Third Year
Watson, *Theological Institutes* (Parts II & IV)
Pearson, *On the Creed*
Taylor, *Ancient and Modern History*

Fourth Year
Butler, *Analogy, with Teft's Analysis*
Upham, *Mental Philosophy*
Whately, *Logic*
Whately, *Rhetoric*

Hodgins also lists the principal texts in the basic courses offered
by the Baptist church, the Canadian Presbyterian church (the Free
church), the Church of Scotland (the Kirk), the Church of Rome,
the Church of England, and the Congregational church. The Methodist
list is representative in its emphasis on ecclesiastical history,
the evidences of Christianity, biblical criticism, and doctrine.
For example, the Baptists main texts were Paley's *Natural Theology*,
Wayland's *Moral Science*, Paley and Wilson's *Evidences of Christianity*,
Ernesti's *Principles of Interpretation*, Butler's *Analogy*, Jahn's
Biblical Archaeology, and Giesler's *Ecclesiastical History*. But
the Baptist student also studied the Hebrew Bible and the Old and
New Testaments in Greek. Greek and Hebrew were required by all
the Protestant denominations except the Methodists. The Presby-
terians and Anglicans also required that some attention be given
to Chaldee, Syriac, and Arabic.
    In 1860 the basic two-year course required for licensing in the
Anglican church was offered in faculties or departments of divinity
or theology at Bishop's, Trinity, and King's College, Windsor.
The professors of divinity at the other two King's Colleges had
disappeared with the creation of the secular universities of New
Brunswick and Toronto. The only other faculty of theology in
English-speaking Canada was at Queen's, but Acadia had a theolo-

gical institute. The principal independent theological colleges were Knox, established at Toronto by the Free Church Presbyterians in 1844, the Congregational College of British North America, an 1860 merger of Congregational Colleges at Toronto and Halifax, the Pine Hill Theological College at Halifax, an 1860 merger of Presbyterian colleges at Halifax and Truro, and Queen's College at St John's, Newfoundland, an Anglican college founded by the first Bishop of Newfoundland, A.G. Spencer, in 1841.[9] A theological course extending over three years was also provided for Baptists of Upper Canada by the Canadian Literary Institute at Woodstock.[10]

MEDICINE

Canadians were not faced with the problem of providing facilities for the training of doctors until the 1820s. During the French régime, the medical needs of the colony were supplied by surgeons attached to the military forces and by hospitals at Quebec and Montreal, founded in 1639 and 1644 respectively. British military surgeons replaced the French during the early years of British rule, but the situation remained unchanged. The coming of the United Empire Loyalists to the Maritime provinces in the 1780s brought a number of doctors to supplement the military surgeons who had been stationed at Annapolis Royal as early as 1710 and at Halifax from the time of its founding in 1749. When immigration shifted from the Maritimes to Upper Canada at the turn of the century, the medical contingent was again prominent. Until 1820 the main problem was to ensure that only qualified persons were permitted to practise, for there were many unscrupulous in addition to well-meaning quacks who were prepared to offer their services to a gullible public. In these circumstances the granting of the right to practise had been delegated by the government to medical boards established in each of the colonies which were to conduct examinations and to issue licences. Initially the work of these boards consisted of assessing the credentials of men who had received their training in Europe or in the United States, but by 1820 the supply of immigrant doctors was dwindling and the need for native-born recruits was apparent. The medical boards were manned by the leading doctors in each colony; consequently, at the time that the first Canadian medical schools were established, entry into the profession was controlled by the profession itself.

A school of medicine implies the participation of at least two instructors and the provision of some clinical facilities. We must find some other term to describe the activities of a number of individuals who in Montreal, Kingston, and York (Toronto) offered lectures of the type advertised in the *Montreal Gazette* on 20 January 1821:

FREE TO THE PUBLIC!!!
Dr. W.W. Sleigh proposes delivering a few lectures on those
affections which proceed from diseased states of bowels and
liver and satisfactorily prove that ninety-nine diseases out
of a hundred have their origin in those parts; further, will
particularly notice the common mistake of calling a disease
in the liver a consumption. Female patients are particularly
invited, and to render the company a select one, none will be
admitted without a ticket to be had at Dr. Sleigh's house on
giving their names.

Whether the Talbot Dispensatory, near St Thomas in Upper Canada,
at which Charles Duncombe lectured on the Theory and Practice of
Medicine and John Rolph on the Anatomy and Physiology of the Human
Body should be regarded as a medical school depends upon one's
view of the adequacy of its clinical facilities, but the question
is academic since it was in existence less than two years (1824-25).[1]
There can be no doubt, however, concerning the Montreal Medical
Institution which opened on 10 November 1823 and which, as the
Faculty of Medicine of McGill University since 1829, has continued
to the present day. It began with 25 students and a faculty of 4,
all trained at the University of Edinburgh: William Caldwell
(principles and practice of medicine), William Robertson (midwifery and diseases of children), Andrew Holmes (chemistry, pharmacy, and materia medica), and John Stevenson (surgery, anatomy,
and physiology). The leading spirits were Stevenson and Holmes,
who had offered lectures at the Montreal General Hospital in 1822-
23 and who had formally proposed a school on the University of
Edinburgh model in October 1823.
    Because it had a strong and devoted staff with access to the
clinical facilities of a hospital from the outset, the Montreal
Medical Institution quickly established itself as a sound medical
school. The Institution became the faculty of medicine of McGill
University in 1829, but until 1860, when McGill assumed financial
responsibility for the faculty, the university's involvement was
nominal and the faculty was in effect a proprietary school. The
initial agreement between the Montreal Medical Institution and
McGill University was a marriage of convenience, entered into by
both parties with a view to practical advantage. The medical
school would benefit from an association which would enable it to
grant degrees to its students, while McGill by becoming technically
a teaching institution would become legally entitled to the funds
it had inherited from James McGill's will.[12] Originally located
near the Montreal General Hospital, the faculty of medicine moved
to the campus in 1844, shortly after the commencement of instruction in arts. The facilities were entirely inadequate and in 1851
the faculty of medicine moved back to the city into a building
constructed not by the university but at the expense of the individual members of the faculty. Despite such difficulties, the
instruction provided was steadily improved and expanded. Departments of clinical medicine, clinical surgery, institutes of medicine,

medical jurisprudence, and botany were added in the 1840s. In 1860, when the university at long last assumed financial responsibility, the enrolment was 109. But another twelve years were to elapse before the medical school would return permanently to the McGill campus and become the influential force it has been ever since.

The difficulties experienced by the McGill medical school led to the establishment in 1851 of a rival English-language school in Montreal, the St Lawrence School of Medicine.[13] McGill's success, on the other hand, inspired the founding of two French-language schools, l'Ecole de médicine et de chirurgie de Montréal in 1843[14] and l'Ecole de médicine de Québec.[15] The St Lawrence School ceased to function after four or five years but the two French-language schools proved to be permanent. Within a year of the chartering of Université Laval, l'Ecole de médicine de Québec became its faculty of medicine, while l'Ecole de médicine et de chirurgie de Montréal became associated with the Montreal branch of Université Laval in the 1870s and thus was the direct forerunner of the faculty of medicine of Université de Montréal. English-speaking Protestants were prominent in the establishment of both these French-language schools.

The needs of medicine featured prominently in the protracted discussions which led to the opening of King's College, Toronto, and that institution offered a degree program in medicine when it was finally launched in 1843.[16] In the same year, however, John Rolph opened a rival school in Toronto, which in 1853 was incorporated as the Toronto School of Medicine.[17] Rolph, who in addition to having been involved with Charles Duncombe in the short-lived Talbot Dispensatory, had offered instruction to a restricted number of students in his own home at Toronto from 1832 to 1837, had just returned to Canada from exile in the United States to which he had hurriedly repaired following the collapse of Mackenzie's rebellion in 1837. After the closing of King's College in 1849, Rolph's school was for a short time sole possessor of the field in Toronto. But in 1850 the Upper Canada School of Medicine was formed by six local doctors,[18] and a faculty of medicine was authorized at the University of Toronto. But by the terms of the new University of Toronto Act of 1853 the university's functions were specifically limited to examining and granting degrees; instruction was to be provided by proprietary schools like Rolph's and the Upper Canada School of Medicine. However, for the proprietary school there were advantages in having more direct access to the degree-granting power, and this resulted in an outbreak of faculties of medicine. In 1852, the Upper Canada School became Trinity's faculty of medicine, in 1854 Rolph's became Victoria's faculty of medicine, and in the same year a faculty of medicine was instituted at Queen's.[19] In none of these cases was the relationship between faculty and university other than nominal. The universities assumed no financial responsibility and the professors continued to collect fees. But there was constant bickering over the question of control. The Trinity experiment lasted only two years. The complete staff resigned in 1856, three of them reappearing in 1871 when Trinity established a faculty for the second time. Four of Rolph's lecturers resigned in 1856 and promptly re-established the Toronto School of Medicine, which then affiliated with the University of Toronto. Rolph, however, found replacements which enabled Victoria's faculty to continue to function until 1874. In 1866 the Queen's professors, after twelve years of muddle, reorganized as the Royal College of Physicians and Surgeons of Kingston, an institution independent of Queen's University but affiliated with it.

As a result of these varied efforts, 469 medical degrees had been awarded by Canadian universities by 1860: McGill 245, King's College, Toronto, 1, Toronto 26, Victoria 111, Trinity 12, Queen's 58, Laval 16. The course of studies was essentially the same wherever the degree was taken, since it had to accord with the requirements for licensing, and these were essentially the same in each of the colonies. The arrangements at McGill, as outlined in the 1860 calendar, are representative. Candidates for the degree of Doctor of Medicine and Surgery were required to undergo 'three trials': a matriculation examination normally taken during the first session of attendance ('Students ... will be examined in Classics and in English or French Composition, the standard being such as may from time to time be determined by the Faculty'); an oral examination on 'a thesis or inaugural dissertation, written by himself on some subject connected with Medical or Surgical science, either in the Latin, English, or French Language'; and a general examination, either oral or by written papers, on all branches of medical and surgical science. The general examination was divided into two parts, the Primary (anatomy, chemistry, materia medica, institutes of medicine, zoology or botany), which could be taken at the end of the third year, and the Final (practice of medicine, surgery, midwifery, medical jurisprudence). Students were also required to submit proof that they had studied medicine for at least four years, had attended lectures for at least three sessions of six months, and had 'attended during twelve months in the practice of the Montreal General Hospital, or that of some other Hospital approved by the University.'

LAW

A categorical statement about the state of legal education in Canada a century ago was made by the editor of the *Canadian Law Journal* in 1855:

> Existing laws afford no guarantee of fitness. A young man whose only qualification for entering the study of law, is ability to read and write, may be articled to an Attorney; - spend five years copying and serving papers or idly kicking his heels against the office desk, or in doing the dirty work of a disreputable practitioner. At the end of that time, armed with a certificate of service, he claims to be sworn in as an

Attorney of Her Majesty's courts, and is sworn in accordingly. He may know nothing whatever of professional duties, may, in fact, be grossly illiterate and deficient in every acquirement that would enable him to act with safety and advantage for his client; and yet the law entitles him, simply on proof of service under articles, to undertake the most important duties of an Attorney.[20]

As we shall see, the situation was not quite as bad as this blunt statement declared; the would-be attorney was subject to some kind of examination and was not automatically granted professional status. But, as we shall also see, the basic criticism was justified - existing laws did not afford any guarantee of fitness to practise. There were plenty of 'fit' lawyers in Canada in 1856, and many of them were capable of introducing their articled clerks to the theory and practice of law. But there was no guarantee that they would do so, and there was no guarantee that a student would be articled to a lawyer who was both qualified and prepared to take his teaching duties seriously.

The fault lay with the profession itself since for many years before 1860 it had had effective control of admission to the practice of law. In Nova Scotia - and this appears to have been equally the case elsewhere in the Maritimes - the candidate had to serve five years of apprenticeship in the office of an attorney and then pass an examination before a judge and two barristers. In Upper Canada he was subject to the regulations of the Law Society of Upper Canada established in 1797 by an Act of the legislature which specified that no one should be permitted to practise unless he had been 'entered of and admitted to the said Society as a student of the laws ... have ... standing in the books of the said Society for and during the space of five years ... have conformed himself to the rules and regulations of the said Society and ... have been duly called and admitted to the practice of law as a Barrister according to the constitution and establishment thereof.' In Lower Canada le Barreau de la Province de Québec had not been established until 1849; prior to this time a procedure dating back to an ordinance of 1785 had been in force, whereby after five years of apprenticeship the candidate was examined in the presence of the chief justice by two reputable lawyers. Commencing in September 1849, however, the authority was vested in le Barreau, and its officers - and not as heretofore the governor general - signed the commissions.[21] In 1847 control of entry to the profession of notaire was assigned to the notariat.[22]

In each of the colonies some special recognition was given to the university graduate. In Nova Scotia the period of apprenticeship was reduced to four years for the holder of a recognized degree. In Lower Canada the same privilege was afforded not only to the graduate but also to the candidate who had completed the full course at a classical college. In 1837 the Law Society of Upper Canada ruled that a graduate of a British university or of the proposed University of King's College at Toronto could be called to the bar after being on the society's books for three rather than five years. The same privilege was extended to graduates of Queen's, Victoria, and 'other universities in Upper Canada' in 1847. But in all cases the holder of a university degree was required to take whatever professional examinations were specified.

No attempt to provide formal instruction in the law is recorded in the Maritimes before the establishment of the faculty of law at Dalhousie University in 1883. In Lower Canada the situation was not much better until the establishment of le Barreau in 1849. A course of lectures was offered at Quebec in 1826 by Louis Plamondon and was apparently well received by a number of students. It was not, however, repeated; a motion in the legislature to provide funds for a house in which such lectures could be given was not seriously considered. Four years later it was suggested that an association which in 1828 had founded a lawyers' library in Montreal should expand its activities to include supervision of qualifications for admission to the bar, but the committee appointed to study the matter came to the conclusion that, since most of the lawyers of the province were not members of the association, it was preferable to leave the question of acceptability to the individual lawyer. Nonetheless, the more enlightened lawyers of the province, both French and English, were dissatisfied with the existing arrangements - and so, it may be added, were the more enlightened students. One of the problems was that too many candidates were presenting themselves, and this was in the interest neither of the profession itself nor of the community at large. In 1838 a serious, though unsuccessful, campaign was launched to establish le Barreau. One of the arguments advanced in favour of such a step was that the instituting of a proper and rigorous course of study would have the effect of diverting to other and equally important pursuits a considerable number of young men who had no particular talent for or interest in the law. Too often parental pressure, based on the belief that law, medicine, and theology were the only sure paths to financial or social security, was the real reason for their entering upon the study of the law. But, insisted the editor of *Le Canadien*, a Montreal newspaper, on 3 September 1838: 'l'experience a prouvé qu'il n'etait ni de l'interêt de la jeunesse, ni de celui du pays de laisser aux parents seuls le choix d'un état pour leurs enfants. Notre société canadienne a trop besoin d'hommes instruits dans les différentes branches d'industrie, pour qu'il ne soit pas à propos de modérer la manie qui pousse tout le monde vers les professions savants.'[23]

The situation did improve after the establishment of le Barreau in 1849 though not through any direct action on the part of that body. In 1851 F.M. Bibaud commenced his courses of law lectures at the recently founded Collège Ste Marie, an 'Ecole de Droit,' which continued until 1867.[24] In 1852 McGill's charter was amended to permit the establishment of a faculty of law. The same year saw the chartering of Université Laval, with provision for a faculty of law. Both universities offered the B.C.L. degree and could boast by 1860 of 32 and 16 graduates respectively.

In both instances the degree program was admirably designed. At Laval the central emphases were on civil and Roman law, a total of 684 lectures being scheduled over the three years for the former and 312 lectures, also distributed over three years, for the latter. By 1860 it had not proved possible to obtain a qualified lecturer in international law but there were regularly scheduled courses in civil procedure (50 lectures), commercial law and maritime law (108), criminal law (72), and droit des gens (not specified). Students were also expected to attend the public lectures offered by the faculté des arts in 'la philosophie et les lettres.' Not all the courses offered by the faculty's five-man staff were available each year and only the professors of civil and Roman law were in attendance regularly.

The McGill course, also offered by a five-man part-time staff, was predicated on the belief that theory and practice must be happily balanced:

> The Educational officers of this Faculty have felt that the Law of Lower Canada, though in many of its details purely local, retains, as its leading characteristics, the noble and imposing features of the civil law, and that the principles established in the Roman jurisprudence still form the groundwork of many of its departments. The lectures, therefore, though prepared with especial reference to the law of Lower Canada, have been as far as consistent with their primary object, divested of any purely sectional character and are made to inculcate such comprehensive principles, as form, to a great extent, the basis of every system of jurisprudence.

Translated into terms of specific courses, this statement in the 1860-61 *Calendar* (and repeated for many years thereafter) meant contracts and also real estate and customary law in all three years, public and consitutional law and civil law in the first two, the origin and history of the laws of England, France and Lower Canada in the first, legal bibliography in the second, and criminal law, leases, and international law in the third. This was, for its time, a very sound course, and there is little reason to doubt that the students (in 1860-61, 23 in the first year, 11 in the second, 13 in the third) were well instructed. However, aside from reducing the term of articling by one year, their university studies had no bearing on their qualifications as professional lawyers. This was equally the case with the 36 students registered that year in the B.C.L. program at Laval. Hence the enrolment at both institutions was relatively small. Neither course catered to the needs of the notary.

In 1855 the Law Society of Upper Canada appointed four lecturers - in mercantile law, equity jurisprudence, real property, and the law of landlord and tenant - and all students were required to attend such lectures as were offered.[25] Hitherto, the Law Society had contented itself with the supervision of examinations at the beginning and end of the period of articling and with ensuring that students were properly registered on the society's books for the requisite number of terms. That the society considered itself firmly ensconced in the tradition of the law as a learned profession is suggested by a resolution adopted in 1820 establishing the entrance requirements:

> Whereas the present state of this Province affords the means of obtaining that education which is necessary to the Liberal study and Practice of the Profession of the Law and which will secure to the Province a learned and honorable Body to assist their fellow subjects as occasion may require and to support and maintain the constitution of the Province ... It is resolved by the Society that after this Term all persons presenting themselves to the Society for their approbation previous to their admission upon their Books, shall be required to give a written translation in the presence of the Society of a portion of one of Cicero's Orations or perform such other exercises as may satisfy the Society of his acquaintance with the Latin and English composition ...[26]

Since, as the society was well aware, there was in Upper Canada in 1820 no college and only a handful of grammar schools, it can be said that the society was indulging in wishful thinking; its real convictions are perhaps better illustrated by the fact that a resolution of 1825 to extend the admission requirements to include 'a general knowledge of English, Grecian and Roman History,' and 'some reasonable portion of mathematical instruction' did *not* pass.[27] In 1846 when the requirements had been raised to include British history *or* geography and the first three books of Euclid, a proposal to add French was defeated.[28] In 1860 the requirements for admission were below those for the university.

However, there had been some progress in developing a program for the student who had been admitted. By a regulation of 1828 all students were required to be in residence at York (Toronto) for four terms; this was an attempt to guarantee familiarity with court procedures by forcing the students to attend the courts. A bar examination was instituted in 1831, the candidates being examined orally on the principles of the law of England, the science of special pleading, the law of evidence, the law relating to trials at *nisi prius*, and the practice of the courts. In 1854, by which time the bar examination had become partly oral and partly written, the candidate was examined on the following texts:

Stephen, *Commentaries*, Vol. I, Book 2
Blackstone, *Commentaries*, Vol. I, Chapters 2-13
Goldsmith, *Equity*, Parts 1 and 2
Smith, *Contracts*
Smith, *Mercantile Law*
Taylor, *Evidence*
William, *Real Property*
Stephen, *Pleading*

Archibold, *Queen's Bench Practice* or Smith, *Chancery Practice*
Public Statutes Relating to Upper Canada and the Roles and
Orders of the Courts.

Additional texts were cited for those who wished to qualify for
the 'Call with Honors,' for example Volume IV of Stephen's
Commentaries and Coote's *On Mortgages*, but none of these was
characterized by a primary concern with the theory as opposed to
the practice of law. It was a far cry from either the Laval or
the McGill course of study.

The society had done its modest best to urge the establishment
of a university at Toronto and its influence underlay the decision
to establish a chair of common and civil law when King's College,
Toronto, was at long last opened in 1843.[29] The first appointee
to the chair, W.H. Draper, did not accept the appointment, but
lectures were offered by W.H. Blake (1844-47) and by G.S. Connor
(1848-49). The chair disappeared with the abolition of King's
College on 31 December 1849, but a faculty of law was authorized
for the University of Toronto which came into existence on 1
January 1850. However, the faculty of law was never constituted,
and by an act of 1853 the university's functions were limited to
examining and degree granting.

Nonetheless the university established an LL.B. program and a
number of degrees were granted by 1860. The first year of the
three year course, which was based on normal university matriculation, was the first year of Arts - Latin, Greek, rhetoric,
English literature, history, logic, moral philosophy, and political
economy. Two years of study of legal texts followed:

II	III
Hallam, *Constitutional History*	Cox, *British Commonwealth*
Bentham, *Theory of Legislation*	Mitford, *Pleading & Equity*
Smith, *Manual of Equity Juris-*	Archibold, *Landlord & Tenant*
prudence	Addison, *Contracts*
Smith, *Mercantile Law*	Westlake, *Conflict of Laws*
William, *Real Property*	Burton, *Compendium of the Law*
Bowyer, *Civil Law*	*of Real Property*

However, the final examination was based on still other texts,
some highly practical and some theoretical: Snyder, *Vendors and
Purchasers*; Jarman, *Wills*; Taylor, *Evidence*; Blackstone,
Commentaries Vol IV; Sander's edition of *Justinian's Institutes*;
and - under the heading of Roman Jurisprudence - the forty-fourth
chapter of Gibbon's *Decline and Fall of the Roman Empire* and
four chapters of Arnold's *Rome*. It was also possible in 1860 to
obtain the LL.B. by a special examination if one held an M.A. or
was a barrister of seven years' standing. In this case, the texts
were confined to law as a matter of first principles, the student
selecting six tests from a list which included Hallam, Bentham,
Sanders, Gibbon and Arnold of those already noted and as well
Cicero, *De Legibus*, Aristotle, *Politics*, Vattel, *Law of Nations*,

Wheaton, *International Law*, Lieber, *Political Ethics*.

By 1860 two other universities in Upper Canada were offering a law degree on essentially the same bases - Trinity a B.C.L. since 1853 and Victoria an LL.B. commencing in 1860. Trinity listed two lecturers in law on its staff, but Victoria confined itself to appointing examiners. In 1862 Queen's University at Kingston also established a short-lived Faculty of Law.

ENGINEERING

The preamble to the Royal Charter of Incorporation granted to the Canadian Institute in 1851 can be said to be the manifesto of the advocates of applied science in Canada:

> Whereas William E. Logan, John O. Brown, Frederick F. Passmore, Kivas Tully, William Thomas, Thomas Ridout, Sandford Fleming, and others of our loving subjects in our Province of Canada, have formed themselves into a Society for the encouragement and general advancement of the Physical Sciences, the Arts and Manufactures, in this part of our Dominions; and more particularly for promoting the acquisition of those branches of knowledge which are connected with the Professions of Surveying, Engineering, and Architecture: being the Arts of opening up the Wilderness and preparing the country for the pursuits of the Agriculturist, of adjusting with accuracy the boundaries of Properties, of improving and adorning our Cities and the habitations of our subjects, and otherwise smoothing the path of Civilization; and also being the Arts of directing the great sources of Power in Nature for the use and convenience of man, as the means of production and of traffic both for external and internal trade, and materially advancing the development of the Resources and of the Industrial Productions and Commerce of the Country; and have commenced the formation of a Museum for collections of Models and Drawings of Machines and Constructions, New Inventions and Improvements, Geological and Mineralogical Specimens, and whatever may be calculated, either as Natural Productions or Specimens of Art, to promote the purposes of Science and the general interest of society, and have subscribed and collected certain sums of money for these purposes.[30]

At the time the Charter was granted there was no instruction of an advanced nature being offered in any of these subjects anywhere in Canada. But considerable progress was made during the next nine years. In 1860 three universities had well-organized two-year courses and an agricultural college had been established in Quebec.

Even before the Canadian Institute's Charter was granted, though not before steps had been undertaken to secure it, the University of Toronto had advertised for a professor of civil engineering.[31] Nothing resulted immediately from this announcement, partly because of technical difficulties raised by certain of the applications but mainly because of the uncertain status of the University pending the reorganization of 1853; the two-year course eventually offered at University College was not announced until 1857 and the first students did not enrol until 1859, by which time its neighbour, Trinity, was offering lectures on surveying and fortifications. In 1852 Sir Edmund Head, the lieutenant governor of New Brunswick, began to advocate a course in civil engineering at King's College, New Brunswick; in 1853 he provided funds for lectures and practical instruction; and in 1854, following some preparatory lectures in mathematics by William Brydone Jack, a three-month course of lectures on engineering was given by McMahon Cregan, a prominent railroad engineer.[32] Later that year the Royal Commission recommended a two-year course in civil engineering and land surveying.[33] In 1859 a one-year certificate course in civil engineering and surveying (including 'the principles of architecture') was introduced, and the first certificate was granted in 1862 by what had then become the University of New Brunswick. At McGill, Principal Dawson's thirty popular lectures of 1855[34] led to the establishment of a two year diploma course in 1857, the first diploma being granted in the following year. The course was temporarily discontinued in 1863 (owing to a dearth of candidates) but was successfully and permanently revived in 1871. Latin was not required for admission to these special engineering courses but French was. For the most part the course of study was a special arrangement of regular arts courses. The program at Toronto is representative:

First Year
Euclid, Bk. XI., Props. 1 to 21; Statics and Dynamics; Astronomy; English; French; Chemistry and Chemical Physics; Elementary Mineralogy and Geology

Second Year
Hydrostatics, Optics and Acoustics; Applied Chemistry; Mineralogy and Geology

AGRICULTURE

The quite substantial development of engineering education in the 1850s was due in large measure to its distinguished and forceful advocates. Sir Edmund Head was the lieutenant governor, and the founding fathers of the Royal Canadian Institute were prominent citizens and men of affairs. No such advocates appeared to plead the cause of agriculture. However, the needs of the farmers were very much in the minds of members of the legislatures. In 1830, Upper Canada authorized a grant of £100 for importing livestock, grain, useful implements, etc. to any district agricultural society which itself raised £50 for these purposes, an action which not surprisingly encouraged the development of such societies –

there were 61 by 1859. A provincial agricultural association was incorporated in 1847, and in 1850 boards of agriculture were established for both Lower and Upper Canada. An Act to Make Better Provision for the Encouragement and Promotion of Agricultural and Mechanical Science of 1857 was a further sign of the times. As early as 1843 a bill introduced, but not passed in the Upper Canada legislature, had specified agriculture as the one subject which must be taught at the provincial university.[35] In 1851 there was a proposal to convert King's College, New Brunswick, into an agricultural school, and the Royal Commission of 1854 recommended the offering of a special course in agriculture. The practical outcome of these varied actions and proposals was the introduction of special two year courses at McGill (1856) and Toronto (1857) and the opening of a government supported school of agriculture in association with the classical college of Ste Anne-de-la-Pocatière (1859).[36] In each case the practical details of farming received due attention; for example, at McGill the lecturers dealt with such subjects as chemical and mechanical properties of soils, organic and inorganic constituents of plants and manures, rotation of crops, tillage, domestic animals, and orchard and garden culture. The courses were by no means unworthy of a university. The professor of agriculture at Toronto might refer in his course on the practice of agriculture to such mundane matters as weeds, blight and its remedies, butter and cheese-making, and principles of the lease, but he also lectured on management of property, theory of rent, and the relations of political economy to rural affairs.

The bias against trade training was very strong. When asked by the Select Committee investigating the affairs of the University of Toronto in 1860 whether he thought there should be a professor of agriculture in University College, Egerton Ryerson replied:

> I certainly think not. I think anyone who wishes to learn Agriculture would learn more with Hon. Mr. Christie on his Farm, in six months, than he would learn for three years with a Professor of Agriculture in Toronto University. In the list of subjects in the University Calendar, I find 'the Practice of Manuring, the Management of Stock, Construction of Farm Buildings, Dairy Management,' etc. I do not think any practical instruction on such subjects can be given in a University.[37]

More important, perhaps, the special courses failed to attract students. The course at McGill was transferred to the Normal School in 1863. The course at Toronto was withdrawn in 1864. Only at Ste Anne, where practice had always predominated over theory, did the agricultural course attract a sizable student body. It was not until the 1880s and 1890s that agriculture established itself as a recognized field in Canadian higher education.

GRADUATE STUDIES, TEACHER TRAINING, COMMERCE

To complete the record, brief reference must be made to three
other fields of professional education. There were no graduate
studies in Canada in 1860. Most of the colleges granted the M.A.
degree, but the requirements, following the British model, involved
no course work. Sometimes, as at Victoria, the M.A. was granted
to a B.A. of three years' standing who submitted a letter of
application and 'whose mental improvement and moral character
have appeared satisfactory to the authorities of the university,'
but normally, as at McGill, the B.A. of three years' standing
submitted a thesis 'on any literary, scientific, or professional
subject approved by the Faculty.' Two universities - Laval and
McGill - were theoretically involved in teacher-training since
they were technically responsible for normal schools, but in both
cases the connection was entirely nominal and in neither was the
instruction provided by university staff.[38] Finally, McGill had
offered since 1856 a special course of commerce designed 'for
students desirous of devoting themselves for one or two sessions
to the collegiate studies more immediately connected with commercial pursuits.' This was a special grouping of regular arts
courses with English composition, arithmetic and algebra, mathematics and natural philosophy, chemistry, natural history, modern
languages and history coupled with commercial law, general principles of the law of contracts, and a series of lectures on such
topics as insurance, bills and notes, and partnerships.

NOTES TO CHAPTER 5

1 J.W. Dawson, *The Duties of Educated Young Men in British
   North America* (1864), 19
2 See above, chapter 3.
3 The provincial grant to the University of New Brunswick was
   in the amount of $8,844.48 from 1828 to 1905.
4 H. Provost, 'Historique du Séminaire de Québec, *Rev. Univ.
   Laval*, 17 (1963), 591. Provost has modernized the spelling
   and punctuation. The act is reprinted in his *Le Séminaire
   de Québec: documents et biographies* (1964), 1-3.
5 Grand Séminaire de Montréal, *Centenaire 1840-1940* (1941);
   L. Pouliot, 'La Première Ecole de théologie à Montréal: Le
   Séminaire St. Jacques (1825-1840)' *Sciences Ecclesiastiques*,
   6 (1954), 237-47
6 J.L. Bergevin, *Université d'Ottawa: vocations sacerdotales
   et professions liberales, 1848-1928* (1929), 12. See also G.
   Carrière, *L'Université d'Ottawa 1848-1861* (1960), 45-8.
7 T.W. Allen, *Trinity University Review*, June 1902, 84
8 H.Y. Hind, et al., *Eighty Years' Progress of British North
   America* (1864), 442. Hodgins also lists the additional texts
   prescribed each year for 'honours.'

9 J.W. Falconer and W.G. Watson, *A Brief History of Pine Hill Divinity Hall* ... (1946), 1-15; D.C. Masters, *Protestant Church Colleges in Canada* (1966), 84-7

10 Hind, *Eighty Years' Progress*, 439-42

11 E. Seaborn, *The March of Medicine in Western Ontario* (1944), 261-3

12 H. MacLennan, ed., *McGill: the Story of a University* (1960), 39-43. McGill did not offer instruction in any subject other than medicine until 1843.

13 J.G. Heagerty, *Four Centuries of Medical History in Canada* (1928), II, 119-20

14 E.J. Auclair, 'L'Ecole Victoria de Montréal,' *Trans. Royal Society Canada 1938*, section 1, 1-20

15 C.-M. Boissonault, *Histoire de la Faculté de Médicine de Laval* (1953), 135-43

16 C.M. Godfrey, 'King's College: Upper Canada's First Medical School,' *Ontario Medical Rev.*, 34 (1967), 19-22, 26

17 M.A. Patterson, 'The Life and Times of the Hon. John Rolph ...,' *Med. Hist.*, V (1961). There is no detailed history of the Toronto School of Medicine.

18 G.W. Sprague, 'The Trinity Medical College,' *Ontario Hist.*, 58 (1966), 63-98

19 H.P. Gundy, 'Growing Pains: the Early History of Queen's Medical Faculty,' *Historic Kingston*, 4 (1954-55), 14-25

20 *Canada Law Jour.*, 1 (1855), 163

21 F.J. Audet, 'Les Débuts du Barreau de la Province de Québec,' *Cahiers des Dix*, 2 (1937), 207-35

22 A. Vachon, *Histoire du notariat Canadien, 1621-1960* (1962), 79-96

23 Quoted by Audet in 'Les Débuts,' 229

24 E.-F. Surveyer, 'Un Ecole de droit à Montréal avant le code civil,' *Rev. Trimestrielle Can.*, 6 (1920), 140-50

25 W.R. Riddell, *The Legal Profession in Upper Canada in its Early Periods* (1916), 47-9. Riddell's is a notably disorganized account of legal education in Ontario to 1889 but it is also the fullest account, particularly if the notes are taken into consideration.

26 Riddell, *Legal Profession*, 39

27 Ibid., 41

28 Ibid., 46

29 J.M. Young, 'The Faculty of Law' in W.J. Alexander, ed., *The University of Toronto and its Colleges* (1906), 149-67

30 W.S. Wallace, ed., *The Royal Canadian Institute Centennial Volume* (1949), 131

31 C.R. Young, *Early Engineering Education at Toronto* (1958), 9-14

32 A.F. Beard, 'The History of Engineering at the University of New Brunswick,' in A.G. Bailey, ed., *The University of New Brunswick Memorial Volume* (1950), 76-9

33 See above, chapter 3.

34 See above, chapter 4.

35 J.G. Hodgins, ed., *Documentary History of Education in Upper Canada*, VI, 72

36 F. Létourneaù, *Histoire de l'Agriculture au Canada français* (1950), 238-41; J.G. Chapais, 'Notes historiques sur les écoles d'agriculture dans Québec, '*Rev. Canadienne*, 17 (1916), 336-67

37 Hodgins, *Doc. Hist.* (1906), XV, 117

38 By 1860 normal schools had also been established in Upper Canada (1847), New Brunswick (1847), Nova Scotia (1855), and Prince Edward Island (1856).

6

Scholarship and Research

J.L. Myres, the historian of learned societies, has said that three
things are necessary for the effective prosecution of research:

Opportunities for intercourse and conference among men of good-
will, good eyes and good sense;

Means for circulation, as well as compiling, the voluminous
records of research, to preclude all but the most necessary
duplication of experience;

Storehouses, perhaps even lumber rooms, where the *curiosa naturae*,
curiosities or rarities which defied explanation now, might be
kept at hand till the crucial instance or happy conjecture came.[1]

More recently a Canadian scholar, Millar MacLure, has specified
four requirements: 'Apart from such qualities of industry, intelligence and taste as he may possess or acquire, the "producing" scholar
needs four conditions to flourish: a first-class library, or access
by way of travel, film, photostat or facsimile to the holdings of
other libraries; a learned community, or "institute," in which to
associate with his fellows; recess from full-time undergraduate
teaching; and means of publication.'[2] Faraday had a simpler formula: 'There are three necessary steps in useful research - the
first to begin it, the second to end it, the third to publish it.'
   No one can read extensively in the history of the Canadian universities without becoming convinced that these institutions were
blessed in their early days with an extraordinary number of men of
good-will and good sense; that many of them were also gifted with
good eyes is borne out by publications in the fields of botany and
geology. The Canadian record of research and scholarship up to
1860 is at the very least respectable, as the names of Dawson,
Logan, and Garneau bear witness. When we consider the difficulties
under which these early scholars laboured, the record of achievement
can be regarded as remarkable. There were almost no opportunities

for personal contact with scholars in other universities, no such thing as interlibrary loan, a very limited number of scholarly journals, none with a wide circulation, and no large museums or libraries.

The first step is to begin it - to find the time for study and contemplation. "My work during all the years of my college life in Montreal,' said Principal Dawson, 'included about twenty lectures weekly, besides the care of the management and interests of the institution, and frequent efforts for its extension and enlargement.'[3] The teaching load of every Canadian professor in the nineteenth century was a heavy one, and the demands on his time for committee work and student counselling appear to have been as time-consuming as they are today. As we have seen, he was almost invariably lecturing in more than one field, and he received no assistance from graduate students. He was not, it is true, troubled by the necessity of supervising the work of graduate students, but by the same token he lacked the stimulation to develop his own research which such supervision naturally provides. More often than not, he also lacked the stimulation of contact with fellow-workers in the field. His was the day of the one-man department, his the day of the isolated community. Consider the position of Loring Bailey, who was appointed professor of chemistry and natural science at the University of New Brunswick in 1861:

The isolation, more particularly from scientific centres and scientific co-laborers, has always been a great draw back in my position - there being not more than two or three persons in the whole Province, and *none* in Fredericton, who know anything or care anything about the pursuits in which my pleasure is chiefly sought. However, I have the satisfaction of knowing that I work in a comparatively unexplored field and hope to lay a good foundation here, upon which in the future others may build.[4]

Bailey remained at Fredericton until his retirement in 1909, and his bibliography contains over one hundred scholarly papers. He was fortunate in that his field of research (botany and geology, not chemistry) could be pursued in isolation and without reference to large libraries.

President Brydone Jack's statement at the University of New Brunswick Encoenia of 1876 is one of several indications that Canadian scholars were early aware of the importance of research and also of the conditions necessary for its effective prosecution:

To render the University popular and attractive it must be able to show that it is progressive. It must be provided with all the best modern appliances for rendering its course of study effective and interesting. Its apparatus, library, museum and laboratory must receive the additions which from time to time become necessary. Its course of study must also be made more varied and complete to keep pace with the requirements of the age. The grand object to be attained is the widening of the sphere of education imparted, the bringing within the scope of

University instruction every branch of human knowledge, and the making of it more thorough, searching and progressive. It should be the ambition of every up-to-date University to make provision for the endowment of scientific research, so that men able and willing to devote their time and talents to original investigations and the prosecution of fresh discoveries in the branch of their study in which they have become famous may meet with due encouragement.[5]

But Jack was also aware of the local facts of life. 'I do not presume,' he continued, 'to compare this University with any of the wealthy long-established institutions to which I have referred. With us it is still the day of small things, and for many years we must be content to follow afar off, humbly and laboriously in their footsteps.' We have earlier referred to the inadequacies (or non-existence) of laboratory facilities for undergraduate instruction in science;[6] if the professor lacked equipment for the teaching of elementary science, he was not likely to have the more elaborate equipment required for his own research. Nor was the position of his colleague in arts much better; few college libraries had as many as 5000 volumes. The largest was Laval's - 28,000 volumes in 1863, including 2000 in law, 4000 in medicine, 8000 'in the different branches of science and literature,' and 14,000 in theology. This figure was provided by J.G. Hodgins who compiled the number of volumes in the libraries of Upper and Lower Canada 'from the best sources at our command' for his articles in *Eighty Years Progress of British North America*.[7] His other figures include McGill 8000, Bishop's 4000, Grand Séminaire de Montréal 2500, Toronto 15,000, Knox 4000, Trinity 3500, Queen's 3000, Ottawa 2000, St Michael's 1500, Victoria 1000.

Of course, for normal purposes, a small library was sufficient. 'The ordinary text-books used in education, the classical authors in various languages, the books of reference in common use, are not so numerous as to be beyond the reach of any College, or even of many private individuals,' John Langton, vice-chancellor of the University of Toronto, told the Select Committee of 1860:

But there is another class of Books which you will not find there, consisting principally of Books of Reference of a more special character, not so often used it is true, but as essential when occasions for consulting them occur; and those numerous periodical publications issued by learned and Scientific Bodies in various parts of the World, in which almost all new views and discoveries first make their appearance, and, without access to which, a Scholar, or a Man of Science, in this Country would have to remain contented with his ignorance, until, years after all Europe had been turning their attention to something new, he gathered the information from some digest, published in a more popular and accessible form. Such publications, often of a very costly kind from their limited circulation, can only be found in a Public Library; and, until Canada possesses such a collection, she must be content to remain in a position of inferiority, ill adopted to her growing wealth and intelligence.[8]

There was no such reference library in Canada in 1860. Nor was there a national museum, though the need for one had been suggested by William Logan, director of the the Geological Survey, in his annual report of 1852, in which he asked 'whether a growing country like Canada could not afford to anticipate what its future importance may require in the nature of a national museum and at some future time not far distant erect an appropriate edifice specially planned for the purpose.' But nothing was done to implement the suggestion until 1872 when a start was made towards organizing a dominion archives in the Department of Agriculture at Ottawa.[9]

But though there was no dominion archives in 1860 to house documents relating to the history of Canada, no national museum (or lumber room) to store the *curiosa naturae*, and no national library in which to place the learned journals, appropriate materials were being gathered, and periodicals which would occupy an honourable place on the unbuilt shelves were being published. The Literary and Historical Society of Quebec had been established in 1824 and had published *Transactions* in 1829, 1837, 1855, and 1857. The Natural History Society of Montreal, established in 1827, began to publish the *Canadian Naturalist and Geologist* in 1857. The Royal Canadian Institute began publication of the *Canadian Journal* in 1852. In addition, a number of medical journals had had short runs, particularly in Montreal where the *Journal de Médecine de Québec* (Jan. 1826 to April 1827) was followed by the *Montreal Medical Gazette* (April 1844 to March 1845), *British America Journal of Medical and Physical Science* (1845-52 and 1860-62), *Lancette Canadianne* (1847), *Canadian Medical Journal* (1852-53) and the *Medical Chronicle* (1852-59); at Toronto the *Upper Canada Journal of Medical, Surgical and Physical Science* was published from April 1851 to September 1854. The Botanical Society of Canada, organized at Kingston in 1860, published its *Annals* from 1860 to 1862. Other professional journals were the *Journals of Education for Upper Canada* and *for Lower Canada*, instituted in 1848 and 1857 respectively, and the *Canadian Agriculturist*, which began publication in 1848. Journals such as the *Literary Garland* (1838-57), the *Maple Leaf* (1847-49), and the *Anglo-American Magazine* (1852-55) provided an opportunity for essays if not foot-noted articles in the fields of literary criticism and history.[10] Of all these the most significant for scholarship and research were the publications of the Literary and Historical Society of Quebec, the Natural History Society of Montreal and the Royal Canadian Institute.

During the French régime an académie des sciences had enjoyed a brief existence through the encouragement of Comte de La Galissonière, an enlightened governor (1747-49), who had also attempted unsuccessfully to persuade the French king to establish a printing press in the colony.[11]

The most learned society in French Canada was also sponsored by a governor, but as its name suggests and as the preamble to

its charter proclaims, its primary interest was in historical
rather than scientific research:

> Whereas an Association of divers of our loving subjects in the
> City of Quebec in the Province of Lower Canada, has been formed
> ... under the name of the 'Literary and Historical Society of
> Quebec' for the prosecution of researches into the early history
> of Canada, for the recovering, procuring, and publishing,
> interesting documents and useful information, as the Natural,
> Civil and Literary History of British North America, and for
> the advancement of the Arts and Sciences in the said Province
> of Lower Canada, from which public benefit may be expected.[12]

Nor was it primarily an assembly of French Canadians. Conceived
by Lord Dalhousie, it originally consisted of English-speaking
residents of Quebec, but in 1829 it absorbed a very similar but
French-speaking organization founded in 1827, the Society for
Promoting Literature, Science, Arts and Historical Research; consequently the list of 'our loving subjects' in the charter of 1831
includes the names of a dozen French-Canadians including F.-X.
Garneau. In due course, historical research did become the
society's main concern; collections of *Historical Documents* were
published in 1838, 1840, and 1843, and the *Transactions* of 1837
and 1855 contain many papers on the language and customs of the
North American Indians. However, with the exception of the first
president's inaugural address (J. Sewell, 'The Early Civil and
Ecclesiastical Juridical History of France') and a paper by J.F.
Perrault on a contemporary problem ('Plan Raisonné d'éducation
générale et permanente'), the contents of the first two *Transactions*
(1829, 1831) were in the field of natural science. They include
significant geological reports by H.W. Bayfield and F.W. Baddeley.
The society maintained a general interest in science after this
initial activity was replaced by a concentration on the original
objectives. Its petition of 1841 was instrumental in persuading
the government to establish the Geological Survey in 1842.[13]
    The view of the founders of the Canadian Institute[14] that some-
thing more than a general interest in science was urgently needed
was clearly stated in the editorial which ushered in the first
volume of *The Canadian Journal: A Repertory of Industry, Science
and Art, and a Record of the Proceedings of the Canadian Institute:*

> It can scarcely be denied that the pursuit and cultivation of
> the Physical Sciences has made comparatively little progress in
> Canada, and by no means attained the established place which
> might have been looked for at this stage of our history. It is
> true that two Societies, directed more or less to this subject
> have existed in Lower Canada for more than twenty years - the
> Literary and Historical Society of Quebec, founded in 1824, and
> the Natural History Society of Montreal founded in 1827, but we
> have the highest authority for inferring that the latter at
> least has not as yet realized the expectations of its zealous

founders, nor can the last Report of the authorities of the former, be deemed entirely satisfactory.[15]

The editor, H.Y. Hind, went on to diagnose the failure of the existing societies and to prescribe the new Institute's remedy:

It rather appears too, and we refer to this, because it is the evil which it has been principally sought to avoid, in the constitution of the Society just referred to, that the objects expressed by the titles Natural History Society and Literary and Historical Society, are too special to be able to stand alone in this country at present. They do not include a multitude of objects in which much of the most active talent in the country is engaged, for example, those involved in the professions of the Engineer, the Artist, the Surveyor, the Architect, all of them represented by Societies of high standing in Great Britain, and therefore capable in their nature of extending the basis of similar bodies here ... We may hope that an attempt to unite under one roof and in one organization a full representation of the active mind of the community, may be more fortunate.[16]

This practical bias is reflected both in the original membership of the Canadian Institute ('men distinguished in Science and Arts, residing in the Province' were admitted as honorary members, but full, corresponding, and student membership was limited to those actively engaged as land surveyors, civil engineers or architects) and in the contents of the *Journal* under Hind's editorship (1852-55). Typical original communications were 'Notes on the Geology of Toronto' (H.Y. Hind), 'On the Probable Number of the Indian Population in British America' (J.H. Lefroy), 'Gas Patents' (H.H. Croft) and 'On the Provincial Currency' (J.B. Cherriman). Papers read at the meetings of the Institute in 1852 included such practical presentations as 'On the Use of the Telescope, as applied to Field Practice,' and 'A Review of the Several Clauses in the Surveyor's Act of 1849.' But a marked change occurred with the New Series of the *Canadian Journal* initiated under the editorship of Daniel Wilson in January 1856. In his preliminary address, Wilson announced that there were genuine students of science in Canada and that they urgently required a medium of communication which would 'furnish a means of intercourse among themselves, as well as an interchange of thought and discovery with the scientific world at large':

The advancement of Canada in commercial and agricultural prosperity during recent years, is without a parallel in the history of the British Colonies; and there is abundant reason for believing that it is even now only on the threshold of a career of triumphant progress. It must be the desire of every well-wisher of the province, that this advancement in industry and material wealth should not be unaccompanied by some corresponding manifestations of intellectual vitality. There is no reason why

Canada should not have her own literature and science, as well as her agriculture and commerce; and contribute her share to the greatness of the British Empire by her mental as well as her physical achievements. Already the published Reports of the Magnetic and Meteorological Observatory have made the name of Toronto familiar to European savants; and the labors of the Provincial Geological Survey, under the guidance of Mr. Logan, have contributed results, the scientific value of which is universally recognized. But, meanwhile, such students of science as Canada has, stand, to a great extent, isolated in relation to each other, and look mainly for the appreciation of their labors to their scientific brethren in Europe. If Mr. Logan meets with copper or coal in the course of this geological survey, he communicates it to Canada, and all her journals give welcome circulation to the fact; but if palaeontological researches among our Canadian strata disclose novel truths in relation to the structure of the *Graphalite*, he goes to Paris or to London with the discovery, and communicates it to his scientific brethren - as Mr. Dawson originally published his Acadian Geological observations, - through the medium of English Societies' Transactions. Thus the science of Canada has, as yet, no recognized or independent existence, and its students, if they would place themselves in *rapport* with those of other lands, can only do so by a sacrifice analogous to the naturalization by which a foreign emigrant attains to the privileges of American citizenship.[17]

The contents of the first issue of the New Series (January 1856) represented a widening of the range of subject matter but also a deepening of the level of approach:

Displacement and Extinction Among the Primeval Races of Man
(Daniel Wilson)
On Some New Salts of Cadmium and Iodides of Barium and Strontium
(H. Croft)
Remarks on a Canadian Specimen of the Proteus of the Lakes
(J.G. Hodgins)
On the Value of the Factor in the Hyrometric Formula
(Capt. A. Noble)
Notes on Some Points in the Anatomy of the Leech
(James Bovell)
Coleoptera Collected in Canada
(William Couper)

These papers and Wilson's Preliminary Address occupy the first 38 pages of a 96-page issue. The remaining space is devoted to Reviews (of Dawson's *Acadian Geology*, Longfellow's *The Song of Hiawatha*, Todhunter's *A Treatise on Analytical Statics*, etc.) and Scientific and Literary Notes, arranged under seven departments presided over by the members of the editing committee, whose titles indicate that the 'honorary members' as distinct from the 'full members' had taken over control:

1 *Geology and Mineralogy:* E.J. Chapman, Prof. of Geology & Mineralogy, University College, Toronto
2 *Physiology and Natural History:* James Bovell, M.D., Prof. of the Institutes of Medicine, Trinity College, Toronto
3 *Ethnology and Archaeology:* Daniel Wilson, LL.D., Prof. of History and English Literature, University College, Toronto
4 *Agricultural Science:* H.Y. Hind, M.A., Prof. of Chemistry, Trinity College, Toronto
5 *Chemistry:* Henry Croft, D.C.L., Prof. of Chemistry, University College, Toronto
6 *Mathematics and Natural Philosophy:* J.B. Cherriman, M.A., Prof. of Natural Philosophy, University College, Toronto, and Rev. G.C. Irwing, M.A., Prof. of Mathematics and Natural Philosophy, Trinity College, Toronto
7 *Engineering and Architecture:* F.W. Cumberland, C.E., and Alfred Brunel, C.E.

Each issue of the four volumes edited by Wilson (1856-59) followed the pattern set in the opening issue and the pattern was continued under E.J. Chapman, who succeeded him as editor in 1860.

Hind was correct in stating that in 1852 the Natural History Society of Montreal had not realized the expectation of its zealous founders, but he would not have made the same statement ten years later. Shortly after J.W. Dawson's arrival in Montreal in 1855 as principal of McGill, interest in the society was revived and a focus given to its activities by the publication of a journal. The first volume of the *Canadian Naturalist and Geologist* (1857) was entirely the work of E.W. Billings, a staff member of the Geological Survey, but the second volume (also 1857), which added *and Proceedings of the Natural History Society of Montreal* to the title, was a normal journal edited by a committee of the society, which included Dawson, Billings and T.S. Hunt, the professor of chemistry at Laval who was also Chemist to the Geological Survey. Its annual volumes continued until 1883 when the *Proceedings* of the Natural History Society of Montreal began to be published separately.

The most significant papers in the three journals we have discussed were in the fields of biology and geology, where in the nineteenth century the accurate description of natural phenomena could still be the basis for important advances. Since the time of Jacques Cartier and Samuel Champlain, Canada had offered a rich field of investigation to the natural scientist, and this had been appreciated throughout the French régime, to which the world of science owes the contributions of such men as Michael Sarrazin, Peter Kalm, and Jean-François Gaultier.[18] Interest in botany and zoology continued under the British régime, but the major effort was in the field of geology. Sir William Logan's *The Geology of Canada*, published in 1863 but based on studies undertaken by Logan and his staff over a twenty-year period commencing with his appointment as director of the Geological Survey of Canada in 1843, is the most important publication by a Canadian scientist in the period under review. The significant work of Principal Dawson in the field of palaeobotany was also well advanced by 1860. But most scientists were drawn towards the practical application of their specialties in a new and growing country. This was particularly true of the chemists, who tended to apply their knowledge to agriculture and mining and to use it to supplement the work in geology. Thus James Robb, the professor of chemistry and natural history at the University of New Brunswick, was the first president of the Provincial Society for the Encouragement of Agriculture and he contributed a geological map of New Brunswick for a volume entitled *The Agricultural Capabilities of New Brunswick*, Henry How, professor of chemistry and natural history at King's College, Windsor, published *The Mineralogy of Nova Scotia* (1869), and as has been noted Thomas Sterry Hunt, professor of chemistry at Laval, worked for years on the staff of the Geological Survey.

But while the descriptive sciences and the applications of chemistry offered fruitful fields for Canadians in the mid-nineteenth century, the experimental sciences of chemistry and physics made little headway. The situation at New Brunswick was typical:

> Though Robb and Bailey successively occupied the Chair of Chemistry and Natural Science during seventy years, at no time was there any marked development in the teaching or practice of chemistry as such ... In an isolated and undeveloped country ... it is not to be expected that the experimental sciences would flourish, whereas the study of the geology and biology of the region offered attractive possibilities. Chemistry ... and to a large extent Physics – remained a necessary but subsidiary course in the curriculum, handicapped by lack of apparatus and contact with the tremendous developments going on in the outside world.[19]

The researches of Robb and Bailey were in botany and geology, not chemistry. Experimental chemistry was one of the few fields to which H.H. Croft, professor of chemistry at the University of Toronto from 1843 to 1880, did not turn his considerable talents. Nothing resembling modern research in physics occurred in Canada until the 1880s. But the pages of the early volumes of the *Canadian Journal* contained a number of papers in the field of pure mathematics, notably by George Paxton Young and J.B. Cherriman.[20]

Such publications as made claim to scholarship in the humanities up to 1860 in English-speaking Canada were the works of Englishmen and Scots who had come to Canada as professors, for example the Rev. John McCaul, whose *Britanno-Roman Inscriptions* of 1863 was a compilation of earlier papers, some of which had appeared in the *Canadian Journal* between 1858 and 1860, Daniel Wilson, whose *Memorials of Edinburgh in the Older Time* (1847) and *Archaeology and Prehistoric Annals of Scotland* (1851) had been published before his arrival in Canada, and James Beaven, professor of divinity in King's College, Toronto, and from 1850 professor of metaphysics and ethics at the University of Toronto, whose *Elements of Natural Theology* appeared in 1850 and an edition of Cicero's *De Finibus* in 1853. Egerton Ryerson's comment to the Select Committee of 1860 on Wilson's efforts was an indication of the value he attached to such work:

> He, to be sure, has published a book, and it was a book upon 'relics,' a book about antiquities ... He has a peculiar affinity for subjects of that description and in his leisure moments in this Country has devoted himself to disembowelling the Cemetries of the Indian Tribes in seeking up the Tomahawks, Pipes and Tobacco which may be found there and writing essays upon them.[21]

Native Canadians like Ryerson tended at times to be so thoroughly involved in the political and religious controversies of the day as to be incapable of understanding the timeless world of scholarship. Sir John Bourinot had this in mind when analysing Canada's intellectual strengths and weaknesses in 1893. The Canadian experience, he argued, more closely resembled that of Virginia than of New England:

> Statesmanship rather than Letters has been the pride and ambition of the Old Dominion, its brightest and highest achievement. Virginia has been the mother of great orators and great presidents, and her men of letters sink into insignificance alongside of those of New England. It may be said, too, of Canada that her history in the days of the French Régime, during the struggle for responsible government, as well as at the birth of confederation, gives us the names of men of statesmanlike designs and of patriotic purposes. From the days of Champlain to the establishment of the confederation, Canada has had the services of men as eminent in their respective spheres, and as successful in the attainment of popular rights, in moulding the educational and political institutions of the country, and in laying broad and deep the foundations of a new nationality across half a continent, as those great Virginians to whom the world is ever ready to pay its meed of respect. These Virginia statesmen won their fame in the large theatre of national achievement - in laying the basis of the most remarkable federal republic the world has ever seen; whilst Canadian public men have laboured with equal earnestness and ability in that far less conspicuous and brilliant area of colonial development, the eulogy of which has to be written in the histories of the future.[22]

In French Canada up to 1860 much of the energy which might have been expended in scholarship and research had to be directed to the prosaic task of providing text-books for the schools and colleges. The question of text-books had never posed a problem for the colleges in the English-speaking colonies since a supply of appropriate works was readily available through the British

and American markets. But French-speaking students required
French language texts, and these the British and American markets
did not supply. Appropriate texts were available in France, but
normal relations with Paris, abruptly severed in 1760, were not
effectively resumed until the 1850s.

Wade and others have shown that French Canadians were by no
means ignorant of intellectual and literary developments in France
during the first half of the nineteenth century,[23] but they have not
altered the general picture of cultural isolation. The ideas of
the French Revolution remained anathema to the Roman Catholic
church, which controlled education at all levels. In any event,
text-books, particularly in science and mathematics, were hard to
obtain and there was a compelling need for such works as J.-B.
Meilleur's *Traité de Chimie* (1833) and Langevin's *Traité de Calcul
Différentiale et Intégrale* (1848).[24]

French Canada also produced a number of useful books of the type
represented by Bouchette's *Description Topographique de la Province
du Bas Canada* (1851), a compilation of factual information which
does not, however, constitute either scholarship or research.
Nonetheless, such works directed attention to the problems facing
French Canada in the early nineteenth century, problems that lay
deeply rooted in the past and were being probed simultaneously
by amateur antiquarians like Jacques Viger, the founder of the
Société Historique de Montréal and the first president of the
Société St Jean Baptiste, whose unpublished manuscript material
had reached forty-four volumes at the time of his death in 1858.
Both Viger and Bouchette stand symbolically behind Francois-Xavier
Garneau, whose three-volume *Histoire du Canada depuis sa découverte
jusqu'à nos jours* (1845-48) is the most important work of the
period by a French Canadian and a work whose significance, if not
its scholarship, far outweighs Logan's *The Geology of Canada*.
The themes enunciated by Garneau would occupy the minds of French
Canadian intellectuals for decades to come and would establish the
direction of French Canadian scholarship well into the twentieth
century.

NOTES TO CHAPTER 6

1 J.L. Myres, *Learned Societies: a Lecture delivered in the
   Library of the Department of Education at the University of
   Liverpool 4th November, 1922* (1922), 18
2 M. MacLure, 'Literary Scholarship' in C.F. Klinck, ed.,
   Literary History of Canada (1965), 531
3 R. Dawson, ed., *Fifty Years of Work in Canada ... Being
   Autobiographical Notes by Sir William Dawson* (1901), 108-9
4 Letter of L.W. Bailey to W. Rogers, President, Massachusett's
   Institute of Technology, in J.W. Bailey, ed., *Loring Woart
   Bailey* (1925), 72-3

5 W.O. Raymond, *The Genesis of the University of New Brunswick with a Sketch of the Life of William Brydone-Jack. President, 1861-1855* (1920), 28

6 See above, chapter 4, 53-4.

7 H.L. Hind, *et al.,* *Eighty Years Progress of British North America* (1864), 475, 508-24

8 J.G. Hodgins, ed., *Documentary History of Education in Upper Canada* (1906), XV, 168

9 See below, chapter 18, 322-3.

10 Other general journals of the 1840s and 1850s, all short-lived, were *Revue Canadienne: journal scientifique et littéraire* (Montréal, 1845-48), *Repertoire national: ou Recueil de literature canadien* (Montréal, 1848-50), *Colonial Protestant; Journal of Literature and Science* (Montreal, 1848-49), *British Colonial Magazine* (Toronto, 1852-53), *Provincial or Halifax Monthly Magazine* (Halifax, 1852-53). Longer lasting were three denominational publications: *Presbyterian* (Montreal, 1848-75), *Presbyterian Witness* (Halifax, Toronto, 1848-1925), *Wesleyan* (Halifax, 1838-1907).

11 M. Wade, *The French Canadians 1760-1945* (1955), 27

12 Literary and Historical Society of Quebec, *The Centenary Volume, 1824-1924* (1924), 17

13 A geological survey was first proposed in 1832 by John Rae, the economist, in a petition to the House of Assembly of Upper Canada: B.K. Harrington, *Life of Sir William Logan* (1883), 122 ff.

14 See above, chapter 5, 72.

15 *Can. J.*, 1 (1852-53), 2

16 Ibid., 2-3

17 *Canadian J. Industry, Science and Art*, n.s. 1 (1856), 1-2

18 L.E. Pariseau, 'Canadian Medicine and Biology during the French Régime' in H.M. Tory, ed., *A History of Science in Canada* (1939), 58-68

19 F.J. Toole, 'The Scientific Tradition' in A.G. Bailey, ed., *The University of New Brunswick Memorial Volume* (1950), 73

20 For Young, see J.A. Irving and A.H. Johnson, 'Philosophical Literature to 1901' in C.F. Klinck, ed., *Literary History of Canada* (1965), 435-6.

21 Hodgins, *Doc. Hist.*, XV, 269

22 J.C. Bourinot, 'Our Intellectual Strength and Weakness: a Short Review of Literature, Education and Art in Canada,' *Trans. Royal Society Canada* 1893, section 2, 4. See also Bourinot's *The Intellectual Development of the Canadian People* (1881).

23 Wade, *The French Canadians*; C. Galarneau, *La France devant l'opinion canadienne (1760-1815)* (1970).

24 L. Lortie, 'Les Mathématiques de nos ancêtres,' *Trans. Royal Society Canada* 1955, section 1, 31-45; *Le Traité de chimie de J.-B. Meilleur* (1937)

1890

The operations of McGill are now so extensive and complicated that the dangers of disintegration and isolation have become greater than any others, and the Principal must always be the central bond of union of the University, because he alone can know it in all its parts and weigh the claims, needs, dangers, difficulties and opportunities of each of its constituent faculties and departments.

Principal Dawson, 1893

7
The Royal Society of Canada, 1882-1890[1]

For three days at the end of May in 1890 professors from five Canadian universities sat together in the Railway Committee Room of the House of Commons in Ottawa. They were assembled not as professors but as fellows of the Royal Society of Canada, which was holding its annual meeting in the room where it had been born nine years earlier. The papers presented concerned problems other than those to which the members had primarily directed their minds during the previous nine months; for the time being 'La Femme dans la société moderne,' 'The American Bison,' and 'Drift Rocks of Central Ontario' took priority over such perennial questions as compulsory Latin, the hiring of staff and, since women had by now been admitted to some of the universities, the relations of young men to young women. Doubtless there was occasion to discuss such problems informally, for the society's schedule was a sensible one - there were no evening sessions and the day's business began at 10:00 A.M. But though higher education was not the subject of formal discussion, this assembling of professors from different institutions was a significant event. Their predecessors of 1860 met only to present evidence against each other before committees of the legislature.

The five universities represented were Dalhousie, Laval, McGill, Queen's, and Toronto. The only member attending from Toronto was President Daniel Wilson although three of Wilson's colleagues were also fellows of the Royal Society; E.J. Chapman (mineralogy and geology), Ramsay Wright (natural science), and James Loudon (mathematics and physics). The McGill delegation included the familiar figure of Principal J.W. Dawson (geology) as well as four professors: G.P. Girdwood (chemistry, J.C. Murray (philosophy), Alexander Johnson (mathematics and natural philosophy); and D.P. Penhallow (botany). Two McGill Fellows were absent - H.T. Bovey (dean of applied science) and B.J. Harrington (chemistry and mineralogy), while still another McGill professor, T.W. Mills (physiology), was one of two persons elected to membership at the closing session.

The other, Charles G.D. Roberts, was professor of English literature, political economy, and logic at King's College, Windsor.
Representing Laval were T.-E. Hamel (physique), J.-C.-K. LaFlamme
(minéralogie et géologie), C. Tanquay (archéologie), and H. Verreau
(histoire du Canada). From Queen's had come its principal, G.M.
Grant, its chancellor, Sanford Fleming, and two professors, John
Watson (philosophy) and N.F. Dupuis (mathematics). Dalhousie was
represented by George Lawson (chemistry) and J.G. McGregor (physics),
who at 30 had been the youngest of the 80 persons named as charter
fellows of the Royal Society in 1882. The University of New
Brunswick was the only other university which in 1890 had a fellow
of the Royal Society on its staff, but L.W. Bailey (biology) was
among the absentees.

As originally constituted, the Royal Society consisted of 20
fellows in each of four sections: French literature, with history,
archaeology and allied subjects; English literature, with history,
archaeology and allied subjects; mathematics, chemical and physical
sciences; and geological and biological sciences. According to
the constitution, the fellows were to be persons resident in the
Dominion of Canada or in Newfoundland, who had published original
works or 'memoirs of merit' or had rendered eminent service to
literature or to science. The fellows were expected to take their
responsibilities seriously: 'any member failing to attend three
years in succession, without presenting a paper, or assigning
reasons in writing satisfactory to the Society, shall be considered
to have resigned,' but the category of retired member was authorized
for those who wished to withdraw - William Osler became a retired
member in 1885 on moving from McGill to the University of Pennsylvania. Unfortunately not all the inactive fellows were as prompt
as Osler to make room for new blood, and this created a problem
for the society since it had a restricted membership. The council
(or executive) referred to this problem and to the general question
of restricted membership in the report it submitted to the society
at the opening session:

In the case of a Society with a limited membership of eighty
members, the average attendance can hardly ever exceed fifty
under the most favourable circumstances, unless it were possible
for all the members to give up their official or professional
duties at the demand of the Society. For instance, this year
the Honorary Secretary has received a letter from Professor
Bovey in which he communicates his regrets that, on account of
his absence in England on business connected with the Science
Faculty of McGill University, he will be unable to be present
at this meeting. Mr. Gilpin, Inspector of Mines in Nova Scotia,
is also unable to be with us in consequence of his presence being
imperatively required, during this week, by the Executive government of the Province, to give them the benefit of his advice and
assistance with respect to the reorganization of the Board of
Examiners of candidates for certificates as underground managers
of mines. While it is quite true that these cases illustrate

the difficulties that necessarily prevent a large meeting, there are, at the same time, other reasons which operate to a minor degree in the same direction. For instance, several gentlemen have, from time to time, left the Dominion, and made their home in other countries, without even informing the Secretary of their change of residence. It would be well for each section to inquire carefully into the circumstances of the continual absence of members and into all matters which may affect the practical usefulness of a section. It is absolutely indispensable, all must admit, that this Society should be a working body, and not a purely honorary institution. In the case certainly, of those gentlemen who have left the country to pursue a career of usefulness elsewhere, it would be well to consider whether they should not be placed on the list of retired members as a recognition of their actual work in the Society. It has also been suggested that the limitation of membership to eighty in all, or twenty in each section, might be advantageously enlarged to one hundred in the aggregate, or twenty-five in each section. It is only necessary to look over the list of literary and scientific workers throughout Canada, to see that a number of gentlemen who might be most efficient members, are kept out of the Society for years in the absence of sufficient vacancies. Should the membership be enlarged as suggested, it would not be necessary, nor indeed advisable, to fill up the quota of each section immediately, but only as proper cases of election suggest themselves clearly in the interest of science and literature. The Council do not make any special recommendation on this point, but simply direct attention to a matter worthy of consideration and debate. It must always be remembered that the great object of the Royal Society is to give currency to the best scientific and literary thought of the Dominion. It would be unfortunate if strict rules of election and a limitation of membership should give the Society a degree of exclusiveness which may, in a measure, practically diminish its usefulness as a dominion institution.[2]

At its final session, the society decided to take action. Two delinquents were placed on the list of retired members 'as a recognition of their work while active members of this Society,' and it was decided to permit sections to admit one additional member in any year in which a vacancy was not created by normal means, a new maximum being set at 25. But these steps were taken too late to permit new fellows to be chosen to replace the two delinquents, and in one section the required number of votes was not obtained by any candidates proposed to fill a normal vacancy. Hence the total was 77 fellows in 1890 rather than 80.

The decision to extend the membership of the Royal Society to a theoretical maximum of 100 was a sensible rather than a revolutionary step and it did not constitute abandonment of the principle stated by its first president, J.W. Dawson, in 1882:

It would be a mistake to suppose that this Society should include
all our literary and scientific men, or even all those of some
local standing. It must consist of selected and representative
men who have themselves done original work of at least Canadian
celebrity. Beyond this it would have no resting-place short of
that of a great popular assemblage whose members should be
characterized rather by mere receptivity than by productiveness.[3]

Burpee has stated bluntly that some of the original fellows were
men of mediocrity.[4] An analysis of the membership of 1890 confirms
this view and also indicates that some of the persons elected
between 1883 and 1890 could be similarly described. But from the
outset candidates had been carefully screened and it is not easy
to identify a Canadian scholar or scientist of stature in 1890 who
was *not* a member of the Royal Society. A thirty per cent representation was a reasonably accurate indication of the contribution
which the universities and colleges were making to the advancement
of literature and science in Canada in 1890. The fact that the
bulk of the academic contingent was contributed by five universities is also a reasonably accurate indication of the comparative
strength of the 20 degree-granting institutions in operation at
that time.

It was certainly fitting that a society whose object was the
promotion of literature and science in the Dominion of Canada
should have been born in a railway committee room, for in the last
third of the nineteenth century the railway was the key to the
development of Canada and, indeed, to its survival as a nation.
In 1882 Canada consisted of seven provinces, only four of which
approximated their present geographic size. The dominion had been
formed in 1867 when the colonies of Canada, New Brunswick, and
Nova Scotia entered into a union; Upper and Lower Canada, the two
divisions of the older Canada, taking the names of Ontario and
Quebec. In 1870 the territories of the Hudson's Bay Company were
ceded to the new dominion and the Province of Manitoba was created
out of a tiny portion of this vast area. The crown colonies of
British Columbia and Prince Edward Island entered the dominion
in 1871 and 1873. At this time Ontario, Quebec, and Manitoba were
half their present size, and large stretches of land separated
British Columbia from Manitoba, and Manitoba from Ontario. The
completion of the Intercolonial Railway in the 1870s effectively
linked the Maritime provinces with Ontario and Quebec, but the
retention of British Columbia in the federation and the development
of the West depended upon the building of a transcontinental railway, a task that was not accomplished until 1885. It was fitting,
too, that the society should have been born and have its headquarters in Ottawa, the capital of the new dominion. No fewer
than 21 of the 1890 fellows were residents of Ottawa, in almost
all instances civil servants in the growing number of government
departments and agencies. Eight of these were associated with the
Geological Survey.

The Royal Society itself was contributing in two ways to the development of Canada as a national entity. First, it acted from the time of its establishment as a national organization which could deal on even terms with such organizations as the British Association for the Advancement of Science and the National Academy of Science of the United States of America. Second, it acted as a connecting link for the efforts of local societies devoted to the advancement of literature and science. Such organizations could become affiliates of the Royal Society, in which case their delegates could attend the annual meeting and space would be provided in the *Proceedings* for a report on their activities during the preceding year. The list of affiliate societies in 1890 is worth recording, both as an indication of the Royal Society's far-reaching influence and as an indication of the considerable increase in the number and range of local societies. Only those identified by an asterisk were in existence in 1860:

Society of Canadian Literature of Montreal
* Natural History Society of Montreal
Numismatic and Antiquarian Society of Montreal
The Society of Historical Studies, Montreal
La Société Litteraire et Musicale de Montréal
* The Literary and Historical Society of Quebec
The Geographical Society, Montreal
* Institut Canadien, Québec
The Ottawa Literary and Scientific Society
The Ottawa Field Naturalists' Club
* L'Institut Canadien Français d'Ottawa
* The Hamilton Association for the Promotion of Literature, Science and Art
Wentworth Historical Society, Hamilton
Murchison Scientific Society, Belleville
The Entomological Society of Ontario, Belleville
* The Canadian Institute, Toronto
The Natural History Society of New Brunswick
The Nova Scotian Institute of Natural Science
The Nova Scotia Historical Society
The Natural History Society of British Columbia

The Royal Society's chief instrument in co-ordinating the scientific and literary efforts of Canadians and in establishing Canada as a force in the world-wide pursuit of knowledge was the publication and distribution of its *Proceedings and Transactions,* made possible by an annual $5000 grant from the dominion government. The society had decreed in 1883 that copies of the *Transactions* should be sent to:

All members who have paid their subscriptions
All Associated Societies
Such foreign Societies as may be selected by the Council

The Lieutenant-Governors of the Provinces of the Dominion and
Newfoundland
The Members of the Privy Council of Canada
The Chief Justice and Judges of the Supreme Court of Canada
The Speakers of the Senate and House of Commons
The Chief Justices of each Province
The Premier of each Province
The Speakers of the Legislature of each Province
The Minister or Superintendent of Education in each Province
The Universities, the Library of Parliament and the Libraries
of Provincial Legislatures

Five hundred copies were being sent by 1890 to societies and institutions outside Canada, 73 going to England, 10 to Ireland, 7
to Russia, 5 to New South Wales, and 3 to Ecuador.

> During the year now closing, the distribution has been extended
> over Central and South America. We could not obtain the requi-
> site information concerning Brazil owing to the Revolution last
> fall, but it is now on hand. The information concerning Mexico
> was defective but we have recently completed the required list
> of institutions. Niçaragua we have also correct information
> about. At next distribution we can include all these.
>   With the above exceptions and those of Guatemala and Venezuela
> we believe we have sent the Annual Transactions over the whole
> civilized world. Of these two last places we can get no accu-
> rate information.[5]

The Canadian people have never spent $5000 to such good effect.
   The original members of the Royal Society were nominated by the
governor-general, but the selection was made by a committee of whom
J.W. Dawson, P.-J.-O. Chauveau, and J.G. Bourinot were the most
influential figures.[6] It is generally agreed that their choices
included all the scientists and scholars of distinction resident
in Canada at that time. An analysis of the background of the
charter members tells us something about the state of Canada's
culture in 1882.
   Approximately half of the charter members were Canadian born
(37 out of 80), but the figure is in one sense misleading since
all but one of the members of Section I (French Literature with
history, archaeology and allied subjects) were born in Canada and
the exception, P. DeCazes, had emigrated at the age of 9. There
were 7 native Canadians in each of the scientific sections, but
only 4 in Section II (English Literature, with history, archaeology
and allied subjects). Of the 60 members of Sections II, III, and
IV, 32 had been born and educated in the British Isles.
   Almost all the fellows in Section I had completed the classical
course at one or other of the classical colleges and eight had
studied at the Séminaire de Québec. Three had attended Laval,
eight had been called to the bar, and three were ordained priests.
The most influential members in the first decade of the life of

98

the Royal Society were P.-J.-O. Chauveau, president 1883-84, and the Abbé H.R. Casgrain, President 1889-90.

In contrast, only four members of Section II were born in Canada, though three others arrived early enough to receive their education in this country. Only three held Canadian university degrees, J.G. Bourinot a B.A. from Trinity, R.M. Bucke an M.D. from McGill, and G.T. Denison an LL.B. from the University of Toronto. Most held degrees from British univerisites: G.M. Grant, W. Lyall, J.C. Murray, John Watson, Daniel Wilson, and G.P. Young from the Scottish; George Murray and Goldwyn Smith from Oxford; and John Reid from Queen's College, Belfast. Six were ordained ministers; only one was a lawyer. In this section the most influential members were university presidents - Daniel Wilson, president 1885-86, and G.M. Grant, president 1890-91.

In the two science sections, the Canadian and British elements were about equally distributed, but the Canadian born contingent was particularly strong among the younger members. Of the nine members of these sections who were under forty in 1882, seven were Canadians: H.A. Bayne, E.G. Deville, B.J. Harrington, J.G. McGregor, G.M. Dawson, J.-C.-K. LaFlamme, and William Osler. With the exception of LaFlamme all studied at universities outside Canada. In terms of undergraduate degrees, McGill was represented in the two sections by six fellows; Dalhousie, Laval, Queen's, Toronto, and King's College, Windsor, by one each. The group included Ph.D.s or D.Sc.s from Breslau, Göttingen, London, and Yale. Five of the first nine presidents of the Royal Society were drawn from these two sections: J.W. Dawson (1882-83), T.S. Hunt (1884-85), T.-E. Hamel (1886-87), George Lawson (1887-88), and Sandford Fleming (1888-89).

Had the Prince of Wales made a second royal tour in 1890 he would presumably once again have received addresses from many of the universities and colleges of Canada. It can also be assumed that he would have received an address from the Royal Society of Canada and that it would have been characterized by optimism. This would have been justified by the record of actual achievement. The society was in a flourishing state: the eight published volumes of its *Transactions* had established its reputation throughout the civilized world; its relations with local societies throughout the dominion were excellent; and its collective opinion was listened to with respect by the government. It is questionable, however, whether optimism and a sense of achievement would have characterized the addresses of the colleges and universities. Endowments from private individuals during the previous 15 years had greatly improved the position of Dalhousie, McGill, and Queen's. In 1887 a solution had at long last been found to the 'University of Toronto Question' in a reorganization which enabled denominational colleges to enter into federation with the provincial university to the mutual advantage of all concerned. Laval had firmly established three of its four faculties and had worked out a satisfactory relationship with the collèges classiques. But none of these universities was receiving anything like adequate support from public funds, and Sir Robert Falconer's general assessment of the position of higher education in the 1880s made fifty years later was sound:

> The universities had no contact with one another. Most of them had been conceived, born, and nourished for sectarian purposes, and all were very poor. Because they were poor, they were ill-nurtured, and were as a rule at odds with one another. Professors were badly paid, libraries were meagre, laboratories were few and scantily equipped, museums hardly existed. The provincial treasurers harassed by other demands for which they were afraid to tax their constituents, took advantage of the divided interests of the colleges to refuse aid impartially to all.[7]

Falconer's reference to the provincial treasurers is significant. By the terms of the British North America Act of 1867, the responsibility for education was assigned specifically and exclusively to the provinces; the universities, therefore, could expect no direct assistance from the federal government. In the one field where the federal government had entered the realm of higher education, it was in actual competition with the universities, since the Royal Military College, which it had established in 1876, offered a course in engineering. The position of the universities and colleges was further complicated by the tendency of the provinces in the 1870s and 1880s to establish separate institutions for advanced training in agriculture and engineering. For a number of reasons, then, the universities found it difficult to obtain the funds necessary to offer the kind of curriculum which many professors regarded as essential:

> No regard for the old system of academic drill can blind our eyes to the fact that the educational problem and University work have undergone an immense transformation. The physical and so-called practical sciences have come to the front with multiplied claims and attractions that cannot be resisted, and should not be resisted ... Every university worthy of the name must not only furnish instruction in what is known of the sciences, but should, if possible, make provision for original investigations. And beyond all these, we must have such subjects as comparative philology and comparative religion, together with the study of what Macaulay calls the most splendid and the most durable of the many glories of England, our own magnificent English literature, now taking a well-deserved position in the curriculum of every University.[8]

So said President Nelles at the Victoria University Convocation of 1885.

But without adequate funds how could new chairs be established and how could 'the physical and so-called practical sciences' be properly taught? The growing conviction that a college which relied entirely on denominational support could not command the

funds required for a university course worthy of the name led
Victoria into federation with the University of Toronto in 1889,
and by 1890 the same conviction was beginning to lead the denominational colleges then comprising the entire teaching force of the
University of Manitoba to a similar conclusion. Elsewhere, however, denominationalism was strongly entrenched; and poor, under-
nourished colleges continued to offer the relatively inexpensive
curricula of the 1860s, with consequences which Falconer also
described in his 1932 review: 'Higher education was defective in
facilities for the study of the sciences, just the subjects which
would appeal to the youth of a new country calling them to explore
it; coming ill-prepared from poor schools to stereo-typed curriculum of the universities, they found themselves outmatched by
teachers who had enjoyed the advantage of a classical education
in the homes of an old civilization.'[9] As we shall see in the
following chapters the curricula of 1890 were by no means as
stereotyped as this comment would suggest. Falconer was specifically referring to the position of the universities in 1882, the
year in which the Royal Society was founded. A number of notable
changes took place in the following eight years, and these altered
the situation significantly.

NOTES TO CHAPTER 7

1 The *Proceedings and Transactions of the Royal Society of Canada*
   1882-90 are the basic reference. The origins of the society
   are described by the first president (J.W. Dawson) in his
   presidential address (*Proc.* 1882-83, lii-lvii;) by V. Morin,
   'Les Origines de le Société Royal,' *Cahiers des Dix* 2
   (1937), 157-98; and by several writers, notably R.A. Falconer
   and L.J. Burpee in Royal Society of Canada, *Fifty Years Retrospect: Anniversary Volume, 1882-1932*, (1932). Falconer's
   chapter in the latter volume is the address he gave as president
   of the Royal Society in 1932 under the title 'The Intellectual
   Life in Canada as Reflected in its Royal Society'; it is also
   published in the *Proc.* for that year. A number of other presidential addresses, each published in the *Proc.* for the year in
   question, have dealt with the aims and early achievements of
   the Royal Society: F.G. Marchand, 'The Origin and Aims of the
   Royal Society,' 1898; W.C. Clark, 'The Work of the Royal Society
   in Canada,' 1900; Alexander Johnson, 'Our Semi-Jubilee and
   Canada,' 1906; J.P. McMurrich, 'The Royal Society of Canada:
   its Aims and Needs,' 1923; H.M. Tory, 'A Study of the Organization
   and Work of the Royal Society of Canada,' 1940; W.S. Wallace,
   'Planning for Canada,' 1941; Jean Bruchesi, 'Regards sur le
   Société Royale du Canada,' 1954; E.W.R. Steacie, 'Science and
   the National Academy,' 1955; W.A. Mackintosh, 'These Seventy-
   Five Years,' 1957. For biographical details about the fellows
   of the Royal Society, see the obituaries published in the *Proc.*
   in the year of or the year following their death.

2   *Proc.* 1890, vii
3   *Proc.* 1882–83, x
4   Burpee, *Fifty Years Retrospect*, 2
5   *Proc.* 1890, v
6   Morin, 'Origines,' 168–77
7   Falconer, 'Intellectual Life,' 10
8   Quoted by C.B. Sissons, *A History of Victoria University*, (1952), 172
9   Falconer, 'Intellectual Life,' 11

8

Institutional Development

The single bright feature in the history of higher education in
the Maritime provinces in the late nineteenth century was the
development of Dalhousie University, an institution that existed
only on paper in 1861 but which by 1890 occupied a stronger position than any Canadian university except McGill, Queen's, and
Toronto. Otherwise the picture was one of mere survival and modest
consolidation. The only permanent casualty of the period was the
University of Halifax, an examining and degree-granting institution established by the legislature of Nova Scotia in 1876 and
abolished in 1881.[1] However, St Mary's was closed in 1881
following the withdrawal of all provincial grants to Nova Scotia
institutions and did not reopen until 1902. On the other hand,
two new institutions had been added to the list: St Joseph's at
Memramcook, New Brunswick, which received a provincial charter
in 1868 and began to grant degrees in 1888, and Collège Sainte-
Anne at Church Point, Nova Scotia, a French-language collège
founded in 1890 by the Eudist fathers; it obtained a charter in
1892 though it did not begin to exercise its degree-granting
powers until 1903.

   Perhaps there was more progress than is suggested by the phrase
'modest consolidation.' Acadia, under the presidency of J.M.
Cramp (to 1869) and A.W. Sawyer (1869-97) established itself as
a sound liberal arts college, but it is revealing to note that
it was not in a position to assign a professor solely to the subject of physics until 1891. King's College at Windsor ventured
into the field of engineering in 1872, but its staff in 1890 -
arts and theology as well as engineering - numbered seven. Mount
Allison, which became the University of Mount Allison College in
1886, added a faculty of theology in 1875 and in 1891 was to set
up a conservatory of music, but devastating fires in 1866 and
1882 prevented any major advance. St Francis Xavier obtained its

charter in 1866 and steadily developed its arts course, but the development of greatest significance at Antigonish was the establishment in 1883 of a women's college which affiliated with St Francis Xavier in 1894. The continued excellence of the University of New Brunswick staff could not compensate entirely for the indifference of the legislature upon which it was almost completely dependent for support. The annual grant from the province remained at the constant figure of $8,844.48 from 1828 to 1906; this probably explains why the university was not able to establish a four year arts course until 1887 or a chair of physics until 1889. One is tempted to regard as symbolic the fact that the account of the historical development of the University of New Brunswick published in the 1890 *Calendar* makes no reference to any event subsequent to 1860.

The basic problem at all these institutions was inadequate financial support. Until 1881 the legislature of Nova Scotia made small grants to a half dozen institutions in the province but in that year withdrew support from all institutions of higher education. New Brunswick restricted its meagre support to the provincial university. The colleges had, therefore, to depend upon the contributions of their individual supporters. The modest position which these institutions occupied in 1890 - modest, certainly, in relation to the hopes they had entertained thirty years earlier - was evidence that something more than denominational enthusiasm and the efforts of devoted staff was needed to keep pace with the increasingly complex nature of university education. The same point was proved by the development of Dalhousie into a genuine university, for the secret of its success lay in the fact that it had found independent sources of financial support and that it had escaped from the coils of denominationalism.

Ironically, however, it had been denominational enthusiasm that led to the revival of Dalhousie in 1863. When the two Presbyterian bodies in the Maritimes entered into union late in 1860, committees were appointed to discuss the reorganization of Dalhousie College, whose board of governors had held no meetings since the closing of the Dalhousie High School in January of that year. The deliberations of these committees eventuated in a new Dalhousie University Act of 1863, which incorporated a suggestion proposed by Principal Dawson of McGill that denominations be represented on the board of governors in proportion to their support of endowed chairs. When the college reopened in November 1863, its 60 students were taught by a staff of six, three of them nominated by the Presbyterian church which assumed the responsibility for their salaries. There were numerous petitions to the legislature in 1864, especially from Acadia, to repeal the new Act, but these were unavailing, and the college quickly established itself as a sound institution, principally because it had a strong staff. Two of the original six, the Rev. William Lyall (philosophy) and George Lawson (chemistry and mineralogy), would subsequently be among the charter members of the Royal Society of Canada. Lyall and Lawson were still serving Dalhousie

in 1890, and so were the Rev. John Johnson (classics), who did
not retire until 1894, and the Rev. Charles Macdonald (mathematics)
who died in office in 1901. A fifth of the original six professors,
the Rev. James Ross (philosophy) was Dalhousie's principal until
his retirement in 1885.[2] In 1864, a tutor in modern languages
was appointed, one Louis Pujol who was dismissed in February 1865;
his successor, John Liechti, retired as professor of modern languages in 1906. Another strong appointment was made in 1865, James
DeMille, professor of rhetoric and history until his death in
1880. Blessed with this solid, and, as events proved, long-serving
staff, Dalhousie made steady progress between 1865 and 1880; a
medical faculty was organized in 1868, a program for an honour
B.A. was introduced in 1873, authority to accept other colleges
as affiliates was obtained in 1875, and a faculty of science was
established in 1878. Part of this progress was made possible by
a gradually increasing provincial grant and part by a five year
fund-raising campaign (1870-75) which produced a small but permanent endowment. However, the continued opposition of the denominational colleges of Nova Scotia to any suggestion that resources
be pooled under Dalhousie's direction, as well as their perennial
protests at Dalhousie's apparently preferred position, led the
legislature in 1876 to create the University of Halifax, whose
degrees, on the University of London model, would be open to students from Acadia, King's, Mount Allison, St Mary's, and St Francis
Xavier, as well as Dalhousie. This aberration lasted until 1881,
but by that time Dalhousie was on the road to independence.
    Between 1879 and 1884 George Munro, a Nova Scotian who had be-
come wealthy as a publisher in New York, gave $350,000 to Dalhousie,
partly for matriculation scholarships, but principally for endowed
chairs: physics (1879), history and political economy (1880),
English literature and rhetoric (1882), constitutional and international law (1883) and metaphysics (1884). In addition, three
other endowed chairs - classics, modern languages, chemistry -
were made possible in 1882 by the $65,000 willed to Dalhousie by
Alexander McLeod. These chairs attracted first-rate scholars,
for example, J.G. McGregor to Physics, John Forrest (who succeeded
Ross as Principal in 1885) to history and political economy,
J.G. Schurman (the future president of Cornell), W.J. Alexander
(who would found the school of English studies at Toronto) to
English literature, and R.C. Weldon (who would establish the
Dalhousie faculty of law in 1883) to constitutional and inter-
national law. The moral of all this has been drawn by Professor
Harvey:

Not only were standards set and traditions created, by 1887,
but the endowments of Munro, McLeod and [Sir William] Young
[Chairman of the Board, 1848-84, whose gifts are estimated at
$68,000] had made the University independent of those small and
precarious provincial grants which had always evoked denominational ill-will and were constant factors making for instability
of policy. But, when appeals for assistance were no longer made

to the Government, sectarian bitterness tended to disappear, and the Dalhousie Idea was free to make its contributions on its merits.[3]

True enough: but the time would inevitably come when private endowment would prove inadequate to produce the funds necessary for the operation of a modern university, and progress would once again depend on assistance from the government.

QUEBEC

On a scale that was smaller only because fewer institutions were involved, the Maritime experience between 1860 and 1890 was repeated in English-speaking Quebec; Bishop's, the small denominational college, had difficulty in holding its own, whereas McGill, the institution which had escaped from denominationalism and could draw on a few wealthy men for substantial endowment funds, made striking progress.

Where King's at Windsor had ventured into engineering, Bishop's at Lennoxville ventured into law and medicine. But Bishop's faculty of medicine was situated at Montreal and its faculty of law at Sherbrooke; essentially both were proprietary schools, since neither was effectively under the control of the university at Lennoxville. The full-time teaching staff at Bishop's – for arts and theology – numbered five in 1890. A year later it was augmented by the appointment of a 'Lecturer in the Faculty of Arts.' St Francis College at Richmond remained a junior college in affiliation with McGill, a status also achieved by Morrin College, a Presbyterian foundation established at Quebec in 1862, and Stanstead Wesleyan College, which had been established as a secondary school at Stanstead in 1819. But McGill, like Dalhousie and for precisely the same reasons, had moved steadily forward. Its greatest strength was its location in Montreal, which through the deepening of the St Lawrence ship canal and the improvement of its harbour facilities had become an important transatlantic port. Montreal was also a great railroad centre and, partly because of the failure of two of the leading Upper Canada banks in 1866 and 1867, it had become the banking capital of Canada. All this had led to a considerable development of industry and to a much increased population. More important in our context, it had made possible the existence of a group of industrialists whose fortunes, though modest in comparison with those of their American counterparts like Carnegie, Rockefeller, and Vanderbilt, were unparalleled elsewhere in Canada. Principal Dawson was able to convince a number of these men, notably William Molson, Peter Redpath, Thomas Workman, Sir William Macdonald, and Sir Donald Smith (later Lord Strathcona) that McGill deserved their support. McGill also received generous support throughout this period from both the graduate body and the citizens of Montreal; appeals for funds in 1871 and 1881 were well received. Consequently the problems that faced Dawson in the final year of his principalship (1893) were utterly different from those facing him when he assumed office in 1855. The great need now was less for money than for the effective coordination of the university's wide-ranging activities: 'The operations of McGill are now so extensive and complicated that the dangers of disintegration and isolation have become greater than any others, and the Principal must always be the central bond of union of the University, because he alone can know it in all its parts and weigh the claims, needs, dangers, difficulties and opportunities of each of its constituent faculties and departments.'[4]

The major units over which Dawson presided in 1890 were five faculties (arts, medicine, law - all established by 1860 - applied science (1878), comparative medicine and veterinary science (1888); three affiliated arts colleges (Morrin, St Francis, Stanstead); four affiliated theological colleges (Congregational College since 1865, Presbyterian College since 1868, Wesleyan College since 1880, the Diocesan (Anglican) College since 1880); the McGill Normal School; and the Donalda Special Course in Arts - the regular arts course provided in separate classes for women. No doubt Dawson had his difficulties in the year 1890. They were, however, of a very different order from those which faced the presidents of, for example, Bishop's and Acadia.

In French Canada, despite two significant developments since 1860 (at Montreal the establishment in 1876 of a largely independent branch [La Succursale] of Université Laval, and at Quebec the reorganization of the faculté de théologie in accordance with the terms of the papal bull, 'Aeterni Patris,' of 1879), the position of higher education was far from satisfactory. Superficially, Laval's position in 1890 was impressive. Its four faculties had sizable staffs; 18 professors in law, including 9 at Montreal; 30 in medicine, including 19 at Montreal; 31 in arts, including 17 at Montreal; and 15 in theology, including 9 at Montreal. Its affiliates included grand séminaires at Sainte-Anne, Chicoutimi, Rimouski, Montréal, and Québec; two professional schools (Ecole vétérinaire française de Montréal and Ecole polytechnique de Montréal), and 16 collèges classiques. The latter included 8 of the collèges so designated in 1860 - Petit Séminaire de Québec, Collège de Montréal, Nicolet, St-Hyacinthe, Sainte-Thérèse, Ste-Anne-de-la-Pocatière, L'Assomption, and Trois Rivières; 6 of the 1860 collèges industriels - Joliette, Rigaud, Lévis, Sainte-Marie de Monnoir, Sherbrooke, and Rimouski; the Collège Laurent founded in 1847 but not categorized in 1860; and Petit Séminaire de Chicoutimi, established in 1864. The ninth 1860 collège classique, Collège Sainte-Marie, was still very much in evidence; by the terms of the papal decree (*Jamdudum*) of 1889, which greatly increased the independence of the Montreal Succursale, the Collège Sainte-Marie was given the right simply to present its candidates for the Laval degrees, which the faculté des arts would then be automatically obliged to grant.

But closer examination reveals serious weaknesses. Higher

education in French-speaking Quebec was still dependent on the financial support of the Roman Catholic church; the province's contribution was almost entirely confined to the support of technological
training - the Ecole polytechnique and the Ecole vétérinaire.
Except in theology graduate studies were non-existent. The faculties of law and medicine were staffed by part-time professors. As
for the state of the faculty of arts, the situation as described
in the 1890 *Annuaire* can only be described as plaintive: L'enseignement complet de la faculté des Arts, conduisant à la Maîtrise ès
Arts, n'est pas encore organisé, faute d'élèves. Vu le peu de
ressources que présente le pays comme encouragement à la recherche
de ce grade, il est peu probable que cet enseignement soit organisé
de sitôt d'une manière sérieuse.' The fear that it would be some
time before the master's program would be organized was well founded;
the same statement appears *without change* in the *Annuaire* of 1920.
The truth of the matter was that the faculty's efforts in 1890 as
in 1860 were restricted to the supervision of examinations for
the classical college course, the offering of cours publics at
Quebec for the general public and for students in law, medicine,
education (at l'Ecole normale), and arts (the final year of philosophie), and to the provision of cours privés for students in
philosophie at the Petit Séminaire de Québec in the subjects prescribed for the final B.A. examination.

Moreover, despite the papal decree of 1889, there remained a
serious rift between Laval at Quebec and the branch at Montreal,
a reflection in part of the ancient rivalry of the two cities, in
part of the conflicting ambitions of the two dioceses, and in part
of the division within the Roman Catholic church between the pro-
ponents of ultramontanism (Quebec) and gallicanism (Montreal).[5]
This rift would continue to inhibit the development of higher
education in French-speaking Canada until the branch became the
completely independent Université de Montréal in 1919.

ONTARIO

The most important date between 1861 and 1890 in the history of
higher education in Upper Canada - or Ontario as it would henceforth be called - was 1 July 1867. By the terms of the British
North America Act, which created the Dominion of Canada on that
date, responsibility for education was assigned to the provinces.
One of the first actions of Ontario's first government was to
announce that the annual grants to denominational colleges, which
in some cases had been granted since 1842, would be stopped at
the end of 1868.[6] This meant that colleges like Queen's, Trinity,
and Victoria would have to obtain increased support from private
sources if they were to survive as independent institutions. The
opportunity to enter into affiliation with the University of
Toronto remained open, but as yet there was little enthusiasm for
this alternative. At Trinity, for example, a committee appointed
to consider the question of affiliation in 1870 reported 'that

the measure was surrounded by so many difficulties and open to so
many grave objections that it was one that should not be entertained.'7 The committee agreed that the financial problem was
also serious and that steps should be taken to improve the financial position of the College; specifically they recommended 'the
greatest possible retrenchment in expenditures, the conversion of
wild land and other property into cash, and the realizing of debts
and monies due the College.' At Queen's and Victoria rather more
practical measures were adopted to improve the financial position
of the college - the launching of campaigns to raise $100,000.
Through the efforts of Principal Snodgrass, Queen's raised this
sum during 1869, but it took Victoria four years to reach the same
objective. However, in both cases the income from $100,000 did
little more than offset the loss of the government grant: in 1867
Victoria and Queen's had received $5000, Trinity $4000, Regiopolis
$3000, St Michael's $2000, Ottawa $1400, and Assumption $1000.8
Much more money than this was needed if the institutions were to
be maintained as universities worthy of the name.

Finance was becoming a problem for the University of Toronto
as well. Initially its difficulties had appeared to be removed
by the recognition of its exclusive right to the old King's College
endowment; but this income was fixed, and by 1883, when its inadequacy had become obvious, the university decided to appeal to the
legislature for further financial assistance. Though the immediate
response to this proposal was vigorous protest from the denominational colleges, the ultimate result was the Federation Scheme of
1887.9 Between 1883 and 1887 a series of conferences was held,
involving at different times and on different occasions representatives of Toronto, Queen's, Victoria, St Michael's, Knox, the
Congregational College of British North America (despite the fact
that it had moved to Montreal in 1864), Wycliffe College (an
Anglican theological college established at Toronto in 1877), and
the Toronto Baptist College (the theological work of the Canadian
Literary Institute had been transferred under this name to Toronto
in 1881). These prolonged discussions culminated in the University
Federation Act of 1887, which reestablished the University of
Toronto as a teaching institution. This had immediate repercussions
in the field of professional education. A faculty of medicine was
organized in 1887 by the simple process of absorbing a proprietary
school, the Toronto School of Medicine. By the terms of the
Federation Act, the School of Practical Science, which the province
had established in a building constructed on the university campus
in 1878, entered into affiliation, and the university thus acquired
in fact, though not until 1901 in name, its faculty of applied
science. In 1889 a faculty of law had been established but the
decision of the Law Society of Upper Canada in the same year to
establish its own law school resulted in the withdrawal of the
faculty in 1894.

The most important feature of the Federation Act was the division
of labour within the faculty of arts between the university and
federating colleges. In general terms, the university would be

responsible for all instruction in the physical, natural, and social sciences, while the colleges, which for this purpose would include the non-denominational University College, would provide instruction in the humanities.[10] A university entering into federation was required to place in abeyance its rights to grant degrees in all subjects except theology, but it could still maintain a complete and independent theological college and it could be thoroughly involved in the undergraduate program in arts by offering the very subjects which were in terms of physical equipment the least expensive to teach. The Federation Act of 1887 was merely permissive so far as the denominational universities were concerned, but it was given almost immediate effect by the decision of Victoria to enter federation. This decision, taken officially in 1890, was consummated by the physical removal of Victoria from Cobourg to Toronto in 1892. In due course, two other institutions entered into federation, Trinity in 1904 and St Michael's in 1910. The relations of St Michael's College to the University of Toronto between 1881, when it became affiliated, and 1910 are too complex to detail here.[11] Technically, it became a federated college in 1887 but it did not undertake to provide instruction in 'college subjects' until 1907. Trinity had no relation to the University of Toronto until 1904. Finally, Knox and Wycliffe, which had entered into affiliation in 1885, became federated theological colleges in 1890; such colleges confined their work to theology and were not involved in the arts program.

Three of the Ontario institutions which participated in the discussions which led to the act of 1887 did not enter into association with the University of Toronto. One was the Congregational College of British North America which, being located in Montreal, was not really concerned. A second was the Toronto Baptist College. The Baptists, traditionally opposed to joint action by church and state in the field of education, obtained a charter for a university of their own in 1887 and McMaster University, uniting the undergraduate branch of the Canadian Literary Institute at Woodstock and the theological work of the Toronto Baptist College opened its doors on the edge of the University of Toronto campus in 1890. The third and most important exception was Queen's, with Trinity and Victoria a leading participant in the discussions, where it was represented by its principal, the Rev. G.M. Grant. At the time of his installation in 1877, Grant had stated in clear terms his view of the proper relation of the various universities and colleges of the province. There should be one provincial university and the denominational colleges should not seek provincial support:

As far as provincial action was concerned, it was surely well, it seems to me, that Ontario should devote the whole endowment accruing from the land set apart for university education, to one good college, rather than fritter it away on several institutions. If others are in existence from local, denominational, or other necessities, let the necessity be proved by the sacrifices their friends are willing to make for them, and the real extent of the necessity by the survival of the fittest. The existence of one amply endowed from provincial resources will always be a guarantee that provincial educational interests shall not be sacrificed to the clamours of an endless number of sects and localities, and the guarantee also of the efficiency of the various colleges, the provincial college included.[12]

In effect Grant was giving up the claim of Queen's on the old King's College endowment - despite the legislature's action in cancelling the grants in 1868, the claim had never been abandoned officially - and he went on to state his belief that Queen's should also free itself from the financial support which it had received since its inception from the Colonial Committee of the Church of Scotland. In Grant's view, Queen's should rely solely on the sacrifice of her friends. He immediately launched a campaign which raised over $150,000 by the end of 1878, sufficient to provide $30,000 for a new building (contributed by the citizens of Kingston), $70,000 to endow two chairs, $30,000 to replace the Church of Scotland grant, and $20,000 for a library and other uses. This was sufficient to make provision for separate chairs of mathematics, natural history, chemistry, and physics, as well as an assistant in classics and a lecturer in political economy. But it was still not enough. In 1883 Grant persuaded the alumni to guarantee an annual sum of $7800 for five years, and in 1887 he led another campaign, this time realizing $260,000, including a donation of $6000 from the student body. In consequence, between 1888 and 1891 separate chairs were established in history, English literature, modern languages, mental philosophy, moral philosophy, Greek, Latin, and political economy. By 1890, Queen's had a very strong faculty of arts, for Grant's appointments, which included James Cappon in English, Adam Shortt in political economy, and John McNaughton in Greek, were excellent. Up to this point, theology excepted, Queen's had shown little interest in professional education, but a change was about to take place. In 1892 the Royal College of Physicians of Kingston would again become the faculty of medicine, and in 1893 a school of mining and agriculture would be established.

Not all the institutions in Ontario were involved in the federation discussions. The history of Regiopolis, which received a charter in 1866, is obscure throughout this thirty-year period, but it is known that the cutting off of the government grant in 1868 was a severe blow, from which, as an aspiring university, it never recovered.[13] At Windsor, Ontario, the Basilian fathers reopened Assumption College in 1870, offering initially the first six years of the classical college course; by 1890 the two years of philosophy had been added. The University of Western Ontario, with which Assumption would affiliate in 1919, had also been established prior to 1890. Theological differences between the Diocese of Toronto, whose high church leanings were reflected in the theological training provided at Trinity College, and the

Diocese of Huron, whose doctrinal views, reflected the Irish
Protestant propensities of Benjamin Cronyn, its first Bishop, had
led in 1863 to the incorporation of Huron College at London.
Courses in divinity, modern languages, and classics with mathematics
were offered in 1864. Though the enrolment was never large, the
effort was sufficiently successful to warrant the forming of an
association of the professors and alumni of Huron College in 1877
'to establish a University and University College to facilitate the
obtaining of the highest scholastic training and instruction in
evangelical truth for the future clergy of this diocese and Dominion,
and to meet the educational wants of the fast-developing West by
supplying it with an undenominational School of Arts, Law, Medicine,
and Engineering.[14] In 1878 an Act of Incorporation was obtained
for the Western University of London, and in 1881 lectures were
begun in arts, medicine, and theology, Huron College having become
the faculty of theology. One B.A. was granted in 1883, but in 1885
Huron College withdrew from affiliation and the arts faculty was
suspended; it did not reopen until 1895 when Huron once again became affiliated. However, the faculty of medicine, actually a
proprietary school independent of the university senate, carried
on and the Western University granted degrees in medicine in 1883
and steadily from 1885 on. In 1890 there were twelve graduates.
A faculty of law was also established in 1885, with a dean,
registrar, 8 lecturers and 38 students; but the refusal of the
Law Society of Upper Canada to accept the examination results as
fulfilling any part of the requirements for qualification to
practice law in the province of Ontario led to the cancelling of
lectures in 1886.

   The difficulties of a college which had to rely entirely on
denominational support from 1868 on are well illustrated by the
University of Ottawa, which had obtained its charter in 1866.
In the persons of its superior, the Rev. J. Tabaret, and two of
his colleagues, Rev. L.P. Paquin and Rev. J.B. Balland, Ottawa
had during the 1870s and 1880s three of the most progressive
professors in Canada. In 1874 they introduced a new program of
studies which aimed 'at practical utility, as well as thoroughness
and approved method, in the several courses.'[15] The mathematical
and science elements in the classical course were strengthened,
and a civil engineering course was introduced. But the change
was something more than a re-arrangement and expansion of the
curricula; it also reflected a new conception of the role of the
professor:

   The *university* method of giving to each professor a special
   branch, replaces the system previously followed, in which the
   professors had each the sole and entire charge of a class, and
   so taught various branches; a system which did not sufficiently
   favour the due development of special talents, tastes, and
   aptitudes of professors. The present method, besides ensuring
   more perfect knowledge on the part of the professor, and there-
   for more rapid progress for the student, is far more attractive

for both. The professor is not distracted from his favourite
study by others, for which he has no taste and which he could
but teach superficially or imperfectly, and the student is
delighted to find each of his professors brimful of his subject,
an enthusiast, so to speak, thereon, and enjoys the additional
advantage, no inconsiderable one, of seeing many able men come
in turn with their varied stores of learning, and each with his
own peculiar way of imparting it.[16]

But despite this enthusiasm, the civil engineering course had to
be suspended in 1880, and again, after reopening, in 1885, osten-
sibly for want of students, but fundamentally for lack of the
facilities which would attract a substantial student body. Nor
in 1890 was the end of difficulties in sight; as we shall see,
Ottawa's attempt to establish a sound course in science was to
be again frustrated in the period 1900-5.[17]

Denominational enthusiasm, progressive ideas, and financial
embarrassment were also demonstrated at Albert College during
the quarter-century of its existence as a university. The
Belleville Seminary, which had opened in 1857, obtained a charter
as Albert College in 1866. By 1876 it had established faculties
of arts, theology, law, music, and engineering, and a department
of agriculture which offered a two-year diploma course. The basis
for the latter was the Hastings Professorship of Mining and Agriculture, established by the County of Hastings in 1869. To provide these remarkably varied offerings in 1883-84, Albert College
had a staff of eight, one of whom doubled as rector of the Albert
College Grammar School and a second as principal of its Commercial
Department, which offered a one-year course in spelling, grammar,
arithmetic, mensuration, penmanship, book-keeping, business correspondence, and banking. It is perhaps just as well that following
the union of the Methodist churches of Canada in 1884 Albert College
reverted to the status of a secondary school, its undergraduates
transferring to Victoria College at Cobourg.

THE WEST

At a meeting open to all university graduates held in Regina on
10 September 1890, the following motion, proposed by the Anglican
bishop of Saskatchewan and Calgary, was adopted: 'In the opinion
of this meeting the establishment of one university for the whole
of the North-West Territories based on principles that would permit the affiliation of collegiate institutions for all the denominations in the Territories would be the best means of promoting
the interests of higher education in the North-West.'[18] Since
the population of the North-West Territories at the time of the
meeting was under 10,000, it is not surprising that this gathering
produced no immediate results, but the spirit of Bishop Pinkham's
motion that there should be a single degree-granting institution
for the whole area was accepted fifteen years later when the

provinces of Alberta and Saskatchewan were carved out of the North-West Territories. The same principle was adopted by the Province of British Columbia, whose legislature in 1890 approved an Act ... to Establish One University for the Whole of British Columbia. It would be twenty-five years before a university of British Columbia was actually established but, in the interim, degree-granting privileges were denied such institutions as Whetham College at Vancouver (1890-93) and Columbian Methodist College at New Westminster (1892-1927).[19] Such powere were also denied two institutions located in what would become the Province of Saskatchewan, Emmanuel College[20] at Prince Albert, established in 1882 and ultimately an affiliated theological college of the University of Saskatchewan, and Lansdowne College,[21] which failed to establish itself at Portage La Prairie in 1890.

The principle of a single degree-granting university for a province had already been adopted in Manitoba. The preamble to the bill which created the University of Manitoba in 1877 declared that it was desirable 'to establish one university for the whole of Manitoba.' As W.L. Morton has shown, discrepancies between the versions of the Act printed in French and English make it difficult to decide whether the original intention was to create an institution that would never be anything but an examining and degree-granting body or whether the establishment of an institution on the then University of London model was regarded as a necessary first step, to be followed ultimately by the assumption of teaching responsibilities.[22] In any case, this issue was not raised until 1889; initially all instruction was provided by affiliated colleges. In 1877 three colleges were in a position to provide instruction in arts: Roman Catholic and French-speaking St Boniface (which had been offering a full classical course since 1866), Anglican St John's (which had been offering work in arts and theology since 1866), and Presbyterian Manitoba College (which had begun to offer work beyond the secondary level shortly before its removal from Kildonan to Winnipeg in 1874). During the legislative session of 1877 two other colleges were incorporated - Trinity College, sponsored by the Episcopal Methodists and Wesley College, which, as the Wesleyan Institute, had been established by the Conference of the Wesleyan Methodist Church in 1873; and provision was made for their affiliation with the University of Manitoba when they could demonstrate that they possessed adequate staff. The union of the Methodist churches in 1884 resulted in a pooling of re- sources, and Wesley College became a fourth affiliated arts college in 1888. Prior to this, the Manitoba College of Medicine (1883) had entered into affiliation and, after consultation with the Law Society of Manitoba, the university had instituted exami- nations for the LL.B. degree and outlined a reading course. But one Manitoba institution remained outside the fold. In 1879 the Baptists had established Prairie College at Rapid City in the western part of the province. It was operated in conjunction with a proprietary institution called McKee Academy. Prairie College was closed in 1890 when the McKee Academy moved to Brandon, where it was henceforth known as Brandon College. In 1899 the

114

Baptists assumed full responsibility for Brandon College and in due course they would challenge the policy of a single degree-granting university for the whole province.

As of 1890 the University of Manitoba had granted 136 degrees in arts, 5 in law, and 31 in medicine. Each arts college taught its own students, and all students sat for the university examinations. A course of study satisfactory to the Protestant colleges, whose bias was towards the tradition of the liberal arts college, and to Roman Catholic St Boniface, long a collège classique, had been adopted, and relations between the colleges were harmonious. This harmony was made possible by good will on all sides, but it was facilitated by the fact that the curriculum was basically a rigorous training in classics and mathematics. The sciences received little attention. However, by 1889 the claims of science were much stronger than in 1877; locally, they were being provided with a sharp focus by the requirements of the Manitoba College of Medicine. In the fall of 1889 a committee appointed to consider the advisability of the university undertaking to provide instruction in some subjects recommended that university chairs be established in natural science, mathematics, and modern languages. A second committee made similar recommendations, and the university council then decided that chairs in chemistry, geology and physics, biology and physiology, mathematics, and modern languages should be established and that the government should be requested to amend the University Act to permit the university to undertake instruction in such subjects as the council recommended. However, these proposals were not satisfactory to St Boniface, whose leader, Archbishop Taché, now discovered and called attention to the discrepancies in the French and English versions of the 1877 Act. 'I would never,' he declared, 'have consented that the College of St. Boniface should join and become an integral part of a University in which teaching would be imparted without any control which could protect the students of our college in their religious belief.'[23] There was also the practical problem that the establishment of university chairs would require the provision of substantial provincial funds, and these the government was not anxious to provide. The combination of denominational opposition and government reluctance resulted in a delay of 15 years before the council's recommendations of 1889 were implemented, and then only through the generosity of Lord Strathcona, whose gift of $20,000 in 1904 made it possible to appoint professors of botany, physics, chemistry, mathematics, and physiology. But long before this, the Protestant colleges agreed among themselves to pool their resources and to teach science for the university if it would supply space and equipment for teaching and examining. The appropriate arrangements were made in 1890, and from then until 1904 science instruction at the University of Manitoba was provided in this unofficial form.

It is apparent from this review that higher education in Canada was greatly extended in the thirty-year period from 1861 to 1890. To the considerable number of institutions already in existence

in eastern and central Canada at the beginning of this period
were added Dalhousie, St Joseph's, and Collège Sainte-Anne in
the Maritimes, Assumption, McMaster, and Western in Ontario, and
(since essentially it was an independent university) the Montreal
branch of the Université Laval as well as a number of classical
colleges in Quebec. Even more striking was the expansion to the
west - by 1890 a reasonably complex university for Manitoba, a
number of small and not necessarily permanent colleges in the
territory that would become the provinces of Alberta and
Saskatchewan, and in British Columbia. If the short-lived Whetham
College at Vancouver is taken into account, it could be said that
by 1890 higher education stretched from coast to coast.

Higher education was also extended to women during this period.
It will be recalled that Mount Allison had been the pioneer in
this field, a B.Sc. having been granted to Miss Grace Lockhart
in 1875.[24] Nine other institutions had followed this lead by 1890,
Victoria in 1883 (one M.D.-C.M.), Acadia (one B.A.), and Queen's
(four B.A.s) in 1884, Dalhousie (one B.A.) and Toronto (five
B.A.s) in 1885, Trinity (one Mus.Bac.) in 1886, McGill (eight
B.A.s) in 1888, Manitoba (one B.A.), and New Brunswick (one B.A.)
in 1889. In all cases students were admitted to the university
some years before the first degree was earned - at Queen's, for
example, in 1878, where the first fully matriculated women entered
in 1880. Though there was a good deal of concern about the consequences of admitting women to the same classes as men, good sense,
as well as force of circumstances in the form of limited financial
resources, made common classes the general rule. McGill was the
exception, a parallel set of lectures being offered in the Donalda
Special Course in Arts, financed from the income of a $120,000
endowment donated by Sir Donald Smith. The special problems attendant on the provision of instruction in such subjects as anatomy
to classes composed of both men and women led in 1883 to the
establishment of two medical colleges for women, the Ontario
Medical College for Women at Toronto, and the Kingston Women's
Medical College at Kingston.[25] The extension of the privileges
of higher education to women did not apply to any Roman Catholic
institution until 1897 when four students registered at the
affiliated Mt St Bernard College were awarded the B.A. degree by
St Francis Xavier University.

Mention of the establishment of the two medical colleges for
women is a reminder that there was during this period a considerable expansion of facilities for higher education taking place
outside the universities. Neither of these colleges had degree-
granting powers; they were professional schools which prepared
students to qualify as medical practitioners, the necessary degree
being awarded by the University of Toronto or Queen's University
on the basis of examinations set and marked by those institutions.
Comparable schools had been established by 1890 in a number of
other professional fields, sometimes under private auspices, but
normally by governments. We shall deal with such developments
in chapter 10, which is concerned with professional education in

116

the year 1890. But in order to complete this outline of the development of higher education in Canada between 1861 and 1890 we shall note here that the following institutions were established during this period: the Ontario Veterinary College at Toronto in 1862, the Ontario Agricultural College at Guelph in 1874, the Royal College of Dental Surgeons at Toronto in 1875, the Royal Military College at Kingston in 1876, the Montreal College of Pharmacy in 1875, the Ontario College of Pharmacy at Toronto in 1881.

NOTES TO CHAPTER 8

1 During the six years of its existence, the University of Halifax granted 10 degrees, 7 of which were *ad eundum*: 4 LL.B.s, 1 M.A., and 2 M.D.s. It also granted 1 LL.B. and 1 B.Sc. 'by private study' and 1 M.B. to a student prepared at the Halifax Medical College.
2 The sixth member of the original staff, Thomas McCulloch, son of Dalhousie's first president, died in 1865. He was professor of physics.
3 D.C. Harvey, *An Introduction to the History of Dalhousie University* (1938), 109
4 J.W. Dawson, *Thirty Eight Years at McGill* (1893), 22
5 See A. Lavallée, *Québec contre Montréal: la querelle universitaire 1876-91* (1974)
6 Material bearing on the government's action, including the arguments pro and con advanced in the debate in the legislature, is to be found in J.G. Hodgins, ed., *Documentary History of Education in Upper Canada* (1907), XX, 208-21 and XXI, 33-54, 245-59. For details about the grants provided between 1842 and 1868, see R.S. Harris, 'The Evolution of a Provincial University in Ontario' in D.F. Dadson, *On Higher Education* (1966), 21-3.
7 T.A. Reed, ed., *A History of the University of Trinity College* (1952), 74
8 Grants of $750 were also provided for the Toronto School of Medicine, the Trinity Medical School, and the Royal College of Physicians and Surgeons, Kingston.
9 The fullest accounts of the events culminating in the Federation Act are provided by N. Burwash, 'A Review of the Founding and Development of the University of Toronto as a Provincial Institution,' *Trans. Royal Society Canada* 1905, section 2, 37-98; and C.B. Sissons, *A History of Victoria University* (1952), 271-409. See also W.S. Wallace, *A History of the University of Toronto* (1927), 114-39; and W.L. Grant and F. Hamilton, *Principal Grant* (1904), 271-94.
10 The subjects actually assigned to the colleges were English French, German, Semitics, Latin, Greek, ancient history, and moral philosophy or ethics. Italian, Spanish, modern history, and the history of philosophy were nominated university sub-

jects. For an explanation of the inconsistencies, see Wallace, *History*, 130-1.

11 E.J. McCorkell, *Henry Carr - Revolutionary* (1969), 17-19
12 Grant and Hamilton, *Principal Grant*, 208-9. The address, which was published in full in a number of newspapers, is summarized, with many excerpts, 205-15.
13 L.K. Shook, *Catholic Post-Secondary Education in English-Speaking Canada* (1971), 24-6
14 J.J. Talman and R. Talman, *Western, 1878-1953* (1953), 1
15 University of Ottawa, *Prospectus 1878*
16 University of Ottawa, *Calendar 1878*
17 See below, chapter 14.
18 A.S. Morton, *Saskatchewan: the Making of a University* (1959), 8
19 Columbian Methodist College was authorized by the legislature in 1893 to grant degrees in theology. Its work in arts continued for many years in association with the University of Toronto with which, through the influence of the now federated Victoria University, it had become affiliated in the early 1890s. On the theological side Columbian is one of the ancestors of the Union Theological College which affiliated with the University of British Columbia in 1928. For Whetham and Columbian, see H.T. Logan, *Tuum Est: A History of the University of British Columbia* (1958), 13-14, 86.
20 J.E. Murray, 'The Early History of Emmanuel College,' *Sask. History*, 9 (1956), 81-101
21 Little is known of Lansdowne College. W.L. Morton, *One University: a History of the University of Manitoba* (1957), 27, notes that it opened at Portage la Prairie in 1890, failed to establish itself, and was closed after a short life.
22 Morton, *One University*, 22-3
23 Taché to Sir John Drummond, 28 December 1889; quoted by Morton, *One University*, 45
24 See above, chapter 2, 11.
25 On both the women's medical colleges, see C. Hacker, *The Indomitable Lady Doctors* (1974).

9
Arts and Science

By 1890 a number of Canadian universities possessed faculties of
law, medicine, and theology, and a few could boast of faculties
in other professional fields, notably engineering. But in the
case of law and medicine, the relationship of the professional
faculty to the university remained a largely nominal one, with the
university exerting little control over the day-to-day activities
of what in effect were proprietary schools; and in the case of
theology and engineering the professional faculty could hardly be
called independent of the faculty of arts since the professors
were also (and primarily) members of that faculty. Hence, the
faculty of arts in 1890 remained the dominant one in the Canadian
university, and its activities continued to be the chief concern
of the university's president. He, in turn, dominated the faculty
of arts, for the day of the responsible dean had not yet arrived.

   Though largely confined to supervising the affairs of the faculty
of arts, the president could not complain that time hung heavily
on his hands, since the activities of this faculty were extensive;
they included whatever offerings the university provided in the
fields of adult education and graduate instruction. At Ottawa and
at Dalhousie, diploma courses in commerce were offered under the
rubric of arts, and at Dalhousie there were also two or three year
courses in journalism, technology, and pre-medicine. A number of
institutions offered a B.Sc. program, others a B.L. program, one
a Ph.B. program. Furthermore, the B.A. program, which was the
principal undergraduate offering, was in almost all cases not one
program but two: a pass, general, fixed, or ordinary course (to
give it its various titles), and an honour course, with in some
cases different standards of admission and in all cases different
standards of achievement and different courses of study. Important
as the honours programs were, they involved only a small proportion
of the students. Since the majority of the students took the
general B.A. course, it is to that program we shall turn initially.

THE GENERAL B.A.

There were four types of general B.A. in the Canadian universities
in 1890. One was the classical course offered in the Roman Catholic
colleges - normally an eight year program, but at University of Ottawa
and at certain classical colleges (for example, Joliette and Rigaud)
of seven years duration. A second was the course offered at King's,
Bishop's, and Trinity, the Church of England colleges which continued to follow the Oxford and Cambridge pattern of the three year
B.A. The other two types of general B.A. were both four year programs, but they were distinguised from each other by the fact that
in one case the course of studies was prescribed from beginning to
end, while in the other the student was permitted a considerable
degree of freedom in the selection of subjects to be studied in
the final two years. It is to be noted that in this fourth type
the principle of election did not apply to the first two years and
in general this was equally true of the first year at Bishop's,
King's, and Trinity, which offered a three year B.A. The classical
college course was entirely prescribed.

One explanation for the dominance of the principle of prescription was offered by Principal Dawson at the opening of the 1891
session at McGill: 'We have not arrived at the stage when, as in
Germany, the student may select his course of study for himself,
nor even at the wide range of choice recently allowed in some of
the universities of the United States, nor should we until the
preparatory training of matriculation shall have been greatly advanced.'[1] Though no one would contest the superiority of the
standards achieved in the German gymnasium over those that obtained
in the North American secondary schools in the 1880s, it is a moot
question whether, as Dawson appeared to imply, the American freshman was better prepared at this time than was his Canadian counterpart. There were other reasons, both practical and philosophical,
to explain the failure of Canadian institutions to answer the call
to the elective system sounded by President Eliot of Harvard in his
inaugural address in 1869. For one thing, the Canadian honour
courses provided an alternative to the elective system for those
students who were ready for specialization. For another, the
elective system, to be effective, required a much larger teaching
staff than most Canadian universities could afford in 1890, a
practical consideration which also explained why so many American
institutions continued along the traditional path. But more
important still, there was in Canada, with its strong English,
Scottish, and Roman Catholic traditions, a belief in the soundness
of the traditional program. Many Canadians were prepared in 1890
to defend a fully prescribed curriculum on philosophic grounds.

Dawson was right, however, in recognizing that an undergraduate
course of studies must be based on matriculation requirements.
By 1890 these were essentially the same for all Canadian institutions. The usual requirement was standing in five subjects -
classics, mathematics, English, history with geography, and either
a science or a modern language. Classics meant Latin *and* Greek

a typical prescription (McGill's) being Greek Grammar, Latin Grammar, *Aeneid* Book I, 1-300, Caesar's *Gallic Wars* Book I, and Xenophon's *Anabasis* Book I. Dalhousie permitted the substitution of French *or* German for Greek, but the more usual substitution for Greek was French *and* German (Manitoba, Queen's) or French *and* physics (Mount Allison, Queen's). Mathematics, like Latin, was universally required - papers on arithmetic, algebra (to simple or quadratic equations) and geometry (the first three or four books of Euclid). Only McGill, Acadia, and New Brunswick required French, and only the latter two required a science. English was a standard requirement but did not necessarily involve English literature. At McGill the prescription - again quite typical - was: writing from dictation, a paper on English grammar including analysis, a paper on the leading events of British history, an essay on a subject to be given at the time of the examination. Frequently the subject for the English was based on specified literary texts, and many universities, including those in Ontario, required an additional paper on set texts, a practice which by 1900 would be universal. History was often included under English, as at McGill, but was increasingly emerging as a separate subject; normally the matriculation requirement included attention to ancient as well as British history and the phrase 'and the geography related thereto' commonly appeared.

There was no matriculation examination as such in the classical course since this was a seven or eight year program embracing the secondary and undergraduate years. At Laval the B.A. was awarded to the student who obtained two-thirds of the total points possible at both the Examen des Lettres (taken at the end of the sixth year) and the Examen des Sciences (end of the eighth). The subjects and points were as follows:

Lettres
une version latine (18 points)
une version grecque (18 points)
un thème latin (18 points)
l'histoire universelle, l'histoire du Canada et la Géographie
  (28 points, including 4 for answers in English on Canadian
  history)
les principes et l'histoire de la littérature et de la Rhétorique
  (20 points)
une composition littéraire (36 points)

Sciences
philosophie intellectuelle et morale (30 points)
physique et chimie (24 points)
mathématiques et astronomie (24 points)
histoire naturelle (12 points)

At Ottawa, which offered the classical course in seven years, mathematics and science were prescribed in all years, but Latin and Greek were completed by the end of the fifth; and the final two years were devoted to philosophy, mathematics, and physics. The subjects for the Intermediate Examination, equivalent to the Examen des Lettres, were Greek, Latin, English, French, history and geography, mathematics (arithmetic, algebra, trigonometry), and geology; those for the Final Examination, logic, metaphysics, moral philosophy, political economy, astronomy, mechanics, and experimental physics. An essay on a philosophical subject was a further requirement at the Final Examination.

The Laval program represented no substantial change from that prescribed in 1860, but it was being offered in many more colleges, not all of which were entirely satisfied with the arrangements. The thirty-year period was marked by continual discussions (and arguments) as to how the papers should be set and marked, high-lighted by Congrès des Collèges de l'Enseignement Secondaire in 1880 and 1890.[2] At the latter a proposal that the university examinations be limited to those in philosophy, mathematics, and 'les devoirs de la composition' was passed by a vote of 8 to 7, but since this did not represent the required two-thirds majority it was not implemented until 1891, when the Congrès reassembled. The change was welcomed by the colleges since it simplified procedure and reduced the functional authority of Laval, but it had no effect on the course of study, or on the over-riding importance of exami-nations in the eight year course. The association with Laval was of great benefit to the colleges since it was a guarantee that standards would be high, but it militated against experimentation in the curriculum and it concentrated attention on the passing of examinations rather than on education *per se*. The problem has been well stated by the historian of Collège de l'Assomption:

L'affiliation universitaire, en 1880, apportera aux études le bienfait incomparable de la sanction du baccalauréat; mais ne faut-il pas regretter qu'elle ait du même coup étouffé maintes initiatives, où la plume des écoliers trouvait à s'exercer librement dans une féconde originalité? Saisis désormais par le cauchemar des examens universitaires, les élèves et leur maîtres devront tous porter le joug d'une programme d'études plus précis, impitoyablement uniforme et duquel il ne leur sera guère loisible de s'écarter.[3]

Freed from the nightmare of examinations and in a position to act without reference to an outside authority, Roman Catholic colleges like Ottawa, St Joseph's, and St Francis Xavier were quicker to introduce minor changes in the course of study. But their convic-tion that the time-honoured course was essentially sound deterred them from making major changes.

The theory behind the program of the three Church of England colleges which offered the general B.A. degree in three years was stated in the King's College *Calendar*:

The object aimed at in the Arts Course is to impart a good general
education, while every facility is afforded for the prosecution
of special studies. Accordingly, every matriculated student ...
is required to attend the Lectures of all the Professors until
he has passed his Responsions. After this he is at liberty to
select three or more of the subjects lectured on to form the
subjects of his B.A. examination. If the student be desirous of
taking Honours at his B.A. Examination he can do so in any one
or more of the subjects lectured on after passing the ordinary
Examination.

Responsions, normally taken at the end of the first year, involved
examinations in classics, English literature, divinity, mathematics,
chemistry and physics, and either French or German. For the B.A.
examination, the student could offer any three of classics, English
literature, mathematics, divinity, natural science, modern languages,
and economics and history. At Bishop's the course was more
thoroughly prescribed: divinity, Latin, Greek, French, and English
in all three years, mathematics and either history or Hebrew in the
first two, chemistry or political economy in the second and third,
and three subjects studied for a single year - physics in the first,
logic in the second, and natural science (or additional mathematics)
in the third. Trinity, on the other hand, introduced the principle
of election in the first year:

I
divinity, Latin, Greek or French & German, mathematics, physical
science, 1 of natural science, French, German, Hebrew
II
divinity, Latin, Greek or French & German, 1 of mathematics or
mental philosophy, physical & natural science, 2 of history,
French, German, Hebrew
III
divinity, Latin, Greek or French & German, 1 of mathematics,
philosophy, science, modern languages, English history & literature, Oriental languages.

At Trinity women students were also permitted to substitute Italian
for Greek and, even more surprising, harmony for the mathematics
of the First Year.
Of the ten institutions offering the B.A. in a four year course,
five had introduced the principle of options in the upper years and
five continued to prescribe all or almost all of the subjects in
all four years. At Manitoba, which as an examining and not a
teaching university organized its programs in terms of examinations
rather than courses, there were no options at all; students were
required to write examinations in Latin, Greek, French, English,
mathematics, history, and chemistry at the Previous Examination
(end of second year) and in Latin, Greek, English, French, mathe-

matics, science, history, and philosophy at the Final B.A. Examination. New Brunswick, Victoria, and Acadia permitted a choice only among languages. McMaster also permitted a choice among languages and as well two minor options in the fourth year - history or science of education, civil polity or evidences of Christianity. Since McMaster's B.A. program was introduced in 1890, presumably after study of various possibilities, it is of particular interest as an example of the four year prescribed course:

I
Latin, 2 Languages, English, mathematics, Bible
II
Latin, 2 languages, English, physics, chemistry, history, mental science
III
Latin or Greek, 1 language, English, physics, history, mental & moral science, civil polity, science of education, Bible
IV
Latin or Greek, 1 language, English, physics, mineralogy & geology, history or science of education, civil polity or evidences, logic.

The program offered in the remaining five institutions was not radically different. At Toronto, Latin, English, and languages were prescribed for four years, and there were compulsory courses in mathematics, physics, chemistry, history, and philosophy in one or other of the first two years; the student's freedom of movement was limited to selecting two of history and political science, philosophy, and physics in the third year, and two of political science, philosophy, and mathematics and physics in the fourth. Dalhousie, however, prescribed only three of five subjects in the third year (Latin or Greek, physics, history) and none in the fourth, where five of 18 subjects were to be selected. Mount Allison prescribed a language (not necessarily Latin), English, and logic and psychology in the third but only ethics in the fourth, the student choosing one of six options in the third and three of seven in the fourth to fill out his program. Queen's, which maintained the Scottish practice of dividing all subjects into junior and senior and did not insist upon a particular order in which subjects were taken, required the junior and senior courses in Latin, Greek or Moderns, English, philosophy, mathematics, and physics, and two of 14 other 'subjects,' for example, junior and senior history, junior and senior political science, first year honours English; alternatively, a student could substitute an additional subject from the list of 14 for senior Latin and for senior Greek or Moderns. Finally, McGill had adopted the terminology of 'groups.' Greek or Latin and natural philosophy were required in the third and fourth years and moral philosophy in the fourth, to which the student added three subjects in each year, one to be chosen from a list headed 'Literature, Etc.' and one from a list headed 'Science.'

The resemblances among these four types of B.A. program are more striking than the differences. In all cases there is a heavy emphasis upon languages – four years of Latin is normal – and an insistence that the student devote attention to English, history, all branches of philosophy, and to mathematics and science. The traditional certainly outweighs the experimental. But there was one B.A. program, which, though entirely prescribed, revealed a thoroughly experimental approach to the curriculum. This was the course offered at Acadia.

During the first term of his freshman year the Acadia student took four courses – Latin, mathematics, French, physics – and attended a series of weekly lectures delivered by the president. After Christmas, mathematics was continued, but Greek replaced Latin, French became an elective study except for those who had decided to substitute modern languages for Greek throughout the course, and history and English were begun. In the second and third years, Latin and Greek were scheduled in each of the four terms, with French (first term) and German (second term) constituting an option for Greek. The Roman and medieval history of the first year was followed by later medieval and modern history in the first term of the second. English was continued in each term, but with a decreasing number of class hours – 3, 3, 2, 1; there were also monthly essays in all four terms and a special examination in literature and a rhetorical exhibition at the end of the second year. Mathematics continued to occupy four hours a week in each term, but by the third year it had become physics – the six term prescriptions were plane and sold geometry, algebra, general geometry and differential calculus (or acoustics and general chemistry), survey and navigation, and astronomy and mechanics. An hour was devoted to physiology throughout the second year, three hours to chemistry in the second term of the second year, and five hours to geology and mineralogy in the first term of the third. In addition, there was an hour of practical ethics throughout the second year and courses in logic, psychology, and political economy in the second term of the third year. Thus, by the end of the third year, there had been systematic and detailed study of Latin, Greek or French and German, mathematics, science (chemistry, physics, geology, mineralogy, physiology), history, English, and the students had been introduced to philosophy. They were now prepared for a final synthesizing year.

The final year at Acadia involved three courses in each term, psychology, evidences of christianity, and constitutional history in the first, and metaphysics, moral philosophy, and political science in the second. All were four hours a week except political science, which was two. In addition, the students attended four lecture courses in the first term – on classical literature, English literature, French and German literature, and the history of mathematics. In the second term they devoted a good deal of time to preparing two substantial essays, one (termed a thesis) which they were required to read to the staff and student body

and a second which they had to read to the university senate.
Clearly this was a course with a beginning, middle, and end, one
that had been carefully designed by the faculty and which emphasized
the unity of knowledge.

B.Sc., B.L., AND Ph.B.

In the year 1890, two Canadian universities awarded bachelor's
degrees in science - Laval, which granted seven B. ès Sciences,
and New Brunswick, which granted two B.Sc.'s. Laval also granted
sixteen B. ès Lettres and Dalhousie two B.L.s. No university
granted a Ph.B.
   The latter as a degree twice granted by Mount Allison - in 1882
and 1887 - to students who wished to substitute modern languages
for classics in the four year B.A. course. The Ph.B. disappeared
from the Mount Allison *Calendar* in 1894, and has never been granted
by any other Canadian university. In effect it was the same degree
as the B.L. which Dalhousie granted between 1887 and 1901 to 19
students who had taken French and German in place of Latin and
Greek in the regular B.A. course. At Ottawa, the B.L. was awarded
on a different basis - to students who, having matriculated in
arts, had successfully completed the linguistic, historical and
philosophical parts of the B.A. course but not the mathematical.
'In the Intermediate Examination, candidates for B.L. are exempted
from higher algebra, analytical geometry and analytical trigonometry and in the Final Examination ... from calculus, physical
astronomy and the mathematical part of physics.' Fifteen students
completed this program between 1881 and 1890. The Ottawa arrangement was a variant of the practice adopted at Laval for many years
of awarding the B. ès L. to students who achieved two-thirds of
the required marks at the Examen des Lettres but less than two-
thirds (though more than one-third) at the Examen des Sciences.
The single B.L. granted by St Joseph's in 1888 was equally a
consolation prize representing a 50% average on all examinations
with at least 25% on each paper rather than the 66% average, with
33% on each paper, required for the B.A.
   The early history of the B.Sc. degree is even more complex since
it could represent a standard that was higher, lower, or equivalent to that represented by the B.A. At Laval it was of a lower
standard, being awarded to students who obtained the requisite
two-thirds average at the B.A. Examen des Sciences but had fallen
below the required average at the earlier Examen des Lettres. At
Mount Allison, which awarded six B.Sc.s between 1864 and 1878,
the course of study was three years in length in contrast to the
four required for the B.A. The Ottawa B.Sc. also represented a
program shorter than the B.A., the degree being awarded to students
who completed a special three-year course which they entered after
three years of Ottawa's seven-year classical course. This special
course, which included two years of Latin and an impressive amount
of English, French, history, and political economy, omitted Greek,

reduced the amount of philosophy, and expanded the science element particularly on the practical side. Unfortunately, the course attracted few students; only one graduate is recorded prior to 1890.

But while the B.Sc. awarded at Laval, Ottawa, and Mount Allison was of a lower academic quality than the B.A. granted by the same institutions, the degrees of this type which had been granted by Queen's and New Brunswick were at the postgraduate level. In the late 1870s, Queen's granted the B.Sc. to three students who had distinguished themselves by obtaining first class honours in the honours departments of mathematics and natural philosophy and of chemistry and natural science or, oddly enough, in logic, metaphysics and ethics, with second class honours in classics and in history, rhetoric and English literature; the degree disappeared in 1880 with the introduction of an earned M.A. and D.Sc. A similar situation obtained at New Brunswick. Prior to 1889, the B.Sc. was awarded to a B.A. of six years' standing who wrote examinations in chemical and mechanical philosophy and in natural science, and one degree was awarded on this basis - in 1885. The two B.Sc.s which were awarded in 1890 were granted to B.A.s of two-years' standing who had submitted an appropriate thesis. But in 1891 the regulations were again changed and the degree was equated with the honours B.A., the candidate being required to obtain honours in the three science departments. Still another arrangement had been introduced by King's, Windsor - a four year course (in comparison with the King's three-year B.A.) based on matriculation in Latin, English, and mathematics - but not Greek.

Still to be mentioned are the two B.Sc. programs which, by placing the B.Sc. on a parity with the B.A., set the pattern that would be universally adopted in the twentieth century. Such a course had been announced in a confident manner by Victoria in its *Calendar* of 1875:

This Course of study is designed to meet the growing necessities of our country, and the growing preferences of our times. Heretofore, the College Halls have been frequented chiefly by men who intend to enter the *learned professions*, strictly so called. The Arts Course must still attract these men, and furnish the most suitable discipline and culture for clergymen, lawyers, physicians, teachers etc. There are, however, many young men who look forward to the occupations of engineering, surveying, mining, navigation, architecture, etc. etc., - occupations full of promise in our country's future. Men with such expectations have hitherto, very generally, shunned Universities, and perhaps not without reason, when the Course in Arts was the only one open to them. Now, however, will be found in the Scientific Course the most profitable preparatory discipline for these pursuits, and at the same time a wide and liberal culture, such as will qualify the Graduate in Science for the highest social and political stations.

The course offered at Victoria in 1875 and which underwent only minor adjustments in the succeeding years was a heavy one, but there can be no doubt that it was well designed to achieve the two stated purposes – a knowledge of science in its theoretical and practical aspects, and a broad liberal education:

I
mathematics, botany, history, English, physics
II
mathematics, logic, political economy, history, English, French
III
mathematics, inorganic chemistry, zoology, mineralogy, geology, organic chemistry, French, German, civil polity, philosophy
IV
astronomy, surveying and navigation, biology, analytical mechanics, determinative mineralogy, English, German, ethics, philosophy

The courses were in most instances those offered to the B.A. student of the equivalent year, and initially the admission requirements were identical with those for the B.A. But despite the removal of classics from the matriculation requirements in 1876, there was never more than a handful of students – for the six years commencing in 1875: 2, 2, 6, 9, 8, and 11. Evidence of the quality of the course may be deduced from the fact that eight of the eleven students registered in 1880 already had a B.A.

This program disappeared with the entry of Victoria into federation with the University of Toronto in 1892. Dalhousie had established a similar program in 1878, but again the response of students was discouraging – there was a total of five graduates between 1880 and 1884. In the latter year, the course was temporarily suspended. It was reactivated two years later, but the first graduate of the revived course did not qualify until 1892. The course that he successfully completed was the following:

I
French or German, botany, mathematics, inorganic chemistry, English
II
The Language continued, practical chemistry, mathematics, English literature, logic and psychology
III, IV
The Language not taken in the first two years, physics, advanced mathematics or organic and practical chemistry and (in the fourth year) one of the following: French, German, history, political economy, organic or medical chemistry, practical chemistry, practical physics, metaphysics and ethics.

As will be seen in the following chapter, neither this program nor that of Victoria bore a close relationship to the courses of study offered to engineering students at this time.

THE HONOURS B.A.

It is likely that the failure of the B.Sc. degree to gain substantial stature by 1890 was due in part to the fact that an opportunity
for considerable specialization in the sciences was available in
the honours B.A. program. Since this program equally provided for
specialization in the humanities and, to the extent that they had
been developed, the social sciences, it also offers an explanation
for the relative inflexibility of the Canadian general B.A. course
at this time. President Eliot's young man who knew what he wanted
and was prepared to pursue it in depth could in Canada satisfy his
intellectual desires in an honours course. At the same time, it
was recognized that the honours program was appropriate to only a
limited number of students. Thus, while McMaster University felt
it necessary to provide for honours in its B.A. program when it
commenced to offer instruction in 1890, President T.H. Rand made
it clear that the main object of the faculty of arts was to provide a sound course for the average student: 'The Arts Department
offers to its students a well-balanced general course of 4 years,
only those students being permitted to take honors who are able
to reach and maintain, without undue effort, a standard of 75%.
This arrangement places honors within reach of only well-qualified
students.'[4] McMaster's decision to make provision for honours was
partly based on practical considerations. The category of *specialist*
had been introduced in the secondary schools of Ontario, and professional advancement, both within a school system and within the
Provincial Department of Education, required the possession of a
specialist certificate, granted only to those who possessed an
honours B.A.[5] The University of Toronto had long since committed
itself to a heavy emphasis on the honours course; if the other
Ontario universities wished to have their fair share of the best
students, it was necessary for them to offer courses which would
qualify graduates for the specialist certificate; otherwise, all
the high school principals and department heads would be Toronto
graduates and likely to encourage their students to go to Toronto.
The experience of Queen's in the 13 years following Principal
Grant's assumption of office in 1877 is indicative of how circumstances forced the partial abandonment of Queen's theoretical
devotion to general education in arts and science:

One of the points at issue between Toronto and the outlying
universities was the comparative merits of the special and the
fixed courses. Speaking broadly, University College laid stress
on honour work, and to give students opportunity to pursue
certain lines with some thoroughness, permitted them to omit
certain other studies, or at least to be content with a slighter
acquaintance with them. The outlying colleges prescribed a
fixed or balanced course, which all were obliged to take. It
provided an excellent general education, but nowhere gave specialized instruction, while the Univeristy College honour
courses took students a respectable length into the department

of their choice, at the risk, as the outlying colleges invariably pointed out, of leaving them ill-informed on other essential subjects. The honour course met with the approval of the provincial department, as well as of the general public, and the absence of honours in the degrees of the outlying institutions was one reason for the preponderance of Toronto men in the high schools. Grant now moved toward the honour course by instituting a system of options which at first enabled students to lean towards the side of the curriculum which their tastes caused them to prefer. The tendency continued as the staff was increased, until at length Queen's carried the principle of specialization to considerable lengths.[6]

The honours offerings first appear in the Queen's *Calendar* of 1879, with five Departments involved: classics; mathematics and natural philosophy; chemistry and natural science; history, rhetoric and English literature; logic, metaphysics and ethics. In 1884, Victoria, which had permitted 'additional work for honours' in certain subjects since 1861, announced honours courses in classics, mathematics, moderns, Orientals, and English and history. In the same year Trinity added mental and moral philosophy, physical science, and theology (basically Orientals) to the two subjects, classics and mathematics, which it had been offering at the level of B.A. with honours since 1854; Moderns followed in 1888. In 1885, Ottawa introduced a B.A. with honours in classics, English or French literature with history, mental and moral philosophy, mathematics and physics, and natural science.
The carrot of the specialist certificate did not apply in the other Canadian provinces, but other influences, including the Oxford tradition and the example of Toronto, caused almost every Canadian university to introduce some type of honours program well before 1890. Special or honours courses were available at Manitoba from the time of its establishment. At McGill, they had existed in the form of 'courses of study for special honours in classics and mathematics after the ordinary B.A.' in 1858. They appeared at New Brunswick by 1862, at Acadia in 1863, at Dalhousie in 1871, at King's in 1872, at Bishop's by 1882, and at Mount Allison in 1884.
Where an honours B.A. represented additional work at a level beyond that required for the ordinary B.A., it could be said to resemble the M.A. earned by course work, as for example at King's, Windsor or at Ottawa where the student could not sit the examination for a B.A. with honours until he had passed the examinations for the general B.A. Indeed, the degree granted by Queen's to students who obtained first class standing in one of its 14 honour courses was the M.A., while Principal Dawson of McGill had occasion to observe in 1880 that 'after graduation young men can pursue with us what in the United States are called post-graduate courses, by taking for one or two years the honour work in one or more of the courses which they have not pursued as undergraduates.'[7] At McGill the additional work for honours was not introduced until

130

the third year, the student qualifying as a candidate for honours by obtaining first class standing in the honours subject or subjects and at least second class standing in all other subjects. Dalhousie, New Brunswick, Mount Allison, Queen's, and Manitoba also confined honours work to the two final years. Acadia introduced additional work for honours in the second year, and this was the plan that McMaster decided to adopt in 1890. At Bishop's and at Trinity the candidate for B.A. with honours devoted his second and third years to preparing for the honours examination of his third and final year. Only at Toronto and Victoria did the student commence work at the honours level in the first year.

Despite the fact that it offered honours in the first year, Victoria was still doubtful about the theoretical soundness of undergraduate specialization. It had introduced additional work for honours in 1862, prescribing an additional book of Virgil and two of Legendre's *Geometry* in the first year, an additional book of Horace's Odes and of the Iliad in the second, and *Phénomènes Physiques du Corps Vivant* and Macintosh's *Dissertation on the Progress of Ethical Philosophy* in the fourth. But it had also emphasized that breadth rather than depth was the mark of the B.A.:

> The Curriculum is constructed on the principle of encouraging a well-balanced and varied culture, and not with the view of stimulating extraordinary proficiency in particular departments. It will be seen in another part of the Calendar that there are a few *prizes* awarded to special excellence, but all candidates for honors are required to pursue the same course, and the estimate of merit will be based on the aggregate of all the subjects of the curriculum, including pass-work as well as honor-work.[8]

Indeed, the honours candidate, rather than being excused any pass work in deference to his additional obligations in honours, was required to do more pass work than the pass candidate. The latter, in 1862, could if he wished take either French or mathematics in his second and third years; the former had to take both.

By 1890 Victoria had relaxed its requirements to some extent. There were no exemptions in the first two years, but in the third the student could confine himself to the honours work of his own department (classics, mathematics, Orientals, moderns, or English and history) and to the fixed course in natural science, philosophy and, if he were in classics or mathematics, to modern language. In the final year the work outside his department was restricted to astronomy, geology, lithology and ethics. Basically the same arrangement was made at the other universities which concentrated honours work in the upper years; McGill and Dalhousie permitted the student to ignore two pass courses, Mount Allison one, New Brunswick one in the third year and two in the fourth. Manitoba was generous enough to permit the honours philosophy student to ignore pass ethics and logic, and the honours mathematics and physics student to ignore pass physics. But unless the work was already covered by the honours subject, all honours students at Manitoba had to pass general examinations in trigonometry, statics, hydrostatics, physics, ethics, and logic in addition to the paper set by their own department.

What distinguished the Toronto honours system from the program offered at Victoria and the other Canadian universities was that the student was seldom required to study subjects unrelated to his main interest. Normally, all the honours students were required to take the pass English, Latin, and mathematics of the first year, but for the final three years their course of study was that laid down by their honours department with the required pass subjects limited to a small number directly related to the major field. In 1890, for example, the pass requirements for honour classics and for honour mathematics and physics were as follows:

Classics	*Mathematics & Physics*
English I	English I
mathematics I	Latin or Greek I
history I, II	French and German I, II
French or German or Hebrew	chemistry II
I, II	practical chemistry III
philosophy II, III	

The gradual development of the honour course system at Toronto between 1860 and 1890, a matter of some complexity and of many details, was described at length by Ramsay Wright and W.J. Alexander in 1906.[9] The most significant dates are 1877 and 1880. In the Calendar for 1877-78 it was stated that 'there are two ordinary modes of proceeding to the degree of B.A. - Pass and Honour,' and the arrangements for the two types of program were listed separately. Furthermore, provision was made to transfer students who failed to obtain standing in honours to the Pass Course of the next year - an arrangement which tended to emphasize the difference in quality of the two types of course. At this stage there were five honour courses: classics, mathematics and natural philosophy, modern languages with history, natural sciences, and mental and moral science with civil polity. A sixth, Oriental languages, was added in 1888, and in 1891 the list was extended to eight, by the creation of separate departments of political science and of chemistry and mineralogy. The second date of importance was 1880, which marked the arrival of Maurice Hutton as professor of classics. Under Hutton's guidance the honours course in classics was gradually changed from a heavy but largely disparate grouping of courses into a tightly knit sequence which gave as much attention to the thought and life of Greece and Rome as to the languages in which its history, literature, and philosophy were recorded.[10] In the course of time Hutton's influence was reflected in the organization of the other honours courses in the humanities and social sciences.

SPECIAL OFFERINGS

The activities of the faculty of arts and science in the field of
adult education will be described at the end of this chapter and
in graduate education in chapter 11. There remains to be mentioned
here a number of miscellaneous undertakings by particular institutions. Some of these were directly related to the B.A. program,
for example the special arrangements adopted by Acadia and Queen's
to facilitate the taking of a degree by the practising teacher,
or the Special Arts Course for Women provided at McGill. Others
were supplementary - for example the classes in gymnastics and in
elocution which, for a fee, McGill students could avail themselves
of, or the lectures in political science which Trinity arranged
for J.G. Bourinot to offer during the 1890-91 session. Finally,
there were a number of diploma or certificate courses of two or
three years' duration.
Dalhousie was particularly prominent in this latter field. It
offered a three year course 'Preparatory to the Study of Technology' and two year courses in liberal arts, journalism, commerce,
and pre-medicine. In all cases these were groupings of regular
arts or science courses, the timetable having been so arranged
as to make them available 'for the benefit of students who may
wish to spend but a short period of time at the University.'
Thus the student in journalism took in his first year French,
English literature (both first and second year courses), history
(both third and fourth year courses), and either logic and psychology (a second year course) or political economy (a fourth year
course). In his second year he took French, advanced English
literature, ethics, political economy or metaphysics, constitutional history and constitutional law. If he attended regularly
and passed the examinations, he was granted a certificate 'stating
the nature of the course pursued and the degree of success attained.' The commerce course offered at Ottawa was not comparable
to Dalhousie's, being essentially a secondary school course with
a heavy emphasis on practical banking and accounting procedures.
The efforts of Queen's to assist the extramural student in the
B.A. program were impressive. Such students were required to
register in October and obtain class tickets for any subjects in
which they wished to be examined in the following April or
September. These tickets were to be forwarded to the professor
who was responsible for marking the essays and exercises which
the student was required to submit at specified dates. Regular
classes would be held during July and August in any subject for
which ten students were prepared to register at $10.00 each. If
$200 could be guaranteed, the university would send a lecturer
in May or June to any centre in Ontario or Quebec. Finally, the
examination could be written wherever five students were assembled.
The Donalda Special Course in Arts was introduced at McGill in
the fall of 1884, Sir Donald Smith having donated $50,000, the
endowment from which to be used to provide 'separate and distinct'
arts classes for women. The funds were sufficient to provide for

the first and second year courses only, but in 1886 Smith increased
the sum to $120,000 and 'the Course' was extended to the third and
fourth years. The program was precisely the same as that authorized
for men - the same courses of study, the same examinations, and
in most if not all cases the same lecturers. It was not, however,
practical to provide honours courses to two parallel sets of students, and consequently the Donalda who wished to take honours
was required to take her honours courses in the company of men.
This latter experiment appears to have been a success.

Having now reviewed the organization of undergraduate programs
provided in the faculties of arts in 1890, it is time to turn to
the offerings of individual departments. Technically, it is
inappropriate to talk of departments at this time since in almost
all cases a single person was responsible for the instruction
provided in any given subject; indeed, many professors were responsible for two subjects. No faculty of arts as yet numbered
as many as 20 full-time instructors, and most numbered less than
10. Because the numbers remained small and because the president
had little else to concern himself with except the activities of
the faculty of arts, there was as yet little need for a dean.
As previously noted, the president himself fulfilled the functions
of dean.

In all but five cases, the president was a clergyman, and
normally he taught philosophy or divinity. The lay presidents
included the only two scientists in the group, J.W. Dawson of
McGill (geology and natural history), and Thomas Harrison of
New Brunswick (mathematics). The other laymen were Daniel Wilson
of Toronto (history), T.H. Rand of McMaster (science of education,
ethics and civil polity), and J.R. Inch of Mount Allison (philosophy). Only Rand, Wilson, and the Rev. John Forrest of Dalhousie
(history and political science) could be described as social
scientists, and this only by stretching either the term or the
imagination. Political science and economics, as well as psychology, were only just emerging as subjects separate from philosophy.
Indeed, if one were to assign history to the humanities and
include political science and economics under philosophy, it
would be possible to say that in 1890 there were no social scientists on the staffs of Canadian universities. However, the recent
appointments of Adam Shortt as lecturer in political science at
Queen's and W.J. Ashley as professor of political economy and
constitutional history at Toronto were an indication that a new
era was about to dawn. *About to dawn* is, nonetheless, the proper
phrase; the relative importance of the humanities, social sciences,
and sciences in 1890 can be seen in Table 1 (page 136) where the
full-time appointments to the staffs of the faculty of arts at
three small and three large universities are listed.

HUMANITIES

Despite the strong position occupied by Latin and the rising
prominence of the modern languages, particularly English, the

most notable arts subject in 1890 was philosophy. Still embracing
economics, political science, and psychology in most institutions,
it occupied the key position in the upper years of the B.A. course.
This had long been the situation in the classical course offered
by the Roman Catholic institutions; in 1890 it was almost equally
true of the protestant and non-denominational universities. Admittedly, few institutions went so far as did Acadia, whose final
synthesizing year consisted almost exclusively of courses in the
various branches of philosophy, but all, with the single exception
of King's, prescribed at least one and normally several courses.
The usual arrangement was to prescribe logic and psychology in
the second or third year, and ethics, metaphysics, and political
economy in the third or fourth. The history of philosophy was
normally reserved for honours students. Since King's prescribed
a full course in divinity in each of its three years, the exception noted is more nominal than real.

The closing years of the nineteenth century were in fact the
heyday of philosophy as an undergraduate subject. Its chief rivals
in the traditional course, classics and mathematics, were subjects
with which the students were thoroughly familiar by the time they
had matriculated, and both suffered in popular appeal from the
disciplinarian approach which too often characterized instruction
in the subject in both the high school and college. Philosophy,
in contrast, was a fresh subject, and furthermore it was often
brilliantly taught; John Watson of Queen's, George Paxton Young
of Toronto, J. Clark Murray of McGill, William Lyall of Dalhousie
were from all accounts great teachers and there were many more.
In the Roman Catholic colleges, a new enthusiasm for scholastic
philosophy had been engendered by the promulgation of the papal
bull, *Aeterni Patris*, by Pope Leo XIII in 1879. The fact that
philosophy was essentially an upper year subject and frequently
taught by the president gave it additional prestige. Furthermore,
its future rivals - history, English, the modern languages, the
individual sciences - were still endeavouring to establish themselves, while others such as economics, political science, and
psychology were still under the wing of philosophy. However,
this was soon to change. By 1890, the handwriting was on the
wall; the new subjects *were* emerging and philosophy's monopoly
was far less-embracing than it had been 10 years earlier. By
1920, the subject no longer occupied a central position in the
B.A. program except in the Catholic colleges.

The chief comment to be made about the position of classics in
1890 concerns the declining status of Greek. Latin was in an
extraordinarily strong position; it was universally required both
at matriculation for the B.A. course, and in the freshman and
sophomore years, and more often than not in the junior and senior
years. In contrast, it was now quite normal to matriculate without Greek and to substitute one - or frequently two - modern
languages throughout the B.A. course. On the other hand, Greek
had been strengthened by the establishment of separate chairs
for Greek and Latin at Queen's and at Toronto, with the result
that, while proportionately fewer students were studying Greek,

TABLE 1
Full-Time Appointments in Arts and Science, 1890–91[a]

	Full-time Staff	Humanities	Social Science	Science[b]
King's, Windsor	6	Classics Modern Languages Divinity[c] (P) English/history/economics		Math–Physics Chemistry–Geology
New Brunswick	6	Classics–history English–French Philosophy–political economy		Math (P) Physics Chemistry–natural science
Dalhousie	8	Classics Modern languages English Metaphysics–ethics	History–political science (P)	Math Physics Chemistry–mineralogy
Queen's	15	Latin Greek Classics (asst. prof.) Modern languages Mental philosophy Moral philosophy English Hebrew[c]	History Political science (lecturer)	Math Astronomy Physics Chemistry–mineralogy Natural Science (lecturer)
McGill	13	Classics Classics (asst. prof.) English (also lecturer in history) English (lecturer) French German (lecturer)		Math–physics Chemistry–mineralogy Botany Geology–natural history (P) Geology (lecturer)

TABLE 1 continued

	Full-time Staff	Humanities	Social Science	Science[b]
		Philosophy		
		Orientals		
Toronto (including University College but not Victoria College)	18	Greek	History-ethnology (P)	Math
		Greek (lecturer)	Pol. econ-constit. hist.	Physics
		Latin (lecturer)		Chemistry
		English		Mineralogy-geology
		English (lecturer)		Physiology
		French (lecturer)		
		German (lecturer)		
		Italian-Spanish (lecturer)		
		Oriental literature		
		Philosophy		

a   Rank is that of Professor unless otherwise noted.
b   Science professors at King's, U.N.B., McGill also offered instruction in applied science or engineering.
c   Also offered instruction in theology.
P   President.

137

those who persevered were exposed to a richer course.

The decline of Greek was counterbalanced by the rise of the modern foreign languages, and in 1890 the scales were at a transitional point; Greek was still required both at matriculation and as a part of some B.A. programs, while a modern language was a matriculation requirement at only three institutions (Acadia, McGill, New Brunswick), and at most institutions students could avoid a modern language by selecting Greek as their second foreign language. Only in the French-speaking institutions (including Ottawa) and at Acadia, Bishop's, King's, and Manitoba was French a specific requirement. The usual procedure was to substitute French *and* German for Greek.

The still tentative position of the modern language department was also reflected in the status accorded to its professors. Only at Acadia, Dalhousie, King's, McMaster, McGill, Mount Allison, and Queen's was there a separate chair for modern languages. At New Brunswick and at Victoria modern languages included English. Toronto contented itself with lecturers in French, German, and Italian/Spanish; Trinity with a lecturer in modern languages *and* philosophy. There was, however, nothing tentative about the nature of the courses taught by the modern language professors and lecturers of this period; literature now received at least as much attention as grammar and composition, and the study of complete texts was a feature of all courses. On the other hand, in 1890 modern languages normally meant French and German. Only at Toronto were Spanish and Italian available in the B.A. program.

Hebrew was often included in the B.A. program as an acceptable second or third language for students intending to proceed to theology. It was normally taught by a professor of Hebrew who was primarily a member of the faculty of theology - as at Queen's, McMaster, and Victoria - or by a professor of divinity - as at Trinity, Mount Allison, and King's. But both Toronto and McGill had full-time professors of Oriental Literature and honour courses in Oriental Languages and Semitics respectively.

The rising subject in the humanities was English. By now universally required at matriculation, it was mandatory in the first year except at Trinity, and often prescribed throughout, as for example at Bishop's, King's, Manitoba, McMaster, New Brunswick, and Queen's. Though still not dignified by a separate chair at some of the small colleges, the claims of English had been generally recognized in the 1880s, a decade which saw the establishment of professorships at Dalhousie, Queen's, and Toronto. By 1890 a lecturer, as well as a professor, was required to meet the increasing instructional demands at the two largest institutions, McGill and Toronto.

A distinctive feature of the work of the Canadian department of English at this time was the integration of the work in literature and composition. These were not regarded as separate subjects, but as different branches of the study of English language and literature. The prescription at McGill is representative:

First Year
Three lectures a week. Until Christmas the work of the class
will partly consist of exercises in English composition. Two
lectures a week will be given to the study of English classics.
Milton's *Comus* and a portion of Bacon's *Essays* have been
selected for the session of 1890-91. After Christmas there
will be a course of about thirty lectures on English Literature
previous to the Elizabethan Period.
Second Year
A period of English Literature, and one play of Shakespeare.
One lecture a week before Christmas; two Lectures a week after
Christmas. During the Session of 1890-91 the leading poets of
the Nineteenth Century will form the subject of the lectures.
Shakespeare - a *Midsummer Night's Dream*
Third Year
A. Chaucer's *Prologue to Canterbury Tales*. Lecture once a week.
B. Rhetoric. Lecture once a week. Textbook: *Bain's Rhetoric*.

This is a program that differs markedly from that being developed
in the American universities at this time. At Michigan, for
example, the two required English courses for the B.A. degree were
one-term courses in practical rhetoric and composition and in
science of rhetoric; the study of literature was postponed until
the second year, and the student was then free to pursue it or
not as he wished. In the United States this bifurcation of liter-
ture and composition produced an emphasis on composition which in
some institutions (Michigan is an example) led to the establishment of separate departments of English Language (or Composition)
and of English Literature, and subsequently to a spawning out of
the former of departments of speech, journalism and, ultimately,
radio and television arts. Until the 1940s when at Sir George
Williams an effectively independent sub-department of composition
was established within the department of English and where the
composition course was compulsory for *all* students, no such development occurred in Canada. Since the 1880s literature and composition have been regarded as allied subjects; composition has been
taught through the process of making detailed corrections on
essays which the student has been required to prepare on aspects
of the work in literature and by the analysis of the prose style
of the authors studied. Thus, at McGill in 1890 the first term
exercises in composition were carried on in conjunction with the
lectures on literary texts, and in the third year the literature
course gave specific attention to the principles of rhetoric.
   Two things are notable about the literature content of the
McGill course (and again it is representative of Canadian practice
at this time); first, the emphasis upon the study of particular
texts, and second, the nature of the literature selected for
study. The texts included the contemporary - in 1890 Browning
and Tennyson were still alive. The concentration upon a relatively
small number of texts meant that the student was not required to
read widely; the McGill student, for example, would have had no

contact with eighteenth century authors. This was, however, the ordinary or pass English course; the student electing honours in English at McGill was required in his third and fourth years to read many additional texts which did expose him to the broad spectrum of English literature, though not of American or Canadian.

The only two institutions in Canada which included courses in public speaking as an integral part of the degree program were two Maritime colleges which had close links with neighbouring New England liberal arts colleges, where the oratorical tradition was strong throughout the nineteenth century. At Acadia, as we have seen, the Rhetorical Exhibition was scheduled at the end of the sophomore year, and the graduation requirement included the oral presentation of a thesis (often called an oration) and a final essay. At Mount Allison, all students were required during their first two years to prepare weekly exercises 'in English Composition or Elocution' and in the final year the student was required 'to write and deliver ... four orations at dates fixed at the beginning of the Session.' Acadia and Mount Allison maintained this tradition for a further 25 years.

Most Canadian universities and colleges did give some attention to oral composition in 1890, and this was particularly true of the Roman Catholic colleges. However, such work was incidental to that devoted to written composition, and the interest was less in the technique of public speaking than in the logic and organization of the argument presented. The only course which was primarily interested in technique was a non-credit course in elocution offered at McGill, but, as the Calendar description indicated, it was more concerned with interpretative reading than with public speaking: 'Voice culture, including exercises for developing the thorax. Rush's philosophy of the voice. Grouping of Speech. Narrative reading and the reading of poetry. Biblical readings. Dramatic reading and declamation.' This course was available to McGill students who were prepared to pay a small fee ($7.50 in 1890) from 1867 to 1899; it was offered in the evening by John Andrew and John Stephen, successively masters of elocution at the McGill Normal School.

SOCIAL SCIENCES

If we adopt the criterion that the emergence of an academic subject as a recognized, independent discipline is marked by the assigning of responsibility for it to a professor who devotes his whole time to that subject, it can hardly be said that any of the subjects now normally grouped in the social sciences had achieved such recognition in the Canadian universities by 1890. Queen's and Toronto had professors of history, but at Toronto the professor was also president of the university, while at Queen's the Rev. George Ferguson had not been relieved of his responsibilities for English until 1888. Mount Allison had a professor of political science, but he was as much concerned with economics and constitutional history as with political theory. The normal arrangement in 1890 was for a professor to be responsible for two subjects - English and history, or history and political science, or political economy and constitutional history, or philosophy and political economy. The social scientist had advanced from a settee to a love-seat; he had still to advance to a chair. The distinction between economics and political science was everywhere blurred. Psychology appeared in the title of a professorship only at McMaster, where it was coupled with philosophy and logic. Anthropology, geography, and sociology had not made an appearance.

Of the 'new' disciplines, history appeared to be in the strongest position. It was normally required for matriculation and it was normally prescribed at some stage in the B.A. course. Introduced at most institutions in the 1860s, usually in association with English, history benefited from the increasing burden of the work in English. At both Queen's and Toronto it was the need to establish a separate chair in English that permitted the occupant of a combined chair to concentrate his attention on history.

In fact, however, history was still suffering from doubts about its suitability as an undergraduate subject. In 1880 J.W. Dawson had discussed the inherent difficulties of history as an academic subject. 'In so far as mere general knowledge is concerned, any educated man can attain this in an easy and delightful manner by his own reading.'[11] On the other hand, 'to attain any fitness for profound or original research, requires a thorough preliminary training more especially in languages and literature, rather than any premature entrance on the direct study of history.' He concluded that history was a subject for the graduate school, where it could be taught by several advanced specialists wholly devoted to particular fields. According to Dawson, McGill's method of dealing with history was 'to exact a certain amount of reading in ancient history from junior students, and to render accessible to senior students a short course in some portion of modern history, as an aid and inducement to farther study after graduation.' Hence in 1890 the attention of the students in classics was directed to the collateral subjects of history, antiquities, and geography, and they were required to write an examination at the end of the first year in Greek and Roman history; among the options available to fourth year students was a lecture course sketching general European history from the fall of the Roman Empire of the West to the discovery of the New World. This course, which met once a week, was offered by the department of English language and literature.

The McGill offering in history was thinner than that provided in most Canadian universities at this time. Thicker and therefore more representative was the program at Queen's. Here the junior class was devoted to ancient history, the senior class to modern history. The Calendar description of the latter indicates the nature of the course:

Lectures on: The Study of History; its methods and purposes
The Rise of Modern European Nations
The Feudal System
The Growth of Towns in the Middle Ages
Commerce in the Middle Ages and the Hanse Towns
The Crusades and their influence on Europe
The Development of Monarchy
The State of Europe before the French Revolution
The British Constitution
Students will also be examined on: Hallam's *Middle Ages* and
Bourinot's *Constitution of Canada*
Books Recommended: Guizot's *History of Modern Civilization*
Guizot's *History of France*
Green's *History of the English People*
Bryce's *Holy Roman Empire*
Freeman's *Growth of the English Constitution*
Kingsford's *History of Canada*
Fortnightly Essays are required.

Two additional courses were provided for students electing to
take honours in history, the first concerned with the principles
of government (with Stubb's *Constitutional History of England*
as the basic text) and the second with the British, American,
and colonial constitutions (Hallam's *Constitutional History of
England*, May's *Constitutional History*, Bancroft's *History of the
Constitution of the United States*).   Again fortnightly essays
were required and again there were recommended texts – Rousseau's
Social Contract and De Tocqueville's *Democracy in America* are
examples.

The coming subject in the social sciences was political science,
which, as J.G. Bourinot pointed out in a paper presented to the
Royal Society of Canada in 1889, had particular and concrete
value, offering as it did the possibility of an adequate training
for the politicians, civil servants, lawyers, and judges who were
needed to cope with the economic and constitutional problems of
an emerging nation.[12] G.W. Ross, the minister of education for
Ontario, arranged for the appointment of W.J. Ashley to the newly
created chair of Political Economy and Constitutional History at
Toronto 'in the earnest hope that I would be able to afford to
the undergraduates of our University a comprehensive course of
training in economics and political philosophy, which would fit
them for dealing with the many social and constitutional problems
which require particular attention in a rapidly expanding country
like Canada.'[13] The same need was being felt in French-speaking
Canada.   'A qui est-il permis aujourd'hui d'ignorer les principes
de le Science Economique, qui interviennent dans toutes les
affaires?' asked the Université d'Ottawa in announcing a new plan
of studies in 1893.   Indeed, it could be argued that the need for
an adequate program in political science was even more urgent in
French Canada, since a failure to understand the full implications
of some of the new doctrines could undermine the faith of French
Canadians and therefore the culture which stemmed from that faith:

A combien de dangereuses erreurs ne sont point exposé les jeunes
esprits qui entreprennent cette étude sans un guide à l'oeil
sûr et au pied ferme? D'un côté le Liberalisme, qui se vante
d'avoir introduit dans le monde économique les deux grandes
idées de liberté et de propriété, mais de liberté sans frein
et de propriété sans devoirs: de l'autre, le Socialisme avec
son principe de l'omnipotence de l'État sur la propriété et
toutes les conséquences qui en decoulent; le Chemin entre ses
deux erreurs est étroit, raide et glissant. Le faire monter
par l'élève sans trébucher et sans verser ni à droite, ni à
gauche, c'est le but que se propose, et, nous osons le dire,
qu'obtient le professeur d'Economic Politique de l'Université
d'Ottawa.

The need, then, was recognized on all sides, for both practical
and philosophical reasons. And as Ottawa and Toronto demonstrated,
something was being done about fulfilling it.

In his Royal Society paper, Bourinot had seen political science
as a means of solving practical problems; hence the priority he
assigned to constitutional history, law, and economics. He was
not particularly interested in political theory. His views were
shared by G.M. Ross and Edward Blake, the persons chiefly responsible for the establishment of the chair at Toronto and for
the appointment of W.J. Ashley to occupy it in 1888. Prior to
this, political science, under the title of civil polity, had
been taught at Toronto by the department of philosophy; the
appointment of Ashley, an historian, represented a clean break,
which was further emphasized in 1889 when Ashley was also appointed
to the newly established faculty of law. The four-year course
offered in this faculty and leading to the LL.B. degree was for
the first three years identical with that offered in the second,
third, and fourth years of the honour course in political science,
and included major courses in elementary economics, history and
criticism of economic theory, economic history, English constitutional history, Canadian constitutional history, public finance,
Roman law, jurisprudence, and the history of English law. Political science proper was restricted to a course entitled History
and Criticism of Political Theories, in which the students examined
the views of Plato, Aristotle, Hobbes, Locke, Rousseau, Burke,
Bentham, Herbert Spencer, and T.H. Green from the appropriate
texts. Neither Ashley nor the faculty of law were at Toronto
in 1895, but the emphases on economics and constitutional history
which Ashley introduced were maintained in the honour course in
political economy under his successor, James Mavor.[14]

Elsewhere in Canada, political science and economics evolved
directly from philosophy, with a consequent heightening of emphasis
on political theory and on abstract economics. This - the normal
situation in the Canadian universities in 1890 - is well illustrated in the program offered at Queen's. The instructor in charge,
Adam Shortt, who would be promoted from lecturer to professor of
political science in 1891, had graduated in philosophy in 1883 and
after three years of study in Scotland returned to Queen's as a

tutor in philosophy in 1886. Gradually taking over the courses
in political science which the professor of philosophy, John
Watson, had been giving since 1878, Shortt was made lecturer on
political science in 1889. Of the two ordinary degree courses
offered in 1890, the junior class was concerned with the principles
of political economy, the basic texts being Marshall's *Economics
of Industry*, Jevons's *Money and Mechanism of Exchange*, and
Cunningham's *Growth of English Industry and Commerce*. The senior
class was a critical examination of the leading theories of the
State and a discussion of the nature of social and political
relations; here the texts were Plato's *Republic*, Locke's *Treatise
on Civil Government*, and Montague's *The Limits of Individual
Liberty*. In the honours course (at Queen's two additional years
of study beyond the junior and senior classes) there was in each
year 'more detailed discussion of Economic, Social and Political
Principles' through critical reading of a dozen or more texts –
examples are Carlyle's *Past and Present*, Arnold's *Culture and
Anarchy*, Marx's *Capital*, and Bagehot's *Lombard Street*.

In Canada the first step towards the separation of psychology
and philosophy occurred in 1892 when the department of philosophy
at Toronto established a psychological laboratory and assigned a
lecturer to full-time work in psychology. In 1890, however,
psychology remained as much a subdivision of philosophy as did
logic, the course with which it was frequently paired. Thus at
McGill, the second year course concerned elementary psychology
in the first term, elementary logic in the second, while in the
third year course the first term was devoted to the logic of
induction and the second to the psychology of cognition. Psychology seldom was scheduled in the final year of the B.A. course,
even for honours students; in 1890 it was regarded not as a subject of importance *per se* but, like logic, as an essential preliminary to the advanced study of ethics and metaphysics.

SCIENCES

In a pamphlet on medical education in Ontario which he published
in 1892, Daniel Wilson, the president of the University of Toronto
demonstrated convincingly that the decision to abolish the
university's faculty of medicine in 1853 had had a most unfortunate
effect on the development of science studies at Toronto. Had the
university been required to make adequate provision for the needs
of medical students in biology and chemistry, it would have been
obligated to develop these and related departments; instead, the
training of doctors had been left to the proprietary schools,
with the result that 'scientific work [has] played a very subordinate part in undergraduate studies.'[15] Fortunately, he continued,
the re-establishment of the faculty of medicine in 1887 had altered
the situation; already the necessary strengthening of botany and
the introduction of physiology and histology had transformed the
old department of natural history into 'an efficient school of

biology.' Much more, of course, remained to be done, for, as he
pointed out, chemistry, physics, psychology and even palaeontology
have relevance for medical studies.

Had Wilson written a companion pamphlet on engineering education
in Ontario, he could, by tracing the history of engineering studies
at Toronto, have produced an equally convincing argument to show
that the development of university science departments was directly
related to the requirements of professional schools. Unless
science was to remain a subject about which a professor lectured,
proper laboratories had to be built. But proper laboratories required a considerable expenditure of money, which could not be
justified unless a reasonable number of students were available
to use them. At Toronto, science had stood still from 1860 to
1878, but in the latter year laboratories were established in
chemistry, geology and mineralogy, biology, and physics in order
to provide for the needs of the students at the School of Practical
Science, which the government had established in 1875 and for which
it provided a building on the university campus in 1878. Three of
the laboratories were housed in this building, but the facilities
were equally available to the students in the faculty of arts.
Consequently, from this time on laboratory work became an integral
part of the science courses taught at the University of Toronto.
By 1890 the science staff at Toronto included professors of
physics (separated from mathematics in 1887), mathematics, chemistry, biology, and mineralogy and geology; fellows in each of these
five subjects; and a lecturer in physiology. The fellow was
'required to assist in the teaching and practical work of the
department; to pursue some special line of study therein; and to
devote his entire time during the Terms to the work of the Department, under the direction of the Professor.' In addition to this,
the seven-man staff of the School of Practical Science included
a professor and a fellow in applied chemistry. It is inconceivable
that a staff of this size could have been justified unless the
responsibilities of the science departments included the provision of instruction for the 91 students registered at the School
of Practical Science in 1890.

At most of the small institutions the staff in science numbered
two or three. Acadia had professors of mathematics and of natural
sciences, Mount Allison professors of mathematics and of chemistry
and physics, Trinity a professor of mathematics and part-time
lecturers in natural and physical science. New Brunswick, which
had recently entered the field of engineering, assigned four of
its faculty of eight to the science side: professors of mathematics, chemistry and natural science, physics, civil engineering.
At Dalhousie, where the requirements of the faculty of medicine
had necessitated the provision of a proper chemical laboratory,
the science staff was limited to three, but it included outstanding
professors of physics (J.G. McGregor) and of chemistry (George
Lawson). Dalhousie's strength was partly the consequence of
endowed chairs. This was also evident at Queen's, where there
were professorships of mathematics, astronomy, chemistry and

mineralogy, and physics; however, Queen's full development in science had to await its entry into engineering in the early 1890s. The only university which could stand comparison in science with Toronto in 1890 was McGill, which had entered the field of engineering in 1871 and whose faculty of medicine was a genuine part of the university. In 1890 McGill had five science professors (mathematics and natural philosophy, chemistry and mineralogy, botany, natural history, engineering) and two lecturers (descriptive geometry, geology). But proper laboratory facilities were not provided until the 1890s.

In 1860 every arts student at a Canadian university was required to do considerable work in mathematics and to attend lectures on most of the sciences. The lectures were at an elementary level and in some instances they resounded with theological undertones. Where there was a remarkable professor, a few students were in a position to carry forward their studies in particular sciences to a reasonably advanced level.

There was both advance and retrogression in the subsequent 30 years. The facilities for students who wished to specialize in science were unquestionably improved at those universities able to establish laboratories and to provide a staff which could devote attention to particular subjects. The honours courses offered at Dalhousie, McGill, Queen's, and Toronto were sound in construction and thorough in treatment. It is questionable, however, whether the presentation of science to the *general* arts student was as effective in 1890 as it had been in 1860. In the interim, of course, conditions had changed; it was a good deal easier in 1860 to explain the elements of the individual sciences and to show their interrelations than would be the case thirty years later. Furthermore, the developments in the humanities and the emerging social sciences were almost as great, with the result that at most institutions some degree of choice was offered the student in the final two years. In 1860 it had been in their final years that the courses in the elements of science for the general arts student were scheduled. By 1890 the likelihood of ever attending lectures in geology, mineralogy or biology was remote for the student who was not specializing in science. The normal fare was two years of mathematics and a course or two in physics and chemistry. Only at the Roman Catholic colleges, where the curriculum was essentially as it had been in 1860, was there still an attempt to introduce every student to the broad spectrum of science.

What is true of the treatment of science when one compares the position in 1890 with that of 1860 is equally true of the arts course as a whole. The opportunities for students who wished to specialize were markedly improved, but the adequacy of the program for the general student could be seriously questioned. In the honours courses, which by 1890 had been introduced in one form or another at every English-speaking Canadian institution, specialization was possible in most areas – classics, modern languages, English, history, philosophy, mathematics and physics, chemistry, natural science. Admittedly, the degree of penetration in any one of these areas was conditioned by the fact that instruction tended to be the responsibility of one man; the day of the department had not yet arrived. But within that limitation - and it was not in 1890 a very serious one if, as was usually the case, the professor was well trained and dedicated - the opportunities were considerable.

In the general, pass, fixed, or ordinary course, however, the opportunities were not remarkable. The classical course in the Roman Catholic colleges had undergone little if any change. The efforts to establish a general course in science (B.Sc.) had been discouraging, as had those to establish an arts course in which modern languages replaced the classical (B.L. and Ph.B.). The elective principle had been generally accepted as governing the organization of the upper two years of the B.A. course, but little thought had been given to the possibility of limited specialization through concentration on a few related subjects in these upper years. Only at Acadia and in the Roman Catholic colleges did a recognizable rationale clearly underlie the general B.A. course.

EXTENSION

Extension work of the type mentioned in chapter 4 as having been offered at Acadia, Laval, McGill, and Queen's by 1860 continued to be provided at these and other Canadian universities in 1890; and it has continued to be provided ever since, appearing now in the form of either university-sponsored lectures to which the public is invited without charge or as non-credit courses offered through a department of university extention or adult education to any one who wishes to pay a nominal fee. The value of such offerings is indisputable whether regarded as a contribution to the general education of the community or as a means of improving the university's image in the minds of those who support it; but it is also beyond doubt that from a purely academic point of view non-credit work has limited value. The justification for a university committing part of its limited resources to such work was also much stronger in 1860 or in 1890 than it is today when so many other agencies are offering lectures of this type.

By 1890 the Canadian universities were well aware of the University Extension Movement which had been launched in England in the 1870s as a means of literally extending the work of Oxford and Cambridge to other centres through the provision of lecture courses and tutorials. This, in the opinion of President Daniel Wilson of the University of Toronto, was the model which should be followed in Canada rather than the one being followed in the United States:

The idea involved in the scheme of University Extension has to be jealously kept in view if we would avoid bringing the whole movement into contempt. Its aim is the organization of syste-

147

matic study and testing examinations. The very term implies
that it is to be under University Guidance and Control; and
one of the foremost dangers to be guarded against, is the re-
production under some meretricious title, of the old Lyceum
lectures, with their sensational fancies and flashy humor.
There will be no scarcity of lecturers volunteering for the
work. As a supplement to the past-time of the concert-room
and the theatre, the popular lecture has its legitimate place;
and in the hands of gifted men, like Emerson and Lowell, had
an earnest purpose in view. Yet, even with such lecturers, there
was nothing systematic. They rather helped to dignify, than to
supersede, the popular humorist. We have no quarrel with Josh
Billings or Mark Twain, so long as they are confined to their
legitimate sphere; and make no attempt to hide their motley
under the doctor's gown. Systematic courses of instruction,
of home-reading, of examination and accredited results, carried
on at the cost of localities desiring to avail themselves of
extra academical teaching, if done under the countenance and
supervision of a carefully selected University board, may not
only prove of inestimable value to a large class outside the
sphere of undergraduate life; but may ultimately react on the
inner life of the University with quickening power.[16]

Wilson's remarks were made at his address to convocation in
October 1891. A year before, a senate committee had been established to make proposals for the organization of extension work
along the lines of the Oxford-Cambridge model, but its efforts,
as we shall see in chapter 15, were not successful, the only
immediate effect being the scheduling of 'Saturday Lectures' by
members of the staff at Toronto and neighbouring towns. A similar outcome occurred at the University of New Brunswick where a
parallel attempt to introduce the Oxford-Cambridge system led in
1891 to the establishing of university extension classes at Saint
John – the university, it will be recalled, was located at
Fredericton.[17] In this scheme, which operated for some years,
the students could if they wished write examinations following
the eight or ten weekly lectures, and if successful were awarded
a certificate. Such certificates, however, carried no credit
towards a degree. Of more significance for the development of
adult education in the universities was the decision of Queen's
in 1889 to make arrangements for practicing teachers to take
courses towards their degree without attending lectures.[18]

NOTES TO CHAPTER 9

1   J.W. Dawson, *The Canadian Student* (1891), 4
2   H. Provost, *Historique de la Faculté des Arts de l'Université
    Laval, 1852-1952* (1952), 31-2, 41-2
3   A. Forget, *Histoire du Collège de L'Assomption, 1833-1933*
    (1953), 172

4   McMaster University, *Opening of the Arts Department October 10, 1890* (1890), 8
5   The development of the specialist certificate is described in R.S. Harris, *Quiet Evolution: A Study of the Ontario Educational System* (1967), 79–83.
6   W.L. Grant and F. Hamilton, *Principal Grant* (1904), 240–1
7   J.W. Dawson, *The Future of McGill University* (1881), 8
8   Victoria University, *Calendar* 1862–63
9   W.J. Alexander, ed., *The University of Toronto and its Colleges, 1827–1906* (1906), 80–91
10 A group of classical graduates, *Honours Classics in the University of Toronto* (1929)
11 J.W. Dawson, *The Future of McGill*, 8
12 J.G. Bourinot, 'The Study of Political Science in Canadian Universities,' *Trans. Royal Society Canada* 1889, section 2, 3–16
13 G.W. Ross to W.J. Ashley, November 1890 quoted in A. Ashley, *William James Ashley: a Life by his Daughter* (1932), 54
14 For Mavor's influence on political economy, see A. Bowker, 'Maurice Hutton, James Mavor, G.M. Wrong: Truly Great Men' (1975).
15 D. Wilson, *Medical Education in Ontario* (1892), 2
16 D. Wilson, *Address at the Convocation of Faculties of the University of Toronto and University College, October 5, 1891* (1892), 16–17
17 See below, chapter 10.
18 See below, chapter 10.

10

Professional Education

The most significant developments in professional education during
the thirty-year period ending in 1890 were in the fields of agriculture, dentistry, engineering, military studies, pharmacy, and
veterinary medicine, and for the most part they took place outside
the universities. It was the federal government that established
the Royal Military College at Kingston in 1876, the government of
Ontario that established the College of Technology at Toronto in
1872 and the Ontario Agricultural College at Guelph in 1874, and
it was the government of Quebec that established l'Ecole polytechnique at Montreal in 1874. A private citizen founded the
Ontario Veterinary College at Toronto in 1862, another private
citizen the Montreal Veterinary College in 1875. The Royal College
of Dental Surgeons (Toronto, 1869), the Montreal College of
Pharmacy (1875), and the Ontario College of Pharmacy (Toronto,
1882) were instituted by associations of dentists and pharmacists.
With the exception of the Royal Military College all these schools
entered into affiliation with a university within a few years of
their establishment, and in due course most of them became faculties of the university in question. But it is important to recognize that the initial stimulus came from without. The only new
field that seriously engaged the attention of the universities
during this period was engineering, and this mainly because it
offered the university the opportunity to develop its facilities
for the teaching of science; then, as now, the line between pure
and applied science was difficult to draw. Thus Toronto maintained
its tiny department of civil engineering until the College of
Technology, renamed the School of Practical Science, was moved
to the campus in 1878; McGill, which had abandoned its engineering
course through lack of applicants in 1863, reintroduced a degree
program for engineers in 1871 and established what proved to be
a permanent faculty of applied science in 1878; King's College,
Windsor, which added Engineering to the title of its Professor
of Mathematics, Natural Philosophy and Astronomy in 1872, insti-

tuted a school of engineering in 1874; Ottawa introduced a three
year civil engineering course in 1874, suspended it in 1880, and
revived it in 1885; and New Brunswick, which had developed its
one year certificate course in land surveying, navigation, and
engineering into a two year diploma course in science by 1871,
established a chair of civil engineering and surveying in 1889.
But, in the main, the interest of the Canadian universities in
professional education throughout this period continued to be
confined to the time-honoured professions of theology, law, and
medicine. It is appropriate therefore to begin an analysis of
professional education in 1890 with a review of developments in
these traditional fields.

THEOLOGY[1]

The number of Protestant theological colleges and faculties of
theology affiliated with universities more than doubled between
1860 and 1890.

Church of England

Queen's College, St. John's Newfoundland	Est. 1841
University of Trinity College, Toronto	Faculty of Divinity 1852
Bishop's University, Lennoxville	Faculty of Divinity 1853
University of King's College, Windsor	Dept. of Theology 1857; School of Divinity 1884, Faculty 1890
Huron College, London	Est. 1863; affil. Western Univ. 1881-85
St John's College, Winnipeg	Theological Tutor 1866; Dept. 1874
Montreal Diocesan College	Est. 1873; affil. McGill Univ. 1880
Wycliffe College, Toronto	Est. 1879; affil. Univ. of Toronto, 1885

Presbyterian

Queen's University	Faculty of Theology 1841
Knox College, Toronto	Est. 1844; affil. Univ. of Toronto, 1885
Presbyterian College, Halifax	Est. 1860
Morrin College, Quebec	Est. 1861; affil. McGill Univ. 1862
Presbyterian College, Montreal	Est. 1867; affil. McGill Univ. 1868
Manitoba College, Winnipeg	Dept. of Theology 1883

Methodist

Mount Allison University	Dept. of Theology 1864; Faculty 1875
Victoria University	Dept. of Theology 1871; Faculty 1873
Wesleyan College, Montreal	Est. 1873; affil. McGill Univ. 1880
Wesley College, Winnipeg	Dept. of Theology 1889; affil. Univ. of Manitoba 1888

151

Baptist

Acadia University	Theol. Inst. 1851-83; Dept. of Theol. 1890
Can. Literary Inst. Woodstock	Theological Course 1860-80
Toronto Baptist College	1881-89 (absorbing work of Can. Lit. Inst.)
McMaster University	Fac. of Theology 1890 (absorbing Toronto Baptist College)

Congregationalist

Congregational College of British North America	Est. at Toronto 1843; transferred to Montreal 1864; affil. McGill Univ. 1865

In addition, Albert University at Belleville, which merged with Victoria in 1884, had a faculty of theology from 1876 to 1883. There were also two short-lived Church of England theological colleges in the area now occupied by the Province of Saskatchewan: Emmanuel College at Prince Albert and Saint John's College at Qu'Appelle.[2] The former began as a school for Indian boys in 1879 but offered a theological course from 1881 to 1886; the latter, which appears to have been as much a cooperative as a theological college - it opened in 1885 with three farm students, three theological students, and some ordained 'farming brothers' - had ceased to exist by 1895.

The vastness of the country was one reason for this proliferation of theological colleges; it explains, for example, the establishment of colleges in western Canada. As we shall see in chapter 16, a half-dozen more would be established between 1890 and 1910. But distance was also a factor in the east as the Baptists were in the process of discovering. In 1883 it was decided to consolidate the theological work at Wolfville and Toronto, since great difficulty was being experienced in providing an adequate staff at both colleges; surely, it was argued, consolidation would guarantee the existence of one strong college which could cater to the needs of Baptists in all provinces. Hence the transferral of the Acadia Theological Department to the Toronto Baptist College in 1883. By 1889, however, it had become obvious that few students from the Maritimes were making the trek to Toronto, and the board of governors of Acadia, under pressure from the Maritime Baptists, resolved to re-establish the Acadia department in 1890.

A second cause for proliferation was the combination (often difficult to disentangle) of rivalry between individual bishops and difference of opinion on doctrinal matters. The personal rivalry between the bishop of Huron and the bishop of Toronto had a great deal to do with the establishment of Huron College at London in 1863, but doctrinal matters were also involved as can be seen from the titles of two of the pamphlets published by interested parties a year or two before the founding of Huron: *Two Letters to the Lord Bishop of Toronto: in Reply to Charges Brought by the Lord Bishop of Huron against the Theological*

Teaching of Trinity College and *The Bishop of Huron's Objections to the Theological Teaching of Trinity College, with the Provost's Reply.*[3] The dispute was essentially a conflict between the High Church and Low Church (or evangelical) elements within the Anglican communion. The teaching at Trinity College represented the former; Huron College was founded to reflect the latter.

A desire for evangelical truth was not, however, confined to those who lived in the Diocese of Huron. There were numerous and influential evangelicals in the Diocese of Toronto itself. In 1869 they formed the Evangelical Association of the Church of England, which in 1873 became the Church Association. This latter group succeeded in establishing a second Church of England theological college in Toronto[4] despite the categorical opposition of the bishop of Toronto, A.N. Bethune, who nearly forty years earlier had been the one-man staff of the Diocesan Theological Institution at Cobourg, the predecessor of Trinity's faculty of divinity.[5] The Protestant Episcopal Divinity School opened in October 1877, and under its principal, the Rev. J.P. Sheraton, who came to Toronto from the Maritimes, it made modest but steady progress; there were nine students in the first class. The situation improved markedly in 1879 with the death of Bishop Bethune and the election of Archdeacon Sweatman of the Diocese of Huron as his successor. Sweatman was a compromise choice. The High Church party sought the election of Provost Whittaker of Trinity College, but he was unalterably opposed by the evangelical wing. The High Church party agreed to accept Sweatman on condition that the Church Association be disbanded, and this was agreed to. There was a movement in 1880 to merge the new school with Trinity's faculty of divinity but this petered out; in the same year the first four graduates of the Protestant Episcopal Divinity School were ordained by Bishop Sweatman. The name Wycliffe College was adopted in 1885, the year that the new college entered into affiliation with the University of Toronto.

A third reason for the increased number of Protestant theological colleges was the changing attitude of the Methodists towards the requirements for the ministry. Though Ryerson had expressed the hope in his inaugural address as principal of Victoria College in 1842 that at no too distant date four years of comprehensive study would be required of candidates for ordination,[6] the practice of pursuing a course of reading while engaged on circuit work continued to be regarded for many years as a satisfactory procedure for the probationer. Learnedness, it was agreed, was not an essential qualification for preaching the gospel; the clear call, determination, and enthusiasm were far more important. In a relatively uneducated society this outlook was sound enough, but by the 1860s such a description was beginning to be inappropriate for the Canadian colonies. The importance of an educated clergy was increasingly stressed at the Annual Methodist conferences but, except at Mount Allison where a department of theology was introduced in 1864, little was done until the arrival from England of the Rev. William Punshon and his appointment as pastor of the

Metropolitan Church in Toronto in 1868. Punshon remained in Canada for only five years, but his influence was immediate and compelling.[7] He constantly emphasized the need for a highly educated clergy and he frequently referred to Victoria College in this connection. There can be little doubt that Victoria's decision in 1871 to provide a theological course was directly related to Punshon's enthusiasm, or that the same influence lay behind the sanctioning of a second Methodist theological college in Montreal in 1873. In 1870 the Episcopal Methodist church authorized a theological department at Albert College, Belleville. Instruction was commenced in 1871 and the transition to faculty of divinity accomplished by 1876. The faculty ceased to exist in 1884 when, following the merger of the Methodist churches, Albert College's university work was transferred to Victoria. Some theological courses, however, continued to be offered at Belleville for the benefit of candidates for the ministry who did not intend to obtain a B.A. degree. The union of 1884 also resulted in the merger of two Methodist colleges in Winnipeg, neither of which had been able by itself to provide sufficient facilities to qualify for affiliation with the University of Manitoba.[8] Affiliation was accorded to Wesley College in 1888 and a theological department was established the following year.

A principal result of this effort of the major Protestant denominations to provide theological training in all sections of the country was that all the theological colleges, faculties, and departments remained small. A staff of three or four was the norm and where there was a university connection some or all of the staff members in theology were also engaged in arts work. In the case of the independent colleges, particularly during the first years, a single professor often carried almost the entire load. At Presbyterian College, Montreal, for example, lectures in exegetics were given by the minister of a local church, but the principal, D.H. MacVicar, gave instruction in mathematics, Latin, Greek, logic, and moral philosophy, besides all the regular subjects of the theological curriculum, particularly systematic theology, apologetics, and church history.[9] Consequently there was little development of specialization in theological studies between 1860 and 1890. In the latter year the course of study was essentially what it had been thirty years before.

Technically there was also a doubling of the number of grands séminaires between 1860 and 1890, since to those at Quebec, Montreal, and Ottawa had been added grands séminaires at Rimouski (1870), Ste Anne-de-la-Pocatière (1871), Chicoutimi (1873), and Trois Rivières (1874). However, these latter, like the grand séminaire that had been at Nicolet from 1855 to 1875 and the one at Ste Thérèse de Blainville which, between 1878 and 1881, was affiliated with Université Laval, were not grands séminaires in the full sense of the term. Each was the creation of the local diocese and each was an extension of an existing petit séminaire. The seminarians enrolled at these institutions were young men who having completed part of their theological studies at Quebec or

Montreal were continuing their studies on a part-time basis while serving as full-time teachers at the petit séminaire. The staff were their senior professors at the petit séminaire and diocesan clergy qualified to provide supervision and guidance for courses required for the degree program established by Laval. Some students may have begun their theological studies at these institutions, but few, if any, would have qualified as priests without spending one or more years at Quebec or Montreal. The subordinate position of these diocesan seminaries is underlined by the fact that by 1890 each was affiliated with Université Laval.

In 1866 Université Laval formally established its faculté de théologie, the staff being drawn from the grand séminaire, and in 1870 the first earned degrees were awarded, two bacheliers en théologie and one licence en théologie. In 1871 two doctorates were awarded. These degrees were authorized both by the civil charter of 1852 and by the authorities in Rome who in 1853 had approved the offering of 'les grades académiques en théologie et dans les hautes sciences sacrées.' The status of the degrees was strengthened in 1876 with the recognition by Rome of Université Laval as officially a *université catholique*. Shortly after the publication of the papal bull, *Aeterni Patris*, the university announced its intention of adopting the program proposed, which called for the basing of philosophical and theological studies on the *Summa Theologica* of St Thomas Aquinas.[10] By this time the Montreal branch of Université Laval had been established and the grand séminaire at Montreal occupied the same position vis-à-vis the university's faculty of theology at Montreal as the grand séminaire de Québec did to the university's faculty of theology at Quebec. By 1890 the university had granted 122 bachelor's degrees, 31 licences, and 5 doctorates. It had also awarded one licence en philosophie - in 1882 to L.-A. Paquet, who in 1884 after two additional years of study at Rome began to offer a course in advanced philosophy in the faculty of theology. It was not until 1893, however, that the licence en philosophie began to be awarded on a regular basis.

In 1889 University of Ottawa was also recognized by Rome as a Catholic university and therefore empowered to grant the highest degrees in theology, canon law, and philosophy. This led in December 1889 and November 1891 respectively to the formal establishment of faculties of philosophy and theology; the first licence en philosophie was awarded in 1891, the first licence en théologie in 1893, the first baccalauréat en théologie in 1894. Doctorates in philosophy and theology were also awarded at this time but in both cases to members of the teaching staff only.

Some theological work may have been carried on informally and periodically at some or all of the English-speaking Roman Catholic colleges established or consolidated during this period: Assumption at Windsor, St Joseph's at Memramcook, N.B., St Michael's at Toronto, St Francis Xavier at Antigonish, N.S., and St Boniface at Winnipeg. But there was no seminary in the Maritimes until the establishment of Holy Heart Seminary in Halifax in 1893, or in Ontario (except at Ottawa) until the establishment of St Augustine's at Toronto in 1913.

LAW

Thirteen Canadian universities granted first degrees in law during the period 1861-90, and five of them granted a substantial number: McGill 378, Laval 344, Toronto 172, Dalhousie 72, and Victoria 71.[11] By 1890 the number of institutions prepared to offer law degrees was increased to 15 by the addition of Ottawa and the Western University at London. Ottawa began to list a three year course in its *Calendar* for 1888-89, J.S.D. Thompson, prime minister of Canada 1892-94, being listed as one of the lecturers. Western established a faculty of law in 1885, offered lectures to 38 students in 1885-86, cancelled lectures half-way through the 1886-87 session, and 'temporarily' suspended the faculty in the summer of 1887. However, this interest in legal education was more apparent than real; there was very little actual teaching of law in the Canadian universities in 1890 or in any of the preceding thirty years. In the majority of cases the university's activity was confined to examining: a course of study for the various degrees was outlined in the Calendar, examiners were duly nominated, candidates sat for periodic examinations, and degrees were awarded. Only Laval at Quebec and McGill had offered a regularly scheduled course of lectures throughout the period, and only three other institutions were offering such a program in 1890 - Laval at Montreal (since 1878), Dalhousie since 1883, and Toronto since 1889. Only at Dalhousie from 1883 and at McGill in 1890 was there a professor employed in the teaching of law on a full-time basis. Admission to practise in each of the several provinces continued to be controlled by the provincial law society and only in Nova Scotia did the Law Society accept the local university's law degree as qualification to practise. It was the combination of this latter provision and the establishment of a fully endowed chair of international and constitutional law that enabled the Dalhousie faculty of law to become the outstanding law school in Canada almost as soon as it opened in 1883. Dalhousie's first graduates received their degrees in 1885. By 1890 it was not only the best but also the largest university law school, with 18 graduates compared with 12 at Toronto, 7 at McGill, and 23 divided between Laval at Quebec and Laval at Montreal.

Dalhousie could not, however, boast of being the largest law school in Canada; that distinction was held by Osgoode Hall in Toronto, the school sponsored by the Law Society of Upper Canada, which registered some 300 students during the session 1890-91. As noted in chapter 5, the Law Society in 1855 instituted lectures for students-at-law, i.e., intending barristers as distinct from intending solicitors who were termed articled clerks. These lectures, normally a series of 12 on each of mercantile law, law of

landlord and tenant, equity jurisprudence, and real property,
were offered by delegated members of the society until 1868, but
attendance was not compulsory. However, a legislative act of
1872 authorized the society to require both students-at-law and
articled clerks to attend readings and lectures. A 'school' was
now established with four lecturers, one of whom was designated
chairman, but in the face of complaints by lawyers outside Toronto
that they were being deprived by this arrangement of their articled
clerks the school was suspended in 1878. It was re-established
in 1881 for a two year period, continued for a further year in
1883, and for a further two year period in 1884. Throughout the
1880s, the society debated whether it should provide for the
professional training of lawyers, or whether it should turn over
this responsibility to the universities. It finally decided not
to involve the universities and consequently in 1889 re-established
what was henceforth called the Osgoode Hall Law School on a permanent basis with a full-time dean and two part-time lecturers.

In his inaugural address, W.A. Reeve, the newly appointed dean,
noted that there was still some difference of opinion among
lawyers as to the comparative merits of the school and the office
in affording the means of education for the practice of law and
therefore doubt in some quarters as to the need for such a school
as was now being established. He argued that both were required.
It was the province of the office to show the student how to do
that which the school had taught him the reason for doing. Certainly one should learn by doing, but 'there still remains the
question how we are to learn whether or not the thing ought to
be done at all.'[12] In describing the curriculum which the school
would offer, he welcomed the introduction of courses in private
international law and in constitutional history, but noted that
the latter was concerned only with Canadian constitutional history.
He expressed regret that neither Roman law nor public international
law received attention. In Reeve's view, these omissions and the
failure to deal with constitutional history in a wider context
were unfortunate. They were however, controlled by circumstance:

> The importance of these studies cannot well be over-estimated.
> Many think that the proper place for them is in a university
> curriculum as being a legitimate part of a liberal education.
> However that may be, in view of the compulsory nature of the
> scheme and the circumstances of the country and profession the
> omissions at all events at present seem justified. The aim
> has been while making liberal additions to the course of study
> to add nothing except what may be justly considered as part of
> the education needed to fit the lawyer to properly practise
> his profession in this Province.[13]

The four year course offered in the faculty of law at the University of Toronto commencing in 1889 was a serious attempt to act
on the principle that the study of law, being a legitimate part
of liberal education, could most properly be taught at a university.

For the first three years the curricula was identical with that
of the last three years of the honour course offered in the
faculty of arts by the departments of history and political science,
the subjects including political economy, constitutional history,
Roman, international, and constitutional law, public finance, and
jurisprudence. In the fourth year attention was concentrated on
more practical matters, with final examinations in contracts,
real property, equity, torts, domestic relations, corporations,
criminal law, commercial law, and conflict of laws.

The faculty responsible for this course, which led to the LL.B.
degree, consisted of the professor of political economy and constitutional history (assisted by a graduate student, termed a
fellow), two part-time professors (Roman law, constitutional and
international law) and nine honorary lecturers. The program was,
however, doomed to failure by the insistence of the Law Society
that attendance at the Osgoode Hall Law School was required of
all potential lawyers. Within a few years the courses of the
fourth or professional year were withdrawn, standing in the
equivalent courses offered at Osgoode Hall being accepted as fulfilling the fourth year requirements for the Toronto degree. The
faculty of law was suspended in 1894.[14]

The attitude of the Law Society also explains why the interest
of the other universities of Ontario in the teaching of law during
this period was either tentative or nominal. The refusal of the
Law Society in 1862 to accept the Queen's LL.B. as the equivalent
of attendance at Osgoode Hall resulted in the withdrawal of lectures in 1864. The brief revival of these lectures from 1881 to
1884 was occasioned by the temporary closing of the Osgoode School
from 1878 to 1881. The Law Society's refusal to accept graduates
of the Western University's faculty of law led to its suspension
in 1886, the second year of its brief existence. The establishment of a faculty at Ottawa in 1888 occurred at a time when it
seemed likely that the Law Society would turn legal education
over to the universities. The decision to establish the permanent Osgoode Law School in 1889 tolled its death knell before it
had produced its first graduate – the faculty was withdrawn in
1896. Three other universities in Ontario – Trinity, Victoria,
and Albert – never got beyond the examining and degree-granting
stage.

The situation was somewhat similar in the province of Manitoba.
In 1877, the year that the University of Manitoba was established
with among other powers that of granting degrees in law, the
Law Society of Manitoba was empowered to make rules for the improvement of legal education. In 1878 the university authorized
a committee to consult with the Law Society and arrangements
were made to provide a reading course leading to the LL.B.; the
course began to be offered in 1883 and four degrees had been
granted by 1890. It was not until 1914 that a law school was
established in Manitoba and then by the Law Society itself.

In the Province of Quebec the universities were more active in
the field of legal education. The faculties of law at McGill

and Laval had an uninterrupted existence throughout the period, the Ecole de Droit founded by F.M. Bibaud at the Collège Ste Marie in 1851 continued until 1867,[15] and Bishop's established a faculty of law at Sherbrooke in 1880. The latter never assumed other than local significance and its existence was brief - the LL.B. was not granted after 1889.

The courses of study at Laval and McGill closely resembled each other since the graduates of both schools had to pass the professional examinations set by the provincial law society before they were admitted to practise. But both courses differed substantially from the courses offered in the other Canadian provinces in the emphasis placed on Roman and civil law, the consequence of Quebec law being based on both the Civil Code and English common law. As the McGill Calendar of 1890 noted, 'No more interesting or attractive legal system exists than that prevailing in this Province, where may daily be seen and studied, not simply theoretically, but in active operation as parts of our law, the three famous systems of jurisprudence - Roman, French and English.'

In 1890, the Laval program (taught both at Quebec and at Montreal) consisted of a stated number of lectures to be taken over a period of three years in seven subjects: civil law (630), Roman law (210), international law (30), procedure (144), commercial and maritime law (108), criminal law (108), administrative law (150). At McGill, the dean was responsible for Roman law, constitutional law, and criminal law; in the course of a 29 week academic year he delivered a total of 95 lectures to students of all three years. His 10 colleagues offered 230 additional lectures each year in the following subjects: real estate (10), commercial law (75), contracts (15), civil procedure (45), notarial law (10), civil law (55), and legal bibliography and history (28). The latter course was a recent innovation concerned with the sources of law in the Province of Quebec and the relations between the English and French elements. The professor of legal bibliography was also secretary of the faculty and librarian - the faculty had recently been bequeathed three important law libraries. All lectures were delivered in the early morning (8:30 to 9:30), or in the late afternoon (4:00 to 5:00, 5:00 to 6:00). A similar timetable was followed by the students of Laval, both at Quebec and Montreal.

In 1890 the dean of law at McGill had become a salaried officer 'whose duty it will be primarily to devote his whole time to the work of the Faculty.' It had been felt for some time that 'while professional men engaged in the active practice of their profession might be relied on to deliver regularly a limited number of lectures on special subjects, they could not be expected to undertake to submit to the serious interference with their business and inevitable interruptions involved in very lengthy courses.' It is questionable, however, whether the giving of one lecture a day at 4:00 or 5:00 P.M. can be said to constitute full-time work. But at Dalhousie the dean, R.C. Weldon, gave three lectures a week at either 11:00 A.M. or 12:00. Furthermore, his chief colleague, Benjamin Russell, who also had the rank of professor and was secretary of the faculty, lectured four or five times a week, usually at 10:00 or 11:00 A.M. The courses offered by the five lecturers, all local lawyers or judges, were scheduled at 3:30 or 4:30 P.M. and in one case at 8:00 P.M. The three year course was organized as follows:

I
Constitutional History (Weldon, 2 lectures a week), Contracts (Russell, 2), Criminal Law (Weldon, 1), Torts (Lecturer, 1), Real Property (Lecturer, 1)
II
Constitutional and International Law (Weldon, 2), Conflict of Laws (Weldon, 1), Negotiable Instruments (Russell, 1), Equity Jurisprudence (Russell and Lecturer, 1), Partnership and Companies (Lecturer, 1)
III
International Law (Weldon, 1), Equity Jurisprudence (Russell and Lecturer, 1), Personal Property (Russell, 1), Evidence (Lecturer, 1), Marine Insurance (Lecturer, 1).

MEDICINE

In all but one respect, the situation of medical education in Canada between 1860 and 1890 was strikingly similar to that of legal education. A comparatively large number of universities was involved - McGill with over 1000 graduates during the period, Trinity, Toronto, Victoria, and Queen's with over 500, Laval with over 300, Bishop's, Western, Manitoba, and Dalhousie with numbers ranging from 114 to 14.[16] An eleventh institution can be included if one takes seriously the single degree granted by the University of Halifax in 1879, a twelfth if the Montreal branch of Université Laval be regarded as a separate institution. But again the relation of the university to the professional school was in most instances nominal rather than real; except at McGill and Laval, instruction was provided by what were in effect proprietary schools, and at Laval the financial contribution of the university was negligible. In the case of Bishop's and Victoria the medical faculty in 1890 was located in Montreal, 100 and 300 miles respectively from Lennoxville and Cobourg. However, again as in law, there were signs of an improved situation towards the end of the period - the development of a first-class medical school at McGill, the establishment of what would in time prove to be sound medical schools at Dalhousie, Western, and Manitoba, and, by the terms of the Federation Act of 1887, the re-establishment of a teaching faculty at Toronto.

But there was one important difference between the situation in medicine and in law. By this time medical training that did not include clinical instruction was unthinkable. The potential lawyer or judge might be left to desultory reading, didactic lectures, and routine clerking, but the potential doctor had to dissect a body, walk the wards, witness and assist in operations. Consequently, medicine *was* taught. Probably most of the schools could be described as inadequate, but at least they were schools in the literal sense. Furthermore, one of them, McGill, had by 1890 become outstanding, and its example had a salutary effect on all the others.

The historical development of the medical schools and faculties during this period is particularly complicated, especially in the case of those located in the cities of Toronto and Montreal where rivalry sometimes produced an almost farcical situation. At Toronto five institutions were involved, though never all at the same time. In 1860 there had been two medical schools - the Toronto School of Medicine and the faculty of medicine of Victoria. Since the Act of 1853 the University of Toronto's activity had been confined to examinations and the granting of degrees. The Victoria faculty, headed by the redoubtable but aging John Rolph, maintained a somewhat precarious existence until 1874, when, four years after Rolph's resignation as dean, it was dissolved. The Toronto School of Medicine, a much better staffed institution, carried on until 1887 when, following the Federation Act of that year which permitted a teaching faculty at the University of Toronto, it became the basis for Toronto's revived Faculty of Medicine.[17] But by 1887 there were two other medical schools in Toronto. Trinity, which had had a medical faculty from 1852 to 1856, revived it in 1870, providing the professors with a building at a cost of $7000 and supporting them for six years with an annual grant of $1200. In 1877, the professors withdrew, incorporating themselves as the Trinity Medical School, an affiliate of Trinity, which once more confined itself to the granting of degrees. In 1888, the Trinity Medical School became the Trinity Medical College and the relation with the university somewhat closer. When Trinity entered into federation with the University of Toronto in 1904, the Trinity Medical College was absorbed into the University's faculty of medicine. The other medical school at Toronto in 1887 was the Ontario Medical College for Women, founded in 1883 as a means of solving certain difficulties felt by male students and faculty to inhere in any attempt to provide medical education on a co-educational basis. The college continued until 1906, by which time apparently the fears of students and professors had been sufficiently allayed and women had become admissible to the Faculty of Medicine of the University of Toronto. Thus, though medical education at Toronto was concentrated in one institution by 1907, in 1890 it was still distributed among three.

At Montreal, medical education was also shared by three institutions in 1890, a reduction of one from the previous year. The McGill faculty had had a continuous and, as we shall see, a splendid development from 1860. In 1871, about the time when McGill began to make its great strides forward, a second English-speaking school was established in Montreal, the stimulus coming from doctors who found themselves outside the McGill orbit; led by Dr. F.W. Campbell, five such doctors prevailed upon Bishop's University at Lennoxville to establish a faculty of medicine at Montreal. In 1905, shortly after Campbell's death, the Bishop's faculty was merged with McGill's.

McGill was one of two medical schools in Montreal in 1860. The other, l'Ecole de Médecine et Chirurgie, founded in 1843, devoted considerable effort between 1860 and 1866 to the search for a university with which it could affiliate in order that its graduates could have a degree, the degree having been a requirement for the right to practise since the incorporation of the College of Physicians and Surgeons of Quebec in 1847. Affiliation was refused by Laval in 1862 and 1864, by Ottawa in 1866. But an agreement was reached in 1866 with Victoria at Cobourg and l'Ecole became the faculty of medicine of Victoria University in Montreal (at this point Victoria also had a faculty of medicine in Toronto). This connection continued until 1890, but it did not resolve all the problems of l'Ecole. With the establishment of the Montreal Succursale in 1876, Laval proposed that l'Ecole enter into affiliation with it, or rather that its staff, together with certain professors which the Laval faculty of medicine would appoint, should become the faculté de medecine of l'Université Laval à Montréal.[18] But unexpected difficulties arose, the outcome being not a single expanded school but two quite separate schools, one affiliated with Victoria and the other with Laval. Then there was an attempt to dispose of the older school by debarring staff and students from the Hôtel Dieu which had long served as its teaching hospital, and by threatening excommunication on the ground of disobedience and association with a Protestant institution. The Pope himself intervened at this point and ordained that l'Ecole should continue. The situation was finally resolved as a result of the new arrangement accorded the Montreal Succursale by the papal bull (Jamdudum) of 1889; the two schools were now merged as the faculté de médecine de Laval à Montréal. But until the establishment of Université de Montréal in 1919, l'Ecole de Médecine et Chirurgie retained independent corporate existence.

The involvement of Université Laval in the problems of medical schools in Montreal may well have exhausted its capacity for the controversial; in any event the development of the faculty of medicine at Quebec was straightforward enough - steady if unspectacular progress and a gradual increase of staff, students, and facilities. Queen's at Kingston, on the other hand, had a difficult time. Never really related to the University in any organic sense, the staff of the faculty resigned in 1866, and incorporated themselves as the Royal College of Physicians and Surgeons of Kingston, an independent institution which then sought and obtained affiliation with Queen's. It was not until 1892 that the college again became the Queen's faculty of medicine; in the interim, Queen's function was limited to examining and degree-granting. In 1880 the Royal College of Physicians and Surgeons announced that women would be accepted as students at the college. In the 1880s, however, the male was as apprehensive in Kingston as in Toronto: the presence in classes of women 'became a source of irritation among the students, and the faculty was obliged to decline to receive any more women students.' This led to a public appeal for funds and, following the donation of a building by the city of Kingston, to the establishment of the Kingston Women's Medical College, which began to offer instruction in 1882-83 and whose first graduates received their medical degree from Queen's in 1884. This college continued until 1895 when the remaining students were transferred to the Ontario College for Women at Toronto.

Finally we turn to the three schools which did not exist in 1860. Two were relatively recent additions - the Faculty of Medicine of the Western University at London, which had admitted its first 15 students in 1882, and the Manitoba College of Medicine whose first 9 students entered in 1883. The Manitoba College was affiliated from the start with the University of Manitoba; the first medical degrees were granted in 1886. Western's first medical graduate received his degree in June 1883 at the end of the school's first session; he was a transfer student from the Trinity Medical School at Toronto. By 1890, the faculty of medicine at the Western University *was* the University, instruction in both arts and law having been withdrawn. Fortunately the faculty had acquired its own building in 1887 and was able to carry on independently.

In 1863, immediately after completing arrangements for the re-opening of its faculty of arts and science, Dalhousie's board of governors raised with the Medical Society of Halifax the question of establishing a faculty of medicine, but the matter was deferred for the time being chiefly because of the difficulty of providing adequate clinical instruction in the Halifax hospitals. By 1868, the hospital situation had improved substantially and Dalhousie did establish a faculty of medicine which at first offered instruction only in the summers, the winter period being left clear for medical apprenticeship or for clinical study elsewhere. A full medical course was offered in 1870 and the first degrees granted in 1872. There were, however, difficulties, particularly with respect to accommodation; the only space available for the practical study of anatomy was 'an attic room reached by a ladder in semi darkness.'[19] These difficulties eventually led the medical members of the faculty (the president and Professor George Lawson who provided instruction in chemistry were also members) to establish themselves as the Halifax Medical College which was incorporated (without degree-granting powers) in 1875 and which subsequently spent $12,000 on a building and facilities. The relationship with Dalhousie was severed in 1876, but was resumed in 1885, following the demise of the University of Halifax, with which the Halifax Medical College had become affiliated in 1876. In 1890 Dalhousie's faculty of medicine was still essentially a proprietary school with the university's responsibility limited to providing instruction in chemistry and botany. It was not until 1912 that the University assumed full control.

With the introduction in the late 1850s of certificate courses at New Brunswick, McGill, and Toronto, engineering appeared in 1860 to be on the point of establishing itself as a recognized university course. But there was no progress at all during the 1860s. The McGill course was withdrawn in 1863 because of a lack of applicants. At New Brunswick, 'attendance was small and the number of students receiving diplomas in Engineering not more than five or six yearly, usually less than this number.'[20] At Toronto, attendance was smaller still; the largest entering class numbered four and only four students had qualified for the diploma by 1870.

There were two reasons for the dearth of applicants, the first being that the subject lacked prestige. John Galbraith, the future principal of the School of Practical Science, entered University College, Toronto, in 1863 but he registered in arts, not in civil engineering. In those days, he later remarked, 'engineering was but a Trade and a person might after serving some apprenticeship present himself for examination by the University examiners and if his test proved satisfactory he would be awarded a diploma by the University.'[21] A student who went to university in the 1860s because he wanted to study some subject at a more advanced level than was available at a high school was not likely to select engineering. The second reason was that the course itself was not an attractive proposition for the young man who wanted to be an engineer. At Toronto most of the applied subjects were removed from the course of study within two years of its introduction - principles of architecture, engineering finance, use of instruments, geodesy, drawing.[22] These changes were made necessary by the failure of University College to appoint a professor of civil engineering. No regular member of the staff was qualified to give instructions in these subjects. E.J. Chapman, professor of mineralogy and geology, had some experience in civil engineering work, but it was inadequate for the task, and students were forced to rely on the prescribed texts and such instruction in engineering technology as they could obtain outside the university. In the middle 1870s some students from the department of civil engineering at University College 'received instruction in Drawing in the downtown non-professional School of Practical Science ... and did very well at it.'[23]

In describing the School of Practical Science as a 'non-professional school,' C.R. Young in the above quotation was referring to the fact not only that it was an institution that did not have the power to grant degrees but also that it was designed to produce technicians or technologists rather than professional engineers. The school had been established by the provincial government in the belief that the development of the provincial economy depended upon a regular supply of well-trained mechanics and technicians and in the conviction that universities were not capable of providing such training. In 1869, the University of Toronto, stimulated in part by the announcement that the County of Hastings had set money aside to endow a professorship of mining and agriculture at Albert University in Belleville, proposed to the government that it be provided with funds to establish a School of Mines and Mining Engineering. The government did not entertain this proposal; nor did it make any attempt to support the efforts that were being made at Belleville. Rather it proceeded to establish a technical school of its own. In January 1871, J.G. Hodgins, the deputy superintendent of education for Ontario, and Alexander Machattie, a medical doctor and chemist, were commissioned to visit institutions in the United States with a view to making recommendations about the development of technical education in Ontario. In a remarkably short period of time,[24] the commissioners visited eight institutions, including Harvard, Yale, Rensselaer, and Massachussets Institute of Technology and produced a report recommending the establishment of a School of Technology which 'in its Teaching, Management and Government should be kept entirely distinct from any other institution.' In particular it should not be associated with any university:

> To attach it as an Appendage to any School, or College for teaching purposes, would be to ensure its ultimate failure. The more efficient the Institution to which it might be attached for these purposes (paradoxical as it may appear), the more certain and speedy would be the failure of the School. Even at the two distinguished American universities of Harvard and Yale, where Scientific Schools exist, their efficiency and success is just in proportion to their entire practical separation for teaching and other purposes from the other parts of the University.[25]

The commissioners' insistence on the complete independence of the proposed institution from any university was partly based on a belief that the university method of instruction was not appropriate for the type of training needed:

> In most of the Institutions visited, the mode of teaching was by conversational Lecture, combined with a daily system of questioning on the lesson of the preceding day. The Students were required to take notes of a certain class of Lectures; but, where practicable, Blackboard Exercises on the part of the whole Class was invariably the chief feature of the daily exercise, or 'recitations' of Students. This was followed by a brief explanation of the Lessons for the next day. At the end of each month, (in some Institutions), and invariably at the end of each half year in all of them, the Students were subjected to a rigid Written Examination, followed, in many cases, by an Oral one, designed to test more fully the personal knowledge of the subject on the part of each individual Student.

The result of the half yearly Examination determined the status as well as the continuance in the Institution of the Student.[26]

At the same time the commissioners appeared to have in mind a four-year course, and they described their proposed course of study as providing for the professional education of architects, civil, mechanical and mining engineers, chemists, metallurgists, and teachers of science.

The commissioners' recommendation that $50,000 be appropriated for the purpose of establishing a college of technology and school of industrial science was accepted by the government almost as soon as the report was submitted and, despite strong criticism from the opposition party, was approved by the legislature in February 1871. In May 1872 the institution was launched in a building in downtown Toronto as a school of technology offering evening classes 'for the special instruction of mechanics and others in Drawing, Natural Philosophy [Physics] and Chemistry.' There were no fees. The initial registration was 181.

By 1878, however, the School of Technology had become the School of Practical Science, located on the University of Toronto campus, and offering three-year diploma courses to full-time students in engineering (civil, mechanical, mining), assaying and mining geology, and analytical and applied chemistry. Four of the six members of its teaching staff were professors at University College. There were no longer any evening classes, but in addition to seven regular students there were 171 occasional students, 23 from medical schools in the city who took chemistry and biology, 38 from the Ontario Veterinary College taking chemistry, and 110 students from University College taking one or more of chemistry, biology, and mineralogy. In 1884 the degree of Civil Engineer was authorized by the University of Toronto Senate for graduates who had spent three years on approved engineering work after completion of the course. With the implementation of the Federation Act of 1887, the science departments of University College were transferred to the University of Toronto, the arrangement between the School of Practical Science and University College came to an end, and the school entered into affiliation with the university. By 1890-91 the enrolment of regular students had risen to 89 and the number of full-time staff in applied science to seven. The school had become, in fact, though not until 1901 in name, the faculty of applied science and engineering of the University of Toronto.

The decision of the Ontario government to establish a school of technology in the early 1870s was paralleled by a similar decision by the government of Quebec, but in this case the government began by requesting a university to undertake the task. So far as French-speaking Quebec was concerned, technical training in the 1860s was restricted to the work that was being done in schools of agriculture and in collèges industriels. There were twelve of these latter in 1867 but they were mainly concerned with commercial training - bookkeeping, elementary accounting, etc.; only two were teaching physics, only one chemistry, and only six drafting.[27] It was not until 1871 that McGill revived its work in engineering, this time in the form of three-year diploma courses in civil engineering and surveying, mining and mining engineering, and practical chemistry and assaying; but for several years before this Principal Dawson had been emphasizing the need for McGill to re-establish its work in the engineering field.[28] In 1869 P.-J.-O. Chauveau, for many years superintendent of public instruction in Quebec but now premier, set aside certain funds for the establishment of an 'école de sciences.'[29] In 1870 the government offered Laval an annual grant of $1200 to provide for cours publiques in science. It was felt at Laval that the need was for courses with a practical orientation and in September 1871 it was announced that courses would be offered in November in agricultural chemistry and in economics. In the same month, the government authorized payment of $1200 to Laval for apparatus and scholarships. The courses were offered in November, but in February 1872 Laval decided to return the grant to the government. One reason was that the amount of the grant was not very substantial. Another was the political furor that had been created by the appointment of François Langelier, a lawyer with radical views, as the lecturer in economics.[30] A third, and probably the most compelling reason, was the fear of government intervention in the affairs of the university. The government asked the university to reconsider the matter but to no avail. In March the rector closed off the correspondence with these conclusive if cryptic words: 'Les changes qui nous forcent à ne pas assumer la responsabilité de fonctionnement de l'Ecole de Sciences que veut fonder le Gouvernement ne soit pas de nature à pouvoir être allegées par le Gouvernement quelle que soit sa bonne volonté à notre égard.'[31]

By this time McGill had established its new courses and the need to provide for comparable opportunities for young French Canadians was even more obvious. Nonetheless, it was not until the fall of 1873 that the government announced that it would establish a school of technology in Montreal. Events moved quickly from this point and in January 1874 classes in what was initially called L'Ecole des sciences appliqués were begun. The project, which was supported by a $3000 government grant, involved a staff of two, offering a three-year diploma course in four divisions: civil engineering, mining and metallurgy, mechanical and metals, and 'les industries diverses.' Of the twelve students who registered in January, six wrote examinations in March and five returned in September, by which time the staff had been increased to four.

In 1875 the institution was transferred to a building of its own as L'Ecole polytechnique. A year later it was recognized by the government as 'sur le même pied que les universités.' Its first five graduates received their diplomas in 1877. In 1887 the government grant was increased to $6000, the school was affiliated to Université Laval, and graduates became eligible

for a Laval degree. Eighteen students were enrolled on a full-
time basis in 1880-81.

By 1890, the School of Practical Science and the Ecole polytechnique were two of the three substantial schools of engineering
in Canada. The third was at McGill, where the courses introduced
in 1871 had been organized within a faculty of applied science
since 1878. In 1890 its 61 full-time students were enrolled
either in a common first year or in one of four departments, civil
and surveying, mechanical, mining, practical chemistry. The basic
degree was the Bachelor of Applied Science (introduced in 1871
and first granted in 1873), but the M.Eng. and the M.App.Sci.
were also listed. The staff of the faculty consisted of five
professors and one lecturer in engineering and six professors
cross-appointed from Arts.

Three other universities were offering an engineering degree
in 1890, but only one of them had granted a degree. This was King's
College at Windsor which had established a school of civil engineering in 1874. Ten students had been granted the B.E. degree,
initially on completing a three year course but since 1880 after
a four-year course. In 1890 W.R. Butler was in charge of the course;
a King's graduate (B.E., 1875, M.E. 1890), Butler was professor of
mathematics, natural philosophy, and engineering, but also registrar and bursar. At New Brunswick a professor of civil engineering
and surveying had been appointed in 1889; the first graduate of
its four year course would receive his diploma (C.E.) in 1892.
Courses in civil, mechanical, and mining engineering were listed
in the University of Ottawa Calendar but no students had been
admitted since the suspension in 1880 of the diploma course
introduced in 1875. The faculty of engineering at Albert University ceased to exist with the merging of Albert and Victoria in
1884. Finally it should be noted that since 1886 Dalhousie had
been providing a three-year diploma course 'preparatory to the
Study of Technology,'[32] and that the course of study at the Royal
Military College centred on engineering.[33]

ARCHITECTURE

In 1890 architecture was regarded as a branch of engineering and
was provided for in two of the three major schools. It had been
taught from the start at Ecole polytechnique: 'le cours de
construction civile donné par M. Haynes, dès le premier temps
n'est pas autre chose [que l'architecture]; ce professeur suivait
le programme de l'Ecole Centrale [de Paris].'[34] At Toronto architecture had appeared more recently. The 1887-88 Calendar advised
students who wished to pursue architecture as a profession to
enrol in the regular course in civil engineering, but indicated
that they would be admitted to certain courses as special students.
The appointment of a lecturer in architecture was considered in
1888 and acted upon in 1890, at which point architecture was
listed as one of the five regular departments in the school.

168

Five students were registered in architecture in 1890, one of
whom obtained his degree in 1891.

AGRICULTURE

In a number of respects the development of agricultural education
in Canada from 1860 to 1890 parallels that of engineering during
the same period. The main development is once again in the provinces of Ontario and Quebec. There would be a very substantial
development of agricultural education in the western provinces
in the succeeding 30 years, but in 1890 the population was just
beginning to be large enough to warrant serious consideration of
the subject; in 1892 the legislature of Manitoba passed an Act
authorizing the founding of an agricultural college. The only
sign of interest in the Maritime provinces came at the very end
of the period with the opening of a small agricultural school at
Truro, Nova Scotia. This occurred in 1888, three years after the
appointment of a professor of agriculture at the Provincial Normal
School at Truro. Once again, as in engineering, the main stimulus
came not from the universities but from the government, and the
main result was the establishment of schools that were independent
of the universities. It should also be noted that the developments in the two fields proceeded without relationship to each
other. In the United States there was a close relationship
between the development of agriculture and engineering since the
terms of the Morrill Act of 1862 required the universities to
'teach such branches of learning as are related to agriculture
and the mechanic arts.'
However, there was one important difference between the approaches adopted towards agriculture and engineering in Canada.
The universities were anxious to assume responsibility for engineering and protested vigorously against the establishment of
separate and government-controlled institutions; they showed no
such desire to provide instruction in agriculture. Laval expressed little interest in a proposal of 1864 that it establish
a model farm and provide science and mathematics courses adapted
to the needs of agriculture.[35] The subject of agriculture is
one of the few that Principal Dawson of McGill did not discuss
publicly. The withering away of the diploma course in agriculture which had been introduced at University College, Toronto in
the 1850s at the same time as the diploma course in civil engineering did not produce a proposal that the government provide
the university with funds to establish a proper school of agriculture; nor did the authorities at Toronto endeavour during the
1870s to convert the agricultural college which the government
established into a university-oriented institution, as they were
successful in doing with the College of Technology. The Ontario
Agricultural College at Guelph had by 1890 developed a degree
level program and was affiliated with the University of Toronto
for degree purposes. But the pressure for this had originated

in Guelph rather than Toronto and the diploma course remained the principal offering.

In the Province of Quebec the development took the form of the establishment of a series of schools of the type represented by the school at Ste Anne-de-la-Pocatière which had opened in 1859.[36] In addition to Ste Anne, which continued to operate throughout the period, schools were established at Ste Thérèse de Blainville (1863-66), at l'Assomption (1867-98), at Richmond (1875-89), and at Rougemont in 1883. The last mentioned school survived for only one year; opened in May, it closed in November 'faute de recrués.' In addition, a school was contemplated at Compton in 1872. In all cases the course offered was of one or two years in length and was at the diploma rather than the degree level.

The government provided small grants in support of these schools, but there was increasingly the feeling that what was really needed was a single well-organized school to provide for Quebec what the Agricultural College at Guelph had been providing for Ontario since its establishment in 1874. Certainly this was the conclusion reached by each of three separate commissions authorized by the legislature in 1877, 1883, and 1887. By 1890 the number of schools had been reduced to two, Ste Anne and Assomption, but less through any action of government than through natural decay. Nor was there any proposal under consideration in 1890 for a single well-developed school or college.

The proposal to establish a provincial school of agriculture in Ontario came from John Carling, the minister of commerce and agriculture who in August 1869 commissioned the Rev. W.F. Clarke, the editor of an agricultural journal, to visit the leading agricultural colleges of the United States and to submit 'an economical and practical scheme for the establishment of an Agricultural College in the Province.'[37] Clarke did visit a number of American colleges as well as the Department of Agriculture at Washington, but in his report submitted in June 1870 he devoted most of his attention to the Massachusetts Agricultural College at Amherst and the Michigan Agricultural College at Lansing. To the latter he awarded the 'palm of superiority': 'in many respects it is essentially worthy of being made a study by those who are anxious to establish on a sound basis, and without extravagant outlay, an Agricultural College in a new and rising Country.'[38] Clarke did not, in fact, submit a concrete proposal for the establishment of a college but one soon emerged on which he commented at length in a memorandum to the provincial secretary in February 1872. By this time it had been decided to locate the college at Guelph (rather than at Mimico, a suburb of Toronto, as had been first proposed) and it was agreed that there would be a model or experimental farm in connection with it. Thus, when classes were begun in May 1874 they were offered at the School of Agriculture and Experimental Farm. The institution was to have two purposes: 'First, to give a thorough mastery of the practice and theory of husbandry to young men of the Province engaged in Agricultural and Horticultural pursuits; and, second, to conduct experiments, tending to the solution of questions of material interest to the Agriculturalists of the Province, and publish the results from time to time.'[39] It will be noted that 'practice' precedes 'theory' in the above statement. The priority given to practice explains in part the locating of the college at a distance from the University of Toronto: 'We have tried the same experiment which has been so often tried elsewhere, with invariably the same result, that is, we have tried to unite an Agricultural School with a literary institution, (the Toronto University), on the theory that an Agricultural Student should combine a Literary Course with an Agricultural one; the result has been failure. The literary has over-shadowed and extinguished the other. The general has overpowered the special.'[40]

The 31 students who entered the college in May 1874 registered for a two-year course, but the diploma could be obtained in one year by those 'who can produce evidence of having assisted in farm operations for at least two summers.' By 1880 when the institution was renamed the Ontario Agricultural College and Experimental Farm, the enrolment was approaching 200. In 1888 the college entered into affiliation with the University of Toronto, which would grant the B.S.A. degree to students who, having completed the two-year diploma course, returned for a third year. Thus, there was provision for mastery of both the practice and theory of husbandry, but the general was not to be permitted to overpower the special.

The second objective of the college - the conducting of research and the publication of results - was taken seriously from the outset. But this objective received more elaborate attention with the establishment in 1886 of the Dominion Experimental Farm at Ottawa. We shall have more to say about this development in chapter 12.

VETERINARY MEDICINE

E.A.A. Grange had been appointed head of a department of veterinary science at the time of the opening of the Ontario Agricultural College in 1874, and his lectures on anatomy and physiology included veterinary pathology, materia medica, and general veterinary subjects.[41] But at the OAC, as at all agricultural colleges both then and now, the reference to veterinary medicine was in the context of animal husbandry and was not designed to produce professional veterinarians. By 1890 there was no lack of opportunity to become a professional veterinary in Canada since four schools had been established for this purpose.

The oldest of these was the Ontario Veterinary College which had been established in 1864. It was a proprietary school, owned and operated by Andrew Smith, a graduate of the Edinburgh Veterinary School, who came to Toronto in 1861 at the invitation of the Board of Agriculture of Upper Canada to take responsibility for the veterinary lectures in a course of veterinary and agricultural lectures which the board had decided to sponsor. A four-week course comprising 26 lectures by Smith and 72 by Professor George Buckland, the professor of agriculture at University College was offered in February and March 1862. These lectures were at a general or elementary level, but in the fall of 1862 Smith offered more advanced instruction in what was called a 'regular' as distinct from a 'familiar' course. The regular course was Smith's project rather than the Board of Agriculture's and with its introduction the Ontario Veterinary College was born.[42] Its faculty in 1862-63 consisted of Smith, Buckland, J.J. Meyrick, who lectured on the horse, and D.N. McEachran, who remained on the staff until 1866 when he moved to Montreal to establish a college of his own.

McEachran was also a graduate of the Edinburgh Veterinary College, but his approach to veterinary education was different from Smith's. Indeed the two men represent in almost classical terms the basic and competing biases not only of veterinary medicine education, but of professional education as a whole: 'Smith did not disregard science ... but he was essentially a practical man whose interest in education was with the veterinary art, not the science of veterinary medicine. McEachran espoused the scientific point of view and called, perhaps long before it was practicable, for higher entrance requirements, for a three-year course, and for a close affiliation with the medical faculty and with research scientists.'[43] In 1876 Smith added a third storey to the building he had built in 1868, and a fourth in 1889, by which time the enrolment was over 300; but he never did add a third year to the two year course which had been established by 1864; nor did Smith encourage the involvement of the University of Toronto or any other university or medical school in the affairs of the college. In contrast, McEachran's Montreal Veterinary College began as a three-months' course of lectures sponsored by the McGill Medical School, offered a three year course from 1875, included William Osler among its staff members, and in 1889 became the faculty of comparative medicine and veterinarian science of McGill University. On the other hand, McEachran was not faced with the necessity of adding storeys to the building he provided from his own funds in 1875; enrolment was always much smaller than at the Ontario Veterinary College; there were 51 students in 1890. With the attainment of faculty status, graduates of the college became eligible for a McGill degree. Forty-seven degrees were granted in 1890, but many of these were to students who had completed the three-year course in the previous 15 years.

High standards were not the only reason for the relatively modest enrolment in veterinary medicine at McGill University in 1890; there was also the factor of competition. The need for French-speaking veterinarians had been in McEachran's mind in 1866 when he began teaching at the McGill Medical School, and lectures were offered in both languages. By 1876 two graduates of what since 1875 had been called the Montreal Veterinary College and also Collège Vétérinaire de Montréal, J.-A. Couture

and O. Bruneau, were in charge of the courses in French and in
1879 they were joined by another graduate, V.T. Daubigny. But
all three withdrew in 1885, Daubigny and Couture to establish a
college of their own, l'Ecole de médicine vétérinaire de Montréal,
which immediately affiliated with Victoria University of Cobourg,
and Couture to establish a third school in Quebec, L'Ecole
vétérinaire de Québec, which affiliated with Laval.[44] In 1886,
Daubigny parted company with Bruneau and established l'Ecole
vétérinaire française de Montréal which affiliated with Université Laval à Montréal. By 1894, however, there was a single
French-speaking veterinary school, L'Ecole de médecine comparée
et de science vétérinaire located in Montreal and affiliated with
the Montreal branch of Laval. Like the Ontario Veterinary College
it was essentially a proprietary school. Like the schools from
which it descended, it offered a two-year course.

ROYAL MILITARY COLLEGE

A proposal to establish a military college in Canada was made in
1816 but nothing came of it until Canada attained dominion status
in 1867.[45] Prior to this, defence was the responsibility of Great
Britian, though there had always been a Canadian militia. In the
1860s a number of schools were established to prepare candidates
for commissions in this voluntary force, but these could properly
be called cadet schools since their function was to provide 'for
the mere mechanical instruction in the minutiae of drill, discipline and interior economy, so as to enable the militia to be
officered by those who would be capable of instructing in drill.'[46]
In 1871, with the withdrawl of British troops from all garrisons
except Halifax, the first regular Canadian units were organized;
these were artillery batteries at Kingston and Quebec, and schools
of gunnery were established at both garrisons. But obviously
something more was needed if a proper permanent force was to be
developed and, particularly since the cadet schools had been
closed down with the withdrawal of the British troops, if the
voluntary militia was to be effectively trained. With this in
mind, the dominion government in 1872 commissioned Lt. Col. H.C.
Fletcher, military secretary to the governor general, to visit
the American Military Academy at West Point and to make recommendations about military training in Canada. Fletcher's Report on
the Military Academy at West Point (1872) and his Memorandum on
the Military System (1873) were the basis for the military college
established at Kingston in 1876. The Royal Military College,
as it was called from 1878, was to be 'somewhat on the model of
West Point' but not a duplicate of it:

> Its purpose, as defined by Act of Parliament, was to impart 'a
> complete education in all branches of military tactics, forti-
> fication, engineering and general scientific knowledge in sub-
> jects connected with and necessary to a thorough knowledge of

173

the military profession.' It was to offer a four-year rather
than a two-year course. It was to train 'scientific' officers
for the engineers and artillery as well as 'ordinary' officers
for the non-technical branches, infantry and cavalry. It would
produce Canadian officers for command and staff appointments,
and so obviate the need to import British regulars, but its graduates would be prepared for civil as well as military employment
because Canada had as yet no need for large numbers of officers.[47]

What was and is distinctive about the Royal Military College is
the attempt to prepare for civilian as well as for military life.
In 1879 a year before the members of the first class received
their diplomas, an agreement was reached with the British War
Office that five commissions in the British army would be made
available each year to graduates of the Royal Military College.
It was assumed that perhaps as many graduates might be absorbed
into the permanent Canadian force, though in fact the number was
much smaller than this - in 1898 only 8 of the 61 officers in the
permanent force were graduates of R.M.C. But many more than 10
graduates were expected each year. The first class to enrol
entered in June 1876 and numbered 18, but a second class of 11
entered in February 1877. The policy of two entries a year was
continued until 1882, following which there was a single entry.
A total of 310 students was admitted to the college between 1876
and 1890, an average of 20 per year. Hence the emphasis on the
opportunities available to the graduate other than as a professional soldier. It was noted in the General Regulations for 1890
that 'the Civil Engineering Course is complete and thorough in all
branches,' that 'the Course of Physics and Chemistry is such as
to lead towards Electrical Engineering and Meteorological Service,
and other departments of Applied Science,' and that 'the obligatory
course of surveying includes what is laid down as necessary for
the profession of Dominion Land Surveyor.' By 1891 arrangements
had been made with the Law Society of Upper Canada to permit graduates of R.M.C. to enter Osgoode Hall Law School on the same
basis as graduates in arts. The possibility of graduates going
on to chartered accountancy and even medicine was also being ex-
plored.
The military element in the course of study was not, however,
neglected. An analysis of a course of study of 1890, as outlined
in the General Regulations, indicates that approximately one-third
of the students' time was devoted to non-academic professional
matters.

DENTISTRY

Provincial or local associations of farmers had something to do
with the establishment of agricultural schools and colleges in the
provinces of Ontario and Quebec and, as we have seen, the Agricultural Board of Upper Canada, which gave grants to local associations,

174

was responsible for bringing Andrew Smith to Toronto, thus paving
the way for the establishment of the Ontario Veterinary College.
In the case of engineering, the influence of the profession on
the development of professional training was limited to that of
particular individuals, partly because it was not until the 1880s
that Canadian engineers began to organize themselves in professional societies. In contrast, the early development of education
in dentistry and pharmacy was entirely due to the efforts of an
organized profession.

By 1892 legislation respecting the practice of dentistry, which
effectively gave to legally constituted provincial associations
of dentists responsibility for determining who should be admitted
to practice, had been passed in all the Canadian provinces -
Ontario (1868), Quebec (1869), Manitoba (1883), British Columbia
(1886), the North West Territories - from which Alberta and Saskatchewan were later created - (1889), New Brunswick (1890), Nova
Scotia (1891), and Prince Edward Island (1891); and in each of
these provinces an association had been formed. In all the provinces except Ontario the profession contented itself with specifying a term of apprenticeship, normally three or four years,
and conducting qualifying examinations, though in Quebec the
provincial association endeavoured to interest both McGill and
Laval in developing a dental course. In Ontario, however, the
profession went the essential step further. It established in
1875 a dental college, which by 1890 was providing a three-year
course which, through the college's affiliation with the University
of Toronto, led to the degree of Doctor of Dental Surgery.

The Act Respecting Dentistry, passed by the Ontario legislature
in 1868, granted the title of Licentiate in Dental Surgery to all
British subjects resident in the province who had been practising
for five years, constituted them as the Royal College of Dental
Surgeons of Ontario, and authorized the board of directors of the
college to act as a provincial board of examiners. The act also
specified that henceforth persons commencing the study of dentistry should serve an apprenticeship of two years and attend one
session at a dental college. In 1868 such a 'college' was established at Toronto by G.L. Elliott but without the approval of the
R.C.D.S. Board, and from it seven persons 'graduated' in 1869.
Though a second session of Elliott's school was announced, it was
not apparently offered, but in 1869 the R.C.D.S. itself opened a
school with instruction in dental subjects being provided by J.
O'Donnell and F.J. Calendar and in medical subjects by the staff
of the faculty of medicine of Victoria College. This venture
collapsed after one year owing to a dearth of students (there were
two graduates) and hence a lack of funds, tuition fees being the
main if not the sole source of revenue. During the next year or
two efforts were made to obtain degree-granting powers for the
college or to obtain the same result by affiliation with the
University of Toronto, but these were unsuccessful.

In 1875, however, the Royal College of Dental Surgeons reopened
its school. It was to some extent a proprietary school since the

fees ($100 for a four-month course) went to the full-time instruc-
tors, but it was under the direction of the Royal College of Dental
Surgeons, which in 1893 assumed full responsibility for it. In the
interim, the course was extended to two sessions in 1876 and to
three in 1892; entrance standards were steadily raised (though full
university matriculation was not required until 1896), and affiliation with the University of Toronto arranged in 1888. In 1890
there was a faculty of six, including both the original professors,
and an enrolment of 71. Twenty five graduates had been awarded the
D.D.S. degree in 1889, 29 in 1890. In the same year the college
became a member of the (American) National Association of Dental
Faculties.

PHARMACY

In Canada the development of professional education for pharmacy
up to 1890 followed a similar pattern to that of dentistry, though
in the case of pharmacy two colleges rather than one had been
firmly established by the end of the period and the basis for two
others had been laid. However, the courses offered were not of
comparable standard to those of the Royal College of Dental Surgeons, the admission requirements being lower and the instruction
confined to a single academic year.
   Pharmacy acts paralleling the Dentistry acts to which we have
referred had been enacted by the legislatures of six provinces by
1891: Quebec in 1870, Ontario in 1871, Nova Scotia in 1876,
Manitoba in 1878, New Brunswick in 1884, and British Columbia in
1891, with the North West Territories following in 1892. The
Manitoba and British Columbia acts made provision for provincial
pharmaceutical associations, all persons practising the profession
at the time of the passing of the act automatically becoming members. Usually, however, an association of pharmacists had been
formed prior to the passing of the Act and usually active lobbying
by the association lay behind the legislation. Pharmacists had
more difficulty than the dentists in gaining recognition as professionals, partly because of opposition from the medical profession; pioneer Canadian doctors followed the British medical tradition of the doctor dispensing his own medicines and their mid-
nineteenth century successors for selfish reasons were loath to
turn over this business to the pharmacists.
   Prior to 1870, the qualifications to practise as a pharmacist
were normally incorporated in medical legislation. The Montreal
Chemists Association was formed in 1864 with the object of changing
an 1859 Act requiring that apothecaries, chemists, and druggists
obtain a diploma from the College of Physicians and Surgeons of
Lower Canada by way of examinations conducted by its board of
governors. Similarly, the Toronto Chemists and Druggists Association was formed in 1867 to protest against proposed legislation
which would have assigned to a medical body responsibility for
granting licences in pharmacy and for controlling the practice of

176

pharmacy. The name of the Toronto group was changed almost immediately to the Canadian Pharmaceutical Society, under which title it launched in 1868 the *Canadian Pharmaceutical Journal*, dedicated to strengthening Canadian pharmacy through education, communication, and co-operative endeavour. In 1870 the Canadian Pharmaceutical Society became the Ontario College of Pharmacy, but the journal continued under its original name; since 1923 it has been the organ of the Canadian Pharmaceutical Association, the national professional organization.

In the winter of 1868-69, the Ontario College of Pharmacy made arrangements for pharmacy apprentices to take chemistry classes two evenings a week at no cost to themselves at the Toronto Mechanics' Institute. During the following twelve winters, E.B. Shuttleworth, one of the founders of the Ontario College of Pharmacy, offered instruction in chemistry twice weekly in his own home to a handful of apprentices, the numbers ranging from 3 to 11.[48] In addition, after the establishment by the government of the College of Technology (later the School of Practical Science), the Ontario College of Pharmacy made arrangements for its apprentices to receive regular instruction at the college, but this remained a somewhat *ad hoc* venture until 1882 when the college itself opened a school in rented quarters with Shuttleworth as principal. However, little practical work could be offered until 1887 when the college took possession of a newly constructed building with appropriate laboratories. In 1887 the course, now compulsory for apprentice pharmacists, was extended to six and a half months, the admission requirement being approximately junior matriculation. By 1890 there was a teaching staff of four. In 1892 the College affiliated with the University of Toronto and its graduates became eligible for a Bachelor of Pharmacy degree. The degree program was not made compulsory as a qualification to practise pharmacy and was not extended to two years until 1927, although this had been suggested as early as 1894.

The needs of pharmacy students were among those catered to in the cours privés offered by the faculty of arts of Laval University in 1860, and some instruction was provided at Montreal from 1868 on, initially under the auspices of the Montreal Chemists and Druggists Association and subsequently of the Pharmaceutical Association of the Province of Quebec after its incorporation in 1870. But there was no regularly offered and systematically developed course until the establishment of the Montreal College of Pharmacy in 1879. For the first nine years all instruction was in English, but with the appointment of French-speaking professors of chemistry and materia medica in 1888, what was in effect a parallel course in French became available. In 1906 the French-speaking professors withdrew to establish l'Ecole de pharmacie de l'Université Laval à Montréal and in 1917 the Montreal College became a department of pharmacy within the faculty of medicine of McGill. In 1890, however, the Montreal College was not related to any university.

Attendance at a course of lectures was one of the requirements for licensing specified in the 1878 Act which established the Pharmaceutical Association of Manitoba as the licensing body in that province, but ten years passed before this provision could be implemented. In 1888, a professor of St John's College was engaged to give lectures in chemistry, and by 1889 an arrangement had been made with the Manitoba Medical College whereby pharmacy students were admitted to appropriate classes. This arrangement continued until 1899 when the Pharmaceutical Association established the Manitoba College of Pharmacy, which three years later entered into affiliation with the University of Manitoba.

In 1890 the Nova Scotia Pharmaceutical Society, which had become responsible for licensing in 1876, approached the Halifax Medical College (at this stage independent of Dalhousie University) with a view to the establishing of a Master of Pharmacy degree course which would be accepted as the requirement for certification in the province. Such a course was instituted in 1890 but the degree was not *required* for licensing. Systematic education in pharmacy for the Maritimes had to await the establishment in 1911 of the Nova Scotia College of Pharmacy in space provided by Dalhousie University.

MUSIC

Four Canadian universities offered degrees in music in 1890 – Bishop's, Ottawa, Trinity, and Toronto; none provided any instruction. Their role, and equally that of Albert University which had a faculty of music for some years before its merger with Victoria in 1884, was confined to examining, and the *Calendar* statement was limited to specifying the requirements to qualify for the Bachelor of Music and Doctor of Music degrees. For the B.Mus. there were First Year, Second Year, and Third Year Examinations, at the last of which the candidate was also required to present an exercise. At Bishop's, the exercise was to be 'in at least four parts with an accompaniment for the organ, piano or string band.' The Doctor of Music degree required three years of study beyond the B.Mus., and a more complicated exercise; at Bishop's, 'in six parts with orchestral accompaniment.'

The only university that had granted a substantial number of music degrees was Trinity, which awarded 89 between 1886 and 1891. Many of these were granted *in absentia*. In 1885 Trinity appointed a registrar resident in England and arranged for the examinations to be taken simultaneously in London and Toronto, and subsequently arrangements were made for the examinations to be written in New York. By 1890 British professors of music were protesting against these Canadian degrees, and Trinity ceased to accept candidates in Great Britain in 1891.[49]

In the late 1880s, four conservatories of music were established, one at Sackville, N.B., one at Hamilton, Ontario and two at Toronto. The proposal for the conservatory at Sackville came from the Alumnae Society of the Mount Allison Ladies College, who

petitioned the university board of regents to this effect in 1888.[50]
The board did provide $3000 and the conservatory was established
in connection with the Ladies College over which the board also
presided. In 1913, a Bachelor of Music program was introduced at
Mount Allison. At Toronto the Toronto Conservatory of Music was
established in 1886 by Edward Fisher, and the Toronto College of
Music in 1888 by F.H. Torrington. The first of these opened in
1887 with 200 pupils and it entered into affiliation with Trinity
in 1888. The Toronto College of Music became affiliated with the
University of Toronto in 1890. By 1896 both institutions were
affiliated with the University of Toronto, as was the Hamilton
Conservatory established in 1889.

TEACHER TRAINING

Normal schools continued to provide for the training of elementary
school teachers in 1890 and the universities' only involvement was
the purely nominal connection that McGill and Laval had with the
normal schools that bore their names. Towards the end of the
period, however, the universities, particularly in Ontario, began
to concern themselves with the preparation of secondary school
teachers.
    Egerton Ryerson, as superintendent of education for Upper Canada,
had in the late 1850s endeavoured to provide for the professional
as distinct from the academic preparation of secondary school
teachers, but he was much ahead of his time. His Model Grammar
School was closed in 1863 after five years of operation.[51] The
general view at this time, as for many years thereafter, was that
a university graduate was entirely competent to teach in a grammar
school. It was not until the 1870s that this proposition was
seriously questioned, at which time chairs of education were established in a number of universities in England, Scotland, France,
and the United States to provide lectures on the theory and practice of pedagogy to undergraduate students who were planning to
become teachers.[52] This movement explains in part the listing of
education as an arts and science subject in the 1887 University
of Toronto Federation Act and the inclusion of science of education as a third or fourth year option in the B.A. program introduced at McMaster in 1890.
    It is also of interest to note that Victoria held a summer
school for science teachers in 1878, and that Queen's in 1889
made special arrangements for extramural students to pursue their
studies towards the B.A. without attending classes. These arrangements, which were designed primarily for practising teachers, involved the student registering in October for examinations to be
written in the following April or September, the submitting of
essays and exercises to a designated professor on prescribed dates,
and the holding of examinations in any location where there were
five candidates.
    The most significant development in teacher training remains to

to be mentioned, the consequences of the decision of the Ontario Department of Education in 1885 to introduce the category of specialist teacher.[53] Since 1871 there had been in Ontario two types of public secondary school, the collegiate institute and the high school, with the former receiving a larger annual grant than the latter. To qualify as a collegiate and therefore to become eligible for the larger grant, the school had to have four teachers and at least 60 students studying classics. For this latter provision there was substituted in 1885 the requirement that a minimum of four masters should be specially qualified in classics or mathematics or natural science or modern languages including English. To qualify as a specialist, the candidate was required to pass certain examinations set by the department on professional matters and to produce evidence of a certain standard of achievement in the academic subject. To prepare candidates for the professional examinations, training institutes were provided at certain collegiates during the autumn term. The potential high school teacher attended the collegiate and received instruction from the principal in the teaching of high school subjects, observed the experienced teachers, and under supervision did some teaching himself. Of the 184 students who attended the institutes during the five years they were offered (1885-90) more than three-quarters qualified as specialists.

The significance of this for the universities was that the academic qualifications for the specialist certificate became identified with the requirements for the honour as distinguished from the pass B.A. This process was not completed until 1898 when graduation from an honour course became a requirement for specialist standing, but it had begun to develop by 1890 and it partly explains the emphasis that all Ontario universities placed on honours work from this time on.

COMMERCE, PHYSICAL EDUCATION, NURSING

To conclude this chapter we shall refer to developments in three other fields which in the twentieth century would occupy a significant position in Canadian higher education. One of these, commerce, had made its appearance as early as 1860, but had made no progress in the intervening years. There had been a substantial development of commercial education at the secondary level in Ontario and Quebec, but the only university offering in 1890 was the two-year diploma course at Dalhousie. There was nothing in Canada comparable to the Wharton School of Commerce established at the University of Pennsylvania in 1881.

A number of Canadian universities in 1890 employed an instructor of gymnastics to supervise the modest gymnasium that had been built to give instruction to students who were prepared to pay a small fee. Usually the instructor was an army sergeant, but McGill's appointment in 1887 was James Naismith, a graduate of McGill, who in 1891 at Springfield, Massachusetts, invented the game of basketball. By 1890 McGill also had appointed a part-time gymnastics or physical education instructor for its women students. Naismith resigned in 1890 and was replaced by Robert Tait MacKenzie, who had obtained his B.A. from McGill in 1889 and was by this time enrolled in medicine. MacKenzie has been called the father of physical and health education in America and as we shall see in chapter 16 he developed his basic ideas at McGill in the 1890s.

The following observation on nursing was made by Sir William Osler: 'When I entered the Montreal General Hospital, where I began the study of medicine in 1868, we had the old-time nurses. They were generally ward servants who had evolved from the kitchen or from the backstairs into the wards.'[54] Had Sir William entered the Hôtel Dieu de Montréal or the Hôtel Dieu de Québec in 1868 he probably would have had a different experience, since nursing in these hospitals had been carried on for two centuries by devoted and from all accounts well-trained nuns. With this exception, his statement is a reasonably accurate description of the state of nursing in 1868. Florence Nightingale's work had begun in conjunction with the St Thomas Training School for Nurses in 1860, but her model, the financially and administratively autonomous 'Nightingale School,' was not introduced into Canada until 1874, when Dr Mack's Training School was established at St Catharines, Ontario. A more important event was the establishment of a school of nursing by the Toronto General Hospital in 1881 since it, rather than the Nightingale School, proved to be the model generally adopted in Canada. By 1890 there were hospital schools of nursing at Toronto, Montreal, London, Guelph, Winnipeg, Fredericton, Saint John, N.B., Galt, Brockville, Peterborough, Halifax, Charlottetown, and Hamilton. All were operated on essentially the same basis. The 'course' lasted two years but most of the student's time was devoted to practical nursing, including a large amount of bed-making, dusting, serving of meals, bathing of patients, and other non-professional tasks, and to a small amount of private duty nursing in patients' homes (for which the hospital collected fees). Academic instruction, provided by doctors of the hospital and the supervising nurse, was not offered throughout the two years but only in certain months, and the total number of lectures was not large. In 1890 at the Toronto General Hospital 160 lectures were provided during nine months of the two-year course. These were increased to just over 200 - 119 by the medical staff, 84 in practical nursing when, in 1886, the course was lengthened to three years.

NOTES TO CHAPTER 10

1 Reference to all the protestant colleges discussed in this section is made in D.C. Masters, *Protestant Church Colleges in Canada: a History* (1966), 29-132. Master's chapter headings for this period are 'The Golden Years (1829-1867) and 'Changing Ideas (1867-1890).' Institutional histories are listed in the bibliography.

2 Masters, *Protestant Churches*, 99-100. See also L.G. Thomas, 'The Church of England and the Higher Education in the Prairie West before 1914,' *J. Can. Church Hist. Soc.*, 3 (1956), 6-7; and L.N. Murray, 'St. John's College, Qu'Appelle, 1885-1894,' *Sask., Hist.*, 11 (1958).

3 Other items in this pamphlet war are listed under 'Theology' in *A Bibliography of Higher Education in Canada* (1960) and the *1965 Supplement*. The war itself is discussed in T.A. Reed, ed., *A History of the University of Trinity College* (1952), 62-9; and A.H. Crowfoot, *Bishop Cronyn* (1957), 90-7.

4 For the development of Wycliffe, see D. Hague, 'The History of Wycliffe College' in *The Jubilee Volume of Wycliffe College* (1927), 1-60; and J.P. Sheraton, 'History of Wycliffe College' in J.G. Hopkins, ed., *Canada: An Encyclopaedia of the Country* (1898), IV, 222-6.

5 See above, chapter 5, 61.

6 E. Ryerson, *Inaugural Address on the Nature and Advantages of an English and Liberal Education* (1842)

7 For Punshon, see C.B. Sissons, *Egerton Ryerson: His Life and Times* (1947), II, 542-658 (passim).

8 The Conference of the Wesleyan Methodist Church established the Wesleyan Institute at Winnipeg in 1873; this was incorporated as Wesley College in 1877. Trinity College was also incorporated in 1877 at the request of the Episcopalian Methodist Church but it was never opened. W.L. Morton, *One University: A History of the University of Manitoba* (1952), 26-7

9 J.H. MacVicar, *Life and Work of Donald Harvey MacVicar* (1904), 81-2

10 H. Blais, 'L'Enseignement de le théologie au Canada,' *Culture,* 2 (1941), 206-20; C.-O. Garant, 'Le Cinquantenaire de l'encyclique "Aeterni Patris" à Laval,' *Rev. Dominicaine*, 35 (1929), 419-37; H. Bastien *L'Enseignment de la philosophie au Canada français* (1935)

11 See appendix 1.

12 W.A. Reeve, 'Inaugural Address to the Law School, Ontario,' *Can. Law Times*, 9 (1889), 244

13 Reeve, 'Inaugural,' 249

14 J.M. Young, 'The Faculty of Law' in W.J. Alexander, ed., *The University of Toronto and its Colleges* (1906), 149-67

15 E.-F. Surveyer, 'Une Ecole de Droit à Montréal avant le code civil,' *Rev. Trimestrielle Can.*, 6 (1920), 140-50; P. Desjardins, *Le Collège Sainte-Marie de Montréal*, II (1944), 60-102

16 See appendix 1.

17 A. Primrose, 'The Faculty of Medicine' in Alexander, *The University of Toronto and its Colleges*, 175-7

18 A. Fauteux, *Bibliographie de la question universitaire Laval-Montréal 1852-1921* (1922), also in Université de Montréal, *Annuaire* (1922-23), is the best introduction to this contre-temps, the various stages of which are described in L.-D.

Mignault, 'Histoire de l'Ecole de Médecine et de Chirurgie de Montréal,' *Union Médicale*, 55 (1926), 629-63.

19 D.C. Harvey, *An Introduction to the History of Dalhousie University* (1938), 93

20 A.F. Baird, 'The History of Engineering at the University of New Brunswick' in A.G. Bailey, ed., *The University of New Brunswick Memorial Volume* (1950), 81

21 C.R. Young, *Early Engineering Education at Toronto, 1851-1919* (1958), 63

22 Young, *Toronto*, 18

23 Ibid., 19

24 The commission's appointment was dated 12 January 1871; the commissioners' report (reprinted in J.G. Hodgins, ed., *Documentary History of Education in Upper Canada* (1908), XXIII, 1-32) was submitted in January 1871. Cf. Young, *Toronto*, 25-31.

25 Hodgins, *Doc. Hist.*, XXIII, 10

26 Ibid., XXIII, 9

27 L.-P. Audet, 'La Fondation de l'Ecole Polytechnique de Montréal,' *Cahiers des Dix*, 30 (1965), 150-1

28 J.W. Dawson, *Plea for the Extension of University Education in Canada and Especially in Connection with McGill University* (1870)

29 Audet, 'La Fondation,' 156

30 Ibid., 153-8

31 H. Provost, *Historique de la Faculté des Arts de l'Université Laval, 1852-1952* (1952), 26

32 See above, chapter 9, 133.

33 See below.

34 O. Maurault, *Ecole Polytechnique de Montréal 1873-1948* (1948), 51

35 Provost, *Historique*, 26-7

36 For a detailed account of developments in Quebec, see F. Létourneau, *Histoire de l'Agriculture au Canada français* (1968).

37 Documents bearing on the establishment of the Ontario Agricultural College, including Clarke's report, are reprinted in Hodgins, *Doc. Hist.*, XXV (1908), 175-89.

38 Ibid., XXV, 179

39 *Canadian Educational Directory* (1876), 127

40 President of the Provincial Agricultural Association, quoted in Hodgins, *Doc. Hist.*, XXV, 187

41 F.E. Gattinger, *A Century of Challenge: A History of the Ontario Veterinary College* (1962), 55-6.

42 The institution has been known as the Ontario Veterinary College since 1867. Prior to this it was called both the Upper Canada Veterinary School and the Toronto Veterinary College: Gattinger, *Century*, 38.

43 Ibid., 18

44 J. Saint-Georges, '75th Anniversary of the School for Veterinary Medicine of the Province of Quebec,' *Can. J. Comp. Med.*, 25 (1961), 239-42

45 A. Preston, 'The Founding of the Royal Military College ...,'
    Queen's Quarterly, 74 (1967), 399
46 F.J. Dixon, 'Military Education in Canada,' in J.C. Hopkins,
    ed., *Canada: an Encyclopedia of the Country* (1898), IV, 444
47 Preston, 'Founding,' 404
48 E.W. Stieb, 'Pharmaceutical Education in Ontario. I: Prelude
    and Beginnings (The Shuttleworth Era),' *Pharmacy in History*,
    16 (1974), 64-71
49 T.A. Reed, *A History of the University of Trinity College*
    (1952), 98-100
50 R.C. Archibald, *Historical Notes on the Education of Women
    at Mount Allison 1854-1954* (1954), 13
51 R.S. Harris, *Quiet Evolution: a Study of the Ontario Educa-
    tional System* (1967), 72
52 Ibid., 77-8
53 Ibid., 79-83
54 J.M. Gibbon and M.S. Mathewson, *Three Centuries of Canadian
    Nursing* (1947), 146

11
Graduate Studies

The fact that graduate work had become recognized as a function
to be carried on in the Canadian university by 1890 represented
considerable progress from 1860 when there were no graduate students and masters' degrees were granted on the basis of work done
at the bachelor's level, combined with physical survival, avoidance
of jail, the payment of a fee, and some evidence of a continuing
interest in literary or scientific study. Thirty years later,
the M.A. had almost completed the transition from 'automatic' to
earned degree; the Ph.D. had been introduced at several universities (though not as yet in the form it assumed in the twentieth
century); a few other earned degrees had been established (the
M.Sc. at King's and Ottawa, the M.Eng. at King's, the M.App.Sci.
at McGill, the *licence* at Laval); and a number of fellowships had
been established for graduate students. Thus, while the position
of graduate studies could not properly be described as either
satisfactory or permanently defined, it can be said that the ground
had been cleared of weeds and the soil prepared for systematic
cultivation in the early years of the new century.

THE MASTER'S DEGREE

The basic requirement for the M.A. in 1890 was an acceptable
thesis on a literary or scientific subject which had been approved
in advance by the appropriate university department. However, the
thesis could not normally be presented until the candidate had
been a B.A. for three years 'maintaining meanwhile a good reputation' - to use the words of a typical Calendar statement. This
was the position at Acadia, McGill, Mount Allison, and, with
exceptions to be noted below, at Dalhousie and Victoria. Ottawa
and New Brunswick would accept the thesis two years after the B.A.,
Toronto after one.

In addition to the presentation of an acceptable thesis McGill required its M.A. candidates to pass an examination on the major subject, but this requirement was waived in the case of students who had an honours B.A. with at least second class standing. New Brunswick required all candidates to sit for an examination 'on subjects or authors prescribed.' Dalhousie also required an examination, but only for students who chose an alternative route to the M.A., one that substituted for the thesis 'a course of study approved by the Faculty and of about the extent represented by the academic work of a single year.' The movement towards course work as an integral part of the M.A. program was also implicit in the statement issued by McMaster University in 1890 when announcing its intention to offer M.A., Ph.D., and Doctor of Laws degrees: 'On the subjects prescribed for each of these advanced courses lectures will be delivered which will serve to place before the student in a clear and forceable manner the best methods of conducting the investigations undertaken, the points which should receive special attention and the proper conditions and necessary limits of the lines of investigation pursued.' The statement went on to explain that in each course there would be exactly twenty lectures, all offered within the space of seven weeks, 'to permit men who may have entered upon the active duties of life to continue their studies with a view to any of the higher degrees.' Unfortunately, this interesting experiment was not tried out; in 1891 the McMaster senate announced that it was postponing implementation of the advanced degree program 'until the Arts Departments were fully equipped.'

Course work rather than the thesis was the basis for the M.A. at Queen's and Victoria, but the courses offered were at the undergraduate level. At Queen's the M.A. was awarded to the student who had completed one of the 14 honours B.A. courses and in the process or in addition had taken certain specified undergraduate courses; the graduate in English and History, for example, was required to have taken Latin, English, history, and either Greek or modern languages at both junior and senior levels as well as junior mathematics. Victoria had a somewhat similar arrangement for one of the two M.A. degrees it was granting in 1890, the one which it awarded to students who had qualified for an honours B.A. and who had also passed the final B.A. honours examinations in a department *other than* the one in which they had obtained their first degree. But Victoria also granted the M.A. to B.A.s of three years standing who applied in writing and 'whose attainments and moral character were satisfactory to the Senate.'

Two Canadian universities, Manitoba and St Francis Xavier, continued in 1890 to grant the M.A. without the requirement of additional work beyond the baccalaureate, but by 1900 each required either course work or a thesis or both. By 1900 the only 'unearned' masters degree in Canada was that granted by Laval which continued to grant the M.A. on the basis adopted in 1857 when, finding it impossible to establish graduate level courses in the faculté des arts, it announced that the M.A. would be granted to teachers in the classical colleges who had eight years of service and who were occupying the position of prefect of studies or professor of philosophy, rhetoric, belles-lettres, chemistry, or mathematics and physics.[1]

THE Ph.D.

The 1890-91 *Calendars* of three Canadian universities, Mount Allison, New Brunswick, and Queen's, outline a program for the Ph.D. The senate of the University of Toronto had approved a Ph.D. program in 1885, but the degree was not announced until 1897. However, no Canadian university had granted an earned Ph.D. by 1890. The Acadia *Calendar* of 1890 records all the graduates of the university up to that time and among the degrees listed are two types of Ph.D., one called honorary and one without specification. The recipients of the two unspecified Ph.D.s were, at the time they received the degree, professors on the Acadia staff and all the evidence points to the degrees being as honorary as those so described.

Since there had been no graduates of any of these programs, they are of interest only as indicating the attitude adapted towards the Ph.D. at this time. In each case the candidate was required to have an M.A. At Mount Allison, which appears to have interpreted the degree literally as one in philosophy, he was required to pass an unspecified number of examinations (probably two) in which he would be tested on his knowledge of 24 specified works in philosophy and history, the authors including Plato, Kant, Grote, Hallam, and Gibbon. New Brunswick, which required the student to have had the M.A. for three years, prescribed a definite course of study, either 'Literary' or 'Scientific.' The Literary course embraced classics, English literature, modern languages, history, political economy, and philosophy; the Scientific course, mathematics, astronomy, physics, chemistry, natural history, and geology. In either case the candidate had to produce evidence of specialist knowledge in one of these subjects by way of (a) examinations set by the university, and (b) either a thesis embodying original research or a certificate of attendance at a postgraduate course. It was not specified that the course had to be taken at Fredericton.

At Queen's, the requirements for the Ph.D. included the passing of examinations, the submitting of a thesis, and the passage of four years from the obtaining of the B.A. The degree was offered in nine 'courses': classics, modern language and literature, philosophy, and any combination of *two* of English, history, political science, and *one* modern language. Each course was outlined in detail in the Calendar. The descriptions varied in the amount of work required of the candidate, but particularly in modern language and literature, which included French, German, either Spanish or Italian, and comparative grammar of the Romance languages, the demands were heavy. Queen's also offered comparable courses leading to the D.Sc. degree in pure and applied mathematics and in science, i.e., botany, chemistry, geology, and zoology.

FELLOWSHIPS

In 1883 the Royal Society of Canada appointed a committee 'to enquire into and report upon the forms of aid and encouragement given in other countries to young men deemed qualified and desirous to engage in Original Literary or Scientific Work, and to suggest the best means of providing similar aid and encouragement for young men in Canada.'[2] The committee's report, not submitted until 1885 owing to the death of one of its members, consisted largely of a listing of the fellowships available at the leading English, Scottish, Irish, Australian, American, and Canadian universities. The Canadian fellowships listed were at Dalhousie (two Munro tutorships in mathematics and classics tenable for one or two years at $1000 a year), Trinity (one $500 fellowship in biology tenable for up to three years), and University College, Toronto (nine $500 fellowships in classics, mathematics (2), French, German, philosophy, chemistry, biology, and geology tenable for up to three years). The committee noted that it was a requirement of all these fellowships that the holder assist in the teaching offered by the department to which he was assigned and consequently that in no case did the fellowship permit the holder to devote his full attention to graduate work: 'In Canada we have made a beginning but the beginning is small and the few fellowships which our universities possess are in all cases so conditioned that their holders being required to engage in teaching are unable to go abroad.'[3] Nor was the committee optimistic that the situation was likely to improve: 'Our colleges are so badly endowed that all the funds are needed to provide the first requisites of university work, Professorships, Libraries, Museums and Laboratories.'

Had the Royal Society Committee wished to do so, it could have produced evidence of the value of fellowships that permitted the student to go abroad by referring to the record of the Canadians who had been awarded Gilchrist scholarships at the University of London since their establishment in 1868.[4] One of these scholarships, which provided £100 a year for up to three years, was available to the student standing highest amongst those from Canada who had taken the matriculation examination at the University of London, the purpose being to make it possible for the student to prepare for the B.A. or B.Sc. degree of the University of London by attendance either at University College, London, or at the University of Edinburgh. Technically, the Gilchrist Scholarship was for undergraduate not graduate study, but for Canadians at least it was in fact an opportunity to do postgraduate work. Seven of the Canadians awarded Gilchrist Scholarships between 1868 and 1887 had a B.A. at the time they applied, and

six others were undergraduates of at least one year's standing.
A memorandum submitted to the Gilchrist trustees in 1895 by a
group of former Gilchrist scholars noted that many Canadians used
the fellowship as a means of pursuing advanced studies while osten-
sibly preparing for the bachelor's degree. Indeed, in the view
of these scholars, the relative failure of the scheme was a direct
consequence of the requirement to do undergraduate work: 'It was,
we believe, the endeavour first to combine the College courses in
Canada with preparation for the scholarship examination and afterwards to combine the general and at the same time very miscellaneous
work of the B.A. and B.Sc. courses of the London University with
advanced study of special departments which led to overwork, loss
of health and consequent failure to complete courses and achieve
distinction.'[5]

Three of the 18 Canadian winners did, in fact, withdraw from the
program for reasons of ill health and two others died in their mid-
twenties. Four others, however, went on to the M.A. and another
four to the D.Sc. But more important, as evidence of the value
of postgraduate fellowships for Canadian higher education as a
whole, is the fact that nine of the Canadian Gilchrist scholars
returned to Canada to take positions on the staff of Canadian
universities, the majority for their working lifetime:

Date	Name	Subject, Position	University	Years
1871	J.G. McGregor	Physics	Dalhousie	1879-1901
			Edinburgh	1901-1913
1874	W.J. Alexander	English	Dalhousie	1884-1889
			Toronto	1889-1927
1875	J.G. Schurman	English, Philosophy	Acadia	1880-1882
		English, Metaphysics	Dalhousie	1882-1886
		Philosophy, President	Cornell	1886-1920
1877	W.L. Goodwin	Chemistry	Mount Allison	1882-1888
		Chemistry, Engineering	Queen's	1883-1920
		Dean of Applied Science		
1878	S.W. Hunten	Mathematics	Mount Allison	1883-1933
1881	H. Murray	Classics	Dalhousie	1887-1931
1882	W.M. Tweedie	English	Mount Allison	1887-1935
1884	A.W. Duff	Engineering	New Brunswick	1890-1893
		Physics	Purdue	1893-1898
		Physics	Worcester Polytech. Institute	1899-1936
1887	W.C. Murray	Philosophy	New Brunswick	1891-1892
		Philosophy	Dalhousie	1892-1908
		President	Saskatchewan	1908-1939

Three of the nine, McGregor, Goodwin, and W.C. Murray, became fellows of the Royal Society of Canada.

One of the Gilchrist scholars, W.J. Alexander, after spending three years at the University of London returned to North America and after two years of high school teaching registered at Johns Hopkins University where he obtained a Ph.D. in 1883. He was one of 26 Canadians who attended Johns Hopkins between 1881 and 1890, 11 of whom were awarded fellowships and 15 of whom qualified for the Ph.D.[6] Between 1886 and 1891, 11 other Canadians attended Cornell, 7 on scholarships, of whom 6 obtained the Ph.D. All 6 of the Canadians at Harvard in the sessions 1888-89, 1889-90, and 1890-91 were on scholarships. Two Canadians registered at Clark University when it opened in 1889, 8 (as graduate students) at the University of Chicago when it opened in 1892. By 1890, indeed, the ambitious young Canadian academic was more likely to go to the United States for graduate study than to Europe, and this raised for the first time the problem of brain-drain to the south. W.J. Alexander returned to Canada, as did five other Johns Hopkins Ph.D.s of this period who were to play important roles in the development of Canadian higher education during the next forty years - J.C. Fields, A.B. Macallum, J. Playfair McMurrich, Archibald Macmechan, and Charles Saunders, but a number of those who went to Johns Hopkins and to the other American graduate schools subsequently took positions in the United States. The Royal Society committee was right in emphasizing the inadequacy of the graduate fellowships arrangements in the Canadian university, since in a very real sense fellowships are the key to effective graduate programs. But the situation was more serious than they recognized in 1885, and by 1890 it had become more serious still.[7]

While fellowships may be the key to effective graduate programs they are not in themselves a guarantee that a graduate program will be effective; there must also be adequate library and laboratory resources and professors who are not only qualified to instruct at this level but are also in a position to do so. Another fellow of the Royal Society of Canada, William Osler, in pointing out in 1884 that practically no Canadian professors were in a position to undertake research, was also in effect saying that no Canadian professors were in a position to instruct at the graduate level:

> It is one thing to know thoroughly and be able to teach well any given subject in a college, it is quite another thing to be able to take up that subject and by original work and investigation add to our stock of knowledge concerning it, or throw light upon the dark problems which may surround it. Many a man, pitchforked, so to speak, by local exigencies into a professional position has done the former well, but unless a man of extraordinary force he cannot break the invidious bar of defective training which effectually shuts him off from the latter and higher duties of his position. We have, however, many men in our colleges with good records as investigators, and we hear

from them but seldom on account of the excessive drudgery of teaching which the restricted means of their college compel them to undertake. The instances are few indeed in our universities in which a professor has but a single subject to deal with, and those which do exist are in subjects of great extent and often subdivided in other colleges. In looking over the list of branches taught by a single professor in some of our colleges, we may indeed say with Dr. O.W. Holmes that he does not occupy a *chair* but an entire *settee*. If Canadian scholarship is to be fostered, if progress in science is to be made, this condition of things must be remedied, and we may confidently hope will be, as years roll on ... But unless the liberality of individuals is manifested in the manner of the late Mr. Johns Hopkins of Baltimore, we shall have to wait long for a *fully equipped* Canadian university. The Government of Ontario, however, has now the opportunity to put Toronto University on a proper basis, and do a great work for the intellectual life of this country. And it can consistently do so, as the Institution is a State foundation and is under State control, and the condition of the local Exchequer is plethoric.[8]

Osler, it will be noted, was hopeful that state support would soon enable at least one Canadian university to be fully equipped. Unfortunately, the University of Toronto had to wait until 1905 and 1906 for the government of Ontario to place it financially 'on a proper basis.' Certainly, neither it nor any other Canadian university was in such a position in 1890 and this in large measure explains the tentative nature of graduate studies in Canada at this time.

NOTES TO CHAPTER 11

1 H. Provost, *Historique de la faculté des arts de l'Université Laval, 1852-1952* (1952), 9
2 'Report of the Committee on the Encouragement of Original Literary and Scientific Work,' *Proc. Royal Society Canada* 1885, xxix-xli
3 Ibid., xii
4 The history of the scholarship is recorded in R.A. Falconer, 'The Gilchrist Scholarships: an Episode in the Higher Education of Canada,' *Trans. Royal Society Canada* 1933, section 2, 5-13.
5 Falconer, 'Gilchrist Scholarships,' 10
6 For the statistics of Canadians attending graduate schools presented in this paragraph I am grateful to Peter N. Ross, who has obtained the information for a University of Toronto Ed.D. thesis on the development of the Ph.D. at the University of Toronto.
7 The number of Canadians attending American graduate schools increased markedly in the 1890s - over 30 at Johns Hopkins,

over 50 at Cornell, over 60 at Harvard, over 80 at Chicago. In a number of instances - J.G. Hume and C.E. Saunders (Harvard, Johns Hopkins); W.L.M. King (Chicago, Harvard); J.P. McMurrich (Clark, Johns Hopkins) - the same individual attended two institutions.

8   Unsigned editorial, *Canadian Medical & Surgical Journal* (January 1884), quoted by H. Cushing, *The Life of Sir William Osler* (1925), I, 209

12
Scholarship and Research

In 1893 the president of the Royal Society of Canada, J.G. Bourinot, in his presidential address attempted to assess the position of literature, education, and the arts in Canada, the title of his paper being 'Our Intellectual Strengths and Weaknesses.'[1] The following year his successor, G.M. Dawson, attempted to provide a similar assessment of the Canadian situation with respect to scientific investigation.[2] Together these two essays provide a basis for defining the state of scholarship and research in Canada at this time.

It is significant that neither address devoted much attention to the universities as centres of research and scholarship, and also that the majority of the persons mentioned by Bourinot and Dawson as contributing to Canada's intellectual strength were not university professors. Dawson, it is true, specifically stated that he was primarily concerned with applied research, i.e., research 'tending more or less directly to the development of natural resources and advantages,'[3] and consequently that he would not allude to 'the numerous educational institutions in which a scientific training is given nor to the results which have accrued from the individual labours of scientific workers throughout the country, though in many cases these have been of the most creditable and important character.'[4] Nonetheless, his was a review of the various *institutions* engaged in scientific work and investigation in Canada and the omission of the universities is revealing. Bourinot was concerned among other matters with studies in the fields of history, political science, and literary criticism, and his analysis indicates that in these fields at least the universities were not making much of a contribution.

Bourinot, indeed, had difficulty in matching Dawson's claim that individual Canadians had produced scholarly work that was of an *important* character:

I cannot boast that we have produced a great poem or a great
history which has attracted the attention of the world beyond
us and assuredly we find no noteworthy attempt in the direction
of a novel of our modern life; but what I do claim is, looking
at the results generally, the work we have done has been sometimes above the average in those fields of literature - and here
I necessarily include science - in which Canadians have worked.
They have shown in many productions a conscientious spirit of
research, patient industry, and not a little literary skill in
the management of their material.[5]

Bourinot's concentration on novels, poems, plays, history, biography, and literary criticism in his assessment of Canada's intellectual life at this time was a necessary response to the facts
of the case; there were no works by Canadians in economics or political science or psychology or sociology to which he could refer.

APPLIED RESEARCH IN GOVERNMENT DEPARTMENTS

In the area of applied research the Canadian position in 1890 was
both creditable and important, and for this, as Dawson made clear,
the credit lay with government, primarily the federal government.
He concluded his review of what had been done to encourage scientific investigation in Canada by noting that some provincial
governments had provided grants to local scientific societies and
that provincial museums had been established in Nova Scotia (1868)
and British Columbia (1886); but nine-tenths of his space was devoted to describing the activities of agencies or departments of
the federal government - the Geological Survey, the Meteorological
Service, the Dominion Lands Survey, the Experimental Farms, and
the Department of Marine and Fisheries.
   As we have seen in chapter 6, the Geological Survey was well
established by 1860. Throughout the ensuing three decades its
work was greatly expanded, partly as a consequence of the expansion of the country to the Pacific. One of the conditions specified by British Columbia when agreeing to become a province in
1871 was that its territory would receive the immediate attention
of the survey.[6] The full-time professional staff of the Geological
Survey by 1890 numbered 18, 8 of whom were members of the Royal
Society.[7] Though not formally organized until 1871, the Meteorological Service of Canada can also be said to extend back to 1860,
since it had developed from the work initiated at the observatory
in Toronto established by the British government in 1841 and taken
over by the government of Upper Canada in 1853 when the British
staff was recalled to London.[8]
   Under its first Director, G.T. Kingston, a part-time professor
at the University of Toronto who had been in charge of the Toronto
Observatory since 1855, and his successor (from 1880) Albert
Carpmael, a service that was truly national was rapidly developed.
By the time Dawson spoke in 1894 it involved over 400 stations

194

reporting regularly to the central office in Ottawa, including 29 reporting daily by telegraph data relevant to weather forecasting. In 1883 the observatories at Saint John, N.B. and Quebec and the McGill Observatory at Montréal were placed under the jurisdiction of the Meteorological Service. Both Carpmael and G.T. Girdwood, a professor of chemistry at McGill who was in charge of the McGill Observatory were fellows of the Royal Society.

The Dominion Lands Survey, of which another Royal Society fellow, E.W. Deville, was director, was also organized in 1871 in connection with the opening up of the western provinces, and its initial concern was with the surveying of Manitoba and the North West Territories.[9] In 1884 its work was extended into British Columbia in connection with the building of the C.P.R. and in 1890 the complex task of surveying the Canadian Rockies was under way.

In 1886, an act respecting experimental farm stations was passed and W.E. Saunders, another Royal Society fellow, who had been commissioned in 1885 by the minister of agriculture to develop a detailed plan for the encouragement and development of the agricultural resources of Canada, was appointed director.[10] By 1890 a central farm had been established at Ottawa, with divisions assigned to animal husbandry, cereals, chemistry, entomology, field husbandry, and horticulture, and branch farms had been established in the Maritimes (Nappan, N.S.), in Manitoba (Brandon), in the North West Territories (Indian Head in what is now Saskatchewan), and British Columbia (Agassiz).

In concluding his review of the several branches of scientific research carried out by the government, Dawson felt that 'allusion must be made to several comparatively late undertakings begun under the auspices of the Department of Marine and Fisheries.'[11] These included a hydrographic survey of the Canadian portion of the Great Lakes begun in 1883 and the commencement of systematic tidal observations in 1890. However, it was not until 1898 that the department established the Board of Management (which in 1912 became the Biological Board of Canada and later the Fisheries Research Board of Canada) and not until 1899 that the first biological station was established.[12]

All these government activities had a practical orientation and the mandate issued to men like Saunders, Carpmael, and Deville was to carry on applied rather than basic research. The line dividing pure and applied research in the nineteenth century (as in the twentieth) was a difficult one to draw, and the publications of the professional staff engaged in these services included many papers of a theoretical nature. Some of these appeared in the *Transactions of the Royal Society of Canada* and in the journals or proceedings published by other learned societies, such as the Canadian Institute and the National History Society of Montreal, but some, too, were published in the official reports and studies of the government agencies. Furthermore, these government publications made available a great deal of factual information which was needed if scientists in particular fields were to carry on studies of a fundamental nature. Moreover, two of the agencies,

the Geological Survey and the Experimental Farms, were also concerned with the collecting and preserving of geological, biological,
archaeological and other specimens, and the first of these had been
formally charged by legislation in 1890 with responsibility to
develop and maintain a national museum. The importance of such a
museum was emphasized by G.M. Dawson in his 1894 address, and he
lamented the fact that the government had not yet provided a suitable building for the collections: 'This museum should be of a
national character, and there is every reason to hope that when
it is undertaken, its plan will include provision for all the
valuable collections which have been or may be made by the several
department governments so that it may form in effect a representation of the resources, the history and the various lines of activity of the whole country.'[13] Dawson's hopes, unfortunately, were
not realized until 1913.

LEARNED AND PROFESSIONAL SOCIETIES

The establishment of the Royal Society of Canada was unquestionably the most important institutional development in Canada during
the period 1861-90 so far as research and scholarship were concerned. It was an organization with a national rather than a
local membership, and almost from the outset one with an international reputation. No other body could make this claim. Indeed, the fact that almost all the other learned societies in
Canada entered into affiliation with the Royal Society was evidence of its pre-eminent position.
    Of the societies which could be described as well established
in 1860, three continued to operate through the period and to
carry on a publishing program, though each had problems of dwindling membership and inadequate funds. The least successful was
the Literary and Historical Society of Quebec, which increasingly
confined its attention to historical subjects.[14]
    The Natural History Society of Montreal published a journal
throughout the period, but more often than not there were fewer
issues than were advertised to appear; in 1869 the title was
changed from the *Canadian Naturalist and Geologist and Proceedings
of the Natural History Society of Montreal* to *The Canadian Naturalist and Quarterly Journal of Science,* and in 1883 to the
Canadian Record of Science. The Canadian Institute (of Toronto)
continued to publish the *Canadian Journal* until 1878, but thereafter confined its publication activities to an annual volume of
Proceedings, retitled *Transactions* in 1890. The range of subjects
dealt with in the Canadian Institute's publications, it should be
added, was comparable to that of the Royal Society of Canada, some
notable scientific papers being included but also papers in such
areas as local history, anthropology, economics, and archaeology.
The wide ranging interests of the Canadian Institute were reflected
in the fact that between 1885 and 1890 it established sections
concerned with biology, architecture, geology and mining, philology,

196

photography, and history.[15] The effectiveness of the Canadian
Institute and the Natural History Society of Montreal during these
years is partly explained by the heavy involvement of a number of
professors from, respectively, the University of Toronto and McGill.
There was no similar involvement of professors from Laval in the
work of the Literary and Historical Society of Quebec.

Of the new societies established between 1861 and 1890 the most
important (other than the Royal Society of Canada) from a scientific point of view was the Entomological Society of Canada founded
by William Saunders in 1863, whose journal, *Canadian Entomologist*
established in 1868, has now been published for over a century;
but there were other scientific societies whose existence was of
great importance in stimulating interest and encouraging effort
at the local level in centres other than Montreal, Toronto, and
Ottawa: the Natural History Society of New Brunswick (1862) commenced publication of a *Bulletin* in 1882; the Nova Scotia Institute
of Natural Science (1862) which from time to time published *Proceedings and Transactions*; the Historical and Scientific Society
of Manitoba (1879), whose *Transactions* were regularly published
from 1882 to 1906; and the Natural History Society of British
Columbia (1890) which published *Papers* in 1891 and a *Bulletin* from
1891 to 1910.

On the non-science side, the new societies were almost entirely
concerned with history, and primarily with local history: New
Brunswick Historical Society (1874), which published *Collections*
(of documents) in 1884; Nova Scotia Historical Society (1878),
Collections (1878); Montreal Historical Society (1889), *Transactions*
from 1899 to 1917; and the Pioneer and Historical Society of the
Province of Ontario (1888), which became the Ontario Historical
Association in 1898, and the publisher of *Papers and Records*...
from 1899. Local history, it should be noted, was very much a
concern of the Historical and Scientific Society of Manitoba.

PROFESSIONAL JOURNALS

We noted in chapter 6 the existence in 1860 of a number of journals concerned with law, medicine, agriculture, and education.
Relatively few of the journals mentioned survived to 1890 but there
were plenty of new ones in the fields of law, medicine, and education, and journals concerned with architecture, dentistry, and
pharmacy had also made their appearance. Generally speaking, the
stimulus for all these professional journals came not from the
profession itself but from one or more individual practitioners
and in some instances, the law journals for example, as a purely
business proposition. In the case of medicine, most of the journals were edited and financed by doctors who were connected with
one or other of the medical schools but in no case was there any
involvement of the university with which the school was affiliated.

None of the medical journals of 1860 survived more than a few
years, but about 20 new ones were launched in the next 30 years.[16]

More than half of these ceased after one or two issues, but five
had long and honorable runs, and one, *Union Médicale* (1872), has
celebrated its centenary. The *Canada Lancet* (originally the
Dominion Medical Journal) was published regularly from 1868 to
1922, the *Canadian Practitioner* (originally the *Canadian Journal
of Medical Sciences*) from 1876 to 1924, the *Canadian Medical
Record* (originally the *Montreal Medical Journal*) from 1872 to 1904.
The Maritime Medical News, established late in the period at
Halifax, ran from 1888 to 1910 when it was absorbed within the
Canadian Medical Association Journal. Also worthy of mention are
the Montreal General Hospital's *Pathological Reports*, issued
periodically from 1876 to 1902 and the medium through which many
of William Osler's early investigations were reported.

   The Upper Canada Law Journal and Local Court Gazette (1855) continued to be published as the *Canada Law Journal* (from 1864) until
1922 and the *Lower Canada Jurist* from 1865 to 1891, but neither of
these nor any of the half-dozen other law journals which were instituted between 1861 to 1890 could be described as being concerned
with the philosophic as distinct from the technical aspects of the
law. Canadians had to wait until the 1920s for a proper law journal.

   Both the *Journal of Education for Upper Canada* and the *Journal
of Education for Lower Canada* ceased publication in the late 1870s,
a year or two after the reorganizations which removed the superintendents of education from the scene, but the journalistic
vacuum was filled by a number of new publications originating in
Toronto (*Canadian School Journal*, 1877-87; *Educational Monthly of
Canada*, 1879-1905; *Educational Weekly* 1885-87, *Educational Journal*
(1887-97), or Quebec *Enseignement Primaire*, 1878-1968; *Educational Record of the Province of Quebec*, 1881-1965). These new
journals, however, concerned themselves almost exclusively with
matters related to the elementary and secondary schools rather
than with educational matters in general as had been the case with
the journals which Egerton Ryerson and P.-J.-O. Chauveau had edited.

   George Beers, a Montreal dentist, edited the *Canadian Journal
of Dental Science* from 1868 to 1879, and 10 years later, established the *Dominion Dental Journal*, which continued until 1934
when it was absorbed within the *Journal of the Canadian Dental
Association*.[17] Both the journals edited by Beers were comparable
in content to the typical medical journal of the time. The first
publication concerned with architecture, *Canadian Architect and
Builder*, which ran from 1888 to 1908, was more a trade journal
than a professional one.

JOURNALS OF OPINION AND UNIVERSITY PUBLICATIONS

One of the striking weaknesses of the Canadian intellectual scene
in the 1860s and 1870s was the absence of journals concerned with
literature, politics, and cultural matters in general.[18] The
absence is complete for the 1860s and is only partially relieved

in the 1870s by the *Canadian Monthly and National Review* (1872-78)
and its successor *Rose Belford's Canadian Monthly and National
Review* (1879-82). The situation improved somewhat in the 1880s
with *The Bystander* (1880-83, revived 1889-90), *The Week: a Canadian Journal of Politics, Science and Literature* (1883-96), and
Saturday Night (1887-   ). But with one exception there was no
Canadian journal in 1890 comparable to *Queen's Quarterly* (1893-)
or *Canadian Magazine of Politics, Science, Art and Literature*
(1893-1939).

The exception was *Le Canada Français*, a quarterly published
under the direction of a Comité de Professeurs de l'Université
Laval for four years, 1888-91. This was an ambitious undertaking,
each issue running to about 200 pages, including a 50-page supplement of previously unpublished historical documents. Original
work published was to be paid at the rate of 50 cents a page,
though authors were warned in the Prospectus which appeared at
the beginning of the first issue to be 'patient' on the matter of
payment until the review was well established. Concerned generally
with *religion, philosophie, histoire, beaux-arts, sciences*, and
lettres, the review would, however, centre attention primarily on
the French Fact in North America and would operate within the
context of the Catholic church - 'L'Eglise et la Patrie seront
les deux grands amours de nos coeurs.' The one subject excluded
would be politics:

> Avec le concours de nos collaborateurs nous voudrions pouvoir
> étudier tout particulièrement (1) le mouvement religieux et les
> oeuvres qu'il enfante dans les diverses parties du monde, (2)
> le mouvement social et les graves questions économiques qui
> bientôt, peut-être, mettront en péril l'avenir des sociétés;
> (3) le mouvement scientifique et littéraire, et les rapports
> de la science et de la littérature contemporaines avec la
> religion.
> Pour suivre la voie droite dans ces questions délicates et
> nouvelles, nos écrivains ne seront pas en peine: ils n'auront
> qu'à inspirer des grandes vérités proclamées à notre époque par
> nos illustres pontifes Pie IX et Léon XIII, et marcher à la
> lumière des flambeaux allumés par ces grandes intelligences
> assistées du Saint-Esprit.[19]

The range of articles is represented by the following from the
first issue - with the exception of N. Legendre, all the authors
were professors at L'Université Laval:

M.E. Methot, Le Jubilé de Sa Sainteté Léon XIII
A.H. Gosselin, Rôle Politique de Monseigneur de Laval
T. Chapais, La Bataille de Carillon
H. Casgrain, Coup d'oeil sur l'Acadie avant la Dispersion de
          la Colonie Française
N. Legendre, Le Réalisme en Littérature
J.-C.-K. Laflamme, Métallurgie électrique

No explanation is given in the final issue for the cessation of publication in 1891.

In 1889 the first of four volumes in a University of Toronto Political Science series was published, *The Ontario Township* by J.M. McEvoy. This series and *Le Canada Français* are the only examples of the involvement of Canadian universities in scholarly publication up to 1890.

In 1894, the Royal Society of Canada published a volume containing the bibliographies of its members, both living and dead.[20] There is not much doubt that this records almost every publication of scholarly or scientific substance produced by a Canadian between 1861 and 1890. Many of the bibliographies are extensive: 200 items are listed for William Saunders, 178 for C.J.S. Bethune, 111 for Benjamin Sulte, 90 for Robert Bell, 67 for J.G. Bourinot (who edited the volume). The quality of the scientific papers of men like Saunders, Osler, J.G. McGregor, D.P. Penhallow, and Robert Bell is indicated by the fact that some of their papers appeared in the most reputable British and American journals. One notes, however, that the chief publications of a substantial number of the members of the scientific sections were school text books - James Loudon, *Algebra for Beginners*, Ramsay Wright, *An Introduction to Zoology for the Use of High Schools*, W.L. Goodwin, *Textbook in Chemistry*, N.F. Dupuis, *Synthetic Solid Geometry* (and five others). The international world of science did not benefit from such efforts, but young Canadians did. Someone had to do this job.

For Sections I and II, those concerned with the humanities and social sciences, Bourinot's assessment is close to the truth: 'a conscientious spirit of research, patient industry and not a little literary skill in the management of their material.' The only scholar in the humanities and the social sciences with an international reputation in his field in 1890 was John Watson, Professor of Philosophy at Queen's University, whose *Kant and his English Critics* and *Schelling's Transcendental Idealism* had been published (in Scotland) in the early 1880s. Watson's principal publications lay in the future, but by 1890 he had made a start.[21] The same can be said for Canadian scholarship in general.

NOTES TO CHAPTER 12

1   J.G. Bourinot, 'Our Intellectual Strengths and Weaknesses: A Short Review of Literature, Education and Art,' *Trans. Royal Society Canada* 1893, section 2, 3-36. See also Bourinot's *The Intellectual Development of Canada* (1881).
2   G.M. Dawson, 'The Progress and Trend of Scientific Investigation in Canada,' *Proc. Royal Society Canada* 1894, lii-lxvi
3   Dawson, 'Progress,' liii
4   Ibid.
5   Bourinot, 'Intellectual Strengths,' 28

6 M.Y. Williams, 'The Earth Sciences and the Royal Society of Canada,' *Trans. Royal Society Canada* 1961, 67

7 The full-time staff figure is taken from the annual report. Part-time staff of the survey included a number of university professors who were active in the summer. A photograph by William Notman of the staff of the Geological Survey in 1888, reproduced in E. Hall, ed., *Early Canada: a Collection of Historical Photographs of Officers of the Geological Survey of Canada* (1967), includes 46 persons, among them F.D. Adams of McGill, J.-C.-K. Laflamme of Laval, and L.W. Bailey of New Brunswick.

8 Dawson, 'Progress,' lvii

9 Ibid., lix

10 For the establishment and early development of the Experimental Farm, see *Canada, Fifty Years of Progress on Dominion Experimental Farms, 1886-1936* (1936). Saunders's report appeared as an appendix to the Minister of Agriculture Annual Report for 1885 and was separately published as *Agricultural Colleges and Experimental Farm Stations with Suggestions Relating to Experimental Agriculture in Canada* (1886).

11 Dawson, 'Progress,' lxii

12 H.B. Hackey, *History of the Fisheries Research Board of Canada* (1965), 29-45

13 Dawson, 'Progress,' lvi

14 The publications of the Literary & Historical Society of Quebec between 1861 and 1890 included five series of historical documents dated 1861, 1866/67, 1871, 1875, and 1877.

15 W.S. Wallace, ed., *Royal Canadian Institute Centennial Volume* (1949), 153-4

16 'Medical Journals' in H.E. Macdermot, *One Hundred Years of Medicine in Canada* (1967), 156-66

17 D.W. Gullett, *A History of Dentistry in Canada* (1965), 291-3

18 A review of nineteenth-century journals in the English language is included in H.P. Gundy, 'Literary Publishing' in C.F. Klinck, ed., *Literary History of Canada* (1969), 174-88. See also for journals in both languages 'Literary Magazines' in N. Story, ed., *Oxford Companion to Canadian History and Literature* (1967).

19 A.B. Routhier, 'Le Canada Français: son but et son programme,' *Canada Français, 1* (1888), 10-11

20 J.G. Bourinot, *Bibliography of the Members of the Royal Society of Canada* (1894)

21 Watson's achievement is assessed by J.A. Irving and A.H. Johnson in 'Philosophical Literature to 1910' in C.F. Klinck, ed., *Literary History of Canada*, 436-42.

1920

WHEREAS the Dominion Government does not in any way contribute to the support of higher education in the Dominion and WHEREAS the majority of the Universities of the Dominion are almost wholly dependent for their maintenance and development on gifts from private citizens ...

Preamble to Resolution adopted by the
Conference of Canadian Universities,
17 May 1920

13
The Conference of Canadian Universities, 1911-1920

Representatives of Canadian universities and colleges met together for two days in May 1920 at Université Laval in Quebec City to discuss a variety of problems related to Canadian higher education. They did so in a formal context, this being the seventh meeting of the National Conference of Canadian Universities.[1]

The first attempt to promote joint action by a group of Canadian universities occurred in 1891 when a conference, convened by the minister of education for Ontario, was held at Queen's University in Kingston to discuss university extension work. It was attended by representatives of most of the Ontario universities and of McGill, and one of the conclusions reached was that there should be a Canadian association for the extension of university teaching. Such an association was formed but it met only once - at Toronto in 1892, the delegates on this occasion including a representative from the University of New Brunswick. The Queen's conference of 1891 did lead, however, to joint action with respect to extension work in both Ontario and Quebec. In Quebec a committee on University Extension involving McGill, Laval, and Bishop's met on several occasions during the next few years, and in Ontario, though no committee was formally established, similar discussions were held. By 1900, however, this movement had died out.[2]

In 1903 there occurred an event which could have brought the National Conference of Canadian Universities into being a decade before it was in fact constituted. This was the Allied Colonial Universities Conference held at Burlington House in London, England on 9 July and organized by Sir Gilbert Parker, a Canadian, who had been living in England since 1897 and who had been a member of the British Parliament since 1900.[3] Fourteen Canadian universities were represented at this conference.

Lord Bryce, who was chairman of the morning session, began the proceedings by explaining the purpose of the gathering, which he described as 'the first Conference of the kind that has ever been held': 'We are met to consider what we can do to enable the uni-

versities of the British world to help one another, and to develop
their functional activities partly by combination and partly,
where there is room for that method, by specialisation also.'[4]
This was quite a task to undertake in a single day but the committee in charge made it possible by presenting two resolutions
for approval, one at the beginning of the morning session and
one at the beginning of the afternoon session. The discussion
therefore was always focused on a specific question, and, since
many of the speakers were men of great distinction (Bryce, R.B.
Haldane, Lord Kelvin, Oliver Lodge, Henry Roscoe, Sir William
Ramsay), the proceedings make remarkably good reading. The resolutions, both of which were passed unanimously and without amendment, were these:

> That ... it is desirable that such relations should be estab-
> lished between the principal teaching Universities of the Empire
> as will secure that special or local advantages for study, and
> in particular for post-graduate study and research, be made as
> accessible as possible to students from all parts of the King's
> Dominions.

> That a Council, consisting in part of representatives of British
> and Colonial Universities, be appointed to promote the objects
> set out in the previous Resolution.

Resolution 2 went on to name particular persons as members of a
committee to establish the council, among them Bryce, Kelvin,
Lodge, Gilbert Parker, and Lord Strathcona (Donald Smith), the
chancellor of McGill and the Canadian high commissioner, London.
    There is no record of this council ever having met.[5] Nor was
there any reference to it in the proceedings of the Congress of
the Universities of the Empire which was held at the University
of London in 1912; this is surprising since the objectives of
the 1912 congress were essentially the same as those of the 1903
conference and since Parker was a member of the organizing committee. It is also odd that the Allied Colonial Conference was
not referred to by any of the Canadians who in 1911 and 1915 organized the National Conference of Canadian Universities, since
a number of them attended it. One suspects, however, that the
1903 conference had positive effects, both in England and elsewhere. The fact that some of those who attended the conference
of Canadian universities held at McGill University on 6 June 1911
were not strangers to one another and had in fact been over the
same ground on an earlier occasion may well explain why the first
Canadian universities conference was not the last.
    The meeting at McGill in 1911 was arranged by its principal,
William Peterson, and Robert Falconer, president of the University of Toronto, who at the request of the committee which was
by this time organizing the congress to be held in London the
following year, invited the presidents of the Canadian universities to meet together for the purpose of discussing the congress

agenda. Invitations were sent to 19 universities: Acadia, Alberta, British Columbia (at this time operating as McGill University College of British Columbia), Bishop's, Dalhousie, King's, Laval, McGill, McMaster, Manitoba, Mount Allison, New Brunswick, Ottawa, Queen's, St Francis Xavier, St Joseph's, Saskatchewan, Toronto, Western Ontario. All but two accepted (Acadia and King's) and all but four attended - at the last moment the representatives of Alberta and Manitoba were unable to be present.

The conference began with a statement by R.D. Roberts, university extension registrar at the University of London, who had been appointed secretary of the congress, outlining the history of the movement that had culminated in the decision to hold a congress and the subjects proposed for discussion at it. He stressed the tentative nature of the proposed agenda and pointed out that 'it was open to any University or group of Universities to suggest other questions than those mentioned in the programme for consideration.'[6] His audience took him seriously, and, though the London Congress was kept constantly in mind, the discussion took the form of a general review of the problems of higher education in Canada, some of which, for example the conducting of examinations in music, were local problems which would not have been of any interest to professors or vice-chancellors from Oxford, Melbourne, and Bombay. Most of the problems were ones facing universities wherever they were located (matriculation standards, graduate work, exchange of professors) but, quite properly, they were consistently discussed in the context of the Canadian situation. At the end of the day it was agreed that the Canadian delegates to the 1912 Congress should meet in Montreal on their way to London if this was felt to be either necessary or desirable by a committee consisting of Peterson, Falconer, Professor James Cappon of Queen's, and the Reverend Gaspard Dauth, vice-rector of Université Laval at Montreal. No meeting was held in 1912, but two of the members of this committee, Peterson and Falconer, were instrumental in calling a second conference.

The second conference of Canadian universities was again a one-day affair, the representatives of 15 universities meeting at the University of Toronto on 1 June 1915. The delegates were presented with a program which called for discussion of the following topics:

A. Standards for Degrees - undergraduate, professional, and postgraduate
    (1) Matriculation
    (2) Length of course for degrees
    (3) Honor courses
    (4) Postgraduate work
B. Transfer of Students
    (1) Equivalents in curricula
    (2) Good standing required from students
    (3) Evaluation of certificate issued by Education Department

     (4) Relation of University degrees of the several Provinces
         to Professional Societies
C. Student Life
     (1) College Athletics
     (2) Officers' Training Corps
     (3) Halls of Residence and rules for resident students
     (4) Greek Letter Societies
D. Administration
     (1) Sources of Income of Canadian Universities
     (2) Methods of Appointment and Promotion
     (3) Form of Permanent Organization of Conference

The conference began by dealing with A (1) - Matriculation. This provoked 'considerable discussion,' but eventually a committee was appointed 'to examine into existing systems, including standards, and report.' The delegates dealt with the next topic, Length of Courses, in the same fashion, again concluding discussion by the appointment of a committee 'to investigate and report.' It was now time for lunch. The afternoon was devoted to appointing further committees - on organization (of the conference), on legal education, on medical education, on engineering education, on graduate work in general, on graduate work in agriculture in particular. There was no time to discuss any of the topics listed under C (Student Life) or those dealing with finance and appointments under D (Administration). The speakers at the dinner tendered to the delegates by the University of Toronto after the conference had adjourned tended to emphasize the need to develop strong graduate schools and the 'importance of the Universities of Canada co-operating more closely for the development of a truly national spirit.'[7]

It will come as no surprise to learn that the conference was extended to two days in 1916, or that most of the time at this and succeeding conferences was devoted to receiving and discussing reports submitted by the various committees that had been appointed and which would subsequently be appointed. Most of the committees were concerned with matters bearing on instruction and research, and reference will be made to certain of their reports in succeeding chapters. With respect to these 'academic' committees, all that needs to be emphasized here is that the conference gave about equal attention to problems related to (a) arts and science, (b) professional education, and (c) graduate study and research.

Of more immediate concern is the work of the conference in these early years on its own organization and in its relations with other bodies, notably the dominion government. A committee on organization was appointed at the 1915 conference. It submitted a draft constitution at the 1916 conference, which was approved with some amendments in 1917, and slightly amended in 1918. The constitution was a curious document, at least so far as membership was concerned. Twenty-eight institutions were named as members, one of which, Nova Scotia Agricultural College, did not have degree-granting powers. Université Laval at Quebec and Université Laval at Montreal were recognized as separate institutions, though the latter did not become the Université de Montréal until 1919. St Michael's, Trinity, and Victoria were included as members but were listed 'under' the University of Toronto, with which they were federated, as were the Ontario Agricultural College, which was a University of Toronto affiliate, and Osgoode Hall Law School, which was not. Brandon College was included 'under' McMaster. No criteria were given for membership, and no provision was made for the admission of new members. The constitution stated the number of delegates an institution could send to the annual conference, specified that there would be a conference each year, and provided for a fee of $10.00 to be paid by each institution to the conference for each delegate to which it was entitled. Provision was also made for sectional meetings – Eastern (the universities in the Maritime provinces); Central (Ontario and Quebec); Western (the four western provinces). No sectional meeting has ever been held. At the 1920 meeting the conference decided that since most of the delegates would be attending the Second Congress of the Universities of the Empire in 1921, the Canadian conference should not meet until 1922.

For the next twenty years the National Conference of Canadian Universities met at 2-year intervals. It did not become much involved with government until 1918 when it became concerned with the rehabilitation of World War I veterans. It is true that as early as 1915 some of its committees, for example the committee on graduate work in agriculture, began to discuss various matters with government departments at both federal and provincial levels. In 1916 the conference petitioned the dominion government with respect to the status of Chinese nationals attending Canadian universities, and in connection with compulsory military drill it appointed a committee 'to endeavour to harmonize university relations with the Government, and to take such action with regard to military matters affecting universities as they may consider necessary.' This committee did not find it necessary to report in 1917. But in 1918 the conference became concerned about the action (or the inaction) of the government with respect to veterans and much of the time of its meetings in 1919 and 1920 was concerned with these and allied matters.

The agenda of the 1920 conference, which was organized in three sessions, included a paper on forestry education presented by the director of the school of forestry established at Laval in 1910. There was also a presentation on the subject of military training by two invited guests, one representing the inspector general of military forces in Canada and one representing the Canadian Officers Training Corps. But most of the time was devoted to the reports of the nine committees which had been established at earlier conferences. Two of these were *ad hoc* committees with specific terms of reference, the committee to correspond with British and French universities and the committee to interview the premier on the education of soldiers. The other seven could be described as standing committees on academic affairs: matriculation, medical education, legal education, engineering education, graduate work in Canada, graduate work in agriculture, education for foreign trade and service, university co-operation in scientific and industrial research. The names of these committees reflect the subjects which were of compelling interest to the Canadian universities in the year 1920.

The conference passed a single resolution in the course of its deliberations, one that reflected a particular concern of the Canadian universities at this time:

That WHEREAS, the Dominion Government does not in any way contribute to the support of higher education in the Dominion, and WHEREAS the majority of the Universities of the Dominion are almost wholly dependent for their maintenance and development on gifts from private citizens; THEREFORE resolved that the Conference of the Universities of the Dominion respectfully petitions the Dominion Government to so amend the Income Tax Act that provision may be made ... for the exemption from income tax of any gift to a Canadian University.[8]

The constitution provided for an executive committee of five to act for the conference between meetings. Having passed the above resolution, the executive was directed 'to consider the advisability of memorializing the Governments of the several provinces with regard to the question of ear-marking a certain percentage of the money received as succession duties, for the purposes of the Universities' and empowered it to carry out the idea 'if it should be found practicable.'

By 1920, then, the National Conference of Canadian Universities was an organization which, in addition to meeting regularly to discuss the development of Canadian higher education, acted as the recognized spokesman for the universities of Canada at home and abroad. The contrast with the situation in 1890 when the universities had no form of organization at either the national or the provincial level is striking, and nothing more clearly indicates the change that had taken place in Canadian higher education in the intervening thirty years.

NOTES TO CHAPTER 13

1 The Conference of Canadian Universities (CCU) was named the National Conference of Canadian Universities (NCCU) in 1916. In 1958 it became the National Conference of Canadian Universities and Colleges (NCCUC), and in 1964 the Association of Universities and Colleges of Canada (AUCC). The proceedings of each of its meetings have been published, but until the 1950s without indication of the place of publication. Until 1958 responsibility for editing the proceedings rested with

the secretary-treasurer of the conference, and the individual
issues were printed in the city in which he was located. On
all matters bearing on the organization, see G. Pilkington,
'A History of the National Conference of Canadian Universities,
1911-1961.'

2 J.R. Kidd, *Adult Education in the Canadian University* (1956),
38-9.

3 'Official Report of the Allied Colonial Universities Conference
Held at Burlington House ... on July 9, 1903 ..., *Empire Review*,
6 (1903), 65-128. Prior to the conference there was published
at London a 32-page pamphlet entitled *The Allied Colonial
Universities Conference* which announced the program, stated
the two resolutions which would be considered by the delegates,
and reported the replies of the twelve universities in the
United Kingdom to certain questions posed to them by the organizing committee concerning the number of colonial students
in attendance and any special arrangements made for such students.

4 'Report Allied Colonial Conference,' 73

5 The 1903 conference is briefly discussed in E. Ashby, *Community of Universities: an Informal Portrait of the Association
of Universities of the British Commonwealth 1913-1963* (1963),
1-4. According to Ashby there was talk of another conference
in two years' time, 'but nothing came of this and nothing more
appears to have been done to promote cohesion among Commonwealth universities until 1909.'

6 *CCU Proc.* (1911), 5

7 Ibid. (1915), 18

8 *NCCU Proc.* (1920), 16

14

Institutional Development

THE MARITIMES

In 1921 the Carnegie Corporation of New York invited William
Learned of the Carnegie Foundation for the Advancement of Teaching
and Kenneth Sills, President of Bowdoin College in Maine, to visit
the educational institutions of the Maritime provinces 'with a
view to suggesting a constructive policy for the treatment particularly of the institutions that had applied for aid.'[1] During
the previous 10 years the corporation had received requests for
aid from Acadia, Dalhousie, King's, Mount Allison, New Brunswick,
and St Francis Xavier, and had made grants to Acadia ($30,000 for
its library in 1906, $75,000 for a faculty pension fund in 1920),
St Francis Xavier ($50,000 for a professorship of French in 1919),
and Dalhousie ($40,000 for a science building in 1912, $20,000
to repair damages caused by the Halifax harbour explosion of 1917,
$500,000 for development of the medical school in 1920).[2] Several
institutions had suggested the benefits to be gained from a general survey, and early in 1921 the corporation had been formally
invited to undertake such a study by the Province of Nova Scotia.
Learned and Sills conducted their visits in October and November
of that year, and their report, which was published by the corporation in 1922 under the title *Education in the Maritime Provinces*, is a detailed description of higher education in the
Maritimes at this time, one which began with an analysis of the
strengths and weaknesses of the seventeen institutions visited
and concluded with a proposal that higher education in the Maritime provinces be completely reorganized. The plan that Learned
and Sills recommended will be discussed in detail in chapter 20.
Basically it called for a concentration of higher education at
two centres: Halifax and Fredericton. King's, Acadia, Mount
Allison and St Francis Xavier would transfer their university
work to Halifax where, in association with Dalhousie, they would
become federated colleges of a University of the Maritime Provinces.

The existing campuses at Windsor, Wolfville, Sackville, and Antigonish would be used entirely for secondary school purposes. The
University of New Brunswick would remain an independent institution at Fredericton but would cooperate closely with the University at Halifax. The remaining institutions would become affiliates of one or other of these universities or revert to a
secondary school status.

Learned and Sills had something good to say about almost every
institution they visited. In general they were impressed by the
quality of the teaching staff and also by the management skills
of those in charge. But they were appalled by the conditions in
which the professors were required to teach and by the complete
inadequacy of the funds at the disposal of the presidents and
governors. They noted that so far as the degree-granting institutions were concerned government support was limited to the
annual grant made by the Province of Nova Scotia to the Nova
Scotia Technical College ($50,000) and by the Province of New
Brunswick to the University of New Brunswick ($25,000). This
meant that all the other universities were entirely dependent
upon student fees and endowment. But the combined endowment of
Acadia, Dalhousie, King's, Mount Allison, and St Francis Xavier,
which together enrolled about 1700 students, was substantially
less than that of any *one* of three New England colleges, Amherst,
Bowdoin, and Williams, none of which enrolled more than 500
students. Furthermore, where Amherst, Bowdoin, and Williams
concentrated on the liberal arts, the Maritime colleges also
offered courses in professional subjects. In the commissioner's
view it was doubtful that any of these colleges was providing
adequately for the needs of *all* their students, and it was certain that they were not providing adequately for the needs of
the one million people who lived in New Brunswick, Nova Scotia,
Prince Edward Island, and Newfoundland. What particularly dis-
turbed Learned and Sills was the unsatisfactory condition of
elementary and secondary education in the four provinces. The
basic problem here was the low quality of the teachers, and this
indicated the need for an improvement of teacher training. But
none of the universities was concerned with the training of
teachers. Furthermore, in an attempt to increase the income derived from students fees, the universities were undermining the
standards of secondary education by admitting freshmen who had
not fully matriculated.

It is worth emphasizing that the Learned-Sills report was entitled *Education in the Maritime Provinces of Canada*, not Higher
Education in the Maritime Provinces of Canada. Over and over
again the authors comment on the obligation a university has to
its constituency, and the complete reorganization they proposed
was based less on what they felt was good for the institutions
concerned as on what they felt was good for the people of the
Maritime provinces whose interests the institutions had been
established to serve.

Dalhousie they found to be the largest, best equipped, and

most important institution.[3] Compared with the other major universities in Canada (and Dalhousie was, in 1920, a major institution) it was not very large - 679 students, of whom 159 were in medicine, 68 in law, and 55 in each of dentistry and engineering. Faculties of medicine and dentistry had been established in 1911 and 1912 respectively through the absorption of the Halifax Medical College, hitherto an affiliate, and of the Maritime Dental College, which had been established and immediately affiliated with Dalhousie in 1908. There had been a faculty of engineering from 1906 to 1909, but it had been abolished with the establishment of the Nova Scotia Technical College as the single institution in Nova Scotia offering the final two years of engineering; engineering students at Dalhousie, as at Acadia, King's, St Francis Xavier, and Mount Allison, were enrolled in the first three years of a five year course. Dalhousie also had three affiliates: Mount Saint Vincent Academy, a Roman Catholic women's college established at Halifax in 1914 which offered the first two years of arts and science; the Maritime College of Pharmacy which had been established with the university's cooperation in 1911; and the Halifax Conservatory of Music. In 1920, the University was in the process of occupying a new 52-acre site a mile away from its old 8-acre campus, which was being turned over to the faculty of medicine, but at this stage only the library, a science building, the law school, and the first floor of an arts building had been constructed. The arts building had been temporarily converted into a gymnasium, and the arts departments were temporarily housed with law. The faculty of law did not obtain full possession of its building until the 1950s.

This considerable expansion had been made possible by gifts totalling $2,600,000 since 1890, the most substantial of which were the $500,000 grants received in 1920 for the development of the faculty of medicine from both the Carnegie Corporation and the Rockefeller Foundation.[4] General campaigns in 1912 and 1920 had raised $400,000 and $439,000 respectively. But relatively little of this money had been used to strengthen the undergraduate program in arts. Learned and Sills noted that in 1920-21 'only one person gave instruction in the entire group of Historical, Political, Social and Economic Sciences, and one person taught all the Psychology and Philosophy.' No courses were offered in education.[5]

The next largest university in the Maritimes in 1920 was Acadia with 330 students; 86 in engineering, 3 in theology, 18 categorized as special, and the remainder in arts and science. Acadia impressed Learned and Sills as being sound and well managed: 'the entire establishment gives everywhere the impression of thrift and skilful handling.'[6] It also was one of only three institutions which had anything to recommend it with regard to physical equipment:

There is nothing approaching a satisfactory provision for Science instruction except the beginnings to be found at

214

Dalhousie. The only elements worth mentioning at any of the other institutions are the Library at Acadia, which is a good start, or would be if it possessed larger reading and reference facilities, and the art collection and building at Mt. Allison, which could become the basis of good collegiate instruction in Fine Arts.[7]

Nonetheless, Acadia was not one of the two institutions which struck Learned and Sills as being 'a genuine college' - it was, like all the others except Dalhousie, and 'to a lesser extent,' St Francis Xavier, more properly described as a collegiate insti- tute.[8] This was because the campus at Wolfville comprised, in addition to the college, an academy and a ladies seminary, both of which had more students than the university. The academy was a secondary school for boys (Grades VIII-XI), with a commercial department (Grades XI and XII); the ladies seminary 'a combina- tion music, art and business school [which] offers also the usual secondary academic subjects.'[9] Learned and Sills felt that the mixing of secondary and higher education at such institutions as Acadia, Mount Allison, and King's was inhibiting the proper develop- ment of both. In their view an important advantage of consoli- dating higher education at Halifax was that the institutions re- maining at Wolfville, Sackville, and Windsor would be in a posi- tion to concentrate upon becoming outstanding secondary schools, and they would immediately have the increased physical faculties needed to make this possible.

Mount Allison, which had 262 students, was found to be 'fairly prosperous financially' but physically in very bad shape:

The buildings and equipment ... are seriously defective. The one adequate structure is the Men's Residence ... All univer- sity activities are crowded into Centennial Hall and a small Science building. The library (18,000 volumes) is stowed away in several different places, and part of it is totally inaccess- ible ... The physical situation is such as to make the erection of a library, a science hall and a women's residence imperative if the university is to remain where it is.[10]

If, however, the university were moved to Halifax, the vacated premises could profitably be used by the Ladies College (over 400 students) and by the Academy for Boys (over 200 students).

King's College at Windsor was in even worse shape physically than Mount Allison since its main building had been totally des- troyed by fire in 1920: 'With the main building gone the College has a chapel, a large convocation hall used now for a dining hall above and a library below, and a small wooden dormitory in which classes are held. The library is fairly large but is not kept up. It is open but two afternoons a week, and the most valuable books were found boxed and piled near the main entrance for ready re- covery in case of another fire.'[11] This was the situation in which the 73 students in arts, the 18 in engineering, and the 4

in theology found themselves in the fall of 1921. Their class-
mates in law were not much better off; they attended classes in
the late afternoon and evening in various courtrooms and two
rented rooms in Saint John, New Brunswick. In 1892 a group of
lawyers in Saint John had established a proprietary law school
which King's had agreed to accept as its faculty of law after the
University of New Brunswick had declined to do so. 'The Dean was
paid $350 by the university at Windsor, which is then reimbursed
in the same amount from Saint John. The balance, after certain
expenses are paid, is divided among the teachers.'[12]

No reason except the obvious one has been given for the University of New Brunswick's refusal to adopt the Saint John Law School
in 1892. Certainly New Brunswick could have used a few more students; in 1891 its enrolment was 77. This had risen to 105 in
1900 and to 177 in 1920. Its provincial grant was increased from
$8844.48 to $14,000 in 1906 to permit the extension of its work
in engineering and the introduction of a course in forestry; in
1911 it was increased to $17,000, in 1913 to $20,000, and in 1919
to $25,000. With no endowment to speak of, New Brunswick was en-
tirely dependent upon the provincial grant and student fees.

The institution in the Maritimes which had made the most progress between 1890 and 1920 was St Francis Xavier at Antigonish,
even though its full-time enrolment remained relatively small –
194 – and most of the development occurred following the assumption of the presidency by the Rev. Hugh MacPherson in 1906.[13]
MacPherson, who continued as president until 1936, laid the
foundation for the outstanding work which St Francis did in the
area of adult education in the 1920s and 1930s by building up a
strong academic staff during the first dozen years of his régime.
Staff members were sent to complete their graduate training at
American universities, and alumni and friends of the university
were encouraged to endow professorships – English, history, geology in 1907, Gaelic in 1908, classics in 1913. A chapel was
built in 1910 but also a science building, a gymnasium in 1916
but also a library. The $50,000 received in 1920 from the Car-
negie Corporation for a chair in French carried with it a commitment that the university would provide a similar amount for a
chair of education. To Learned and Sills 'its courses appear[ed]
sound, and its aims well defined and of high standard.' But they
also were impressed by the university's sense of dedication and
its concern for problems whose locus extended beyond the limits
of the campus:

The college has recognised and endeavoured in an original and
effective manner to fulfill its educational obligations to its
constituency. It has organized and conducts each year a 2-
months People's School for untrained adults, which has been
notably successful. Its interest in the problem of providing
rural teachers for its vicinity takes the practical form of
offering scholarships based on service in such schools.[14]

216

Of the institutions not yet mentioned which were in existence
in 1890, about all that one can report is survival: St Joseph's
at Memramcook, St Mary's at Halifax, Collège Ste Anne at Church
Point, and St Dunstan's at Charlottetown. The latter obtained
degree-granting powers in 1917 but did not begin to exercise them
until 1941.

Two other institutions were given degree-granting powers during
this period, the Collège du Sacré Coeur at Caraquet, New Brunswick,
in 1900 and the Nova Scotia Technical College at Halifax in 1907.
The former, a classical college established by the Eudist Fathers
in 1899, granted 28 degrees between 1904 and 1915, when following
a disastrous fire it was moved to Bathurst, New Brunswick. The
Nova Scotia Technical College was opened in 1909 and granted its
first degrees in 1910. Learned and Sills, who described it as
'well officered and adequately equipped for its strictly limited
function,' noted that its establishment, which included among its
by-products the withdrawal of faculties of engineering at Dalhousie
and St Francis Xavier and the dropping of plans to establish
others, was a striking example of the positive gains to be derived
through cooperation by Maritime institutions.

The report also referred to five other institutions, the normal
schools at Fredericton, New Brunswick, and Truro, Nova Scotia,
the Nova Scotia Agricultural College at Truro, and two colleges
which later became chartered universities, St Thomas College at
Chatham, New Brunswick and Mount St Vincent Academy at Halifax.
St Thomas College was described as a 'boys school of not more than
junior college grade';[15] it obtained degree-granting powers in
1934. Mount St Vincent was offering the first two years of arts
and science in affiliation with Dalhousie University and became
a degree-granting institution in 1925.

QUEBEC

The most important event in the history of higher education in
French-speaking Canada between 1890 and 1920 was the granting of
a charter to the Montreal branch of Université Laval in 1919.
This necessitated reorganization at Quebec quite as much as at
Montreal, and the changes paved the way for the emergence of a
new conception of the role of the French-language university in
Canada. But while the signs of this new attitude had already
begun to reveal themselves in structural terms at Montréal by
1920 and at Laval by 1921, many years were to elapse before the
reorganization would be completed and the new role clearly defined.
The faculties of letters, sciences, social sciences, and philosophy which both universities wished to establish in 1920 were
not in all cases organized until 1940, and it was not until 1960
that all of these were functioning with the effectiveness their
founders had in mind. In many respects the position of Laval and
Montréal in 1920 was similar to what it had been in 1890. The

same was true of the two English-speaking universities in the Province. Bishop's remained a small college, McGill continued to be a large and important university.

During the first 10 years of this period Bishop's struggled to become a university in fact as well as in name by developing programs of a professional nature. In 1893, at the urging of the Association of Dental Surgeons of the Province of Quebec, it agreed to provide some lectures for dental students through the agency of its faculty of medicine in Montreal, and in 1896 a department of dentistry was established at Montreal with students proceeding to a Bishop's D.D.S. degree.[16] This venture came to an end when the Bishop's Medical School became part of McGill in 1905. The absorption of its medical school also ended Bishop's always tenuous relationship with medical education; its equally tenuous connection with legal education had ended with the suspension of the faculty of law at Sherbrooke in the early 1890s. In 1898 a course of lectures in the art of teaching was introduced, 'with the view of qualifying graduates of the University for Academy [secondary school teaching] diplomas';[17] but within a few years the Calendar stated that this course would only be given if a sufficient number of candidates applied. Apparently there were enough in 1920-21, since 11 of Bishop's students in that year were in education. But the total enrolment at Bishop's in that year was 71.

A good case can be made that in 1890 McGill was the leading university in Canada. The argument would be based on the strength of its science departments and of its professional faculties, particularly medicine and applied science. On the arts side the position was less impressive; in the humanities and in the emerging social sciences at least three other universities, Dalhousie, Queen's, and Toronto, were stronger. The appointment of William Peterson, a distinguished classicist, as principal in succession to the polymath scientist J.W. Dawson in 1895 suggested that McGill would now turn its attention to strengthening its arts departments, but this was not in fact what happened.[18] McGill's development continued to emphasize the areas in which it was already strong, as is indicated by the list of major buildings constructed on the main campus during this 30-year period, Engineering 1893, Physics 1893, Library 1893, Chemistry and Mining 1898, Royal Victoria College (a women's residence) 1898, Medicine 1901, Engineering 1909 (replacing the 1893 building destroyed by fire in 1907), Student Union 1911, Medicine 1911 (replacing the 1901 building also destroyed by fire in 1907), Stadium 1920. In addition a second campus was established for Macdonald College at Ste Anne-de-Bellevue on the west extremity of Montreal in 1907, with facilities for agriculture, household science, and teacher training; the McGill Normal School moved to this campus, and for the first time became an integral part of the University's operation.[19]

This extensive building program, made possible by gifts from individual donors like Sir William Macdonald, greatly increased McGill's physical facilities for both teaching and research and enabled it to expand its offerings in the area of professional education not only into agriculture and household science but, towards the end of the period, into dentistry, nursing, and social work as well. By 1920, it was unquestionably Canada's most famous university, the institution from which Sir William Osler had graduated and where he had done his early teaching, where Sir Ernest Rutherford had conducted his Nobel prize-winning experiments in radiation physics, and where Stephen Leacock taught economics and political science, when he was not writing his humorous books. The fame of McGill also owed something to the enthusiasm of the many Americans who had been attracted to and graduated from its medical school.

While the chartering of the Université de Montréal was the most significant event in French Canada during this period, it was by no means the only event of importance. There was a steady expansion of facilities for higher education with respect to both liberal arts and professional training. Five new colleges offering the complete eight year course to the B.A. were established between 1890 and 1920, bringing the total to 22, and six other colleges were founded which provided a six-year program, with their graduates proceeding to another college for the final two years of philosophy. More significant still, provision was made in 1908 for women students to obtain the B.A. with the opening at Montreal by the Congregation of Notre Dame of what was initially called l'Ecole d'enseignement supérieur pour les jeunes filles, and from 1925 Collège Marguerite-Bourgeois.[20] This institution confined itself to preparing students for the two examinations set by the university, lettres (at the end of the sixth year) and sciences (at the end of the eighth); the first four years of the eight-year classical course had to be provided for girls elsewhere, and this led to the establishment of convents offering what was called enseignement primaire supérieur. Between 1911 and 1920 11 of these schools were established, each of which was recognised as an affiliate of Laval. Also granted this status were two other schools for girls which concentrated on household science, and six for boys which provided enseignement secondaire moderne, a course approximately paralleling the first six years of the classical course, but without Latin and Greek. The consequence of all these developments was that in 1919 Université Laval's influence extended to all forms of secondary education in the province. With the establishment of Université de Montréal, there was a division of affiliates between the two universities, those located in the dioceses controlled by the Archbishop of Montreal becoming affiliates of the new university. Of the existing classical colleges six remained affiliates of Université Laval,[21] while 13 entered the Université de Montréal orbit; the latter included l'Ecole d'enseignement supérieur pour les jeunes filles, and the two Jesuit Colleges at Montreal which enjoyed special status, Collège Ste Marie and Loyola.[22] A papal decree of 1889 had authorized Collège Ste Marie to present its candidates for degrees without the necessity of writing the examinations set by the university; the same

privilege was extended to Loyola when it was established as an
English-speaking college in 1896.

The expansion of professional education took place chiefly at
Montreal. At Quebec the principal institutional development was
the establishment of an Ecole d'arpentage (surveying) in 1907 and
of an Ecole forestière in 1910, which were merged as L'Ecole
d'arpentage et de génie forestier in 1919. In both cases the
funds to establish and maintain the institution were provided by
the government. Two agricultural schools also affiliated with
Laval, Institut Agricole d'Oka, established in 1892 by a religious
order, the Trappists, in 1908, and l'Ecole d'Agriculture de Ste
Anne-de-la-Pocatière in 1912. With the establishment of the
Université de Montréal, Oka's affiliation was transferred to the
new university, but Ste Anne continued as an affiliate of Laval
and in 1940 became its faculty of agriculture. These several
affiliates were attached to the faculté des arts; in 1920 Laval
continued to have only the four traditional faculties, arts, law,
medicine, theology. However, the basis for two new faculties
were laid at this time with the establishment in 1921 of l'Ecole
normale supérieure and l'Ecole supérieure de chimie. Designed
in the first instance to provide for the needs of secondary school
teachers, these developed respectively into the faculté des
lettres in 1937 and the faculté des sciences in 1938.

According to the Act establishing the Université de Montréal,
the University consisted of faculties and schools which were completely integrated (fusionnées) and of schools (or even faculties)
which were affiliées, agrégées, or annexées. An école agrégée
was the same as an école affiliée except that it was located outside the Province of Quebec; in both cases the University established the course of study and set the examinations. In the case
of an école annexée the University approved the course of study
and was involved in the examination process. Ecoles annexées
were completely independent so far as finance was concerned.
Initially there were six faculties and six schools, three of the
schools being annexée. The faculties were théologie, droit,
médecine, philosophie, lettres, sciences, the first three being
carryovers from the period of association with Laval, and the
latter three new creations. The écoles fusionnées, which had
been founded either by individuals or by a professional association, were l'Ecole de médecine vétérinaire, an affiliate since
1893, l'Ecole de chirurgie dentaire founded in 1894 and affiliated
since 1904, and l'Ecole de pharmacie, established and affiliated
in 1906. Of the three écoles annexées, two had been established
by the government, l'Ecole polytechnique in 1874 and l'Ecole des
hautes études commerciales in 1907, and the third, Institut
agricole d'Oka, had been supported by an annual government grant
from the outset. It will be noted that there was no faculté des
arts. The classicial colleges, including l'Ecole d'enseignement
supérieur pour les jeunes filles were classified as écoles
annexées. In practice, however, the term école annexée has always been used at Université de Montréal to designate institutions

primarily concerned with instruction at a sub-matriculation level.
In the 1920-21 *Annuaire* the classical colleges, Ecole polytechnique, Ecole des hautes études commerciales, and Institut agricole
d'Oka were listed as *affiliée*.

ONTARIO

In 1890 the prospects for rapid and effective development of
higher education in Ontario were bright. A new university,
McMaster, had just opened in Toronto with the largest initial
endowment in Canadian history. Ottawa had been accorded the
status of a Catholic university by papal decree in 1889. Victoria
had decided to pool its resources with those of the University of
Toronto and was in the process of moving from Cobourg to Toronto.
Queen's, having decided in 1885 not to enter the proposed confederation, succeeded in the next three years in raising the substantial sum of $260,000, which enabled it to further strengthen
an already strong faculty of arts. Trinity, which had also declined to enter into federation with the University of Toronto,
was well-accommodated and seemingly in a position to carry on its
limited operation indefinitely. Most important of all, a solution
had been found to the University of Toronto question which successive legislatures had been struggling with for half a century.
The Federation Act of 1887 re-established the University of
Toronto as a teaching institution and at the same time, through
its arrangements for federated and affiliated status, provided
a satisfactory university connection for theological colleges
like Knox and Wycliffe, for professional schools such as those
that had been established by the dental and pharmacy professions,
and for the engineering and agricultural colleges which the
government itself had established.
But 1890 proved to be a false dawn. During the next 15 years
the bright prospects faded one after the other. McMaster had a
$1 million endowment, but its campus measured only 250 feet by
250 feet. Not all of the endowment was immediately available
and the purchasing power of the funds was reduced over the years
by deflation and overly conservative investment. McMaster made
progress but slowly. Ottawa had financial problems throughout
the 1890s, but in 1901 realized the dream it had been entertaining
for a quarter of a century - a science building which would enable it to provide properly for science and engineering. However, in 1904 Ottawa's main building was destroyed by fire and
the science hall was required for other purposes. Trinity now
found it expedient to enter into federation with the University
of Toronto in 1904. Western Ontario revived its faculty of arts
in 1895 but was constantly in a state of financial crisis; in
1904-5 its income was $3502, its expenditures $4444. In 1893
Queen's received a $5000 grant from the province to establish a
school of mines, and by 1905 the government had contributed over
$250,000 to what was in effect the university's faculty of engi-

221

neering; but Queen's had been frustrated in its attempts to establish schools of veterinary medicine and forestry.[23] In 1902 Principal Grant died. A year earlier he had finally convinced the board of trustees and the general assembly of the Presbyterian Church of Canada that the university should become independent of the church, and that the faculty of theology should become a separate institution, controlled by the church and affiliated with the university. But within a month of Grant's death, opposition to the proposal began to develop. Queen's did attain its independence but not until 1912, and in the meantime it remained a denominationally controlled institution and therefore ineligible for government grants. Support for the Kingston School of Mines, which was technically an affiliate of Queen's, was funnelled through an independent board.

Queens' chief rival in Ontario, the University of Toronto, was, if anything, in an even more unsatisfactory position. Its authorities had assumed that the government would provide substantial support on a continuing basis for the 'new' university created by the Federation Act, and this seemed a justifiable assumption in the light of a second Act passed in 1887 which 'authorized the Lieutenant-Governor-in-Council to defray the current expenses of the said University of Toronto and University College, including in both cases, the care and maintenance and ordinary repairs of the property assigned for their use.'[24] But this clause was interpreted by the government as signifying only that it must approve all expenditures charged against the university's general income fund. Aside from odd grants provided to meet emergency and other extenuating circumstances, government support during the 10 years following the 1887 Act was meagre. Thus, the university was forced to draw on its endowment funds in order to finance new buildings in these years (Biology, 1888; Library, 1892; Gymnasium, 1894; Chemistry, 1895) and to provide for new professorships.

In 1897 the government agreed to pay $7000 a year to the university, and in 1901 it began to provide annual grants to the science departments, and to make up any deficits incurred in the normal operating budget. But these were *ad hoc* measures which made it difficult for the university to carry on its existing programs and impossible for it to develop new ones. The great need for funds to further the institution's development was one of the main reasons for the appointment in 1905 of a Royal Commission on the University of Toronto.

The Commission report was submitted in April 1906, and as a result of its recommendations the government decided to turn over to the board of governors a sum equal to 50 per cent of the provincial succession duties to meet operating expenses. In addition to this welcome aid, in the previous year legislation had been passed which provided nearly $500,000 to be used for construction of long-needed plant facilities: a physics building, a convocation hall, men's residences, annexes to the women's residence and to the science building, and the relocation of the Toronto General Hospital. Meanwhile, in 1906 President Loudon

222

had submitted his resignation, and now with adequate financing and a new executive head, the Rev. Robert Falconer, the university was able to undertake academic expansion into new fields which the Royal Commission had prescribed: a faculty of household science (1906), a faculty of education for training secondary school teachers (1907), and a faculty of forestry (1909). The 1906 University Act, passed as a result of the Royal Commission Report, had implemented the commission's recommendation that the School of Practical Science become a completely integrated part of the university as the faculty of applied science and engineering. The faculty of medicine now had excellent facilities on both the medical and clinical sides. With the federation of Trinity in 1904 there were three arts colleges, and with the development of a full arts program at St Michael's between 1906 and 1910 the number was raised to four.[25]

This golden period came to an end in 1914 when not only did a world war check the progress of all Canadian universities, but the province decided to limit the amount of the annual grant to $500,000 in the event that 50 per cent of the succession duties exceeded this amount. By 1920, the university was once more in financial trouble. Part of the rationale for the government's decision to place a ceiling on support for the University of Toronto was that it was beginning to recognize some obligation to help finance two other Ontario universities.

In 1912, Queen's became independent of the Presbyterian Church and, thereby, in the government's view, eligible for grants. It had, as we have seen, been receiving money indirectly through the Kingston School of Mines since 1893 and since 1907 had received a grant for the faculty of education which had been established that year at the request of the government. An additional grant was received in 1912 for a public health medical laboratory, and in 1913 an amount was included for the faculty of arts. The total grant in 1913 was $74,000, in 1915 $127,000, in 1919 $176,000, or $256,000 if an $80,000 grant to the Kingston General Hospital with which the medical faculty was functionally related is included.

A similar pattern had developed at Western University in London. In 1908 it became independent of the Church of England and in 1910 received a $10,000 grant for its institute of public health. In 1917 the grant included an amount for the faculty of medicine and for the faculty of arts as well as for the institute of public health. In 1919 the total grant had risen to $84,000. At this point the government decided to review the whole question of university grants, and a royal commission on university finances was appointed in October 1920. Its report,[26] presented in February 1921, recognized that the government's first responsibility was to support the University of Toronto ('it is a primary obligation upon the Province to make the Provincial University worthy of the intelligence, wealth and resources of the Province') but also that, since Queen's and Western were providing a special service for the eastern and southwestern districts of Ontario, they also should receive regular and substantial assistance.

As we shall see in chapter 20, this view was adopted as government policy.

In 1920 close to 90 per cent of the students in Ontario universities were registered either at Toronto or Queen's, whose respective enrolments were 5073 and 1503.[27] Western, which did not adopt the name University of Western Ontario until 1923, had 331 - 192 in arts, 132 in medicine, 7 in nursing. The remaining two universities, McMaster and Ottawa, which at this stage offered only arts and theology, had enrolments of 259 and 192.

The basis for two other Ontario universities was laid during the latter half of this 30-year period and a significant development occurred in the evolution of a third. In 1919 Assumption College at Windsor and the Ursuline College at Chatham entered into affiliation with Western.[28] Ursuline College was moved to London in 1920 and, though remaining technically an affiliate, as Brescia College, it became an integrated part of the University of Western Ontario. Assumption remained at Windsor and after 34 years as one of Western's arts colleges became in 1953 Assumption University of Windsor. In 1911 there was established at Waterloo the Evangelical Lutheran Theological Seminary which in 1914 began to offer a secondary school course leading to senior matriculation in what was initially called Waterloo College School.[29] In 1923 the first year of arts was offered in the Waterloo College of Arts, and as Waterloo College this institution became affiliated with the University of Western Ontario in 1925. In 1959 it became Waterloo Lutheran University (renamed Wilfrid Laurier University in 1973). Finally there was established at Sudbury in 1913 a classical college whose first graduates received their B.A.s from Laval in 1922. In 1960 it became Université de Sudbury, one of the institutions which joined together to form the federated Laurentian University.[30]

THE WEST

Prior to 1903 applications having been made by denominational bodies to the Legislative Assembly of the North West Territories for the incorporation of colleges with degree-granting powers, the Hon. F.W.G. Haultain, Premier of the Territories, who was also Minister of Education, introduced in that year a bill making provision for the establishment of one University and one only for the Territories, in order to avoid a repetition of the evils which by reason of competing institutions had been experienced by the Eastern Provinces. This bill was enacted by the Legislative Assembly without opposition and received general approval from the public.[31]

This statement appeared in the report of a committee consisting of the presidents of the universities of Saskatchewan, Toronto, and Dalhousie which the Province of Alberta appointed in 1914 to advise it whether a second university should be established in that

province. The provinces of Alberta and Saskatchewan had been
created out of the North West Territories in 1905, and one of the
first acts passed by the legislature of Alberta was that establishing a provincial university. This act was passed in 1906.
In 1907 H.M. Tory, a professor of mathematics at McGill, was
appointed president, and in 1908 the University opened in rented
rooms in Edmonton with a faculty of 5 and a student body of 45.
Initially there was a single faculty, arts and science, but by
1914 there were two others, law and applied science, and also a
department of extension. The enrolment was 418. By this time,
too, the university was occupying its own campus on the outskirts
of the provincial capital. Although Edmonton was the capital, it
was rivalled in size by Calgary, 200 miles to the south, whose
influential inhabitants had argued that, since Edmonton had been
chosen as the seat of government, Calgary should be the seat of
the provincial university. When this argument failed, a movement began to have a second university at Calgary.[32] In 1911
the legislature authorized the incorporation of a Calgary college
but denied it degree-granting powers. Nonetheless Calgary
College opened in 1912, with 4 professors and 24 full-time students, and it was still operating (17 full-time students) in 1914;
hence the appointment of a Royal Commission. The commission
recommended that for the time being university work in the province be concentrated at Edmonton but that an institute of technology and arts be established at Calgary. However, by this time
World War I had broken out, and, discouraged by the commission's
report, the sponsors of Calgary College closed its doors, thus
ending the existence of an institution that had been reported to
the Congress of the Universities of the Empire in 1912 as one of
the 'lusty babes of this spring.'[33]

Saskatchewan, the other province created in 1905, followed an
almost identical course. An act establishing the University of
Saskatchewan was passed by the legislature in April 1907; W.C.
Murray, a professor of philosophy at Dalhousie University, was
appointed president in August 1908; and the university opened in
September 1909, also in rented quarters, also as a faculty of
arts and science, also with a faculty of five, but with 70 registered students rather than 45. By 1914, when President Murray
was serving on the Calgary College Commission, the University of
Saskatchewan had faculties (which it has always called colleges)
of arts and science, agriculture (1912), and law (1913), schools
(departments) of engineering (1912) and pharmacy (1914), an enrolment of 406, and a campus on the outskirts of the city of
Saskatoon. As in Alberta, the location of the single provincial
university was a problem, since once again there were two important centres, the other being Regina, which had been selected as
the capital. However, this matter was settled by the board of
governors in 1909 in Saskatoon's favour. Interest in developing
a university at Regina did not revive until the 1920s.

Another major question was decided in 1908; whether Saskatchewan
should follow the example of Ontario and Manitoba in having its

225

agricultural college on a campus of its own, thus making it effectively independent of the provincial university, or whether the
college of agriculture should be located on the main campus and
made an integral part of the provincial university. The board of
governors proposed the latter alternative after sending a committee of board and senate members on a month's tour of American
universities. Their report did not, however, convince the minister
of agriculture, who decided to send his deputy minister on a similar trip. When the deputy minister returned with the same recommendation, the minister not only agreed to the proposal but turned
over to the college of agriculture the extension work which his
own department had been carrying on since 1905. He also released
two of his most senior officials, one of whom was the deputy
minister, to serve as professors.[34]

Failure to agree as to where the provincial university should
be located was a major reason why British Columbia, an older and
more populous province than Alberta or Saskatchewan, did not
establish its university until 1915. A university of British
Columbia had been authorized by an act of 1890 but the act lapsed
before the university had been legally constituted, a direct
consequence of delays resulting from the efforts of Victoria,
the capital city located on Vancouver Island, and Vancouver, the
larger city situated on the mainland, to be selected as the site.[35]
However, in 1899 a beginning was made when first year courses in
arts were offered at the Vancouver High School. The Vancouver
School Board had arranged for the high school to become an affiliate of McGill University in Montreal, with McGill prescribing
the courses of study and being responsible for the examinations.
In 1902 the scheme was extended to the second year of arts at
'Vancouver College' and first year arts courses became available
at 'Victoria College,' the Victoria School Board having arranged
for its high school to be affiliated with McGill on the same
basis. The next step was the establishment of McGill University
College of British Columbia in 1906.[36] This was an institution
incorporated in the Province of British Columbia with its own
board of governors (all British Columbia residents except McGill's
principal) and its own staff. The courses offered were basically
those offered in comparable courses at McGill. The intention was
for McGill University College to provide the full course in arts
and the first two years of applied science, with the B.A. degree
being granted 'locally' to those who completed the fourth year.
In 1906-7 the first two years of arts and the first year of
applied science were provided, in 1907-8 the second year in
applied science was added, and in 1908-9 the third year of arts.

Many people in British Columbia were doubtful about the wisdom
of this venture from the time it was first proposed. They could
see the practical value it would have in providing higher education for young people of the province, but they also saw that it
gave the government an excuse to postpone indefinitely the establishment of a full university. A movement to revive the University
of British Columbia Act 'so far as it needs revival' and to provide

an endowment for a provincial university was begun within days of the passing of the McGill University College Act.[37] This led to the passage in 1907 of An Act to Aid the University of British Columbia by A Reservation of Provincial Lands, which provided that lands not exceeding 2 million acres be set aside within three years for this purpose, and in 1908 of An Act to Establish An University for the Province of British Columbia.

The passage of this latter act checked the development of the plans to make McGill University College a degree-granting institution. It was now obvious that its fate was to be that of a caretaker institution, 'waiting patiently until her successor was ready to relieve her.'[38] The fourth year of arts never was offered, though the period of waiting lasted for seven years. Much time was spent in choosing a site (1908-10), in selecting a president (1910-13), in holding a competition for an architect (1912), in selecting a chancellor and members of senate, and in appointing members of the board of governors (1912-13), and in drawing up and then pruning an operating budget (1913-15). But in September 1915 the University of British Columbia did open, and the McGill University College went out of existence. Many of its students, of course, were among the 379 who registered at the new university, and some of its faculty were included in the original University of British Columbia staff of 34.

Like Alberta and Saskatchewan, British Columbia opened in rented quarters:

> In 1914 the Legislature voted $500,000 and the Government promised $1,000,000 for the following year, thus enabling the Board to proceed with the actual work on the university. The clearing of the site (at Port Grey) was completed and necessary grading done; the steel and concrete work of the Science Building was completed, the Deans of Agriculture and Applied Science and some professors were appointed, and in general the necessary preparations were made for beginning University work in the fall of 1915.
>
> Upon the outbreak of war in 1914, the Board of Governors, feeling that it would be shortsighted and unpatriotic to commit the public to a large capital expenditure and heavy fixed charges when every available dollar in the country might be required in the struggle to preserve the rights and liberties of free peoples, decided to withhold the contract for the completion of the Science building, to make no further contracts or appointments to the staff, and to postpone large expenditures on the library and grounds. By this action the grant for the year largely reverted to the Provincial Treasury and the people were not committed to a heavy outlay in 1915.[39]

This may have been patriotic; it certainly proved to be shortsighted. The cornerstone of the science building was not laid until 1923 and no buildings on the Point Grey campus were occupied until 1925. The postponement meant that the university would not be adequately housed for ten years. It also meant that the university was in no position during its first decade to develop the range of courses which, as the capstone of the provincial educational system, it was anxious to provide. In 1920 its offerings were limited to arts and science, engineering, agriculture, and nursing; the faculty of agriculture became operative in 1917 and a course for graduate nurses was introduced in 1920, but attempts to establish programs in commerce and forestry were not successful. In contrast, both Alberta and Saskatchewan, in addition to offering instruction in arts and science, engineering, and agriculture, had also developed programs in law, pharmacy, accountancy, and home economics, and in Alberta's case in medicine and dentistry as well.[40] The development of both institutions had been checked by the war; programs that had been introduced had to be withdrawn and plans to institute others postponed. But, because the universities were well organized and adequately housed prior to the war, they were able to act quickly and effectively as soon as it was over.

In 1920 the University of British Columbia had more students than either the University of Alberta or the University of Saskatchewan, but it was not as well organized and it did not have the sense of confidence that comes from a clear sense of purpose and strong leadership. British Columbia's problems had been further compounded in 1918 by the death of its first president, F.F. Wesbrook.[41]

The University of Manitoba, though established in 1887, did not have a president until 1913, and this symbolized, if it did not fully explain, the difficulties that the university experienced between 1890 and 1920. The story is a complex one, involving at least eight legislative acts and a series of commissions of enquiry, one of which established some kind of record by producing three separate and conflicting reports. It has been admirably told in W.L. Morton's *One University: a History of the University of Manitoba*. Morton's chapter headings outline the basic plot: 'The Struggle for a Teaching University (1889-1904),' 'The Years of Growth (1904-1910),' 'The Years of Deadlock (1912-1917),' 'The University and The Province (1917-1922).'

In 1890 the University of Manitoba was an examining and degree-granting institution with all instruction being given in the constituent colleges or affiliated schools, but the three Protestant colleges were pooling their resources to provide a single class in the science subjects.[42] In 1892 the University Act was amended to permit the university to teach, but the informal arrangement continued until 1900 when a faculty of science was formally established and the university agreed to pay half the salaries of the three professors concerned. However, the struggle for a teaching university did not end until 1904 when, following the agreement of Lord Strathcona to donate $5000 for four years for general purposes, the university was in a position to appoint professors of botany, physics, chemistry, mathematics and physiology.[43]

During what Morton calls 'The Years of Growth,' teaching in science was consolidated and expanded, instruction in engineering begun, and university professors of English, history, and political economy appointed. The university now had three professional schools as affiliates: the Manitoba Medical College since 1883; the Manitoba College of Pharmacy, established and affiliated in 1902; and the Manitoba Agricultural College. An act providing for the establishment of an agricultural college had been passed in 1903, and the college had opened in 1906 on its own campus on the outskirts of Winnipeg and at some distance from the centre of the city where the colleges were located. The Manitoba Agricultural College became an affiliate in 1907.

It withdrew from affiliation in 1912, and this signalled the beginning of the 'Years of Deadlock.' The University Act had been amended in 1911 to permit the appointment of a president, but a bill had also been proposed by the University Council which would create a university on the Toronto model with a board of governors and a senate, basic control shifting from the colleges to the university. As could be expected, this proposal was disturbing to some persons in the colleges. It was also disturbing to the Manitoba Agricultural College which feared that it would be absorbed by a fully operative provincial university, particularly since there had been discussion for several years of locating the university on a site adjacent to the college. The government apparently shared these fears since, after arranging for disaffiliation, it gave the college the right to grant its own degrees.

The deadlock was broken in 1917 with the passage of the University of Manitoba Amendment Act which, as Morton points out, was misnamed since it created a new institution on the model proposed in the 1911 bill. The actual turning point came in 1915 when the Conservative party was replaced by the Liberals. In 1916 the Manitoba Agricultural College again became affiliated, the degrees it had granted in the interim being converted into University of Manitoba degrees. It remained, however, a separate institution until 1924.

By 1920, the University of Manitoba was a provincial university in the full sense. Its colleges were now affiliates rather than constituents, and as a university - distinct from a collection of colleges and professional schools - it offered a wide range of programs, including all subjects in arts and science. It had absorbed the Manitoba Medical College, which became its faculty of medicine in 1918, and the Manitoba College of Pharmacy, which became a department in arts and science in 1914. A faculty of arts and science had been established in 1917, a faculty of engineering in 1920. Since 1913 there had been a department of architecture, and since 1914 an effective relationship with another affiliate, the Manitoba Law School, founded by the Law Society of Manitoba in that year after consultation with the University.

A number of theological colleges were established in the western provinces between 1900 and 1920, almost all of which became affi-

liated with one of the provincial universities; reference to these
will be made in the Theology section of chapter 16. But to complete the record of the development of higher education in the west
from 1890 to 1920, three other institutions must be mentioned.

The most important of these was Brandon College, which became
Brandon University in 1967. Tenuously related to a secondary
school which had been established first at Rapid City, Manitoba,
and then at Brandon in the 1880s, it effectively dates from 1899
when it was reorganized by the Western Baptist Union. Classes
were begun in arts and theology in 1900 and a new building occupied in 1901. The institution had some relationship with the
University of Manitoba in connection with matriculation examinations, but, from the standpoint of Brandon, not a very satisfactory one, and this led first to an unsuccessful attempt to attain
a charter in 1906 and in 1911 to affiliation with McMaster University, then located in Toronto. In 1920, 120 students were registered in arts, and one in theology.

Between 1907 and 1915 there was also a Baptist college at
Summerland, British Columbia.[44] This was Okanagan College, basically a secondary school but offering first and second year work
in arts from 1909 on to a small number of students. In 1910 it
became an affiliate of McMaster, but the numbers remained small.
It was closed in 1915.

Columbian Methodist College established at New Westminster, B.C.,
in 1892 deserves special mention because, from the closing of
Whetham College in 1893 until the opening of the first year arts
course at Vancouver High School in 1899, it was the only institution offering university work in British Columbia.[45] It was affiliated with the University of Toronto and offered instruction in
arts and theology, but it was also a ladies college and a secondary school for boys. It suspended its theological work from 1915
to 1919, but after resuming it for four years yielded this field
to another Methodist theological college and concentrated on secondary school work.

THE FEDERAL GOVERNMENT

The Royal Military College at Kingston continued to operate
throughout this period. There was no basic change in the character of the school or in its academic program despite the fact that
in 1897 the course was reduced from four to three years. The four
year course was re-established in 1920.

The dominion government can also be said to have been responsible
for establishing another institution during the period under review.
This was the Khaki University of Canada, which operated in England
in 1918 and 1919. The president of Khaki University was the ubi-
quitous H.M. Tory, who after organizing the establishment of
McGill University College of British Columbia had gone on to become the first president of the University of Alberta. At the
invitation of the Y.M.C.A., Tory made a survey of its educational

program for soldiers in England and France during the summer of
1917. His report was enthusiastically received by the Y.M.C.A.
which proceeded to raise $500,000 to finance the scheme proposed,
and by the government, which gave the project moral, administrative, and official support. The project was not confined to university work, but a Khaki University was established in September
1918 at Ripon, which in the course of the next twelve months provided first and second year courses in arts, science, commerce
and engineering for some 2000 men. There was also a Khaki University Theology College. The scheme was supported by the National
Conference of Canadian Universities, all of whose members agreed
to accept credits earned at Khaki University.

The government support of Khaki University was in striking contrast to its reaction to proposals, advanced by the National
Conference of Canadian Universities among others, that veterans
who wished to resume or begin university studies should be given
financial support. In November 1918 the government authorized
the granting of loans to a maximum of $500 to disabled veterans
in need of assistance to pursue a course of study interrupted by
war service, and some months later this was extended to all veterans. But these were loans repayable within five years and they
did not apply to veterans who had not yet begun their studies.
The arrangements were very different from those made by the Canadian government for the rehabilitation of veterans of World War II,
which were based on the premise that the veteran should be posi-
tively encouraged to obtain more education and not merely assisted
in completing the studies he had already begun.

NOTES TO CHAPTER 14

1 W.S. Learned and K.C.M. Sills, *Education in the Maritime
   Provinces of Canada* (1922), vii
2 R.M. Lester, *Review of Grants in the Maritime Provinces of
   Canada and Newfoundland 1911-1933* (1934); also S.H. Stackpole,
   Carnegie Corporation Commonwealth Program 1911-1961 (1963)
3 *Education in Maritimes*, 18
4 All benefactions to Dalhousie University from 1863 to 1938
   are listed in the *Calendar* for 1940-41, 2-7
5 *Education in Maritimes*, 18
6 Ibid., 23
7 Ibid., 31
8 Ibid., 31
9 Ibid., 21
10 Ibid., 24
11 Ibid., 17
12 Ibid., 16
13 W.X. Edwards, 'The MacPherson-Tompkins Era of Saint Francis
   Xavier University,' *Can. Catholic Hist. Assoc. Report 1953*,
   49-65
14 *Education in Maritimes*, 25

15 Ibid., 27

16 E.H. Bensley, 'Bishop's Medical College,' *J. Can. Med. Assoc.*, 72 (1955), 463-5

17 D.C. Masters, *Bishop's University: The First Hundred Years* (1950), 75

18 E.A. Collard, 'Sir William Peterson's Principalship, 1895-1919' in H. MacLennan, ed., *McGill: The Story of a University* (1960), 73

19 For the development of the new campus, see J.F. Snell, *Macdonald College of McGill University - a History from 1904-1955* (1963).

20 Sister Lucienne Plante, 'La Fondation de l'enseignement classique féminin au Québec 1908-1926,' unpublished thèse de licence en lettres, Université Laval, 1967

21 Petit Séminaire de Québec; Petit Séminaire de Nicolet; Collège de Ste-Anne-de-la-Pocatière; Petit Séminaire de St-Germain de Rimouski; Petit Séminaire de Chicoutimi; Collège de Lévis. Three colleges located outside Quebec remained in relationship with Laval as collèges agrégés: St Dunstan's at Charlottetown, P.E.I., an affiliate since 1892; Collège des Pères Jesuits, Edmonton, Alberta (1917); and Collège de St Pierre, Gravelbourg, Saskatchewan (1919).

22 Petit Séminaire (or Collège) de Montréal; Séminaire de St-Hyacinthe; Séminaire de St Thérèse de Blainville; Séminaire de l'Assomption; Séminaire de Joliette; Collège de St-Laurent; Collège Bourget (Rigaud); Séminaire St-Charles Borromée (Sherbrooke); Collège Ste-Marie, Loyola; Ecole de l'Enseignement Supérieur

23 F.E. Gattinger, 'Veterinary Instruction at Queen's and O.A.C.,' *Can. Veterinarian J.*, 3 (1962), 174-7; J.W.B. Sisam, *Forestry Education at Toronto* (1961), 9-18

24 R.S. Harris, 'The Establishment of a Provincial University in Ontario' in D.F. Dadson, ed., *On Higher Education: Five Lectures* (1966), 28

25 E.J. McCorkell, *Father Carr - Revolutionary* (1969), 17-19

26 Royal Commission on University Finances, *Report of ... Toronto* (1921), 2 vols. The chairman of the commission was H.J. Cody, a member of the 1906 Royal Commission on the University of Toronto and minister of education for Ontario in 1918-19. The briefs submitted by Queen's, Western, and Toronto, which are included as appendices to the report, provide detailed information about their position in 1920 and their development in the period covered by this chapter.

27 The enrolment figure for the University of Toronto does not include students in affiliated colleges such as Ontario College of Pharmacy and Royal College of Dental Surgeons. It does include students in the federated arts colleges.

28 J.J. Talman and R.D. Talman, *Western - 1878-1953* (1953), 130-2

29 Ibid., 132-4

30 A. Plante, *Vingt-cinq ans de vie française: le Collège de Sudbury* (1938)

31 *Report of the Royal Commission Appointed to Consider the Granting of Degree-conferring Powers to Calgary College* (1915), 4

32 P.E. Weston, 'A University for Calgary,' *Alberta Hist. Rev.*, 11 (1963), 1-11

33 Congress of the Universities of the Empire, *Report of Proceedings* (1912), xxi

34 C. King, *The First Fifty: Teaching, Research and Public Services at the University of Saskatchewan 1909-1959* (1959), 28-30

35 H.T. Logan, *Tuum Est: a History of the University of British Columbia* (1958), 1-11

36 Ibid., 21-9

37 Ibid., 32

38 Ibid., 24

39 *U.B.C. Calendar 1920-21*, 21

40 At Alberta engineering was withdrawn for a period during World War I.

41 Wesbrook, dean of medicine at the University of Minnesota at the time of his appointment in 1913, was a man of great ability, enthusiasm, and charm. The succession of setbacks which he and the university experienced during the next five years are recorded in W.C. Gibson, *Wesbrook and his University* (1973).

42 See above, chapter 8, 115.

43 W.L. Morton, *One University: a History of the University of Manitoba 1877-1952* (1957), 62

44 K. Imayoshi, 'The History of Okanagan Baptist College, 1907-1915,' unpublished B.D. thesis, McMaster University, 1953

45 Little has been written about Columbian Methodist or Whetham Colleges; see Logan, *Tuum Est*, 13

15
Arts and Science

An analysis of full-time enrolment in the Canadian universities and colleges for the session 1920-21 reveals that just over 10,000 undergraduates were registered in professional courses and just under 10,000 in 'arts, pure science, letters and philosophy,' the category used by the Dominion Bureau of Statistics to describe students in arts and science.[1] However, some of the students reported as being in professional courses were the responsibility of a faculty of arts and science since the course they took was offered by a department of that faculty - physical and health education and social work are examples. Faculties of arts and science were also responsible for the 690 graduate students reported as being enrolled on a full-time basis in 1920-21; there were as yet no schools or faculties of graduate studies and almost all graduate work was supervised by departments in arts and science. In addition, at most universities the faculty of arts and science was deeply involved with students attending summer schools and at many with the supervision of what the Dominion Bureau of Statistics described as 'pre-university' work; in 1920-21 ten degree-granting institutions reported an enrolment of an additional 10,000 students in 'courses leading to matriculation and other preparatory courses.' It is probably fair to say that in 1920 two-thirds of the teaching offered in the Canadian universities was the responsibility of the faculty of arts and science.

But it is also important to recognize that faculties of arts and science in 1920 were, with very few exceptions, units of modest size. More than half the 37 institutions which reported enrolments in this area had fewer than 200 students. The only very large faculty of arts was at Toronto, which had 3196 students, but here the students were divided among four colleges. There were also college units at Laval, Montréal, and Manitoba. The other institutions with as many as 400 students in arts and science were British Columbia 676 (with an additional 75 at Victoria College), McGill 537, and Queen's 446. All of these institutions and many others as well had a dean of arts and science and he, rather than the president, 'ran' the faculty; by 1920 Canadian university presidents had enough *university* problems on their hands to keep them fully occupied. But in no case were the administrative duties of the dean sufficiently heavy to warrant more than a slight reduction of his teaching load. The fact that the numbers were relatively small also meant that the day of the large department had not yet arrived. All of the larger institutions and many of the smaller were organized on departmental lines, but only a handful of departments numbered as many as ten full *and* part-time members.

Admission to university was still by way of either junior matriculation or senior matriculation except at those institutions which retained the classical college system. Junior matriculation admitted to the first year, senior matriculation to the second year, of a four year course leading to the general B.A. or B.Sc.; in other words senior matriculation, taken in a secondary school, and first year arts and science were alternative routes to the second year. In our analysis we shall disregard senior matriculation as a separate entity and speak only of a first year. To be admitted to this first year the universities required standing in five subjects: English, history, mathematics, Latin and one other. Greek was never required though it could be offered in place of Latin. Only four institutions, Acadia, Dalhousie, St Francis Xavier, and Saskatchewan, required two languages, Icelandic being an acceptable offering at Saskatchewan. Only five institutions, British Columbia, Dalhousie, New Brunswick, St Francis Xavier, and Saskatchewan, required a science.

THE GENERAL OR PASS B.A.

The student was almost always required to take five courses in each year. In the first year, three of the five were invariably prescribed: English, a language, mathematics; and usually a fourth - another language or a science. In the second year, English, the language of the first year, and one other course were usually prescribed. - In the universities east of Manitoba, Latin or Greek was prescribed for two years and more often than not a second language as well. The western universities specified only a language for two years, though Saskatchewan also prescribed first year Latin. At all universities a science, usually physics, was normally required in the first year. History was a first or second year requirement only at Alberta, British Columbia, Manitoba, McGill, and New Brunswick. Nowhere was a freshman or sophomore required to take a social science other than history. The Roman Catholic colleges continued to prescribe religious knowledge in each year of the course as did King's, Bishop's, and Acadia. New Brunswick, McMaster, St Francis Xavier, and Western prescribed philosophy in the second year. There were no first or second year courses, prescribed or optional, which could be described as interdisciplinary. The following programs were representative:

Acadia
  I Latin, a language, English, mathematics, biblical literature,
    1 of 4 sciences
  II Latin, the language continued, English, biblical literature,
    2 courses chosen from science, mathematics, a language
British Columbia
  I English, a language, history, mathematics, 2 courses chosen
    from languages and sciences
  II English, the language continued, 3 other courses

The arrangements for the first two years as outlined above were
based on three principles: that the student should be exposed to
subjects in a number of disciplines (the principle of distribution),
that he should study at least one subject in depth (the principle
of concentration), and that he should have some choice in deciding
which courses he would take (the principle of free election). The
same three principles underlay the arrangements for the final two
years of the General B.A. program.

In the larger universities the principle of free election had
by 1920 been extended to the choice of subjects in which the student was required to concentrate, and to the choice of those by
which he would fulfil the distribution requirements; and there
was also a tendency to begin the upper year program in the second
year. At Queen's, for example, the subjects for the final three
years were divided into three groups: (a) language and literature, (b) mathematics and science, (c) philosophy, history, political and economic sciences; and the student was required to select
his courses from at least two groups and to take five courses in
one subject (his major) and four in a second subject (his minor),
the latter being 'related' to the subject selected as the major.
At Saskatchewan he was required to take either history or economics and either philosophy or education before he graduated, and
in his last two years to take either six courses in one subject
or four in one and three in another. Similar arrangements were
in force at each of the other large English-speaking institutions,
Alberta, British Columbia, Manitoba, McGill, and Toronto.

Because the smaller universities had smaller staffs, they had
to organize their more limited human and physical resources more
rigorously; consequently, they tended to prescribe the subject or
subjects of concentration and also the method of fulfilling the
distribution requirement. Thus at Western, English was prescribed
in all four years (the student's major), history in the third and
fourth (his 'related' minor), and philosophy was required in the
third year (distribution). At McMaster, English and a language
were required for four years (double major), history in the last
two (minor), philosophy in the second (distribution). At St
Francis Xavier English was required for four, Latin for the first
three, philosophy for the last three. In the interests of distribution, Dalhousie required that a student take courses in history

and philosophy, while New Brunswick prescribed philosophy in the second year, chemistry (the student's third science course) in the third. Acadia made the fourth year entirely elective, but prescribed history, economics, psychology, and education, and two philosophy courses in the third.

Concentration and distribution are devices aimed at providing focus and pattern to the studies undertaken by a student in an arts and science course. They are intended to ensure that the student has a balanced academic diet - soup, main course, dessert rather than, cafeteria-style, only a main course or only a selection of soups or of desserts. Another device to attain the same end is to prescribe a course specifically designed either to provide focus and pattern to the course of study as a whole or to relate the studies the undergraduate is pursuing to the larger world into which he will graduate. Two of the smaller universities offered such courses in 1920.

The Western University at London prescribed three courses at the outset of the student's undergraduate program, two designed to develop specific skills which it was believed would be useful to the student in all his courses and one designed to provide perspective with respect to the larger world. The skills courses were public speaking and library science, the former partly intended to develop the ability to express oneself in seminar and discussion class, the latter specifically designed to introduce the student to the library and to 'research' procedures. The third course, public health and bacteriology, was thus described in the Calendar:

A series of 15 lectures is given to students of the first year dealing with public health, preventive medicine and hygiene, and describing the essentials of bacteriology so far as applicable to modern life. The modern methods of handling and preventing infectious diseases, the hygiene of water, milk, food and flies, the physiological principles involved in and the significance of ventilation, foods and feeding, water supplies, sewage disposal, vital statistics, infant mortality, etc. ... Technicalities are avoided, the aim being not to train public health specialists but to give such information as any educated person should have concerning the great advances of modern public health in order that he or she may be able to understand and fit in with them. The ordinary infectious diseases are described as to their appearance and symptoms so far as would be useful to the ordinary life of a private citizen.

At Mount Allison there was also a modest attempt to introduce the freshman to the world of study since meetings of the compulsory first year course in English were pre-empted on half a dozen occasions in order that members of staff and especially invited visitors could lecture on aspects of university life and work. But a more significant undertaking was the course called Evidences of Christianity which was prescribed for all students in the graduating year: 'The object of this course is to assist the student near the end of his undergraduate career to review the grounds of his religious faith in the light of his maturer knowledge, and co-ordinate his beliefs with the facts and principles with which his scientific and other studies have made him familiar.' Such a course was clearly a carry-over from an earlier period; under some title it would have been included in almost all B.A. programs in 1860 and in many in 1890. Probably its basic objectives were pro-vided for at a number of other universities in 1920 in religious knowledge and philosophy courses. No doubt, too, universities other than Mount Allison provided formal or informal lectures in-tended to introduce the student to university work – the descrip-tion of a course in a Calendar is after all the barest of outlines. Nonetheless, it is of some significance that the calendars of very few English-language Canadian universities at this time reflected in their description of the courses of study for the B.A. degree a conscious attempt to provide focus and pattern.

THE CLASSICAL COLLEGE COURSE

In 1902 a basic reform of the classical college course was insti-tuted in France which resulted in the establishment of four parallel programs leading to the degree, each providing for dif-ferent combinations of specialization: Latin and Greek, Latin and Sciences, Latin and Modern Languages and Literatures, Sciences and Modern Languages and Literatures.[2] There was no similar development in French Canada. The course of study and the regu-lations for qualifying for the B. ès Arts, B. ès Sciences, and B. ès Lettres were essentially the same in 1920 as in 1890. How-ever, a number of additional colleges had been established, inc-luding one for women, and the course was therefore available to a larger number of students.

The failure to make significant changes in the course did not reflect any lack of concern on the part of those responsible for it. The Congrès d'Enseignement Secondaire of 1890-91 was followed by similar gatherings in 1901, 1906, 1911, 1914, and 1917, and at each of these there was prolonged discussions of the content of the course as well as of the administrative arrangements.[3] In-creasingly from 1906 on, the argument was advanced that, while the course was admirably designed for students who were capable of and interested in specialization in classics and philosophy, it did not provide adequately for the student who was capable of and interested in specialization in mathematics and science. And surely French Canada had to have engineers and scientists if it were to function effectively in an industrialized economy. Unfor-tunately, as Maheux has pointed out, the classical college course was so closely identified with the survival of French Canadian values that the slightest suggestion of change in its structure immediately placed educators and patriots on the defensive.[4] There would have been no problem if there had been an alternative form

238

of secondary education, but such an alternative was only beginning
to emerge at the end of the period. In the meantime the classical
course retained its traditional form. Not until the mid-1920s was
there a strengthening of its mathematics and science component.

Another subject frequently discussed at the congrès was the
quality of instruction provided in the classical colleges. Almost
all the instruction was given by ordained priests or seminarians -
in 1911 of a teaching staff of 543 only 15 were laymen, in 1921
only 38 of 676.[5] This meant that the preparation of most teachers
was the completion of the classical course itself and some theological training. Hence the movement to establish écoles normales
supérieures at the universities which would offer academic and
professional training for clerical teachers and provide a program
that would attract lay teachers into secondary school teaching.
This movement did lead in 1920 to the establishment of the Ecole
normale supérieure and l'Ecole de chimie at Laval and the faculté
des sciences and the faculté des lettres at Université de Montréal.[6]

By 1920 the Bachelor of Philosophy degree had disappeared from
the Canadian higher education scene except at Ottawa where it was
granted at the end of the third year of the four year arts course
to students who obtained an 80% average. The B. ès Sc. and the
B. ès L. continued to be offered in the French-speaking universities as alternatives to the B. ès Arts for graduates of the classical course. In the English-speaking universities the B.L. degree
had also been dropped, but the B.Sc. was in the process of establishing itself as the degree granted to students in arts and science
who specialized or concentrated in science rather than arts.   A
relatively small number of B.Sc.s were granted in 1920, 14 by Laval
and 26 by 9 English-speaking institutions. The former, however,
included three of the four western universities as well as McGill
and Dalhousie. At the other major universities the B.Sc. was
reserved for students in professional courses.

HONOURS COURSES

The offering of an honour B.A. as well as a general B.A. was a
distinguishing feature of Canadian higher education in 1890 since
provision was made for both types of degree at most English-
speaking institutions and at all the larger ones. The beginnings
of honour courses can be traced back to 1860, but the programs
did not become clearly defined until the 1880s. The period 1890
to 1920 was one of consolidation in the older universities and
of adoption in the new. It was also a period in which a distinction developed between two types of honour course, one requiring
four years of study beyond junior matriculation and one requiring
five.

In the Maritime provinces and in Quebec, the universities which
had developed honour courses by 1890 continued to offer them,
with the exception of King's whose arts enrolment in 1920 stood
at seven. At Acadia, Dalhousie, New Brunswick, and McGill, honours

work was confined to the third and fourth years, a high standard being required in the work of the first two years (80% at Acadia) and certain first- and second-year courses being prerequisite to admission to particular honour courses. Most of the honour courses offered at these universities involved two subjects rather than one – English and French, English and German, English and philosophy, rather than English pure and unconfined. The honour student was required to take more courses than the student in a general course, had to achieve a higher passing standard, and in some cases was required to write comprehensive examinations and submit a graduation thesis. At Mount Allison the arrangements were similar, but honour work began in the second year. Bishop's continued to offer an honour degree in three years from junior matriculation.

In Ontario, where the development of honour courses was stimulated by the requirement of an honour B.A. for the secondary school specialist teaching certificate, an honour program was offered at four of the five universities in 1920. Ottawa's courses had not been accepted by the Department of Education as fulfilling the academic requirements for the specialist certificate and it had temporarily withdrawn from the field, but the Queen's and McMaster courses had been recognized as equivalent to Toronto's in the 1890s and Western's achieved the same status in 1908. At Toronto, McMaster, and Western, the honour degree required four years of study from senior matriculation and the student entered the honour program at that point. Queen's advised candidates for an honour degree to spend five years from junior matriculation, but made it possible for the student to complete the course in four years by taking extra subjects.

There was some increase in the number of courses offered at Queen's, McMaster, and Western, but the striking development was at Toronto which increased the number of its honour courses from 9 to 23 during this period, as can be seen from the following list in which the year in which the course was first offered has been placed in parentheses:

	1891-92	*1920-21*
Languages	Classics (1877)	Classics Greek and Hebrew (1904)
	Oriental Languages (1888)	Oriental Languages Oriental Languages – Greek Option (1918)
	Modern Languages & History (1877)	Modern Languages (1893) French, Greek, Latin (1920)
Humanities and Social Sciences	Modern Languages & History (as above)	English & History (1895) Modern History (1895)

	Philosophy (1877)	Philosophy Philosophy, English or History (1919) Psychology (1920)
	Political Science (1891)	Political Science
Science	Maths. & Physics (1877)	Mathematics & Physics Physics (1904)
	Natural Science (1877)	Biology (1904) Biological & Medical Sciences (1920) Physiological & Bio- logical Sciences (1910)
	Chemistry & Mineralogy (1891)	Chemistry & Mineralogy Chemistry (1904) Geology & Mineralogy (1904)
Other		Commerce & Finance (1909) Household Science (1907) Household Economics (1920)

This considerable increase was achieved partly by the subdividing of existing courses, partly by new combinations of subjects, and partly by expansion into new fields, some of which, for example oriental languages, philosophy, and psychology, had no connection with the high school teaching certificate. While it is true to say that the specialist certificate stimulated the development of honour courses by creating a demand for them on the part of would-be teachers, the courses themselves were not designed with the classroom needs of teachers in mind. They were intended to provide a liberal education through the intensive study of a number of related subjects. This being the case, there was no reason for confining the program to subjects which happened to be taught in the secondary school.

The three new universities of the West introduced honour courses within a few years of their establishment, Saskatchewan in 1910, Alberta in 1911, British Columbia in 1920. In each case the system adopted was that of the eastern universities rather than of Ontario, honour work being confined to the final two years and not requiring an additional year of study. At Manitoba, however, the Ontario pattern was adopted in 1923 when, as the first step in a reorganization of the curriculum in arts and science at both undergraduate and graduate levels, honour courses requiring a fifth year of study were introduced. There was no reference to honour courses in Manitoba's 1920-21 *Calendar*. The earlier honour courses had disappeared with the introduction of major and minor requirements in the B.A. program in 1911.

It could be argued that this section should be entitled 'Business' or 'Business Administration' and that it should be included in the following chapter which deals with the development of profes- sional education from 1890 to 1920. But most of the programs described by O.D. Skelton in a paper on University Preparation for Business presented to the National Conference of Canadian Universities in 1923 led to a Bachelor of Commerce degree, many were offered as courses in Commerce and Finance, and with one exception all were supervised by a faculty of arts and science.[7] At the Université de Montréal the work was provided in the Ecole des hautes études commerciales, which had been established by the Quebec government in 1910 and had entered into affiliation with Université Laval à Montréal in 1915. But, with this one exception, the considerable development of education for business which oc- curred between 1900 and 1920 took place within the faculty of arts, usually as an expansion of the work of the department of political economy. This gave to the undergraduate program in 'business' a theoretical rather than a practical orientation which on the whole it has retained ever since.

The development at the University of Toronto, the first insti- tution to enter this field, is in many respects typical. At the urging of the Canadian Manufacturers' Association and the Toronto Board of Trade a two-year diploma course in commerce was introduced in 1901. It was intended 'to supply facilities for the training of young men who desired to turn their attention to domestic and foreign commerce, banking or those branches of public service, e.g. trade consularships, in which a knowledge of business is essential.'[8] It was also seen as a means of preparing teachers for commercial classes in the secondary schools. But it was not seen as a uni- versity course in the full sense: 'The course has been limited to two years of study in order to meet the requirements of stu- dents who cannot spend a longer time in preparation. Such stu- dents as are able to complete a four years' course of study will find in the Arts course in Political Science a curriculum corres- ponding in some important respects with that prescribed for the diploma in Commerce.'[9] The actual subjects prescribed were, how- ever, regular arts and science courses including English and a modern language for two years and first year physics and chemistry. On the business side there was a first year course in actuarial science, an introductory course in economics and, in the second year, courses in economic geography and history, banking and public finance, transportation and commercial law. By 1909 this had become a four-year course leading to a B.A. degree called Commerce and Finance, with Latin prescribed both at matriculation and in the first year. For several years provision was made for the work of the last two years to be taken on an extramural basis while working in a downtown office, but by 1920 this interesting experi- ment had been abandoned and, in terms of organization, the course was indistinguishable from any other honour course. Its heavily theoretical bias was underlined by the fact that in 1920 a second four year course was established by the faculty leading to the B.Comm. degree. The courses were similar, that leading to the B.A. degree emphasizing finance and that leading to the B.Comm. emphasizing commerce. But in 1923 the courses were merged, the B.Comm. being awarded on completion of what was essentially the old B.A. course.

Two year diploma courses were also introduced at Manitoba in 1904, at McGill in 1914, and at Alberta in 1916. The course at Manitoba, which does not appear to have always been offered, was largely an evening operation. Among other things, it provided instruction in chartered accountancy. The Alberta course was designed for chartered accountants, and led to a diploma in accountancy which fulfilled the requirements of the Intermediate and Final Examinations of the Institute of Chartered Accountants of Alberta. The same emphasis characterized the work at Saskatchewan, which appointed a professor of accounting in 1914, who began in 1917 to give evening courses for students preparing for the provincial chartered accountancy examinations. In 1920 a school of accounting (in the faculty of arts and science) was established, offering a four year course to a Bachelor of Science in Accounting degree, which in conjunction with two years of apprenticeship in an office qualified the holder to practise as a chartered accountant in Saskatchewan.

The diploma course at McGill had developed by 1917 into a three year course leading to a B.Comm. degree. This was offered in a school of commercial studies, like the schools at Alberta and Saskatchewan a subdivision of arts and science but with rather more independence. At McGill the emphasis was entirely practical, as can be detected in the policy statement contained in the 1920 Calendar:

In all subjects the work will be, as far as possible, of a practical nature. Thus the English courses will include a drilling in letter-writing, précis-writing, and the preparation of reports. The French, German and Spanish courses will aim at imparting facility in speaking as well as writing, and will consider the special phraseology employed in business correspondence. The mathematical and scientific courses will deal in the fullest manner with applications to industry, commerce, and finance. In the lectures on History, Political Economy, and Commercial Law, the aim will be in the first case to trace the growth and development of modern ideas and institutions; next, to impart a knowledge of those general economic principles which are necessary to a full understanding of other subjects; in the third instance, to give the student such an acquaintance with the law as may be of real service in everyday business transactions. Finally, in Accountancy, the conditions and methods imposed by the increasing complexity of commercial, industrial and financial organizations will be considered in detail.

The staff of the School consisted of an assistant professor of accountancy and an assistant professor of economics. The degree exempted the holder from the Junior and Intermediate though not the Final Examination for the licence to practise as a chartered accountant in the Province of Quebec, as did the University of Toronto degree for the comparable licence in Ontario.

Three other English-speaking universities entered the field at the very end of the period. Dalhousie established a four year B.Comm. course in 1920, and in the same year Western appointed a lecturer in accounting, who offered elementary and advanced courses in accounting and also courses in such subjects as business organization and principles of advertising in the honour course offered by the department of commercial economics; the real development of Western's course in business administration began, however, in 1922 with the appointment of E.K. Morrow, a graduate of the Harvard Business School, as professor of economics. But the basis for Queen's important work in this field had been laid by 1920 with the introduction through the efforts of O.D. Skelton and W.C. Clark of a well-developed and wide-ranging program in 1919. The B.Comm. was offered in eight areas: general business, banking and finance, accounting and auditing, commercial specialist (for high school teachers), foreign trade, public service, secretarial work, and social service. Over 40 separate courses were outlined in the *Calendar* though it was made clear that not all of these would be offered each session. The problem of obtaining qualified staff to provide for advanced work in all these areas and the lack of student demand for some of them led within a few years to the replacement of this elaborate and, for undergraduates, highly specialized program by a general course with provision for some specialization in certain areas, notably accounting. The 1920 program is nonetheless of considerable interest, and not least for the inclusion of training for social workers as a responsibility of a school of commerce and business administration.

The programs described thus far were a response to the need felt in all parts of English-speaking Canada for young men specially prepared for a variety of tasks related to the development of Canada as an increasingly industrialized nation. The same need was felt in French-speaking Canada but with even greater force. Without exception, the programs developed in English-speaking Canada during these 20 years were an expansion of the work of a department of political economy, and it can be assumed that the degree courses offered by these departments prior to the introduction of courses specifically labelled *commerce* provided some kind of university preparation for business. According to the University of Toronto, the curriculum of its course in political science in 1901 corresponded 'in some important respects with that prescribed for the diploma in commerce'; and that curriculum had been available to students for 12 years. But in the French-speaking universities there was no honour course in political science and there was very little political science and even less economics in the classical course which led to the B.A. The limitations (as distinct from the weaknesses) of the classical course were, indeed, advanced as one of the strongest arguments for establishing an Ecole des hautes études commerciales.[10] The virtues of a thorough grounding in the classical languages and philosophy were admitted, and it was equally admitted that such an education was a fine basis for the 'liberal' professions of law, medicine, and theology. But though French Canada had enough lawyers, doctors, and theologians, it had very few bankers, economists, actuaries, accountants, business men. The existence of a school of the type proposed would divert some of the intelligent young men who were, for want of any alternative rather than from a sense of vocation, swelling the ranks of the three old professions. As the *Annuaire* of the Université de Montréal would still be saying in 1920: 'L'enseignement de l'Ecole s'addresse d'abord à tous ceux qui préfèrent se tourner vers les carrières commerciales ... au lieu d'aller se joindre à ceux déjà trop nombreux qui encombrent actuellement toutes les carrières liberales.'

Because the Université Laval had no department of political economy either at Quebec or Montreal, there was no obvious base for the development of commerce courses within the university. Hence, at the turn of the century when the Montreal Chamber of Commerce became as convinced as the Toronto Board of Trade that facilities for training young men in domestic and foreign commerce were urgently needed, pressure to do something about the situation was brought to bear not on the local university but on the government, and the model proposed was that of the professional schools of commerce which had been established during the late nineteenth century in France, Germany, and Belgium. It was some years before the government took action, but in 1907 l'Ecole was incorporated and in 1910 it opened with 32 students, all on government bursaries, in a building built with government funds.

The original students, who came from the Ecole normale Jacques-Cartier or from commercial colleges, or in some instances from the public elementary schools, were 'assez mal préparés,' and this continued to be the case for some years - it was not until 1916 that a graduate of a classical college enrolled at l'Ecole.[11] The basic course was of three years' duration, leading initially to a diploma, but from 1917 on to a B. ès sciences commerciales degree. The scarcity of academically qualified applicants led to the introduction of a one-year preparatory course in 1914. By 1920 l'Ecole's offerings included, in addition to this preparatory course and the cours regulier, a variety of evening programs, including diploma courses for actuaries, accountants, and bank employees. L'Ecole had not by any means realized the hopes of its founders, but it was firmly established and in a position to make substantial progress during the next decade.

At Quebec, Université Laval had been offering evening courses leading to a certificate in commercial law since 1908 and in accounting since 1918. A proposal in 1913 to establish a chair in actuarial science was not implemented.

HUMANITIES

In 1920 arts and humanities continued to be almost synonymous
terms in the Canadian universities. In the English-speaking institutions science had made substantial progress, and in a faculty
of arts and science now occupied the position of full partner.
Arts, however, remained the senior partner, and in arts the dominant subjects were in approximately the order named: English,
Latin, philosophy, history, and French. Historians continued to
regard themselves as humanists rather than as social scientists
and their subject as one whose value lay in yielding perspective
rather than evidence. The only 'pure' social sciences that had
gained clear recognition were economics and political science,
but they were regarded as related rather than separate disciplines -
it was still the day of political economy. In the French-speaking
institutions the position of the humanities was stronger still,
as strong indeed as it had been in 1890. Science there had not
as yet made substantial progress, history was equally biased towards the humanistic side, and economics and political science
had only begun to establish themselves with the founding at
Université de Montréal in 1920 of l'Ecole des sciences sociales,
economiques et politiques.

In French-speaking Canada there had also been no change in the
relative importance of the various humanistic subjects. Greek
continued to be prescribed in the classical course, the only exception being at l'Ecole de l'enseignement supérieur, where the
young girls were required to substitute a modern language for Greek
on the grounds that the latter was beyond their capacity. This
view was hotly protested by the authorities at L'Ecole and by the
girls themselves, and Greek was made a requirement for their degree in 1923. Latin, French, and English continued to be the core
of the classical course for the first six years and philosophy the
centre of attention in the final two.

In the English language institutions there were important changes
in the position of individual subjects. Classics lost ground,
though not as much as had been gloomily predicted at the turn of
the century. By 1920 Greek had long since ceased to be a required
subject and with the exception of some of the Roman Catholic colleges Latin had ceased to be required in the final two years.
But it *was* required at matriculation and for the first two years
in all the Eastern universities. Philosophy had also suffered a
decline. It was no longer as it had been in 1890 the key subject
in the arts course at all institutions, and at most of the larger
universities (Dalhousie, McGill, Toronto, the four Western universities) it had disappeared from the list of prescribed courses.

The two subjects which had gained in importance were modern
languages and English. Moderns effectively meant French *and*
German; not even at McGill and Bishop's was French prescribed at
matriculation or in the B.A. course. Indeed the only general
courses for which French was a requirement were those leading to
the B.Sc. where both French and German were required. Most students

did in fact choose French as the subject to fulfil the language requirement since it tended to be taught at most secondary schools, whereas its chief rivals, German and Spanish, were taught at relatively few.

To the extent that there was a core subject in the arts and science program in 1920 it was English, which was universally required in the first two years of both the B.A. and the B.Sc. program and which at a few institutions was prescribed in all four years. At many of the universities which had faculties of engineering and agriculture, the department of English by this time was also providing separate courses, usually for two years, prescribed by these faculties for their students. One hesitates, however, to call English a core subject since the sequence of courses was not designed, as the upper year courses in philosophy were in 1890, to provide a coordinated view of the studies that constituted a liberal education. English was a required subject partly because it was a means of giving attention to the practical skills involved in preparing written essays and reports, which were required in all arts and in some science subjects.

This was a special problem for the new universities of the West, particularly Alberta and Saskatchewan, where secondary schooling was almost as recent an innovation as higher education. The University of Alberta *Calendar* of 1911-12 announced that:

> Immediately after registration, all matriculants, whether they submit accredited certificates or not, are required to write a theme, the subject to be chosen from a list provided by the Professor. Should this theme fall below a standard of average excellence, the student will be required to take a special course in composition. No credit towards the degree will be given for this work, but students assigned to it must comply with its conditions and show satisfactory improvement in composition before they can advance to their degree.

The first-year English course at Alberta assigned two hours a week to composition, with lectures on rhetoric, study of models of exposition, argument, description and narration, regular weekly themes, supplemented by class-practice in sentence structure, paragraph structure, and oral themes. But the course also devoted two hours a week to English literature from its beginnings to 1700, and the professor of English literature taught the course as a unit. In the following year, one hour was devoted to composition, with fortnightly themes, and three to English literature from 1700 on. This was the typical Canadian pattern in 1920. There were no courses concentrating solely or primarily on problems of oral and written composition as did the rhetoric course usually prescribed for freshmen in American colleges at this time.

Partly because the emphasis on composition was subordinated to that on literature, relatively little attention was devoted to public speaking. Western's introduction of a one hour course in this subject was not a complete innovation; Mount Allison had its

senior oration, the public speaking course which Queen's had prescribed in 1910 as part of senior English was still offered as an
elective in 1920, and several courses for engineers and agriculture
students emphasized oral work. But it was an innovation. Two
universities, McGill and Queen's, offered electives in advanced
English composition which provided some opportunity for creative
writing. Literature, it can be added, was almost always English
literature. The chief exceptions were a course in Canadian-
American literature which had been introduced at McGill in 1907
and a course in Canadian literature introduced at Queen's in 1917.

While classics and philosophy had lost ground in terms of their
importance as integral elements in the general B.A. program, they
can also be said to have made progress since 1890 as concentration
or honour subjects. Greek may have disappeared as a prescribed
subject and the number of students choosing it may have dramatically declined, but the honour course in classics at the University of Toronto and at several other universities was expanded
and refined, and there was always a small number of gifted candidates. Honour courses in philosophy, or in philosophy and English,
or history, or a modern language also became standard offerings,
and there was comparable development in English, in French, and
in German. Apart from Toronto there was no development in Italian
and very little in Spanish until its inclusion in the Ontario high
school course of study in 1918. Courses in Icelandic were introduced at the University of Manitoba (Wesley College) in 1901 and
in Gaelic at St Francis Xavier in 1907.

SOCIAL SCIENCES

It is tempting to say that by 1920 the social sciences in the
Canadian universities had emerged as an area of study comparable
to the humanities and the sciences, and some evidence can be produced to support the statement. Economics, political science,
and psychology had attained recognition as disciplines distinct
from philosophy. Courses in geography and sociology were offered
in a number of institutions. As a subject of study, history was
increasingly seen as a means of understanding the problems of
contemporary society rather than as a discipline necessary to the
cultural and intellectual development of the individual. At most
institutions students in the faculty of arts were required in the
interests of the distribution principle to take at least some
courses in subjects other than language and literature or mathematics and science.

However, at least as much evidence can be produced in support
of the argument that the faculty of arts and science continued to
be at this time an organization whose name accurately reflected a
twofold division of disciplines. The distribution requirement in
the area other than languages and science could normally be met
by taking courses in philosophy or history. The number of historians who considered themselves to be humanists was at least as

248

large as the number who considered themselves to be social scientists. None of the new disciplines was offered in the secondary school, with the result that the only exposure to social science at the first or senior matriculation year level was in the normally required course in history. Only the larger universities had departments of history and of political economy, and none had departments of economics *and* political science or of geography or of psychology or of sociology. Political science was invariably associated with economics or with history or with philosophy, psychology with philosophy. Frank Underhill's appointments at the University of Saskatchewan were symptomatic - professor of history and lecturer in political science.

Underhill's position was symptomatic rather than typical. In 1920 relatively few Canadian professors lectured in more than one discipline; one was an historian or an economist or a political scientist or a psychologist, though rarely at this stage a sociologist and never a geographer or an anthropologist. Geography was taught either by economists or by geologists. With the single exception of Sir Bertram Windle, a distinguished British medical doctor who in 1920 was appointed as a part-time professor at St Michael's College at the University of Toronto, no one offered instruction in anthropology.

In the case of history and political economy, the continuing identification with the humanities rather than with the sciences was partly the result of the attitude and training of the men (there were no women) who constituted the teaching staff. Most of the historians and political scientists had taken their advanced training at Oxford, while most of the economists had entered the field in their late twenties or early thirties following a switch of interest from philosophy or some other subject. Stephen Leacock had taken modern languages as an undergraduate and had taught them at a secondary school for nearly a decade before moving to Chicago for doctoral work in economics, while O.D. Skelton had devoted his time until the age of 27 to classics. Several of the first professors of history and of political economy were clergymen, G.M. Wrong, the effective founder of the Toronto 'School of History,' for example, and A.L. McCrimmon, the first occupant of the chair in political economy at McMaster. K.W. Taylor's comment on the founding fathers of Canadian economics could be applied with equal validity to the founding fathers of Canadian history and political science:

[They] were all far more than economists, and none of them started off their university careers as economists. They lived, of course, in a less specialized age. Shortt, Skelton, Mavor, and Leacock throughout their careers could almost equally well be described as historians or political scientists. McCrimmon of McMaster and Keirstead of New Brunswick were equally well qualified as philosophers and theologians. Mavor, who was head of the Toronto department from 1892 to 1922, never held a university degree until Toronto conferred upon him an honorary Ph.D. in 1912.[12]

Both Leacock and Skelton took their doctorates at the University of Chicago in the early years of the century and, particularly from 1910 a number of young Canadians followed this identical path, though frequently, as in the case of Harold Innis, after an interruption caused by World War I. However, the consequences of such exposures to a less philosophically oriented approach to the study of economics were not apparent in the Canadian universities until the 1920s. In the case of history, the Oxford influence continued to be the dominant one until the 1930s as Chester Martin, head of the Toronto department, noted in 1932:

> It is the fashion in some quarters to disparage the so-called research schools in the United States. The 'schools' may not as yet have written 'great history'; but a Canadian who contemplates the enthusiasm of these young scholars on one side of the boundary and the morass of conventional Canadian history on the other, is apt to reflect upon the revolution which has indubitably taken place before our eyes, during the last decades or two, in the recorded 'history' of the United States. How much of this has been due to unrecorded toil in the quarries of lilliputian research? At any rate, the thing has been done. Nobody will ever again have the hardihood to write the desperate nonsense that used to pass for sober history fifty years ago in the United States.[13]

This continuing bias towards a British and philosophical approach (as distinct from an American and 'scientific' one), combined with a dearth of Canadian material that could be used in history and economic courses, was reflected in the undergraduate curriculum of 1920, which continued to emphasize European rather than North American history and the theory of economics rather than its application. This was unfortunate since, though Canadian history did receive attention in the English language secondary schools and in the first four years of the classical college course, it was not a senior matriculation subject and was missing from the final years of the classical college course. Economics, it should be added, was not a secondary school subject. However, Canadian history, and particularly the history of French Canada, began to receive substantial treatment at both Université Laval and Université de Montréal towards the end of the period through the annual lecture courses offered at the latter by Abbé Lionel Groulx from 1915 and by Thomas Chapais at the former from 1916.[14] Particularly in Groulx's case the approach was not restricted to political and constitutional developments but embraced intellectual and cultural matters as well.[15]

Throughout most of this period the position of psychology was similar to that of political science, being administratively associated with another discipline, in this case philosophy. At the very beginning of the period, shortly after the appointment of J.M. Baldwin as professor of philosophy at the University of

Toronto, a psychological laboratory was established within the department, in which until 1909 August Kirschmann, a graduate of Wundt's Leipzig laboratory, carried on fundamental research and conducted seminars on the 'new psychology.' This experimental emphasis was continued at Toronto following Kirschmann's return to Germany and was expanded during World War I as the result of the work by E.A. Bott on the rehabilitation of muscularly disabled war veterans. By 1920 the staff in psychology at Toronto numbered seven; five were in the department of philosophy and two at St Michael's College, where psychology was taught as a branch of scholastic philosophy. By this time, too, an honours course in psychology had been developed, but it was not until 1927 that an independent department of psychology was established. Such a step had been taken at McGill in 1924.

World War I, in R.B. MacLeod's phrase, 'brought Canadian psychology fully to life' through the recognition of its usefulness in such matters as personnel selection and training as well as in the area of rehabilitation. By 1920 its functional independence of philosophy was generally accepted in all the non-Catholic institutions, though in no case had this acceptance been recognized administratively. Prior to World War I, however, with the exception of Toronto and McGill, where a psychological laboratory had been established in 1910, psychology was effectively a branch of philosophy. Fortunately the new subject was given considerable encouragement by the heads of the leading departments of philosophy - John Watson at Queen's, John MacEachran at Alberta, William Caldwell at McGill and G.S. Brett at Toronto. The latter had a great reputation in the field of academic philosophy as both teacher and scholar, but it is of some significance that his most distinguished work was his three volume *History of Psychology* published between 1912 and 1921.[16]

By 1920 courses in economic or commercial geography had been offered for some years in at least two universities, Toronto (from 1906) and Montreal (in l'Ecole des hautes études commerciales from 1910) and in that year were introduced at McMaster; in 1915 a course in physical geography was offered at the newly opened University of British Columbia by the geologist and dean of arts, R.W. Brock, who was no doubt influential in the establishment of a department of geology and geography at British Columbia in 1922. Rather more universities offered courses in sociology than in geography by 1920, but nothing resembling a program in this subject could be said to have been offered until the appointment by McGill of C.A. Dawson as an assistant professor in 1922.

An anthropological division was established in 1910 at the Victoria National Museum in Ottawa (re-designated the National Museum of Canada in 1927), with Edward Sapir, an outstanding American scientist and linguist, as director, but at this stage the University of Ottawa was in no position to take advantage of his presence. The attitude of the academic world towards anthropology in 1920 has been eloquently described by Watson Kirkconnell:

In 1919, I almost became an anthropologist. Wide reading in
the field had aroused my interest and with the prospect of im-
minent release from the armed forces I had resolved to register
at Columbia for a doctorate in the somatological aspects of the
science. On the personal advice of Edward Sapir ... I made a
special trip to New York in April 1919 and sought the advice of
the head of the department, Dr. Franz Boas ... In a candid burst
of pessimism, he urged me to stay out of professional anthropology. Such a department was regarded as a frill by North American
universities and was the first to get the axe whenever times
grew hard. It would be folly to proceed, for I should run a
great risk of starving. I took his warning and went no further.[17]

The argument for the development of the social sciences throughout these 30 years was based in large measure on the recognition
that Canada needed to expand its industrial capacity, and this was
recognized by a number of French Canadians, notably Léon Gérin,
Errol Bouchette, and Edouard Montpetit, who, aware of the dominant
position occupied by English-speaking Canadians - and Americans -
in the province's economy, realized that French Canada must produce in quantity its own economists, political scientists, and
sociologists as well as soundly trained businessmen and journalists.[18]
The views of these men were influential in the establishment of
Ecole des hautes études commerciales, with funds provided by the
provincial government, in 1907. Unfortunately, lack of financial
resources at Laval prevented that university from expanding its
program at Quebec, and the same restriction applied at its Montreal
branch which became the Université de Montréal in 1919. However,
one of the first actions of the new university was to establish
an Ecole des sciences sociales, économiques et politiques. But
this did not occur until 1920.
Outside the universities, on the other hand, there was a considerable degree of activity, particularly from 1900 on, as a
consequence of the papal encyclical *Rerum Novarum* of 1891, which
outlined a program of social action for the Roman Catholic church.[19]
The first organization established to implement the directions of
this encyclical was La Societé d'économie social et politique by
two priests at Quebec in 1905. A more important development was
the establishment of Action social catholique initially at Quebec
in 1907 but in 1911 transferred to Montreal, placed under the control of the Jesuits, and reorganized as l'Ecole sociale populaire,
modelled on similar écoles, which by this time had been established
in various European countries. The activities of Ecole social
populaire included conferences, workshops, study groups, and the
publication of pamphlets and were popular rather than scholarly
in nature. A more scholarly approach was characteristic of Les
Semaines sociales du Canada, again on a European model, which was
described by its founder, Father Papin Archambault, s.j. as 'une
chaire ambulante de Sociologie Catholique dont le but specifique
est le diffusion de le Doctrine social de l'Eglise.' But it, too,
was not established until 1920.

SCIENCES

By 1920 there was provision in all the English language institutions for solid instruction at the undergraduate level in mathematics and the basic sciences (botany, chemistry, geology, physics,
zoology), including at all but the small denominationally controlled
institutions the opportunity for sufficient specialization to enable the student to proceed to graduate studies, which by this
time were offered on a systematic basis at McGill and Toronto.
Adequate provision for science had been made from the outset at
the three new provincial universities of the West - Alberta,
Saskatchewan, and British Columbia - though the disruption of the
building plans at the latter caused by the outbreak of World War I
prevented the University from implementing by 1920 the complete
program it had expected to introduce in 1915. At Manitoba, university professorships in the sciences had been instituted during
the first decade of the century. At all four universities, the
provision for faculties or schools of agriculture and engineering
either strengthened the case for science appointments in the
faculty of arts and science or provided a source of expertise on
which that faculty could draw, though this was less obviously the
case at Manitoba for agriculture because of the location of agriculture and arts and science on different campuses.

The staff in the sciences inevitably varied in size in accordance
with the size of the institution, but, at least in the context of
undergraduate instruction, there appears to have been little variation in the academic qualifications of the individuals concerned.
In 1920 Acadia had only six full-time staff members on the mathematics-science side (biology 2, chemistry 2, mathematics 1, physics 1) out of a faculty of arts and science total of 16, but
their qualifications were comparable to the 12 out of a faculty
total of 29 at Saskatchewan or of the 26 out of the total of 51
at McGill. It will be noted that there was no staff member in
geology at Acadia and that botany and zoology were grouped under
biology. The situation was the same at Saskatchewan - no staff
listed under geology, four under biology. At McGill, which had a
large enrollment in engineering in 1920, the faculty of arts and
science's department of geology and mineralogy had four full-time
staff members and there were departments of botany and zoology
with two and three staff members respectively.

With respect to laboratory facilities and access to scientific
journals, the same generalizations can be made - adequate arrangement in the small institutions, good, and in the case of McGill,
Queen's, and Toronto very good arrangements in the larger institutions.

In the French-language universities the teaching of science was,
until 1920, effectively restricted to what was offered in the
classical colleges by (with a few notable exceptions) inadequately
qualified teachers working in ill-equipped laboratories. It was
not until 1920 that a faculté des sciences was established at
Montréal and that the basis of the faculté des sciences which was

253

established at Laval in 1937 was laid through the founding of an Ecole supérieure de chimie; and as we shall see in chapter 21 both of these new foundations were preoccupied to a very substantial extent during the next decade with the training of teachers of science for the classical colleges. Cyrias Ouellet dates the origin of 'la vie scientifique au Canada Français' from the year 1920, and his view is shared by all other French Canadians who have written on the subject.[20] This is not to denigrate the work of Ecole polytechnique in the area of applied science, or to overlook the genuine contributions to the advancement of individual sciences which were made by individuals connected with Université Laval at both Québec and Montréal prior to this date. It is, rather, to define the difficulties under which the French Canadian scientist had to work in the late nineteenth and early twentieth centuries. As Ouellet eloquently puts it, in almost all instances he was working effectively alone and without apparent encouragement: 'Isolement du monde extérieur, structure mentale axée sur des valeurs qui ont la pernicieuse propriété de se suffire à elles-mêmes, sensibilité negative à l'égard d'une industrialisation d'origine étrangère, absence totale de cadres, voilà quelques éléments d'un cercle vicieux dont la solidité est bien éprouvée.'[21]

EXTENSION

Between 1910 and 1920 all of the Western universities established a department of agricultural extension and began the practice of providing short courses and demonstrations designed to assist farmers and their wives to solve the practical problems of agriculture and household science. They were led by Saskatchewan in 1910 just one year after it had become operational. The policy adopted by the institutions was often referred to as the Wisconsin Idea because it had been most fully developed at the University of Wisconsin in the late nineteenth and early twentieth century. According to the theory, the university's role was to make available its resources to all the citizens whose taxes supported it. This conception of the university was voiced by the founding president of the University of Alberta, H.M. Tory, at the first convocation in 1909. In his inaugural address he declared that 'the modern state university has sprung from a demand on the part of the people themselves for intellectual recognition' and 'the people demand that knowledge shall not be the concern of scholars alone ... The job of the extension department is to find out from the people what the university can do for them beyond the classroom and the laboratory.'[22]

Tory's intention on assuming the presidency of Alberta was to establish a department of extension at once, but it was not until 1912 that he was in a position to institute Canada's first department of extension, as distinct from a department of agricultural extension. When it was established, its activities included not only the provision of practical assistance to the farming community, but also lectures on subjects such as literature and political science. Indeed, lectures of this type were offered by the university faculty, and even by Tory himself, for some years before the so-called practical work was begun.[23] This pattern was repeated at British Columbia following its opening in 1915, i.e. popular lectures preceding practical ones. At Saskatchewan, the department of agricultural extension soon recognized that the citizens of that province had cultural needs as well as practical problems. In meeting these needs, the department drew upon the resources of the University's college of arts and science.

As was noted in chapters 4 and 9, the offering of public lectures and of non-credit courses had been characteristic of a number of Canadian universities for many years before 1890. In fact, the policy advocated by Tory had been adopted by the Ontario Agricultural College in the 1880s when, following the accession of James Mills to the presidency, courses and demonstrations of a practical nature had been systematically and vigorously provided throughout Western Ontario by O.A.C. staff members.[24] In the 1880s, too, the School of Practical Science at Toronto offered evening courses of an equally pragmatic nature, and in 1894, some years after its affiliation with the University of Toronto, courses were given to prospectors and miners in two northern Ontario communities, Sudbury and Rat Portage.[25]

In 1889, Queen's University had undertaken to make arrangements whereby individuals not resident at the University during the academic year could obtain credit towards a B.A. This had been decided in the interests of practising teachers, who thereby could continue their formal education while carrying on their profession. Throughout Ontario and Quebec, the development of adult education at the universities from 1890 to 1920 consisted largely of the expansion of these two services - the offering of public lectures on a variety of subjects by staff members, and the provision of courses leading to a degree or a certificate for practising teachers. The period saw little activity in the field of adult education on the part of the Maritime universities, though in 1920, with the founding of the People's School at St Francis Xavier University, a new type of university extension work was begun.

In 1891, the minister of education of Ontario convened a meeting of representatives of the universities of the province to consider the general question of university extension and the specific question of whether it would be desirable and possible to coordinate the work of the several universities in this field.[26] At the meeting, to which representatives of Bishop's, McGill, and New Brunswick were also invited, it was decided to organize a Canadian association of the extension of university teaching, and the first meeting of this organization was held in January 1892. It also proved to be the last. During the next few years a committee on university extension involving the three universities of Quebec - Bishop's, Laval, and McGill - met periodically, presumably for the purpose of coordinating their activities, but in Ontario, and at least by 1900 in Quebec, universities pursued their own individual paths.

Considerable progress was made, particularly in Ontario. From 1895 on, a systematic scheme of Saturday morning public lectures became a regular feature of the University of Toronto's program, and what were, in effect, lecture bureaus were established at McMaster, Queen's, Toronto, and Western Ontario to provide lectures on demand, for a minimal fee, to groups and communities throughout the province. The most important development, however, was in the area of credit courses either for a degree or for a teaching certificate. The Queen's extramural degree program was continued, the chief matters of note in this connection being the introduction in 1909 of a requirement that the candidate spend one year as a full-time student, and the addition of a summer school in 1910 at which credit courses were offered. In 1905, the University of Toronto, encouraged by the Provincial Department of Education which had been giving courses in the summers in its normal schools since 1900, established a summer school in order to provide for school teachers who now required certificates to teach such subjects as art, household science, and nature study. By 1907, courses carrying a credit towards the B.A. were also being offered at the summer school. In 1907, a faculty of education was established at Toronto, and it soon assumed effective responsibility for the pedagogical courses, leaving the faculty of arts with the degree work, which by 1913 involved the preparation and marking of correspondence assignments undertaken by the students during the preceding winter. Meanwhile (1905-16), the university had begun to give both pedagogical and arts courses in a teachers' course offered in the late afternoons during the academic term. Attendance in the courses carrying credit towards a degree was never large (33 in 1907-8, of whom 30 were women); by 1912-13 the numbers had dwindled to 11 and in the next three years no courses were offered. However, they were revived in 1916-17, and in 1919 the first two extramural graduates received their degrees.

Up to this time supervision of these winter and summer courses, and also of the Saturday morning lectures and the Workers Educational Association classes which were introduced in 1918, was the responsibility of the University of Toronto. However, with a reorganization of the education faculties at Toronto and Queen's in 1920, at which time both were replaced by the Ontario College of Education, Toronto was freed of responsibility for the pedagogical courses. But by this time, extension activities had expanded sufficiently to warrant the formation of an extension department and this was undertaken in 1920. The title of the new division was the Department of University Extension and Publicity. The inclusion of 'Publicity' is a reminder that at Toronto, as elsewhere (for example, the universities of the West), there was general recognition that extension work in all its varied forms represented the most effective means of acquainting the public with the important work the universities were doing. Queen's established a department of extension in 1921, as did Western Ontario, which had also instituted a summer school in 1918.

By 1920, the four western universities were also offering certificate courses for teachers and had made provision for part-time students to earn credits towards a degree in arts and science. In each case, this represented a cooperative effort by the university and the provincial department of education. The sequence of events at Saskatchewan was typical. In 1914, the Department of Education requested the university to hold a summer school at which courses in teaching methods, financed and directed by the department, would be offered in agriculture, art, household science, nature study, and elementary science. In 1917, the university was asked to assume responsibility for the organization and management of the pedagogical courses, and in the same year it offered courses for degree credit. Following the same model, summer schools were established at Alberta in 1919 and at British Columbia and Manitoba in 1920.

Mainly because in 1907 teacher training became the responsibility of Macdonald College, provision of pedagogical courses played no part in the development of McGill's summer school. However, McGill was the first Canadian university to launch a summer school on a permanent basis. Courses carrying credit towards a B.A. were offered in the summers continuously from 1899, and, within a few years, certificate summer courses in surveying and other engineering subjects were being offered by the faculty of applied science. The first Canadian course in library science was also introduced by way of a summer course at McGill in 1904.[27]

NOTES TO CHAPTER 15

1 Dominion Bureau of Statistics, *Statistical Report on Education in Canada 1921* (1923), 110-11
2 C. Garnier, 'Education in France' in *Yearbook of Education 1932* (1932), 830-2; G. Milhaud, 'French Educational Philosophy' in *Yearbook of Education 1936* (1936), 820-2
3 H. Provost, *Historique de la Faculté des Arts de l'Université Laval, 1852-1952* (1952), 41-8, 67-70
4 'The Future of the Faculty of Arts,' *National Conference Canadian Universities Proceedings* (1942), 123-5
5 Fédération des Collèges Classiques, *Notre réforme scolaire* II (1963), 166
6 Provost, *Historique*, 77-9; A. Pouliot, 'La Faculté des Sciences,' *Rev. Univ. Laval*, 6 (1952), 378-9; E. Chartier, 'La Faculté des Lettres,' *Action Universitaire*, 11, no. 10 (Juin 1945), 35-40; A. Léveilleé, 'La Faculté des Sciences,' ibid., 41-5
7 *NCCU Proc.* (1923), 69-77
8 *University of Toronto Calendar 1901-2*, 272
9 Ibid.
10 R. Rumilly, *Histoire de l'Ecole des Hautes Etudes Commerciales de Montréal* (1966), 15-26
11 Ibid., 47

12 'Economic Scholarship in Canada,' *Can. J. Econ. Pol. Sci.*, 26 (1960), 8

13 'Fifty Years of Canadian History,' in W.S. Wallace, ed., *Royal Society Fifty Years Retrospect* (1932), 68

14 Thomas Chapais's initial appointment as a professor of history at Laval was in 1879, but it was not until 1916 that he offered instruction on a sustained basis.

15 A convenient introduction to the work and influence of Groulx is provided by G.F.G. Stanley in 'Lionel-Adolphe Groulx: Historian and Prophet of French Canada' in L.L. Lapierre, ed., *Four O'Clock Lectures* (1966), 97–114.

16 On Brett, see J.A. Irving, 'The Achievement of George Sidney Brett,' *Univ. Toronto Quart.*, 14 (1945), 329–65.

17 *A Slice of Canada: Memoirs* (1967), 30

18 On Gérin, see J.-C. Falardeau, 'Léon Gérin: His life and Work' in Lapierre, *Four O'Clock Lectures*, 59–76: on Bouchette and Montpetit, see A. Faucher, 'Edouard Montpetit,' ibid., 77–96.

19 M. Tremblay and A. Faucher, 'L'Enseignement des sciences sociales au Canada de langue français,' in *Royal Commission Studies* (1961), 191–3

20 *La Vie scientifique au Canada Français* (1964), 13. See also L. Lortie, 'Les Débuts de l'ère scientifique' in L. Lortie et A. Plouffe, eds., *Au Sources du présent* (1960), 90–104.

21 *Vie scientifique*, 16

22 Quoted in E.A. Corbett, *Henry Marshall Tory: Beloved Canadian* (1954), 100

23 The trials and tribulations, but also the triumphs, of the pioneer extension lecturer in the West are delightfully described by E.A. Corbett in his *We Have With Us Tonight* (1957).

24 A.M. Ross, *The College on the Hill* (1974), 40–2

25 C.R. Young, *Early Engineering Education at Toronto 1851-1919* (1958), 104–5

26 For a detailed account of this conference and its consequences, see A.M. Tough, 'The Development of Adult Education at Toronto before 1920,' M.A. thesis, University of Toronto, 1962.

27 See below, chapter 16, 295.

16

Professional Education in 1920

> While it is, of course, the old-established faculties that give
> the University its character, it would be a mistake to genera-
> lize as to the dilution of the University idea by the multitude
> of attached departments and the part-time teaching which contri-
> bute to the attendance in these immense institutions. New stars
> being drawn into the orbit of the older planets make an impres-
> sive constellation. There are schools of agriculture, education,
> commerce, dentistry, pharmacy, journalism, nursing; there are
> thronged conservatories of music; summer-sessions for six weeks
> and extension courses on almost every conceivable subject. The
> educational sky is thickly studded; nor can one venture to
> prophesy as to what feeble star may be travelling fast towards
> this cluster of schools and faculties. Are the Osteopaths, who
> ask a surer scientific foundation for their skillful massage,
> within recognition? Or have the Chiropractors a hope of regu-
> larizing their manual dexterity? What about the Optometrists
> who think that a little more optics will help them to fit glasses
> better?[1]

This statement is taken from a paper presented by the president
of the University of Toronto to the Second Congress of the Universities of the Empire which was held at the University of Oxford
in the summer of 1921. Sir Robert Falconer's paper was one of
five presented at an opening session given over to the discussion
of how much of a university's efforts should be devoted to liberal
or general education and how much to professional education or
training. The question was one which it was very pertinent to ask
with respect to higher education in Canada at this time. It was
obviously a matter of concern for the relatively large and well-
established universities like McGill and Toronto which had begun
to experience the problems of the multiversity as early as 1890,
but because they too had become 'multi-faculty' it was just as
much a problem for old but still relatively small institutions

like Dalhousie, Laval, Manitoba, and Queen's and for the new and fast-growing institutions of the west. In 1920-21 the University of Alberta had only a handful more than 1000 students, but it was involved with engineering, law, accounting, dentistry, pharmacy, household economics, and theology, as well as arts and science at both undergraduate and graduate levels.

A layman might well have been puzzled by Falconer's question, or rather surprised at the failure of the assembled delegates to give him a simple and straightforward answer. Surely by referring to the functions which as a university it was equipped and authorized to perform, a university could decide whether or not it should offer a course for osteopaths. The trouble was that the universities themselves were not clear as to what these functions were. In 1905, some laymen had pointed this out to the Royal Commissioners who were then investigating the university of which Sir Robert was about to become president.

> We think that the University as the head of the educational institutions of the Province, should direct in greater measure than at present the course of technical and commercial education, higher and lower.

> We find it difficult, however, to come to a clear understanding of what the University really is. The older and newer tendencies with regard to the University organization and work seem still in conflict. At present the University seems to us to be a loose federation of technical and professional schools. We are not aware that there are any general conditions, constituting a basis or reflecting a principle according to which any technical or other school may enter and form a part of the real Cultural University. Without desiring to reduce the prominence given to cultural work in University instruction, we think it advisable for you to determine as definitely as possible the organic relation of the various federated branches to the cultural heart of the University. This would help greatly in clarifying the organization of technical instruction, and assist in co-ordinating this instruction as carried on by higher and lower schools, and of preventing overlapping. In this way, the country would know better what technical instruction to expect of our University, and in the end of each grade of school as well.[2]

The royal commissioners of 1906 had taken notice of these remarks of the Canadian Manufacturers' Association, and their report was a serious and on the whole successful attempt to define the role of a publicly supported university. They did concern themselves with the proper relationship of the various branches of the university to each other, and they did place their seal of approval on professional education as such. Their report appears to have had an important influence on the universities which were about to be established in the West. At Alberta, Saskatchewan, and

British Columbia instruction in agriculture, law, pharmacy, and other professional subjects was recognized as a proper and important function of the university from the outset.

In actual fact the position of professional education in the Canadian universities in 1920 was less muddled than Falconer's rather facetious questions about optometry, chiropractic, and osteopathy might suggest.

So far as academic legitimacy was concerned, the position of engineering, agriculture, forestry, veterinary medicine, and dentistry was now as firm as that of law, medicine, and theology. By 1920, household economics, nursing, social work, and commerce were on the point of being admitted to the club. The somewhat ambiguous position of pharmacy was mainly the consequence of the failure of the pharmacists themselves to decide what academic standards were required for admission to the profession. And, assuming financial support could be found, there was a willingness to consider other new areas - library science at McGill, journalism at Montreal. The two areas where there did appear to be a genuine muddle were music and education.

But before turning to Falconer's new stars, what of his older planets, law, medicine, and theology? The brief answer is that in 1920 medicine was of central importance, but theology and law remained on the periphery.

THEOLOGY

With the single exception of Morrin College, the Presbyterian foundation at Quebec City which was closed in 1899, all the Protestant theological colleges, departments, and faculties which were operating in 1890 were still active in 1920, though several had shut down temporarily during World War I. An additional eleven colleges had been established, all but one of them in the western provinces:

Church of England

St Chad's College, Regina, Sask.	Est. 1907; affil. U. of Sask., 1910
Emmanuel College, Prince Albert, Sask.	Reest. 1906; affil. U. of Sask., 1910
Anglican Theological College, Vancouver	Est. 1920, incorporating Bishop Latimer College (1910) and St Mark's College (1912); affil. U.B.C. 1922.

Presbyterian

Presb. Theol. College, Saskatoon, Sask.	Est. 1914; affil. U. of Sask., 1913; Renamed St Andrew's College 1924
Robertson College, Edmonton, Alberta	Est. 1910; affil. U. of Alberta 1913

Westminster Hall, Vancouver, B.C.	Est. 1908; merged with Ryerson College (Methodist 1923) in 1925 as Union College of B.C.; affil. U.B.C. 1924

Methodist

Alberta College, Edmonton	Est. 1903; Theological Dept. 1909; affil. U. of Alberta 1909
Columbian Methodist College, Vancouver	Est. 1892; theological work assumed by Ryerson College 1923

Baptist

Brandon College (1899)	Est. 1899; Dept. 1902; affil. McMaster Univ. 1911

Lutheran

Evangelical Lutheran Seminary, Waterloo, Ont.	Est. 1911; affil. (as Waterloo College) U. of Western Ontario 1925
Lutheran College & Seminary	Est. at Edmonton 1913; moved to Saskatoon 1914. Seminary status 1920; affil. U. of Sask. 1925

This brought the Church of England total to 10, the Presbyterian to 9, the Methodist to 6, the Baptist to 3. A Congregational College of British Columbia was incorporated in 1914 but the project was dropped.

The consequence of this further proliferation of colleges was that the position of Protestant theological education remained in 1920 what it had been in 1890 and 1860 - a very large number of very small colleges. The Dominion Bureau of Statistics figures for 1920-21 report an enrolment of 173 theological students in nine Church of England institutions (there was no report from St John's College, Winnipeg), with 59 of them at Wycliffe. Over 50 staff members were listed for these nine institutions, no doubt many on a part-time basis and some involved with instruction in arts as well as with theology. The contrast with the Toronto Bible College, an institution of a very different type, is striking; in 1920-21 it had an enrolment of 477, including 330 women, and a staff of six.[3] Seven women were reported at the theological colleges, three at McMaster and two each at Queen's and Trinity.

Masters shows that there was an expansion and liberalization of the theological curriculum during these 30 years; by 1920 most courses of study included comparative religion, religious education, missions, and sociology.[4] Nonetheless, not much progress could be expected so long as a small staff attempted to cover the whole field for a handful of students. Staff could be increased in either of two ways: by a denomination concentrating its theological work at a smaller number of institutions or by cooperation between colleges of different denominations located on or near the same campus. There was no attempt to pursue the first of these alternatives between 1890 and 1920, but in 1912 three separate experiments in inter-denominational cooperation were initiated. Two of these were in the West and involved the Presbyterians and the Methodists. At Winnipeg, Wesley College and Manitoba College had been cooperating to a limited extent in the field of arts and science instruction since 1890. In 1912 it was proposed that they cooperate in offering the Bachelor of Divinity degree. Such a course was instituted in 1913 but was withdrawn a year later, partly owing to dissatisfaction on the part of some of the Wesley students, but mainly for reasons connected with the relationship of the separate colleges with the University of Manitoba.[5] In the same year there was the launching of a common theological course for the students at Alberta College (Methodist) and Robertson College (Presbyterian), both of which were located on the University of Alberta campus. This cooperation continued until the merging of the two colleges, first as United Theological College of Alberta and then as St Stephen's College following the establishment of the United Church of Canada in 1925.[6]

The other experiment was at Montreal and involved four denominations.[7] Under the aegis of McGill University, its four affiliated theological colleges entered upon a cooperative scheme which ultimately (1948) led to the establishment of a common Faculty of Divinity. Each of the four colleges, Montreal Diocesan College, Presbyterian College, Wesleyan Theological College, and Congregational College, continued to teach 'denominational theology,' but all general theological subjects were taught by the appropriate member of a combined staff which in 1920 numbered 16.

The main development in the Roman Catholic church during this period was the establishment of English-speaking seminaries. Prior to 1890 all theological education had been concentrated at Quebec, Montreal, and Ottawa though some theological training was carried on in other seminaries both *grand* and *petit*, and in the mother houses of the various religious orders.

The first of these was the Holy Heart Seminary established by Archbishop O'Brien in Halifax in 1895. This institution was in the charge of the Eudist fathers whom O'Brien had earlier invited to establish Collège Ste Anne at Church Point. Apparently O'Brien originally had in mind a parallel college for his English-speaking constituents, but he was persuaded by the Eudist fathers in France to establish a seminary which would provide training for diocesan clergy in all the Maritime provinces. In 1920, the Holy Heart Seminary had a staff of seven and an enrolment of 92.

St Augustine's Seminary at Toronto was founded by Archbishop McEvoy 'to train priests for English-speaking dioceses of both eastern and western Canada.' Designed to accommodate 100 students, it opened in 1913 in a splendid building made possible by a $500,000 donation from Sir Eugene O'Keefe. In 1920-21 it had a staff of nine and 131 students and was already in need of the addition which was provided in 1926. A number of students came from the western provinces.

At the three French-language universities the period saw a further development of the faculté de théologie with the organization of programs leading to the licence and the doctorat in both theology and canon law. In 1920 the enrolment at Montreal was 299 with a staff of 15, at Laval 168 with a staff of 13, at Ottawa 67 with a staff of 12.

LAW

A committee on legal education to consist of one representative from each university having a law school was appointed at the Second Conference of the Canadian Universities in 1915. This should have given it a membership of seven, three from universities that had law schools in 1890 (Laval, McGill, Dalhousie), and four from universities that had established schools in the interim (King's, which acquired a school at Saint John, N.B. in 1892; Alberta, which established a faculty in 1912; Saskatchewan, which established a college in 1913; and Manitoba, which established the Manitoba Law School in conjunction with the Manitoba Law Society in 1914). In fact, eight persons were named to the committee; King's was not represented but Ottawa and Toronto were, though neither university had a school or faculty of law. Four Canadian law schools were not represented on the committee since they had no connection with the conference; these were the schools established by provincial law societies - Osgoode Hall at Toronto (1889), Wetmore Hall at Regina, Saskatchewan (1913), and the schools at Vancouver and at Victoria in British Columbia (1914).
    The committee reported to the conference at each of its next four annual meetings, the membership remaining constant except for the addition of a representative from Université de Montréal, which became independent of Laval in 1919. At the 1916 Conference the report was limited to outlining the requirements for admission to practise in the various provinces,[8] but in 1917 the committee presented its recommendations on three matters which had been referred to it by the conference:

(1) That steps should be taken to procure the further recognition of University examinations by the Provincial Law Societies, so as to put an end to the present duplication of examinations.
(2) That a preliminary course of two years in Arts should be required as a condition of admission to the Law Schools - such condition being both educationally desirable and having the further advantage of bringing the Canadian schools up to the standard required by the Association of American Law Schools.
(3) That legal studies should be admitted to the Arts course as a distinct course of study leading to the B.A. degree.[9]

The implementation of these proposals would have established law as a university discipline in the full sense. The first was designed to have the degree accepted as the academic requirement

264

for the right to practise, the second to ensure that the student
of law had a sound general education before he entered upon his
legal studies, and the third to further the development of law as
an academic subject as distinct from a professional subject. Unfortunately, the committee's recommendations were essentially negative. The suggestion that law courses be included as optional
subjects in the B.A. program 'was generally received with favour,'
but the committee members were not prepared to make recommendations
about either of the first two proposals; in their view, the varying
circumstances of the different provinces inhibited the recognition
of university examinations by provincial law societies while 'objections to the suggestion that the 2 years in Arts be required
for admission to the law course were sufficiently strong to cause
the Committee to abandon the idea.'

It could have been argued, and probably was, that the universities by themselves were unable to take the steps necessary to improve the situation. Admittedly they could do something about
establishing law as a subject in the B.A. program, but only the
provincial law societies could authorize the degree as a requirement for admission to practise and in default of this requirement
only the provincial law society could ensure that all qualifying
lawyers had a sound general education. All that the conference,
as representing the Canadian universities could do, was to continue to make its views known to the provincial law societies. The
committee's report was therefore approved and the members were
instructed 'to watch the general proceedings of the Canadian Bar
Association at a meeting to be held in Winnipeg on the 29th of
August next, and to report anything of interest to the next conference.

But were the universities in such a helpless situation? In 1918
the conference was told bluntly by R.W. Lee, dean of the faculty
of law at McGill, that the fault lay with the universities themselves and that the remedy did lie within their powers. Lee was
now the chairman of the committee and he announced that there was
nothing to report since the Canadian Bar Association had not met
in 1917. But he went on to say that legal education in Canada
was in an unsatisfactory condition because the instruction of students was largely in the hands of judges and practising lawyers,
'who although they may be excellent judges and practitioners are
not necessarily good teachers and, in any case can give only a
small part of their time to the University.' What was the point
of complaining about the quality of the work in the non-university
schools, if the same conditions applied in the university schools?
Then he said:

> As regards the relation of university law schools to the pro-
> fessional bodies, he considered that the best course to follow
> would be to conduct legal education in the university on such
> efficient lines that the Bar Associations would not hesitate to
> admit the graduates of these law schools to the practice of their
> profession without further examination, and that the most effec-

tual method of raising the standard of legal education in university would be to recognise legal studies as an integral part of the work of a University and to appoint professors at salaries sufficient to command their whole time and attention.[10]

In other words if we put our house in order, perhaps the provincial law societies will do likewise. And the way to put the university house in order was to appoint a sufficient number of persons who were in a position to give their whole attention to this task.

At the time Lee spoke there were only six full-time teachers of law in Canada, two at Saskatchewan and one each at Dalhousie, McGill, the Manitoba Law School, and Osgoode Hall. The situation did improve in the next few years. McGill appointed its second full-time professor in 1919 and its third in 1920. Dalhousie its second in 1920 and its third in 1921. By 1924, Manitoba and Saskatchewan also had three full-time staff members. The presence of three full time staff members was, it may be noted, one of the qualifications for admission to the Association of American Law Schools.

When the Canadian Bar Association did resume its annual meetings in 1919, it appointed a committee on legal education for the purpose of considering how orderly affairs were in the provincial law society houses. The committee did not report until 1923, but it was able at that time to report a general improvement in the standards required for admission to the law schools of the various provinces, which in part resulted from pressures brought to bear by the Canadian Bar Association itself.[11]

There was, then, in the early 1920s a considerable improvement in the conditions pertaining to legal education in Canada. But in 1920 this dawn was only beginning to break. In most respects the situation was the same as it had been in 1890. There had been no essential change in the three-year degree course and, aside from an increase in day-time lectures at some institutions and an increasing use of the case method in most, there had been no substantial change in the instruction offered.[12] A number of universities had introduced law courses in the B.A. program, most notably Toronto, where seven courses were listed in Roman, constitutional, and international law.

MEDICINE

Among the many debts that Canada owes to Andrew Carnegie was the decision of the Carnegie Foundation for the Advancement of Teaching in 1909 to include Canadian medical schools in the survey of medical education which it commissioned Abraham Flexner to conduct. Flexner's report is credited with transforming medical education in the United States from an art into a science. The effect on Canadian medical education was comparable.

In Flexner's view medical education in 1909 was, on the whole, better conducted in Canada than in the United States: 'In Canada conditions have never become so badly demoralized as in the United States. There the best features of English clinical teaching had never been wholly forgotten. Convalescence from a relatively mild over-indulgence in commercial medical schools set in earlier and is more nearly completed.'[13] However, Western University at London he found to be 'as bad as anything on this side of the line,' while Laval, both at Quebec and Montreal, and the Halifax Medical College, an affiliate of Dalhousie, he described as 'feeble.'[14] Two of the remaining schools, McGill and Toronto, were 'excellent,' while Queen's and Manitoba 'represent a distinct effort toward higher ideals.' Flexner felt that Canada's needs could be met by 'the four better English schools [McGill, Toronto, Manitoba, Queen's] and the Laval Department at Quebec,' but he was doubtful about the future of Queen's, owing to the limited clinical facilities available in a town the size of Kingston. He did not say in so many words that any of the schools should be closed.

Five basic criteria were used to evaluate the medical schools surveyed by Flexner: admission standards, laboratory facilities, clinical facilities, the involvement of full-time staff, and the relation of the school to a university. The latter was crucial; in his view the medical school must be an integral part of the university with which it was associated and the university must accept financial responsibility for it. He had no fixed requirements for the number of full-time staff, but he was suspicious of any school that had none. His approach to the subject of admission standards and of laboratory and clinical facilities was pragmatic rather than doctrinaire. The essential questions were not the number of years of schooling or the availability of particular types of equipment, but rather whether students were prepared for medical studies and whether the facilities were adequate to provide the training required.

So far as admission standards were concerned, Flexner was generally satisfied with the requirements of all the Canadian schools with the exception of Western.[15] He was unhappy about laboratory facilities at Dalhousie and Western (both of which he described as 'wretched'), and about clinical facilities at Dalhousie ('feeble'), Queen's ('limited'), Western ('entirely inadequate'), and Laval at Montreal ('meagre'). The clinical facilities at McGill were 'excellent,' the laboratory facilities at Toronto 'among the best on the continent.' Only McGill, Toronto, and Queen's had full-time professors, and only at McGill, Toronto, and Laval at Quebec were the medical schools organically related to the university.

One of the effects of the Flexner report in the United States was the closing down of a substantial number of medical schools. In almost all cases these were proprietary schools with no university connection, or only a nominal one. No schools were closed in Canada despite the fact that five of the eight could be described as proprietary in the sense that they were owned by a group of individuals. But in no case does it appear that the school was proprietary in the sense of being operated with a view to making money. The most likely candidate, the school at Western, was certainly not a profitable business; in 1912 the 'proprietors' offered to sell the school to the university for $25,871, this being the amount of money they estimated they had invested over the years in unpaid lectures and in cash.[16] Moreover all five schools had a quite definite relationship with a university, albeit by Flexner's standards an unsatisfactory one. The value of this relationship now became apparent in the speed and relative ease with which all five schools became integrated medical faculties. This process was completed at Dalhousie in 1911, at Queen's and Western in 1913, at Laval in Montreal in 1919 (with the establishment of the Université de Montréal), and at Manitoba in 1920.

In each case the integration of the medical school within the university led to a marked improvement of the financial position and hence to a strengthening of the academic staff through full-time appointments, and to the provision of proper laboratory and clinical facilities. On behalf of its medical faculty, a university could appeal to the provincial government, to the city in which it was situated, and to American foundations like Carnegie and Rockefeller for financial support, and such appeals were made with considerable success during the ten-year period 1912-1922. Had Flexner made a second survey in 1921 the weakest adjective he would have used to describe the laboratory and clinical facilities would have been 'adequate.' He would also have reported satisfaction with the admission requirements at Western.

By 1920, the bases for two additional medical schools had been laid in the West. A faculty of medicine was established at the University of Alberta in 1913, designed to offer initially a pre-medical year and the first two (medical) years of a four year degree course, with the students proceeding to Manitoba, McGill, or Toronto for the two clinical years and internship. Instruction in the first medical year was begun in 1915. Commencing in 1916 some clinical instruction was provided in the second year, the facilities of the Strathcona City Hospital, built on the campus in 1912-13, being used for this purpose. Construction of a medical building was begun in 1920, a dean of medicine was appointed in 1922, and the full four year medical course became available in 1923. At Saskatchewan this pattern was repeated, though on a slower schedule. A professor of bacteriology was appointed in 1919, a college of medical sciences offering two pre-medical and two medical years was instituted in 1926, a university hospital was built in 1955, and the full four year course was offered in 1956.

The two schools found by Flexner to be 'excellent' in 1910 were much more deserving of that description in 1920. McGill's medical building, destroyed by fire in 1907, was replaced by a new building with more modern facilities in 1911. A $1,000,000 laboratory building was provided in 1922. At Toronto, where a medical building had been completed in 1902 and where the Trinity Medical College had been absorbed in 1904, the main 'physical' development was in the working out of functional arrangements for clinical teaching with the Toronto General Hospital (relocated close to the campus in 1912) and several other hospitals. By 1921 Toronto had appointed two full-time clinical professors, Dr Duncan Graham in medicine and Dr C.L. Starr in surgery. In 1919 it extended the undergraduate medical course to six years from five. McGill followed this move in 1921 as did Queen's in 1922.

Another important development of the post-Flexner decade was the expansion of medicine into the field of public health and hygiene. Institutes of Public Health were established with provincial government support and in association with the medical school at Western in 1910 and at Queen's in 1912. At Toronto, the Connaught Medical Laboratories were established in 1914. In conjunction with them a department of hygiene in the faculty of medicine offered a diploma course in public health. This would lead in 1926 (with Rockefeller Foundation assistance) to the establishment of a school of hygiene. Public health was also receiving attention by 1920 at each of the other medical schools.

ENGINEERING

By 1920 it was generally recognized in North America that the education of engineers was as much a responsibility of the university as was the education of medical doctors. Integrated faculties of engineering (or of applied science and engineering) were a normal feature of all the larger Canadian universities. The exceptions were Université Laval which did not offer engineering and Université de Montréal, where the 'faculty,' l'Ecole polytechnique, was an affiliated institution financed independently of the university. In Ontario the two engineering schools established by the government had been taken over by universities, the School of Practical Science by the University of Toronto in 1906 and the Kingston School of Mines by Queen's in 1916. Engineering had been offered at each of the new universities of the West virtually from the beginning (Alberta 1908, Saskatchewan 1912, British Columbia 1915), and had been introduced at Manitoba in 1907. At all four universities it enjoyed faculty status by 1921.

The most interesting development in engineering education during the period occurred in the Maritime provinces. In 1889 the University of New Brunswick had established a chair of civil engineering and surveying and had begun to offer a diploma course. The latter was expanded to a degree program in 1899 and a building for engineering and physics was contructed in 1901. By 1907 there were three professors, a course in electrical as well as civil engineering was offered, and provision had been made for the M.Sc. In 1920, there were almost as many students in engineering at New Brunswick as in arts, and there were substantially more in the faculty of applied science, including forestry, than in the faculty of arts.

269

But it was a very small faculty - 52 students in engineering, 32 in forestry - compared with the numbers at Toronto (805), McGill (659), and Queen's (397). At the turn of the century it appeared that there would be a number of such schools of engineering in the Maritimes. The School of Engineering at King's College, Windsor, established in the 1870s was still operating. In 1899, St Francis Xavier established a department of engineering; in 1902, Dalhousie established a school of mines which in 1906 became a faculty of engineering; in 1903, Acadia began to offer the first two years of a four year engineering course; in 1904 Mount Allison established the McClellan School of Applied Science. But in 1907 the legislature of Nova Scotia, convinced that the needs of the province and of the Maritime area in general were not likely to be adequately provided for by a series of small schools, particularly with respect to research, passed an act establishing 'an institution for the purpose of affording facilities for scientific research and instruction and professional training in civil, mining, mechanical, chemical, metallurgical and electrical engineering or any departments which may from time to time be provided.' This was the Nova Scotia Technical College, a degree-granting institution which would offer only the final two years of the undergraduate course, arrangements having been made with Acadia, Dalhousie, King's, Mount Allison, and St Francis Xavier to confine their efforts to the work of the first three years of a five-year course from junior matriculation. Sums of $100,000 were provided by the government in 1907 and 1909, and in the latter year the college was opened in its own building with a staff of three and an enrolment of nine. In 1920 there was a staff of seven and an enrolment of 33, with about 150 students registered in engineering at the five affiliated universities.

Nova Scotia's concern about technical education in the early 1900s was not confined to the provision of training at the professional level and for the development of research; the legislature passed a Technical Education Act in 1906 which made some provision for the training of technicians and technologists. Nor was this concern peculiar to Nova Scotia. In 1909, the Ontario Department of Education commissioned its chief director, John Seath, to submit a plan for the development of technical education in the province. This he did in a report entitled *Education for Industrial Purposes*, published in 1910. In the same year the federal government appointed a Royal Commission on Industrial Training and Technical Education, which produced a three-volume *Report* in 1913. Both of these reports led to action, the first by way of the Industrial Education Act of 1911, which authorized the offering of technical courses in the Ontario secondary schools, and the second through two acts which provided federal funds to the provinces on a matching basis for the development of vocational training. One of these acts, the Agricultural Instruction Act, was passed in 1913, but the passage of the second, the Technical Education Act, was delayed by the outbreak of World War I until 1919; its effects consequently had hardly begun to reveal themselves by 1920. However, it was already apparent by 1920 that the effect of both reports was to provide for the development of technical education by an expansion of secondary school facilities rather than by the establishment of separate institutions created for the purpose. From 1910 to 1950, technical education in Canada other than in the fields of agriculture, art, and music tended to be provided in a secondary school context, and this is one reason for the relatively late development in Canada of community colleges and technical institutes. With respect to engineering, this had the effect of producing many chiefs and relatively few indians. In 1920 there was ample provision for the training of the professional engineer in Canada, but very little for the training of the support staff he needed to function effectively as a professional.

By 1920, the undergraduate program in engineering had become standardized in the sense that all institutions offered a four year course for students entering with approximately the same academic preparation. The program offered by the individual universities varied mainly in the specializations offered, the smaller confining themselves to two or three of civil, mechanical, electrical, and mining, and the larger (Ecole polytechnique, McGill, Queen's, Toronto) offering all of these and chemical as well. Queen's and Toronto also offered a course in engineering physics, while architecture was still a division of engineering at McGill, Toronto, and l'Ecole polytechnique. At all institutions the first year was effectively a common one and at some specialization was reserved for the final two years. In all cases the course was demanding in terms of class hours, and, aside from English and economics, not characterized by much attention to subjects whose immediate relevance to the practice of engineering was not obvious. At the larger institutions there was a growing interest in research and in graduate work, but the facilities for the former remained meagre and the number of applicants for the latter small.

ARCHITECTURE

A total of twelve degrees in architecture were granted in 1920 by Canadian universities, four each by McGill and Toronto, three by Montreal, and one by Manitoba. They were awarded on completion of a five year course from junior matriculation offered in a faculty of engineering, except at Manitoba where the professor of architecture appointed in 1913 had been assigned to the faculty of arts (in 1921 the architecture course was transferred to the faculty of engineering). At Manitoba the degree was Bachelor of Architecture; elsewhere it was B.Sc.

It is not surprising that, though accepted as a recognized subject for university study, architecture had not at this time obtained independent status but continued as a department within engineering. The number of graduates at Toronto, which granted its first degree in 1892, had never exceeded seven in any year, and no degrees were granted in eleven of the years between 1892

and 1920. A similar situation obtained at McGill, which established its course in 1896, granted its first three degrees in 1899,
awarded none from 1900 through 1905, and granted no more than nine
degrees in any year prior to 1920. Manitoba did not award a degree until 1919. The development of Manitoba's program was held
back by World War I; this was also the case at Alberta and indeed
at Toronto and McGill, which between them had only two graduates
in 1918 and 1919.

The degree course at Montreal was offered at the affiliated
Ecole polytechnique, which had been offering instruction in architecture since its establishment in 1874. In 1909, l'Ecole underwent a reorganization, and architecture became one of the institution's two basic divisions. Until 1919, the graduate received a
certificate, but with the establishment of Université de Montréal
degrees were authorized and the first three awarded in 1920. At
this time the staff numbered five, the majority having been trained
at the Ecole des Beaux-Arts in Paris. The course, however, had as
strong an engineering component as had those at McGill, Manitoba,
and Toronto. But in 1923 the staff was transferred *en bloc* to
l'Ecole des Beaux-Arts which the provincial government had established at Montreal in that year, and thereafter the program increasingly resembled the design-oriented approach of the school
at Paris.

The question of whether there should be more emphasis on design
and less on such subjects as strength of materials was periodically
raised at the English-language universities by both faculty and
practising architects, particularly at Toronto, where between 1905
and 1912 a proposal to establish a faculty of fine arts was several
times advanced. In 1920, however, the engineering element remained
dominant.

FORESTRY

Between 1907 and 1910, degree courses in forestry were established
at three Canadian universities - Toronto, New Brunswick, and Laval -
and in 1921 a fourth degree program was introduced at the University
of British Columbia. Nearly 50 years were to pass before there
would be a fifth. The sudden burst of activity in the first decade
of the century is worthy of note, as is the leadership displayed
by the universities in this particular branch of professional
education. J.W.B. Sisam has remarked: 'In contrast to most other
professions in which the members themselves first join in associations or societies to provide training facilities for new recruits
with the universities only gradually taking over this responsibility,
forestry training in Canada began at once in the university
without the support of an established profession and without a
background of experience and tradition.[17]

One reason for this is that in the early 1900s there was no
established forestry profession in Canada; at the time the Toronto,
New Brunswick, and Laval schools were being established there were

no more than a half-dozen Canadians who had professional training
in this field. Another is the enlightened view of government at
both federal and provincial levels; in the case of New Brunswick
and Laval, the provincial government took the initiative in establishing the school, the universities being assured at the outset of adequate financial support. Toronto, however, actively
sought the assignment, partly at least out of self-interest; it
was fully aware that the Ontario government was seriously considering a proposal to provide the funds for the establishment of
a faculty of forestry at Queen's.

Nevertheless, the need for professional foresters in Canada at
this time was obvious, both to conserve one of the nation's richest
natural resources and to develop the lumber and the pulp and paper
industries. This need was reflected in 1900 in the formation of
the Canadian Forestry Association, with financial support from
the federal government and the provinces of Ontario, Quebec, and
British Columbia. By the end of the year the membership was 369.
The objectives of the Canadian Forestry Association were: 'the
preservation of the forests for their influence on climate, fer-
tility and water supply; the exploration of the public domain and
the reservation for timber production of lands unsuited for agriculture; the promotion of judicious methods in dealing with
forests and woodlands; re-forestation where advisable; tree
planting in the plains and on streets and highways and the collection and dissemination of information bearing on the forestry
problem in general.'[18] Sisam's statement is inaccurate in one
sense. The C.F.A. was an association and it was active in the
development of the early Canadian forestry schools, but it was
not a 'normal' professional association. Few of its members were
working foresters and it did not provide any training facilities
within its own organization as other early professional associations often did. However, an association of professional foresters was formed in 1908, the Canadian Society of Forest Engineers,[19]
which became the Canadian Institute of Forestry in 1950. Its
first president, B.E. Fernow, had been appointed dean of the faculty of forestry at the University of Toronto on 28 March 1907.

Fernow, without question the most influential figure in the
development of forestry education, not only in Canada but in North
America,[20] might well have been appointed dean of forestry at
Queen's University. In 1894 he had had discussions with W.L.
Goodwin, director of the Kingston School of Mines, while attending
a meeting of the Royal Society of Canada as one of several representatives of American learned societies. Goodwin, on returning
to Kingston, convinced the senate of Queen's, with which the
School of Mines was affiliated, that 'something should be done in
forestry education,' but lack of funds prevented any concrete
action.[21] In 1901, however, the board of governors of the School
of Mines invited Fernow to Kingston to give a lecture at a conference called to discuss the forestry problem, and a few months
later it arranged for the amendment of its act of incorporation
to provide for the inclusion of forestry among the subjects to be

taught. In January 1903, Fernow gave a course of ten lectures on forestry at Queen's and later that year the senate approved a four-year B.Sc. degree in forestry. But the University of Toronto was also by this time interested in expanding its offerings and in that same year its senate authorized a three-year diploma course modelled in part on that of the Yale Forest School, which had been established in 1900. The Toronto course was described in some detail at the 1904 meeting of the Canadian Forestry Association in a paper presented by President James Loudon,[22] and in the discussion that followed attention was drawn both to the proposed Queen's course and to the fact that instruction in forestry had been given at the Ontario Agricultural College for ten years. Indeed, it was suggested that if the older universities of the province could not agree as to what ought to be done, 'the founding of a nice modest little school of forestry at Guelph in connection with the School of Agriculture' would provide a simple solution. The association declined to indicate any preference for the establishment of a school at any one of the institutions but it did pass the following resolution: 'that the Ontario Government be and hereby is requested to make an appropriate grant for the operation of a Provincial School or Schools of Forestry.'[23] The government, however, took no action until 1906 when, following the defeat of the Liberals in the 1905 election and the appointment of a Royal Commission on the University of Toronto, the Conservative government accepted the report of the Royal Commission, which included a recommendation that a faculty of forestry be established at the University of Toronto.

The Toronto faculty was inaugurated in the 1907-8 session with five students undertaking a four year course to the B.Sc.F. degree under the direction of two full-time staff members, Fernow and A.H.D. Ross, and a part-time lecturer, E.J. Zavitz, who for several years had been a lecturer in forestry at the Ontario Agricultural College. By 1910, the enrolment had risen to 40 and the staff to four, two of whom, C.D. Howe and J.H. White, had appointments as joint lecturer in Forestry and Botany. White was the first graduate of the faculty (in 1909) but he also held two other Toronto degrees, a B.A. in honour science (1904) and an M.A. (1907). The enrolment dropped drastically during World War I (nine students in 1917), but was back to 'normal' (55) by 1920 when C.D. Howe replaced Dean Fernow, who had reached retirement age. Of the first 41 graduates 31 were initially employed by the Dominion Forestry Branch. By 1920, the faculty was also offering the professional degree of Forest Engineer (F.E.) and a six-year program which led to the B.A. *and* the B.Sc.F. degree. The latter, which had been introduced in 1910, was withdrawn in 1921.

A resolution passed at the New Brunswick Forest Convention in February 1907 led to the opening of a second school at the University of New Brunswick in September 1908.[24] An act authorizing the school was passed by the legislature in the spring of 1908 and the government provided an annual grant of $2500 to establish a chair. R.B. Miller, a Master of Forestry from Yale, was appointed and occupied the position, that of professor in the department of applied science, until 1919. In 1918, the staff was doubled by the appointment of an instructor in charge of practical work. The degree was the B.Sc.F., awarded after four years from junior matriculation, with the first year taken in common with civil and electrical engineers. Thirty-two students were enrolled in 1920-21.

In 1905, the Quebec premier, Jean Lomer Gouin, persuaded the Quebec government to send two students, G.-C. Piché and Avila Bédard, to the Yale Forest School for two years.[25] Both became members of the six-man staff of the Ecole Forestière established by a legislative act on 4 June 1910, Piché being named director. Ten days later the Ecole became an affiliate of Université Laval. Instruction began in September with twelve students enrolled, seven of whom received a diploma in 1912 on completing a two year course. Ten of the students were on full bursaries.[26] The school was associated with the faculté des arts but was financially independent of the university; for 1910-11 it received a $4000 grant, which was increased to $5000 in 1911 and to $10,000 in 1918. In 1919 it was merged with l'Ecole d'arpentage, which had been established by the government on a similar basis in 1907, as l'Ecole d'arpentage et de génie forestier; Piché retired as director but remained as a faculty member and Bédard assumed the directorship of the combined school. The relationship with the government and with the university remained unchanged, but henceforth students took a three year course leading to the B. ès Arpentage and then a one year course to the degree of Ingénieur Forestier. Eighteen students were enrolled in 1920-21.

A plan for the development of the University of Saskatchewan sketched by President Murray in 1908 shortly after his arrival in Saskatoon included a school of forestry within a college of agriculture.[27] This appears to be the only reference to forestry by anyone at any of the prairie universities until the 1960s. At British Columbia, however, there was an unsuccessful effort by both the board and the senate in 1917 to establish a school of forestry,[28] and in 1918 and 1919 a two term 'Short Course in Forestry' was offered to about forty veterans of World War I.[29] 'Unencumbered by prerequisites, fees or examinations,' it is said to have been both a success and a direct encouragement for the establishment of a department of forestry in the faculty of applied science in 1921. British Columbia awarded its first B.Sc. in forestry two years later.

AGRICULTURE

Until 1911 the only institution granting degrees in agriculture was the University of Toronto, which since 1888 had been awarding the B.S.A. to graduates of the degree-course offered at its affiliate, the Ontario Agricultural College at Guelph. But in 1911 degrees were also granted by Manitoba, McGill, and Laval, and by 1920 Alberta, Montréal, and Saskatchewan also had agriculture graduates and British Columbia had students in the third year of a four year degree program. This considerable expansion resulted from the opening up of the West and the general recognition of the need for a systematic development of the physical and human resources of rural Canada. Except in French Canada, the new faculties or schools of agriculture tended also to be involved with home economics (or household science) and with the training of teachers for the rural schools. They were also much concerned with extension work, frequently in cooperation with the provincial department of agriculture. In all cases the expansion was made possible by financial support from government - the provincial governments from the outset, and, following the passage of the Agricultural Act of 1913, the federal government as well.

The development of the Ontario Agricultural College during this period was both steady and substantial. The degree-course was increased from three years to four in 1902 and at the same time the admission requirement was raised to full junior matriculation. However, the latter led to a decline in enrolment and after a year or two the requirement of junior matriculation was removed. In actual fact admission to the degree course followed completion of the two year diploma course, which continued to be offered. Students completing it with a 50% overall average and 60% in English were admitted to the third year of the degree course. In 1920 the junior matriculation requirement was re-introduced and a clear separation drawn between the two year and four year programs.

In 1903 the Ontario Normal School of Domestic Science at Hamilton was transferred to the O.A.C. campus as the Macdonald Institute, in effect a home economics department offering a two year certificate course in domestic science, a two year diploma course for professional housekeepers, and over the years a variety of shorter courses. Beginning in 1904, the Provincial Department of Education began to offer summer courses for teachers at the Macdonald Institute. Initially the courses were designed for elementary school teachers, the subjects including nature study, school gardens, manual training, and household science. In 1909 a course qualifying a person to teach agriculture in the elementary schools was introduced and in 1913 a comparable course for high school teachers was added.

The consequence of these developments was that by 1929 the Ontario Agriculture College, including the Macdonald Institute, was in Canadian terms a large and complex institution with more than 2000 students in attendance. However, over 800 of these were summer school students, about half as many were taking short (e.g. two week) courses during the winter, and 368 were at the Macdonald Institute. Of the 741 full-time students in agriculture about one-third could be considered as actual or potential degree level students. Fifty nine B.S.A.s were awarded in 1920.

The addition of household science and teacher training to the offering at Guelph was an attempt to implement the ideas advocated by J.W. Robertson in what became known as the Robertson-Macdonald Movement.[30] Robertson, who had joined the staff of the Dominion

276

Experimental Farms after some years as a professor at O.A.C.,
became convinced in the late 1890s of the importance of nature
study and manual training in the education of young children, of
the need to consolidate schools in the rural areas, and of the
importance of scientific agriculture for the farmer and of training
in household science for his wife, and he was able to persuade
William Macdonald to devote a considerable portion of his considerable wealth to the promotion of these ends. The Macdonald
Institute at Guelph was the latter's contribution to the cause
in Ontario. His contribution to the cause in Quebec was Macdonald
College, which opened in 1907 at Ste Anne de Bellevue.

With Robertson as first principal, the college, which immediately
became the faculty of agriculture of McGill University, had three
components: a school of agriculture, a school of household science, and a school for training teachers. That education rather
than agriculture was at the heart of the enterprise is made clear
in the 'stated' purposes: '(1) The advancement of education; the
carrying on of research work and investigation, and the dissemination of knowledge; all with particular reference to the interests
and needs of the population in rural districts. (2) The provision
of suitable and effective training for teachers, and especially
for those whose work will directly affect the education in schools
in rural districts.'[31] The B.S.A. degree was available from the
start and was first awarded in 1911. But, as at O.A.C., a two
year diploma course constituted the first half of the degree program. Junior matriculation was, however, an additional requirement for admission to the third year. In 1920, 503 students were
enrolled, of whom 137 were in the degree course in agriculture.

In 1907 the situation with respect to agricultural education
in French Canada was almost as bad as it had been in 1890, which
was worse than in 1860. There were two small ill-equipped schools
of agriculture in Québec in 1890, one at Ste Anne-de-la-Pocatière
and one at Assomption, both offering a two year diploma course.
The latter was closed in 1898, but, in 1893, the provincial government prevailed upon the Trappist fathers at Oka to establish an
Ecole de pomologie et d'agriculture which it subsidized to the
extent of $2000 annually for the next 15 years. Complaints about
its inadequacies led to a thorough reorganization in 1908 when,
as l'Institut agricole d'Oka, it became affiliated with Laval.
At the same time, the government grant was increased to $5500.
By 1910, a full four year course leading to a degree had been developed and the first three degrees were awarded the following
year. L'Institut was further strengthened by an annual $2000
grant from the federal government, beginning in 1912. In 1919,
with the establishment of Université de Montréal, its affiliation
was transferred there.

In 1912 the school at Ste Anne-de-la-Pocatière was provided with
a new building in place of the one it had been occupying since
1859 and it, too, was admitted to affiliation with Université
Laval. However, the new building was not equipped with appropriate laboratories, the library was of more interest to an anti-

quarian than to an agriculture student, and there was a shortage
of trained professors. A serious problem, of equal concern to
l'Institute agricole d'Oka, was the academic qualifications of
the entering students: of the 62 students who enrolled in 1913
only two had matriculated, and Louis Fortin, who enrolled in 1914,
described himself as the first classical college graduate to enrol
at Ste Anne in its whole history.[32] By 1920, however, a great
deal of progress had been made despite a necessarily slow start,
the first year or two having been spent solidifying the existing
two year diploma course. A clear separation was then made between
the three year degree course and the two year diploma course. In
1920 the majority of the degree students either had a B.A. or had
attended a classical or a commercial college, and the staff, most
of whom had been subsidized to attend universities in the United
States or France, were either adequately or well qualified.

In the Maritimes the main development was the emergence of the
Nova Scotia Agricultural College offering a two year diploma and
the usual variety of short courses in both summer and winter.
The origins of this college date back to 1885 and the appointment
of a professor of agriculture at the Provincial Normal School at
Truro. In 1892, a separate building, to be designated the School
of Agriculture, was provided. In 1893 a School of Horticulture
was established at Wolfville by the Nova Scotia Fruit Growers'
Association, but when its building was destroyed by fire in 1898
it was relocated at the farm which the Normal School had acquired
in 1888. In 1905 the two schools were united as the Nova Scotia
College of Agriculture. The college, which also had a domestic
science department, was maintained by the provincial government.

The most dramatic developments occurred, as would be expected,
in the four western provinces, each of which established a faculty
or college of agriculture in the ten year period 1906-15. What
was unusual was the very different means which were adopted to
arrive at the same ends.

A proposal that Manitoba establish an agricultural college was
made as early as 1884 by the lieutenant governor of the province
at a University of Manitoba convocation, and in 1892 the Legislature passed an act authorizing such a step.[33] But the necessary
funds were not available, and no concrete action was taken until
1900 when, following an election campaign in which the successful
Conservative party proposed the establishment of an agricultural
college, a royal commission was appointed to make appropriate
recommendations. The commissioners visited various American universities in the midwest and the Ontario Agricultural College at
Guelph, and in their report, which was tabled in 1902, they recommended that the O.A.C. pattern be followed, i.e., a college
independent of the provincial university. Their justification of
this position, and W.L. Morton's comment on it deserve to be quoted:

In its report it recommended the establishment of an agricultural college. Farmers, it affirmed, are made, not born.
'Farming is now a profession, and farmers should have the

278

advantage of professional instruction, quite as much as lawyers and doctors.' The college should be established as a separate institution, apart and distinct from the University of Manitoba: '... your Commissioners think that education in agriculture for young men from the rural districts, should be so given by a separate college, that they may not be side-tracked or alienated from the farm ...' This was to introduce into the development of the University of Manitoba a new and, as it was to prove, a disturbing tradition, that of the separate agricultural college, exemplified in the Ontario Agricultural College at Guelph and in the earlier American schools of agriculture. It was a tradition which sprang from the fear rural people entertained of the drawing power of the city in the years after 1870 when the industrial and urban revolution was creating the great cities of North America, to the depression and disadvantage of agriculture and rural life. The new tradition was to become the strongest and most significant in the history of the university, one which, in its ultimate consequences, was to go far towards determining the character and fate of the university.[34]

The report was accepted by the government and steps immediately taken to implement it; a site was acquired on the western outskirts of Winnipeg (the University of Manitoba colleges were all in the centre of the city) and funds were voted to construct a building. In 1904 an act creating the Manitoba Agricultural College was passed and in 1906 the college opened with a staff of four and a student body of 85. For the first two years only a two year diploma course and a number of short courses were offered, but in 1908 the College entered into affiliation with the University of Manitoba, which authorized a B.Sc. in Agr. degree; this was a five year program with the diploma course constituting the first two years, an arrangement that posed problems for the college in its relations with the university since the requirement for admission to the diploma course was substantially lower than university matriculation. On the whole, however, relations were cordial and for the next several years the college made good progress. It introduced a home economics program in 1910, began extension work in 1911, and in 1914 had a full-time staff, including those in home economics, of 46.
In 1912 the college was moved to a new location at Fort Garry, eight miles to the south of downtown Winnipeg, and its original site was turned over to the university. In at least one sense this was an advantageous step for the college - the original site was too small to provide for an adequate experimental farm - but it caused friction and, in conjunction with continuing arguments over admission standards, resulted in the withdrawal of the college from affiliation. For the next four years the graduates of the B.Sc. program received their degrees from the Manitoba Agricultural College. In 1915, the Conservative government was defeated at the polls and the principal of the college, who was closely associated with the outgoing premier, was forced to resign.

Affiliation was resumed in 1916. In 1919 junior matriculation was made a requirement for admission to the diploma course. This raised the standard of the degree course but it also resulted in a sharp decline in enrolment. In 1920 the full-time enrolment in agriculture, both degree and diploma students, was 203. By 1924, when the college became an integrated faculty of the University, the full-time enrolment was down to 69.

The first order of business of the board of governors of the University of Saskatchewan in January 1908 was to choose a president, and it is significant, first that one of the matters on which candidates interviewed were asked to express their views was the place of agriculture in the university, and second that the response of W.C. Murray, the man chosen to be president, was: 'the College of Agriculture must be regarded as the sheet anchor of the University.'[35] Another question which faced the board was whether a college of agriculture should be an organic part of the university or, like the Ontario Agricultural College, an independent affiliate. The latter arrangement was favoured by the minister of agriculture, W.R. Motherwell, an O.A.C. graduate.[36] The board favoured integration, but before recommending it sent a three-man committee, including Murray, to investigate universities in the United States. In contrast to the Manitoba royal commissioners, they recommended that the O.A.C. pattern *not* be followed:

> We believe that union will prevent both the waste due to separate institutions and the demoralizing rivalry which too frequently appears between them. Union will also secure for the teachers trained in the University the advantages of courses in Agriculture and Domestic Science, and will in this way greatly facilitate the introduction of the teaching of Agriculture into our Public and High Schools. While union will place at the disposal of the students of Agriculture the literary, social, and scientific advantages of the University, it will also bring the University students into close touch with Agriculture and quicken their interest in the great industry of the Province.[37]

The minister, however, was still not convinced, and he sent his deputy minister, W.J. Rutherford, also an O.A.C. graduate, whom he had recruited from the Manitoba Agricultural College with a view to his becoming head of a separate agricultural college in Saskatchewan, to visit the same American universities. When Rutherford reported that he agreed with the committee's recommendation, Motherwell endorsed the proposal and from then on gave it his unqualified support. This included the releasing of Rutherford and the other senior official in his department, John Bracken, from their duties so that they could accept appointments as professors in the college, and the turning over to the college the extension work of his own department.

Rutherford and Bracken were appointed to the staff in 1909, the former as dean and professor of animal husbandry, and the latter as professor of field husbandry. The college did not open until 1912, but the interim was devoted to careful planning of the program and the physical facilities, which included an experimental farm. The program would consist of a diploma course (three sessions running from November to March), a degree course (four years to the B.S.A. from junior matriculation), extension work, and pure as well as applied research. Initially only the degree course was offered - to 70 students in September 1912; however, in 1914, the diploma course was added and enrolled 60 students. In 1920, 68 students were registered in the degree program, which by this time provided specialization in agricultural engineering, animal husbandry, and field husbandry. There were 108 in the associate course, and the full-time staff of 20 was divided among departments of animal husbandry, agricultural engineering, dairying, field husbandry, and soil science. Horticulture was added in 1921 and farm management in 1925. There was also an active research program.

In Alberta and British Columbia the development of agriculture in the provincial university proceeded more easily (though also more slowly), principally because the institutions were not required to provide a diploma course.

In Alberta this need was supplied by provincial agricultural schools established at Olds and Vermilion in 1913. The staff of the faculty of agriculture, which was established in 1915, was able from the start to concentrate on its B.S.A. program and on research. Two courses leading to a degree were offered, a three year course for graduates of the provincial schools and a four year course for those with junior matriculation. It was also possible to take a combined course of six year's duration leading to B.A. and B.S.A. degrees. A department of home economics was established in 1918 with responsibility for a B.H.Ec. degree. From the time of the establishment of the university in 1908, there had never been any question but that a faculty of agriculture would be established and it is a little surprising that seven years passed before instruction was provided. Some time was required, of course, to provide the required facilities, but the main explanation lies in the fact that at the outset Alberta concentrated on establishing a strong faculty of arts and science, upon the resources of which the faculty of agriculture was able to draw in due course. This, as well as its freedom from a concern with a diploma course, gave its program a particularly strong academic character.

In British Columbia the question of a separate agricultural college was raised but a report by the Commissioner of Dominion Agricultural Instruction in 1913 recommended that the Saskatchewan rather than the O.A.C. pattern be followed.[38] L.S. Klinck was appointed dean of the faculty of agriculture in 1914, a year before the university was opened for instruction. For the first two sessions he confined his teaching to a course on the scientific basis of agriculture available to third and fourth year students in arts and science. The B.S.A. program was introduced in

1917 with seven students registered. The first degrees were granted at the end of the 1920-21 session, at which time the enrolment was 51 and the full-time staff numbered 11. While not involved with a diploma course, the staff did offer short courses both on campus and in various parts of the province. In 1919-20, 640 students were registered in 10 such courses.

VETERINARY MEDICINE

Two universities granted degrees in veterinary medicine in 1920, Université de Montréal (6) and University of Toronto (5). In both cases the students were enrolled in an affiliated institution, financially independent of the university, L'Ecole de médecine vétérinaire de la Province de Québec and the Ontario Veterinary College. The courses were four years in length from junior matriculation or its equivalent. At Montréal, the degee was docteur en médecine vétérinaire (though a bachelor's degree was granted at the end of the second year); at Toronto, a B.V.Sc. At the latter a D.V.Sc. was available to the B.V.Sc. of three years standing who submitted an acceptable thesis 'embodying the results of an original investigation conducted by himself on some subject approved by the Senate.'
    L'Ecole de médecine vétérinaire was the sole survivor of four veterinary colleges operating in the Province of Quebec in 1890. By 1894 the three French-language colleges had been reduced to one, L'Ecole de médécine comparée et de science vétérinaire located in Montréal. In 1899 it was taken over by the provincial government which thereafter provided an annual grant, in partial recompense for which the minister of agriculture was entitled to nominate 25 students each year as 'boursiers.' Renamed and reorganized, l'école was subject to inspection by the minister of agriculture, whose representative, along with a representative of the minister of agriculture at Ottawa and two nominees of the Collège des médecines vétérinaires de la Province de Québec, was present at the final degree examinations. In 1918, the course was lengthened from three to four years, and in 1919, with the establishment of the Université de Montréal, l'école's affiliation was transferred from Laval to that institution.
    The Ontario Veterinary College became an affiliate of the University of Toronto in 1897 but degrees were not granted until 1910 following the extension of the course from two to three years. In 1897 letters patent were issued incorporating Andrew Smith (the founder and principal of the College), his son and three other persons as the Ontario Veterinary College Ltd., a clear indication of the proprietary nature of the institution. But though a proprietary school, the college had periodically been in receipt of public funds ($289 in 1866 for salaries, $2000 in 1880 for a museum and library are examples), and authority to practise veterinary medicine rested not with the college but with the legislature. An Act Respecting Veterinary Surgeons of 1895 stated

'that the present Veterinary College established by the Agricultural
and Arts Association [which had been created in 1868] is hereby
continued for the instruction and examination of pupils in anatomy,
physiology, materia medica, therapeutics, chemistry, and as to the
breeding of domesticated animals, and may exercise such powers as
have been delegated to the said College by the said Agricultural
and Arts Association.' During the next 10 years there was continual criticism of the standard represented by the diploma, particularly by the Ontario Veterinary Association, which in 1903 recommended that the course be lengthened to three years. In 1905 the
O.V.A. submitted a brief to the Royal Commission on the University
of Toronto urging the government to take over the college and trans-
form it into a faculty of comparative medicine of the University
of Toronto with Andrew Smith as dean. The commissioners did recommend in 1906 that the Ontario Veterinary College be taken over
by the government on the same basis as the Ontario Agricultural
College, that the University of Toronto establish a degree course
'at least as thorough and advanced as those provided in the leading
universities of the United States,' and that the 'new' college be
not only affiliated with the university but located in close
proximity to it. Satisfactory arrangements were made with Smith,
and in February 1908 he surrendered the Ontario Veterinary College
Ltd. charter and the college became a public institution.
  Under the new principal, E.A.A. Grange, an O.V.C. graduate of
1873, who had taught veterinary science at O.A.C. from 1874 to
1882 before going to the Michigan Agricultural College to establish a department of veterinary science, the course was lengthened
to three years and the college physically moved to a location near
the University of Toronto campus. The lengthening of the course,
combined with the effects of World War I, resulted in a sharp decline in enrolment (169 graduates in 1908, 93 in 1918). Grange retired in 1918 and was succeeded by another O.V.C. graduate, C.D.
McGilvray, who promptly increased the length of the course to
four years (1918), raised entrance requirements to full junior
matriculation (1919), and had the B.Sc. and D.Sc. degrees introduced (1919). In 1922 the college was relocated once more, this
time on the campus of the Ontario Agricultural College at Guelph.
  As noted earlier, veterinary science was included in the course
of study at the Ontario Agricultural College in 1874, and it has
continued to be an integral part of the O.A.C. course of study
ever since. This is not surprising, granted the obvious connection between veterinary medicine and animal husbandry. Indeed all
Canadian faculties or schools of agriculture have offered lectures
on veterinary medicine in their degree courses within a few years
of their establishment. Certainly in 1920 veterinary medicine was
taught at O.A.C., McGill (Macdonald College), Montréal (Institute
agricole d'Oka), Laval (Ste Anne), and the four Western universities, as well as at the Ontario Veterinary College and l'Ecole
médecine vétérinaire de la Province de Québec.
  Veterinary medicine was not taught at Queen's University in 1920
but it was offered for a brief period in the 1890s, and the Univer-

sity had granted one degree in this field in 1898. The institution established by the Ontario government at Kingston in 1893 was a school of mining and agriculture. The School of Mines, which eventually became the faculty of applied science of Queen's University, was the first and most important concern of its organizers but a school of dairying was established in 1894 and, connected with it, a veterinary school in 1895. The latter offered a two year diploma course and also a 'post graduate' course; on completion of the latter in 1898, W. Rowson was awarded the degree of Doctor of Veterinary Medicine and Surgery. Rowson was one of seven students in the school in 1897-98. The following year there were five, including a single freshman; the school was closed at the end of that session. The Dairy School continued until 1908, when, following the destruction of its building by fire, the work was transferred to a provincial school at Kemptville controlled by the Department of Agriculture.

HOUSEHOLD SCIENCE

In 1891 W.W. Andrews, Professor of chemistry at Mount Allison University, proposed the teaching of 'domestic chemistry' on the grounds that 'education of this kind would raise the kitchen to the dignity of a laboratory and would add charm of scientific interest to the housewife's tasks.'[39] The suggestion, made in a pamphlet entitled 'Mount Allison's Possible Forward Movement,' was taken up by the alumnae society of the Mount Allison Ladies College. At their annual meeting held later that year the members expressed their hearty concurrence with 'the proposal to establish a Scientific Cooking School,' but it was not until 1903 that classes in household economics were taught at Mount Allison. By that time a half-dozen schools of household (or domestic) science had been established in Canada.

The main stimulus for this burst of activity, most of which occurred between 1897 and 1903, did not stem from the desire to provide scientific cooking schools for the actual or potential housewife but from the need to provide teachers of domestic science for elementary schools, while the stimulus itself came from women rather than from professors of chemistry. In 1893, a number of Canadians attended the World's Congress of Representative Women held at Chicago, and on their return they organized the National Council of Women of Canada, which at its first annual meeting in April 1894 resolved that: 'the National Council of Women of Canada do all in its power to further the introduction of industrial (or manual) training for girls into the public school system of Canada, believing that such training will greatly conduce to the general welfare of Canadian homes, and that copies of this resolution be sent to the ministers of education of each provincial government.'[40]

That same year the School Act of Ontario was amended to permit school boards to add domestic science to the course of study, and in 1897 regulations for introducing domestic science into the public schools of Ontario were issued by the Department of Education. Regulations were also laid down concerning the qualifications for domestic science teachers. This led to the instituting of lectures in domestic science at the Ottawa and Toronto Normal schools in 1898 and to the establishment in 1900 of the Normal School of Domestic Science and Art at Hamilton and the Victor School of Household Science and Arts at Toronto. In 1904, the Normal School at Hamilton was transferred to Guelph as the Macdonald Institute of Home Economics in association with the Ontario Agricultural College where it offered for the next 50 years a two year diploma course qualifying the holder to teach domestic science in the elementary schools and also a two year Professional Housekeepers' course 'designed to aid those women who desire to become matrons and skilled housekeepers.' The Victor School, renamed the Lillian Massey School of Household Science and Art in 1901, also offered a two year 'normal' school course until 1913, but from 1902 on its main concern was with a degree program in household science authorized by the University of Toronto in that year on the urging of President Nathaniel Burwash of Victoria University, with which the University of Toronto was then in federation.

The program offered at Mount Allison commencing in 1903 was similar to that offered at the Macdonald Institute: a two (and also a one) year 'normal' course qualifying the holder to teach household science in the public schools of New Brunswick; and a housekeeper course for those 'wishing to have scientific knowledge and practice of everything that relates to the home.' Technically, the program was offered not by the university but by the Mount Allison Ladies College, but it was physically located on campus and university staff members were involved in the instruction. When Mount Allison introduced a degree program in 1924, the two year course was incorporated as the first half of the four year program.

An almost parallel development occurred at Acadia. In 1902 a domestic science department was opened at the Acadia Ladies Seminary, offering a two year Normal course and a one-year Homemakers' course. When Acadia established a degree program in 1925, the seminary's work in home economics was taken over by a newly established school of household science.[41] A program similar to that offered at the Acadia Ladies Seminary was also provided from 1901 on at a second institution in Nova Scotia, the Truro School of Domestic Science, an affiliate of the Provincial Normal School.

Turning to the province of Quebec, a School of Household Science was one of the three units provided at Macdonald College when it opened at Ste Anne de Bellevue in 1907.[42] Here the courses were confined to 'homemaking' since teacher training was provided for in another of the college's units, the School for Teachers. The original offerings were one and two year homemaking courses, but by 1910 the two year course was upgraded to a Housekeeper's Course and by 1914 it had been transformed into Institution Administration, with an emphasis on dietetics. This significant development was the work of Katherine Fisher, a 1901 graduate of the Ontario Normal

School for Domestic Science, who joined the Macdonald College staff in 1910 and who, on proposing the establishment of a degree program to McGill's principal, Sir William Peterson, in 1916, was told: 'it just isn't done, Miss Fisher, you can't raise home economics up into higher education.'[43] This may have led to her resignation in 1917, but a year later a degree program was established by McGill, the students taking two years as regular students in the faculty of arts and science before going on to a two year course at Macdonald College. The first B.H.S. was granted in 1922.

In French-speaking Quebec an interest in the science (or art) of homemaking antedated 1890; it can perhaps be traced back to the seventeenth century and Marguerite Bourgeois. Certainly there was *l'enseignement ménager* at the Ursuline convent at Roberval in 1882.[44] In 1909, both the Ecole de Roberval and the Ecole de Saint Pascal, staffed by the Congregation de Notre Dame, became affiliates of l'Université Laval and by 1920 l'Hospice de Saint Joseph in Montreal was in the same relationship with Université de Montréal. The students in these schools were in the age range 15 to 19 and on completion of their course received a diploma rather than a degree. The universities were, however, represented at their final examinations and for the teaching staff of the schools in particular the relationship was important rather than pro-forma.[45]

In addition to McGill and Toronto, two of the western universities were offering a degree in home economics in 1920; Manitoba granted its first degrees in 1918, and Alberta in 1920. Alberta had established a department in 1918 and had arranged for students to obtain a B.Sc. in H.Ec. through the faculty of arts and science or a B.H.Ec. through the faculty of agriculture. The one degree granted in 1920 was a B.H.Ec. Saskatchewan had also established a department of household science in the faculty of arts and science, and by 1920 it was possible to obtain a B.A. with a major in home economics. At Manitoba, a two year diploma course was offered at the Manitoba Agriculture College in 1910, but the degree was not authorized until 1917, the year when the college resumed its affiliation with the university.[46] In 1920 the senate of the University of British Columbia approved in principle the establishing of a department of home economics but postponed action for financial reasons.

President Burwash who, unlike Principal Peterson, believed that home economics could be 'raised up into higher education,' and who was heavily involved in the design of the B.H.Sc. degree program introduced at Toronto in 1902, described the course in these words:

> The course embraces the fundamental elements of a liberal education, and is intended to be as complete and severe, as a discipline, as one of the Honor Courses for the B.A. degree. It differs from these in omitting Latin but in every other respect it requires the same matriculation and examination in languages and literature as the broadest of the Honor Courses in Science

or Philosophy. To this thorough literary training extending over three years it adds Philosophy two years, History and Economics one year, and a selected course of Honor work in science for three years. The Scientific courses chosen are those which lay the foundation for the application of science to the whole sphere of home life. The first three years are fitted out with the practical study of household problems in the light of these fundamental sciences, and the whole completed by a fourth year of research work in some selected branch of science as applied to the economy of the household.[47]

The intent, clearly, was liberal rather than vocational education. Unfortunately, the claims of the professionals soon came into play. One of the graduates of 1907 applied for admission to the university's recently established faculty of education with a view to obtaining a high school teacher's certificate, but was refused admission on the grounds that she did not have first year mathematics and first year Latin. Incredible as it may seem, this fiat was accepted, as was the more logical request that some work in textiles and clothing be included in the program in view of the emphasis given to these subjects in the high school course of study in domestic science; the course of study was revised accordingly. The effect was to reduce the home economics element in the first year to one hour per week and to remove entirely from the fourth year the 'research work' which according to the original plan was to characterize the final phase of the program.
The degree program was offered initially by the Lillian Massey School, acting in this respect as a department of the university, but in 1906, as recommended by the Royal Commission on the University of Toronto, a faculty of household science was established, the school being absorbed therein. This step was encouraged by the offer of Mrs Lillian Massey Treble to provide a well-equipped building for the faculty. The sod was turned in July 1908 and the building completed in 1911. By this time the degree offered was the B.A. (Household Science), which had been authorized in 1906 and first granted in 1907. Nine students had been awarded the B.H.Sc. between 1906 and 1910, but the degree was then suspended until 1924, when it was reintroduced as a program under the full control of the faculty in parallel to a B.A. (Home Economics), control of which rested with the faculty of arts. In 1913 it became possible to obtain a general B.A. with concentration in household science. The faculty discontinued its normal school courses at the conclusion of the 1912-13 session, but at the same time introduced graduate work. An M.A. in nutrition was awarded in 1914.

DENTISTRY

Between 1891 and 1920, schools of dentistry were established at Dalhousie, McGill, and Montréal, and a department of dentistry within the faculty of medicine at Alberta. Together, these enrolled by 1920 between 350 and 400 students. Over twice this number, 890, were enrolled at the Royal College of Dental Surgeons in Toronto, which, though affiliated with the University of Toronto, was operated by the profession and was financially independent of the university. The R.C.D.S. was a very large operation; in terms of numbers of students it was almost as large as the universities of Alberta, British Columbia, or Saskatchewan, and it was substantially larger than Dalhousie; viewed as a faculty, which technically it did not become until 1925, it was exceeded in enrolment only by arts and science and by medicine at Toronto and by agriculture at Manitoba. Its staff, most of it part time, numbered 74 – 24 professors, 7 associate professors, 3 lecturers (in English, French, and chemistry), 2 demonstrators (including the artist C.W. Jeffreys), 7 clinicians, and 31 demonstrators. The basic offering at the college was a five year course from junior matriculation leading to the D.D.S. of the University of Toronto and to the licence to practise dentistry in the Province of Ontario. It also provided a seven month course for dental nurses and, in conjunction with the University of Toronto, combined courses in medicine and dentistry and in dentistry and arts. It was also a pioneer in the continuing education field, extramural lectures being provided for local dental societies.

The R.C.D.S. course of study had been steadily strengthened. In 1892 the course was extended from two years to three, in 1896 junior matriculation was required for admission; in 1907 the course was lengthened to four years, and in 1919 to five. The four year course was retained for several years for the benefit of returning veterans, but this concession was discontinued in 1922. Compulsory indentureship, which in 1890 stood at three years, had been abolished in 1908 and since 1906 there has been joint examinations for the degree and licence to practise. While the teaching staff consisted largely of part-time lecturers, three particularly significant appointments had been made: A.J. McDonagh in 1915 'to what is said to be the first chair in the world for teaching periodontology in a dental school,';[48] Wallace Seccombe in 1916 as head of the first department of preventive dentistry in North America; and H.K. Box as professor of dental pathology and periodontology in 1920. Box, who had just been awarded the Ph.D. in pathology and biochemistry at Toronto, was appointed research professor in 1927.[49]

Since 1896 the R.C.D.S. has been located on College Street in close proximity to the university, first at no. 93 (where additions were required in 1898 and 1902) and from 1910 at no. 230. In 1920, the Ontario government after an initial refusal (based on its policy not to support private institutions which had been in effect since 1868) approved a grant of $100,000 for extension of the building at 230 College Street. That the government should make an exception in this case is testimony of the position occupied by the college at that time.

The move from 93 to 230 College Street was occasioned not by overcrowding but by the wish of the Toronto General Hospital to purchase the property in order to expand the hospital. To strengthen its hand, the college circulated a questionnaire to all Ontario dentists asking specifically whether the school should become an integrated faculty of the University of Toronto. Ninety-five per cent of those responding were in favour of integration. Negotiations with the university followed, but, though the university had no objection in principle to establishing a dental faculty, its financial position did not permit it to do so 'in the forseeable future.'[50] The integration of the R.C.D.S. within the University of Toronto did not occur until 1925.

An act incorporating the Dental Association of the Province of Quebec was passed in 1869, but despite the efforts of George Beers, its long-time secretary, the association (or the Quebec Dental Society as it was often called) was relatively inactive for the next 20 years. In 1889 a new act gave the association power to act as a board of examiners for persons seeking the licence to practise and to prescribe terms of apprenticeship. This led in 1892 to the establishment in Montreal of a dental college of Quebec (also Collège Dentaire de la Province de Québec) with Beers as dean. The plan was for instruction to be given in both English and French and for the medical subjects to be taken at McGill or Université Laval à Montréal. Difficulties arose, however, over affiliation with both institutions, and the result was that arrangements were made in 1893 with Bishop's University for the medical subjects to be taught in its medical school which was located in Montreal.[51] In 1896 the school was formally affiliated with Bishop's, which granted the D.D.S. to graduates of its three year course. This arrangement, which provided instruction in both languages (the Dental College of Quebec had a section française) continued until 1904 when Bishop's medical school was absorbed into McGill's. At this point McGill established a department of dentistry within its faculty of medicine and a four year course was introduced leading to the degree of Graduate in Dental Surgery (G.D.S.). One G.D.S. was granted, but by 1908 the degree of DDS had been substituted.[52] In 1913, A.W. Thornton became the first full-time head of the department of dentistry, and in 1920, when the department was made a faculty, Thornton was appointed dean.

Instruction in the McGill department was in English. However, an école de chirurgie dentaire de Montréal was established in 1904, based on the section française of the Dental College of Quebec, with clinical facilities being provided by Université Laval à Montréal, with which it was immediately affiliated. It too offered a four year course leading to a degree of docteur en chirurgie dentaire (D.C.D.). Designated an école fusionnée in the charter creating the Université de Montréal, it was given faculty status in 1921.

In 1907, the 1891 Act creating the Nova Scotia Dental Association was amended to empower it to establish a school of dentistry. In 1908, the Maritime Dental College was opened in Halifax, five students registering for a four year course. The college was affiliated with both Dalhousie University and the Halifax Medical School.

The latter became the faculty of medicine of Dalhousie University in 1911 and in 1912 the Maritime Dental College was merged with the university as its faculty of dentistry. Three students were awarded the D.D.S. in 1912.

An attempt was made in 1896 by the Manitoba Dental Association to arrange for a course of lectures to be given to prospective dentists by the University of Manitoba but, since at this time the university had no teaching departments, no action was taken. In 1916 an amendment ot the Manitoba Dental Association Act made the University of Manitoba the sole examining body in dentistry. Henceforth, candidates for the licence to practise had to matriculate in arts and successfully pass two sets of examinations, one after having articled for two years and one after having articled for four. Instruction in dentistry was not offered at the University of Manitoba until 1958.

The Province of Saskatchewan adopted the same plan as Manitoba. An amendment to the Dental Act in 1917 gave the university control of the requirements for matriculation in dentistry and responsibility for the prescribing of a curriculum and for the conducting of the appropriate examinations.[53] The defining of the curriculum was, however, to be made in consultation with the Council of Dental Surgeons and three of the five members of the board of examiners were to be nominees of this council. As in Manitoba, there were two sets of examinations: (a) anatomy, chemistry and metallurgy, histology and physiology; (b) bacteriology and pathology, materia medica with therapeutics, medicine and surgery with anaesthesia, operative dentistry, prosthetic dentistry, orthodontia, and practical examination in operative and prosthetic dentistry.

In British Columbia a 1908 act created a College of Dental Surgeons of British Columbia with responsibility for licensing in succession to the Board of Dental Examiners which had been established in 1886. The B.C. Dental Society, which had been active in the 1890s but not thereafter, was reorganized in 1916 and was renamed the B.C. Dental Association in 1920. There was little apparent relationship between the college and the association and this perhaps explains the lack of interest in establishing a school. The movement to provide dental education in British Columbia dates from 1951.

Alberta, on the other hand, made arrangements in 1916 to provide instruction for the basic subjects of a dental course. Two years of dentistry would be provided in the faculty of medicine and the students would then proceed to Toronto or McGill for the final two years. The first three students were accepted into this program in 1918. The first year of arts and science was made a requirement for admission into the two year course in 1921, and by 1924 the department had become a school (though still within the faculty of medicine) and was offering a full dental course. The first D.D.S.s were granted in 1927.

To complete the record it should be noted that a faculty of dentistry existed on paper at the University of Trinity College from 1893 to 1904, during which time examiners in dentistry were listed

in the Calendar and the degree of D.D.S. granted to 43 persons.[54]
However, there is no evidence that any instruction was offered –
several of the Trinity 'faculty' were also members of the staff
of the Royal College of Dental Surgeons. This venture came to an
end with the federation of Trinity with the University of Toronto
in 1904, the degrees granted subsequently becoming Toronto degrees.

PHARMACY

In 1890 there were only two schools of pharmacy in Canada, the
Ontario College of Pharmacy in Toronto and the Montreal College
of Pharmacy. Since neither was associated with a university, they
were in no position to offer a degree program. Thirty years later
there were seven schools, all associated with a university and all
but one offering a degree program. The Montreal College of Pharmacy
had, in effect, been subdivided into two schools in 1906 when the
Quebec legislature granted a charter to an école de pharmacie and
the Montreal school's three French-speaking instructors transferred
to the new institution, which was immediately affiliated with the
Université Laval à Montréal. The Montreal college continued as
an English-language institution but in 1917 became affiliated with
McGill as a department within its faculty of medicine, offering a
one year diploma course which with appropriate apprenticeship
qualified the recipient to practise pharmacy in the province. In
contrast, the école de pharmacie which, with the establishment of
the Université de Montréal, became an affiliated school, granted
a *B. en Pharmacie* degree to students who completed its three year
course with a 60% average or better. It also offered a *D. en
Pharmacie* degree to those who took the third year work a second
time and passed with a 75% average or who submitted an acceptable
thesis. L'école was the largest school in Canada in 1920 with
an enrolment of 171, a number of the students transferring from
Laval after taking their basic science work in Quebec City. The
McGill school, with an enrolment of 39, was one of the smallest,
its numbers exceeding only those at Manitoba (30) and Dalhousie
(24).
   The other large school of pharmacy in Canada in 1920 was the
Ontario College of Pharmacy with an enrolment of 168, including
10 women. In 1892 it had become affiliated with the University
of Toronto, the graduates of its compulsory one year course (for
which the entrance requirement was junior matriculation) thereafter being able to obtain a Bachelor of Pharmacy degree. This,
in conjunction with four years of apprenticeship and a minimum
age of 21, qualified the student to become licensed as a pharmacist. The graduates of its compulsory one year course who had
junior matriculation standing were also eligible for a Bachelor
of Pharmacy degree. However, students could until 1927 be admitted with Grade X standing, and in conjunction with four years
of apprenticeship and a minimum age of 21, could on completion of
the course become licensed as pharmacists. It was not until 1927

that the degree became a requirement for the licence.

By 1890, the Halifax Medical College was offering a one year course to the Master of Pharmacy degree, but this was not required for the licence to practise in the Province of Nova Scotia. There was one graduate in 1893 and subsequently three others. The medical college rejected a proposal of the Nova Scotia Pharmaceutical Association that it establish a faculty of pharmacy in 1905, and in 1909 the association itself began to provide lecture courses for apprentice pharmacists in the premises of the newly established Nova Scotia Technical College. This led in 1911 to the establishment of the Nova Scotia College of Pharmacy and to the offering of a one year diploma course for which the admission requirement was junior matriculation. The following year the Nova Scotia College of Pharmacy was affiliated with Dalhousie and provision was made for a B.Pharm. degree on completion of a two year course from junior matriculation, with Dalhousie providing instruction in the basic sciences. In addition to providing the professional courses for the degree, the affiliated college offered the junior and senior diploma courses which were required to be completed during the four years of apprenticeship, and, in addition to the degree, were a requirement for licensing. In 1917, the New Brunswick Pharmaceutical Association became associated with its Nova Scotia counterpart in the direction and support of the college, which was accordingly renamed the Maritime College of Pharmacy.

The three other new pharmacy schools were established in the prairie provinces. A Manitoba college of pharmacy was formed in 1899 offering a one year program. In 1902, the college affiliated with the University of Manitoba and in 1905 offered the Bachelor of Pharmacy degree for a one year course combining university and college work. In 1914, the college was absorbed by the university as a department in the faculty of medicine, the basic offering being a two year course to a diploma rather than a degree. However, in 1920, a B.Sc. in pharmacy was authorized for a four year program from junior matriculation, the first year being identical with that for the B.Sc. in the faculty of arts and science.

Schools of pharmacy were established at the University of Alberta and the University of Saskatchewan in 1914, and, though both began by offering a one year certificate or diploma course, provision was soon made for a four year B.Sc. program, in each case similar to that introduced at Manitoba in 1920. Saskatchewan continued to offer a one year diploma course until 1924, when it extended it to two years, a step Alberta had taken in 1919; total full-time enrolment at Saskatchewan in 1920 was 61, at Alberta 43. At none of the prairie universities was the degree required for licensing in 1920.

Although there was a substantial increase in the number of schools during the thirty-year period (1850-1920), the standards achieved in contrast to dentistry were not impressive. At several institutions there was a single full-time staff member. Under the circumstances it was understandable that research was not a subject to which any of the schools could direct serious attention.

NURSING

With two exceptions no university in Canada had been directly involved in the education or training of nurses prior to the year
1920, responsibility for this having rested for over 30 years with
schools of nursing established in individual hospitals of which
there were 70 in 1910 and over 150 in 1920. These hospital schools
of nursing offered a two or three year course, for which the admission requirement was more often than not below the junior matriculation level but from which the graduate emerged prepared to
sit the provincially authorized examinations leading to certification as a registered nurse. The exceptions were the universities
of Western Ontario and Toronto. At the former lectures to nurses
in training at Victoria Hospital in London as well as to undergraduates in arts had been provided since 1913 by the institute
of public health established in that year and becoming the faculty
of public health in 1917. At the University of Toronto, a course
in medical social service offered by its department of social service had been included among the lectures taken in the senior year
by nurses in training at the Toronto General Hospital. At least
three provincial associations had appealed to universities to
establish nursing programs, the University of Toronto by the
Graduate Nurses Association of Ontario in 1905, the University of
Saskatchewan by the Association of Registered Nurses of Saskatchewan
in 1917, the University of Manitoba by the Manitoba Association of
Graduate Nurses in 1919; in no case had the appeal been successful.
But in 1920, five universities entered the field almost simultaneously: British Columbia with a degree course; Dalhousie,
Toronto, and Western Ontario with one year diploma courses in
public health for R.N.s; and McGill with two one year diploma
courses for R.N.s, one in public health and one designed to prepare R.N.s as supervisors and teachers in hospital schools of
nursing. All these projects were made possible by financial
assistance provided by provincial branches of the Canadian Red
Cross, $5000 being provided for each of five years to British
Columbia, McGill, and Toronto primarily for staff salaries, $7800
to Western Ontario between 1920 and 1924 for general purposes,
and $4000 in each of 1920 and 1921 and $7500 in 1922 to Dalhousie
in the form of 20 annual scholarships.
   With the exception of the Dalhousie program which was withdrawn
at the end of the 1922-23 session, all these programs took root
and were continued by the universities concerned after the withdrawl of the initial Red Cross support. During the period of
Red Cross involvement, McGill introduced a third diploma course
in hospital administration (in 1921), and Western Ontario (in
1923) followed British Columbia's lead in establishing a degree
program. Twenty years were to elapse before degree programs were
established at McGill and Toronto, but their origins date from
1920.
   The B.Sc.N. program introduced at British Columbia in 1919 set
the pattern for the degree programs established in other Canadian

universities over the next 20 years. Patterned on the existing American model, it was a five year program from junior matriculation, with the first two years and the fifth spent at the university and the summer between the first and second years and the whole of the third and fourth spent at the Vancouver General Hospital in what was to all intents and purposes the hospital's R.N. program. On completion of the course, the graduate received both the degree and certification as a registered nurse.

Though not directly involved in nursing education, Manitoba since 1913 and Saskatchewan since 1917 had been responsible for the registration examinations specified in the legislative acts establishing the Manitoba Association of Graduate Nurses and the Association of Registered Nurses of Saskatchewan.

SOCIAL WORK

As was the case in the United States and Britain, organization of programs in social work did not occur in Canada until the first decade of the twentieth century. Except for some lectures arranged by a group of individuals at the University of Manitoba in the winter of 1902-3, there was no attempt to introduce social work as a field of study until 1914, when a department of social service was set up at the University of Toronto.

This development had resulted from the activities of two voluntary associations composed largely of women: the Social Science Study Club organized in 1911, and the Social Workers Club established in 1912. At a meeting held in 1913 attended by representatives of these groups and by President Falconer of the University of Toronto, a resolution advocating the establishment of a training program for social workers was adopted and subsequently forwarded to the board of governors of Toronto. Fortified by the knowledge that one of the members of the Social Science Study Club, Mrs H.D. Warren, was prepared to provide the funds required for the services of a full-time director, the proposal was approved and the program introduced in the fall of 1912, with an American, Franklin Johnson, as director.

The basic program offered was a one year diploma course involving lectures and field work, but any of the courses could be taken on a part-time basis. In the first year only 11 of the 293 students were on a full-time basis. In 1918, a two year diploma course was introduced, and, by 1920, 5 persons had qualified for the two year diploma, while 100 had earned the one year 'certificate.' By this time also, specialization was possible in case work, community organization, child welfare, settlement work, industrial investigation, mental hygiene, and medical social work. The department also offered monthly public lectures throughout the academic year and provided special short courses for particular groups, the Neighbourhood Workers Association, for example.

McGill established a department of social work in 1918 with Howard T. Falk as director, the program at the outset being

financed by the Joint Board of Theological Colleges, the Graduates'
Society, and two individuals. It also began by initially offering
a one year diploma course, but as of 1923 there was a two year
diploma course and a one year certificate course. In 1922 the
name was changed to the School for Social Workers.

Two other English-language institutions were providing some
instruction in social work in 1920: Manitoba which offered a
series of social welfare courses consisting of 18 weekly lectures
on economics and 9 each on psychology, mental hygiene, social
work and social progress, and child welfare; and Queen's which
included social service ('Preparatory for work in philanthropic
and community service') as one of the eight fields of specialization in its business administration program leading to the B.Comm.
degree.[55] In French Canada, a direct concern with social work
began with the formation of the Ecole des sciences sociales,
economiques et politiques at the Université de Montréal in 1921.

LIBRARY SCIENCE

In 1911 Acadia University appointed the librarian as instructor in
library science, and in 1920 two credit courses were offered in the
B.A. program: library methods, consisting weekly of two hours
of lectures and four of laboratory practice, and history of libraries and library administration, demanding a one hour lecture
and four hours practical work. Apart from these developments,
Canadian university involvement in the training of librarians
was limited to summer courses offered on the campuses at McGill
and Toronto.

The McGill program was first offered in 1904 at the instigation
of the university librarian, C.H. Gould, a friend of Melvil Dewey,
at that time director of the New York State Library School at
Albany. Initially a four-week course, it was subsequently extended
to six weeks and was offered periodically during the next years -
in 1905, 1907, 1910, 1911, 1913, 1914, and 1920. In 1919, Gould
was succeeded as librarian by G.R. Lomer, who almost immediately
proposed the establishment of a full year course but was not successful in obtaining his objective until 1927.

In Ontario, the initiative was taken by Walter R. Nursey, the
inspector for public libraries for Ontario, who organized a four
week summer course under the auspices of the Provincial Department
of Education at the Toronto Model School in 1911. In 1912, the
course was held at the University of Toronto Library and in 1913
was conducted by Hester Young of the University of Toronto Library
staff. The aim of the course, for which there were no required
qualifications or fees, was to prepare people to carry on the
daily routines and services of the public libraries and to be
familiar with the Public Library Act under which they functioned.
In 1917, the course was extended to two months and in 1919 to three
months, by which time it was referred to as the Ontario Library
Training School. In 1921 an entrance examination was required
unless the applicant had senior matriculation.

Except for McGill, where the School for Teachers at Macdonald
College was responsible for the training of teachers for the
Protestant schools of Quebec, the universities of Canada were not
involved in the training of elementary school teachers in 1920.
This was done in normal schools, which had no connection with the
universities, unless as in the case of Saskatchewan they could be
affiliated. There was a single normal school in Prince Edward
Island, New Brunswick, and Nova Scotia, two in each of Manitoba,
Saskatchewan, and British Columbia, three in Alberta, seven in
Ontario, and twelve in Quebec. The total normal school enrolment
in 1920 was 6035.

In six of the nine provinces, the normal qualification for
teaching in the public high schools was a university degree and
a training course at a normal school or, as in Ontario, at a college of education. In the four western provinces, the training
course was four months, in Ontario nine, in Nova Scotia six weeks.
For its permanent certificate, the Protestant Central Board of
Examiners of the Province of Quebec required a university degree,
two courses in education which could be taken in the process of
obtaining a bachelor's degree, the Strathcona Certificate Grade
B, awarded after completion of a course in physical training which
could also be taken during an undergraduate course, and 50 half
days of practice teaching; but a second class certificate was
issued to those who completed a nine month diploma course offered
at Macdonald College, for which the entrance requirement was two
years of arts and science.

There were no public secondary schools in Roman Catholic Quebec
at this time. In New Brunswick the qualification for high school
teaching was a one year course at a normal school from senior
matriculation, and in Prince Edward Island a two year course at
Prince of Wales College, for which the admission requirement was
below the standard of junior matriculation. There were no official requirements for teaching in the relatively small number of
private secondary schools in English-speaking Canada, but most
teachers held a bachelor's degree. In the classical colleges
of Quebec the bachelor's degree was the minimum requirement.

Concern for the quality of teaching in the classical colleges
which was carried on almost exclusively by priests and seminarians,
whose qualifications were limited to the B.A. and their theological
studies, led Camille Roy to propose the establishment of an école
normale supérieure at Laval, but his efforts were unsuccessful
until 1920 when one was set up within the faculté des arts. However, two attempts were made by Laval prior to 1920 to provide
additional academic and some pedagogical instruction for practising teachers. The first was between 1903 and 1906 when a professor of French literature was appointed, and the successful
completion of his courses earned a certificate d'études littér-
aires. The second try was in 1918 when instruction leading to
a diplôme de grammaire was authorized for students who had comp-

leted courses introduced that year by Abbé Arthur Maheux.[56] At Montreal an Institut d'enseignement moderne et de pédagogie was founded in 1919 to provide comparable instruction for members of religious orders, and this became an école annexée with the establishment of Université de Montréal in 1919, at which time five religious orders were involved. The faculté des lettres and the faculté des sciences established by Université de Montréal in 1920 functioned basically as écoles normales supérieures for the next 20 years.

McGill, as we have seen, was involved in the training of secondary school teachers by way of providing two education courses offered at Macdonald College which were accepted as credits for the B.A. degree. From 1898, Bishop's University at Lennoxville had also been prepared to enable its graduates to meet the requirement of the two education courses, its method being to provide a course of lectures on the art of teaching. These were offered periodically, but the demand was not great. By 1920, it was arranged that the lectures would be delivered every third year, but only if, in the opinion of the college council, a sufficient number of students were prepared to register. Courses in education were also offered for credit in 1920 at Acadia and New Brunswick, the former giving five courses in psychology and education, and the latter a single course in the psychology or philosophy of education. In both cases the courses were offered under the auspices of the department of philosophy.

The province which had devoted the most attention to the training of secondary school teachers was undoubtedly Ontario; it had begun to certify teachers as early as 1885.[57] In 1890 an Ontario School of Pedagogy was established at Toronto by the Department of Education, and for the next seven years it offered a 14 week course in the fall consisting largely of lectures on educational psychology, the history of education, school organization and management, and the methodology of teaching particular subjects. Some of the methodology lectures were given by University of Toronto professors. The weakness of this course, which did lead to a certificate, was that little or no provision was made for practice teaching, and this led to the replacement of the Ontario School of Pedagogy in 1897 by the Ontario Normal College at Hamilton, the course being extended to a full academic year and including practice teaching in the Hamilton schools. The training of high school teachers was one of the subjects dealt with by the Royal Commission on the University of Toronto appointed by the government in 1905, and among whose recommendations was the establishment of a faculty of education at the University of Toronto. In 1907 the Ontario Normal College at Hamilton was discontinued and faculties of education were established at both Toronto and Queen's, each to be directly supported financially by the Department of Education. The department did provide an adequate building for the Faculty at Toronto in 1910, the facilities including a functioning school (the University of Toronto Schools) offering the secondary school grades and convenient opportunities for supervised practice teaching. The department did not, however, make similar provision for the faculty at Queen's and, though both the university and the Kingston School Board were cooperative, the faculty throughout its 10 year history operated under the most difficult circumstances. Its history came to an end in 1919 when the government decided to centralize secondary school teaching preparation at the faculty at Toronto, which was renamed the Ontario College of Education. For the next 45 years all Ontario high school teachers were required to take a one year course at this institution.

PHYSICAL AND HEALTH EDUCATION

Robert Tait McKenzie, who was appointed instructor in gymnastics at McGill in 1890, is generally regarded as the most important figure in the development of physical and health education in North America, but the bulk of his contribution was made at the University of Pennsylvania, where he served as professor of physical education and director of the department of physical education from 1904 to 1931.[59] It was in the 1890s at McGill, however, that he developed his ideas. A medical student at the time of his appointment as instructor in gymnastics, he obtained his M.D. in 1892, and, in 1895, was given a second part-time appointment as assistant demonstrator in anatomy. In 1896 he was appointed medical director with responsibility for the supervision of the health of all students. All students were henceforth required to take a medical examination, and the gymnastics program was expanded. But McGill was not in the position to offer McKenzie the kind of appointment which the Pennsylvania professorship represented and it is not surprising that he resigned. Nonetheless, McGill continued to take physical education seriously, particularly with respect to women. In 1902, Miss V.M. Holstrom was teaching gymnastics at the Royal Victoria College (for women). In 1906 all first year women students were required to take a weekly two hour class in gymnastics, in 1907 all second year women were required to take a one hour class weekly, and in 1908 the second year requirement was increased to two hours and a one hour course was also required in the third year. This program was the responsibility of Ethelmary Cartwright, a graduate of the Chelsea College of Physical Education in England, who had been appointed director of physical education for women in 1906. By 1910 Miss Cartwright was prepared to offer a full four year course in physical education.

In the summer of 1912 a four week summer course for physical education teachers was offered at McGill by Miss Cartwright under the auspices of the Protestant School Board's Teacher Training Committee. The course was also given during the 1912-13 session, arrangements having been made for a diploma certifying the holder to teach as a specialist in physical education in the Protestant elementary schools to be issued on completion of three summer or winter sessions. In 1913 a course consisting of twenty 1 1/2 hour lectures on the principles and practices of physical education and qualifying for the Strathcona Trust certificate was offered to fourth year men and women. A second diploma course called massage and remedial gymnastics was introduced in 1914 to meet the need for trained masseuses. In 1916 the two diploma courses were expanded to full one year programs and in 1919 to full two year programs, at which point responsibility for them was assumed by the university. The staff in physical education in 1920 consisted of Miss Cartwright, physical director for women, Miss Georgina Wood, assistant physical director for women, F.W. Harvey, who had succeeded Tait McKenzie as university medical Officer in 1904, and A.S. Lamb, director of the department of physical education. Lamb, who in 1912 had been appointed an instructor in gymnastics on graduating from Springfield College, and in 1916 physical director, had by this time obtained his M.D. degree.

At this point, a demonstrable need for persons trained in physical education was provided by the establishment of the Strathcona Trust. This was a program initiated by the dominion government to encourage physical and military training in the elementary and secondary schools.[60] In 1908 the Province of Nova Scotia had agreed to participate in a plan developed by the Department of Militia whereby the efforts of the province to encourage schools to organize cadet corps and to introduce rifle shooting and physical training as extracurricular activities would be supported by the government which would provide the necessary equipment, funds to pay bonuses to the teachers, and instructors to enable the teachers to qualify as instructors in these subjects. The terms of the agreement with Nova Scotia were so phrased that any other province could also participate, and by 1912 all provinces were 'enrolled.' Hearing of the scheme in 1909, Lord Strathcona, who in the 1880s as Donald Smith had provided the funds for the Donalda Course for Women at McGill, offered to provide a trust fund of $500,000 to aid in its promotion, an offer which the government had no difficulty in accepting. The program was actually financed by the 4% interest which the government agreed to pay on the trust funds, and the amount distributed was not remarkably large - about $20,000 each year. The provinces received an amount proportionate to their population, with 80% being spent in the elementary schools and 20% in the high schools. Fifty per cent was devoted to physical training, 35% to military drill, and 15% to rifle shooting. From a physical education standpoint the scheme was of dubious value, as people like Miss Cartwright had occasion to point out[61] - were military personnel really knowledgeable about how physical education should be taught? But the scheme did serve to arouse general interest in physical education and in programs for training physical education instructors.

At the University of Toronto the senate established a diploma course for men in 1900 and a 'programme' for women in 1901, and a three year course leading to a certificate (at a fee of $2 a year) was outlined in the 1902-3 Calendar. During the first five

years, five men and one woman qualified for the certificate.
They had one predecessor, F.W. Wood, who during his undergraduate
years had voluntarily assisted the sergeant major in charge of
gymnastics.[62] Wood planned to be a high school teacher and knowing
that teachers with experience in physical education were in demand
he reasoned that it would be to his advantage to have some concrete
evidence of his ability to instruct in this field. He went to see
the president, James Loudon, and asked for some tangible recognition of the service he had rendered the university. After due
consideration he was granted a diploma in gymnastics and physical
drill a year after his graduation in 1899.

With the appointment of Dr J.W. Barton as physical director in
1908, the course was reduced to two years and the certificate
became a diploma in physical training, but it was revised again
in 1912, following the appointment of Miss Ivy Coventry as director of athletics for women. Lectures were now given one hour a
week over four years, and there were three hours of practical
work each week. The nature of the course in 1920 can be seen
from the calendar outline of the fourth year program:

Theory
Prescription of Exercise: remedial gymnastics; spinal curva-
ture; special apparatus; massage and thermal agents
Physical Department Methods: organization; administration;
gymnasium construction and equipment; swimming pools; playgrounds; extension work
History of Physical Education

Practice
For Men – Pedagogy: common faults in teaching; assignment of
exercise for classes of various grades; nomenclature; calisthenics, apparatus; gymnastic and athletic competition; rules
of competition scoring; practical extension work; supervision
of classes outside the University
For Women – Pedagogy: supervision of classes outside the
University; mutual instruction in Swedish exercises and gymnastics; calisthenics, apparatus; technique of dancing; marching
tactics; gymnastic and athletic games; continuation of class
instruction in artistic drills; fencing; swimming and life-
saving.

Also available in Toronto in 1920 was a two year diploma course
leading to an elementary school teaching certificate offered by
the Margaret Eaton School of Literature and Expression, which had
been established in 1901 as the School of Expression by Emma Scott
Raff and which had adopted the longer name in 1906 when Timothy
Eaton provided a building for the school in honour of his wife.
The concerns of the School of Expression were the interpretation
of literature, the problem of voice production, and the promotion
of physical education, but by 1915 the Margaret Eaton School had
two basic departments, dramatic art and physical education. With

respect to the latter department the 1915-16 Calendar stated:

A recognition of physical education as an essential in the curriculum of every school and college has created a demand for
thoroughly qualified teachers. Through the rapidly increasing
interest in the establishment of playgrounds and recreation
centers throughout the country, the demand for trained instructors and workers exceeds the supply. The aim of this department is to provide young women with a thorough training which
will enable them to take advantage of these opportunities for
service as teachers and supervisors of physical education in
all its phases.

The two year course in physical education leading to a teacher's
diploma was introduced in 1916. In 1918 increased enrolment in
the school, mainly in the department of physical education, required the acquisition of a second building at Yonge and McGill
Streets which became the headquarters for the physical education
program. Known as the Margaret Eaton School Extension it had an
adequate gymnasium and a 'sanitary swimming tank.'
The two other Canadian universities offering instruction in
physical education in 1920 were Alberta and Saskatchewan where
physical training had been, in theory, a requirement in all degree
programs since the establishment of the institutions in 1908 and
1909 respectively. However, in each case some years passed before
instruction was provided. At Saskatchewan, Miss Clare Hamilton
was appointed instructor in physical education for women in 1914,
and at Alberta, D.F. MacRae and Christine Fabb were appointed
director and assistant director of physical education in 1919.

MUSIC

For the first two decades of the twentieth century instruction
in music in Canada continued to be provided by conservatories
rather than universities, though the latter continued to grant
degrees to students of the conservatories that were affiliated
with them. At the end of the period, faculties of music were
established at Toronto (1918), and at McGill (1920), but the
McGill faculty was essentially a renaming of the McGill Conservatory which had been founded in 1904. Typically, at both Toronto
and McGill the principal of the conservatory became the dean of
the new faculty.
Although the Toronto College of Music, the Toronto Conservatory
of Music, and the Hamilton Conservatory of Music were all dis-
affiliated in 1918, the local examinations in music conducted by
the Toronto Conservatory from one end of the country to the other
continued to be called the University of Toronto Local Examinations.
In 1921 legal control of the conservatory was assumed by the university. Degree candidates were required to have matriculated,
and examinations rather than courses continued to be the basis

301

for awarding the Bachelor of Music and Doctor of Music degrees.

In the Maritimes, three universities were offering music degrees, Dalhousie in conjunction with the Halifax Conservatory, established in 1898, Mount Allison since 1913 in association with the Mount Allison Ladies College, and Acadia since 1917 in conjunction with the Acadia Ladies Seminary. In none of these institutions including McGill and Toronto, was it possible for a student to obtain credit for a music course in the B.A. program. In 1920 the approach of Canadian universities to general as opposed to professional education in music was confined to the offering of concerts, organ recitals, and the occasional public lecture. An apparently serious attempt to provide something more substantial was made by Queen's University for three years commencing in 1901, when a course of 30 lectures was offered to students for a cost of $1.50 and to the public for $3.00.

In the Province of Quebec, the Académie de musique de Québec, formed in 1868, was affiliated with Université Laval from 1909 to 1914, but no degrees were granted. Interest in sacred music developed, however, in the faculté de théologie, following the publication of the papal encyclical *Motu proprio* in 1903; J.-R. Pelletier, a priest at the Séminaire de Québec, was sent to Rome and Paris in this connection. His subsequent efforts led to the establishment of a department of sacred music in the Ecole de musique which the université founded in 1922. Two schools of music were associated (annexée) with the Université de Montréal in 1920: the Schola cantorum, and the Ecole de musique Nazareth, which had been established in 1861 to provide for the training of the blind. The Conservatoire national de musique, founded in 1905, also became an école annexée in 1921.

NOTES TO CHAPTER 16

1 R.A. Falconer, 'Old Wine in New Bottles' in Second Congress of the Universities of the Empire, *Report of Proceedings* (1921), 17-18
2 Submission of the Technical Education Committee of the Canadian Manufacturers' Association to Royal Commission on the University of Toronto in *Report* (1906), 167
3 For the history of the bible college of Canada, see H.W. Boon, 'The Development of the Bible College or Institute in the United States and Canada since 1880 and its Relation to the Field of Theological Education in America,' unpublished doctoral dissertation, New York University, 1950.
4 D.C. Masters devoted chapter 5 of *Protestant Church Colleges in Canada* (1966) to the period 1890-1920. He entitled it 'The Onset of Liberalism.'
5 Masters, *Protestant Colleges*, 154-9
6 Masters, *Protestant Colleges*, 167. See also *Calendar of Alberta (Methodist) and Robertson (Presbyterian) Theological Colleges affiliated to the University of Alberta*, session 1918-19

7   O. Howard, *The Montreal Diocesan Theological College: a History from 1873 to 1963* (1963), 59-64. Also see below, chapter 28, 529-30.

8   *NCCU Proc.* (1916), 28-30

9   *NCCU Proc.* (1917), 53. The committee's report is at 58-60.

10 *NCCU Proc.* (1918), 9

11 Canadian Bar Association, 'Legal Education in Canada,' *Can. Bar Rev.*, 1 (1923), 71-84

12 For comment on the Canadian attitude towards the case method and also for a description of the Osgoode Hall Law School from 1890 to 1920, see S. Denison, 'Legal Education in Ontario,' *Can. Bar Rev.*, 2 (1924), 85-92

13 A. Flexner, *Medical Education in the United States and Canada* (1910), 13

14 The quotations in this paragraph are drawn from pages 325-6 of *Medical Education*, which includes reasonably detailed comments on each of the Canadian schools. The accuracy of some of Flexner's statements was challenged by some schools in the pages of volume 1 (1911) of The *Journal of the Canadian Medical Association*: 'Queen's and the Carnegie Report,' 62-4; the 'Halifax Medical College,' 64-70; and 'Medical Teaching in Halifax,' 983-5; 'The Vindication of Laval,' 354-6; 'Manitoba Medical College,' 988-91; 'Western University,' 993-4. See also J.J. Talman and R.D. Talman, *Western - 1878-1953* (1953), 78-9. Talman reports 'the local tradition' - that Flexner did not himself visit London but admits that 'some of his remarks have a ring of actual observation.' Flexner admitted inaccuracies in his report on Laval at Montreal: in a statement published in the February 1911 issue of the *American Medical Association Journal* he confessed to have misunderstood the legal position of the Montreal school and stated in what respects the information bearing on Montreal in the report was inaccurate. But while Flexner's details may in some cases have been wrong, his conclusions appear to have been consistently right. The authorities at the Canadian schools were quick to point out inaccuracies in the report but they were almost as quick to act on the recommendations that the report contained.

15 The basic requirement in the English-speaking schools was the same as for admission to the first year of arts and science; in the French-speaking schools it was completion of the classical course. The medical course was five years in length, except at Western where it was four.

16 Talman and Talman, *Western*, 79

17 J.W.B. Sisam, *Forestry Education at Toronto* (1961), 26

18 A.D. Rodgers, *Bernhard Eduard Fernow* (1951), 383

19 The question of whether or not membership in the Canadian Society for Forest Engineers should be restricted to professional foresters is discussed by Rodgers, *Fernow*, 431-3.

20 The over 600 pages of Rodgers's study provide ample evidence to support this statement.

21 W.L. Goodwin, 'Forestry Education in Canada,' *Report of Fourth Annual Meeting of the Canadian Forestry Association* (1903), 89. See also Sisam, *Forestry Education*, 10-11.
22 J. Loudon, 'Education in Forestry,' *Report of the Fifth Annual Meeting of the Canadian Forestry Association* (1904), 42-5. The C.F.A. had been informed of Toronto's interest in forestry education by Professor J.H. Faull during the discussion arising from Professor Goodwin's paper in 1903.
23 Ibid., 52
24 H.E. Videto, 'The Growth of Forestry at the University of New Brunswick' in A.G. Bailey, ed., *The University of New Brunswick Memorial Volume* (1950), 87-8
25 Université Laval, *Cinquantenaire de l'enseignement des sciences forestières a l'université Laval 1910-1960* (1960)
26 In 1911 the course was increased to three years, the first of which was largely devoted to practical work. The students took lectures in September and October and from Easter to mid-May. The intervening months and also May and June were spent in the field. This practical program was discontinued in 1914 and a two-year course reestablished. G. Maheux, 'Un Demi-Siècle en Rétrospective 1910-1960,' *Forêt et Conservation*, 26 (1960), 8, 14-15.
27 A.S. Morton, *Saskatchewan: the Making of a University* (1959), 44
28 H.T. Logan, *Tuum Est: A History of the University of British Columbia* (1958), 66
29 G.A. Garrett, *Forestry Education in Canada* (1971), 22
30 For an account of the Macdonald Robertson Movement, see J.F. Snell, *Macdonald College* ... (1963), 35-41
31 Ibid., 58
32 L. de G. Fortin, 'La Faculté d'Agriculture,' *Rev. Univ. Laval*, 7 (1952), 131
33 The best account of the development on the Manitoba Agricultural College is to be found at various points (see index) in W.L. Morton's *One University: a History of the University of Manitoba* (1952). More details are provided in University of Manitoba Faculty of Agriculture and Home Economics, *Golden Jubilee 1906-1956* (1956).
34 W.L. Morton, *One University*, 58-9
35 A.S. Morton, *Saskatchewan*, 37
36 A.R. Turner, 'W.R. Motherwell and Agricultural Education 1905-18,' *Sask. Hist.*, 12 (1959), 81-96. See also W.P. Thompson, *The University of Saskatchewan* ... (1970), 43.
37 C. King, *The First Fifty: Teaching, Research, and Public Service at the University of Saskatchewan* (1959), 29
38 *Tuum Est*, 47
39 E.C. Rowles, *Home Economics in Canada* ... (1964), 73. The words quoted are Mrs Rowles's, though the phrasing may be Andrews's; no copy of the pamphlet is extant and her citation is based on handwritten notes. As the following notes indicate, this whole section draws heavily on Mrs Rowles's book, which

is concerned with the programs at Acadia, Macdonald College, Macdonald Institute, Mount Allison, Saskatchewan, and Toronto.

40 Ibid., 11

41 The Acadia Ladies Seminary was closed in 1926 and its programs in fine arts and music were also taken over by the university. Initially there was a school of household science and fine arts, but within a year there were separate schools of household science and of music. Ibid., 70

42 For the early development of Macdonald College, see J.F. Snell, *Macdonald College of McGill University - a History from 1904-1955* (1963), 35-84, particularly 65-7, 81-2.

43 Rowles, *Home Economics*, 60

44 A. Tessier, *L'Enseignement ménager dans la Province de Québec* (1943)

45 For an explanation of Laval's concern with institutions offering education at the elementary school level, see the section on 'Couvents' in the address of the recteur (Mgr François Pelletier) at the Séance de Clôture, 17 June 1920 in Université Laval, *Annuaire 1920-21*, 274-5.

46 The degree course, to consist of the two year diploma course followed by three 5 1/2 month terms, was authorized by the Board of Governors of the Manitoba Agricultural College in 1915 and presumably was accepted by the University of Manitoba when the college resumed affiliation in 1917. J.H. Wilson, 'A History of Home Economics Education in Manitoba, 1826-1966,' unpublished M.Ed. thesis, University of Manitoba, 1966

47 Burwash's statement appeared in the form of a letter published in the Lillian Massey School of Household Science Calendar for 1903-4.

48 D.W. Gullett, *A History of Dentistry in Canada* (1971), 129

49 Box, on the point of moving to Edmonton to establish a practice following graduation in 1915, was offered a $1000 fellowship by the R.C.D.S. to pursue studies in pathology in the faculty of medicine at the University of Toronto. From 1916 on he had a half-time appointment in the department of pathology of the R.C.D.S. J.H. Johnson, 'The History of Dental Research in Canada,' *J. Can. Dent. Assoc.*, 18 (1952), 315

50 Gullett, *History of Dentistry*, 137-8

51 For the somewhat confused and confusing history of the Bishop's Dental School, which had seven deans between 1896 and 1904, see in addition to Gullett, 86-7, 101-2, M.A. Rogers, 'Faculty of Dentistry, McGill University,' *J. Can. Dent. Assoc.*, 31 (1965), 311-12, and 'The Dental Profession and Bishop's College,' *Canadian Medical Record*, 24 (1896), 241-5.

52 Though the D.D.S. degree was authorized by McGill in 1908 and was listed thereafter as the degree to be awarded, the diplomas issued until 1918 read 'Doctoris in Arts Dentalis Scientia.' Thereafter the diploma carried the words 'Doctor of Dental Surgery.'

53 The decision to request the government to place responsibilty for the conducting of the licensing examinations in the hands

of the University of Saskatchewan was made by the Council of
the College of Dental Surgeons of Saskatchewan following a
dispute which arose in 1916 over the employment of non-regis-
tered assistants by a prominent member of the College. See
L.J.D. Fasken, 'History of Dentistry in Saskatchewan,' *J. Can.
Dent. Assoc.*, 18 (1952), 359.

54 Gullett, *History of Dentistry*, 82-3
55 A.C. McGregor, *The Department of Social Science, University
of Toronto, 1914-1940* (1940), 10-11
56 Low enrolment combined with shortage of staff led to the withdrawal of the eight-option offering within several years.
57 R.S. Harris, *Quiet Evolution: a Study of the Educational
System of Ontario* (1967), 79-83
58 'M. Lebel, La Faculté des Lettres de Laval,' *Rev. Univ. Laval*,
6 (1952), 450
59 A.S. Lamb, 'Tait McKenzie in Canada,' *J. Health and Recreation*, 15 (1944), 69-85; and J. Day, 'Robert Tait McKenzie:
Physical Education's Man of the Century,' *Can. Assoc. Health
Physical Education and Recreation J.*, 33, no. 4 (April-May
1967), 4-17
60 F. Consentino and M.L. Howell, *A History of Physical Education in Canada* (1971), 26-30
61 E.M. Cartwright, 'Physical Education and the Strathcona Trust,'
The School, 4 (1916), 306-10
62 W.F.R. Kennedy, 'Health, Physical Education and Recreation
in Canada: a History of Professional Preparation' (1955)

17
Graduate Studies

The problem of graduate work was one of the matters discussed at
the first Conference of Canadian Universities held at Montreal
in June 1911. Indeed, 'the desirability of increased facilities
for Post Graduate Study' was one of the reasons for convening the
1912 Congress of the Universities of the Empire, and it was the
need to plan the agenda for the British meeting that provided the
impetus for holding the Canadian Conference.[1] Prior to 1911 the
Canadian universities, *collectively*, had not been seriously concerned with provision for graduate studies, although *individual*
institutions such as Queen's, Toronto, and McGill offered opportunities for graduate work in various fields.

By 1915, when the National Conference of Canadian Universities
(the NCCU) next convened, the problem of providing adequately for
graduate work was on everyone's mind. Two of the working committees struck by this second conference were a committee of graduate
work and one on graduate work in agriculture. The decision to
establish the latter body appears to have been based on the fact
that no graduate work in this field was offered anywhere in Canada.
This was noted in the report of the committee to the 1916 conference, as was the need for substantial numbers of persons with
advanced training in this field to serve on the staff of university faculties of agriculture and in government departments.
The committee, chaired by President Walter Murray (Saskatchewan),
made this recommendation:

> The Minister of Agriculture at Ottawa should be requested to
> take steps to make available for the training of graduate stu-
> dents the resources of the scientific branches of the Depart-
> ment, and also to arrange for such work with the Agricultural
> Colleges of the Dominion. In the event of such being done,
> the hope was expressed that the opportunities thus afforded
> might be made more readily available by the establishment of
> scholarships.[2]

The recommendation was duly approved by the conference and the
committee encouraged to pursue this line. Murray's report to the
1917 conference made no reference to the response of the minister,
but the committee now proposed that a system of scholarships and
fellowships in agriculture be established similar to those recently provided by the Advisory Council for Scientific and Industrial Research (National Research Council) for students in the
basic sciences, and that these awards be administered by a committee of agricultural experts appointed by that council. The
NCCU approved these recommendations and instructed its secretary
to transmit them to the ministry of agriculture 'with the cordial
support of this Conference.'[3] In 1918 it was reported that,
'under the conditions of the war, money could not be diverted for
this purpose.' The committee was now instructed 'to refer the
question back to the Provincial Departments of Agriculture with
the recommendation from this Conference that money for the establishment of scholarships for the purpose indicated should, by
agreement with the Dominion Government, be taken out of the grants
given to the Provinces under the Dominion Agricultural Act, and
that such money should be handed over to be administered by the
universities.'[4] With the exception of Saskatchewan which assigned
funds for one graduate scholarship, the provincial governments
proved to be no more accommodating than the federal government.
The committee was, however, able to report to the 1920 conference
that arrangements were being made to establish master's degrees
in agriculture at McGill (Macdonald College), British Columbia,
and Saskatchewan.[5] There were no further reports from this committee, and, in fact, it was discharged in 1923.

When it was appointed, the NCCU committee on graduate work had
representatives from 14 different universities who concerned
themselves almost entirely with the Ph.D. Their report to the
1916 conference 'showed that as regards Masters' degrees, the
differences between programs are so slight as not to call for any
special comment.'[6] With respect to the Ph.D., however, the position was not satisfactory. The only programs offered were those
at McGill and Toronto and there were complaints that seemingly
well-qualified graduates of other Canadian universities were not
invariably accepted as candidates. But the two great needs of
Canadian graduate schools were scholarships and increased library
facilities. 'It was through these that the American Universities
were able to attract so many of our Canadian graduates.'[7]

In order to offset this American threat, the conference appointed
a special committee to correspond with British and French universities with a view to making arrangements that would increase the
number of students from Canada pursuing their graduate studies in
these two countries, and it instructed the members to examine ways
and means whereby the graduate facilities of Canadian universities could be pooled so that a student need not be confined to
any particular institution for the whole of his studies. At the
1917 conference it was reported that the British and French universities had reacted favourably to the Canadian suggestion and

would see what could be done. But there was a war going on, and
obviously not much could be accomplished until it was over. The
committee had two recommendations: that Toronto and McGill should
coordinate their doctoral programs in the interests of providing
as wide a range of doctoral level courses as possible, and that
a systematic campaign be launched to establish a large number of
scholarships and fellowships so that qualified students from all
Canadian universities could pursue their graduate work at Toronto,
McGill, and ultimately other institutions in Canada. It was noted
that the National Research Council had announced that 20 studentships of $600 each and 5 fellowships of $1000 would be awarded in
the 1917-18 session. Actually, four studentships of $750 and
three fellowships of $1000 were given out that year.

The 1918 report of the NCCU committee on graduate work in Canada
centred on the negotiations carried on with Toronto and McGill.
It was stated

> that there was a possibility of a good measure of co-operation
> being effected between these two universities so that a candi-
> date for the degree could, if he wished, spend part of his time
> at McGill and part at Toronto. A proposal to confer a double
> degree was, however, not entertained by the University of
> Toronto; and as McGill had no scholarships in connection with
> its Graduate School, whereas Toronto had, a difficulty would
> arise under this head. This difficulty, however, could probably
> be removed by the establishment by McGill of a number of scholar-
> ships for this purpose.[8]

These hopes were not realized. There was no report from the committee in 1920, and by 1922, when the conference next met, alternative solutions to the problem were being proposed. This will
be alluded to in chapter 23. The question arises, what exactly
was the position of graduate studies in Canada by the year 1920?
First, at the M.A. level.

THE MASTER'S DEGREE

The committee on graduate work stated in 1915 that the standards
and requirements for the Master's degree were basically the same
from one end of the country to the other. The chief exception was
at Queen's where an M.A. was granted to graduates of an Honour B.A.
course who obtained first class standing. (An Honour B.A. was
granted to the graduate with second or third class standing.)
But in 1919, Queen's introduced a one year M.A. program for which
the Honours B.A. was an admission requirement. Hence, throughout Canada in 1920 the normal requirement for the M.A. was an
Honours B.A. (or B.Sc.), a year of full time study in a particular
subject, and a thesis. Since at almost all Canadian universities
the Honour B.A. required an additional year of study beyond the
General B.A., the M.A., in effect, required five years of study

beyond senior matriculation, or six years beyond junior matriculation. This was a year more than was required in the United States where the normal pattern was completion of Grade 12, four year B.A., one year M.A. Also established as a Canadian norm by 1920 was the requirement of two years of study for the M.A. for the student with a General B.A.

The differences between the various M.A. requirements were, however, more than 'slight' and they do call for comment here. A thesis was not mandatory at Dalhousie, St Francis Xavier, and British Columbia, or for candidates in the social sciences at McMaster. At St Francis Xavier the program involved courses from two 'correlated' departments; at Dalhousie it could be in two 'allied' departments; Manitoba, British Columbia, and Bishop's specified a minor as well as a major subject; and McGill required two minors, though only the major subject had to be pursued beyond the undergraduate level. A number of universities (Dalhousie, St Francis Xavier, British Columbia, McGill) permitted their own graduates to substitute private study over two years for the year of full-time study.

At all the larger institutions the requirements for the master's degree in the sciences and mathematics were comparable to those for degrees in the humanities and social sciences. At some, the University of Toronto for example, the M.A. was awarded in 'science' subjects; at others the M.Sc. rather than the M.A. was granted for work in this area. A few other master's degrees had been introduced recently, the M.Comm. at Queen's, the M.A.Sc. (Master of Applied Science) at Toronto (for students in engineering), the M.Sc. in Agriculture at Saskatchewan. Toronto and Queen's had also introduced a master's level program with a bachelor's title, the B.Paed. (Bachelor of Pedagogy). The degrees of Civil Engineer (C.E.), Mining Engineer (M.E.), Mechanical Engineer (M.E.), Electrical Engineer (E.E.), and Chemical Engineer (Chem.E.) which Toronto had been offering since 1891 also represented work at the master's level, being awarded to Bachelors of Applied Science who had spent three years in professional practice and had submitted an acceptable thesis. In contrast, the degree of Ingénieur Civil awarded by Université Laval from 1889 was a first degree.

B.PAED. AND D.PAED.

The B.Paed. and also the D.Paed. had been introduced at Toronto in 1894 as a result of the Provincial Department of Education's concern about the quality of its inspectors and principals. At this time there was no faculty of education at the University of Toronto. To be admitted to the university's B.Paed. program the candidate had to have a B.A. and a permanent teacher's certificate, and to obtain the degree he had to pass written examinations in five areas: psychology with/its application to pedagogy, the science of education, the history and criticism of educational systems, school organization and management, and methods in English.

310

mathematics, and one other subject. A list of recommended books
was provided but no instruction or even counselling was offered.
To obtain the D.Paed. the candidate had to have the B.Paed. and
a specialist teacher's certificate in one of five areas (classics,
natural science, etc.), have taught 'successfully' for ten years
and have passed a different set of examinations in the five areas
of the B.Paed. program. Both degrees had the advantage of reducing the number of years of teaching experience required to qualify for the school inspector certificate issued by the provincial department. A thesis was added to the requirements for the
D.Paed. in 1897, the year in which the University of Toronto
launched its Ph.D. program; presumably it had been decided that
a thesis should be required in all doctoral programs.

With the establishment of faculties of education at Toronto and
Queen's in 1907 certain changes were made in the requirements for
the B.Paed. and D.Paed. degrees, which were now offered by both
universities. The 'courses' were revised 'in sympathy with later
movements in education,' the methods examination was dropped, and
it was no longer necessary to take all the examinations in the
same year. Furthermore, the staff at each faculty would provide
guidance to candidates. It was not, however, until 1914 that
either university offered any instruction, and then only in the
form of summer courses, two of the four courses being offered in
alternate years at one or other of the universities. When, in
1919, the faculty of education at Toronto became the Ontario
College of Education, Dean W.A. Pakenham in his report on the
final session of the faculty noted that 62 students had been registered for courses in pedagogy, two had obtained the D.Paed.,
and 20 had completed part of the requirements for either the
B.Paed. (4) or the D.Paed. (16). In addition, 10 students were
registered for an M.A. in educational theory. The time had come,
he argued, for the university to give much more serious attention
to the support of graduate work in education: 'The registration
... calls attention to the rapidly growing demand in Canada for
courses in education. The demand is so varied and so strong that
the University cannot afford longer to neglect it in the organization of the teaching staff and course of instruction in the
Faculty of Education. It must act immediately or American universities will train the education experts of Canada.'[9]

THE DOCTORAL DEGREE

The requirements for the Ph.D. and D.Sc. degrees outlined in the
1890-91 Calendar at Queen's continued to be listed for the ensuing 30 years, the only significant change being the addition
of Old and New Testament language and literature to the list of
subjects in which the Ph.D. could be obtained. Between 1904 and
1910 there were three Ph.D.s awarded, all in philosophy; in 1921
there was one in history, and in 1925 one in physics. It can
hardly be said that a doctoral program was being offered by Queen's

in 1920. However, such programs were available at McGill and Toronto.

Though approved by the senate in 1885, a program for the Ph.D. was not introduced at Toronto until 1897.[10] At McGill the Ph.D. program was initiated in 1906.[11] The requirements were essentially the same at both institutions and reflected the pattern of the leading American universities adopted after two decades of debate following the establishment of Johns Hopkins University in 1876. This called for three years of full time study beyond the B.A. or B.Sc.,[12] a major subject, two minor subjects, one 'outside' major, a reading knowledge of French and German, a comprehensive examination in the major field, and a thesis representing an original contribution to scholarship or scientific knowledge.

The emphasis at both Toronto and McGill was on the conducting of research; there was no concern at all for preparation for college teaching. James Loudon who was largely responsible for the introduction of the Ph.D. at Toronto, had this to say to the Royal Society of Canada in 1902:

As to the ultimate scientific value of what has already been accomplished in the way of research under the influence of this recent movement [the rapid development of graduate programs in the U.S.A.], there is room for a qualifying remark. It must be remembered that much of the graduate work referred to does not mean actual research, the course for the Ph.D. in many cases being no higher than the honours B.A. course with us. What is required to remedy this unsatisfactory condition is that the Ph.D. be given only on the German plan, and that the main test therefore, a research, be published. When this condition becomes absolute there will be material for the world's judgment as to the amount and quality of the contribution to the advancement of knowledge.[13]

Prior to introducing the Ph.D. program, McGill had provided for two other earned doctorates, the D.Litt. and the D.Sc., but these followed the European rather than the American model.[14] Available from 1899 on, these degrees were awarded to M.A.s of at least five years' standing who had distinguished themselves 'by special research and learning in the domains respectively of literature or philosophy and of science.' Candidates were required to submit either a thesis or a published work. No D.Litts were awarded by McGill during the next 15 years, but by 1920, five D.Sc.s had been awarded; two in physics in 1915; and one each in mathematics and applied mechanics in 1917; and one in physiology in 1920.

While the number of doctorates, including the D.Sc., granted by McGill and Toronto up to and including the year 1920 was relatively small, 15 and 47 respectively, the range of disciplines is impressive: botany, chemistry, geology, mathematics, physics, and zoology at both institutions; physiology and applied science at McGill; dentistry, English, psychology, philosophy, and semitics at Toronto.

312

The doctorate in philosophy and that in theology were both
listed under 'Post-Graduate Courses' in the University of Ottawa
Calendar for 1920-21; in each case there was a simple statement
that the program of theses could be obtained from the dean of the
faculty concerned.[15] In 1912, the faculty committee at Laval
drew up specific conditions for the Ph.D., but there were only
one or two applicants during the next eight years. The main concern of Laval at this point was with the *licence*.

THE LICENCE

As we have seen[16] the M.A. (Maître-ès-arts) had been awarded
by Laval to certain teachers in the classical colleges since the
1860s and seven persons received the degree on this basis in 1920;
but there was no reference to the M.A. in the *Annuaire* for 1920-21
except on page 112, where it is identified in parentheses as being
equivalent to the newly introduced licence-ès-lettres. Two years
before, at the instigation of Arthur Maheux, a diplôme de grammaire had been established to provide pedagogical training for
the teachers of the first four years of the classical course,
almost all of whom were young priests (some still seminarians)
whose educational qualifications consisted of the B.A., obtained
by completing the classical course and their theological studies.
In some instances the teacher of the 'literature' classes of the
classical course had a licence-ès-lettres from a European university and the teachers of the philosophy classes frequently had a
licence en philosophie or en thélogie from Laval, but in both
cases this required two years and considerable expense and in any
event was not directly relevant to the teaching situation in which
these young men were placed:

> Ne serait-il donc pas possible de trouver, pour nos professeurs
> de grammaire, un mode de préparation qui exige moins de temps
> que la licence, qui présente moins de difficultés, qui soit
> proportionné à l'enseignement qu'ils auront à donner? Oui,
> cela est possible: établissons un examen que nos jeunes profes-
> seurs pourront aisément préparer dans leur loisirs et sous la
> direction des maîtres expérimentés qu'ils ne manqueront pas de
> trouver dans leur collège. Cet examen sera, si l'on veut, un
> certificat d'aptitude à l'enseignement des langues classiques,
> un *diplôme de grammaire*, qui pourra devenir un acheminement
> vers la licence-ès-lettres.[17]

Maheux's program was introduced and the first two diplomas were
awarded in 1919. More important it proved to be a step towards
the establishment of the licence-ès-lettres, which was established in September 1920: this was a two year program for B.A.s,
essentially of private study but with detailed instructions being
provided by the faculté des arts. Later, in 1920, a further step
was taken with the decision to establish in September 1921 an
école normale supérieure with specific responsibility for 'la

313

formation pédagogique des professeurs de l'enseignement secondaire' and with a staff of seven including Maheux. The director until 1927 was Mgr François Pelletier, rector of Laval from 1915 to 1921, who in company with Camille Roy had been urging the establishment of such a school for almost 20 years.[18]

In 1920 Laval also granted licences in theology, canon law, philosophy, and law. The licence en droit was simply the bachelor's degree with high standing, but the other three licences involved at least a year of additional study beyond the first degree. The licence en théologie was available in 1890, having been established along with bachelors and doctors degrees in 1871. The licence en droit canonique (there was also a doctorate) had been available since 1901. Of more significance is the licence en philosophie. In 1884 L.-A. Paquet, who had been sent to Rome for doctoral studies following Laval's decision to reorganize its theological teaching in accord with the directives of the papal encyclical *Aeterni Patris*, began to lecture on the *Somme Théologique* of St Thomas Aquinas in the faculty of theology, and in 1893 he began to give lectures designed to prepare candidates for the licence en philosophie, a degree which had been established some years earlier. This program required two years of study beyond the B.A., the final examinations being based on 40 philosophical theses. Between 1894 and 1920, 129 licences en philosophie were awarded by Laval, but during this period the number of lectures offered in connection with the program was small - two a month on the average - and the candidates were all in holy orders.[19] But about 1920 laymen began to apply for admission and to accommodate them a second set of lectures was offered. This led to a much expanded program and in 1926 to the establishment of an école supérieure de philosophie and in 1936 of a faculté de philosophie. The licence en philosophie, it should be added, was similar to the licence ès lettres since one of its chief purposes was to prepare candidates to teach philosophy in the classical colleges.

The degrees offered by Université Laval were of course available to students at the Montreal branch from the time of its establishment, and many of the programs were continued at the Université de Montréal when it became an independent institution in 1919. The licence en droit, for example, was awarded by Montréal in 1920 on the same basis as at Laval in 1919. Partly because it was new, the university was able to move more quickly along the path on which Laval was clearly heading. Its original faculties included lettres, philosophie, and sciences, each, among other things, with responsibility for developing programs designed to be of assistance to classical college teachers. The faculté des sciences, for example, offered in 1920 a licence ès sciences program which provided for specialization in mathematics, physics, chemistry, and the natural sciences, while in the faculté des lettres the licence was for many years the main concern. The licence was seen as catering to two rather different needs, and therefore two routes towards its acquisition were provided: 'La licence est proprement un titre supérieur à enseigner dans les hautes classes des collèges secondaires, écoles assimilées, académies, etc et surtout dans certaines chaires dans l'université.' This was the licence d'enseignement, and the program leading to it required study of the languages basic to the classical course (French, Latin, Greek, and at least one modern language) and French Canadian literature and history.[20] But the licence was also 'un titre d'honneur ... une attestation de haute culture complètement désinteressée'; consequently for the licence de culture only two subjects were compulsory - French and Latin - three other subjects being chosen from Greek, pedagogy, history of art, history, history of Canada, geography, Canadian literature, a modern language. Both courses were two years in length and had the same admission and graduation standards.

FELLOWSHIPS

The lack of fellowships for graduate students was cited along with inadequate library facilities as one of the two basic reasons for the weakness of graduate studies in the Canadian universities by the National Conference of Canadian Universities' graduate committee in 1916. That the situation had not improved by 1920 can be seen by noting the fellowships available at the only two universities with substantial graduate programs. Toronto could offer four open fellowships (i.e., for study in any field), two in political economy, one in anatomy, one every second year in one of the medical sciences, and eight teaching fellowships which involved the giving of some elementary instruction in the classroom or laboratory - two in mathematics, three in physiology and biochemistry, one in pathology, and two in botany; each of these was worth about $500, with the open fellowships also covering tuition. Demonstratorships and assistantships were also available with an honorarium of about $500 in physics (10), chemistry (7), botany (7), and pathological chemistry (2). McGill had two open fellowships, one at $750 and one whose amount had not yet been announced, one in political economy at $650 and two in medicine (the proceeds from $10,000 and $25,000 trusts). No doubt there were some demonstratorships and assistantships available as well.

The list of scholarships and fellowships in the McGill Calendar for 1920 began with a reference to the Rhodes scholarships and to the Science scholarships granted by Her Majesty's commissioners for the exhibition of 1851. McGill students were, of course, eligible for these scholarships, but since they involved study in the United Kingdom the awards could not be said to have advanced graduate studies in Canada; indeed they may have indirectly hindered them by attracting first-class Canadian students. The 1851 scholarships provide evidence of the quality of Canadian undergraduate education in science. These scholarships, which were for study at any university in the world, normally for two years, were awarded to candidates nominated by selected universities in the British Commonwealth. McGill and Toronto were included in the original list of 20 universities, each to make a nomination in alternate years commencing with McGill in 1891. In 1893 Queen's and Dalhousie were added, again on an alternating basis. These four universities continued to be the only Canadian nominators in 1920. In 1895 two British and in 1897 one Australian student chose to study at McGill, and in 1895, 1897, and 1914 McGill or Toronto students studied briefly at their own university before going off elsewhere. About half the Canadian holders returned to Canada to take up what proved to be permanent appointments in Canadian universities, among them W.P. Thompson (Saskatchewan), R.W. Boyle (U.B.C.), E.F. Burton (Toronto), and Otto Maass (McGill).

NOTES TO CHAPTER 17

1 *CCU Proc.* (1911), 9
2 *CCU Proc.* (1916), 22
3 *NCCU Proc.* (1917), 25
4 *NCCU Proc.* (1918), 22. The Dominion Agricultural Act of 1912 assigned $10 million over a ten-year period to the provinces.
5 *NCCU Proc.* (1920), 6
6 *CCU Proc.* (1916), 23
7 Ibid., 23-4
8 *NCCU Proc.* (1918), 11
9 W. Pakenham, 'Report of the Dean of the Faculty of Education,' *University of Toronto President's Report 1919-20*, 18
10 For the twenty year struggle to establish the Ph.D. at Toronto, see P.N. Ross, 'The Ph.D. Degree at the University of Toronto,' unpublished doctoral dissertation, University of Toronto, 1972.
11 S.B. Frost, 'The Ph.D. Degree,' *Bulletin of Educational Procedures* (McGill University), no. 11 (February 1967)
12 The original requirement at Toronto was for at least two years of study beyond the B.A. This was increased to three at the same time that the language requirement was introduced in 1911.
13 J. Loudon, 'The Universities in Relation to Research,' *Trans. Royal Society Canada* 1902, vi
14 So far as departments were concerned the distinction between the Ph.D. and D.Sc. at McGill is not evident. By 1920 Ph.D.s had been granted in botany, chemistry, and zoology, D.Sc.s in mathematics, physics, physiology, and applied geology. Both degrees had been granted in geology.
15 Following the tradition of the European universities with respect to doctoral degrees in theology and philosophy, the candidate was among other things required to take a position on various philosophical issues. These issues were formulated as a list of theses.

16 See above, chapter 11, 186–7.
17 Université Laval, *Annuaire 1920–21*, 112
18 M. Lebel, 'La Faculté des lettres de Laval,' *Rev. Univ. Laval*, 6 (1952), 448–52. Camille Roy proposed the establishment of an école normale supérieure in 1902: H. Provost, *Historique de la Faculté des Arts de l'Université Laval, 1852–1952* (1952), 55.
19 E. Trépanier, 'La Faculté de Philosophie,' *Rev. Univ. Laval*, 6 (1951), 174–5.
20 Among the texts listed for detailed study in the Canadien-Français section of the licence program are Groulx, *Rapaillages*; Rivard, *Etudes sur les parlers de France au Canada;* Montpetit, *Survivances françaises;* Garneau, *Histoire du Canada;* Frechette, *Legend d'un peuple*.   It must be noted, however, that excerpts from these texts rather than the whole volumes were assigned.

18
Scholarship and Research

In October 1920, the Ontario government appointed a royal commission 'to enquire into and report upon a basis for determining the financial obligations of the Province' to the three universities, Toronto, Queen's, and Western, which were now receiving annual government grants, and 'to recommend such permanent plan of public aid to these universities as shall bear a just and reasonable relationship to the Legislative grants to primary and secondary education.[1] The commission requested the institutions in question to provide full information 'on their financial resources, and needs, on their academic work, on the number of their student body, and on any matters of general University policy on which it might be deemed desirable to consult them.' Briefs were also solicited from educational, industrial, scientific, and other public bodies. Volume II of the report, published in 1921, contains the statements of the three universities as well as the briefs submitted by a number of individuals and alumni groups and by two public bodies, the Workers' Educational Association and the Royal Canadian Institute.

The university briefs were unusually lengthy and presented clear and detailed reports, not only of their individual situations, but, by extension, of many other contemporary Canadian universities. Each brief emphasized interest in research and scholarship, described actual achievements in these areas over the previous 10 to 20 years, and listed the publications of staff. Reasons were also given for any apparent lack of progress. The factors that had inhibited research and scholarship in Canada's universities were detailed in the brief from the Royal Canadian Institute.

The main thrust of this brief was that not only was there a lack of serious attention to both the 'course in general and the direction of research in particular,' but that university departments were under-staffed. Professors were so overloaded with instructional tasks that they were unable to attend to their own research projects. They were underpaid and there were insufficient funds available for them to carry out research, especially in surgical medicine. This was causing many Canadians to forsake their medical research in their own country for better prospects in the United States. Furthermore, there was no organized means for doing pure research in science outside of the universities, other than the Dominion Observatory; and, beyond the Transactions of the Royal Society of Canada or the Royal Canadian Institute, there was a dearth of 'Canadian organs for the publication of scientific results,' and no 'highly specialized scientific societies such as existed in Britain and the United States.'[2]

The concern here, obviously, was with research rather than scholarship, but, as will be noted, the situation in the humanities and social sciences was, if anything, worse than in the sciences. Before turning to that subject, the state of research facilities to be found in the universities, the various government agencies, and in the National Research Council will be described.

THE UNIVERSITIES

According to the president of the Royal Canadian Institute, J.C. Fields, the failure of the universities to undertake the basic research which, in his view, was so badly needed in Canada was not due to any lack of competent persons to do it, but to the unwillingness or inability of the institutions to give these individual researchers the time or facilities to get on with the task. Of these, the time factor was the most important. According to Fields, 'the equipment is sufficient in some departments, in others inadequate.' He must have been alluding to the relatively few institutions carrying on scientific research at this time. In a survey of the Maritime universities undertaken only two years later, W.S. Learned and K.C.M. Sills found that 'except for the beginnings at Dalhousie,' the equipment for science instruction was completely inadequate.[3] Elsewhere in Canada, too, it was still a time of beginnings. L'Ecole supérieure de chimie at Université de Montréal was not organized until 1921, and, since 1904, the science building of the University of Ottawa had housed the entire university. The arts and science work of the Western University at London was still being carried on in the old Huron College building, and McMaster continued to operate in the single building constructed in the 1880s. It must be remembered, as well, that the building plans at the universities of Alberta, Saskatchewan, and British Columbia were interrupted by World War I and that instruction at Manitoba in 1920 was being carried on in a variety of locations in Winnipeg. On the other hand, the position with respect to facilities for science instruction and research at McGill, Toronto, and Queen's had improved immensely since 1890.

At McGill it was the excellence of the facilities in the physics and engineering buildings erected in 1893 that had persuaded

Ernest Rutherford to accept an appointment there in 1897, and it was in the McGill laboratories that he and Frederick Soddy carried on the research which earned Rutherford the Nobel prize in 1908.[4] As we saw in chapter 14, the building program at McGill was maintained until 1914 thanks to the generosity of various donors.

In 1890 there were three instructional buildings at the University of Toronto: University College, the School of Practical Science, and a small building, Moss Hall, occupied by the faculty of medicine. By 1920, there were more than a dozen, including separate buildings for chemistry, physics, electrical engineering, and mining. There was sufficient equipment available in the medical laboratores in 1921 and 1922 to enable Frederick Banting, Charles Best, and J.B. Collip to carry out the research that won Banting a Nobel prize. It would seem that the inhibiting factor in achieving results in research was as Fields insisted not lack of equipment, but of time. Both Rutherford and Banting were able to dedicate themselves almost entirely to their research activities, and similarly, during World War I, a number of professors, for example J.C. McLennan having been freed from teaching duties also produced fundamental research of outstanding quality.[5]

Both McGill and Toronto, by 1920, were committing a portion of their funds for support of research. For instance, at Toronto the board of governors established a special fund of $15,000 in 1916 to be used for medical research and to establish a school of engineering research in the faculty of applied science. Other such grants were later approved: however, as with McGill, private donations continued to be the main source of research money. It was a gift from a member of the board of governors at Toronto which made possible the establishment of the Connaught Antitoxin Laboratories[6] (later to be renamed the Connaught Medical Research Laboratories). The proceeds arising out of the manufacture of sera and antitoxin by the laboratories were placed in a special research fund which by 1920 amounted to over $100,000. Money also came from the provincial government for support of the Connaught Laboratories to the extent of an annual grant of $3750 between 1917 and 1927.

At Queen's, the Kingston School of Mines became the faculty of applied science in 1916 and this resulted in the addition of buildings to house mechanical and electrical engineering, physics, geology and mineralogy, and chemistry and chemical engineering. Like McGill and Toronto, Queen's, by 1920, was also using part of its operating funds for the support of research. In 1919 a research professorship in science to be held either in the department of physics or chemistry was established, and the first incumbent, A.L. Hughes, was able to spend all his time on research, except for two or three lecture sessions per week.[7] Courses for the training of research physicists and research workers in biochemistry, bacteriology, and biology had also been provided, and the board of trustees had established a system of grants for research in the departments of physics, chemistry, bacteriology, and botany, to be administered by a standing committee on scientific

research. This was reported to be 'the first attempt in Canada
to organize a concerted movement among the scientific departments
of a university to stimulate increased activity in this important
field. The grants are made to purchase apparatus, books, and
supplies and for the employment of assistants for the routine
work. The plan serves the double purpose of encouraging the work
and of training workers.'[8] The Queen's trustees also recognized
'the pressing importance of social and economic issues,' and consequently were allotting funds to support an investigation into
the organization, method, and policies of organized labour in the
West, and another into the economic and financial phases of the
western rural cooperative movement.

GOVERNMENT AGENCIES

The brief presented by the Royal Canadian Institute to the 1920
Ontario Royal Commission on government financing of universities
echoed in many respects the 1894 paper that G.M. Dawson read to
the Royal Society on the subject of scholarship and research in
1890.[9] Like Dawson's presentation, this one called attention to
the excellent work in the area of applied research being carried
on by various government agencies. The work of the Geological
Survey had continued to expand, indeed to such an extent that it
had become necessary to restrict its responsibilities; in 1907 a
Mines Branch parallel to the Geological Survey was initiated
within the Department of the Interior with responsibility for
investigations related to the mining and metallurgical industry;
in 1920 the survey no longer had the Victoria Memorial Museum
under its umbrella since, as of 1913, the collections were housed
in a separate location.[10] By 1920 the Dominion Experimental Farm
System embraced 21 branch farms, 7 sub-stations, 2 tobacco stations, and 86 illustration fields.[11] The work of the Meteorological Service of Canada had also expanded, but it was no longer responsible for the observatories. A chief astronomer for the
Dominion had been appointed in 1890, and, as of 1909 there was
a Dominion Observatory at Ottawa with a 15-inch reflector; in
1918 a 73-inch reflector was built for the Dominion Astro-Physical
Observatory at Victoria, B.C.
    While the relations between the universities and these govern-
ment agencies had always been cordial, there was no official connection; it was a matter of individual professors becoming involved in the work of an agency. There was, however, an official
and functional relationship between the universities and two new
agencies which had been established by 1920: the Biological Board
of Canada (1912) and the Forest Products Laboratories of the
Department of the Interior.
    The Biological Board of Canada (which became the Fisheries
Research Board of Canada in 1938) was actually established in
1898, when at the instigation of a committee including representatives from Dalhousie, Laval, McGill, Queen's, New Brunswick,

321

and Toronto, the minister of Marine and Fisheries authorized the establishment of a Marine Biological Station which would be administered by a special board consisting of one or more representatives from the department and one representative from each of the universities which had supported the petition for its establishment.[12] These universities continued to be represented on the Biological Board of Canada and a representative of the University of Manitoba was added in 1915.

From 1899 to 1907 a 'portable' laboratory was operated each summer at various locations on the Atlantic coast and in the mouth of the St Lawrence River in which professors and students from the universities involved carried out research. In 1908 a permanent station was established at St Andrew's, N.B. - the Atlantic Biological Station - and in the same year the Pacific Biological Station was established at Nanaimo, British Columbia. Prior to this a Georgian Bay biological station had been launched by a $1500 grant by the Department of Marine and Fisheries in 1901. By 1920 the Department of Marine and Fisheries had also established a laboratory at Ottawa.

The first Forest Products Laboratories to be established by the Forestry Branch of the Department of the Interior was located in Montreal and was associated with McGill University from the outset - the testing work of its division of timber tests, for example, was carried out in the strength of materials laboratories at McGill.[13] When the Department established a second laboratory at Vancouver in 1918, a similar relationship to the University of British Columbia was developed.

The work of all the agencies so far mentioned was of actual or potential value to scientists in a wide range of fields, and the government through these agencies was making it easier for Canadians to carry out research. But the publications program of the Experimental Farms did not solve any problem for the professor of history or French literature. By 1920, however, the federal government had established two agencies which greatly enhanced the possibilities of significant scholarship in the humanities and social sciences. The beginning of both the Public Archives of Canada and the Dominion Bureau of Statistics can be traced to the 1870s, but their effective establishment dates from 1904 and 1918 respectively.

An archives branch was established of all places in the Department of Agriculture in 1872, but the dominion archivist, Douglas Brymner, was not assigned responsibility for any government documents.[14] These became in 1875 the concern of a records branch established in the Department of the Secretary of State under a keeper of the records, Henry J. Morgan. Both Brymner and Morgan did useful work in assembling and publishing materials of various kinds, but their collections were not conveniently available to interested scholars. In 1898 a commission recommended the merging of the two offices and following Brynmer's death in 1902, this was done. Arthur Doughty was appointed dominion archivist *and* keeper of the records in 1904. In 1912 the connection with the

Department of Agriculture was severed and Doughty was given the status of a deputy minister. An adequate archives building was not provided until 1926, but by 1920 historians, economists, and others were going to Ottawa to work in the Public Archives.

R.H. Coats was appointed dominion statistician in 1915 and the Bureau of Statistics was formally established as a branch within the Department of Trade and Commerce in 1918, with responsibility to 'collect, abstract, compile and publish statistical information relative to the commercial, industrial, social, economic and general activities and conditions of the people.'[15] Statistics of various kinds had, of course, been collected and published since early in the nineteenth century, but it was not until Coats took charge that Canadian statistics became systematic and reliable.

At the provincial level, the most significant development occurred at the very end of the period. This was the establishment of a scientific and industrial research council by the Province of Alberta 'to promote the development and natural resources of the Province.' From the outset, the university had been associated with the Alberta Research Council which, in 1920, supplied funds for two research professorships.

THE NATIONAL RESEARCH COUNCIL

In *The Inner Ring: the Early History of the National Research Council of Canada*, Mel Thistle carries the NRC story forward from 1916, when it was established by the federal government, to 1935, three years after the opening of the council's laboratories in Ottawa. The book is largely concerned with the long and bitter struggle to establish these laboratories which were fundamental to the fulfilment of the purpose for which the council had been created, i.e., the development of industrial research in Canada. 'Canada already had reasonable facilities to serve the primary industries of agriculture, mining, fishing, forestry; the need was mainly to provide for those secondary and manufacturing industries that had begun to emerge. Neither the young industries themselves nor the universities could hope to do it; this left government as the only possible progenitor.'[16] Through earlier references to the work of such agencies as the Geological Survey and the Experimental Farms we have evidence to support the statement that research in agriculture, mining, fishing, and forestry was being pursued. One of the first actions of the newly established council was to send out a questionnaire to the principal firms in Canada to find out how much industrial research was being carried on by industry itself. Of the 2400 firms that replied to the questionnaire, only 37 reported that they had research laboratories and only 83 reported that they employed anyone for purposes even remotely connected with research.[17] The survey revealed that 'apart from salaries, the total amount expended in 1916 for research by all firms listed did not exceed

$135,000.' In the Royal Canadian Institute brief to the Royal Commission on University Finances in 1921, it was stated that 'industrial research in Canada on any considerable scale would seem to be confined to those commercial concerns which are more particularly interested in the production of rubber goods, pulp and paper, acetic acid and acetone and in the smelting of certain ores (copper, zinc and iron).'[18] It was pointed out that 'American firms, having Canadian branches, do all their research work in the United States.' There was evidence, then, that 'the young industries themselves' could not hope to do it. Our references to the facilities for research in universities indicate that, though there were competent researchers available at most universities, relatively few universities provided the conditions under which effective research work could be carried out.

There was, however, another reason for creating an agency to undertake industrial research rather than having it done at the universities. What was meant at this time by the term *industrial research* is what is now called *development*. This is made clear in a memorandum prepared by the chairman of NRC in 1919 in which he argued that the universities should confine themselves to pure and applied research:

The problems in pure and applied science are clean cut, of general and permanent interest and their solution may have far reaching industrial application while those which concern industrial research though they are of importance and, therefore, to be undertaken, are, in the great majority of cases, narrower in scope and are not therefore likely to develop fully a capacity for research in the student. Of the vast majority of problems of industrial research some are of local interest only, others there are whose solution may lose value because of some discovery in pure science, while others of them are insoluble until discoveries in pure science make the solution available. On the general principle of utility as well as because of ideals the student who is training for industrial research should during that period concern himself with problems in pure and applied science.[19]

So far as industrial research was concerned the role of the universities was to provide the training in pure or applied science which would prepare students to do industrial research: 'to train them inadequately, thereby giving them a false idea with a very limited outlook, is to defeat the hopes of those in the industries who are looking to scientific research to help them in the new and trying conditions which confront these industries. When an individual firm provides a laboratory for research, those engaged to staff that laboratory should be genuine, highly trained researchers and not amateurs or tyros in research.' The memorandum from which these quotations are drawn was one 'Regarding the Communications of the Principal and the Registrar of Queen's University on the Proposed National Research Institute of Canada,' and was in response to a letter to the acting prime minister in which Queen's opposed the plan to establish government laboratories. What Queen's actually was against was the allocation of funds to any body other than the universities. Since, as the questionnaire had demonstrated, there were few trained industrial researchers in Canada, the first problem facing the council was to stimulate the production of trained researchers; and as the only place that they could be trained was at the universities it was clearly necessary to build up the graduate schools. Because McGill and Toronto were the only two universities with fully developed graduate programs, much of the effort of the council during 1917 and 1918 had been directed to ways and means of strengthening these institutions. Queen's felt that it was not receiving its proper share of the funds available and that the building of government laboratories would render its position even worse.

Queen's, however, was not the only university that could be accused of acting out of self interest. The chairman of the council had almost as much difficulty with McGill and Toronto in his efforts to persuade them to coordinate their programs. All the universities had financial problems, and they looked upon the National Research Council with a mixture of suspicion and greed.

Nevertheless, the establishment of the Council was of almost immediate benefit to the universities since, in its efforts to stimulate graduate studies and research of all types, it instituted a policy of making grants to graduate students and to professors engaged in research. The student awards took the form of bursaries (for students entering upon graduate work), scholarships (for students with at least one year of graduate studies), and fellowships (for students who had demonstrated beyond question their ability to carry on research). Three fellowships ($1000) and four scholarships ($750) were awarded for 1917-18. The awards for the next three years were:

Year	Fellowships ($1000-1500)	Studentships ($750)	Bursaries ($500)
1918-19	3	5	-
1919-20	5	18	6
1920-21	5	10	8

The total expenditure (including 1917-18) was $41,250. In 1918 the council had made provision for 25 student grants but, largely for reasons connected with the war, there was only a handful of applicants. The expectation in 1919 was that the number would be increased to 50 and eventually to 100, but this latter hope was not realized until the late 1940s. There were 42 awards in 1921-22, 53 in 1931-32.[20]

There was also at the outset a lack of applicants for the council's grants for assisted research to professors, but this problem was removed with the return to peacetime conditions.

In 1918-19, awards totalling $19,519.96 were made to W.P. Thompson of the University of Saskatchewan, A.A. Porter and Alfred Stansfield of McGill, and Louis Bourgeois of L'Ecole polytechnique at Montreal. In 1919-20, the total rose to nearly $40,000 and in 1920-21 to over $60,000.[21]

According to Thistle, the struggle to achieve the central laboratories 'took place in a unique arena, arranged in four concentric circles.'[22] The Inner Ring of his title refers to the members of the National Advisory Council. The next two circles are the cabinet ministers who sat on the Privy Council Committee on Scientific and Industrial Research, to which the advisory council reported, and the senior civil servants of the various government departments in Ottawa. 'The Outer Ring was composed of industrial groups, universities, and provincial governments, shading off into the public at large.' Actually the universities were involved at two points rather than one, since six of the nine members of the council - the Inner Ring - were university professors or presidents. Furthermore, the two most influential figures on the council during the first 25 years were A.B. Macallum, the full-time chairman from 1916 to 1921, and H.M. Tory, the full-time president from 1928. The extremely close relationship of the National Research Council with the Canadian universities, was symbolized by the decision of the National Conference of Canadian Universities in 1929 to admit the National Research Council to its membership.

SOCIETIES, JOURNALS, AND UNIVERSITY PUBLICATIONS

The lack of outlets in Canada for the publication of scientific results was one of the reasons cited in the Royal Canadian Institute's brief in 1921 for the unsatisfactory condition of Canadian science, and was attributable, in part, to the absence of specialized journals and of specialized societies. The Transactions of the Royal Society of Canada and of the Royal Canadian Institute were not enough; nor, it was implied, were the Royal Society of Canada and the Royal Canadian Institute themselves enough. The position was more serious than was portrayed in the brief, since though it continued to publish its *Transactions*, the emphasis of the institute had been consciously changed about the time that its name had been altered from the Canadian Institute to the Royal Canadian Institute (1914), and by 1920 it was no longer primarily interested in publishing original papers of a scientific nature. During 1910, attendance at meetings ranged from 10 to 40, and tea was served, since it was felt that this would enable those present to become better acquainted with one another:

> ... practically no original papers were then being submitted
> to the Institute. The programme was prepared by the Secretary,
> the President simply presiding, and the rule was to get some
> local speaker to address the meeting on a subject that might

be of some interest. The Programmes were made out generally
from month to month. Since the Institute had no funds, they
could not bring any lecturers from outside, but if it was known
that a distinguished lecturer was in the city, he was asked to
address the meeting.[23]

About 1913 its council decided that the Institute should shift
its ground: 'It was now felt that instead of lectures on abstract
subjects which were not interesting to the public, popular lectures
should be instituted to awaken the public to the necessity of
scientific research, which (outside of academic circles) was almost unknown in Canada. It was with this thought in mind that the
campaign for scientific research was launched through the development of popular lectures.' These lectures did prove popular, indeed they still do, and the campaign for scientific research had
practical and long-range results. In 1914, the council proposed
the establishment within the institute of a bureau of scientific
and industrial research, and in 1915 such a bureau was instituted
'with a Council composed of representatives of the universities,
the boards of trade, and other institutions.' The historian of
the Royal Canadian Institute, W.S. Wallace, states that it is
difficult to establish the extent to which the actions of the
institute were influential in bringing about the creation of the
National Research Council in 1916, but he is no doubt right in
saying that it was 'most influential.'[24] In any event by 1920
the Royal Canadian Institute was not primarily a learned society.

There had been no change in the policies of the Royal Society
of Canada, and in 1920 it occupied much the same position in
Canadian intellectual life as it had in 1890. Its membership
had doubled, and there were now five sections rather than four,
the original Geological and Biological Science section (IV) having
been divided in 1918 into Geological Sciences including Mineralogy
(IV) and Biological Sciences (V). There were also 12 corresponding
members and 27 retired members. Five of the charter fellows remained on the active list and five others were listed as retired.
The title of Sections I and II had been expanded to 'French' (and
'English') Literature, History, Archaeology, Sociology, Political
Economy and Allied Subjects.

In three of the five sections the university representation
continued to constitute about one-third of the membership. But
in Section III (Mathematical, Physical and Chemical Sciences),
with 29 professors out of 39, and Section V, with 20 professors
out of 29, the universities predominated. There were now fellows
from Alberta (2), British Columbia (4), Manitoba (4), Saskatchewan
(1), as well as from Dalhousie (6), McGill (15), New Brunswick
(1 - L.W. Bailey, a charter member), Queen's (4), and Toronto
(34). The 12 university members of Section I, 6 of whom could
be described as full-time, were evenly divided between Université
Laval and Université de Montréal. Neither Laval nor Montréal
had a fellow in any of the science sections. With the exception
of Stephen Leacock, the McGill fellows were in the science sections.

The *Proceedings and Transactions* of the Royal Society continued
to be published annually through a grant from the federal government.   This amounted to $5000 from 1883 to 1913, but in 1914 it
was increased to $8000 in the light of increased publication costs.
This was reduced to $4000 from 1918 to 1920 and publication would
not have been possible in 1920 if the National Research Council
had not contributed $3000 for that purpose.   The $8000 federal
grant was restored in 1921, but the NRC continued to support the
Royal Society for the next seven years.[25]

Fifteen of the 20 local societies affiliated with the Royal
Society of Canada in 1890 continued to be listed as associated
societies in 1920 and 30 others are included in the list reproduced below.   Though the majority were in Ontario and Quebec,
all provinces except Alberta and Saskatchewan were represented.
Only 4 of the 45 had a national constituency (Canadian Forestry
Association, Historic Landmarks Association of Canada, Royal
Astronomical Society of Canada, United Empire Loyalists Association of Canada), and the great majority had a local rather than
a provincial membership.   Only four regularly published papers
of a scholarly or a scientific nature: the Royal Canadian Institute, the Entomological Society of Ontario (which continued to
publish *Canadian Entomologist*), Ontario Historical Society (which
had been publishing its *Papers and Records* since 1899), and the
Nova Scotia Historical Society (whose *Report and Collections* had
been appearing since 1879).

Societies Affiliated with Royal Society of Canada 1920
(Asterisk indicates similar status in 1890)

British Columbia
* Natural History Society of British Columbia

Manitoba
Manitoba Historical and Scientific Society

New Brunswick
Miramichi Natural History Association
* Natural History Society of New Brunswick
New Brunswick Historical Society
New Brunswick Loyalists Society

Nova Scotia
* Nova Scotia Historical Society
* Nova Scotia Institute of Science

Ontario
Canadian Forestry Association
Club littéraire canadien-français d'Ottawa
Elgin Historical and Scientific Institute
Elgin Historical and Scientific Institute Women's Auxiliary
* Entomological Society of Ontario
* Hamilton Association for the Promotion of Science, Literature
  and Art

328

Hamilton Ladies College Alumnae
Hamilton Scientific Society
Historical Landmarks Association of Canada
Historical Society
Huron Institute
* Institut canadien-français d'Ottawa
Lundy's Lane Historical Society
Niagara Historical Society
Ontario Historical Society
* Ottawa Field Naturalists' Club
Peterborough Historical Society
Royal Astronomical Society of Canada
* Royal Canadian Institute
Toronto Astronomical Society
United Empire Loyalists' Association of Canada
Waterloo Historical Society
Women's Canadian Historical Society of Ottawa
Women's Canadian Historical Society of Toronto
* Women's Wentworth Historical Society

Prince Edward Island
Natural History and Antiquarian Society of P.E.I.

Quebec
* Antiquarian and Numismatic Society of Montreal
Cercle littéraire et musical de Montréal
* Institut canadien de Québec
* Literary and Historical Society of Quebec
Microscopical Society of Montreal
* Natural History Society of Montreal
Quebec Society for the Protection of Plants from Insects
and Fungus Diseases
Société d'économie sociale et politique de Québec
Société de géographie de Québec
Société du parler-français au Canada
* Société historique de Montréal

Included in this list of affiliated societies is the Canadian
Forestry Association, established in 1900. This is a reminder
that a substantial number of national associations concerned
with particular professions had been established between 1900
and 1920

Association	*Date*
Canadian Library Association	1900
Canadian Dental Association	1902
Canadian Pharmaceutical Association	1907
Royal Architectural Institute of Canada	1907
Canadian Nurses Association	1908
Canadian Society of Forest Engineers	1908
Canadian Public Health Association	1910
Canadian Bar Association	1914

Canadian Society of Technical Agriculturalists	1920
Canadian Institute of Chemistry	1920
Royal College of Physicians and Surgeons of Canada	1920

In addition, the Canadian Medical Association, which had been
founded in 1867 but which had no continuous membership until its
incorporation in 1909, became from this time on a well-organized
and active body; the *Journal* of the Canadian Medical Association
began publication in 1910.   Journals were also published by the
Canadian Dental Association (*Oral Health*, 1911-), Canadian
Forestry Association (*Forestry and Outdoors*, 1905-25), Canadian
Nurses Association (*Canadian Nurse*, 1905-), Canadian Public
Health Association (*C.P.H.A. Journal*, 1910-).   Three of these
journals, *Forestry and Outdoors, Canadian Nurse,* and *Oral Health*,
were largely devoted to professional rather than scientific matters, but the *Canadian Medical Association Journal* was a genuine
learned journal.[26]
   In many cases these national associations developed from professional associations which had been organized in particular
provinces, in others the establishment of a national association
resulted in the organizing of one or more provincial bodies.   The
number of these provincial associations is too extensive to list.
The following are examples: Ontario Library Association, 1901;
College of Veterinarian Surgeons of the Province of Quebec, 1902;
Law Society of Saskatchewan, 1907; Manitoba Association of Architects, 1914; Registered Nurses Association of Nova Scotia, 1909.
   In striking contrast to the marked development of professional
associations was the apparent lack of interest in establishing
societies based on academic disciplines.   The only society of
this latter type to be established during this period was the
Royal Astronomical Society of Canada organized in 1902 from the
base provided by the Astronomical and Physical Society of Toronto
which had been meeting since 1890 and began to publish its *Journal*
in 1907.[27]   There was also an attempt in 1913 to establish a
Canadian Political Science Association.[28]   Some 40 Canadians attended the meetings of the American Economic Association in 1912
and at a lunch meeting to which they had been invited by O.D.
Skelton of Queen's University they resolved to found a Canadian
association.   The association did meet for three days in 1913
and the papers presented were duly published. But the association
did not meet in 1914 and the matter was dropped until 1929.
   The lack of scientific and scholarly journals was to some extent compensated for by the publication by McGill, Queen's, and
Toronto of research studies undertaken by their staff and students;
it was 'to fill the need for a journal' that in 1910 the departments of history and political science at Queen's began to issue
a series of *Bulletins*, of which 59 were issued between 1911 and
1930. Queen's faculty of medicine issued eight *Publications*
between 1909 and 1914, and in 1912 its department of philosophy
published *Bulletin I*.   There were no others. *University of Toronto
Studies* began to appear in 1897 with Papers from the Chemical

Laboratories, of which 110 had been published by 1920. There
were also University of Toronto Studies in physics (62 papers by
1920), geology (10), biology (18), anatomy (3), physiology (30),
pathology (4), medicine (11), philosophy (1), psychology (9),
philology (11), history and economics (11). Technically, the
series of *McGill University Publications* did not begin until 1921
but those listed from that date include papers issued from as
early as 1896 in botany, chemistry, engineering, geology, mineralogy, metallurgy, medicine, philosophy, mathematics, physics,
and zoology. Many of the McGill and Toronto papers were reprints
of articles that had appeared in American or European journals
and a number were Ph.D. theses. One of the University of Toronto
Studies was *Review of Publications Relating to Canada*, which
appeared annually from 1896 to 1919. Following the establishment
of the *Canadian Historical Review* in 1920, the Review of Publications continued as a regular feature of the new quarterly.

The first Canadian university press also emerged during this
period.[29] In 1901 the University of Toronto purchased two small
printing presses and hired a printer to produce its examinations,
calendars, and official notices, and in 1904 R.J. Hamilton, who
had since 1897 been manager of the Students' Book Department,
was appointed book-keeper of the press. By 1910 the 'Press' was
located in the university library and was in the binding business,
and in 1911 it produced a book for private distribution. A year
later *A Short Handbook of Latin Accidence and Syntax* by J.H.
Fletcher of the department of classics was published and sold to
students as a textbook. Officially designated the University of
Toronto Press in 1915, it was authorized in 1919 to have a publishing department (which was not to incur a deficit of more
than $2000) and in 1920 it was provided with a small building of
its own. By this time it had published six books.

The period was also marked by a succession of attempts to establish university quarterlies and monthlies, in some cases by
the institution itself, in others by a group of professors. In
a number of cases these were what would now be called alumni
magazines designed, as the first issue of *The McGill University
Magazine* expressed it, 'to chronicle the progress of the University and to stimulate a feeling of corporate rather than nominal
unity.'

The first publication of this type was the *McMaster University
Monthly*, which began in 1891 and continued until 1930; by 1905,
however, editorial responsibility had been assumed by undergraduates and the quality of the articles had declined. Other examples are the *University of Toronto Monthly* (1901-47) and the
Revue Trimestrielle Canadienne published by the Ecole des hautes
études commerciales from 1914 to 1957. The *Queen's Quarterly*
(1893-) was launched as a journal of this type but gradually
de-emphasized its interest in Queen's University in favour of a
general concern for Canadian political and cultural problems.
By 1920 it had a national rather than a local orientation.[30]

The *McGill University Magazine*, a quarterly, also reduced its

reporting of undergraduate and alumni activities after the first
half-dozen issues and perhaps in doing so reduced its appeal to
its initial subscribers. In 1906 it ceased publication but was
immediately replaced by the *University Magazine*, a venture sponsored by three universities, McGill, Toronto, and Dalhousie, each
of which was represented on the Editorial Committee. *The
University Magazine* was, however, the creature of its editor,
Andrew Macphail, a part-time professor (of the history of medicine)
at McGill and one of Canada's great editors.[31] Under his direction
it became the leading periodical of political and literary comment
in English Canada. *The University Magazine* ceased publication in
1920, but in a sense was continued by one of the three sponsoring
universities since *The Dalhousie Review* began publication in 1921
with the same basic editorial policy.

Attempts were made by the University of Toronto in both 1893
and 1895 to establish a literary quarterly but both were short-
lived. More successful in this line was the University of Ottawa
which published *Revue Littéraire de l'Université d'Ottawa* from
1900 to 1906 and *University of Ottawa Review* from 1898 to 1915.
However, it was not until 1931 and the establishment of *Revue
de l'Université d'Ottawa* and the *University of Toronto Quarterly*
that the objectives the two universities had in mind were realized.

The first university quarterly had been established by l'Université Laval in 1888, but it had suspended publication in 1891.[32]
In 1902 it was revived, though without the university's official
sponsorship, as *La Nouvelle France: revue des intérêts religieux
et nationaux*. It continued until 1918 when, this time as a 'publication de l'Université Laval' it was merged with *Parler Français*,
a journal established in 1906 by La Société de Parler Français
as *Le Canada Français*. The objectives of the new journal combined
those of an alumni magazine and a journal of ideas.

A somewhat similar development had occurred in Montreal with
the establishment, first of *L'Action Sociale* (1907), then of
L'Action Catholique (1915), and then of *L'Action Française* (1917),
though in this case Université de Montréal (as it would become in
1919) was not officially involved. We are concerned here with
two journals rather than three or one since, though *Action Sociale*
became *Action Catholique* and continues to be published under this
name, *Action Française* was a new venture. However, the first
editor, Omer Heroux, had been a frequent contributor to the earlier journals and professors from Université de Montréal and
Laval were active in all three. The importance of *Action Française* as a journal dedicated to the advancement of the interests
of French Canada as a unit within or if necessary independent of
Canada as a whole is of great significance in the political and
intellectual life of the nation, but its significance dates primarily from 1920 when l'Abbé Lionel Groulx assumed the editorship.
Consequently it will be dealt with in chapter 24.

LIBRARIES - ART GALLERIES - MUSEUMS

Since scholarship and research in the humanities and social sciences depends to so considerable an extent on the availability of the materials housed in libraries, art galleries, and museums, the relative strength of the resources available to Canadians in these areas at any time is of significance in assessing the achievement of scholars in these fields. In 1920 the situation was substantially improved over that of 30 years earlier but it was not impressive.

The number of volumes held in all the 'public' libraries of Canada in 1921 is reported in the Dominion Bureau of Statistics' *Annual Report on Education Statistics in Canada for 1922*, the information being presented province by province and according to type of library, of which university libraries is one category:

Province	Number of volumes	Number of universities	Universities
Prince Edward Island	7,500	1	St Dunstan's
Nova Scotia	127,000	4	Acadia, Dalhousie, Nova Scotia Tech., St Francis Xavier
New Brunswick	39,000	3	Mount Allison, University of New Brunswick, St Joseph's
Quebec	327,000	4	Bishop's, Laval, McGill, Montréal
Ontario	392,000	7	McMaster, Ottawa, Queen's, Toronto, Trinity, Victoria, Western Ontario
Manitoba	29,000	1	Manitoba
Saskatchewan	25,000	1	Saskatchewan
Alberta	25,000	1	Alberta
British Columbia	39,000	1	British Columbia

Undoubtedly some of these figures are misleading; one suspects, for example, that the libraries of theological colleges and seminaries associated with particular universities are not included and in the case of the Grand Séminaire at Quebec, this would represent a very sizable number of volumes. Nonetheless, the figures indicate that the majority of Canadian universities had very modest libraries at this time and that none had a collection comparable to those of the leading universities in the United States.

In 1890 only Nova Scotia had taken steps to organize provincial archives, but, by 1920, three other provinces had followed: Ontario, which established a bureau of archives in 1903, British Columbia, which appointed an archivist in 1908, and Quebec which established its Provincial Archives in 1920. We have already referred to the development of the Public Archives of Canada during this period and noted that its extensive collection was not made effectively available until 1926.[33]

The position with respect to art galleries was similar to that of archives: a recently established (1907) but inadequately housed National Gallery at Ottawa, and respectable though undistinguished galleries at Sackville, New Brunswick (the Owens Museum of Fine Art, 1894), Halifax (Nova Scotia Museum of Fine Arts, 1909), Montreal (Montreal Museum of Fine Art, 1912), and Toronto (Art Gallery of Toronto, 1916). The dates in each case refer to the opening of a permanent building.

In 1903, Frederick Merrill of the New York State Museum at Albany undertook a survey of natural history museums in the United States and Canada, and his report[34] provided details of 21 Canadian collections, five of which were the property of local societies (Natural History Society of Saint John, Historical and Scientific Society of Manitoba are examples), nine of universities or colleges (Acadia, King's, New Brunswick, Laval, McGill, Queen's, Toronto, Victoria, Ontario Agricultural College). There were also provincial museums at Halifax, Toronto, and Victoria, B.C. The most substantial collection was that of the Geological Survey of Canada in Ottawa. The collections at Laval, McGill, Queen's, and Toronto, as well as that of the provincial museum at Victoria, were solid.

Merrill's report on the University of Toronto refers to three separate museums, Geological and Mineralogical, Biological, and Ethnological, four if one includes that of the federated Victoria University. By 1920 these four physically separated collections and also that of the Provincial Ethnological Museum had been consolidated as the Royal Ontario Museum in a $400,000 building opened in 1914.[35] The museum was the responsibility of a board of trustees largely drawn from the University of Toronto's Board of Governors but also included the provincial ministers of education and mines. The heads of its divisions of archaeology, geology, mineralogy, palaeontology, and zoology had academic appointments at the university.

HUMANITIES AND SOCIAL SCIENCES

The two fields in which it can be said that a substantial body of scholarly work was produced by Canadians up to 1920 are those of philosophy and history, and in the case of the latter the statement applies primarily to the immediately preceding 10 or 15 years. There is nothing of significance to report in the fields of classical or oriental studies, modern foreign languages including English, economics (other than in the historical context), political science, sociology, anthropology, or geography. G.S. Brett's three-volume *History of Psychology* (1912-21) was certainly a contribution in the field of psychology, but Brett was a professor of philosophy. Furthermore, he had completed most of the work on these volumes before he came to Canada. Two other philosophers deserve mention, John Watson, who continued to produce works of international importance, notably *The Philosophy of Kant Explained* (1908), and *The Interpretation of Religious Experience* (1912). In the field of thomistic studies L.-A. Paquet's six-volume *Disputationes Theologicae seu Commentaria in Summum Theologicam D. Thomae* (1893-1903) was in its time a major contribution.

In the field of history, there were no Canadian scholars with an international reputation comparable to that of Brett, Watson, or Paquet, but there was an impressive body of work. Almost all of it, as one would expect, was concerned with Canadian history, and much of it was based on the documentary material which by the early 1900s had been collected and organized in the various archives and in many cases published by provincial and local historical societies.

NOTES TO CHAPTER 18

1 Province of Ontario, *Report of Royal Commission on University Finances* (1921), I, 3
2 *Royal Commission Report*, II, 146
3 W.S. Learned and K.C.M. Sills, *Education in the Maritime Provinces of Canada* (1922), 31
4 As noted in a letter to Principal Peterson, Rutherford's only dissatisfaction with McGill was its isolation from the European scientific community: 'the determining factor in deciding to go to Manchester was my feeling that it is necessary to be in closer contact with European Science than is possible on this side of the ocean.' Commenting on the destruction of the Engineering Building in 1907, he said that it was one of the first, if not the finest engineering laboratories in America. A.S. Eve, *Rutherford* (1939), 155-6. For a review of Rutherford's work at McGill and the subsequent work of his colleagues (H.T. Barnes, H.L. Bronson, R.W. Boyle, A.S. Eve, Otto Hahn, F.J. Soddy, et al.), see A.N. Shaw's obituary notice in *Proc. Royal Society Canada* 1938.
5 H.H. Langton, *Sir John Cunningham McLennan: a Memoir with a Chapter on his Scientific Work by E.F. Burton* (1939)
6 R.D. Defries, *The First Fifty Years 1914-1955, Connaught Medical Research Laboratories, University of Toronto* (1968)
7 *Royal Commission Report*, II, 98
8 Ibid.
9 Langton, *Sir John Cunningham McLennan*, chapter 13

10 J.C. Miller, *National Government and Technical Education in Federated Democracies: Dominion of Canada* (1940), 431-41

11 Dominion of Canada, *Fifty Years of Progress in Dominion Experimental Farms 1886-1936* (1939)

12 M.S. Rigby and A.G. Huntsman, *Materials Relating to the History of the Fisheries Research Board of Canada* (1958)

13 G.S. Garrett, *Forestry Education in Canada* (1971), 16

14 W.K. Lamb, 'Archives' in *Encyclopedia Canadiana* (1957)

15 Miller, *National Government*, 456-65

16 M. Thistle, *The Inner Ring* (1966), x

17 Ibid., 159

18 *Royal Commission Report*, II, 146

19 Thistle, *Inner Ring*, 57

20 Miller, *National Government*, 480

21 Thistle, *Inner Ring*, 70-1

22 Ibid., x

23 W.S. Wallace, *Royal Canadian Institute Centennial Volume* (1951), 161. The quotation is from a memorandum prepared for Wallace by John Patterson, Honorary Secretary, 1911-15.

24 Wallace, ibid., 163

25 Miller, *National Government*, 518

26 Several of the associations began to publish journals in the early 1920s: *Scientific Agriculture* 1921, *Canadian Bar Review* 1923, *Royal Canadian Architectural Institute Journal* 1924.

27 R.J. Northcott, 'The Growth of the R.A.S.C. and its Guiding Mentor C.A. Chant,' *Royal Astronomical Society Can. J.*, 61 (1967), 218-25

28 K.W. Taylor, 'Economic Scholarship in Canada,' *Can. J. Econ. Pol. Sci.*, 26 (1960), 6-18

29 E. Harman, 'Founding a University Press,' in her *The University as Publisher* (1962), 19-58

30 D.D. Calvin, 'Queen's Quarterly 1893-1943,' *Queen's Quarterly*, 50 (1943), 117-29

31 C. Berger, *The Sense of Power* (1971), 47

32 See above, chapter 12, 199-200.

33 See above, chapter 18, 322-3.

34 F.J.H. Merrill, 'National History Museums of the United States and Canada,' *New York State Museum Bulletin*, 62 (1903)

35 For the beginnings of the Royal Ontario Museum, see C.T. Currelly, *I Brought the Ages Home* (1956).

1940

The day of science has arrived
Alfred Thompson, M.P.

19

The Conference on
Canadian-American Affairs
1939

The incident chosen to introduce the 1921-40 section of this history of higher education in Canada is a conference attended by 61
Canadians and 90 Americans at St Lawrence University in upper New
York State from 19-22 June 1939. One of a series of conferences
on Canadian-American affairs held between 1935 and 1945, it demonstrates three of the more important developments in Canadian
higher education during this 20 year period: (1) the emergence
of economics, history, and political science as academic disciplines of central importance; (2) the recognition by government
of the professor as expert; (3) the involvement of Canadian professors in large-scale research projects. Reference to this event
also provides an opportunity to note the generous assistance
rendered to Canadian higher education during the 1920s and 1930s
by the Carnegie Corporation of New York and other American philanthropic bodies.

The 1939 Conference on Canadian-American Affairs was one of
four such conferences sponsored by the Carnegie Endowment for
International Peace, which were held alternatively at St Lawrence
University and at Queen's University in Kingston at two year intervals commencing in June 1935.[1] A fifth conference dealing
specifically with educational problems was held under the same
auspices in 1938 at the University of Maine.[2] Each of these
events provided an opportunity for discussion of the relations
of the two countries to each other and was viewed by the Carnegie
people as part of a larger enterprise upon which, at the urging
of James T. Shotwell, they had entered in 1934. Shotwell, a
Canadian who in 1908 was appointed a full professor of history at
Columbia University, became heavily involved in the work of the
Peace Conference at Paris at the close of World War I.

In 1924, he became a trustee of the Carnegie Endowment for
International Peace and director of its division of economics and
history. In the latter capacity, and acting on the suggestion of
J.B. Brebner, a Canadian-born fellow member of the Columbia depart-

ment of history, he proposed in 1933 a large-scale study of the relations of the United States and Canada.[3] Shotwell argued that there was at least as much to be learned about the maintenance of peace and the avoidance of war from the experience of countries between whom there was not the slightest possibility of war arising as from those who had a long record of active conflict. The proposal was approved by the Carnegie authorities, and Shotwell proceeded to arrange for the preparation of a series of monographs by American and Canadian scholars, 25 of which were published between 1936 and 1945 under the general title, 'The Relations of Canada and the United States.'[4]

As Shotwell was later to observe in his autobiography, it was the combination of the published studies and the opportunity for direct, personal contact and detailed discussion which made the whole Carnegie-sponsored project worthwhile. The conferences, he said, set a precedent:

> These were unique occasions. There was nothing new in the holding of Canadian-American conferences by lawyers, bankers, labour unions, professional or businessmen. But those were relatively limited to special professionals or technicians. This was the first time in the history of Canada and the United States that representative citizens of both countries met together to take stock of the fundamentals in their inter-relationship in all the varied fields of intellectual, economic, social and political activity.[5]

At the closing luncheon of the 1939 conference, French-speaking delegate Seraphin Marion, secretary of Section I of the Royal Society of Canada, made a reference to another benefit which accrued from the conference:

> I will be going back to French Canada with a message. If there is one conclusion ... that can be drawn from these very interesting and illuminating conferences, it is this: If the world is going to be saved at all, it will be saved by co-operation, and co-operation means contact. Well, that law applies also to relations between French Canada and English Canada, and French Canada and America. It is often stated that French Canada is very provincial in its outlook. But if that state of affairs exists, is it not due in large measure to the fact that very often in the past French Canadians were left to themselves? That state of affairs has changed, and my message to French Canada will be that among the intelligentsia of English-speaking Canada and the intelligentsia of the United States there is nothing but very strong feelings of sympathy and friendship for French Canada. Even if I had no other message to bring to French Canada I think it would have been worthwhile coming here.[6]

On the less positive side, the Canadian historian A.R.M. Lower who attended four of the conferences told the 1939 gathering that there was a serious limitation in such meetings:

There is a considerable degree of unrealism in a meeting such
as this in that we are all ... on the outside looking in. We
are not the people that determine policy. We do not determine
the course of events. We may conjure up great schemes and have
great thoughts, but the day-to-day business of politics goes
on, and somebody sitting in a government office decides what is
going to be done about it. While our exploratory surveys are
all very well in their sight, and possibly useful to some of
them, it is the people in the government offices who make the
decisions. Policy is made in capitals by politicians, who as
a rule are not very acutely aware of what people such as we are
talking about.[7]

Despite Lower's pessimism, however, it is likely that, as a result
of the opportunities for interchange provided by these meetings,
the politicians in Washington and Ottawa were in a better position
to learn what academics like Lower and his colleagues were 'talking
about.'
    Who were the people attending the conferences? The delegates
at the 1939 meetings were, on the whole, typical of all previous
groups: two-thirds of them were university professors, and the
great majority of these were historians, political scientists,
or economists. The American academic contingent came almost exclusively from the eastern states, whereas the Canadians were
from universities located in all parts of the country.[8] A number
of the Canadians attending the 1939 Conference would play key
roles in Canadian higher education during the next 25 years, among
them J.A. Corry and W.A. Mackintosh of Queen's; D.G. Creighton
and H.A. Innis of Toronto; F.R. Scott of McGill, and K.W. Taylor
of McMaster. Three other prominent figures of the 1950s and 1960s,
V.W. Bladen and F.H. Underhill of Toronto, and N.A.M. Mackenzie
of New Brunswick and British Columbia attended at least two of
the other conferences. There were few French-speaking academics
simply because the social sciences did not begin to develop in
the French-speaking universities until the late 1930s.
    Of the Americans present who were not academics, most were from
New York or Washington, and they were chiefly economists and financial consultants. The United States minister to Canada was in
attendance as were a senator from Utah, senior officials from the
Department of Commerce and the Tariff Commission, and a handful
of industrialists. On the Canadian side there were relatively
few people from business and industry or from government (W.C.
Clark, deputy minister of finance and formerly a professor at
Queen's, and W.A. Riddell, head of the legation at Washington,
were the principal government representatives), but government
agencies were well represented - Canadian Broadcasting Corporation,
Dominion Bureau of Statistics, National Research Council, Public
Archives of Canada - as were such national organizations as the
League of Nations Society, the Canadian Institute for International
Affairs, and the Royal Society of Canada. Years later, the irrep-
ressible Arthur Lower commented that 'Canadians were there in
full force (their expenses were paid!), but the Americans who

turned up were mostly either ex-Canadians or second-string men.[9]

What were the topics of discussion at the conferences? At the opening session of the 1939 conference, Shotwell reminded the delegates of the inevitable shift of interest from purely North American problems to those of world-wide significance which had recently occurred, but he also emphasized that many of the research projects, which by this time were well underway, had made it clear 'that it was no longer possible to state, let alone understand, the problems of Canadian-American relations unless we looked overseas as well.'[10] In the course of the 1939 sessions, a number of addresses were given on a variety of subjects. For example, a paper was delivered by the American under-secretary of commerce, E.J. Noble, on 'The North Country and its Trade Relations,' and another by H.M. Tory, the current president of the Royal Society of Canada, on 'Intellectual Co-operation between Canada and the United States.' The main topics of discussion, however, were North America in the World Today, North American Political Interests, Defense and External Obligations, Trade Control, and International Fiscal Controls. This focus on international relations was a change from that of the conferences held in 1935 and 1937.

The proceedings of all the meetings were published, and it may be presumed that the participation of even a small number of senior civil servants was a guarantee that copies would be widely circulated in government offices in Ottawa and Washington. If one examines the planning and execution of the report of the federal government's 1939 Royal Commission on Dominion-Provincial Relations, the Rowell-Sirois Report,[11] there is evidence that not only was the commission prepared to listen to the views of academics, but also that it initiated a whole series of pilot projects to serve as a basis for the final Report, and that these were largely researched and written by university men. Both the titles of the studies and their authors point to a new awareness of the importance of the various disciplines in the social sciences. Of the dozen specific projects commissioned, seven were published as appendices to the final royal commission report: 'British North America at Confederation,' by D.G. Creighton; 'Difficulties of Divided Jurisdiction,' by J.A. Corry; 'The Economic Background of Dominion Provincial Relations,' by W.A. Mackintosh; 'Legislative Expedience and Devices Adopted by the Dominion and the Provinces,' by L.M. Gouin of Ecole des hautes études commercial, Université de Montréal, and Brooke Claxton, part-time lecturer in law at McGill; 'Labour Legislation and Social Services in the Province of Quebec,' by Esdras Minville (Montréal); 'Public Assistance and Social Insurance,' by A.E. Grauer (Toronto); 'National Income' by D.C. McGregor *et al.* (Toronto).[12] With the exception of Minville and Grauer, all of these people had attended one or more of the Canadian-American conferences, as had two other contributors to the commission studies, Carl Goldenberg, a part-time lecturer in law at McGill and F.A. Knox of Queen's.

From the above, one could justly infer that the pattern of involving academics in high-level attacks on national problems was
a direct fall-out of the Carnegie-sponsored conferences on Canadian-
American affairs.

It was stated at the beginning of the chapter that reference to
these conferences provided an opportunity to give due credit to the
generous benefactions provided over many years by American philanthropic foundations to Canadian higher education. From a financial
standpoint the sponsoring of the Canadian-American conferences was
one of the least expensive of the projects undertaken by the network of Carnegie foundations in the interests of strengthening the
Canadian universities between 1920 and 1940. Support for the whole
undertaking amounted to approximately $180,000, of which approxi-
mately $25,000 was spent on the conferences and $155,000 on the
preparation and publishing of the 25 volumes.[13] Both of these
projects, in theory at least, were of as much value to the United
States as to Canada; they should not, therefore, be regarded primarily as a 'Canadian' expenditure. In any event, Canadians benefited immeasurably from other Carnegie ventures during this period.
Grants in direct support of Canadian higher education exceeded
$6 million; close to $2 million was given in retirement allowances
for Canadian professors or pensions for their widows through the
Carnegie Foundation for the Advancement of Teaching and the Teachers
Insurance and Annuity Associaton funds, over $4 million in direct
grants was awarded to 37 Canadian universities and colleges (Table
2), and over $600,000 was given to organizations other than degree-
granting institutions for work related to Canadian higher education
(Table 1).[14]

Almost every Canadian university was in receipt of a grant; of
the members of the National Conference of Canadian Universities
only Nova Scotia Technical College and three non-degree granting
institutions, Brandon College, Royal Military College, and Nova
Scotia Agricultural College, are missing from the list. In about
half the cases the total grant was under $10,000 and consisted of
a set of the material prepared as audio or visual aids for the
teaching of fine art or music or a grant for library purchases,
but in eight instances the grants exceeded $100,000 and in the
case of the grants to Dalhousie and King's arising out of their
agreement to enter into federation exceeded $2 million. The grants
in support of research were small, but they included one of $8000
to Frederick Banting 'for work on the effect of the extract of
pancreas in the treatment of diabetes.' Three universities received emergency grants in 1932 to meet crises produced by the
Depression: Acadia ($10,000), Alberta ($50,000), St Francis Xavier
($10,000). The grants to Memorial University College of Newfound-
land enabled this institution to become firmly established. Perhaps the most significant benefactions, however, are those listed
in Table 1 under the category of 'Teaching Program'; these were
grants designed to support new developments in the academic program, particularly in the fields of adult education and fine art,
but also in child study, library science, medieval studies, and

music. In the 1930s, when Canadian funds were in short supply, seed money of this type was of enormous importance to institutions which were in danger of losing confidence in their future.

Comparable assistance to Canadian higher education was rendered during these years by the Rockefeller Foundation, but principally in the areas of medicine and public health, with the result that a much smaller number of individual institutions benefited directly. The chief beneficiaries were McGill and Toronto (approximately $1,000,000 each), Alberta, Dalhousie, Manitoba (over $500,000), and Montreal ($375,000).[15]

TABLE 1
Selected Carnegie Corporation Grants to organizations related to Canadian higher education 1920/21-1940/41 ($)

Advisory Group on Canadian College Libraries (1932)	2,552
American Assoc. for Adult Education (grants to Cdn. students 1932)	6,000
American Assoc. for Adult Education (organization of Canadian Association for Adult Education	10,000
American Assoc. of Dental Schools (study of dental ed. 1930-33)	30,000
American Council on Education (Modern Foreign Language Study, 1924-26)	89,000
American Library Assoc. (fellowships Cdn. librarians, 1931-39)	32,100
American Library Assoc. (survey of libraries in Canada, 1930)	10,000
Canadian Association for Adult Education (1936-41)	65,000
Canadian Bureau for the Advancement of Music (1931-36)	38,000
Canadian Council for Educational Research (1939)	10,000
Canadian Institute for International Affairs (1933-41)	26,500
Canadian Museums Committee (fellowships, grants in aid 1932-42)	39,925
Canadian Social Science Research Council (1940-41)	14,800
Learned-Sills Study of Education in Maritime Provinces (1921-24)	5,575
Maritime Provinces, Central Advisory Committee on Education (1924-41)	20,754
National Conference of Canadian Universities (visiting lecturers)	16,000
National Gallery of Canada (1931-41)	64,649
Royal Canadian Institute (International Mathematics Congress, 1924)	6,500
Royal Society of Canada (support 1927, scholarships 1931-41)	163,000
Workers Educational Assoc. of Canada (1936-41)	18,500
Workers Educational Assoc. of Ontario (1929-33)	22,500
TOTAL	691,325

TABLE 2
Grants to Canadian Universities by Carnegie Corporation 1920–40

	Library ($)	Art ($)	Music ($)	Teaching program ($)	Research ($)	Endowment and general ($)	Total ($)
Acadia	15,000	5,000	2,500	5,000 Adult Education 11,200 Fine Art	5,000 Math.	275,000 Endowment 10,000 General (1932)	328,700
Dalhousie	61,000	5,000		4,000 Pathology 8,000 German 50,000 Medicine	6,214 Medicine 1,500 Astronomy	190,000 General 500,000 Medicine 400,000 Endowment 125,000 Geology	1,350,714
King's	3,000					600,000 Endowment (8 chairs) 197,500 General	800,500
Memorial	8,000	5,000	1,325	4,000 Summer session 7,500 Equipment		260,000 General 7,500 Scholarships	293,325
Mount Allison	4,500	5,000	2,550	5,000 German		10,000 General (1932) 125,000 Chemistry	152,050
New Brunswick	4,500						4,500
Prince of Wales College	4,500					75,000 Economics & Sociology	79,500
St Dunstan's	1,800						1,800
St Francis Xavier	4,500			70,000 Adult Education		10,000 General (1932)	84,500

TABLE 2 continued

	Library ($)	Art ($)	Music ($)	Teaching program ($)	Research ($)	Endowment and general ($)	Total ($)
St Joseph's	1,000						1,000
Bishop's	4,500						4,500
Laval	6,000						6,000
McGill	15,000		2,250	135,800 Library Science 19,000 Adult Education 25,000 Chinese Studies		5,000 Establishment of International Labour Office	202,050
Montréal	8,000						8,000
Ecole des hautes études commerciales	3,000						3,000
McMaster	6,000		2,250	48,500 Fine Art			56,750
Ottawa	4,500						4,500
Queen's	15,000	5,000	2,550	5,600 Museum 12,500 Music	9,000 Science 23,000 Biochemistry		72,650
Toronto	17,000	5,000	1,150	44,800 Fine Art 4,800 Physics 14,500 Child Study	29,000 Medicine 24,500 Physics 30,000 Educational 16,500 Linguistics		187,250

TABLE 2 continued

	Library ($)	Art ($)	Music ($)	Teaching program ($)	Research ($)	Endowment and general ($)	Total ($)
St Michael's				33,000 Medieval Studies			33,000
Trinity	6,000						6,000
Victoria	15,000				2,000 Eng. Lit.		17,000
Western	15,000		2,550	12,500 French 10,000 Music			40,050
Assumption	2,400						2,400
Brescia	1,500						1,500
Waterloo	2,400						2,400
Ontario Agric. College					4,250 Poultry		4,250
Manitoba		5,000	2,550	50,000 Arts & Science 10,000 Adult Education			67,550
Saskatchewan	9,000	5,000	5,000	50,000 Arts & Science 33,000 Music 4,500 Physics 10,000 Adult Education	2,500 Biology 2,500 History		121,500
Campion College	1,500						1,500
Luther College	2,400						2,400
Regina College	3,000	2,000	2,500	15,000 Music			22,500

TABLE 2 continued

	Library ($)	Art ($)	Music ($)	Teaching program ($)	Research ($)	Endowment and general ($)	Total ($)
Alberta	15,000	5,000	2,500	56,000 Fine Art 2,500 Museum	10,000 Medicine 3,000 Math. Teaching	50,000 General (1934)	144,000
Mount Royal College							
St Joseph's College	15,000					100,000 Building	15,000 100,000
British Columbia	15,000	5,000	2,500	30,000 Adult Education 10,000 Grad. Studies	10,000 Attendance at Confe- rences		72,500
Victoria College	3,000						3,000

1 A.B. Corey, R.G. Trotter, and W.W. McLaren, eds., *Conference on Canadian-American Affairs ... 1939 Proceedings* (1939). The proceedings of the 1935 and 1937 conferences were edited by the same three persons and were published by Ginn in 1935 and 1937 respectively. The proceedings of the 1941 conference were edited by Trotter and Corey and published by Ginn in 1941.

2 R.L. Morrow, ed., *Conference on Educational Problems in Canadian American Relations ... 1938 Proceedings* (1939)

3 J.B. Brebner's suggestions were made in a paper entitled 'Canadian and North American History,' presented to the Canadian Historical Association in May 1931. (Can. Hist. Assoc., *Report of the Annual Meeting ... 1931*, 37-48). For Brebner's subsequent involvement in the project, see D.G. Creighton's introduction to the Carleton Library edition of Brebner's *North American Triangle: The Interplay of Canada, the United States and Great Britain* (1966), originally published in 1945 as the final volume in the series.

4 J.T. Shotwell, ed., *The Relations of Canada and the United States*, 25 vols. (1936-45).

5 Shotwell, *The Autobiography of James T. Shotwell*, New York: Bobbs Merrill, 1961, 293. See also Shotwell's remarks in Trotter and Corey, *Conference ... 1941 Proc.*, 5-7.

6 S. Marion, *Conference ... 1939 Proc.*, 220

7 Corey, Trotter, and McLaren, *Conference, 1939 Proc.*, 153

8 Ibid., 153

9 A.R.M. Lower, *My First Seventy-Five Years* (1967), 196

10 Corey, Trotter, and McLaren, *Conference ... 1939 Proc.*, 4-5

11 The government initially appointed N.C. Rowell, chief justice of Ontario, and Mr. Justice T. Rinfret of the Supreme Court of Canada as co-chairmen, but the latter resigned three months later for reasons of health. Joseph Sirois, a lawyer and part-time professor of constitutional and administrative law at Université Laval, was then appointed a member of the commission in place of Rinfret, and Rowell was named chairman. In November 1938 Rowell also resigned for reasons of health and Sirois was named chairman. Two of the other members of the commission were university professors: R.A. MacKay, professor of government at Dalhousie, and H.F. Angus, professor of economics at British Columbia. The remaining member was the journalist J.W. Dafoe.

12 Canada, *Report of the Royal Commission on Dominion-Provincial Relations* (1940). The seven research studies cited in the text, identified as appendices 2-7, were separately published by the King's Printer as was 'A Summary of Dominion and Provincial Public Finance Statistics,' identified as appendix 1. Eleven other research studies became available in mimeographed form.

13 Letter of S.H. Stackpole, Director, Commonwealth Program,

Carnegie Corporation of New York, to R.S. Harris, dated 18 September 1972

14 Letter of S.H. Stackpole to R.S. Harris, dated 3 October 1972, gives $1,888,000 as the amount paid by the Carnegie Foundation for the Advancement of Teaching to Canadian professors and to their widows between 1920 and 1940. The details of grants to Canadian institutions and organizations listed in tables 1 and 2 are taken from S.H. Stackpole, *Carnegie Corporation Commonwealth Program 1911-1961* (1963) and R.M. Lester, *Ten Years Catalog of Grants, 1941-51* (1951). In some instances items in the Stackpole volume cover a grant stretching over several years commencing in the 1930s and extending beyond 30 June 1941; reference to the Lester volume permits one to determine how much applied to the period 1920/21-1940/41.

15 Rockefeller Foundation, *Annual Reports* (1920-39)

20
Institutional Development

One of the most apparent changes characterizing higher education in Canada between 1920 and 1940 was the significant increase in enrolments. As indicated in Table 1, the numbers of students rose from 23,418 to 37,225, i.e. by 58%. These figures include Osgoode Hall Law School, Nova Scotia Agricultural College, and Royal Military College which did not have degree-granting powers in 1940, as well as a number of theological colleges not associated with any university. They reflect the larger proportion of women attending university, 16% as opposed to 24%, and a quadrupling of students in the markedly expanded area of postgraduate study. In arts and science, including commerce and secretarial sciences which in 1940 in most institutions were offered by the faculty of arts and science, the student population almost doubled during these years. However, there was only a modest increase in the professional fields. In fact, four of the major faculties, dentistry, law, medicine, and pharmacy, had substantially fewer admissions. Of the fields which by 1920 were well established, only agriculture, engineering, forestry, and veterinary medicine experienced any growth in the next two decades, and in the latter two the numbers remained relatively small.

The most striking progress occurred in the programs of special interest to women: education, household science, nursing, social work, library science, physical and occupational therapy, the last mentioned being a field that had not been offered in any Canadian institution at the beginning of the period. Indeed, if the programs catering to women were disregarded, the numbers in undergraduate professional programs would be almost the same in 1940 as in 1920. On the other hand, the largest single increase, by a factor close to 10, was in graduate studies outside of arts and science. In 1940, almost as many students were engaged in graduate work in agriculture, dentistry, engineering, medicine, and one or two other fields as had been undertaking graduate studies in the academic disciplines in 1920.

TABLE 1
Full-time enrolment Canadian institutions of higher education

Faculties	1920-21			1930-31	1940-41		
	Men	Women	Total	Totals	Men	Women	Total
Arts & Science	6,405	2,667	9,072	16,828	12,300	5,334	17,634
Commerce	361	11	372	883	1,015	175	1,190
Sub-totals	6,766	2,678	9,444	17,711	13,315	5,509	18,824
Agric. (deg.)	845	11	856	889	1,347	26	1,373
Agric. (dip.)	415	–	415	370	389	–	389
Architecture	48	1	49	137	86	10	96
Dentistry	1,253	23	1,276	380	462	6	468
Education	68	88	156	618	297	380	677
Engineering	2,851	3	2,854	3,554	4,368	13	4,381
Forestry	103	–	103	136	173	–	173
H.Sc. (deg.)	–	100	100	639	–	790	790
H.Sc. (dip.)	–	342	342	928	–	634	634
Law	1,076	41	1,117	845	678	19	697
Library Science	–	–	–	42	–	52	52
Medicine	3,108	148	3,256	2,521	2,780	160	2,940
Nursing	• –	122	122	301	–	510	510
Phys. Health Ed.	–	22	22	76	5	123	128
Physio-Occ. Therapy	–	–	–	56	–	174	174
Pharmacy	529	33	562	512	372	40	412
Social Work	13	72	85	110	22	124	146
Theology	2,095	41	2,136	2,231	2,393	36	2,429
Vet. Medicine	116	–	116	122	241	4	245
Sub-totals	12,520	1,047	13,567	14,867	13,613	3,101	16,714
Grad. (Arts & Science)	261	108	369	1,300	1,079	323	1,402
Grad. (Other)	37	1	38	241	309	20	329
Sub-totals	298	109	407	1,541	1,388	343	1,731
Grand totals	19,584	3,834	23,418	34,119	28,272	8,953	37,225

Source: Dominion Bureau of Statistics, *Higher Education in Canada* 1946-48, 48-53.

Reference to the 1930-31 figures in Table 1 reveals that most of the enrolment increase took place during the first 10 years and it may be speculated that the development of Canadian higher education was seriously affected by the Depression. However, it is apparent that the major decline in enrolment in law, medicine, and dentistry took place in the 1920s, that the gains in agriculture and veterinary medicine occurred during the 1930s, and that the advance in commerce, engineering, forestry, and household science was steady over the two decades. The professional fields most adversely affected by the Depression were architecture and pharmacy. However, what is significant about these figures is that the steady advance made during the 1920s in arts and science, education, and graduate work was arrested by the Depression, the 1940-41 figures in these areas being only fractionally higher than those of 1930-31. The Depression also checked the expected development of such new fields as library science, physical and health education, and social work. Commenting years later on the effect of the Depression on McGill, D.L. Thomson noted:

> The effect upon the University was indirect rather than direct, salaries were cut, but then prices fell; and on the whole the teaching staff suffered less and had more security than those in other professions; enrolment kept up, because there were no jobs to tempt young people not to come to college. On the other hand, it was next to impossible, both economically and psychologically, to take bold forward steps in such troubled days. There were developments here and there, of course; but on the whole it would not be unfair to say that, for one reason or another, McGill marked time during the thirties.[1]

It is perhaps not surprising that only two institutions obtained degree granting charters during this period, Mount Saint Vincent at Halifax in 1925, and St Thomas in Chatham, New Brunswick, in 1934. Another college, Sir George Williams in Montreal, was established in 1929, but it did not have degree-granting privileges at its inception. Created on the base of the educational program initiated by the Y.M.C.A. in the 1870s, it was offering by 1935 full programs in arts, science, and commerce, and in 1936 began to award degrees.[2]

This, then, was the general outlook in Canadian higher education from 1920 to 1940; what specific institutional developments occurred in the various regions?

THE MARITIMES

The report of the Carnegie-sponsored investigation of the Maritime institutions which W.S. Learned and K.C.M. Sills carried out in

the fall of 1921 prompted the conclusion that 'advantages ...
comparable with those of McGill ... and Toronto, or of the best
New England institutions' were not available to Maritimers, and
would not be until the resources of the several institutions were
consolidated. A specific scheme was proposed whereby a single
Maritime university would be established on the Dalhousie campus
at Halifax, of which King's, Acadia, Mount Allison, New Brunswick,
St Francis Xavier, and Dalhousie would become constituent colleges.
This would entail the removal of five of the six institutions to
Halifax, at a cost of approximately $4.5 million, but the Carnegie
Corporation was prepared to contribute $3 million to effect the
plan. The report argued that provincial governments were more
likely to contribute to the upkeep of an institution which had no
denominational associations and that it would be appropriate for
the federal government to offer either an annual subsidy or an
endowment grant in support of this venture.[3]

The initial reaction to the proposal was on the whole favourable, but by the end of 1923 St Francis Xavier and Acadia had
decided not to participate, and Mount Allison had announced that
it would have to defer a decision for several years pending the
settlement of the Church Union question.[4] This left only Dalhousie and King's, the end result being a federation of these
institutions, made possible by a Carnegie grant of about $1 mil-
lion. King's, which had lost its main building by fire in 1920,
moved to the Dalhousie campus where, henceforth, it cooperated
in offering arts and science courses in addition to carrying on
its own theological program.

With the aid of two grants ($375,000 from Rockefeller and $200,000
from the Carnegie Foundation), Acadia constructed a new building
to house classrooms, offices, and an auditorium. Its student body,
by 1940, was 417, as opposed to 330 in 1920, and instruction was
offered in arts and science, education, pre-engineering, household science, music, secretarial science, theology, and graduate
studies. The household science and music programs represented
expansion of the offerings at the Acadia Ladies College which had
been absorbed in 1926; art courses at the college were similarly
developed to degree level in a department of fine art in the
faculty of arts and science. The work in education, which consisted of a qualifying year for graduates leading to the Nova
Scotia Superior First Class Licence, was introduced in 1935,[5]
while secretarial science was first offered in 1936.

The position of the three other universities which had declined
to federate with Dalhousie was much the same as that of Acadia.
Mount Allison enrolled 344 students in 1940 in contrast to 262 in
1921 and these were distributed among arts and science, pre-
engineering, household science, secretarial science, music, and
graduate studies. Education was offered, but there were no students registered in the 1940-41 session. The theological program
had been transferred to Pine Hill Divinity Hall in 1925, there
had been a reorganization of the music and fine art programs, and
education and secretarial science had been introduced in 1934

354

and 1935 respectively. St Francis Xavier began to provide for both household science and music in the late 1920s, but the music program was withdrawn in 1936: the main effort here was in the field of adult education, a department of university extension having been set up in 1929. New Brunswick in 1940 had a total enrolment of 364, compared to 177 in 1921, divided among arts and science, pre-engineering, household science, and graduate work. A faculty of law had been added in 1924 by taking over a proprietary school formerly associated with King's College, Windsor.[6] In 1923 the provincial government had provided funds for a physics and chemistry building and had increased the annual grant to $50,000: both moves were indirect results of the Carnegie proposal, reflecting as they did the government's renewed belief that the development of higher education should take place within the boundaries of the province.

The chief beneficiary of the Carnegie plan was, of course, Dalhousie which, in addition to gaining the very adequate building provided for King's on its campus as well as a handful of arts and science students, received over $800,000 in grants from the corporation between 1923 and 1940. The figure would be doubled if one included the grants to King's: $600,000 for the endowment of eight chairs in arts and science and $197,000 for expenses related to the Halifax move. In addition, in 1920 Dalhousie had received a $500,000 grant from the Carnegie Corporation for its medical school. It was also given substantial amounts from the Rockefeller Foundation over this 20-year period which went towards support of the medical school, epidemiology, an Institute of Public Affairs (1936), and a study of morbidity in Nova Scotia (1937-38). A sum of $439,000 was raised in the 1920 centennial campaign and $300,000 was donated for a women's residence in that same year. Donations totalling over $1 million were provided by private citizens and corporations between 1920 and 1940, but there were no direct provincial operating grants.[7]

As a result of these benefactions, Dalhousie was able to improve its physical facilities and to strengthen and expand academic and research programs. Three buildings were completed in 1923, a medical science laboratory, a women's residence, and the law school, but lack of additional space made it necessary for the latter to be occupied by arts and science for the next quarter century. An extension to the women's residence was opened in 1927, an auditorium and a gymnasium in 1932, and a medical and dental library in 1939. The Nova Scotia archives were housed on the campus in 1929, thanks to the provincial government. A program for postgraduate work in fisheries was established in cooperation with the Fisheries Research Board of Canada in 1928, and, paralleling the other provincial institutions of higher education, arrangements were made with the department of education for a teacher training course in the early 1930s. The academic focus, however, was on strengthening the existing programs, particularly those related to arts and science and medicine. The full-time staff in arts and science increased from 20 to 40 between 1920 and 1940. In terms of enrolment, however, the situation was very similar to that of 1920. There were now 749 full-time students, whereas in 1920 there had been 679.

Despite having attained degree-granting status in 1925, Mount Saint Vincent College continued to cooperate with Dalhousie throughout this period, its affiliation remaining in effect until 1941. In 1940-41, there were 154 students registered in arts and science, education, household science, music, and secretarial science. A degree program in library science was introduced in 1938, but attracted no students in 1940-41. At this time the college was the second largest of the five degree-granting institutions in Halifax, King's being the smallest with 8 students in theology and 46 taking an arts and science degree at Dalhousie.

St Mary's, like Mount Saint Vincent, continued to offer secondary school work. In 1940-41 there were 138 students registered in arts and science, commerce, and engineering. Since 1913, the college had been under the control of the Christian Brothers of Ireland and, despite Rome's formal disapproval, it had been enthusiastic about the Carnegie proposal and remained so. Hence, between 1924 and 1927, and again in 1933, serious attempts were made to work out an affiliation arrangement with Dalhousie.[8] These came to nought for a variety of complex reasons which culminated in the withdrawal of the Christian Brothers in 1940, and the re-opening of the college in the fall of 1940 under the auspices of the Jesuits.

What is now Memorial University of Newfoundland was established in 1925 as Memorial University College in a $400,000 building provided by the colonial government. (Newfoundland did not join Confederation until 1949 and thus was still a colony of Great Britain.) The Normal School which had opened the previous year moved to the same premises. The Carnegie Corporation had agreed in 1924 to provide $15,000 for each of five years to support the development of a junior college on the strength of the government's guarantee to provide $5000 annually. Subsequent grants from the Carnegie Corporation brought its contribution by 1940 to over $400,000. From the start the college offered the first two years of arts and science (there was one student in the second year in 1925-26), and in 1940 over half of the students enrolled were in this program. The remainder were normal school students taking a one year teacher training course.

In 1940, there were five other degree-granting institutions in the Maritimes offering what was in effect a classical college course to small student bodies: St Joseph's, 98; Collège Ste Anne, 81; Sacré Coeur, 65; St Dunstan's, 55; and St Thomas, 77. The latter had offered only the first two years of arts and science until 1934, when it added the third and fourth years; in 1936 it began to grant its own degrees. Students at St Dunstan's received their degrees from Université Laval until 1941 when the college began to exercise the powers it had been granted in 1917.

356

Like Dalhousie, McGill began the 1920s with a successful fund
raising campaign to mark its centenary, and throughout the period,
especially in the 1920s, received generous support from the
Carnegie and Rockefeller foundations and private donors. The
centennial endowment fund produced over $5 million, and, in com-
menting on the death of Principal Arthur Currie in 1933, the
chancellor noted that McGill's income from all sources had increased during Currie's 13-year principalship from $1 million to
$2 million. Much of the money went into buildings and equipment:
a biology building in 1922; a dental clinic and library extension
in 1923; a pathological institute in 1924; renovations to the
arts building in 1926; a pulp and paper institute in 1929; a new
Royal Victoria College building in 1932; a neurological institute
in 1934. Thus, the general excellence of McGill's physical plant
was maintained. There were also a number of first-rate academic
staff appointments[9] and a noteworthy increase in the quantity and
quality of holdings in the various libraries. In 1940, McGill's
excellence was by no means to be measured solely in terms of
physical plant. However, Thomson's observation that, because of
the Depression, the university marked time during the 1930s is
accurate. Indeed, it could be said to have fallen back a step
or two since programs in social work and pharmacy were discontinued in 1932, and, in 1933 the graduate program in Chinese studies introduced in 1930 was withdrawn. After 1936 full-time enrolment figures included students in library science and physical
and health education. Nonetheless, over the two decades in question, student numbers in general decreased slightly, from 2947
to 2771, largely because of much reduced admissions to medicine,
law, engineering, dentistry, and music. On the other hand, arts
and science registration had doubled and the number of graduate
students had quadrupled.

Bishop's University doubled its registration between 1920 and
1940, rising to a total of 107 in arts and science, education,
and theology. The numbers of full-time students at Sir George
Williams was also modest at this time, 154 in arts and science
and 38 in commerce, but over 500 were registered in degree courses
in its evening college. Under the sponsorship of the Y.M.C.A.,
the college had since the 1870s offered secondary school subjects,
and in 1925 it began to admit women to the student body. In 1929
senior matriculation was offered, and this, in the protestant
English-speaking sector of Quebec, was equivalent to first year
arts and science. In 1931 the program was extended a further
year, and diploma courses in arts, science, and commerce were
offered. In 1932, the day division was inaugurated with 76 students. By 1934, seven students had fulfilled the requirements
for the two year diploma, and the decision was made to move to a
full degree program. This posed a problem; did the college which
had not secured a charter from the provincial government have
the authority to grant degrees? Consultation with a legal firm

rendered the 'unequivocal' and firm judgment that 'the act of
incorporation of the Y.M.C.A. of Montreal gave all the authority
required by the laws of the province to give instruction of college grade and to confer degrees and grant diplomas.'[10] Hence,
the degree programs were initiated and in December 1936 the first
two degrees were granted. It was to be another decade before the
National Conference of Canadian Universities saw fit to accept
the legal decision and to allow Sir George Williams to become a
bona fide member of the family of Canadian institutions of higher
learning.

Two pages of the 1940-41 *Annuaire* of Université Laval are devoted to the benefactors of the institution, the persons or organizations that had provided financial support since its establishment in 1852. They are grouped under eight headings, the
first quite properly being the Séminaire de Québec. No figure
is given, but it is pointed out that for a very long time the
séminaire had been almost alone in sustaining the university:
'Il a dépensé des sommes considérables pour la construire,
l'aménager et payer ses déficits annuels.' The next two items
refer to the public campaignslaunched in 1902 and 1920 which
raised, respectively, $116,000 and $2 million. The fourth heading
refers to Le Gouvernement de la Province de Québec. In 1910 the
government gave an annual grant for the Ecole d'arpentage et de
génie forestier. Initially $4000, the amount was raised to $5000
in 1911, to $10,000 in 1918, and to $15,000 in 1923. In 1920 it
contributed $1 million to the university's general campaign.
Another grant of $25,000 was made in 1913 and between 1931 and
1939 a total of $300,000 was provided for such developments as
l'Institut de biologie, l'Ecole des mines, and 'pour fins géné-
rales.' Other donations mentioned were: $50,000 from the Knights
of Columbus in 1920 to establish a chair in French literature;
$25,000 from Sir William Price in 1921 for scholarships for science
students; and $100,000 from G.-E. Amyot in 1925 to establish a
chair in science. The final item, Autres Bienfaiteurs, represents
a statement of faith concerning the future of Laval: 'C'est à
ces concours généreux que l'Université Laval doit son existence
et la place très grande qu'elle occupe aujourd'hui dans la vie
intellectuelle du Canada. Ses développements se mesurent néces-
sairement aux ressources dont elle dispose. Elle a fait de grands
progrès depuis 1920; elle se propose d'en faire du plus grands
encore, si on veut bien continuer à lui venir en aide.'
   In 1920 the institution retained the European organization it
had adopted when it was founded in 1852: faculties of law, medicine, theology, and arts, the latter embracing everything that did
not clearly fall under the others. Consequently, the faculté des
arts included within its orbit l'Ecole d'agriculture at Ste-Anne-
de-la-Pocatière, l'Ecole d'arpentage et de génie forestier, and
two newly established schools, Ecole normale supérieure, and Ecole
de chimie. It was also responsible in 1920 for the licence and
doctorat in philosophy, even though most of the instruction was

provided in the faculté de théologie. This pattern continued for
the next 10 years with all new schools being established within
the faculté des arts: Ecole de musique, 1922; Ecole de pharmacie,
1924; Ecole supérieure de philosophie, 1926. However, in 1932,
the latter became the faculté de philosophie and in the following
year a faculté de droit canonique was instituted which, in conjunction with the faculté de philosophie and a reorganized faculté
de théologie, provided the full range of ecclesiastical faculties
called for by the papal decree of 1931, *Deus Scientiarum Dominus*.

In 1937, facultés des lettres and des sciences were set up to
absorb the work previously carried on in Ecole normale supérieure
and Ecole de chimie. At this point, the Ecole d'arpentage was
transferred from arts to sciences, but Ecole d'agriculture remained
under arts until 1940 when it became an independent faculty. By
1940, the faculté des sciences had established three other schools,
Ecole des mines et de géologie, 1937, Ecole de pêcheries, 1938,
and Ecole des gradués, 1938: the latter, within two years, became
an independent unit responsible for graduate studies throughout
the university. What in 1944 would become the faculté des sciences
sociales was also initiated during this period, initially as an
école des sciences sociales, politiques et economiques offering
evening courses to part-time students, but from 1938 as an école
des sciences sociales within the faculté de philosophie offering
degree programs in four areas: sociology, economics, industrial
relations, and social work. In a technical sense these developments greatly reduced the burden on the faculté des arts, but
in actual practice this was not so. By 1940, the 10 classical
colleges affiliated with Laval (including St Dunstan's in
Charlottetown, P.E.I. and a Jesuit college in Edmonton, Alberta)
had been joined by 14 others including 7 women's colleges. The
faculty also supervised the instruction in 6 women's colleges,
which confined their work to the first four years of the classical course, and in the affiliated Ecole de pharmacie and Ecole
de musique. After 1931, there was a third affiliate, the Ecole
supérieure de commerce which, in 1940, was offering both the
licence and the baccalaureat. The faculté des arts was also responsible for the B. en sciences hospitalières which was awarded
after a three-year course taken at one of 13 affiliated hospital
schools.

Although by 1940 Laval had more faculties than Université de
Montréal, the latter had not been standing still since it had
gained its independence from Laval in 1919. In 1920 it had established six faculties: theology, law, medicine, lettres, sciences, philosophy. By 1940 it had added two others: chirurgie
dentaire, which obtained faculty status in 1921, and arts, established in 1927 with responsibility for the classical college
course and for programs for teachers. The conseil of the faculté
des arts consisted of the superiors of the affiliated classical
colleges but it was 'assisted' by the University's comité permanent
sur l'enseignement secondaire; there were 11 affiliated colleges
in 1927 and 10 more by 1940, including 4 colleges for women and

2 outside the province, Campion College in Regina, and Collège Saint-Christophe located on St Pierre and Miquelon, two islands in the Gulf of St Lawrence which still were part of France. An application from the Ecole de pharmacie for elevation to faculty status was not approved in 1924 on the grounds that admission requirements were below standard. The faculté de philosophie became operative in 1923-24 and both it and the faculté de théologie were reorganized in the 1930s in accord with the papal encyclical *Deus Scientiarum Dominus* of 1931. Women were admitted to the faculty of medicine in 1924, and a year later an Ecole d'hygiéne sociale appliquée (public health nursing) was established under its supervision; initially financed by the Metropolitan Life Insurance Company, the school became a department of the faculté de médecine in 1938. Despite their name, the facultés des lettres and des sciences functioned throughout the 1920s and 1930s principally as écoles normales supérieures providing courses for secondary school teachers: however, the faculté des sciences did establish a M.Sc. program in 1933 and was responsible from 1920 on for a pre-medical year (prescribed also for dentistry and optometry students) which led to a certificate d'études physiques, chimiques et naturelles (PCN).

The Ecole des hautes études commerciales, one of the major affiliates of Montréal, revised its basic program in 1923 and established a program leading to the licence en sciences commerciales (or comptables) in 1925. The Ecole polytechnique introduced courses leading to the licence and the doctorat en science appliquée in 1927. In 1928, the Ecole de médecine vétérinaire was transferred from Montreal to Oka where it henceforth operated in close relationship with the Institut agricole. The Ecole des sciences sociales et politiques, which was established in 1920, developed two year degree programs in economics and sociology and a one year diploma course in journalism. In 1925, the Ecole d'optométrie (founded in 1910) became an affiliate after agreeing to require the P.C.N. course as a condition for admission to its two year course leading to the baccalauréat en optométrie et optique. In 1937, an école des bibliothécaires was set up as an école annexée offering a sequence of 192 lectures over a nine month period in a program leading to a diplôme de bibliographie et de bibliothéconomie.

In 1919 the government of Quebec had given a grant of $1 million to Montréal[11] and this had helped to launch the latter as an independent institution. However, a major requirement of the new university was an adequate campus. It had inherited from Laval a collection of buildings, some of which were very inconveniently located. A series of disastrous fires in 1919 and 1922 further complicated Montréal's 'housing' problem, but in 1922 the City of Montreal came to the rescue. As an additional contribution to the launching of the university, it donated sixty acres of land in the heart of the city. An architect was appointed in 1924, a foundation stone laid in 1928, and construction of a single but commodious building begun in March 1930. But in December 1931, with 75% of the work completed, construction was suspended in the face of the realities of the Depression. It remained suspended until 1941.

Plans to complete the building were, however, reactivated in 1937, at which time the provincial government was prevailed upon to provide, first a capital grant of $3 million to be used to complete and furnish the building and to liquidate outstanding debts, and second an annual operating grant of $600,000.[12] This step was accompanied by the passing of an act in 1938 which placed responsibility for the affairs of the university for the next 10 years in the hands of the Société d'administration de l'Université de Montréal whose seven members were charged with the task of completing the building and expanding the academic program. The act also required the government to provide up to $500,000 for capital costs in addition to an annual operating grant of at least $400,000 Thus the construction was resumed in 1941 and the building was officially opened in 1942. It accommodated all faculties except theology, but most of the affiliated schools, notably Ecole polytechnique and Ecole des hautes études commerciales, remained at their existing premises, as did the schools of agriculture and veterinary medicine.

By 1940, in terms of complexity of organization and range of offerings, both Laval and Montréal were comparable to McGill and Toronto; and if one takes into account their involvement with teacher training, including the écoles ménagères, the structure of the French-language institutions was more complicated and their range broader. However, it has to be noted that much of the organizational development at Laval took place in the late 1930s, and that at Montréal in particular the physical plant was not comparable to that of McGill or Toronto. Furthermore, their operating budgets were significantly smaller.

ONTARIO

In October 1920 the Ontario government appointed a Royal Commission on University Finances 'to enquire into and report upon a basis for determining the financial obligations of the Province towards the University of Toronto and the financial aid which the Province may give to Queen's University in Kingston and the Western University of London,' and to recommend a 'permanent plan of public aid to said universities as shall bear a just and reasonable relation to the amount of the legislative grants to primary and secondary education.'[13] Four months later the commissioners submitted a report recommending that all three universities be provided immediately with substantial grants for capital purposes - $340,000 for Queen's, $800,000 for Western, $1,500,000 for Toronto[14] - and that all three should henceforth receive annual grants for operating purposes, the amounts to be reviewed at five-year intervals. For the first quinquennium they proposed a grant to Queen's of $275,000 for each of the first two years

and $300,000 for the next three and to Western of $200,000 for
the first two and $250,000 for the following three. Such grants,
it was agreed, would enable these two universities to provide
services needed in the eastern and southwestern sections of the
province beyond what the provincial university at Toronto could
be expected to provide. However, the first concern of the commissioners was with the University of Toronto: 'it is a primary
obligation upon the Province to make the Provincial University
worthy of the intelligence, wealth and resources of the Province
... nothing but a University of the first rank should be the crown
of our educational effort.'[15] In particular they were convinced
that there must be at Toronto 'a strong centre of well-organized
post-graduate work.' They recommended that the basis for the
annual grant to Toronto should be 50% of the succession duties
averaged over three years as recommended by the Royal Commission
of 1905-6. The government had adopted this formula in 1906 but
had replaced it in 1914 by a fixed $500,000 annual grant. The
commissioners pointed out that had the formula been maintained
the university would have received between 1914 and 1920 an additional $1.3 million and that if this had happened it would not
now be necessary for them to recommend a special grant of $1.5
million for buildings.

   The Ontario government did not accept this recommendation. It
decided instead to continue to provide an operating grant for the
University of Toronto on an annual basis. Over the ensuing 20
years the amount of the annual grant averaged $1,500,000, approxi-
mately one-third the amount that would have been allocated had the
succession duty formula been followed; this explains in part the
failure of the University of Toronto to develop 'a strong centre
of well-organized post-graduate work' by 1940.[16] However, the
government did act on most of the commissioners' other recommendations. On the capital side, Western Ontario was granted the
$800,000 proposed - and an additional $200,000 - which enabled
it to establish itself on its present campus, Queen's was immediately granted $155,000 and received an additional $545,000
between 1923 and 1932, while Toronto was granted $6 million
between 1922 and 1940. The annual operating grant to Western
was initially $205,000, rose to $300,000 in 1930, was $260,000
in 1940, and totalled over $5,000,000 for the twenty years. At
Queen's it began at $210,000, rose to $400,000 in 1930, was
$250,000 in 1940, and totalled $5,500,000. These were impressive
amounts when compared with the support provided by the government
of Quebec to the universities of that province.

   Full-time enrolment at Toronto in 1940 was not significantly
larger than in 1920, about 5000 in contrast with 4000, disregarding
the numbers attending off-campus affiliates such as the Ontario
Agricultural College and the Ontario College of Pharmacy. One
major affiliate, the Royal College of Dental Surgeons, had become
an integrated faculty of dentistry in 1925, and its 225 students
(representing almost one quarter of the increase) were now included in the Toronto figures as were students in two new programs,

362

library sciences and physical and occupational therapy. There had been a sharp decline in enrolment in medicine, from 1127 to 747 but most faculties, including arts, showed a modest increase. Since the university had raised its entrance requirements significantly, the fact that there was a general increase rather than decline in numbers is worthy of note.

During the 1920s, most of the professional faculties at Toronto systematically increased their entrance requirements with the result that by 1930 senior matriculation rather than junior matriculation was the normal basis for admission to the first year. Commencing with the 1931-32 session, senior matriculation was also required for admission to the first year of the faculty of arts. Prior to this, at Toronto as at most universities in English-speaking Canada, one could enter the first year with junior matriculation or the second year with senior matriculation. The decision to require senior matriculation did not lengthen the time taken to acquire the B.A. since the four year general course was simultaneously reduced to three and for some years senior matriculation had been required for admission to the four year honour courses, but it did mean that henceforth almost all students attending the University of Toronto spent five years in secondary schools rather than four. By the early 1950s, the other Ontario universities had adopted the same requirements, and almost all Ontario high schools offered a five year course.

At Queen's, there were no major developments between 1920 and 1940, and again no sharp increase in admissions. Total enrolment rose from 1500 to 1700, with the great majority of students continuing to register in its faculties of arts and science, applied science, and medicine, and in its school of commerce and administration. A handful of students were enrolled in graduate studies and in theology.

At Western Ontario, there had been two important developments: the move of arts and science to the new campus in 1924, and the building up in the 1920s and 1930s of a strong department of business administration on the model of the Harvard Business School but at the undergraduate level. Enrolment increased substantially from 331 to 1323, but almost half of the 1045 arts and science students were at one of the three affiliated institutions: Assumption College at Windsor, 309; Waterloo College at Waterloo, 81; and Brescia College, which had moved from Chatham to the London campus, 65.

During the early 1920s McMaster University pondered what it should do: remain at its absurdly small campus on the edge of that of Toronto; enter into federation with Toronto; or move either to another location in the city or to another urban centre. In 1928 it was decided to move to Hamilton, the actual re-locating to take place two years hence, and $2 million was raised by public subscription to effect the plan. A donation of $500,000 offered by the City of Hamilton was refused on the grounds that it would compromise the Baptist principle of the separation of church and state in education. By 1940, McMaster was well established on its new site where it continued to concentrate on programs in arts and science (474 students) and theology (30).

At the University of Ottawa, though the numbers remained comparatively small (342 in arts, 23 in commerce, 53 in nursing, 14 in library science, 100 in graduate studies), there was some restructuring and expansion during the 1930s, with the result that the institution was in a position to develop into a major university in the late 1940s. Most of the graduate students were in the faculties of theology, canon law, and philosophy which, like those at Laval and Montreal had been reorganized following the publication of the papal encyclical *Deus Scientiarum Dominus* in 1931. In 1929, a reorganization of the faculty of arts was begun; in 1932, St Patrick's College became a constituent college within the faculty; and by 1940 the three affiliated classical colleges of 1920 had become 16, including 7 in Saskatchewan and 2 in Alberta. During the 1930s, the faculty also established schools of music and elocution (1931), political science (1936), and library science (1938), and in 1940 it organized a degree course in nursing in conjunction with Ecole d'Youville, an affiliate since 1931.

During the fall and winter of 1938–39, a committee of the Ottawa Y.M.C.A. held a number of meetings to discuss ways and means of expanding facilities for higher education in the City of Ottawa. The plans were set aside with the outbreak of World War II, but were reactivated in 1941. The outcome was the establishment of Carleton College in the fall of 1942.

THE WEST

One of the facts of life about the history of higher education in Canada is that relatively little attention has been paid to the period 1920 to 1940. Part of the explanation is that most Canadian universities are very old or very new, having been founded either in the nineteenth century or since 1945. For most of the older foundations there are centennial histories, written between 1920 and 1955, and these provide a relatively detailed account of the institutions during their formative years and up to World War I, but they tend to be less detailed in dealing with what was at the time of writing the recent past, no doubt to some extent because it was so recent. In contrast, the histories of the four western provinces, three of which were founded in the early twentieth century, do give detailed attention to the 1920s and 1930s which, at these institutions, *were* the formative years; consequently it is to Morton's history of Manitoba, Logan's history of British Columbia, and Thompson's history of Saskatchewan that one can most profitably turn for insight into life at a Canadian university during these two decades.[17] Each deals, for example, with the effects of the Depression on professors' salaries and student fees, and, since the consequences of the Depression were very much the same in all Canadian universities, a reading of

the appropriate chapters of Morton, Logan, or Thompson is an indication of what was occurring at Dalhousie, McGill, Toronto, and
all the others.

Thompson begins his chapter on the Depression by noting that
the Province of Saskatchewan was more severely affected by the
depressed economy than any other part of Canada. At a time when
the financial well-being of the province was almost completely
dependent on grain production, there was one crop failure after
another, and the government directed many of its urgent economies
towards the university.[18] Thompson goes on to note, first the
steady and substantial decreases in annual government operating
grants, from $676,727 down to $398,000 in the years 1930-34;
second the gradual but proportionately lower increases ranging
from $400,154 to $501,232 over the period 1934-39; and third the
fact that the government provided no capital grants at all during
the 1930s. The effect of this reduction of support on an institution which had virtually no endowment or any source of revenue
other than student fees was drastic. Nevertheless, the university
not only survived but made more advances during the decade than
the other western universities, with the exception of Alberta.
The explanation of its relative success in dealing with the emer-
gencies occasioned by the Depression lies in the sound organization that had been developed by 1920 and in the excellence of the
leadership provided by its first president, W.C. Murray, who
remained in office until 1938. It is clear from Thompson's account that Murray, more than anyone, was responsible for the institution emerging 'in better condition that might have been expected under the circumstances.'[19]

During the 1920s Saskatchewan established three new schools
within the college of arts and science: medical sciences, offering the pre-clinical years of a medical course (1926); education, providing a one year secondary school certificate program
(1927); and household science (1928) which, as an extension of
the department formed in 1917, offered the B.H.Sc. degree. Programs in arts and science were also expanded in a geographical
sense by authorizing in 1924 the affiliation of denominationally
or publicly controlled institutions offering first year work; by
1929 there were eight of these junior colleges. Four of these
were at Regina: the United Church's Regina College, two Roman
Catholic Colleges - Campion for men and the Sacred Heart Academy
for women - and a Lutheran college. There was also a Roman
Catholic college, St Peter's, at Muenster, Lutheran colleges at
Outlook, and at Moose Jaw, and one public institution, Moose Jaw
Central High School. During the 1930s these institutions enabled
many students who could not finance a year at the university in
Saskatoon to obtain first year standing. However, the colleges
had their financial problems, and by 1940-41 only Campion, Regina,
St Peter's, and Lutheran College at Regina continued to offer uni-
versity level work.

By 1940, Regina College was a branch of the university. Financial problems had threatened its closure in 1934, but a $50,000

grant from the Carnegie Corporation enabled the university to take the college under its wing. At the same time, Regina College was providing, in addition to a high school course which culminated in senior matriculation, a number of diploma courses in art, agriculture, household science, and music, the latter being organized within a conservatory of music. A school of fine art was established in 1936, but neither it nor the conservatory offered degree programs in 1940.

The modest advances of the 1930s included the establishment of three additional programs (College of Music 1931, School of Physical and Health Education 1931, and School of Nursing 1938), and brought to 14 the total number of programs offered by the university. Full-time enrolment of 2034 was the highest in its history. (There had been 657 in 1920-21 and 1403 in 1930-31). Forty-three of the arts and science students were registered at St Thomas More College, established on the Saskatoon campus in 1936 by the Basilian fathers, but the institution did not enjoy any financial support from the university.[20]

The University of Alberta, like that of Saskatchewan, was most fortunate in its leaders during the early years of its development. The first president, H.M. Tory, resigned in 1928 to become president of the National Research Council, but he had given strong direction during his tenure, and he had a highly competent successor in R.C. Wallace who had been on the staff of the University of Manitoba since 1910.

The enrolment in 1940-41 was 1851, slightly less than Saskatchewan's, but in 1937 Alberta followed Toronto in insisting upon senior matriculation for entry to first year. Prior to this, students could enter second year from Grade XII (senior matriculation). The most important development of the 1920s was the extension of the medical program to a full degree course, a process completed by 1924. The only new program was a secondary school teaching course similar to that of Saskatchewan; first offered in a school of education within the faculty of arts and science in 1928, it became the responsibility of a faculty of education in 1939. However, three of the departments in arts and science which were responsible for programs introduced at the end of World War I had by 1940 expanded into schools; nursing 1924, household science 1928, commerce 1928. In 1931 Mount Royal College, a United church secondary school in Calgary, having extended its work to the first year level, became an affiliate of the University of Alberta. Another new affiliate was the Roman Catholic St Joseph's College which had received a $100,000 Carnegie grant to assist it in putting up a building on the university campus. Its students were registered in the faculty of arts and science but received credit for courses in history and philosophy taught by the staff of the college.[21] The most significant innovation at Alberta was the establishment of the Banff School of Fine Arts, which had also come into being thanks to a Carnegie grant.[22]

In contrast to Alberta and Saskatchewan, the University of British Columbia was plagued by disorganization and ineffective

366

leadership until at least 1934. The immediate problem in 1920 was that of accommodation, no action having been taken on the resumption of construction at its permanent campus since the suspension of activity in 1914. Largely because of the efforts of students and alumni in one of the most dramatic campaigns in the history of higher education in Canada,[23] the government was persuaded in 1922 to provide $1.5 million for construction of buildings at Point Grey, and by the end of 1925 the university was for the first time adequately housed. In the same year, a department of education within the faculty of arts and science was set up and in 1929 a two year diploma course in social work was introduced by the department of economics, sociology and political science. Efforts to establish programs in music, fine arts, oriental languages, law, and home economics were not successful. Nonetheless, by 1929, as Logan points out, the university seemed clear of its troubles. Located on the site at Point Grey, it could accommodate just over 1500 students, and in the light of positive encouragement from both the public and the government, there were firm hopes for continued progress. Already it had been decided to add two extensions to the science building, to put up an arts building, and to provide temporary accommodation for forestry and home economics on the campus. 'The government grant for ... 1929-30 of $625,000 was, in relation to the students served by it, the most generous ... made until the 1950's.'[24]

However, even before the Depression struck, the optimism had faded. A change of government in 1928 resulted in the appointment of an unsympathetic minister of education. Then a muddled presentation of the 1930-31 budget estimates further complicated relations between the university and the government. Although suspicions of mishandling of public funds, especially in connection with the faculty of agriculture, were not in 1929 substantiated by an official investigation, the government curtailed its financial support of the university.[25] In 1932, new budget irregularities led to a further investigation by the Supreme Court, and eventually a new university act was passed which clearly enunciated the powers and responsibility of the president, the senate, and the board; the latter, henceforth, would include three senate representatives. This had the effect of improving the internal and external outlook of the university; however, the shortage of funds continued to hamper progress. Grants slowly improved from the low of $250,000 in 1932-33, but the $425,000 of 1939-40 was still less than the amount allotted in 1931-32.

The enrolment picture improved quickly; between 1930 and 1934 it had fallen from just over 2000 to 1646, but by 1937-37 there were 2100 students and close to 2500 by 1940-41. By this date the accommodation on the Point Grey campus was anything but adequate. It is not surprising under all these adverse circumstances that no new programs were introduced at the University of British Columbia during the 1930s.

Manitoba suffered from lack of firm leadership as had British Columbia, and the questions of location and space were major concerns. Three alternate solutions were proposed: remain in downtown Winnipeg close to the affiliated colleges; take over the Tuxedo site recently vacated by the Manitoba Agricultural College which had been relocated at Fort Garry; acquire land adjacent to the latter and establish a new campus there. The choice depended to some extent on the answer to a second basic question, that of the long-term relationship of the University to the Agricultural College. This was resolved in 1924, when, in accord with the recommendations of a royal commission, the government decided to amalgamate the two institutions, the college becoming the university's faculty of agriculture and home economics. However, it was not until 1929 that the decision was made to move to Fort Garry, and then only on a partial basis. The faculties of law and medicine would remain in downtown Winnipeg, as would the first and second years of arts and science; only the third and fourth years of arts and science and the other professional faculties would be relocated. This arrangement, which went into effect in 1932 following the construction of an arts and science building, was a divisive one as far as the faculty of arts and science was concerned, since it separated the students into junior and senior divisions.

In company with every Canadian university, Manitoba suffered throughout the 1930s the usual effects of the Depression, a substantial decrease in government grants, but it also experienced an additional financial blow. In August 1932 it was discovered that it had lost almost all its endowment of close to $1 million through the criminal actions of the chairman of its board of governors perpetrated over a period of 30 years. John A. Machray was appointed board chairman in 1924, but he retained the position of honorary bursar of the university, which he had held since 1916, and he continued to be the head of the law firm which since 1906 had been responsible for the university's investments. In these interlocking positions and with the assistance of one of the law firm's accountants he had been able to falsify the accounts over this extraordinary period of time. A Royal Commission on the Impairment of University Funds which the government appointed in 1933 found Machray and his accountant primarily responsible for the disaster, but it was also critical both of the government for appointing him chairman of the board while he was also, in effect, its investment agent, and of the comptroller-general of the province for failure to carry out an annual financial audit.[26]

The only positive outcome of this sordid affair (hardly any of the money was recovered) was a new university act approved in April 1933 which assured that in future the financial affairs of the institution would be properly administered and strengthened the hand of the president by making him a member of the board. In 1934, J.D. McLean reached retirement age and was succeeded by Sidney Smith who remained for the next ten years. For the first time, Manitoba had the kind of leadership it required. Between 1935 and 1940 a faculty of education was established, the foundations for a college of music were laid, a B.Comm. degree was introduced, and a course in interior decoration was added to the offerings of the faculty of engineering and architecture. A systematic program of adult education was also embarked upon.

The four affiliated arts colleges of 1920 were reduced to three in 1940 by the merger of Wesley and Manitoba as United College, but two others had been added, St Paul's College in Winnipeg and Brandon College in Brandon. The latter had become an affiliate in 1939 and in 1940-41 enrolled 69 students in arts and science. In the previous year, the Baptist church had notified the Brandon Board of Trade of its inability to provide further support for the institution.[27] The board appointed a committee to study the problem. One of the members was a local businessman named A.P. Mackenzie who was prepared to offer support to the college if the government would agree to provide an annual grant. Negotiations were carried on over several months, and Mackenzie finally agreed to give $50,000, while the government provided $22,500 annually for 20 years. The city of Brandon, for its part, promised to assign one mill on the tax rate to the college. On becoming affiliated with Manitoba, Brandon terminated its former association with McMaster.

St Paul's College was organized in 1926 by the Roman Catholic archbishop of Winnipeg as a classical college, the staff initially being provided by the Oblate order.[28] The Oblates withdrew in 1931, the year the college entered into affiliation, and for the next two years the staff was drawn from the diocesan clergy. In 1933, the Jesuits assumed responsibility for it. As in the case of St Boniface, the course in scholastic philosophy offered by St Paul's was accepted for credit by the faculty of arts and science. By 1940, both St Boniface and St Paul's had developed women's divisions through association with St Joseph's Academy and St Mary's Academy, respectively.

THE FEDERAL GOVERNMENT

Aside from its increasing involvement in research, which will be discussed in chapter 24, the federal government's activities in higher education during the 1920s and 1930s were limited to a continuing direct responsibility for the Royal Military College. However, during this period, it also became involved in what now would be called post-secondary education through its grants in support of technical education to the various provinces. This will be discussed in the following section.

The Royal Military College remained open throughout World War I, but from the outset it was placed on a war-time footing, with the gentlemen cadets leaving to accept commissions in the British or Canadian armies shortly after becoming 18, the minimum age for obtaining a commission.[29] This normally permitted a 12 or 18 month stay at the college, and the course of study was adjusted accordingly. However, an emphasis on academic education as distinguished from military training was maintained, and the abbre-

viated R.M.C. program differed substantially from that provided
in the several officer's training camps that were established.
It is also notable that in 1916 action was taken on a proposal
first made in 1913 to appoint a director of studies who, rather
than the commandant, would be responsible for the curriculum;
commandants, it was noted, seldom remained in office for more
than four years; they tended to be interested primarily in the
military training aspects of the course of study; and frequently
they stressed matters associated with their own particular branch
of the service.[30] In 1917 changes were made in the entrance
examinations which brought them into line with those for junior
matriculation, the normal basis for admission to university.
Still another indication that the basic interest of the college
was in education rather than in training was the commencement in
1917 of discussions as to the advisability of extending the regular course from three to four years.

The decision to return to a four year course was made shortly
after the conclusion of World War I and came into effect in 1920.[31]
At the same time the government approved a proposal to expand the
capacity of the college to 300 cadets. However, during the next
20 years the enrolment remained fairly steady at about 200. One
explanation was that funds were not provided by the government
to increase the college's physical capacity to accommodate more
students; on the other hand, there was little evidence that there
was an urgent demand for more places. The course of study had
limited appeal on the academic side, and graduates who did not
wish to pursue a military career faced a problem in becoming
qualified as engineers. In 1922, the college's entrance examinations were withdrawn and junior matriculation became the basic
admission requirement, but the political necessity of accepting
some students from all provinces made it difficult to provide a
first year course that was intellectually as stimulating as it
was designed to be. The necessity of giving due attention to
military matters made it difficult to strengthen the academic
program in mathematics and science in the light of the changes
that were being made in the engineering courses at the universities. As a result, by the mid 1930s McGill, Queen's, and Toronto
were no longer prepared to admit graduates to the fourth year of
their degree programs. However, in 1937 there was a major revision of the course of study, all students taking the same subjects
in the first three years but in the final year specializing in
one of five branches of engineering or taking more advanced work
in English, French, history, political economy, and international
affairs.[32] Henceforth 'specially recommended' graduates were admitted to the fourth year of particular university courses and
'recommended' graduates to the third.

JUNIOR COLLEGES AND INSTITUTES OF TECHNOLOGY

Although the first junior college in the United States was not
established until 1902, by 1920 there were over 200 and by 1940
over 600. By contrast, in 1940 no institution in Canada included
the name junior college in its title. However, nine institutions
were offering the first two years of a four year B.A. or B.Sc.
degree program and might therefore have been so described. These
were Memorial University College in Newfoundland, Prince of Wales
College in Charlottetown, Alma College in St Thomas, Ontario,
Mount Royal College in Calgary, Victoria College in Victoria,
B.C., and the four affiliates of the University of Saskatchewan
which were still offering senior matriculation and second year
work, Campion, Luther, St Peter's, and Regina. But none of these
colleges confined itself to the work of the first two years in
arts and science and all but two of them were affiliates of a
particular university. Memorial, Prince of Wales, and Victoria
were also normal schools; Regina was on its way to becoming what
the Americans by this time were calling a community college (an
institution offering vocational as well as liberal arts courses);
and the other five were primarily secondary schools. The total
number of students registered in arts and science in these nine
institutions was fewer than 500, about 2% of the Canadian total.
    Interest in the junior college movement during the 1920s and
1930s is reflected in the inclusion of the topic on the agenda
for the annual meeting of the National Conference of Canadian
Universities both in 1925 and in 1934, as well as in the arrangements for the affiliation of junior colleges by the universities
of Alberta and Saskatchewan. Nonetheless, the numbers involved,
whether of institutions or students, were remarkably small in
1940, certainly in contrast with those across the American border.
    The explanation of the failure of the junior college movement
to cross what was educationally as well as militarily an unde-
fended border lies partly in the number and location of Canadian
degree-granting institutions and partly in the way in which education was organized in the several provinces. In the Maritimes
there was no need for junior colleges so long as there were
degree-granting institutions at almost every centre of population.
In French-speaking Quebec, as well as in French-speaking communities in several other provinces, the collège classique in association with one of the universities provided a full degree program in literally dozens of small towns. In Ontario and Alberta
what was, in effect, the first university year was offered in the
form of senior matriculation in the majority of secondary schools,
and in all provinces it was possible in some secondary schools to
take senior matriculation and thus qualify locally for admission
to the second university year. If one regarded secondary schools
offering senior matriculation and classical colleges offering the
full eight year course as junior colleges, the Canadian total in
1940 as in the 1970s would be comparable to the American.

Relatively few of the over 600 junior colleges in the United
States in 1940 confined their instruction to the liberal arts;
most offered vocational courses and would be more accurately described as community colleges. There was also a substantial number of institutes of technology, which restricted their instruction to courses of a vocational nature, but at the diploma rather
than the degree level. Canadian institutions of this kind in
1940 were confined mainly to the fields of agriculture and home
economics. The best example was the Nova Scotia Agricultural
College at Truro, but there were also schools of agriculture in
Ontario and Alberta and many école ménagères in Quebec. The only
other examples by 1940 were the école forestier at Duchesnay,
Quebec, and the Provincial Institute of Technology and Art in
Calgary, established in 1923 and 1916 respectively.

But again the small number of institutions apparently involved
in the work is misleading. Considerable effort had been expended
during the 1920s and 1930s to develop technical and vocational
education in Canada both by the provinces and the federal government. The latter, it will be recalled, had appointed a Royal
Commission on Industrial Training and Technical Education in 1910
which recommended that $3 million be assigned annually to the
provinces for 10 years for the development of vocational education.[33] A change of government and the outbreak of World War I
prevented any action being taken by Parliament, but in 1919 an
Act for the Promotion of Technical Education was passed assigning
$10 million to be allocated over a ten-year period for this pur-
pose. The arrangement was that the federal funds would be distributed in proportion to provincial population but also on a
matching basis, the consequences of this latter requirement being
that some of the less wealthy provinces had difficulty in drawing
their full share by the end of the ten-year period. However, the
time limit was extended and by 1940 all these funds had been
used up.

In almost all cases the provinces extended the funds to institute or to develop vocational programs in the secondary schools
both within the day-time course of study provided for regular
full-time students, and in evening courses for adults. In terms
of the number of students registered for both day and evening
courses and the range of subjects offered, the program as it developed between 1920 and 1940 was clearly a successful one, but
it did have the effect of identifying vocational training with
secondary schooling rather than post-secondary education. In
Canada, the movement to establish institutions specifically designed for the needs of students beyond high school age effectively dates from 1945.

NOTES TO CHAPTER 20

1   D.L. Thomson, 'McGill between the Wars' in H. MacLennan, ed.,
    McGill: the Story of a University (1960), 101

2 The degrees were granted by Sir George Williams's Board of Management 'by virtue of the authority vested in it by the Metropolitan Board of the Montreal Y.M.C.A.' (H.F. Hall, *The Georgian Spirit: the Story of Sir George Williams* (1966), 50). See also 47-8

3 A concise but detailed report of the reaction of the institutions and the governments to the Carnegie proposal is to be found in *Canadian Annual Review* (1922), 337-41 and (1923), 400-1.

4 In 1925 the United church of Canada was formed by the merging of the Congregational, the Methodist, and parts of the Presbyterian churches of Canada. Presbyterians not entering the union continued to be members of the Presbyterian church of Canada.

5 Courses in education were offered in the faculty of arts by the department of psychology from 1926 on and graduates who had taken appropriate courses, including one based on practice teaching in the Horton Academy, were able to obtain licences to teach in the provincial schools. In 1934, formal arrangements were made with the Nova Scotia Department of Education for the Nova Scotia Teachers Licence to be awarded to graduates who had also taken the one year education course.

6 See above, chapter 14, 216.

7 Details of all donations to Dalhousie for the years 1921 to 1940 are listed in Dalhousie University *Calendar* (1940-41).

8 L.K. Shook, *Catholic Post-Secondary Education in English-Speaking Canada* (1971), 66-7

9 Thomson, 'McGill between the Wars,' 105-6

10 Hall, *Georgian Spirit*, 47-8

11 The government of Quebec had also given $1 million to the campaigns launched by Laval and McGill in 1920-21. It is instructive to compare the list of major donors to the McGill and Montréal campaigns: these are listed in *Canadian Annual Review* (1920), 656 (McGill) and 653-4 (Montréal). The McGill list includes 11 donations of $100,000 or more, the Montréal list only one. The Canadian Pacific Railway Company gave $250,000 to McGill, $50,000 to Montréal.

12 P. Ranger, 'Le Problème universitaire,' *Action universitaire*, 4 (Septembre 1939), 7-9. See also 'L'Aide du Gouvernement à l'Université de Montréal,' ibid., 5 (Avril 1939, 4-5; and O. Maurault, 'L'Université de Montréal,' *Cahiers des Dix*, 17 (1952), 30-2.

13 Royal Commission on University Finances, *Report* (1921), I, 3. See also R.S. Harris, 'The Evolution of a Provincial System of Higher Education in Ontario' in D.F. Dadson, ed., *On Higher Education: Five Lectures* (1966), 45-9.

14 The figure recommended for Toronto was $1.8 million but of this $300,000 was for the College of Education which was separately financed by the Department of Education. The commission also recommended an additional grant for an extension to the Royal Ontario Museum, in part to house the university's department of geology and mineralogy.

15 Royal Commission, *Report*, 9
16 Harris, 'Evolution of Provincial System,' 48
17 W.L. Morton, *One University: a History of the University of Manitoba, 1877-1952* (1957); H.T. Logan, *Tuum Est: a History of the University of British Columbia* (1958); W.P. Thompson, *The University of Saskatchewan: a Personal History* (1970)
18 Thompson, *Saskatchewan*, 122-3
19 Ibid., 122
20 For St Thomas More College, see Shook, *Catholic Post-Secondary Education*, 341-7.
21 For St Joseph's College, see Shook, *Catholic Post-Secondary Education*, 358-64.
22 For the origins and early development of the Banff School of Fine Arts, see D. Cameron, *Campus in the Clouds* (1956), 1-23.
23 Logan, *Tuum Est*, 90-4
24 Ibid., 109
25 Ibid., 110-11
26 The Machray case is dealt with in broad terms and with sensitivity by Morton, *One University*, 147-52. More details are provided in *Canadian Annual Review* (1933), 147-52. The fullest account is the *Report of the Royal Commission on the Impairment of University Funds*.
27 C.G. Stone and F.J. Garnett, *Brandon College: a History, 1899-1967* (1969), 151-8
28 Shook, *Catholic Post-Secondary Education*, 317-24
29 R.A. Preston, *Canada's R.M.C.: a History of the Royal Military College* (1969), 211-15
30 Ibid., 217-18
31 Ibid., 226-9
32 Ibid., 265-8
33 See above, chapter 16, 270-1.

21

Arts and Science

During the 1920s and 1930s the principal, indeed almost the exclusive, forum for the discussion of higher education in Canada was
the National Conference of Canadian Universities which met for two
or three day 'annual' meetings in eleven of these twenty years -[1]
1922, 1923, 1925, 1927 through 1930, 1932, 1934, 1937, and 1939.
On the average these conferences were attended by 45 persons, almost invariably the president, principal, or rector of the 31
member institutions,[2] frequently the registrar and the deans of
the faculties (other than theology) which were well established
by 1920 - arts and science, agriculture, engineering, law, medicine
- and, occasionally, by professors or administrators who were particularly knowledgeable about a subject (university athletics,
adult education, sabbatical leave, the place of music in the university) which had been scheduled for discussion. It must be
remembered that during this period there was no national organization of university professors (the Canadian Association of
University Teachers was not established until 1951), only a handful
of learned societies, and no journal which concentrated its attention on university problems. The only other organization that was
exclusively concerned with the problems of higher education was
the National Federation of Canadian University Students, established in 1927, but it focused on non-academic matters such as
financial aid and intercollegiate debates.
   With the outbreak of World War II, the NCCU, principally through
the work of its executive committee, very rapidly became the
agency representing the universities vis-à-vis the federal government with respect to matters bearing on the role of the universities in the nation's war effort, and it was transformed almost
overnight from a debating society into a combination of lobby
group and advisory body. Along with its new role, it continued
to debate the issues of higher education. From the time of its
second meeting in 1915 when it became formally organized, the
NCCU had periodically adopted formal resolutions directed to both

federal and provincial governments requesting action which would enable the universities to develop their research capacity and their ability to educate and train a wider range of manpower to a greater extent. These resolutions had been forwarded to the governments in question, but until 1940 they had elicited little response. In fact, up to and including the 1939 meeting, the conference was just what its name suggested – a forum for the discussion of problems which, in the minds of university executives, were of crucial concern to the member institutions.

An analysis of the subjects discussed at the conferences of the 1920s and 1930s reveals that the two issues of primary interest were the undergraduate course in arts and science, and the lack of uniformity in admission standards to undergraduate programs. In the 1920s especially, a good deal of attention was also directed to the need for advancing the cause of scholarship and research and of improving the quality of professional education, including graduate studies; but the main focus was on the faculty of arts and science and on the matriculation examinations. Furthermore, the general attitude was one of preserving the traditions of the past rather than of anticipating the needs of the future. With respect to the arts and science course, the concern was with the position of the traditional subjects – classics, English, history, modern languages, philosophy, the natural and physical sciences. There were no papers presented on economics, psychology, or sociology, although a subconference of economics and commerce teachers was held in conjunction with the annual meeting in 1929.

What the delegates did discuss at conference after conference was the threat of declining academic standards. The prevailing mood is reflected in the 1937 program at which five symposia were held. The topics discussed were: Is the Arts Faculty Losing Ground?; The Effect of Summer Schools on the Standards in Faculties of Arts; Safeguarding Matriculation Standards; The Necessity of Compulsory Latin for Arts Matriculation; and Honours Courses. Each of these was a familiar topic as an examination of earlier agenda will confirm. On several occasions during these years, the Conference directed its attention to the subjects of adult education and junior colleges. Here, too, however, the worry over declining academic standards was apparent.

A regular feature of almost every conference was a report from a committee on matriculation. The universities' concern about matriculation standards during these decades was in some measure the consequence of increased enrolment in the secondary schools following World War I, and of the development in the secondary schools of programs with a vocational emphasis. The latter were regarded by the secondary school authorities as particularly appropriate for students who did not intend to proceed to higher education. It was a fact that the percentage of those going on to university seldom reached 10%, even in large cities where an institution was easily accessible: . therefore, there was considerable justification for the change in high school curricula. However, it was more than a quarrel with the actual curricula in the pre-university sector that prompted the conference, despite any evidence of progress, to insist upon retaining a committee on matriculation. The main bone of contention was the poor preparation of the students entering universities, which was attributed to poor teaching in the elementary and secondary schools, and, by extension, to the failure of the universities to assume any responsibility for the adequate preparation of the teachers in these schools. This issue will be referred to in chapter 22. What follows here is an analysis of the courses of study in arts and sciences between 1920 and 1940.

THE GENERAL OR PASS B.A.

By 1940, senior matriculation offered in the secondary school constituted for many students the first year of a university course, and the B.A. General Course remained as it had been in 1920, i.e., a four-year program with the first 2 years largely prescribed - English, a language, Latin (or Greek) or mathematics, a science, and history or a social science. The students were required to concentrate or major in one or two related subjects in the final two years. At Roman Catholic institutions (Mount Saint Vincent, Ottawa, St Francis Xavier, St Mary's) religion continued to be prescribed in all four years, as did philosophy except at St Francis Xavier where it was required in only the first three. McMaster continued to prescribe history, English, and religion (Bible) for three years and either philosophy of science or religion in the fourth. Western Ontario demanded English and history in both the third and fourth years and at least one course in economics and in psychology as well. Several other universities required that a course in a particular subject or subjects be included in the final two years (the continuation of a language and a course in history at St Francis Xavier, one-term courses in public speaking, hygiene and public health, and religious knowledge at Mount Allison), but at most institutions, including all the larger ones, the upper year student was free to select his subjects without restriction other than the requirement to major in one or more subjects.

With prescription largely limited to the first two years, one of which for many students was taken in high school, there was a growing interest at many institutions in providing optional upper year courses which consciously attempted to interrelate the various disciplines - courses in classics in translation and masterpieces of European literature at Saskatchewan, for example, or an outline of physical science at McGill, a course designed for students not majoring in science. However, with the exception of Sir George Williams, no Canadian institution developed general education courses of the type which many American institutions introduced in the 1920s and 1930s following the success of Columbia College's Contemporary Civilization courses introduced in 1917.[3] From the time that Sir George Williams offered its first degree course (it graduated the first class in 1936) all students were required to include in their course work three pandemic subjects: one in humanities, one in social science, and one in natural science. These were full courses, the range and mood of which were both broad and liberal. The B.A. program at Sir George Williams also demanded four courses in English, three in the social sciences, and two in the sciences; and whether registered for a B.A., B.Comm., or B.Sc., students had to pass a rigorous course in English composition. The Sir George Williams experiment was a genuine attempt to produce a well-rounded graduate as opposed to the more highly specialized product of an honours course, and until they were withdrawn in 1960, the pandemic courses represented the most serious attempt undertaken by any English-speaking Canadian university in the twentieth century to offer a meaningful general degree.

THE B.Sc.

By 1940, faculties of science had been established at Laval and Montréal, but at all other institutions pure science continued to be under the wing of a faculty of arts and science, or in some instances a faculty of arts. Most faculties of arts, or of arts and science, granted the B.Sc. degree to students who specialized (honours course) or majored (general course) in mathematics or science, but some of the larger institutions, for example, British Columbia, Queen's, Saskatchewan, and Toronto, reserved the B.Sc. for degrees in applied fields such as engineering, forestry, and nursing, and awarded the B.A. to all graduates in arts and science. Whichever degree was granted, there were no significant differences in the programs of students who specialized or majored in mathematics or science. The non-science content of the four year program from junior matriculation leading to the general degree almost always included English and either French or German in the first two years and one course in the humanities or the social sciences in each of the final two years. The Roman Catholic institutions prescribed a course in religion in all four years, and Sir George Williams required science students, alongside arts and commerce students, to take the three pandemics in addition to demanding three courses in English, including the one in composition.

At Laval and Montréal, up until 1931, it was the practice to award a bachelier ès sciences (B.S.) to students who, while obtaining the required average (60%) at examinations conducted on the work of the final two years (Philosophie-Science) of the eight year course, obtained only 50% at the examinations held at the end of the sixth year (Belles Lettres-Rhétorique) and a bachelier ès lettres (B.L.) to those who had received 60% on Lettres but only 50% on the final examination. After 1931, all students graduating in the facultés des arts were awarded a B.A.

THE CLASSICAL COLLEGE COURSE

In 1920, the B.A., with minor exceptions, was the basic requirement for admission to all the faculties (arts excluded) at both
Laval and Montréal. Consequently, the majority of freshmen had
completed the classical college course before coming to university. The position remained virtually the same in 1940, but by
then there were more exceptions. For example, an alternative
to the B.A. for admission to the Ecole des sciences sociales,
politiques et economiques and to the faculté des sciences at
Montréal was the diplôme d'études secondaires scientifique ou
commerciales awarded by the department of public instruction to
students who had completed the cours primaire supérieur in one
of the French language public schools.4 This three year course
had been introduced in 1929; hitherto, French-speaking Roman
Catholic students were obliged to pay to attend the private classical colleges if they wished to pursue a path leading to university. It would be many more years before the French-speaking
Roman Catholic sector provided the kind of accessibility to higher
education available to the English-speaking non-Roman Catholics
in the province.

Addressing the NCCU in 1942 in a symposium on the Future of the
Faculty of Arts, Abbé Arthur Maheux referred to two reforms which
he considered to have improved the classical college course since
World War I; first, the quality of the teaching had risen since
the establishment of the école normale supérieure at Laval and
the introduction of comparable programs in the facultés des lettres
and des sciences at Montréal in 1920; and second, more scientific
subjects had been made available to students.5 The last hurdle
had been the more difficult one, he said, because of 'the reluctance of the authorities, the majority of whom were strongly attached to the old system.' However, 'the gallant defenders of
the sciences were to win the war.' Certainly the statement applied to the public schools where by 1940 more attention was being
paid to mathematics, chemistry, and biology. However, a comparison of the course of study in 1920 and in 1940 for each of the
final four years of the classical course hardly suggests that the
war had been won.6 Science received more emphasis at the university examinations; and there had been marked improvement in the
facilities for the teaching of science. But the total number of
hours of instruction devoted to particular science subjects and
to mathematics was essentially unchanged from 1920. Furthermore,
Latin now occupied four hours weekly in the final two years, a
significant increase; there were additional classes in English,
French, history and philosophy; and physical education had been
added to the timetable in all four years. On the other hand,
there had been a marked improvement in the facilities for teaching
the sciences.

In 1922, a legislative act had made provision for an annual
grant of $10,000 to each approved classical college to be devoted

'to the equipment or creation of cabinets and laboratories of science, to the purchase of books, and in general to the perfecting of secondary instruction.'[7] There was also a clause which encouraged the sending of individuals to one of the écoles normales supérieures in order to qualify them to teach at the high school level, and some of the subsidy was to be used for bursaries in this connection.

Despite these improvements, throughout the 1920s and 1930s there was increasing debate about the legitimacy of the classical course. Criticism stemmed in part from the fact that, since the B.A. was the basic requirement for admission to all professional faculties and schools in the French-language universities, the preparation of the students who wished to go on to advanced studies in the sciences or the social sciences (economics, for example) was inadequate. In fact, since 1920 medical students at Montréal had been required to take a special course in physics, chemistry, and mathematics (the P.C.N.) as a post B.A. preliminary to medical studies. But the traditional classical college course was also challenged on philosophical grounds, the argument being that it tended to create an artificial division between arts and sciences and to ignore the fact that genuine culture required a firm knowledge of both. Exclusive or even undue emphasis on either the humanities or the sciences was equally limiting.

Une culture de l'esprit qui reste exclusivement littéraire, tout aussi bien qu'une culture exclusivement scientifique, ne peut décemment s'appeler culture générale. Les vérités scientifiques, les faits et les lois qui les relient entre eux, la mathématique qui est l'expression de ces lois, font partie du capital spirituel de l'humanité, au même titre que les constructions et les analyses de la métaphysique et que les formes de langue par quoi les anciens ont exprimé l'âme humaine et ce qui émane d'elle: opérations, amours, admiration, haines, passions. Tout cela forme le milieu complexe qui enveloppe de toutes parts notre âme raisonneuse et sensible. Vouloir limiter arbitrairement les contacts de l'esprit en formation à certaines ordres de pensées, n'est-ce pas le déformer, le mutiler, j'allais dire le dévitaminer sans retour?[8]

Thus observed Frère Marie-Victorin, the director of Institut botanique de Univarsité de Montréal, in a 1936 article in which he went on to note that what characterized the greatest geniuses (St Thomas Aquinas, Leonardo, Dante, Pascal, Goethe, Pasteur were among his examples) was the harmonious development of 'l'esprit de finesse' *and* 'l'esprit de géometrie.'[9] As Audet has noted, the same basic argument was being made in the 1920s and early 1930s by such prominent French Canadian educators as Emile Chartier, Edouard Montpetit, and Léo Pariseau of Université de Montréal and Adrien Pouliot of Université Laval. By 1940, then, on both theoretical and practical grounds, the cours classique was under attack in a much more vigorous sense than at any time in its history.

HONOURS COURSES

Between 1920 and 1940 there was no basic change in the arrangements for honours courses in the faculties of arts (or of arts
and science) at the individual English-speaking Canadian universities but the number of such courses at most institutions had
increased. It remained possible at Acadia, British Columbia,
McGill, Mount Allison, New Brunswick, and Queen's to obtain the
honours degree in four years from junior matriculation by taking
additional subjects, but at Acadia and Mount Allison advanced
honours courses involving a fifth year of study had also been
established. At Bishop's the honours course, like the general,
was three years in length from junior matriculation. At the remaining institutions - Alberta, Manitoba (which had established
an honours program in 1923), McMaster, St Francis Xavier,
Saskatchewan and Toronto - the honours course required four years
from senior matriculation, i.e., an additional year of study.
The proportion of faculty of arts students taking honours courses
did not change significantly over the period; only at Toronto did
the number approach 50%.
  The increase in the number of honour courses resulted in part
from the splitting of double honours courses (e.g., a course in
English and French) into two separate units, but mainly, as staff
resources increased and new specialties developed, by the creation
of new courses - at Western Ontario, for example, in economics,
history, philosophy, and psychology. The most striking increase
was at Toronto which expanded its offerings from 22 to 30, the
most notable additions being law (1929), sociology (1932), fine
art (1936), music (1939), and geography (1940). One of the more
famous Toronto courses, English and History, which had been established in the 1890s and which had provided the model for a
substantial number of other honour courses both at Toronto and
elsewhere, was withdrawn in 1935 and replaced by separate courses
in English Language and Literature and Modern History. The other
important development at Toronto was the introduction in 1931 of
what was in effect a common first year for the honours courses
in the social sciences (Social and Philosophical Studies) and
also a common first year (Mathematics, Physics and Chemistry) for
the honour courses in the physical and mathematical sciences.[10]
In contrast to all other Canadian universities, where the honours
course effectively began at the second year, students at Toronto
continued to opt for honours on entering the university, but,
with the introduction of these common first year courses, specialization in these areas was effectively postponed to the second
year. Separate classes for general and honours students continued
to be provided in all four years.
  A detailed description and analysis by A.S.P. Woodhouse of the
arrangements for honours courses in all the English-speaking universities as they were offered in 1944-45 (and owing to the war
there had been no changes of any consequence in the previous four
years) is to be found in chapter 4 of *The Humanities in Canada*.[11]
This account is a critical one in the best sense of the term,

identifying both the strengths and the weaknesses of what 20 years
earlier the two American educators, W.S. Learned and K.C.M. Sills,
had described as one of the precious features of Canadian higher
education.[12] It is the weaknesses that require attention here,
representing as they do a challenge to this peculiarly Canadian
approach to liberal education comparable to that levelled by contemporary critics of the classical college course as described in
the previous section of this chapter. The basic complaint was
that 'concentration was purchased at the cost of distribution.'
No matter whether the student 'specialized' in the area of the
humanities or of the social sciences or of the sciences, his studies in a Canadian honours course were so arranged as to ensure a
well-rounded education in the area as a whole rather than in a
single discipline or perhaps two disciplines within it. What the
student could well be ignorant of was any real familiarity with
arts - if he were a student in the sciences - or of the sciences -
if he were a student in the humanities or social sciences. It
was true that the requirements of senior matriculation or of the
first year of a degree course which admitted from junior matriculation involved some exposure to the 'other' areas of knowledge,
and it was also true that most honour students were required in
the later years of the course to take one or more courses outside
their field of specialization in the interests of distribution.
However, such courses, including those offered at the senior matriculation level, were not, as the Sir George Williams pandemics
most definitely were, specifically designed to introduce students
to 'at least some of the disciplines which are not already represented in the student's concentration for honours.'[13] Until
such courses were provided, the adequacy of the Canadian honours
course as a form of liberal education would remain in question.

COMMERCE, BUSINESS ADMINISTRATION, SECRETARIAL SCIENCE

Commerce courses were discussed at the NCCU meetings in 1930 and
1932 and the basic complaint was that such courses tended to draw
off able male students from traditional courses in arts and
science. Certainly in 1940 the B.Comm. and equally the B.A. in
business administration was principally a male preserve, with
less than 10% of the students being women. However, this was to
some extent compensated for by the fact that degree courses in
secretarial science had been introduced at Western Ontario in
1926, at Mount Saint Vincent in 1932, and at Acadia in 1936.
The latter program represented the expansion of a two year diploma
course first offered in 1920. Mount Allison, which had also established a diploma course in the early 1920s, continued to restrict its offerings to a two year course. Since these courses
did provide for the development of purely technical skills such
as typing and filing, they were more open than the B.Comm courses
to the charge of vocationalism, but they too were based on economic theory and economic history. Of the 60 students enrolled in

secretarial science in 1940 at Acadia, Mount Saint Vincent and Mount Allison, 15 were men and 45 were women.[14]

It is difficult to estimate with any precision the number of undergraduates enrolled in commerce or business administration in 1940 because at three of the 14 institutions which reported enrolments in these related fields to the Dominion Bureau of Statistics,[15] students in these areas of specialization were included under arts and science. These omissions were particularly critical since they included two of the largest universities, British Columbia and Toronto, and Western Ontario, which had the most vigorously developed program in business administration in the country. It is clear, however, that there had been a very significant increase in the numbers of commerce students since 1920. A D.B.S. publication of 1946 reported that the number of commerce graduates for the five year period, 1937 to 1941, was three times that of the five year period, 1922 to 1926 (1065 compared to 334).[16]

The argument as to where commerce courses rightfully belonged was hotly debated at the 1930 and 1932 NCCU conferences, and it was questioned whether commerce had any place at all in an arts program. Nevertheless, at the English-language institutions, studies in commerce had first been offered in the faculty of arts and science, either in a department of political economy or in an especially created department or school of accounting. With two exceptions, Saskatchewan which had given its school of accounting the status of a college in 1936, and Queen's which established an independent school of commerce and administration in 1937, the B.Comm. continued in 1940 to be the responsibility of the faculty of arts and science. At McGill where the school of commercial studies had been renamed the school of commerce, the connection with arts and science was retained but, in effect, the school was an independent unit.

An analysis of the courses of study in commerce offered at the English-language institutions in 1940 certainly indicates that they were solidly based on economic history and economic theory and on the mathematical principles underlying accounting; and consequently that criticisms of them would equally apply to the courses offered to students specializing in political economy or applied mathematics. Third and fourth year courses typically included such subjects as money and banking, public finance, corporation finance, labour problems, and the economics of marketing. The chief exception was the honours degree course in business administration at the University of Western Ontario, which in addition to most of the courses in the traditional commerce and finance course offered a range of subjects designed with the future concerns of businessmen rather than chartered accountants in mind: advertising, executive problems, factory management, sales management, business statistics. Western's approach to business administration placed heavy emphasis on the Harvard case history method.[17] Its program included an intensive one-year diploma course in business administration for graduates, essentially a collection of upper year undergraduate courses.

In the French-language universities, the Montréal affiliated Ecole des hautes études commerciales continued to be responsible for programs in this area, while at Laval the Académie commerciale de Québec, established in 1924, became affiliated with Laval in 1931 when a $50,000 grant from the city of Quebec spread over five years provided for a new building. In 1938, the académie was reorganized as Laval's Ecole supérieure de commerce. By 1940, Laval offered the bachelier ès sciences commerciales to graduates of a two year course for which either the B.A. or completion of the cours primaire supérieur was the admission requirement and the licence to students who completed a further year of study. At l'Ecole des hautes études commerciales the basic course, with comparable admission requirements, was of three years duration and led to the licence. L'Ecole also offered special two-year programs for prospective secondary school teachers of commerce and for graduate engineers, lawyers, and agriculturists.

THE HUMANITIES

As the continuing debate at the NCCU meetings during these decades illustrated, there were wide-spread complaints about the inadequate preparation of matriculants in all subjects, but in the case of written English the problem was of concern to all departments. Weak grounding of students in mathematics was a matter of concern for professors of chemistry and physics as well as of mathematics, but not in any functional sense for professors of French or philosophy. On the other hand, every professor no matter what his field was handicapped if his students could not express their ideas clearly on written examinations, essays, or reports. As E.K. Broadus pointed out in the paper he presented to the 1927 NCCU meeting entitled 'Weaknesses in English among Undergraduates and Graduates in Canadian Universities,' departments of English could choose between two methods of developing the students' powers of expression: one was to attack the problem directly by giving instruction in sentence structure, essay planning, etc; the other was for the professor to scrutinize rigorously the essays prepared by students in their literature courses. Broadus advocated the direct approach,[18] but neither in 1927 nor in 1940 was this suggestion acted upon by the majority of university departments of English. In certain professional faculties, courses in composition, both oral and written, were taught, but in the faculties of arts and science, with few exceptions, notably at Sir George Williams, English meant first and foremost English literature, and only secondly, English composition.

By 1940, English was not only the central discipline in the humanities but as well in the university as a whole, the one subject which students in all first degree programs, including those in French-language institutions, were required to take. In the English-language institutions, English was universally prescribed

in the first two years of the B.A. and B.Sc. courses and for one
or more years in such professional courses as agriculture, engineering, and medicine. At St Mary's, Sir George Williams, and
Western Ontario it was required in all four years of the B.A.
course. However, there is no doubt that the universal prescription of English over these decades was based less on its touted
value[19] as a cultural subject than on the guarantee it offered
that some attention in its classes would be paid to the practical
problems of written expression.

In consequence of its solid position as a prescribed subject,
English literature can be said to have flourished during these
years particularly at the undergraduate level. The courses offered
underwent little change, the chief additions being the devoting
of slightly more attention to Canadian literature than in 1920,
and at a few institutions, for example Sir George Williams, the
introduction of courses in dramatic production as distinct from
dramatic literature. There was no change in the number of courses
devoted to public speaking.

In English Canada, the modern languages of French, German,
Italian, and Spanish, were the subject of an exhaustive study at
all levels - elementary, secondary, university - conducted between
1925 and 1927 by the Canadian Committee on Modern Languages as
part of a Carnegie Corporation financed study of the position of
modern languages carried out in the United States by the American
Council on Education. This issued in the publication in 1928 of
a substantial two-volume report which, however, was largely devoted
to problems at the secondary school level.[20] Partly because of
this but also because of the almost immediate onset of the Depression, the study did not appear to have had any striking ramifications in the universities other than to stimulate the use of French
as the medium of instruction in literature courses. As the study
shows, German suffered a decline in the 1920s as a result of its
removal from the secondary school course of study by some provincial departments of education during the first world war. However, by 1940 it had regained its modest pre-war position, its
continuing relevance for scientific research being a factor in
this recovery. Honours courses in Spanish were instituted at
Acadia and Western Ontario. Toronto remained the only university
to offer honours work in Italian.

The study of Chinese language and literature was introduced in
Canada at McGill as a consequence of the loan of a valuable research library of 8000 volumes in 1930, six courses being offered
and an M.A. degree being authorized. This venture was another
casualty of the Depression.[21] McGill was unable to provide the
funds necessary to support, let alone develop, the program and
in 1933 the library was returned to its owner, ultimately to find
a permanent home at Princeton. In 1934, as a result of the development of the Chinese collection at the Royal Ontario Museum,
courses in Chinese art and archaeology began to be offered at the
University of Toronto, but it was not until the late 1940s that
courses in language and literature were developed.[22] Gaelic and

Icelandic continued to be offered as undergraduate courses at St Francis Xavier and Manitoba respectively, the Dutch language was taught at Queen's, and Norwegian at Manitoba and Saskatchewan. No university offered instruction in Russian in 1940.

In the French-language universities, courses in Italian and Spanish were given only at the Ecole des hautes études commerciales. In the classical colleges for girls these two subjects could be taken as an alternative to Greek.

Also in French Canada, as a result both of the content of the classical college course and of the considerable development of graduate degree programs in philosophy and theology, classics, philosophy, and religion retained their position as liberal arts subjects. There was some falling off of Greek studies, but, in contrast to the situation in English Canada, in terms of enrolment it continued to be a 'popular' subject. Watson Kirkconnell estimated that in 1943 'when in the schools of all the rest of Canada there were only a few students taking Greek, there were 12,000 students in the collèges classiques of Quebec enrolled for at least 4 years of Greek ... probably about 6000 actually studying Greek in any one year.'[23]

In the English-language institutions, religion retained its position, continuing to be prescribed in all Roman Catholic and most Protestant controlled institutions, but both Latin and philosophy lost ground. The former continued to be a first year (senior matriculation) subject for many B.A. students since the normal requirement was either Latin or mathematics, but relatively few, except those taking honours classics, continued beyond this level. Philosophy continued to be a prescribed subject at the Roman Catholic institutions though not necessarily in all years; at Queen's and Acadia it was required in second year, and was strongly recommended as a second year subject at Dalhousie. In addition, honours courses in philosophy were developed at most universities, as well as honours courses combining the study of philosophy with that of another subject such as English or history.

The considerable development of the study of fine arts and music, particularly during the 1930s, will be described in the concluding section of the next chapter.

THE SOCIAL SCIENCES

For reasons difficult to determine, there was very little time spent in the area of the social sciences at the annual meetings of the NCCU in the 1920 to 1940 period. Nevertheless, an examination of course enrolments in any of the English-language institutions would reveal that, increasingly, students were choosing a subject or subjects in this area of study as their major or concentration subject, or as one of their options. Psychology in particular had become a popular subject, a fact reflected in the tendency of departments of philosophy to now be designated as departments of philosophy *and* psychology. By 1940, honours courses were available in sociology at McGill and Toronto and in geography at the latter. If one looks carefully, courses in these subjects and in anthropology can be found in the 1940-41 calendars of almost every faculty of arts and science. Economics and political science continued to be combined in a single department, which more often than not was also responsible for the program in commerce and finance or business administration. Student interest in these latter subjects was a further explanation for the increased enrolment in the social sciences generally. Economics, it may be added, was mandatory in all degree programs in agriculture, and along with English it tended to be one of two non-science subjects prescribed in programs in engineering.

So far as admission requirements and prescribed courses at the first (senior matriculation) and second year levels were concerned, there was little if any change in the position of the social sciences between 1920 and 1940. A subject called 'social studies,' based on history and geography but including elements of economics, political science, and sociology through an emphasis on social problems, had been added to the secondary school curriculum in some provinces, but history, and to a lesser extent geography, were the only academic disciplines to which the matriculant could be said to have been consciously introduced. Economics was a required subject in the second year at St Francis Xavier and at Acadia, but these were small institutions which, consequently, had a small staff in the social sciences, and the requirement probably represented a method of ensuring that all students were exposed to the academic area that occupied the ground between the humanities and the sciences. Both McMaster and Western Ontario continued to demand history in all four years of the B.A. program, and it retained its position in the classical colleges.

The increasing importance of the social sciences in general, and also the increasing professional self-consciousness of professors in the various disciplines, were reflected in the organization during these two decades of learned societies in history, in economics and political science combined, and in psychology. The dates of their establishment are significant: the Canadian Historical Association at the beginning of the period (1923), the Canadian Political Science Association at the half-way point (1929), and the Canadian Psychological Association at the very end (1940).[24] Technically the Canadian Political Science Association was founded in 1913 but its development had been cut off by the outbreak of World War I and it had been dormant for fifteen years.[25] Economists were as active as political scientists in both its initial organization and its reorganization, and when it began to publish a quarterly journal in 1935 the title was the *Canadian Journal of Economic and Political Science*. The Canadian Association of Political Economists would have been a more accurate title. Sociologists, it should be added, were eligible for membership from the start. There was also established in 1936 a Canadian committee of the International Geographical Union, and it, along with the CHA, the CPSA, and the CPA were the organizational founders of the Canadian Social Science Research Council, established in 1940 - still another indication of the greatly increased status achieved by the social sciences during these two decades.

The Depression of the 1930s was a factor in this general advance. It exposed the unscientific approach that had characterized the development of the Canadian economy throughout its history, as well as the basic problems in the field of dominion-provincial relations, which were the political legacy of the British North America Act of 1867. It also emphasized the need for expert advice in the resolving of social problems of the type that social scientists were equipped to provide. Evidence of this is seen in the extent to which the Royal Commission on Dominion-Provincial Relations, active from 1937 to 1940, drew upon economists, historians, and political scientists (though not psychologists) to undertake the research studies which were the basis of the Commission's final recommendations.[26] There was, however, another important factor: the availability by 1930 of a substantial body of well-documented material on Canadian economic, political, and social development. K.W. Taylor has noted that in the 1920s some 40 books bearing on Canadian economics were published, a larger number than in the previous century, and that during the 1930s the number tripled.[27] The same phenonemon occurred in the area of Canadian history (including its political science aspects), the output in this case being in large measure the consequence of the considerable development of the Public Archives of Canada by A.G. Doughty who had been appointed dominion archivist in 1904.[28] While these developments are of particular relevance to graduate studies and research and scholarship, they are also of significance in the area of undergraduate education. Courses in Canadian history, in economics, and in political science may have borne the same titles in the calendars of 1940 as in those of 1920, but this does not mean that the content of the courses and the approach adopted by the professors were unchanged.

While honours courses in geography and sociology had been established in at least one Canadian university by 1940, the position of these disciplines was tentative rather than firmly established. The 1920s had seen the appointment of C.A. Dawson, the sociologist, to the staff at McGill (in 1922), but for some years Dawson's main concern was with a program in social work, and it was not until 1926 that an honours program in sociology was offered.[29] An honours course in sociology was established at Toronto in 1932 but ten years later Harold Innis, within whose department of political economy the course was offered, described sociology as 'the Cinderella' of the social sciences.[30] At least as good a claim for this title could have been made for anthropology, in which, despite the appointment by Toronto of T.F. McIlwraith as a lecturer in 1924 and the development of eight courses in the subject by 1940, an honours program had still to be introduced. It was Innis who was chiefly responsible for the initiation of geography at Toronto, a subject he regarded as an

essential component of economic history. Two full-time appointments had been made in this subject area by 1940, the same year
that an honours course was established. Another important development in geography in the English-language section was the setting
up of a department of geology and geography at the University of
Western Ontario in 1938.

In French-speaking Canada, an interesting development occurred
from 1929 to 1939 when Raoul Blanchard of the Université de
Grenoble offered summer lectures at Université de Montréal and
conducted field work throughout the province. From an overall
institutional point of view, however, very little progress in the
furthering of study in the social sciences was made during these
two decades. There were, of course, French Canadian members of
the three learned societies established over the 20-year period,
and scholars from both Laval and Montréal were among those who
contributed to the research program of the Royal Commission on
Dominion-Provincial Relations and to the 25-volume Relations of
Canada and the United States series.[31] However, lack of financial
resources impeded innovation in the field as did the continuing
strong position occupied by the classical college course in French
Canadian higher education.

The establishment in 1920 of Ecole des sciences sociales, economiques et politiques at Université de Montréal appeared to be
an augury that substantial developments were about to take place,
but this did not prove to be the case.[32] The basic program offered by the Ecole for the next 20 years was a two year course
for which the entrance requirment was completion of the Ecole
primaire supérieure course (equivalent approximately to junior
matriculation in the English-language provinces), with the instruction being offered in the evenings by part-time professors.
Outside of the director, there were no full-time staff members
at the école until 1945, despite the fact that the program was
extended to three years in 1940 and the école was transformed
into a faculté des sciences sociales in 1942.

At Laval, an école des sciences politiques et sociales was established in 1932, but here too instruction was offered in the
evenings and both students and staff were part-time until 1938.
In that year the école was completely reorganized with a three
year program being offered to full-time students. This led naturally to the replacement of the école by a faculté des sciences
sociales in 1943. Still another promising development was the
establishment at the University of Ottawa in 1936 of an école des
sciences politiques et sociales, with undergraduate and graduate
sections both designed to provide for specialization in international relations, industrial relations, journalism, and public
administration. Here also there was more promise than fulfilment.
The graduate section was not seriously developed until well after
World War II and the undergraduate program consisted essentially
of the substitution of elementary courses in the social sciences
for the science portion of the classical college course. In 1940,
as in 1920, systematic development of the social sciences in the
French language universities lay in the future.

SCIENCES

Two subjects which came up for perennial discussion at the NCCU
meetings in the 1920-40 period were the inadequate preparation of
matriculants for university level science and mathematics courses,
and the paucity of graduate programs. Further testimony to their
importance is indicated by the fact that these issues were also
the focus of attention in the publications which appear as entries
dated from 1920 to 1940 in the mathematics and sciences sections
of the 1960 *A Bibliography of Higher Education in Canada*. There
was little or no discussion of the content or the quality of the
undergraduate program per se, which suggests that there was general
satisfaction with the B.Sc. program. In the English-language institutions physical facilities had certainly been improved, especially
in the 1920s, and at most institutions the number of full-time staff
in each of the departments had doubled. Botany and zoology tended to
become separate departments and more attention was paid to geology.

A very different situation held in French Canada, though here
too the concerns were related to secondary school preparation for
scientific study and to graduate work. The problem was that in
1920 there was no undergraduate program in French Canada comparable
to that for which a B.Sc. was granted at Acadia or British Columbia.
While the science component of the classical college course had
been somewhat strengthened, the university candidates' grounding
in chemistry and physics, for example, was not of the quality required for the graduate level work which, in conjunction with the
prosecution of fundamental research, it was the express intention
of the newly created faculté des sciences at Montréal and the
Ecole de chimie supérieure at Laval to provide. Consequently,
the effort of those responsible for the development of science at
Laval and Montréal during these two decades was devoted largely
to developing the solid base from which graduate studies could be
pursued. The circumstances were not propitious. There was still
great resistance to any serious reduction of the literary and
philosophical content of the classical college course, there was
a lack of trained French Canadian scientists to staff the new
schools, and physical facilities were inadequate. At Montréal,
two fires in the years 1921 and 1922 destroyed much of the equipment which the faculté had acquired in the short time since its
establishment, and in 1931 it was learned that the university's
building program, which was designed to provide adequately for
its needs, had been postponed indefinitely. The situation at
Laval, was, if anything, worse. Nevertheless, considerable progress was made during the two decades, so that if not by 1940,
at least by 1945, a sound base for graduate work and fundamental
research had been laid at both institutions. Solid basic courses
were developed, particularly in chemistry, biology, and mathematics;
students were provided with the support needed to pursue advanced
studies in France and the United States; and through the activities of l'Association Canadienne Française pour l'avancement des
sciences (ACFAS) established in 1924, a genuine French Canadian

scientific community was gradually developing.[33] However, another
decade would pass before the field of science in the French-
language sector could be said to have reached maturity.[34]

EXTENSION

Prior to 1920, extension work in the universities was largely the
responsibility of the faculty of arts and science. With the creation of departments of extension, the faculties were relieved of
this task and, at the same time, lost control over adult education.
Since expansion of these activities tended to be in the area of
certificate and diploma rather than degree work and to be practical rather than theoretical in orientation, staff members in
the faculty of arts, and academics generally, became increasingly
concerned about the extent to which the university in pursuing
these tasks was departing from its traditional role. This concern
was reflected in the meetings of the NCCU held in 1928, 1929, 1932,
1934, and 1937. On the whole, the expanding work of the universities in the field of adult education received general support.
In 1934, for example, the conference expressed its appreciation
of the work of a separate conference on adult education which had
been held immediately prior to the annual meeting, one which had
concluded with the recommendation that the necessary steps be
taken to organize a Canadian Association for Adult Education.[35]
But it is to be noted that the report on this conference was 'received' rather than endorsed, and the discussion preceding this
action reflected ambivalence on the part of most speakers. A
typical statement was that of President Walter Murray of Saskatchewan, who began his remarks by saying that he spoke as a sinner:

> For many years, he had dwelt with the saints but lately he had
> gone over to the sinners. At Saskatchewan certain university
> classes were given in the evening, the students took the same
> examinations as others, and credits were given. Certain credits
> were also given for work done by correspondence but credit only
> for one year. So far the results had not been bad. He agreed
> that the university is in danger of going beyond its sphere but
> conditions differed. In a sparsely settled territory the uni-
> versity may be the only possible agency. The university can
> do great service by examining for professional bodies and with-
> out in any way, impairing its efficiency. Faced with definite
> situations he thought the university ought not to be too diffi-
> dent.[36]

In a similar but less happily reported vein, President Sherwood
Fox announced that 'he too had tried to be virtuous but that the
University of Western Ontario was now carrying on extension classes
in Windsor, St Thomas, Stratford and other places.'[37] However,
Fox went on to say that the courses were identical with those at
the university and that he thought the work was very much worth-

391

while, and he added that 'financially they were nearly self-sustaining.' This last remark was in many respects the clue to the dilemma which men like Murray and Fox found themselves in. Long before the Depression, the tradition had developed in most Canadian universities that extension work should be financially self-sustaining, with the result that the courses offered tended to be those which could be counted upon to enrol a viable number of fee-paying students. Inevitably this injected a vocational bias to the offerings, and in conjunction with the growing popularity of supposedly 'practically orientated' degree courses such as commerce and business administration convinced many professors and presidents that the traditions and the standards of the university were being undermined by the growing importance of extension work.

However, as President Murray had pointed out, conditions differed from institution to institution. Certainly the community in which St Francis Xavier at Antigonish in eastern Nova Scotia found itself differed markedly from that of Toronto or McGill, and in all the discussions at the NCCU meetings there was unanimous praise for the imaginative and dedicated work which since the establishment of the People's School in 1920 St Francis Xavier had been carrying on through study groups and leadership courses to assist impoverished farmers, fishermen, lumbermen, and miners to solve their problems through cooperative efforts, including the establishment of credit unions.[38] With the establishment of a department of extension in 1929, the Antigonish Movement, as it came to be called, was substantially expanded and by 1940 the university's reputation in this field was international in scope.

The fact that most of the extension work undertaken at St Francis Xavier was specifically not designed for degree credit purposes explained the enthusiasm of academics for the Antigonish Movement where there was suspicion of the activities of most extension departments. The main concern of the faculties of arts and science was the maintenance of degree standards, and this was reflected in the attitude of the universities to Frontier College and to Sir George Williams College. The former, which had been in operation since 1900, applied for and was granted a charter by the federal Parliament in 1923. Clause 10 of the charter authorized the institution to grant the B.A. degree.[39] The NCCU formally opposed the inclusion of this clause on the grounds that the institution lacked the resources, both human and physical, to undertake work of degree standard, and the conference was instrumental in persuading the government in 1933 to amend the charter by withdrawing the degree-granting clause.[40] In the case of Sir George Williams, the conference's attitude was simply to ignore its existence until, seven years after it had begun to grant degrees, it applied for membership.[41] Technically the college dated from 1926 when the educational work which the Y.M.C.A. had been carrying on in Montreal for over half a century was concentrated in an evening high school bearing this name and made available to women. Until 1929 the courses offered were restricted to the first four high school grades, but in that year senior matriculation courses were offered. Second, third, and fourth year courses were subsequently made available and in 1936 degrees were awarded to two students, legal opinion having been obtained that the college's Act of Incorporation entitled it to exercise such power. By this time the college was offering courses in daytime as well as in the evening and day students were attending on a full-time basis. But in 1940 the student body consisted overwhelmingly of part-time students taking evening classes. The only reference in the *NCCU Proceedings* to the existence of this institution up to this time was a passing reference by a student participant (Miss Madeleine Parent of the Canadian Student Assembly) in a symposium on Student Self-Government held in 1939. Miss Parent noted that 'An English College in Montreal (Sir George Williams College) had this year sponsored a series of talks by local French Canadians which were a considerable success.'[42] Granted the amount of attention devoted by the NCCU to adult education at each of its meetings from 1927 on, this is a remarkable fact, one that can hardly be explained on the grounds of ignorance. By this time the Dominion Bureau of Statistics had for years been reporting full-time enrolments at Sir George Williams in arts and science and in commerce in its biennial surveys of higher education in Canada. Moreover, much of the instruction offered at Sir George Williams was provided by staff members and graduate students associated with McGill.

Though universities were among the first Canadian institutions to concern themselves with the education of adults, as the history of, for example, the mechanics' institutes, the Instituts Canadiens, and the provincial departments of agriculture clearly shows, they had never in the nineteenth century enjoyed a monopoly in the field. The involvement of the universities probably reached its highest point between 1900 and 1920, a period during which most institutions developed systematic programs of public lectures. A number of them followed the example of Queen's in offering credit courses for the B.A. degree to part-time students and at an early stage the four western universities assumed responsibility for the short courses and practical demonstrations previously carried out by the provincial departments of agriculture.

Over these decades, there was no slackening of the work of the universities in the extension field: indeed, it increased both in the areas already cultivated and in additional ones such as business administration, commercial affairs, and journalism. Evidence of this is provided by the establishment of departments of extension at McGill in 1927, St Francis Xavier in 1929, British Columbia in 1936, McMaster in 1941, and Queen's in 1942. Summer schools were held at Acadia by 1923, Mount Allison by 1924, New Brunswick by 1929, Bishop's by 1930, and Ottawa by 1933. Still more evidence is provided by the 1934 survey of adult education in Canada conducted under the direction of Professor Peter Sandiford of the Ontario College of Education. The report[43] demonstrated clearly the extent as well as the lack of coordination of the work being carried on by both degree-granting and non degree-granting institutions, and it led to the founding in 1936 of the Canadian Association for Adult Education. A notable feature of this study was the revelation of the use to which radio was employed for adult education. In this area, the universities had led the way, beginning with Queen's which had constructed its own broadcasting station in 1932; by 1932, three other institutions had their own stations - Acadia, Alberta, and Western Ontario, and at least five others, Dalhousie, Manitoba, McGill, Saskatchewan, and Toronto, had made arrangements for regular programming with local publicly owned or commercial stations.[44] But the Sandiford report also revealed how much was being done in the field of adult education by other organizations, including two established for the specific purpose - the Workers' Education Association and Frontier College. These and the university departments of extension were dealt with in the section entitled Institutions Engaged Solely in the Task of Adult Education, which occupies almost one-fifth of the entire document. The chapter on University Departments of Extension is twice as long (34 pages) as any of the other 20 chapters. Reference to the involvement of the universities was also made in other chapters, for example, those devoted to museums and art galleries, summer schools and vacation schools, and classes in agriculture, farm clubs and farmers' institutions, but the overall impression on reading the report is of widespread activity by a great range of federal, provincial, and voluntary agencies, as well as by the universities.

In the two French-language universities of Quebec the offering of public lectures continued to be the main teaching function of the faculté des arts, since instruction for students registered for the B.A. degree remained the responsibility of the affiliated classical colleges. At both institutions, there was a serious effort made to provide opportunities for practising teachers both in the private and the public elementary and secondary schools to increase their academic and pedagogical qualifications by way of evening and Saturday classes. At Laval this work was undertaken by the Ecole normale supérieure and the Ecole supérieure de chimie, both attached to the faculté des arts until the establishment of facultés des lettres and des sciences in 1937, and at Montréal by the facultés des lettres and des sciences established in 1920. Much of the work carried on at Laval and Montréal was of the extension type, and even by 1940 there were relatively few full-time students in the facultés des lettres, philosophie, sciences, or sciences sociales.

NOTES TO CHAPTER 21

1 On the development and concerns of the NCCU for the period 1920-40, see Gwendoline Pilkington, 'A History of the Association of Universities and Colleges of Canada, 1911-1961,' Ph.D. thesis, University of Toronto (1974).
2 Membership in the NCCU increased from 28 to 31 between 1920 and 1940 through the admission of the Royal Military College, St

Dunstan's University, and the National Research Council of
Canada. Delegates in 1920 numbered 39; in 1930, 42; in 1939, 36.

3   For the development of general education courses in the United
    States, see Willis Rudy, *The Evolving Liberal Arts Curriculum:
    a Historical Review of Basic Themes* (1960); and Aston R.
    Williams, *General Education in Higher Education* (1968).

4   For the development of public education at the secondary level
    in the Province of Quebec, see L.-P. Audet, *Histoire de
    l'Enseignement au Québec* (1971), II, 282-91.

5   A. Maheux, 'The Future of the Faculty of Arts,' *NCCU Proc.*
    (1942), 122-8

6   The comparison is based on an analysis of the course of study
    outlined in the Université Laval *Annuaire* for 1920-21 and in
    the *Programme des Etudes 1940* issued by the faculté des arts
    for the cours classique de garçons.

7   The act (12 George V, Ch. 5) is quoted in E. Chartier, 'The
    Classical Colleges of Quebec,' *NCCU Proc.* (1923), 30-1.

8   'La Science et nous,' *Rev. Trimestrielle Canadienne*, 12 (1926),
    426, quoted in Audet, *Histoire*, II, 288

9   Audet, *Histoire*, II, 287-9

10 Throughout this period, honours courses at Toronto were divided
    into four groups: (1) languages; (2) social sciences, including
    history and philosophy, and also fine art and music, for which
    a separate first-year course was provided; (3) mathematics and
    physics, physics and chemistry, physics and geology; (4) 10
    other science courses, including geography and household sci-
    ence.

11 W. Kirkconnell and A.S.P. Woodhouse, *The Humanities in Canada*
    (1947), 58-81

12 W.S. Learned and K.C.M. Sills, *Education in the Maritime
    Provinces of Canada* (1922), 41

13 Ibid., 80

14 Dominion Bureau of Statistics, *Higher Education in Canada
    1940-42*, Part II of Biennial Survey of Education in Canada
    1940-42 (1944), 18

15 Ibid., 15

16 Dominion Bureau of Statistics, *Higher Education in Canada
    1942-44*, Part II of Biennial Survey of Education in Canada
    1942-44 (1946), 11

17 For the development of business administration at Western
    Ontario, see J.J. Talman and R. Talman, *Western - 1878-1953*
    (1953), 175-9

18 *NCCU Proc.* (1927), 79-97. Broadus was invited by the confer-
    ence to develop his ideas further. This he did at the next
    conference in a paper entitled 'A Plan for Dealing with
    Weakness in English,' *NCCU Proc.* (1928), 95-9.

19 See, for example, R.S. Knox, 'The Educational Value of the
    Study of Literature,' *NCCU Proc.* (1930), 56-64.

20 I. Goldstick, et al., *Modern Language Instruction in Canada*
    (1928). See also F.W. Walter, 'Modern Language Teaching in
    Universities,' *NCCU Proc.* (1932), 44-9.

21 H.M. Urquhart, *Arthur Currie: The Biography of a Great Canadian*
    (1950), 310. See also *Canadian Annual Review* (1934), 214.

22 L.C. Walmsley, *Bishop in Honan: Mission and Museum in the Life of William C. White* (1974), 158-69
23 Kirkconnell and Woodhouse, *Humanities*, 93
24 The development of the associations mentioned in this paragraph and also of the Canadian Social Science Research Council is described in chapter 23.
25 See above, chapter 18, 330.
26 See above, chapter 19, 342.
27 'Economic Scholarship in Canada,' *Can. J. Econ. Pol. Sci.*, 26 (1960), 10-11
28 On the importance of the services provided by the Public Archives, see A.R.M. Lower, *My First Seventy-Five Years* (1967), 123-35; and D.G. Creighton, *Harold Adams Innis: Portrait of a Scholar* (1957), 64-5.
29 Commencing in 1922-23 it was possible to take an honours course at McGill in sociology and *one* other subject - English, philosophy, political economy, or psychology.
30 'The Social Sciences: Brief Survey of Recent Literature,' *Can. Geog. J.*, 24 (September 1942), x
31 See above, chapter 19, 340.
32 M. Tremblay and A. Faucher, 'L'Enseignement des sciences sociales au Canada de langue française,' *Royal Commission Studies* (1951), 193-4
33 On ACFAS, see below, chapter 24, 440.
34 See L. Lortie et A. Plouffe, eds., *Aux Sources du Présent* (1960), 90-104.
35 Included as an appendix to the *NCCU Proc.* (1934), 45-8 is W.J. Dunlop's report on the Symposium on Adult Education held at Toronto 23 and 24 May.
36 *NCCU Proc.* (1934), 20
37 Ibid., 21
38 The involvement of St Francis Xavier faculty members in the development of cooperatives antedated the establishment of the People's School by at least a decade. See A.F. Laidlaw, *The Campus and the Community: the Global Impact of the Antigonish Movement* (1961), 61-4.
39 E.W. Robinson, 'The History of the Frontier College,' M.A. thesis, McGill University, 1960
40 Pilkington, 'History of the *NCCU*,' 114-16
41 *NCCU Proc.* (1942), 11-12. The application was denied. Sir George Williams College was admitted to membership in 1947.
42 Ibid., (1939), 52
43 P. Sandiford et al., *Adult Education in Canada: a Survey* (1935). The report, which is in mimeographed form without consecutive paging, is a piecing together of selections from reports submitted by the individuals assigned responsibility for the three Maritime provinces, English-speaking Quebec, French-speaking Quebec, and each of the other five provinces, with a preface and introduction by Sandiford.
44 E.A. Corbett, 'The Use of Radio by the University,' *NCCU Proc.* (1932), 55-60

22
Professional Education

In the area of professional education the problems with which
the National Conference of Canadian Universities chiefly concerned
itself were those of the faculties which by the 1920s were firmly
established: agriculture, engineering, law, medicine, dentistry,
the latter having been included principally as a consequence of
active Canadian participation in the Carnegie Foundation for the
Advancement of Teaching Study of dental education in North America.[1]
Forestry was the subject of a paper given at the 1920 meetings by
Professor Piché from Laval in which he emphasized the urgency of
preserving the forests of Canada, the need to engage in reforesta-
tion on a large scale, and stressed that 'education in this connection is of vital importance.'[2] In 1922, two new standing committees[3] were formed to study the problems in the fields of dentistry and commerce. A paper on 'The University and the Training
of Teachers for Secondary Schools' was presented at this conference. It argued that the training of teachers was quite properly
the work of the universities.[4] Although no standing committee
was ever formed to deal with teacher education, in 1923 it was
suggested that every year, in conjunction with the NCCU meetings,
'a conference of Teachers in some particular department of university instruction should be held ...'[5] A further proposal was
made for a survey of the requirements for teachers' professional
certificates. Some attempt was made to follow through on the
first proposal, and the subject of teacher training would come
up again in 1927 and 1930 with the renewed plea for universities
to take some action towards moving teacher training into the
sphere of higher education. The results were again negative.
  The NCCU *Proceedings* during these two decades have but scant
reference to the oncoming professions of library science, nursing,
physical and health education, physical and occupational therapy,
or social work. What the delegates did debate untiringly was the
threat of declining academic standards generally and in traditional
subjects. As noted in the preceding chapter the five symposia

scheduled during this period were: Is the Arts Faculty Losing Ground?; The Effect of Summer Schools on the Standards in Faculties of Arts; Safeguarding Matriculation Standards; The Necessity of Compulsory Latin for Arts Matriculation; Honours Courses. A glance at programs of earlier meetings suggests that it is unlikely that any new ground was being cultivated.

The question of whether commerce should be regarded as a professional or a liberal arts course was one which occupied the delegates at the annual meeting in both 1930 and in 1932. Papers were presented by F.H. Underhill and C.N. Cochrane which deplored the intrusion of practically oriented programs in the faculty of arts.[6] What seemed to be of most concern to the delegates on both occasions was the fact that commerce courses were luring able male students away from those areas of study emphasizing the humanities, with the result, it was argued, that courses emphasizing classical and modern languages including English were increasingly becoming the preserve of female students. The statistics confirm the fact that there was a large increase in the number of students taking commerce (or business administration) and that the majority were male - 11 men and one woman were awarded the B.Comm. in June 1921, 231 men and 32 women in June 1941; but the figures also indicate an increase in the proportion of men graduating in arts - 823 of 1337 or 61% in 1921; 2242 of 3342 or 66% in 1941. In that year, too, of the 342 who earned a B.Sc., 51 were women.[7]

Enrolment in arts, science, *lettres*, and commerce approximately doubled between 1920 and 1940, the numbers being 9444 and 18,824, respectively. This represented an increase in the proportion of full-time undergraduates in Canadian universities from 43% to 54%, and consequently a decline in the proportion of students in professional programs from 57% to 46%. However, the inclusion of commerce, in the arts and science figures tends to be misleading in the sense that at some universities, notably Western Ontario, business administration was under the umbrella of commerce.

The relative drop in enrolment in professional courses was largely attributable to dramatic decreases in law from 1117 to 697, and dentistry from 1276 to 468, the latter reflecting a deliberate raising of standards for admission. A slight decline in medicine from 3256 to 2940 can also be explained by the strengthening and the lengthening of the course. Pharmacy admissions dropped from 562 to 412, but here the explanation lay in a waning of demand rather than to changes in standards. Enrolment in engineering and forestry went up by 50%, from 2854 to 4381 and from 103 to 173 respectively, while that of veterinary medicine doubled from 116 to 245. There was a tripling of registration in architecture, 49 to 146, but it should be noted that in 1939-40 this had dropped to 89. In agriculture there was a considerable increase in numbers admitted to the degree program, 856 to 1373, but a tapering off of students in the diploma course.

The greatest gains in the professional courses occurred in those which catered exclusively to women: household science went up from 100 to 790, and diploma students in household economics

398

doubled from 342 to 634; nursing, which had become a university course in 1920, increased from 122 to 510. Social work had been introduced in 1920 and its registration rose from 85 in 1920-21 to 146 in 1940-41. In the degree courses in education, student numbers rose from 156 to 677, with the latter figure representing a noticeable drop from the high point of 918 in 1932-33. Three new professional programs were initiated, two of which, library science and occupational and physical therapy, were designed primarily for women. In 1937-38, enrolment in library science was 79 but this had dropped to 52 in 1940-41, at which time there were 121 students in occupational and physical therapy. The third new field, optometry, was offered from 1925 on but only at Montréal, where there were 25 men and no women in the degree course.

THEOLOGY

Numbers of full-time students in theology in the Canadian universities improved slightly from 2136 to 2429 between 1920 and 1940, a decrease on the Protestant side being more than offset by the increase on the Roman Catholic. The latter was due to the inclusion in the 1940 figure of students enrolled in the seminaries conducted by the religious orders.[8] The comparative modesty of these figures is apparent when juxtaposed with the total enrolment in Canadian universities, which rose from 23,418 to 37,269. Of more significance was the decline of the importance of the theological faculty or department in the overall complexion of the Canadian university, whether large or small.

In the French-language institutions the situation was somewhat different. At Laval, for example, theology in 1920 was one of four faculties, whereas in 1940 it was one of nine, but of the new faculties established, those of canon law and philosophy were largely staffed by theologians. At Montréal, theology and philosophy counted among a total of seven faculties; there, however, the existence of seven affiliated or associated schools such as Ecole polytechnique was a reminder of the growing interest in secular studies. A similar picture was developing at the University of Ottawa.

In English-speaking Canada, the faculty of theology or the affiliated or federated theological college continued to be represented on the senate or equivalent body of the university, but the problems of theology were seldom discussed at meetings. The number of Protestant colleges had been somewhat reduced despite the establishment of several new ones, notably Lutheran College Seminary at Saskatoon in 1939 and Toronto Baptist Seminary in 1926.[9] Financial difficulties as well as dwindling enrolments resulted in the withdrawal of theological instruction at Brandon College in 1938. The main reason for the disappearance of colleges, however, was the 1925 consolidation of the Methodist, Congregationalist, and a section of the Presbyterian Churches into the United

Church of Canada. This brought about the mergers of several university theology departments with other theological colleges, for example, the Mount Allison department joined Pine Hill Divinity Hall at Halifax, and two McGill affiliates, Wesleyan and Congregational, became the United Theological College in Montreal. Some Presbyterian colleges retained their identity; for example, Knox at Toronto, and the Presbyterian College at Montreal, although the latter continued to cooperate with other theological colleges affiliated with McGill, and like them would be involved in the establishment of McGill's faculty of divinity in 1948.[10] There was no change in the Anglican community, the same ten colleges continuing to function, though in some cases only with great difficulty.[11] The Anglican Theological College at Vancouver became an affiliate of the University of British Columbia in 1927, and subsequently began to cooperate with other affiliated Protestant colleges which also were located on campus. These moves might be said to represent the first faltering steps towards ecumenism in Canada.

So far as curriculum is concerned, there was little change in the programs offered by the various Protestant colleges during the two decades, though most institutions gave increased attention to the sociological and psychological aspects of parish and missionary work.[12] In the Roman Catholic sphere, both English- and French-language theological courses were revised during the mid-1930s in accord with the directions of *Deus Scientiarum Dominus*, the papal encyclical issued in 1931.[13]

LAW

It was noted in chapter 16 that, though the early 1920s saw a considerable improvement in the conditions pertaining to legal education in Canada, owing largely to the efforts of the Canadian Bar Association, 'in most respects the situation was as it had been in 1890.' Essentially this remained true in 1940 though admission standards had been generally raised. In Quebec the requirement of a B.A. for admission to the bar was extended in 1937 to the notariat and in the same year a degree was made a requirement for admission to the bar in Alberta. Two years of arts and science (including senior matriculation) were required for admission to the university law schools in the other provinces. The Osgoode Hall Law School at Toronto had introduced the same requirement in 1926 but had reverted to the requirement of senior matriculation in 1931 on the grounds that the requirement penalized students from low income families, an argument rendered somewhat suspect by the fact that two years later the annual tuition fees were increased from $100 to $150. The number of full-time staff increased slightly - a fourth full-time staff members was appointed at Dalhousie in 1930, for example. There was some extension of the use of the case method and a number of Canadian case study texts were produced, but lecturing remained the mode of instruction. There were no significant changes in the three year curriculum offered by all schools.

Because the provincial law society continued to control certification and to emphasize the practical aspects of legal training,
the situation from the standpoint of most universities remained
unsatisfactory. There was no real problem at Alberta, Dalhousie,
or Saskatchewan. Even by 1920 the Dalhousie law degree had been
effectively recognized by the Nova Scotia Bar Association as qualifying the holder to practise. In 1923 the Saskatchewan Bar
Association withdrew its school in Regina and assigned responsibility for legal training to the university. Both there and at
Alberta satisfactory arrangements had been developed by the university and the law society with respect to the year of articling
which followed the three years of full-time study towards a law
degree. In Quebec, however, the degree course was regulated by
the law society. At Manitoba, full-time study had been introduced
in 1921, but in 1931 the school, which was entirely controlled by
the Manitoba Law Society, reverted to the system of combining
articling with attendance at early morning or late afternoon lectures. The situation was similar at the University of New Brunswick, which in 1923 had 'taken over' the King's College (Windsor)
Law School located in Saint John. At New Brunswick the problem
was manifested in the fact that lectures provided in the second
and third years of the course were offered to both sets of students in alternate years.
Despite the refusal of the Law Society of Upper Canada to grant
any credit for the legal studies offered at the University of
Toronto, the university continued to pursue the course which in
the 1950s led to a radical change in the arrangements for legal
education in Ontario. In 1930, a department of law was detached
from the department of political economy, and a four year honours
course to the B.A. was established, one which gave heavy emphasis
to philosophy and political economy in three of the four years.
The L.L.B. degree continued to be offered and could be taken by
graduates of the honours course after one additional year. The
department in 1940 had five full-time staff members. At McGill
the L.L.B. degree had been withdrawn in 1924 and the faculty concentrated thereafter on a reorganized B.C.L. program.

MEDICINE

The appointment of full-time clinical professors of medicine and
surgery at McGill, Queen's, and Toronto in the early 1920s, combined with the stimulation of medical research provided by the
Banting discovery of insulin in 1921, suggested that substantial
advances in medical education were about to occur in the universities. But such hopes were not fulfilled. During the remainder
of the 1920s and throughout the 1930s no further full-time clinical appointments were made and the undergraduate curriculum,
though strengthened and refined, changed very little between 1920
and 1940. The period was one of consolidation rather than innovation. The one subject that moved to a major place in the undergraduate curriculum was psychiatry; there was, as well, additional

401

recognition of the importance of preventive medicine or hygiene. In 1925, Toronto introduced a service within its faculty of medicine, which by 1944 had developed into a diploma course in art as applied to medicine, and one which is unique in Canada.

At Saskatchewan, the Alberta pattern of beginning with the two pre-clinical years was implemented in 1926, but, in contrast to Alberta, the full program was not available until the 1950s. As opposed to what would occur from 1945 on, there was at this time no great demand on the part of matriculants for places in medicine. This could have been due to the depressed economy and the high cost and lengthy duration of medical studies. In the late 1930s all qualified applicants were being admitted and the medical course was basically six years beyond senior matriculation, with the final year being one of internship. In the English-language institutions, the medical portion constituted four years, preceded either by two, or in the case of those which admitted at the junior matriculation level, three years of arts and science. Laval and Montréal offered a four year course from the B.A., with the first year devoted largely to the basic sciences since these received inadequate attention in the *cours classiques*.

In 1940-41, McGill had an enrolment of 419, Toronto of 724, and the other seven schools had between 200 and 300 among them. Toronto and Montreal were, in fact, comparable in size since the Toronto enrolment refers to students in the six year program from senior matriculation, whereas the McGill figure included only students in the four medical years. Saskatchewan in 1940-41 had 42 students in its pre-clinical program.

The main advances during the period occurred at the postgraduate level. The establishment in 1926 of a school of hygiene at Toronto with generous grants from the Rockefeller Foundation ($650,000 in 1925 and $600,000 in 1930) allowed for expansion and strengthening of the diploma program introduced in 1914 and, since the school was intimately and in part physically and organizationally connected with the Connaught Laboratories, its establishment had a similar effect in the area of medical research, both theoretical and applied.[14] The attempt to establish a similar school at Montréal in the mid-twenties was unsuccessful, but in 1938 l'Institut de microbiologie et d'hygiène was firmly established. The movement towards provision for postgraduate specialization in the clinical fields was greatly advanced by the chartering of the Royal College of Physicians and Surgeons of Canada in 1929.[15] Such a body, which would have responsibility for certifying specialists in specific fields, had been proposed as early as 1913, but more vigorously in 1920 at a time when the American College of Surgeons was actively 'recruiting' in Canada. However, it took nearly a decade for a scheme to be developed which was satisfactory to the leaders of the medical profession in Canada whose traditional postgraduate orientation was to the United Kingdom or to the United States in a case of English-speaking Canadians and to France in the case of French-speaking Canadians. In 1929, the Royal College was established with an initial membership of 508, almost equally divided between those who were named fellows by virtue of their university appointments and those who were selected on a basis of their experience and prestige. Initially the fellows were either physicians (212) or surgeons (296), but in 1942, following a 1937 request of the Canadian Medical Association, the college agreed to assume responsibility for certification in all fields, for example radiology (in 1937 the Canadian Association of Radiologists proposed to establish a College of Radiology which would be authorized to certify specialists in this field). It was not, however, until 1946 that the Royal College of Physicians and Surgeons of Canada began to conduct examinations. By 1960 it had certified over 8500 specialists in 20 fields, the basic requirement being five years of postgraduate training in the specialty in question.

ENGINEERING

Engineering between 1920 and 1940 was characterized by steady but, on the whole, unimaginative progress. The course of study was extended by one year, and by 1940 the norm was four years from senior matriculation. Enrolment in 1940-41 was 4381, representing an increase of about 1500 over the 1920 figure, the latter having been somewhat inflated by the influx of veterans from World War I. The major gain occurred in the four western universities which in 1920 had only recently established engineering schools; at Saskatchewan the registration had increased from 36 to 503, and at Alberta from 71 to 311. The only new engineering program initiated was at Laval where an Ecole des mines et de géologie was set up within the faculté des sciences when it was created in 1937; in 1940-41, there were 46 students studying for the bachélier des sciences appliquées. The only other schools with modest enrolments were New Brunswick with 113, including those in forestry, and Nova Scotia Technical College with 50 students. The latter continued to offer only the final two years of the engineering course and its enrolment cannot properly be described as modest if the 309 students taking pre-engineering at Acadia, Dalhousie, Mount Allison, St Mary's, and St Francis Xavier are taken into account. All the remaining schools had enrolments of over 200.

There was little variation in the design of the curriculum from one institution to another, other than a larger number of graduating departments in the bigger faculties. The course of study remained scientifically and technically oriented, with English and economics constituting an element of liberal education. The continuing dearth of institutes of technology designed to train technologists as distinct from professional engineers partly accounts for the practical bias of the degree program. The depressed economic outlook explains why relatively few students went on to graduate studies.

ARCHITECTURE

By 1940, there were three universities in Canada offering degrees in architecture, Manitoba, McGill, and Toronto. In all three, the program continued to be offered within the faculty of engineering and, partly for this reason, continued to reflect the practical aspects of architecture. The main emphasis was on construction and building design, and all students were required to gain a certain amount of practical experience before being granted the degree. However, at Manitoba and Toronto the curriculum included courses in town planning and landscape design. At Toronto, the students had the choice of design or structural options in their final two years. All three programs were five years in length, following junior matriculation at Manitoba and McGill and senior matriculation at Toronto, and all led to the B.Arch. degree. In 1940-41 total enrolment was 66: 28 at McGill, 25 at Manitoba, and 13 at Toronto.

The University of Alberta which had offered a four year course to the B.Sc. since 1913 withdrew its program at the end of the 1939-40 session on the retirement of the single full-time staff member. Université de Montréal had withdrawn from the field in 1923 following the decision of the provincial government to establish independent écoles des beaux arts at Montreal and Quebec. At these institutions the traditional French emphasis on design was retained.

FORESTRY

The four forestry schools which had been set up between 1907 and 1921 consolidated their position over the next two decades, but did not enjoy dramatic growth. The total number of degrees awarded annually ranged from 16 to 31, the number at any one institution from 4 to 12. There were still only two full-time members of staff at both New Brunswick and British Columbia in 1937 and five at Toronto. At Laval, L'Ecole d'arpentage et de génie forestière boasted a staff of 12 in 1937, but the school was also responsible for a degree program in surveying. The Laval school was also a self-contained unit providing a complete course of studies, whereas much of the instruction at British Columbia, New Brunswick, and Toronto was provided by cross-appointed faculty.

Nonetheless, there were significant shifts of emphasis in all four schools. In 1937, responsibility for l'Ecole d'arpentage et de génie forestière at Laval was transferred from the faculté des arts to the faculté des sciences, and by 1940 there was a revised degree course extending to four years, with a two year diploma course also being offered. In 1935, a major revision of the curricula in the faculty of applied science at British Columbia brought about a reorientation of the forestry department: 'Logging engineering which hitherto had been the principal preoccupation of the department was no longer emphasized and, with the help of

404

Dr. P.M. Barr of the University of California, a programme of scientific forestry was planned.'[16] At New Brunswick, a forestry and geology building was opened in 1930. At Toronto, admission requirements were raised to senior matriculation standard in 1923, the curriculum was revised in 1933, and first an M.A. and than an M.Sc.F. were offered. At all four of these institutions there were improved arrangements for summer camps.

It may also be noted that in 1923, the province of Quebec established an école de gardes forestières at Berthierville to provide technical training courses for personnel in its department of lands and forests. This diploma-level operation was transferred to Duchesnay in 1935 as l'école forestière, the first of the Canadian ranger schools.[17]

AGRICULTURE

In agriculture, the 1920s and 1930s were years dedicated to consolidation and modest expansion of existing facilities. No new institutions were set up, but at Laval and Manitoba there was significant reorganization within the schools. In 1924, the hitherto independent but affiliated Manitoba Agricultural College became an integrated faculty of agriculture and home economics, while at Laval the school of agriculture operating in the faculté des arts was transferred to the faculté des lettres in 1938 and subsequently was established as a faculty in 1940. Full-time enrolment in the degree programs declined in the mid-1920s but had recovered by 1930 and increased steadily during the 1930s. In the diploma courses registration remained at almost the same level throughout – 415 in 1920-21, 389 in 1940-41.

The major developments of the period were, first, the clear separation of the degree and the diploma programs; second, a considerable increase in the available specialized offerings in the third and fourth years of the degree program; and, third, the introduction of graduate work at the master's level. There were two special developments: first, the creation in 1934 of an institute of parasitology at McGill's Macdonald College, with financial support from the National Research Council; and, second, in 1939 the establishment of an école de pêcheries attached to the Laval school (later faculty) of agriculture and with the support of the provincial government.

All these innovations reflected a steadily growing stress on the scientific as distinct from the practical aspects of agriculture. The retention, in the case of Montréal the introduction, of a two year diploma course in 1927 was an indication of the continuing recognition by the universities of a responsibility to provide adequate training for the practising farmer as well as for the agronomist and the teacher or professor of agriculture. This was a topic of utmost concern to presidents of the Western universities and this was reflected in discussions at NCCU conferences throughout the early part of the period. There was an awareness, however, that the degree and diploma courses served two different purposes, and this is evident in the decision made to provide separate programs for each, rather than accepting the two year diploma as a prerequisite for the degree program. The development of specialization in the final two years of the degree course would not have been possible had not a solid basis of preparation in the basic sciences fundamental to agriculture been laid in the first two years. McGill's decision in 1929 to make completion of the first two years of the B.Sc. program a prerequisite for admission to the third year of the degree course in agriculture was in this sense representative of the view of deans and professors of agriculture but also of university presidents. In the same context, the decision to change the title of the degree from B.S.A. to B.Sc. (Agriculture) in 1934 was symbolic. The interest in developing graduate work, and, concomitantly, research was an inevitable outcome of this recognition of agriculture as a science rather than an art, and here it must be noted that by 1940 doctoral programs were available at both the French-language institutions and, through the University of Toronto, at the Ontario Agricultural College.

VETERINARY MEDICINE

The main change in veterinary medicine between 1920 and 1940 was the moving of the two existing schools from large metropolitan centres to new locations on the campuses of schools of agriculture. In 1922, Ontario Veterinary College was transferred from Toronto to the Ontario Agricultural College at Guelph, and in 1928 Ecole de médicine vétérinaire was moved from Montreal to the Institut agricole at Oka. The changes were principally physical, the schools continuing to be independent institutions financed by government funds separately from the agricultural colleges and continuing to be affiliated with the original parent universities, Toronto and Montréal, respectively. However, there was increasingly close association with the agricultural college, certain courses being taken together by students of both institutions and opportunities being made available for sharing human and physical resources. At each institution the physical facilities were greatly improved, though in the case of Oka not until 1935 when a building providing adequate laboratories was opened. Standards were also raised, a B.A. being demanded for admission to the four year course at the Ecole vétérinaire, and the Ontario Veterinary College course being extended from four years to five beyond junior matriculation, or four years beyond senior matriculation. Even so, full-time enrolment in the two institutions doubled over the 20-year period. In association with the University of Toronto, the Ontario Veterinary College introduced a two year master's program, one year of which had to be spent in some University of Toronto department. The D.V.Sc. degree introduced in 1919 continued to be granted upon completion of an acceptable thesis.

406

Enrolment in household science degree courses across Canada increased over these two decades: in 1920-21 it was 234; in 1924-25,
344; in 1926-27, 344; in 1929-30, 639; in 1936-37, 735; in 1937-
38, 1002; the only year it failed to increase was 1933-34 when
it dropped to 565. In 1940-41, full-time enrolment was 790, and
an additional 634 students were admitted to the two year diploma
courses which Macdonald Institute and a number of other schools
offered.

The programs were continued at the five institutions which had
begun to offer degree courses by 1920: Alberta, Manitoba, McGill,
Saskatchewan, and Toronto. At Saskatchewan, the department had
become a school in 1928, and the B.H.Sc. was substituted for the
B.A. in 1929. Mount Allison and Acadia offered diploma courses
in 1920 which became degree programs in 1924 and 1925 respectively. St Francis Xavier initiated a program in 1929, Mount Saint
Vincent in 1932, and Western Ontario in 1937. A second attempt
to start a degree course at British Columbia in 1929 went as far
as senate approval and the allocation of funds by the government,
but with the onset of the Depression the funds were withdrawn and
were not again included in the estimates until 1943.[18] In 1940,
the senate placed home economics at the top of a list of schools
or departments which it felt should be established.[19]

By 1920, the English-language institutions which had originally
established programs in household science primarily to provide
training for teachers in the elementary and secondary schools had
developed an interest in dietetics. The household science programs of 1940 continued to emphasize these two fields; the typical
four year program provided for specialization in either field in
the final two years. At all institutions the course was firmly
established at the undergraduate level, but, except at Toronto,
there had been neither development in graduate work nor much opportunity for staff to undertake research.

In 1920, Montréal admitted as an école annexée l'Ecole Saint
Joseph, a school operated by the Soeurs Grises, which offered
instruction in household science to secondary school pupils, and
also a training course in the teaching of household science which
was recognized by the Conseil de l'Instruction publique and for
which Montréal granted a diploma. Similar arrangements were made
with five other écoles ménagères for varying periods of time over
the next two decades, three of which continued to be listed as
écoles annexées in 1940. Instruction in these schools was, admittedly, below degree standard. The need to provide adequate
training for the teachers of household science in the elementary
and secondary schools was the basic stimulus for the establishment of the degree programs in the French-language universities
just as it had been 40 years earlier in the English-language institutions.

In 1938, a three year program leading to the baccalauréate en
science ménagère was authorized, principally for the benefit of
students at the Ecole ménagère provinciale which concentrated on

teacher training. The latter became an école annexée in 1937. Laval had been issuing certificates and diplomas in this field since 1917: in 1940, it authorized a degree program to be offered at Institut Chanoine Beaudet in September 1941. The institute was renamed Ecole supérieure de science domestique de Saint Paul and became an affiliate of Laval in 1942.

In 1939, the Canadian Home Economics Association was organized, and in November 1943 it began regular publication of a newsletter which by 1950 became the *Canadian Home Economics Journal*. The aims of the Canadian Home Economics Association were 'to promote the welfare of the Canadian Home and to serve the community life in Canada.' This was in contrast to the Canadian Dietetic Association established in 1935 which had control over the professional education of dietitians through the authority it possessed to accredit and inspect the intern courses that dietitians in most provinces were required to take in order to be registered. At the time of the establishment of the Canadian Home Economics Association, 11 universities were offering degree courses in household science or home economics. One of them, Toronto, could be said to have two programs, since in addition to offering both three year general and four year honours B.H.Sc. programs in its faculty of household science, it cooperated with the faculty of arts in offering a B.A. (Home Economics). Furthermore, since 1926 it had been accepting into the final year of its three year general course students with senior matriculation who had completed the two year diploma course offered at the Macdonald Institute at Guelph. However, relatively few Macdonald graduates availed themselves of this opportunity.

DENTISTRY

In the 1920s enrolment in dentistry dropped sharply from over 1200 in 1920-21 to under 400 in 1930-31, following which it rose only slightly during the 1930s, 468 in 1940-41. The overall effect on the largest of the five schools, that of the faculty of dentistry at Toronto, is reflected in the number of graduates at five year intervals:

Year	Total Graduates	Toronto Graduates
1921	189	140
1926	150	83
1931	90	59
1936	106	59
1941	98	45

At Dalhousie, serious consideration was given to discontinuing the faculty in the mid-thirties.[20] At Montreal, doubtless in response to dwindling numbers, attempts were made between 1926 and 1934 by the faculté de médecine to lower standards for admission to dentistry, but these were successfully resisted by the Collège des Chirurgiens-Dentistes de la Province de Québec.[21] At all schools there was some improvement in the provision of clinical facilities, although not as much as the deans desired. Nonetheless, dentistry did make noticeable progress during the period, and standards were generally improved.

In 1916, the Canadian Dental Association established a research committee, which in 1917 sponsored a competition for the best piece of research on a dental subject. In 1920, the Canadian Dental Research Foundation was set up with the aim of raising $100,000, half from the profession and half from the public. It also assumed the duties of the research committee. Unfortunately, nothing like $100,000 was obtained; nevertheless, some funds for research projects did become available, and in 1933 a second research prize competition was held. In 1927, two $250 fellowships were established at Toronto to enable graduates to do what faculties of medicine would call an intern year, and in 1928 the Ontario government was persuaded to provide for a $1000 research scholarship at Toronto. These fellowships were available from 1928 to 1932, but were a casualty of the Depression. In 1927 Toronto introduced the B.Sc. in dentistry, comparable to the B.Sc. in medicine, which combined a medical course with an honours course in science; there were 39 graduates by 1939. In 1928 an M.Sc. in dentistry was offered; there were graduates in 1934 and 1936. A second dental graduate was awarded a Ph.D. in 1940.

From 1933 on, a bachelor's degree was required for admission to the faculté at Montréal, and by 1940 the four year course was based in all schools on the equivalent of one year of arts and science beyond senior matriculation with a solid emphasis on the basic biological sciences. From an educational standpoint, the great event of the period was the publication in 1926 of *Dental Education in the United States and Canada*, the Carnegie Corporation study undertaken by W.H. Gies, which argued that dentistry was not a technology but a health science, and consequently 'that its expanding role could only be fulfilled if ... [its] educational pattern were based more solidly on the biological sciences, and if prevention and research were prominent features of dentistry.'[22]

So far as core curriculum was concerned, all the Canadian schools cooperated fully with Dr Gies during the five years of his investigaton, and by 1927 had implemented most of his recommendations. Despite various handicaps, a genuine effort was being made everywhere in Canada to develop graduate work and to undertake research.

PHARMACY

There was a general raising of standards in the pharmacy schools between 1920 and 1940, but the situation did not improve markedly except in the prairie provinces. In Manitoba, the two year diploma course became the admission requirement to the four year

B.Sc. course in 1920, and admission to the diploma course was raised in 1936 from junior matriculation to senior matriculation. In 1938, the Manitoba Pharmaceutical Association adopted the degree as the basis for licensing, and thereafter the only offering was a three year B.Sc. course from senior matriculation. In Saskatchewan, junior matriculation was made the requirement for admission to the two year diploma course in 1923, senior matriculation in 1936. In 1940, the B.Sc. remained optional for licensing but, in 1924, completion of the certificate course in effect became the first two years of the degree course, with provisions being made for the graduate of the diploma course to take the additional courses required for the degree. In Alberta, where it was also possible in 1940 to become licensed without a degree, admission to the two year diploma course was also progressively increased, to junior matriculation in 1924 and to senior matriculation in 1935. In 1939, the school of pharmacy was transferred from the faculty of arts and science back to the faculty of medicine, where it had been located from 1914 to 1917.

There was no significant change during the two decades at Dalhousie, the enrolment in 1940 being 14. Laval established a school in the faculté des arts in 1924 offering a three year course similar to that offered at Montréal, but in 1940 it remained small, with only 20 students. Registration at Montréal had dropped from 177 in 1920 to 83 in 1940. At McGill, the department of pharmacy, which had become a faculty offering a three year degree program in 1927, proved to be a casualty of the Depression and was withdrawn in 1937. The Ontario College of Pharmacy lengthened its courses from one year to two in 1927, and in the same year began to have some of the instruction in the basic sciences provided by departments of the University of Toronto. In 1935, the entrance requirement was changed from junior to senior matriculation. A proposal to extend the course to three years was approved by the college in 1939, but this was not implemented owing to the need for extensive enlargement and modernization of a building that had not been altered since 1891. The plan was ultimately superseded by the decision implemented in 1948, to offer a four year baccalaureate course. Enrolment had increased somewhat by 1940, to 220 as opposed to 168 in 1920, but neither here nor at any other pharmacy school was serious attention given to research. This deficiency was, however, becoming more and more a topic of discussion.

OPTOMETRY

Schools of optometry had existed in different parts of Canada for varying periods of time since the 1890s; all were proprietary schools and some were subsidized by optical firms.[23] In 1923 and 1924 there was discussion of the possibility of establishing a single college of optometry for the whole of Canada. Among the institutions approached in this connection was Toronto, but in

May 1924 the Ontario Board of Examiners was advised that the university was not prepared to give an optometry course. It would, however, be willing to provide instruction in such subjects as an independently established college would not be equipped to offer. The Ontario College of Optometry, set up in 1925, proved to be a successful institution, and by 1937 it had developed a three year course of study beyond senior matriculation. This met the requirements for registration specified in a new Optometry Act passed by the legislature in 1936. Instruction in some subjects was given by departments of Toronto, and in 1938 there was discussion of formal affiliation. However, no action was taken, and the college continued to offer a diploma rather than a degree.

Ontario was not the only province in which there was an interest in providing adequate training for optometrists. It was possible in 1940 to obtain a degree in optometry in Canada, and had been for 15 years. In 1910 an école d'optométrie had been set up in Montreal, and in 1925 it became an affiliate of the Université de Montréal, which henceforth offered a bachélier en optométrie et optique. To qualify for the degree, students with acceptable matriculation requirements were required to take the preparatory year offered in the faculté des sciences and a one year course at Ecole d'optométrie. In 1934 the course was extended to two years.

NURSING

When nursing was suddenly introduced to the university scene at five campuses in 1920, two quite different types of courses were offered: a degree program offering an alternative to the course leading to the registered nurse (RN) certificate offered at hospital schools of nursing, and a number of diploma courses designed to provide additional qualifications for the person who had acquired an RN at a hospital school. Both types of program were inspired by the inadequacies of the training provided by the hospital schools. These shortcomings were eloquently if briefly described by Edith M. Dickson in her first report as inspector of the 90 training schools in the Province of Ontario in 1923: 'These training schools were not established with the idea of preparing young women to care for the sick, but rather as a means of providing an economical service to the sick in the hospitals.'[24]

The traditional RN course paid no heed to the problems of public health, hence the need for additional basic education in this field. No attention was paid to the problems of supervising other nurses or of administering the nursing branches of hospitals, hence the need for training of that type. Since the RN course was badly organized and poorly taught, there was a need for nursing education, and for a new approach to the whole process of producing a registered nurse. What was required was a degree program combining practical experience gained in a hospital and community setting with the theoretical approach characteristic of university studies.

The introduction of a degree program at British Columbia was an
effort to offer a better alternative to the RN training programs.
The diploma courses introduced at Dalhousie, McGill, Toronto, and
Western Ontario were attempts to counteract the same deficiencies.
With the exception of Dalhousie's, which was discontinued in 1923,
the diploma programs were continued and expanded at the other three
institutions over the next two decades. Western Ontario added
diploma courses in hospital administration and instruction in nursing in 1925. In the same year McGill extended its nursing education course to two years. In 1928, Toronto added a diploma course
in hospital school administration. By 1940, British Columbia,
whose degree course from the outset had provided final year options
in nursing education and public health, had initiated diploma
courses in both areas. Diploma courses were also offered in most
of the other universities which entered the nursing education field
between 1920 and 1940. A particularly notable example is Montréal
which in 1925 accepted as an affiliate Ecole d'hygiène sociale
appliquée established in that year. By 1930, the école had 55
graduates from its one year program and had demonstrated its capacity and worth. It had difficulty surviving the Depression through
loss or reduction of grants from the original sponsors which contributed more than $34,000 over a trial period of five years.
The donors were the provincial government, $5000; the city of
Montreal, $5000; the Montreal Anti-Tuberculosis and General Health
League, $14,000; and the Metropolitan Life, $10,720. The two
governments reduced their annual support drastically, and the
other two participants in the scheme eventually withdrew. However, an enthusiastic and generous alumni contributed an average
of $1000 a year between 1933 and 1938, and in 1940 the school was
absorbed by the faculté de médecine, becoming the Ecole d'infir-
mières hygiénists. An institut d'hygiène suggested in 1927 did
not become a reality until 1946.

Even more attention, however, was devoted to the problem of the
basic course in nursing; by 1940 eight universities were offering
a degree program and a ninth, Toronto, was providing the preparation for the RN certificate through a four year diploma course.
With the exception of Toronto and the two French-language universities, all the degree programs followed the model adopted by
British Columbia in 1920, with the practical training in the hospital occupying the third and fourth years. St Francis Xavier
provided a minor exception by scheduling the practical work in
the second and third years; its program was introduced in 1926
with the affiliation of Saint Martha's School of Nursing. Prior
to this, Western Ontario had established a six-year degree program
in 1923, which was reduced to five years in 1931, and Alberta had
introduced a five year program in 1924. However, at Alberta the
university's involvement until 1937 when it introduced a public
health nursing option as a final year program was limited to the
provision of the first two years of arts and science, the students
going to British Columbia or some other institution for the final
year. A school of nursing offering a degree program was established

at the University of Ottawa in 1933 following the affiliation in 1929 of the hospital school operated in the Ottawa General Hospital by the Congrégation des Soeurs Grises de la Croix. In 1923 Université Laval began to affiliate some nursing schools in the Province of Quebec but did not authorize the degree of bachelier en sciences hospitalières until 1933. The same degree was made available at Université de Montréal in 1934 in consequence of the recognition of Institut Marguerite d'Youville as an ecole annexée - a year later it became école affiliée. Finally, in 1938, the University of Saskatchewan established a school of nursing within the college of medical science, with the first academic year available at Regina College as well as at Saskatoon and with hospitals in both Regina and Saskatoon being used for the practical training.

Those responsible for what was called the Graduate School of Nurses at McGill had entertained the idea of a degree course in 1920 and between 1928 and 1931 a serious effort was made to introduce a six year undergraduate course. In 1932 McGill's financial difficulties led the board to declare that 'unless the Nurses Association and others interested can raise sufficient money to support the School for a five year period, it will be discontinued a year hence.'[25] The school did survive largely through the financial support of its alumni who raised $20,000 between 1933 and 1938 but, rather than being expanded, the program had to be reduced; the hospital administration diploma course was dropped and the other courses were reduced in various ways. However, in 1940, responsibility for the school was transferred from the faculty of arts to the faculty of medicine, and under its auspices a degree program was introduced in 1944.

At Toronto, the failure to establish a degree course until 1942 was attributable less to financial problems than to the conviction of Kathleen Russell that the American plan which had been adopted at British Columbia was educationally unsound. Appointed director of the department of public health nursing in 1920, she became almost immediately aware of the impossibility of basing an essentially postgraduate professional course in any branch of nursing on the 'undergraduate' training provided in the hospital schools of nursing. This view was fortified by a visit she made in 1923 to several newly established schools of nursing in Europe made possible by a travel grant from the Rockefeller Foundation, and the remainder of her life was largely dedicated to developing an integrated basic nursing course in which the practical experience the nurse had to obtain in the hospital and community setting was organized and supervised by the university rather than by the hospital.

The first step was the establishment in 1926 of a four year diploma course in which the students spent the first year at the university taking basic courses in arts and science, the second and third at the Toronto General Hospital, and the final year at the university taking the diploma course in public health nursing. While strengthening the registered nurse's academic background, this arrangement did little to improve the coordination of the practical and theoretical work. The next step was taken in 1933 when, following discussions dating back to 1929 with the provincial government, the university board of governors, the faculty of medicine, and the Rockefeller Foundation, a school of nursing was established offering a 39 month basic course in which all instruction, both academic and clinicial, was the responsibility of the school's staff. There was continued cooperation with the Toronto General Hospital and other hospitals and agencies, but it was the school rather than the hospital or agency which decided what experiences the nurse in training should have. Throughout the course, the students lived in a residence (Queen's Hall) provided by the government in which Miss Russell herself had an apartment. The project was made possible by a Rockefeller Foundation grant of $85,000 provided over a five year trial period, a substantial portion of the funds being used to enable staff members to improve their academic qualifications. The program was carried on by the university at the conclusion of the trial period, and in 1942 the final step was taken with the establishment of a degree course (four years from senior matriculation) available only to students entering from the secondary schools. The school continued to offer diploma courses to RNs, but any RNs who wished to obtain the degree were encouraged to enrol in the faculty of arts as regular students.

The inadequacies of nursing education in Canada were set out in a survey commissioned by the Canadian Nurses Association and the Canadian Medical Association in 1927, and published under the title *Nursing Education in Canada* in 1930. Professor G.M. Weir of British Columbia carried out the survey and his recommendations were that the number of schools should be radically reduced, that all should be reorganized as publicly controlled institutions and should be supported by the provinces, and that all should be directly associated with universities. The Canadian Nurses Association was enthusiastic about these recommendations but, for pragmatic reasons, decided to concentrate its efforts on improving the course of study actually offered in the hospital schools. This led to some improvement, but a further study of nursing education in Canada in 1940 based on a questionnaire revealed that the 10,025 currently enrolled in the 172 hospital schools of nursing were still in most cases receiving an indifferent training.[26]

The number of schools had been reduced substantially since the publication of the Weir Report (in 1930 there were 218), but 112 of those remaining were administered by hospitals with fewer than 200 beds, the figure proposed by Weir and many other authorities as the absolute minimum required for an effective educational program. Of the 175 superintendents of nurses, only 34 had university degrees and only 48 had diplomas in teaching or administration of schools of nursing; 86 had no training in teaching or administration of any sort. Of the 211 instructors in the schools of nursing, 25 had university degrees, 118 had diplomas in teaching in schools of nursing, 16 had certificates as school teachers, and 8 had taken summer courses at universities. Clearly, in 1940, the need for the universities to provide more and better degree and diploma courses in nursing was urgent.

PHYSICAL THERAPY AND OCCUPATIONAL THERAPY

Prior to 1920 the involvement of Canadian universities in physical
therapy was limited to the courses for masseuses offered at McGill's
School of Physical Education from 1914 on[27] and the locating at
the University of Toronto in 1917 and 1918 of what was known as
the Hart House School of Massage and Orthopaedic Surgery. In
occupational therapy the earliest trining in Canada was provided
at the University of Toronto in 1918-19, when the council of the
faculty of applied science and engineering established short emergency courses to train occupational therapists for the military
hospitals across Canada. World War I and its consequences for
thousands of disabled veterans had, however, clearly demonstrated
the need for therapists and led in 1920 to the founding of the
Canadian Physiotherapy Association and in 1921 to the founding of
the Ontario Society of Occupational Therapists, which proved to be
the nucleus of the Canadian Association of Occupational Therapists
established in 1930.

Efforts by the Ontario Society of Occupational Therapists resulted in the establishment of a two year diploma course in occupational therapy by the University of Toronto in 1926, the course
being administered by the department of university extension.
Three years later a parallel course in physical therapy was added.
Both courses continued to be offered in 1940; the admission requirement was senior matriculation and the programs included two
months of practical work during the intervening summer. Six additional months of internship in an approved institution was required
if the graduate wished to be registered by the Canadian Physiotherapy Association of the Canadian Association of Occupational
Therapists.

SOCIAL WORK

The basic training for social workers in Canada in 1940 was a two
year diploma course for which the admission requirement was a
bachelor's degree. This was available at Toronto, which had withdrawn its one year certificate course in 1923; at the University
of British Columbia, which had established a two year diploma
course in the department of economics, sociology and political
science (in the faculty of arts and science) in 1929; and at the
Montreal School of Social Work, which had been established in 1933
following the withdrawal by McGill (for financial reasons) of its
department of social science in 1932. At all three institutions
'mature' students with some experience in social work were admissible without the bachelor's degree. Though refined and strengthened through the addition of 20 additional years of experience
and more highly qualified staff, the programs were virtually the
same as those offered at Toronto in its two year diploma course
in 1920.

Since 1929 Dalhousie University had been offering a one year
diploma course for which the entrance requirement was the completion of a first year of arts and science (equivalent to senior

matriculation), including courses in economics and sociology. In 1940, however, negotiations were underway for the establishment of the Maritime School of Social Work, which would open in 1941 under the joint sponsorship of four Maritime universities (King's, St Mary's, Acadia, and New Brunswick) offering a two year diploma course. The University of Manitoba was clearly interested in establishing a course in social work but, no doubt because of financial problems, could only call to the attention of its students in a section of its *Calendar* headed Studies in Social Work the appropriateness of specific courses offered in the faculties of arts and science and of agriculture and home economics for persons interested in social welfare activities whether in a professional way or in an advisory capacity.

Training in social work was one of the areas contemplated for the Ecole des sciences sociales, economiques et politiques when it was established at the Université de Montréal in 1921, but the financial problems of the newly established university did not permit the école to do more than offer some courses in sociology. In 1939, however, the archbishop of Montreal, Mgr Georges Gauthier, who, as rector of the university in 1920, had encouraged the development of the école, persuaded the Institut Notre-Dame du Bon Conseil to institute a course in social work, which was offered to some 60 students in the 1939-40 session. The course was continued in the following year and became the base for the Ecole de service social established in September 1941 in the building occupied by the Ecole des hautes études commerciales; in January 1942 it became an école annexée of the university. Its two year program led to the degree of maîtrise en service social to candidates with a bachelor's degree, or to a diplôme en service social to those without a degree.

LIBRARY SCIENCE

The case for providing adequate training for librarians had been convincingly made in 1933 with the publication of *Training for Library Science*, the report of a Carnegie Corporation study by C.C. Williamson, which recommended: that library schools be located at universities rather than following the American pattern of being attached to public libraries; that admission to the program be restricted to university graduates; and that it should be a degree course.[28]

At the University of Western Ontario a department of library and secretarial science was established in the faculty of arts in 1924, and students were able to specialize in either library science or in secretarial science while pursuing a B.A. The secretarial science major was continued, but no new candidates for the library science program were accepted after 1928.

By 1920, both McGill and Toronto had been offering summer courses for some years, and by 1927 had instituted one year diploma programs. The one-year course at the McGill Library School led initially to a diploma, but from 1930 on, the B.L.S. was authorized and only candidates already holding a degree were admitted. In 1940-41, enrolment was limited to 20. The university, except in 1925, continued to provide summer courses, and the Library School organized summer programs of either four or six weeks' duration at Vancouver in 1930, at Quebec, in French, in 1932, and in Prince Edward Island in 1933. In 1941, it offered a summer library institute at the Banff School of Fine Arts. For its first 10 years of existence, the McGill program was financed with the help of a $135,000 Carnegie Corporation grant.

Toronto's one-year course was located in and administered by the Ontario College of Education, and was directly subsidized by the provincial department of education rather than the university. As at McGill, candidates initially received a diploma, but the B.L.S. was authorized in 1937 for students admitted with a bachelor's degree. The same program could, however, be taken by persons possessing senior matriculation, a year of library work experience, and a certificate indicating that they were on leave of absence from a public library.

Three other universities introduced programs in library science in the late 1930s. Mount Saint Vincent established a B.L.S. degree in 1938 the first of which was awarded in 1940. There continued to be only a handful of students registered until the course was withdrawn in 1957. In 1937, a summer course was offered at the Bibliothèque municipale in Montreal which led to the diplôme de bibliothéconomie et de bibliographie. This was normally obtained after two years; courses were given on Saturdays during the 1938-39 session, and on weekday evenings from 1940 to 1942. A total of 66 diplomas had been granted by the end of 1940. In 1942, the Ecole de bibliothécaires was accepted by Montréal as an école annexée. As such it received no financial support from the university, and continued to be located in the Bibliothèque municipale. At the University of Ottawa, evening courses leading to the B.L.S. degree over a four year period were introduced in 1938, the first class graduating in 1942.

TEACHER TRAINING

So far as universities were concerned, the principal developments in teacher training between 1920 and 1940 occurred in the four western provinces. In each case the university's involvement began with cooperation with the Provincial Department of Education in the offering of summer courses for practising teachers. This led in 1923 to the establishment of a department of education within the faculty of arts at British Columbia; in 1927 to the establishment of a college of education at Saskatchewan; in 1928 to the establishment of a school of education at Alberta; and in 1935 to the establishment of a faculty of education at Manitoba. The basic offering in all cases was a one year certificate course for university graduates, but at Alberta, Manitoba, and Saskatchewan,

417

programs leading to the B.Ed. and M.Ed. degrees were also available from the outset, the former requiring three additional professional education courses beyond the certificate, and the latter requiring additional courses beyond the B.Ed. and a thesis. The B.Ed. was not introduced at British Columbia until 1942.

There was no change in Ontario. Here, all secondary school teacher training was concentrated at the Ontario College of Education, which continued to offer a one year certificate course and whose graduate degrees of M.A., B.Paed., and D.Paed. were available through its association with the school of graduate studies at Toronto. By 1940, the Maritime universities of Acadia, Dalhousie, Mount Allison, and Mount Saint Vincent offered a one year certificate course for graduates which the Nova Scotia department of education recognized as the preferred qualification for high school teaching; instruction was available in one man or two man departments in the faculty of arts and science, but the enrolment was minimal, only a total of 21 in 1940-41. There was no change in the situation at Bishop's or at McGill, but the establishment of the Ecole normale supérieure at Laval, and of the Ecole supérieure de chimie, the faculté des lettres, and the faculté de sciences at Montréal at the beginning of the period provided some additional academic preparation for teachers in the classical colleges. There was some, though not a great deal of attention devoted to the practical problems of teaching. Pedagogy was the primary concern of the Institut des Soeurs de la Congrégation de Notre-Dame, established in 1926, and of the Institut pédagogique Saint-Georges set up by the Brothers of the Christian Schools in 1929. These institutions were intended to train women and men teachers (both lay and religious) at the elementary and pre-school levels. Both became affiliates of Montréal, which awarded a bachelor's degree in education to graduates of a three year course, and a licence to those who completed an additional year of study.

PHYSICAL AND HEALTH EDUCATION

Consentino and Howell, in their book *A History of Physical Education in Canada*, entitled the chapter devoted to the 1920-45 period 'From Drill to Fitness: the Degree Institution.' The first half of the title exemplifies the fact that in the area of physical education, the 1920s and 1930s saw a shift of emphasis away from the military orientation which had characterized earlier programs towards a general and scientifically based concern for health. One spoke now of physical *education* rather than physical *training*, and the term physical education was expanded to physical *and health* education. Indeed, the Depression years of the thirties marked the beginning of the movement to include recreation as a problem area associated with physical education. The second part of the chapter heading is less apt. It is true that degree programs were eventually initiated, but the first one did not appear until 1940 at Toronto, and the next at McGill in 1945.

Throughout the 1920s and 1930s, the departments of education in the various provinces re-evaluated the courses of study in the primary and secondary schools, and one of the consequences of this exercise was the expansion, or in some regions the introduction, of courses in health education. Another was that the amount of time devoted to physical education was increased appreciably. These changes necessitated a re-assessment of the course of study in the normal schools and in the secondary school teacher training institutions. There was, inevitably, an increase in the demand for persons qualified to teach physical and health education. In retrospect it is surprising that so many years passed before any degree program was introduced.

The B.P.H.E. degree was authorized by the senate of the University of Toronto in June 1940, and a school of physical and health education was set up in December; the first students were admitted in September 1941. Some of them had transferred from the Margaret Eaton School which had been absorbed into the new school in May of 1941. This move had been devoutly wished for and advocated as early as 1919. The course was three years from senior matriculation and in the first year the students took five full courses in arts and science - anthropology, biology, chemistry, English, and psychology; one hour courses on the history and philosophy of physical education and on elementary hygiene and first aid, and six hours of practical work. In the second and third years, aside from a second year course in chemistry, the curriculum was divided between health education and physical education, with 30 course hours devoted to the former and 26 to the latter. Under health education there were courses in both years in functional anatomy, applied psychology, and health assessment and promotion, and one year courses in mental hygiene and in hygiene and preventive medicine. The 26 physical education hours included 10 devoted to theory and 16 to practice. In subsequent years, the health education emphasis was reduced and the theoretical aspects of physical education were increased, but the close connection between Toronto's school of physical and health education and its faculty of medicine was maintained.

In 1920, at Toronto a diploma course spread over four years had been offered to both men and women. However, the men's section was discontinued in 1925, and in 1927 the women's program was replaced with a one year diploma course which was now included in the new Toronto school. The status of the diploma was upgraded by the decision of the Ontario department of education to make physical education compulsory in the secondary schools.

At McGill, three unsuccessful attempts were made to launch a degree course there before Dr A.S. Lamb finally, in 1945, won the victory. However, in 1940 the basic program was still a two year diploma course which had been given in 1920. Actually, it was a three year course, since completion of the first year of arts had, since 1934, been required for admission; and there was also a one year diploma course for graduates in arts or science. But there had been loss of some ground since both of these programs were now restricted to women.

One of the outcomes of Dr Lamb's earlier abortive attempts to persuade McGill to introduce a degree program was the redirecting of some of his considerable energy into other ways of promoting physical and health education as an honoured profession. He was the leading spirit, for example, behind the organization of a Quebec Physical Association in 1923. His major achievement occurred 10 years later with the formation of the Canadian Physical Education Association. Its journal, now called the *Canadian Association for Health, Physical Education and Recreation Journal*, dates from 1934.

Lamb's colleague, Ethelmary Cartwright, who must also have experienced some frustration at the slow rate of progress towards realizing a school of physical education at McGill, resigned from that institution in 1928, and a few months later became professor of physical education at the University of Saskatchewan. In 1931, she was made head of a school of physical education for women within the college of education. The core offering of the school was a one year diploma course for graduates in arts and science or of household science who also held a teaching certificate. This program lapsed when Professor Cartwright retired in 1947, but was revived and expanded in the 1950s.

The basis for a degree program to be introduced at University of British Columbia in 1946 had been laid in the late 1930s, the pressure in this case coming in 1934 and from students rather than faculty or administrators. A request presented to the university's president in 1934 that an instructor be appointed to give free physical training 'to students so desiring,' led to the appointment in January 1936 of two instructors in the men's and women's divisions of physical education: 72 men and 300 women applied immediately, and by 1936-37 the numbers had increased to 232 and 404 respectively. In the interests of justifying the provision of more facilities, the students, in 1939, made a further demand: that physical training be made mandatory for all students. This was implemented for men in 1940 with the introduction of compulsory military training. In 1944, the student organization, the Alma Mater Society, as well as the Alumni Association and the senate, recommended that a department of physical education be established. The degree program was finally authorized in 1945.

MUSIC

In a paper entitled 'The Place of Music in a University Curriculum' presented at the 1927 meeting of the National Conference of Canadian Universities, Ernest MacMillan described the situation in the Canadian universities, which was precisely the same as it had been in 1920. 'The majority of our universities already recognize the vocational side of music and provide in so far as they

420

are able courses which aim at training the professional musician.
Such courses do not, as a rule, lay emphasis upon performance,
this is more frequently left to purely musical institutions, which
may or may not have university affiliations, but which in practice
are largely independent in their curricula.'[29] He went on to
question whether it was in the interests of the professional musician to obtain his training exclusively in a professional school,
arguing that the musician should be educated in the theory of
music as well as trained in its practice: 'The danger is that
students may come to regard such subjects as harmony and counter-
point as a variety of musical mathematics or even as a sort of
jig-saw puzzle. The real function of such study should be ... to
enable students to think in musical terms, to apprehend a compo-
ser's intentions, to separate essentials from non-essentials, to
view various types of music in historical perspective, and, in
so far as technical knowledge and practice can ensure it to become
composers themselves.' The advantage of the faculty of music over
the professional school was not only that it was considered to be
in a position to give due attention to theory, but also that,
requiring as it did matriculation for admission it ensured that
the student had a reasonably balanced general education and furthermore enabled him to pursue his musical studies in a setting
which was cosmopolitan rather than narrowly provincial. Musicians
should not associate only with other musicians.

What concerned MacMillan more than anything else in 1927 was
the failure of the Canadian universities to pay any attention to
music as a liberal arts subject. It was not available for credit
in any B.A. program, and in his view it had quite as solid a claim
for inclusion as other art forms such as literature. In this connection, there was some improvement by 1940, most notably at
Toronto where an honours course in music was introduced in 1935
and at Saskatchewan where, with the help of a $33,000 Carnegie
grant, a chair of music was established in 1930 for the purpose
of 'not only the provision of advanced instruction for students
entering the music profession, but also the cultivation of a
popular taste and appreciation through public lectures and cooperation with the Provincial and Local Musical Festivals.'
Manitoba accepted music as an elective in the junior division of
Arts and Science in 1930, Saskatchewan in the General B.A. program
in 1931. The cause of general musical education during the 1930s
was advanced by the distribution of Carnegie Corporation music
sets to 14 institutions.[30]

MacMillan was hardly correct in saying that the majority of
Canadian universities provided courses for professional musicians;
nor would his statement have applied to 1940. The B.Mus. continued to be offered as it had been in 1920 at Acadia, Bishop's,
Dalhousie, McGill, Mount Allison, and Toronto, and degree programs
had been introduced at Laval, Montréal, Mount Saint Vincent, and
Saskatchewan. Except at Montréal where 116 students were registered for a degree and at Toronto where there were 28, the numbers
were small: 5, for example, at Dalhousie, and 7 at McGill.

In French-Canada the main development between 1920 and 1940 was
the establishment of graduate degrees (the licence and the doctorat
in sacred music and music generally) at both Laval and Montréal.
Bachelor's degrees were also available to students at the Ecole
de musique established within the faculté des arts by Laval in
1922, and at the écoles annexées at Montréal whose numbers had
been increased by three during the 1930s. An Ecole de musique et
de declamation offering diploma courses was established at the
University of Ottawa in 1933.

FINE ART

In 1920, C.T. Currelly, who was director of the Royal Ontario
Museum and also professor of history of industrial art at Toronto,
offered three courses under the rubric World History, which could
be taken by students of the third and fourth years in the faculty
of arts. One of these was a course on the history of art, and it
was either the only one or one of the very few such courses offered
for credit at a Canadian university. Responsibility for courses
in art was left to the non-degree granting professional schools
such as the school of art and design established by the art association of Montreal in 1882; the Nova Scotia College of Art, set
up as the Victoria College of Art and Design at Halifax in 1887;
the Ontario College of Art initiated as the Toronto Art School in
1876, but renamed and reorganized by the provincial government in
1912; the Winnipeg School of Art originating in 1913; and the
provincial institute of technology and art at Calgary first appearing in 1916. Aside from the Ecole des beaux arts de Québec
set up in 1921, of the Ecole des beaux arts de Montréal in 1923,
and the Vancouver School of Art in 1925, the situation remained
static throughout the 1920s.
By 1940, the position had altered, largely due to the generosity
of the Carnegie Corporation of New York. In addition to providing
its $5000 sets of slides, books, and other visual material to 11
universities, funds were provided to five of them to develop various types of fine art programs. Both McMaster and Toronto received
grants of close to $50,000 over a period of five years for the
purpose of establishing departments of fine art in the faculty of
arts. At McMaster, the department was formed in 1933, and by 1940
it was giving six courses, though students could not take fine art
as a major. Most of the funds were used to provide for the salary
of the professor and although the course was still given after the
termination of the Carnegie grant, it was withdrawn in 1943 when
the professor left for war service. At Toronto, the department
was set up in 1934, and a four year honours course in fine art
was initiated in 1935. More than 30 courses were listed in the
calendar in 1940-41; the staff consisted of three full-time members, a part-time instructor, and a number of cross appointments
from the department of architecture of the faculty of applied
science and engineering. Fine Art was available as a major in

the general B.A. program. Alberta's Carnegie grant of $56,000 was used to launch the Banff School of Fine Arts, which confined its activities to summer school programs. Queen's used its grant to hire Goodridge Roberts as resident artist for three years. With the expiry of the Carnegie support in 1936, the university assumed responsibility for the program, and André Bieler became resident artist with the task of presenting two credit courses scheduled in alternate years. Acadia, had established a department of art in 1928, following its merger with the Acadia Ladies Seminary. The Carnegie funds were used primarily to permit the professor, Walter Abell, to conduct a survey of art activities in the Maritime provinces. Acadia's department of art and aesthetics, which Abell had started in 1928 with two full and two half courses, had been extended to seven full courses by 1940, although not all were offered each year. Four of them were required for a major in the general course and five were mandatory for an honours degree.

Credit courses towards the B.A. were also available in 1940 at Mount Allison, St Francis Xavier, Saskatchewan, and Sir George Williams. Courses in the history of art were, by this time, common in the programs offered for degrees in architecture and, since 1920, there had been a professor of the history of art in the faculté des lettres at Montréal. From 1937 on, moreover, it had been possible to obtain a Bachelor of Fine Arts degree at Mount Allison. This was a four year course with a fairly even distribution between the theoretical and practical subjects. The first two years were taken in common by all students, but the third and fourth year students could concentrate on fine art proper or on preparation for teaching art in the schools.

NOTES TO CHAPTER 22

1 During the 1920s the NCCU's concern with professional education took the form of standing committees which normally presented reports to the conference at the annual meeting. In 1929 there were five such committees (Engineering Education, Legal Education, Dental Education, Medical Education, Graduate Studies and Research), as well as standing committees on Sabbatical Leave, Oriental Studies, Publication of Results of Scholarship and Research, and Athletics. In 1930 the conference discharged all standing committees.
2 *NCCU Proc.* (1920), 20-1
3 Ibid. (1922), 18
4 W. Packenham, 'The University and the Training of Teachers for Secondary Schools,' *NCCU Proc.* (1922), 36-44
5 Ibid. (1923), 16
6 Ibid. (1930), 19-21, 74-80; ibid. (1932), 61-9
7 The statistics in this and the following paragraphs and, with respect to enrolment figures, generally throughout the chapter, are taken from Dominion Bureau of Statistics, *Higher Education*

in *Canada 1940-42,* Part II of the Biennial Survey of Education in Canada 1940-42 (1944) and from *Higher Education in Canada 1944-46,* Part II of the Biennial Survey of Education in Canada 1944-46 (1949).

8 *Higher Education in Canada 1944-46,* 16. See also *Higher Education in Canada 1940-42,* 18-19, where - it should be noted - figures for certain Roman Catholic theological schools are *not* reported.

9 On Toronto Baptist Seminary, see D.C. Masters, *Protestant Church Colleges in Canada* (1966), 188.

10 See below, chapter 28, 530.

11 In 1931 the endowment funds of the Diocese of Rupert's Land were lost through the fraudulent activities of its chancellor, J.A. Machray. See W.L. Morton, *One University: a History of the University of Manitoba* (1957), 147.

12 Masters, *Protestant Church Colleges,* 173-85

13 For a concise account of the reforms proposed by *Deus Scientarium Dominus,* see L.K. Shook, *Catholic Post-Secondary Education in English-Speaking Canada* (1971), 106-7, 217-18.

14 R.D. Defries, *The First Forty Years, 1914-1955: Connaught Medical Research Laboratories* (1969)

15 Part I (pp. 3-49) of D.S. Lewis, *The Royal College of Physicians and Surgeons of Canada, 1920-1960,* is devoted to its 'pre-history' and its initial development (to June 1931).

16 H.S. Logan, *Tuum Est: a History of the University of British Columbia* (1958), 124

17 G.A. Garrett, *Forestry Education in Canada* (1971), 146

18 Logan, *Tuum Est,* 88

19 Ibid., 97

20 J.D. McLean, 'Faculty of Dentistry, Dalhousie University,' *J. Can. Dent. Assoc.,* 31 (1965), 298. See also A.E. Kerr, *The Post-War Years, 1945-63 ... Highlights of the Development of the Period by Faculties* (1963), where McLean notes (29-31) that the faculty received no financial support from any of the Maritime provinces until 1947, that at that point there had been only one full-time teacher in the history of the school, and that none of the part-time teachers was devoting more than one half-day a week to the work of the faculty.

21 P. Hamel, 'Evolution de la dentisterie dans Québec et la région de 1902 à nos jours,' *J. Can. Dent. Assoc.,* 18 (1952), 377

22 R.G. Ellis, 'Faculty of Dentistry, University of Toronto,' *J. Can. Dent. Assoc.,* 31 (1965), 331

23 For the early development of optometry, see E.J. Fisher, 'Optometrical Education in Canada,' *Can. J. Optometry, 29* (1967), 81-98.

24 Ontario, *Report of the Inspector of Training Schools in the Province of Ontario* (1923)

25 B.L. Tunis, *In Caps and Gowns: the Story of the School of Graduate Nurses, McGill University, 1920-1964* (1966), 47

26 A.J. MacLeod, 'Nursing Education in Canada,' *Can. Nurs.*, 36 (1940), 666
27 See above, chapter 16, 299.
28 V. Ross, 'The McGill University Library School,' *Can. Lib. Assoc. Bull.*, 14 (1958), 206-11
29 *NCCU Proc.* (1927), 66-75
30 For details of the Carnegie Corporation's support of the development of music in Canada, see S.H. Stackpole, *Carnegie Corporation: Commonwealth Program 1911-1961* (1963), 39-49; and R.M. Lister, *Music Study Material* (1941).

23

Graduate Studies-1940

While the National Conference of Canadian Universities devoted a
good deal of attention to graduate studies at its meetings from
1915 to 1918, particularly with respect to achieving better cooperation between McGill and Toronto, the two chief centres for such
work, the standing committee appointed to study such matters did
not report in 1919, and in 1920 the conference agenda included
only a discussion of ways and means to encourage British universities to be more accommodating in their response to Canadians
interested in pursuing graduate studies in the United Kingdom.
However, when the conference next met in 1922 papers were presented
by F.D. Adams of McGill and R.W. Brock of British Columbia presenting two new approaches to the solution of the general problem.
Adams advocated the adoption of the German model whereby accredited
students pursued their studies over a three year period at whichever universities could cater to their particular needs, and then
presented themselves for examination for the doctoral degree at
any of the institutions at which they had studied. In this way,
Adams suggested, 'the entire resources of higher education teaching
in the Dominion would be given to every student and a national
system of graduate instruction would thus be brought into being.[1]
Brock proposed the establishment of a national graduate school at
Ottawa, which could draw on the facilities provided by 'specialized
libraries, original research material, certain laboratories, and
highly specialized workers that are not duplicated by any of our
universities.'[2] In the ensuing discussion there was some support
for both proposals and a suggestion that Montreal would be preferable to Ottawa as the site of Brock's national school. But the
only action taken was agreement to devote a full day of the 1923
conference to a full discussion of these and any other proposals.
   The conference did not in fact follow this procedure in 1923,
but on the morning of 15 June the committee on research reported
that it had met to study the Adams and Brock proposals as well as
another put forward by Professor W. Sage (British Columbia). The

latter suggested that all Ph.D. work in any university should come under the aegis of a graduate study board made up of a representative from each institution 'which is ready to undertake Ph.D. work in full or in part.'[3] The committee had found both the Sage and Brock plans unworkable because 'direction and control of the student would not rest definitely with the University to which the student was attached.'[4] The Adams plan was approved in principle, and it was recommended to the conference that a special committee be appointed to work out the details. Seven members were invited to partake in the study, with Adams as chairman. The conference did not meet again until 1925, by which time Adams had ceased to be responsible for graduate work at McGill and was not present at the meeting. A small group from the special committee appeared for a scheduled meeting prior to the conference proper. The outcome of their deliberations was agreement that the special committee should be merged with the standing committee, which should be called the committee on graduate studies and research. This was subsequently endorsed by the conference.

Because of difficulties in finding a suitable time and place for a meeting of the committee prior to the 1927 conference, it did not give a report. However its chairman, R.F. Ruttan of McGill, submitted a memorandum 'Notes on the Master's Degree in Canadian Universities,' in which he stated that it had been suggested to the committee that it would be advantageous if it would confine its work to the requirements for the master's degree. He also reported on the results of a questionnaire on the subject of master's programs which had been completed by 17 of 18 institutions contacted: 'It is interesting to note that the number in attendance is increasing annually, and there is greater uniformity in the requirements for the Master's degree at present than was the case in 1915-16.' However, there was no cause for complacency, the chairman said, because there was no consensus as to the 'significance' or 'function' of the M.A. degree. In the experimental sciences, for example, it seemed to be looked upon as a preparation for the Ph.D. The chairman called for 'a free discussion of the place and function of the Master's degree ... (which) may lead to harmony where at present there is ... discord.'[5]

In 1928 there was again a new chairman, H.M. Tory, and while he reported some progress he stressed the intention of the members of his committee during the coming year to proceed actively with their task in the hope of making concrete proposals at the 1929 conference. The lengthy report presented at that session was discussed by the delegates but was not printed in its *Proceedings*. Then, in 1930, *all* the standing or working committees of the conference were discharged. For the next 12 years the only NCCU committees were the executive and nominating committees. The agenda of the meetings consisted of the presentation and discussion of individual papers; however, this did not mean that the problems of graduate work ceased to be discussed.

Papers on 'Undergraduate Preparation for Post-Graduate Study' (R.A. Falconer), 'Graduate Work at McGill University' (F.C.

Harrison), and 'Graduate Work in Toronto in Non-Scientific Subjects' (G.S. Brett, Toronto) were presented at the 1929 conference, and a very lengthy and at times heated discussion followed which is fully reported in the *Proceedings*. A session on 'Graduate Studies in Canada' was held in 1934, with papers by Brett ('Graduate Studies in the Arts and Sciences'), R.W. Brock, ('In Applied Science'), Robert Newton, Alberta ('In Agriculture'), and C.F. Martin, McGill ('Graduate Facilities in Medicine in Great Britain'). A paper entitled 'Promotion of Research within the University and Inter-University Cooperation' was presented at the 1939 conference by R.W. Boyle of the National Research Council; apparently the longest paper ever printed in the conference's proceedings, it was devoted chiefly to documenting the unsatisfactory state of graduate studies in Canada.

Two points emerge as one reads these presentations and discussions - three if one includes the general impression that the situation was not satisfactory. The first is the failure to achieve any effective coordination of the work being done in the individual institutions; McGill and Toronto continued to pursue their own paths and not to take seriously the complaint of the other universities, particularly those in Western Canada, that their students were being discriminated against when applying to Toronto or McGill. The second point is a more positive one: the conviction that graduate work at both the master's and doctoral levels should be based on the honours B.A. As Brett put it in 1939: 'the difference, in point of development, between undergraduate and graduate work, consists in a change of mental attitude, a progress in which the receptive mood usually carried over from the school into the University gives place to the synthetic, constructive outlook of the more mature mind.'[6] Almost every speaker in this 20 year debate not only agreed with Brett's distinction, but was convinced that the graduate of an honours course was much more likely to have achieved this synthetic, constructive outlook than was the graduate of the cafeteria-style pass or general course.

The development of graduate studies in the Canadian universities between 1920 and 1940 can be seen in broad outline by a comparison of the numbers of full-time students enrolled and degrees granted in the years 1920, 1930, and 1940:[7]

	1920	1930	1940
Graduate enrolment	423	1350	1569
Percentage of total enrolment	1.8	4.1	4.3
M.A.s granted	147	274	258
M.Sc.s granted	30	93	118
Licences granted	41	91	211
Ph.D.s granted	24	46	75
Other graduate degrees granted	6	36	175

One notes a basic tripling in full-time graduate enrolment in the course of the two decades as well as of the ratio of graduate students to undergraduates. There were substantial increases in each type of degree granted but the main increase in the numbers of M.A.s and M.Sc.s had occurred by 1930. The number of doctorates approximately doubled in each decade. The 1930s were marked by a considerable increase in the number of licences and in the number of 'other graduate degrees,' reflecting in the first case the long wished-for introduction of systematized graduate studies in the French-language universities, and in the second the expansion of graduate work into professional fields such as agriculture, engineering, and education.

Detailed accounts of the position of graduate studies in the Canadian universities, particularly with reference to the humanities and the social sciences, are provided in three reports published between 1942 and 1947: W.N. Sage, *Graduate Training in Arts in Canadian Universities with Special Reference to Requirements for the M.A. and Ph.D. degrees*, 1942; J.B. Brebner, *Scholarship for Canada: The Function of Graduate Studies*, 1945; and W. Kirkconnell and A.S.P. Woodhouse, *The Humanities in Canada*, 1947. The Sage and Brebner studies were sponsored by the Canadian Social Science Research Council, which had been established in 1940, and the Kirkconnell-Woodhouse study by the Humanities Research Council of Canada, which had been established with the assistance of the Canadian Social Science Research Council in 1943.[8] The Sage study was based on an examination of the situation in 1942-43, the other two, both of which involved actual visits to the institutions, on the situation in 1944-45; but since there were no essential changes during the war period these reports reflect the situation in 1940.

The Sage study was the briefest and the most factual, with chapters devoted to the requirements for the M.A. and the Ph.D. in the English-speaking universities and for the licence and doctorat in the French-speaking universities, outlining procedures with respect to admission, course work, residence, and thesis. There was also a short chapter on the organization of graduate studies in the individual institutions. The Brebner study was a more philosophical treatment based in part on the details provided by Sage. The Kirkconnell-Woodhouse study, which was both detailed and philosophic, included chapters on graduate studies in the English-speaking and French-speaking universities but also on the general or pass course, the honours course, the classical college course, the position of the humanities in the secondary schools and in the professional faculties, as well as on libraries and on aids to scholarship (journals, university presses, fellowships). A list of the publications completed or in progress by 240 scholars in the humanities was included in an appendix. The authors of all three studies admitted to difficulty in attempting to compare graduate work in the English- and French-

speaking universities. The M.A. was not really comparable to the
licence, nor the Ph.D., offered at Toronto and McGill based essentially on the United States model, to the doctorat offered at
Laval, Montréal, and Ottawa, a fact borne out by the offering by
the French-language institutions of an 'M.A. anglais' and a Ph.D.
Hence, we shall deal separately with the English- and French-
language institutions.

ENGLISH-LANGUAGE INSTITUTIONS

A signficant development at the master's level during the two
decades was the extension of the degree into additional professional fields: architecture (M.Arch. at Toronto), education (B.Ed.
and M.Ed. at Alberta, M.Ed. at Saskatchewan), dentistry at Toronto
(shortly after the integration of the Royal College of Dental Surgeons as the university's faculty of dentistry in 1925), veterinary medicine at Toronto (through its affiliate the Ontario
Veterinary College at Guelph). A special M.Sc. in fisheries was
now offered at Dalhousie, drawing on the staff and facilities of
the Fisheries Research Board of Canada, which had been established
at St Andrew's, New Brunswick in succession to the Biological Board
of Canada in 1928.[9]   A master's degree in agriculture had been
established at Saskatchewan by 1920. By 1940 it was also offered
at British Columbia and McGill, through their faculties of agriculture (the latter located at Macdonald College at Ste Anne de
Bellevue) and at Toronto through its affiliate, the Ontario Agricultural College at Guelph. Toronto continued to offer the B.Paed.
as well as an M.A. in educational theory. The master's degree
in engineering (M.Eng. at McGill, but normally an M.Sc.) continued
to be available at the major institutions as it had been in 1920.
  All the large and most of the medium-sized institutions (e.g.,
Acadia and Western Ontario) offered the M.A. and the M.Sc., though
some institutions, notably Toronto, continued to grant the M.A.
rather than the M.Sc. to students in mathematics and science.
The program had become standardized, a one year course from the
honours B.A. or B.Sc., the applicant with a general pass degree
usually being required to devote an additional year to completing
the requirements for an honours degree. The master's degree was
available in most subjects for which there was an undergraduate
honours course, but in the Maritimes staff resources largely confined the program to the fields of English and history. A thesis
was normally required, as was the concentration on a single subject, but a two subject master's degree could be taken at Bishop's,
British Columbia, Mount Allison, and New Brunswick. Only British
Columbia required a second language (French or German), but the
requirement could easily be met by courses previously taken as
an undergraduate. At Mount Allison arrangements had been made
for the M.A. to be taken during four summer sessions. The M.A.
at Ottawa, a bilingual institution which had not developed an
undergraduate honours course system, was of a different pattern,

430

a two year course involving a major and a minor chosen from five subjects (English, French, history, philosophy, mathematics) and an 80 page thesis. A somewhat similar arrangement applied to the M.A. (Anglais) offered at Montréal and to the Maîtrise en arts en français offered at Laval.

McGill and Toronto continued to be the only institutions providing a fully developed Ph.D. program; in 1940 they granted 32 and 33 degrees respectively and had 100 and 140 students enrolled at the doctoral level. The Ph.D. was now available at McGill in economics and political science, history, and psychology, but there were few candidates, and Toronto continued to be the only institution with substantial doctoral programs in the humanities and social sciences. Two other universities granted a handful of Ph.D.s between 1920 and 1940, Manitoba 8 (all in subjects related to biology or biochemistry) and Queen's 6 (two in history, one each in mathematics, French and German, philosophy, physics). Alberta offered the D.Sc. as an earned degree, the requirement for it being an M.Sc., the passage of seven years from the obtaining of a bachelor's degree, and evidence of original work. McGill had similar arrangements for the D.Sc. and also for the D.C.L. and the D.Litt., though without the requirement of a master's degree. The requirements for the Ph.D. at McGill and Toronto had also become systematized, essentially in conformity with those recognized by the Association of American Universities, of which both institutions had become members in 1927: three years of full-time study beyond the bachelor's degree, a specified number of graduate courses, facility in two languages, the passing of written general examinations in the major field, the inclusion of at least one minor cognate subject, and the completion and oral defence of a thesis 'embodying the results of original investigation' (Toronto) or 'representing a distinct contribution to knowledge' (McGill). Both institutions had also brought graduate studies under centralized university control through the establishment at Toronto óf a school of graduate studies in 1922 and at McGill of a faculty of graduate studies and research in 1923. Alberta established a school of graduate studies in 1938.

FRENCH-LANGUAGE INSTITUTIONS

Until 1930 graduate work at Laval and Montreal was to all intents and purposes confined to providing (a) training for candidates for advanced degrees in theology and scholastic philosophy and (b) additional (to the B.A.) academic preparation for teachers in the classical colleges. The attempt to establish an école normale supérieure at both Laval and Montreal during the first two decades of the century has been described in chapter 16,[10] and by 1920 the objective had been literally achieved at Laval, and in fact if not in name at Montréal with the creation of facultés des lettres et des sciences. In 1921 Laval also established an Ecole Supérieure de chimie, like the Ecole normale

supérieure within the faculté des arts and it too was concerned
with the training of secondary school teachers. Throughout the
1920s the efforts of all four of these divisions were for the most
part, though not exclusively (on the science side there was also
attention given to preparing students for such professional courses
as dentistry, medicine, and optometry) concentrated on upgrading
the classical college teacher academically and in improving his
pedagogical skills. So far as both staff and students were concerned, most of this work was on a part-time basis; Montréal, for
example, had no full-time professors in its faculté des lettres
until 1943, and the majority of students both here and in the
Ecole normale supérieure at Laval were active teachers who, by
attending evening or Saturday classes over a period of years,
were able to qualify for a diploma or a licence. At Montréal the
position changed in 1940 with the establishment of an Ecole normale secondaire at the affiliated Séminaire de Philosophie, which
made it possible for the faculté des lettres henceforth to direct
its attention increasingly to genuine graduate work and research,
the possibilities for which were greatly enhanced in 1942 when at
long last the university's permanent building was completed and
occupied. At Laval, the position changed in 1937 with the establishment of facultés des lettres et des sciences, responsibility
for teacher training remaining with the faculté des arts and the
affiliated teacher training institutions which had been established
in the previous ten years.[11] In 1938 Laval established an Ecole
des gradués within its faculté des sciences, but in 1940 this
school assumed responsibility for graduate work in all divisions
of the university.

By 1940 systematic programs for the licence and the doctorat
had been developed at both Laval and Montréal in theology, philosophy, lettres, science, law, and agriculture and at Laval in
canon law as well. The licence was also available at both institutions in commerce. 'Systematic' is perhaps stretching the term
somewhat in the case of law, since all that was required for the
licence was the taking of some additional courses and for the
doctorat the presentation of a thesis, and in agriculture, commerce, and social sciences where the faculties or schools concerned had only been authorized recently to grant degrees beyond
the baccalaureate and where an additional year of study was the
main qualification. In the other faculties, however, the requirements were specific and rigorous. In theology, philosophy, and
canon law, the requirements accorded with those specified by the
papal encyclical *Deus Scientiarum Dominus* of 1931; in philosophy,
for example, the licence at Montréal required a year of study
beyond the B.Phil. (for which the B.A. was a pre-requisite) and
the presentation of a thesis, while the doctorat required a further year of study and a presentation and defence of a second
thesis. At Laval, two years of study were technically required
for each degree. A still more advanced degree, the maître agrégé
de la faculté de philosophie de Laval was also available to holders of the degree of docteur en philosophie who, after conducting

two years of research at another university, published yet another
thesis on a different subject and successfully defended both it
and 50 propositions covering the whole field of philosophy before
a specially invited jury of specialists in the thesis field. The
doctorat en théologie required five years of study beyond the B.A.
The licence ès sciences required two years of study, involving
three of the six subjects offered (biology, chemistry, physics,
mathematics, geology and mineralogy, mining engineering and metallurgy), the doctorat ès sciences (of which two were granted in
1940) a third year of study and both a major and a minor thesis.
In 1940, Laval established in the faculté des lettres a doctorat
ès lettres which normally was taken only by French-speaking candidates already possessing the licence. Essentially a research
degree and limited to the fields of Greek, Latin, French, French
Canadian and comparative literatures, it required five or six
years for the preparation of a thesis of about 600 pages, which
after being defended had to be published before the degree was
granted. A year or two later Montréal established essentially
the same degree but, in line with its inclusion of history, geography and the history of art in its faculté des lettres licence
program, these subjects were also available to candidates for
the doctorat ès lettres. In the early 1940s, too, both universities established degrees basically for English-speaking candidates
in the faculté des lettres, the doctorat ès arts at Montréal, and
the doctorat de l'Université at Laval requiring only one year of
residential study at the university and a much shorter thesis.
It is significant that these degrees were frequently described
as the 'Ph.D. Américain.' At the University of Ottawa a similar
situation had developed by 1940 except that the advanced graduate
degree work was limited to theology, philosophy, and lettres. It
too offered in lettres M.A.s and Ph.D.s for English-speaking candidates and licences and doctorats ès lettres for French-speaking
candidates.

FELLOWSHIPS

The relatively retarded development of graduate studies in the
humanities and social sciences, particularly at the doctoral
level, in the Canadian universities in 1940 was to a considerable
degree attributable to the lack of scholarships and fellowships
available to students who wished to pursue their advanced studies
in Canada. Ironically, most of the scholarships and fellowships
available to them were specifically for study abroad, notably
the Rhodes scholarships which required attendance at Oxford, the
travelling scholarships established, one for each province, by
the Imperial Order of the Daughters of the Empire, which required
study in the United Kingdom, and a number which could be held in
the United States, France, or some other country, such as the
fellowships established by the Royal Society of Canada in 1931
(with funds provided by the Carnegie Corporation), those periodi-

cally granted by the Massey Foundation, and those granted to Quebec citizens by that province. The only new fellowships of this kind which could be held in a Canadian university were the two established by the Canadian Federation of University Women which were available only to women. Several Canadian universities also provided travelling fellowships for their own graduates, notably British Columbia, Manitoba, McGill, Queen's, and Toronto, but again several of these were specifically for study abroad. In the circumstances it is not surprising that financial support for graduate students in the humanities and social sciences at Canadian universities in the 1920s and 1930s depended largely on funds provided by the institutions themselves, and in the 1930s particularly funds of any sort were in short supply.

In the sciences, the situation was much better owing to the program of assistance for graduate studies provided by the National Research Council of Canada.[12] This program instituted in 1917-18, with *bursaries* for students embarking on a master's degree, *studentships* for students in the first year of a doctoral program, and *fellowships* for students in the second year of a doctoral program provided support in the course of the two decades for at least 500 persons – the exact number is difficult to estimate since many individuals successively received each type of grant as they proceeded through their program. Between 1921-22 and 1940-41 a total of 94 fellowships, 319 studentships, and 499 bursaries were granted at a total cost of $638,842. Both the amount of the grants and the number of awards varied substantially in the course of the two decades, the high point coming in 1930-31 when nearly $60,000 was distributed to seven fellows (one at $1750, one at $1500, five at $1000), 22 students ($750), and 35 bursars ($600). In 1933-34 two fellowships were granted at $550, six studentships at $500, and six bursaries at $450 for a total expenditure of just over $9000. The 1940-41 figure of $31,900 was less than in any year during the 1920s, but it did accommodate a larger number of students than in any previous year except 1939-40: four fellowships ($750), 36 studentships ($650), 22 bursaries ($250). In addition, the National Research Council extended its scholarship program in 1938-39 to provide for postdoctoral fellowships to be held in its own laboratories. There were two such special fellowships (at $1000) in 1940-41.

The bulk of these awards were for study in the fields of chemistry and physics and the institutions at which the students pursued their studies were principally McGill and Toronto. But the students themselves came from almost all the universities in Canada as can be illustrated by reference to the 1940-41 awards which involved students from 16 institutions including Acadia, Bishop's, Montreal, Mount Allison, and St Francis Xavier. It is worthy of special note that 15 of the 63 awards made in 1940-41 were to graduates of Saskatchewan. Of the 63, 26 went to McGill, 11 to Toronto, 2 to Queen's, and one each to Alberta and Laval for doctoral studies, and 6 to each of McGill and Saskatchewan, 3 to each of Manitoba and Queen's, and one to each of Acadia, British Columbia

Dalhousie and Montreal for master's work. Their fields of study were chemistry 29, physics 12, biology 7, biochemistry 5, geology 4, genetics 3, and one each for mathematics, chemical engineering, plant pathology, and physiology.

NOTES TO CHAPTER 23

1 F.D. Adams, 'Graduate Work in the Canadian Universities,' *NCCU Proc.* (1922), 56
2 R.W. Brock, 'Canadian Graduate School,' *NCCU Proc.* (1922), 58
3 'Report of Committee on Graduate Work,' *NCCU Proc.* (1923), 52
4 Ibid., 56
5 R.F. Ruttan, 'Notes on the Master's Degree in Canadian Universities,' *NCCU Proc.* (1927), 125-6
6 G.S. Brett, 'Graduate Work in Toronto in Non-Scientific Subjects,' *NCCU Proc.* (1929), 42
7 W.P. Thompson, *Graduate Work in the Sciences in Canadian Universities* (1963), 31
8 See below, chapter 30, 570-1.
9 See above, chapter 18, 321-2.
10 See above, chapter 16, 296-7.
11 See above, chapter 22, 418.
12 The statistics in this and the following paragraph are taken from J.C. Miller, *National Government and Education in Federated Democracies - Canada* (1940), 476-89 for the years 1920-21 to 1936-37, and from *National Research Council Annual Reports* for the years 1937-38 to 1940-41.

24

Scholarship and Research

'The day of science has arrived.'[1] This remark was made in the
House of Commons on 28 April 1921 by Alfred Thompson, the parliamentary representative from the Yukon and also a member of the
special committee appointed in 1919 to study the development of
scientific research in Canada. The context was the extensive
debate on second reading of the bill introduced in the House to
implement the committee's recommendation that the National Research
Institute be established in Ottawa. This bill, which would have
provided the National Research Council with its own laboratories,
was passed on 10 May, but it was defeated in the senate by a vote
of 34 to 16 on 27 May. Seven years passed before the council was
officially authorized to set up its own laboratories, and it was
not until September 1932 that the building on Sussex Drive in
Ottawa was formally opened. Nonetheless, strong support for
Thompson's assertion of April 1921 had been in the wind, for it
was just three weeks later, on 16 May 1921, that Frederick Banting
and Charles Best commenced their experimental work at the University of Toronto which, within months, resulted in the discovery
of insulin. This important discovery, along with other successful
experiments conducted both in universities and at NRC which focused on pressing problems such as the phenomenon of wheat rust
and the tendency of concrete to lose its cohesive qualities in
very low temperatures, demonstrated the very real value not only
of applied research but of the pure research on which applied
research depended. However, although the National Research Council
was provided with an increased budget to provide more scholarship
programs and there was a dynamic development of its assisted research grants-in-aid program, the effects of the Depression were
soon to take their toll. Gradually support for such activities
declined and they did not come back to 1930-31 standards until
1940. Nevertheless, NRC had received authority to build the
laboratories before the onset of the Depression and the move into
them took place in 1932. Despite drastic budget cuts in the 1930s,

the scholarship[2] and the assisted research programs[3] were maintained at as high a level as possible.

With the establishment of its own laboratories in 1932, the NRC could be said to be in direct competition with the universities since its research activities were not confined to applied as distinct from pure research. The fact that there would be such competition was an argument advanced by those opposing the building of the laboratories. However, relations between the universities and NRC remained on the whole harmonious throughout this period. This is not surprising, perhaps, when one takes into account that the various chief executives of NRC were university men, as were nearly all members of the council.

Although some progress in the area of scholarship and research was made in the scientific fields, the same could not be said of the social sciences or humanities. There was increasing recognition of the validity of fundamental studies in such subjects as literature, history, and economics, but there was little movement towards founding organizations designed to encourage scholarship in the humanities and social sciences until the very late 1930s and not much improvement in the facilities for such work. The Depression, however, revealed weaknesses in the economic and political structure of the nation, and this led to a realization that the studies which economists, historians, and political scientists were equipped to undertake had practical value. It has already been noted that the Royal Commission on Dominion-Provincial Relations appointed in 1937 included a number of studies carried out by academics in its final report, and two professors, H.F. Angus of British Columbia and R.A. MacKay of Dalhousie, were members of the commission.[4] One of the recommendations of this commission was the establishment of an organization for the social sciences paralleling the NRC, and such a body did emerge in 1940 in the form of the Social Science Research Council of Canada. In 1943 a similar organization was initiated for the humanities. But in 1937 such developments were still in the future. Any progress made in scholarship in these two areas was accomplished by individuals working on their own and often under difficult conditions. However, the publication in 1940 of Charles N. Cochrane's *Christianity and Classical Culture* and Harold Innis's *The Cod Fisheries* indicated that there were Canadian scholars in the humanities and the social sciences who on their own ground could approximate the achievements in the sciences.

LEARNED SOCIETIES AND JOURNALS

Among the new activities of the National Research Council during this period was the establishment of the *Canadian Journal of Research*, a quarterly which commenced publication in July 1929. It was referred to approvingly by R.W. Boyle, director of NRC's Physics and Electrical Engineering Division, in the lengthy address he presented to the NCCU at its annual meeting in 1939.[5] Boyle noted that this was the only journal of its type in Canada and that since it dealt exclusively with the natural and physical sciences there was no Canadian medium available to engineers and other applied scientists for the publication of research papers. The consequence was that Canadian scientists were forced to go outside the country if they wished their research to be reported, and this, Boyle argued, encouraged the continuation of the 'colonial mentality' which he believed to be the basic explanation of Canada's failure to stand scientifically on its own feet. Nor, he claimed, was the failure limited to the sciences; the colonial mentality affected all aspects of Canadian intellectual life. Humanists and social scientists were also oriented towards Europe and the United States, with the consequence that problems and issues of particular significance to Canada received too little attention. It was in the national interest to abandon the colonial mentality and what this required was a combination of determination and coordinated effort. These had been lacking in an earlier attempt to solve the problem of scholarly publication:

> Undoubtedly, our old scheme for research publications, discussed years ago, was better than our present practices. It failed to get a start because of our lack of united will and purpose, and of our 'colonial mentality.' In this scheme the Universities, the Royal Society of Canada, and the National Research Council, being unable to achieve the purpose single-handed, were to husband and consolidate their financial resources and establish and maintain under their combined auspices a series of scholarly research journals of unquestioned standard ... Now, with a very few exceptions, we have a lot of little journals, only half good in their way and hardly known outside the country.[6]

The reference to the Royal Society of Canada in this quotation is evidence that Boyle was fully aware of its existence and of its annual *Proceedings* and *Transactions*. Indeed, he was among its fellows and in 1940 would be the recipient of its Flavelle Award for eminent scholarly work in the sciences. However, in his view, as a medium for the publication of scholarly and research papers 'The Royal Society *Transactions* hardly count - and more's the pity.' The explanation lay partly in the fact that the *Transactions* appeared only once a year, a matter of considerable import in the world of science where early publication of research findings is crucial. In addition, the membership of the Royal Society was limited and self-perpetuating; new members were elected by the existing fellows, so that the chances of relatively young candidates, or of scholars of any age in the new fields of sociology or geography being admitted were slight.

In 1939 there were 311 Fellows of the Royal Society of Canada, 36 in Section I (Humanités et Sciences Sociales), 65 in Section II (Humanities and Social Sciences), 80 in Section III (Mathematical, Chemical and Physical Sciences), 61 in Section IV (Geological Sciences), and 69 in Section V (Biological Sciences), the

438

latter having been split off from IV (then called Geological and
Biological) in 1918. University professors predominated in Sec-
tions II, III, and V, constituting approximately 50%, 75%, and
80% of the respective membership of these sections. In Section
I, only 8 of the 36 members were university professors and in
Section V government employees outnumbered academics by 24 to 21.

By 1940 there was a good deal of criticism of the Royal Society
both within its ranks and from the outside. In the science sections the complaints of Boyle were echoed with respect to the
difficulties encountered by young and promising scholars gaining
admission, and on the fact that, embraced within an organization
that included non-scientists, the science members were unable to
speak authoritively on the particular needs of science to government or the general public. With respect to Sections I and II,
it was argued that the existence of parallel groups for the humanities and social sciences, one consisting of French-speaking
Canadians and one of English-speaking Canadians, was divisive
rather than unifying, and that the entrenched position of the
older disciplines - classics,English, history, philosophy, political economy - resulted in only nominal recognition of such
'new' disciplines as anthropology, fine art, Spanish, and sociology.[7]

It is difficult to cite much evidence that the Royal Society
during this period, or indeed during the following three decades,
exerted much influence. It continued to receive financial support from the federal government mainly in order to ensure publication of the *Proceedings* and *Transactions*, but the amount decreased and publication would not have been possible had not
support also been provided by the National Research Council from
1918 to 1928 and in some years by various Canadian universities
and provincial governments. In 1928 the Royal Society received
a $25,000 grant from the Carnegie Corporation as the basis for
an endowment, and this was increased to over $80,000 by 1940.
Another Carnegie grant of $75,000, to be expended over a five
year period, enabled the society to institute travelling fellowship grants for young scholars who were *not* Fellows of the Society,
and in 1937 this support was extended for an additional five years
on a somewhat reduced scale. During this period the society also
established a number of medals to be awarded annually for outstanding scholarship or research in the fields of Science (Sir
Joseph Flavelle Medal, 1924), Imaginative Literature (Lorne Pierce
Medal, 1926), and Canadian History (J.B. Tyrrell Medal, 1927).

Boyle had not been strictly accurate in saying that the *Canadian
Journal of Research* was the only Canadian periodical providing
opportunity for the publication of scientific papers. A number
of journals published prior to 1920 were still operational: the
Journal of the Royal Astronomical Society begun in 1907, and the
Canadian Entomologist initiated in 1868, for example. However,
his reference to 'little journals, only half good in their way
and hardly known outside the country' did apply. With respect
to medical and dental science, on the other hand, there was less

room for complaint. *The Canadian Medical Association Journal* and the *Journal of the Canadian Dental Association*, begun in 1911 and 1935 respectively, the latter arising from a merger of English- and French-language journals, did accommodate scientific papers. Since 1935, too, there had been an annual publication of the *Annales de l'Association Canadienne-Francaise pour l'avancement des sciences* (ACFAS). This organization was initiated in 1924 on the model of societies with similar names in Britain and France, and it was a federation of local societies.[8] Its membership was not limited to societies concerned with science and mathematics, as evidenced by the fact that the Société de philosophie de Montréal and the Société historique de Montréal were among its original members. The Association took some time to become fully functional. It was not incorporated until 1930 and did not begin to hold its annual two day conferences until 1933. However, by 1940 it was firmly established, and either embraced, or at one time had done so, 41 different groups, including some outside of the province of Quebec. In addition to holdings its annual meetings, which like those of the Royal Society met in sections[9] and at which papers were given and then subsequently published in the *Annales*, it sponsored public lectures by visiting professors from abroad, awarded grants in aid of graduate study and publication, and arranged each year for a symposium on an important scientific question. ACFAS was supported by an annual grant of $4000 from the Quebec government.

This period also saw the establishment of a number of national professional associations, particularly in the area of medicine: the Canadian Paediatric Society (1922), the Canadian Dermatological Association (1926), the Canadian Physiological Association and the Canadian Rheumatism Association (1936), the Canadian Association of Radiologists and the Canadian Ophthalmological Society (1937), but none of these had published journals by 1940. The Canadian Association of Social Workers, organized in 1926 began to publish a journal, *Social Worker*, in 1932, and starting in 1933 the *Canadian Journal of Occupational Physiotherapy* was published under the combined auspices of the Canadian Physiotherapy Association (1920) and the Canadian Association of Occupational Therapists (1926). These latter organizations, however, were concerned primarily with problems related to an emerging profession, and their journals could not be described as scholarly. The same may be said of the Canadian Home Economics Association begun in 1939 and of its journal which came out initially in 1950. A number of professional societies set up by 1920 launched journals during this period, for example, *Forestry Chronicle* by the Canadian Institute of Forestry in 1925, and *Canadian Journal of Comparative Medicine and Veterinary Science* by the Canadian Veterinary Association in 1937.

The Canadian Historical Association, having evolved from the Royal Society of Canada in 1922, held its first annual meeting in 1923 with a membership of around 350, of whom about 50 were professional historians on the faculties of various universities. The CHA adopted the practice, introduced in 1921 by the Historic Landmarks Association, also an offspring of the Royal Society, of devoting the majority of the agendas of annual meetings to the presentation of scholarly papers. For the first few years, these presentations were summarized in the annual reports but by 1925 they were appearing in full. By this time, too, the *Canadian Historical Review*, established by the University of Toronto in 1920, provided a quarterly medium for the publication of papers on historical subjects. It had taken over responsibility for the *Review of Annual Publications Relating to Canada* which the university had been issuing since 1896. From 1934 on, the *Annual Report* of the Canadian Catholic Historical Association, established in 1933, provided still another medium for the publication of historical papers.

In the 1920s it seemed likely that learned societies both in the field of English and in that of modern languages would be established but in each case the project aborted. In 1926 the Department of English at the University of Saskatchewan held a two day conference to which professors of English from the universities of Alberta and Manitoba were invited. A similar conference was held at the University of Alberta in 1927. According to Watson Kirkconnell these conferences were a great success: 'As teachers, we discussed such professional matters as remedial English (referred to us by the National Conference of Canadian Universities for study), high school curricula, the proper character of examination papers, and modern philosophies of education. Equally important were scholarly papers in which individuals put some of their special research wares on the table and received the criticism and encouragement of men in their own field.'[10] In 1928, a third English conference was held at the University of Toronto, the delegates on this occasion involving professors from one end of the country to the other. This conference also appears to have been a success, but owing to lack of funds it was the last such meeting until the early 1950s.

Between 1924 and 1927, a group of professors of French, German, Italian, and Spanish were involved in a study that resulted in the publication in 1928 of the two volume *Modern Language Instruction in Canada*. This study was financed by the Carnegie Corporation and was part of a larger study undertaken by the American Council on Education and the American Modern Language Committee. It was a large scale affair involving a general committee and five regional committees. Among the recommendations of the study was the establishment of a modern language journal to publish the results of experimental investigations and to keep teachers abreast of progress made in modern language teaching. The committee recognized that 'the lack of a national organization in Canada makes the founding of such a publication difficult.'[11] The need was so obvious, however, that the committee appealed to the National Conference of Canadian Universities for assistance in establishing a journal 'which would at the same time lay the foundation for a national organization.' Unfortunately, the response of the NCCU was negative: 'The Executive and the Conference feel that it is inadvisable to take any action in connection with an individual journal, pending the adoption of a comprehensive policy on the larger question of the attitude of the Conference towards Canadian journals of scholarship and research. It was felt that it should first evolve a satisfactory policy relating to such journals as might come up for consideration in order that all of the departments of scholarship might be given impartial treatment.'[12] As Robert Boyle had told the conference in 1939, 'our colonial mentality' and 'lack of Will' inhibited the organization from developing any policy with respect to scholarly journals.

In the area of the social sciences, however, considerable progress in the establishment of learned societies and learned journals was made, particularly in the 1930s. At the very end of the period the Canadian Psychological Association was established, and in 1940 issued its first *Bulletin*; though it was not in a position to sponsor a scholarly journal until 1947 when the *Canadian Psychological Journal* was launched. The Canadian Geographical Society was established in 1929 and its publication, the *Canadian Geographical Journal*, was first issued in 1930. The objectives of the Canadian Geographical Society were in the first instance to popularize the subject, and this was reflected in the type of article published in the journal, which was aimed primarily at the general reader rather than the scholar. On the other hand, the foundations of a scholarly organization were laid in 1934 with the formation of a Canadian committee of the International Geographical Union. The greatest progress was made in the area of political economy - economics and political science in most Canadian universities continued to be regarded as twin subjects.

In May 1929 a sub-conference of professors of economics and political science was held during the annual meeting of the National Conference of Canadian Universities, with 22 persons from 11 universities in attendance.[13] Here, the decision was made to revive the Canadian Political Science Association established in 1913 but discontinued with the outbreak of World War I. A small financial base was immediately provided by the agreement of six of the surviving members of the old executive to turn over the $300 remaining in its treasury to the new association. From 1930 to 1934 the association arranged for the publication of the papers presented at its annual meeting, and in 1935 it was in a position to launch the *Canadian Journal of Economics and Political Science*. In 1929, too, a Canadian Society of Agricultural Economists was established from the base provided by the already existing Canadian Society of Technical Agriculturists. However, the *Canadian Journal of Agricultural Economics* did not appear until 1952.

THE SOCIAL SCIENCE RESEARCH COUNCIL

The Social Science Research Council was instigated in 1940 as a
result of long-term manoeuvres to organize scholarship in the
social science disciplines.[14] The idea of providing for a body
which would act in this area as the NRC acted on behalf of the
natural and physical sciences had lain behind the creation by the
Conservative government in 1935 of an Economic Council of Canada.
This body of 16 members was to have the prime minister as chairman and the dominion statistician as secretary, and its mandate
was, in the main, 'to study, investigate, report and advise upon
questions relating to the general trend of social or economic
conditions or to any social or economic problems of Canada, and
to authorize the investigations in that behalf as hereinafter
provided.'[15] However, before the plan could become fully implemented, there was an election and the Liberals took over the
reins of government. One of their first actions was to repeal
the act which had created the council. Other attempts were made
along a variety of lines to establish such a body, but it was
not until May 1939 that a plan was finally accepted. At this
time, a committee was formed to look into the idea, and by
November 1939 a promise of financial support was forthcoming
from the Carnegie Corporation. Professor H.A. Innis of Toronto
who had worked especially hard to get the plan off the ground
was asked to join Professor R.G. Trotter of Queen's in the task
of drafting a constitution for the body. It was decided that
there should be a council of four, representative of the Canadian
Committee of the International Geographical Union, the Canadian
Psychological Association, the Canadian Political Science Association, and the Canadian Historical Association; four associate
members consisting of the dominion statistician, the dominion
archivist, and two other members from federal government departments; eight members-at-large appointed by the council in order
to ensure adequate input from disciplines not already represented
and from various regions of the country; and a secretary-treasurer.
    Professor Trotter became the first chairman, and, at the first
meeting, standing committees on current research, grants-in-aid,
publications, and post-graduate training were set up. The Carnegie
Corporation gave another grant of $5000 in 1940-41 and promised
a similar amount the following year. In 1941-42, the Rockefeller
Foundation offered $5000 for the subsidization of the publication
of scholarly works.

UNIVERSITY PUBLICATIONS

Les Editions de l'Université d'Ottawa was established in 1936
but it had no physical plant until 1946 and could hardly in 1940
be described as a functioning university press. In 1940 the

University of Toronto Press remained the only institution of its kind in Canada. However, since 1920 it had developed substantially[16] and in the academic year 1940-41 published 18 books and four quarterlies, *Canadian Historical Review* (since 1920), *University of Toronto Quarterly* (1931), *Canadian Journal of Economics and Political Science* (1935), and *University of Toronto Law Journal* (1935). Its 1939 *Catalogue* listed over 150 titles exclusive of the series of University of Toronto Studies which as noted in chapter 18 dated back to the 1890s and included as no. 44 of the Physiological Series 'Pancreatic Extracts for the Treatment of Diabetus Mellitus' by F.G. Banting, C.H. Best, J.B. Collip, W.R. Campbell, and A.A. Fletcher. More than half of the titles were pamphlets rather than books, 18 were dissertations for the D.Paed. degree, a substantial number were textbooks, and a number of items were listed as out of print. Nonetheless, by 1930 the press had demonstrated its capacity to produce in efficient if slow-paced fashion scholarly publications which required careful editing and involved complex technical type-setting problems, and by 1940 it was producing such publications in quantity. It had also demonstrated by 1940 that the operating of a printing press and bookstore could produce substantial funds for the subsidization of scholarly publication.

The press had been authorized to undertake a publishing program in 1918 and it had moved out of the library and into its own quarters in 1920. These were initially in a one and a half storey building, but in 1926 the planned three-storey building was completed. The first notable production was the two-volume (1947 pages) *Transactions and Proceedings* of the International Mathematical Congress held at Toronto in 1924, a work of considerable complexity owing to the inclusion of a great variety of mathematical symbols, which it published in 1928 and which it subsidized to the extent of $2000. In 1929 it provided a subsidy of $5000 for *A Catalogue of Vases in the Royal Ontario Museum*. In 1929 it absorbed the University of Toronto Studies, hitherto the responsibility of a university committee, and in 1934 the Students' Bookstore, following the purchase by the university of what had been a private business.

The absence of a press of their own did not, of course, prevent universities from providing support for publication, whether in the form of scholarly or research publications or of publications of a more general interest. The *Queen's Quarterly* continued to be supported by Queen's University, and with the cessation in 1920 of the *University Magazine*, which since 1906 had been a joint enterprise of Dalhousie, McGill, and Toronto, Dalhousie assumed entire responsibility for its successor, the *Dalhousie Review* (1921-). *Revue de l'Université d'Ottawa* commenced publication in 1931, the same year as the *University of Toronto Quarterly*. None of these journals could be described during this period as a scholarly journal in the technical sense, i.e., as a journal specifically directed towards specialists in a particular discipline or group of disciplines, but all were scholarly in tone and

serious in intent. The general aim was hesitantly but accurately
put by the editor of the *University of Toronto Quarterly* in its
first issue: 'The old ideal of a 'gentleman's magazine,' described
by our forefathers as amusing because it was reminiscent of all
the nine muses, and instructive because it was concerned with
serious topics competently treated, - this ideal is still perhaps
the best pattern for a quarterly which is intended to be neither
vocational nor technical and yet remains within the limits of
scholarship and academic interest.'[17]
In the late 1930s two periodicals which do answer the description of a scholarly journal as given above began to appear annually, *Etudes et Recherches* in 1936 and *Mediaeval Studies* in 1939.
The former was published by the Collège Dominicain d'Ottawa,
which had no connection with the University of Ottawa but which
on moving to Montreal in the 1940s became associated with Université de Montréal. *Mediaeval Studies* was published by the Pontifical
Institute of Mediaeval Studies which had been established in 1929
by St Michael's College, a federated university within the University of Toronto.
The departments of business or of commerce in three universities
established journals concerned with matters bearing on problems
related to their professional field: Université de Montréal,
Action Economique in 1925, University of Toronto, *Commerce Journal*
in 1933, and University of Western Ontario, *Business Quarterly*
in 1933. In addition, between 1927 and 1935, McMaster University
published 108 issues of *Canadian Economic Services*. At the
University of Toronto an annual series of *Contributions to
Canadian Economics* was published by the department of political
economy from 1928 to 1934 but was abandoned with the establishment
of the *Canadian Journal of Economics and Political Science*. Of
these only the latter could be described as of a genuinely scholarly character.

ARCHIVES, LIBRARIES, MUSEUMS

Considerable progress was made during the 1920s and 1930s in the
organization and expansion of public archives both at the federal
and provincial levels, and this did have a profound and salutary
effect on historical scholarship, which increasingly became based
on a close and scrupulous examination of original documents.[18]
At the provincial level the development took place mainly in the
four provinces which had established archives by 1920. The Provincial Archives of Quebec, formally established in 1920, was
provided with more adequate quarters in the Provincial Museum at
Quebec City in 1931. In the same year the Public Archives of
Nova Scotia, established formally in 1929 from the nucleus afforded
by an organization dating back to the 1850s, was provided with
its own building on the Dalhousie campus. In Ontario, the Bureau
of Archives (1903) became the Department of Public Records and
Archives in 1923. In British Columbia the Provincial Archives

remained in association with the Provincial Library but was effectively independent and in 1937 began in conjunction with the
British Columbia Historical Association to publish the *British
Columbia Historical Quarterly*. The annual reports of all four of
these organizations included the publication of documentary material.

A.G. Doughty, who had been appointed dominion archivist in 1904,
continued in this position until 1935 and, in association with
Adam Shortt, who had been named chairman of the Board of Historical
Publications of the Public Archives in 1918, was responsible for
the publication of a continuing stream of well-edited documents
(for example the two-volume *Documents Relating to Currency, Exchange and Finance during the French Period* in 1926) and for
creating in the archives itself an atmosphere that facilitated
the work of the increasing number of scholars such as D.G.
Creighton, H.A. Innis, and A.R.M. Lower, who came to Ottawa particularly in the summers to work on the material which Doughty
and his predecessors had gathered. The situation was improved
in 1926 with the construction of a new building following the
recommendation of a royal commission, but progress was inhibited
throughout the 1930s because of the Depression.

In contrast to the general improvement in the public archives
area, no progress at all had been made with respect to the establishment of a national library, despite continued pleas, particularly by L.J. Burpee who had been arguing for a national library
since 1913,[19] and despite the recommendations of a 1933 Commission
of Inquiry into the Library Situation in Canada, organized by the
American Library Association with financial support from the
Carnegie Corporation of New York. Canadian librarians had for
many years been members of this American organization, which
periodically met in a Canadian city. In 1927, at the meeting held
in Toronto, over 300 Canadian librarians were present, and 'the
national library situation was reviewed.' A resolution was adopted
to organize a Canadian library association 'with the object not
of competing with the American Library Association, but of securing
co-operation on all matters affecting the welfare of the library
movement throughout Canada as a whole.'[20] John Ridington, librarian of the University of British Columbia, was named president
and subsequently chairman of the Commission of Enquiry, it being
immediately recognized that the gathering of precise information
about the Canadian library situation was the necessary basis for
any further action. A survey was conducted which involved visits
to all provinces in the summer of 1930, and the report entitled
Libraries in Canada was published by the ALA in association with
the Ryerson Press three years later. However, the Canadian
Library Association was not actually formed in 1929; nor on a
second attempt in 1934 when the ALA was meeting in Montreal.
Such leadership as was provided continued to come from several
of the well-established provincial associations, notably those
of Ontario and British Columbia, both of which submitted briefs
on the need for a national library to the Royal Commission on

Dominion-Provincial Relations, appointed in 1937. The commission did refer to the need for a national library in its report but made no recommendations on the grounds that the subject lay outside the commission's terms of reference. This is, it was noted, 'another example of an educational or cultural activity which, if judged expedient, could be appropriately undertaken by the Dominion Government.'[21] The failure to develop an effective national organization was undoubtedly responsible in part for the inability of the librarians to convince Parliament that, the British North American Act notwithstanding, a national library was 'politically expedient.' As we shall see in chapter 30 the establishment of the CLA in 1946 did mark the beginnings of practical government action in this regard.

The Ridington Report devoted one chapter to university libraries, which was based in part on a questionnaire designed to yield information on total volumes held, numbers of professional and nonprofessional staff, numbers of acquisitions in the preceding year, and annual budget for administrative and acquisition purposes. The response was not very satisfactory; seven of the 21 universities contacted failed to return the forms, the delinquents including three of the major institutions, Laval, Manitoba, and Alberta. Two of those which did, King's College and Montréal, reported that the majority of their books remained in storage pending the provision of adequate library space.[22] Four libraries were reported to have in excess of 100,000 volumes: McGill 411,000 (including 100,000 in the Gest Chinese Collection which it had recently acquired, but which it would within the decade see transferred to Princeton); Toronto, 252,486 in its university library and in the vicinity of 100,000 in its federated universities and theological colleges; Laval 180,000, and Queen's 130,000. British Columbia, Dalhousie, and Western Ontario had in excess of 80,000. The only other university library with as many as 50,000 volumes was Saskatchewan, which reported 51,013. The investigators were impressed by the efforts of British Columbia and Dalhousie to increase their holdings. They were appalled by the small numbers of professional librarians employed except at Queen's, Western Ontario, Toronto, and McGill.

Despite the Depression, there was steady improvement during the 1930s at least in terms of total volumes held. The number of volumes reported in 1940 for McGill (exclusive of its theological affiliates and with the Gest Collection removed) was over 400,000, for Toronto (again excluding the federated universities and theological colleges) 400,000, for Laval nearly 250,000, while British Columbia, Dalhousie (including King's), Manitoba (exclusive of its affiliates), and Ottawa all reported over 100,000.[23] Quantity of books, however, is not necessarily an index of quality.

An attempt to assess the quality of Canadian university libraries was undertaken by Watson Kirkconnell and A.S.P. Woodhouse in their 1945 study of the humanities in Canada, which owing to the general maintenance of the status quo during the war years, is a reasonably accurate picture of the situation in 1940. Their verdict was not an encouraging one. Visits made to the 46 universities and classical colleges which had at least 20,000 volumes in their libraries 'suggest that some of these ... are inadequate even for sound undergraduate work in the humanities.[24] In general the facilities for work in Canadian studies were either adequate or good, but in the English-language institutions, with the exception of Toronto, McGill, British Columbia, and Manitoba the collections in French language and literature were surprisingly weak, and the areas of genuine strength were limited to certain branches of English literature at Mount Allison (ballads), McGill (17th century) and Toronto (Tennyson); Chinese at Toronto (Royal Ontario Museum), Icelandic at Manitoba, and medieval studies at Montreal (Institut d'études mediévales Albert le Grant) and Toronto (Pontifical Institute of Mediaeval Studies).

The comparable survey of the social sciences conducted by J.B. Brebner in the same year did not involve a detailed analysis of library facilities but it yielded the same conclusion; that the facilities were grossly inadequate and that the establishing of a national library with an effective means of making its holdings available to universities and other libraries throughout the country by means of inter-library loan, photocopying, and microfilm was a crying need.[25] As Kirkconnell and Woodhouse put it: 'The greatest single need ... is a Union Catalogue of the holdings of all Canadian libraries. In this as in many other matters, the missing keystone of the Canadian library arch is a National Library of Canada. It is conceivable that no other single project could contribute so much to the intellectual and cultural integration of Canadian life.'[26] Library resources, it must be added, was one area in which the sciences were as badly off as the humanities and social sciences. Here, too, the university holdings were not impressive and the National Research Council's efforts to make its library the nucleus for a national science library by 1940 had had only modest success.[27]

A survey of the museums and art galleries of Canada, similar to that of the Ridington Commission, was undertaken at approximately the same time, also with support from the Carnegie Corporation, by Sir Henry Meirs and S.F. Markham. Their report,[28] published in 1932, revealed a very similar situation: some 125 museums and galleries in the country as a whole, including several dozen in universities, but with a concentration in the four cities of Montreal, Ottawa, Quebec, and Toronto, and few with anything resembling an adequate curatorial staff. A chapter entitled 'Museums and Research Work' called attention to the fact that most publication took the form of the inclusion of papers in annual reports 'but the sum total is painfully small compared with the perfect spate of literature emanating from museums south of the border, and while Canadian museums do well to avoid the too facile type of research there is much of real urgency, especially in the anthropological field, that requires to be done immediately.'[29]

448

INSTITUTES AND CENTRES

The Institut de Radium established at the Université de Montréal
in 1922 was the first such body to adopt that particular designation. It received its impetus from the provincial government
which donated one gram of radium valued at $77,000 to the univer-
sity for cancer research. The institut's activities were enlarged
in 1926 with the construction of a small hospital. In 1938 an
Institut de microbiologie et de l'hygiène was set up at Montreal,
and a significant development occurred at McGill in 1929 with the
establishment of the Montreal Neurological Institute. Dr Wilder
Penfield was brought in as director of the institute and in 1934,
as promised, he was provided with an eight-storey building adjacent to the existing Pathological Institute. From the outset, it
has been concerned with research into the medical and surgical
treatment of disorders of the nervous system. Also in 1929, at
Toronto, the Institute of Medieval Studies was set up by St
Michael's College,[30] and in 1938 the University initiated an
Institute of Child Study under the directorship of Professor
William Blatz. At Dalhousie an Institute of Public Administration
was established in 1936.
  This account of developments in the area of scholarship and research has emphasized the difficulties under which universities
and individuals continued to labour in undertaking scholarly work
and in publishing their results during the period up to and including 1940. The amount of first rate scholarship and research
produced even at the larger institutions was discouragingly small,
and the explanation cannot be fully attributed to the inadequacy
of libraries or museums, the dearth of learned societies and
journals, or even to the paucity of direct financial support.
It could also be ascribed to the fact that most Canadian professors
were underpaid and overworked. The situation was succinctly stated
by J.B. Brebner in 1945 in what amounted to a challenge to the
boards of governors of universities and to the Canadian people
at large:

  Here it must be said that the salaries paid to most Canadian
  scholars and teachers can be described as stupid. They are so
  low, and their recipients are so overworked anyway, that a very
  large proportion of the potential usefulness is continuously
  being poured down the sewer of domestic or other drudgery and
  hack-work for extra income. No Canadian university supports a
  systematic structure of sabbatical leave of absence.
  Enlightened teaching and scholarly imagination and inventive-
  ness *require* leisure and congenial environment. The Spartan
  virtues produced soldiers and sterile Spartan culture. Athens
  knew better. The first Canadian university which adopts sabbatical leave and an enlightened salary policy can very quickly
  outdistance its competitors in Canada and draw abreast of those
  in Great Britain and the United States.[31]

It was not until the NCCU organized a full-fledged publicity campaign in the early 1950s to put pressure on the government and the general public to come to the rescue of the universities that the situation was improved.

NOTES TO CHAPTER 24

1 Canada, *House of Commons Debates*, 28 April 1921, 2701. The references throughout this chapter to the National Research Council (NRC) are largely based on M. Thistle, *The Inner Ring: The Early History of the National Research Council of Canada* (1966).
2 See above, chapter 18, 325.
3 See above, chapter 18, 326.
4 See above, chapter 19, 342.
5 R.F. Ruttan, 'Notes on the Master's Degree in Canadian Universities,' *NCCU Proc.* (1927), 1-7
6 R.W. Boyle, 'Promotion of Research within the University and Inter-University Cooperation,' *NCCU Proc.* (1939), 88
7 In 1940 the membership of Section II included 12 professors of history, 8 of English, 6 of political economy, one of sociology (E.J. Urwick), one of Spanish (M.A. Buchanan), and two archaeologists (D. Jenness of the National Museum, Ottawa, and C.T. Currelly, Director of the Royal Ontario Museum, who held a professorship at the University of Toronto). The only sociologist in Section I was Léon Gerin, elected in 1902.
8 For the early history of ACFAS, see J. Rousseau, 'Les Débuts de l'ACFAS: notice historique,' *Annales de l'ACFAS, 1* (1935), 19-24, and 'L'Oeuvre de l'ACFAS,' *Annuales, 3* (1937), 23-7.
9 At the first congrès in 1933 there were 4 sections: sciences morales; mathématique, physique, chimie; sciences naturelles; pédagogie des sciences. The number increased to 10 (including histoire and géographie, sciences médicales, philologie) in 1934, but reverted to 4 by 1936. In 1940 there were 8 sections: mathématique, physique, chimie; crystallographie, minéralogie, géologie, océanographie, botanique, zoologie, biologie medicale; philosophie; physiologie, pédagogie, histoire.
10 W. Kirkconnell, *A Slice of Canada* (1967), 234
11 I. Goldstick, ed., *Modern Language Instruction in Canada* (1928), I, xxxviii
12 Ibid., xxxix
13 K.W. Taylor, 'The Founding of the Canadian Political Science Association,' *Can. J. Econ. Pol. Sci.*, 33 (1967), 581-5
14 The Economic Council of Canada Act, 1935 (C 25-26 George V, ch. 19). See also J.C. Miller, *National Government and Education in Federated democracies - Dominion of Canada* (1940), 580

15 For the development of the Social Science Research Council, see its *First Annual Report 1940-41*; M.F. Timlin and A. Faucher, *The Social Sciences in Canada: Two Studies* (1968); and R.F. Neill, 'The World of Harold Adams Innis: Content and Context' (1966), 190-9.

16 E. Harman, 'Founding a University Press' in E. Harman, ed., *The University as Publisher* (1961), 2-30

17 *University of Toronto Quarterly*, 1 (1931), 3. The one-page editorial began with the statement that the policy of the editor (A.S.P. Woodhouse) was to have no editorials but 'as this is the first number of a new periodical the rule may be suspended for the occasion so as to permit a brief explanation.' This policy, with rare exceptions, has been followed by his successors.

18 W. Kilbourn, 'Historical Writing 1920-1960' in C.F. Klinck, ed., *A Literary History of Canada* (1967), 496-502; see also K. Windsor, 'Historical Writing to 1920,' ibid., 245-50.

19 L.J. Burpee, 'A Plea for a National Library,' *University Magazine*, 40 (1911), 152-63

20 F.D. Donnelly, *The National Library of Canada* (1974), 39

21 J. Ridington, et al., *Libraries in Canada: A Study of Library Conditions and Needs* (1933), 143

22 *Report of the Royal Commission on Dominion-Provincial Relations* (1940), II, 52

23 The University of King's College had moved to Halifax and entered into affiliation with Dalhousie following the fire which destroyed its building at Windsor in 1921. Construction on the main building of the Université de Montréal had begun in 1931 but was not completed until 1942. See above, chapter 20, 354, 361-2.

24 W. Kirkconnell and A.S.P. Woodhouse, *The Humanities in Canada* (1947), 154-67

25 J.B. Brebner, *Scholarship in Canada: the Function of Graduate Studies* (1945), 77-9

26 Kirkconnell and Woodhouse, *Humanities*, 166

27 Thistle, *Inner Ring*, 351-2. See also Donnelly, *National Library*, 45-6.

28 H.A. Meirs and S.F. Markham, *The Museums of Canada* (1932). A separately published appendix, *Directory of Museums and Art Galleries - in Canada* (1933), provided more detailed information.

29 Meirs, *Museums*, 44

30 For the development of the Pontifical Institute, see L.K. Shook, *Catholic Post-Secondary Education in English-Speaking Canada* (1971), 210-28.

31 Brebner, *Scholarship*, 28

1960

We do not judge it to be the responsibility of this Commission
to recommend how public funds should be provided in support of
universities. We do, however, feel it our bounden duty to call
attention as forcibly as we can to the vital part which the
universities must play in our expanding and increasingly complex
economy, and to the necessity of maintaining them in a healthy
and vigorous condition. The functions of universities touch
every facet of our society. Through the preservation of our
heritage they maintain our way of life, and through the interest
they generate in the arts, they enrich it. They enliven the
perception of social processes and contribute to the orderly
development of social institutions and relations. It is incredible
that we would allow their services to society in these ways to
lapse or to lag. But these contributions are not our direct
concern. We are concerned with the contribution made by the
universities to the increase in the national productivity and
wealth of the country. In relation to this aspect of the national
welfare Canadian universities occupy a key position. They are
the source of the most highly skilled workers whose knowledge is
essential in all branches of industry. In addition they make a
substantial contribution to research and in the training of
research scientists.

> Report of Royal Commission on Canada's Economic Prospects
> (1958), 452

25
The Special
NCCUC Conferences of
1956 and 1961

Among the reports to the annual meeting of the National Conference
of Canadian Universities and Colleges[1] in June 1961 was one from
the chairman of a committee which had been established to organize
a special conference to be held in the following November,
President A.D. Dunton of Carleton University. He began by referring to another special conference which had taken place five
years earlier, in November 1956, and then went on to describe the
plans laid for the second of these special events. His report is
relatively brief and is worth quoting in full since, taken together, these two special conferences represent significant turning
points in the history of Canadian higher education. The fact that
Dunton was president of an institution which did not exist in 1940
is symbolic of the tremendous changes that had occurred during the
1940s and 1950s. Dunton described the first conferences in these
words:

> The NCCU held a special conference in November 1956 to consider
> the urgent problems the universities would face when the enrol-
> ment shot up rapidly, as we knew it was going to do. The deli-
> berations of the conference were given wide publicity, and the
> proceedings, published under the title 'Canada's Crisis in Higher
> Education,' had a good circulation. It was at this special con-
> ference that Mr. St. Laurent, the Prime Minister of Canada,
> announced that he was asking Parliament firstly to double the
> federal grants to the universities, and secondly to set up the
> Canada Council with an initial endowment of $50 million and an
> additional $50 million to be dispersed among the universities
> of Canada for certain capital expenditures.
>
> This was naturally the highlight of the '56 conference, but in
> every way it is generally regarded as having been a success.
> I hope the one we are now planning will also have its highlights
> and be equally successful.[2]

In alluding to the second special conference, Dunton said:

The conference to be held in Ottawa on the 13th, 14th, and 15th
of November will be concerned with 'Canada "Universities in a
New Age."' The problems with which it will deal will differ from
those of 1956. The Programme Committee believes that the most
profitable will be the role the universities could and should
play in the growing activities, national and international, of
Canada. There will certainly be no lack of matters for debate.

Unfortunately, delegates will have to provide their own expenses,
but Imperial Oil Limited of Canada has most generously contributed $3,000 towards the central expenses of hiring a hall,
printing the proceedings, and the provision of a dinner at which
we hope the Prime Minister will speak.

We hope that the papers and discussions will indicate to the
federal and provincial governments, and to Canadian people generally, the important contribution towards Canada's growth and
prestige that the universities are making, and the still greater
contributions they might make.

The title, Canada's Crisis in Higher Education,[3] was an appropriate one for the published proceedings of the first special conference, but it would have been just as appropriate had the document been published 5 or even 10 years earlier. Throughout World
War II, enrolment in the universities remained almost stationary;
a creditable increase in the numbers of women attending, especially
from 1942 on, tended to offset the decline resulting from so many
men enlisting in the armed forces. The following figures tell
the tale:[4]

Year	Full-Time Enrolment	Women
1939-40	35,903	8,155
1940-41	34,817	8,107
1941-42	34,680	8,141
1942-43	35,692	8,423
1943-44	35,132	8,911
1944-45	38,516	10,995

The noticeable leap in 1944-45 is explained partly by the enrolment of over 500 veterans who had been discharged as a result
of war injuries. Very early in the war the federal government
had come to the conclusion, partly as a result of persuasion
from university heads, that, unlike the niggardly treatment of
veterans of World War I, generous support should be offered
those individuals, who, after discharge from the services,
wished either to begin or to continue their studies. In 1943-
44, 68 such veterans enrolled in the Department of Veterans
Affairs (DVA) program which provided full-time university students with tuition fees and a living allowance. In 1945-46,

with the conclusion of hostilities, some 20,000 veterans were registered in the universities, and full-time enrolment jumped to 61,861. As the following table illustrates, there was a further increase over the next two years, and then a gradual falling off as the veterans completed their degrees:

Year	Full-Time Enrolment	Veterans
1946-47	76,237	34,000
1947-48	79,346	29,600
1948-49	75,807	21,800
1950-51	64,036	6,126
1951-52	59,849	2,464

The dedication and resourcefulness with which the Canadian universities coped with a sudden doubling of admissions, and their genuine concern for giving all aid possible to the very different type of student personified by mature veterans is one of the more glorious achievements in their history.[5] However, it was generally recognized that this was an emergency situation, and it was assumed that with the disappearance of the veterans enrolment trends would return to normal. But *normal* proved to be a 75% increase in admissions over the pre-war figures. In 1952-53, with just over 1000 veterans included, the figure was over 60,000 in contrast to the 1938-39 figure of 35,000. There were two explanations: a general increase in the population, from over 11.5 million in 1941 to almost 14 million in 1951, and a growing proportion of the secondary school population continuing their studies at university level, 4.2% of the 18-21 age-group in 1941 and 7.2% in 1951.[6] One could assume, then, a steady rise throughout the 1950s and this proved to be the case; there were between 4000 and 6000 more students enrolled each year between 1953-54 and 1956-57, 8000 more between 1958-59 and 1959-60, and nearly 11,000 more in the 1960-61 session, by which time the total full-time enrolment across Canada had moved up to 107,346.

There was, however, another factor which made the future appear even more formidable, the predictable outcome of the rising birth rate in the 1940s, especially from 1945 on. One could actually count the number of children enrolled in the elementary schools in, for example, 1951, and estimate, on the basis of trend projections of the percentage of such children going on to secondary school and of secondary school candidates going on to university, just how many would be knocking on the doors of university admission officers in 1965. And this was what Dr E.F. Sheffield of the Education Division of the Dominion Bureau of Statistics did. As will be noted later, he brought the data he had thus accumulated to the attention of the member institutions of the NCCU in June 1955.[7]

The expansion of the late 1940s had been made possible by the federal government (again at the instigation of the NCCU) providing a subsidiary grant of $150 to the universities for each

veteran enrolled. Although this could clearly have been construed
as a violation of the Canadian constitution, which assigned all
jurisdiction over education to the provincial governments, it was
rationalized on the basis that it was being given to individual
Canadians, rather than to the institutions. Premier Duplessis of
Quebec, an arch-defender of provincial rights, initially allowed
the universities in his province to accept the grant but made it
clear that he was not thereby setting a precedent.[8] The DVA
scheme, it was argued, did not involve the federal government in
any policy decisions with respect to the kind of education provided. Veterans were free to attend the institution of their
choice and the $150 grant to the institution was not one for which
it had to account. The entire program demonstrated both the value
and the feasibility of federal money being used to support higher
education, and this led the federal government in 1951 to accept
certain recommendations contained in the *Report* of the Royal
Commission on National Development in the Arts, Letters and
Sciences (the Massey Report), a body which had been appointed in
1949 with the Right Honourable Vincent Massey as chairman.[9] Although it was stated in the report that initially the universities
were beyond the terms of reference of the commission and would not
be a part of the survey, as work progressed it became increasingly
clear that they could not be ignored. They were provincial institutions, to be sure, but in the view of the commissioners their
'wider and indeed universal functions' must not be either under-
valued or misconstrued. 'They are local centres for education at
large and patrons of every movement in aid of the arts, letters,
and sciences ... [but] they also serve the national cause in so
many ways, direct and indirect, that theirs must be regarded as
the finest of contributions to national strength and unity.'[10]

In its brief to the commission, the NCCU stated that 'the work
of the Canadian universities is of vital importance to national
development in Arts, Letters, and Sciences to such an extent that
they would be jeopardized or crippled if the activities of the
universities were curtailed.' This view was accepted by the commissioners without reservation as 'the official view of the organization of which all Canadian universities are members.'[11]
The report stated that because unfortunately the universities had
been starved for resources 'the humanities have become poor relations' and this gives rise to great concern.[12] Data presented to
the Royal Commission revealed that 'in the humanities, university
positions are both fewer and less well paid than in the pure or
applied sciences. But the starvation of the humanities is only
one symptom of the problem affecting all departments of these
institutions which, as we have seen, are an indispensable factor
in Canadian life. Our universities are facing a financial crisis
so grave as to threaten their future usefulness. The universities
face the twin spectres of falling revenues and rising costs.'[13]

In order to face financial difficulties the universities had
raised fees, and this the commission deplored on the grounds that
it led to more elitism in higher education by tending to reserve

it for the wealthy. Because it was clear that financial depriva-
tion was affecting not just the universities, but the entire nation, the commission made these recommendations:

(a) That in addition to the help already being given for re-
     search and other purposes the Federal Government make annual
     contributions to support the work of the universities on
     the basis of the population of each of the provinces of
     Canada;
(b) That these contributions be made after consultation with
     the government and the universities of each province, to
     be distributed to each university proportionately to the
     student enrolment;
(c) That these contributions be sufficient to ensure that the
     work of the universities of Canada may be carried on in
     accordance with the needs of the nation;
(d) That all members of the National Conference of Canadian
     Universities be eligible for the federal grants mentioned
     above.[14]

The commission also recommended that a system of scholarships
be implemented and financed by the federal government, but this
and the plans laid for establishing a Canada Council for the
Encouragement of the Arts, Letters, Humanities and Social Sciences
had to await a more propitious moment to be adopted.[15] However,
almost immediately Parliament voted that grants amounting to 50
cents times the Canadian population, approximately $7 million,
be allocated to the provinces according to their respective popu-
lations and then divided among the institutions of each province
in relation to their proportion of the full-time students registered in courses 'at a level more advanced than the university
entrance requirements generally accepted in the Province in question.'[16] The grants were to be paid directly to the individual
universities by the Department of Finance, the eligibility of
institutions and of students within them being determined jointly
by that Department, the NCCU, and the provincial governments.
The Quebec premier, M. Duplessis, now insisted that such grants
were an infringement of provincial jurisdiction and he proposed
that as an alternative the provincial governments be given added
taxing powers which would enable them to provide comparable
grants.[17] However, he was persuaded to postpone discussion of
this idea until the expiry of the existing provincial-federal tax
agreements, which would occur at the end of 1951, and consequently
the Quebec universities were able to accept the grants for the
1951-52 fiscal year, the funds in their case being paid in the
name of a joint federal-provincial commission especially created
for the purpose. The other provinces, including Newfoundland
which had joined Confederation in 1949, were offered the same
arrangement, but none availed themselves of it. By the following
year, Duplessis had decided not to go along with the scheme and,
in lieu of the Quebec universities taking federal money, he made

arrangements for comparable support to be provided from the provincial treasury.[18]

The introduction of the federal grants only partially relieved
the financial distress of the universities, and consequently as
the registration increased without any accompanying increase in
grants, the situation simply deteriorated. Most of the efforts
of the NCCU over the next few years were directed towards persuading the federal government and the nation as a whole to provide
something more than token support. At its November 1948 meeting
the NCCU executive decided to form a committee on finance which
would have 'the widest possible terms of reference to discuss
with appropriate ministers of the Federal Government the financial
problems of the Canadian universities ...'[19] The committee was
made up entirely of executive heads of member institutions, and
it was chaired by Principal F.C. James of McGill. In 1953 it
decided that a high-powered publicity campaign should be waged
by the universities which would awaken public opinion to a recognition of the vital need for more generous federal support for
higher education, and for the provision of a comprehensive scholarship plan along the lines suggested by the Massey Report. A
publicity committee was then appointed, and over the next two
years this group, with the help of a professional public relations
firm, presented the case of the universities to the Canadian nation. Presidents and faculty alike travelled across the country
making speeches mainly to Canadian Clubs, giving talks over the
radio, and writing articles for popular magazines. On each occasion the key phrase describing the subject under review was
'The Crisis of the Canadian Universities.' There was no measurable impact, however, until June 1955 when the statistics gathered
by Dr E.F. Sheffield concerning the enrolment which could be expected over the next ten years were unveiled at the NCCU annual
conference.[20] The situation was obviously critical. If Sheffield's
projections were accurate, full-time university enrolment would
double within 10 years. The NCCU publicity committee promptly
sent the Sheffield paper to every weekly and daily newspaper in
Canada, and in November 1955, having been assured of adequate
financial aid from the Carnegie Corporation, the NCCU executive
decided to hold a special conference to discuss the 'crisis in
Canadian higher education.'

Under the chairmanship of Claude Bissell, at this time president of Carleton College, the committee laid plans for the meeting
to which would be invited spokesmen from the non-academic community - businessmen, industrialists, government department heads,
and labour leaders. In Bissell's view, this move would give the
conference an authority that it might not otherwise have possessed.[21]
As it turned out, all NCCU member institutions sent delegates and
there were 17 representatives from various departments of the
federal government, 5 from provincial governments,[22] 17 from
national organizations including a number of industries, and an
impressive delegation from the United States, including J.A.
Perkins and Stephen Stackpole of the Carnegie Corporation. The

460

fact that Prime Minister St Laurent agreed to address the conference lent an even more auspicious character to the occasion.

In arranging the program, the planning committee agreed not to
limit it 'to a narrow statistical and financial analysis.' The
predicted increases in enrolments would be used as a backdrop
'for the analysis of fundamental education issues.' A total of
15 papers was presented on 5 major issues: Educational Structure;
Technological and Scientific Education; The Use of Human Resources;
Problems in Securing Staff; and Finances. The papers were of a
consistently high order and their organization by major topic was
both logical and cumulative, and the text was enhanced by photographs, the most interesting of which portrayed the joyous reaction of the delegates to the announcement by the prime minister
that the existing federal grants would be doubled immediately to
$1.00 per head of population, and that the long and eagerly anti-
cipated Canada Council which had been recommended in the Massey
Report would be established. It would be endowed with $50 million
for university capital expenditures and another $50 million to be
used for development of the humanities and social sciences.

At the same time as he announced the grant, Mr St Laurent requested that the NCCU take over responsibility for their distribution for reasons which he explained at some length.

As you know, according to the present formula, these grants are
distributed by the federal government directly to individual
universities recognized as such by the provincial governments.
In the province of Quebec, the authorities saw fit to allow
this aid to be accepted for the first year only, because they
feared that this was a first step towards encroachment on the
exclusive jurisdiction of provincial legislatures in the field
of education. It was also feared in certain circles that the
federal government might interfere with the freedom of universities. That was certainly not our intention nor the intention
of Parliament nor do I think it could happen. In order to dis-
sipate these fears and to make it abundantly clear that we do
not intend to tamper with the freedom of any individual institution, we are proposing to hand over the monies voted by
Parliament each year for that purpose to the National Conference
of Canadian Universities which would divide it up and distribute
it. In this way, the federal government would have no contact
with any individual institution. We think that this system
will prove a sufficient guarantee for all our universities,
which should be completely free from any kind of interference.
If the NCCU decides to assume this new responsibility, we will
ask for authority to enter into an agreement with the Conference
in order to carry out this arrangement.[23]

The NCCU was agreeable to assume this responsibility beginning
in the fiscal year 1957-58, and this meant two things: first,
the organization would have to become an incorporated body in
order to handle legally all the funds, and secondly, it hastened

the moment which so many of the members had waited for when there would be a permanent home established for the organization, most likely situated in Ottawa. Because membership up to this time had consisted of institutions rather than individuals, there had to be a change in the constitution, and, in fact, in order to circumvent many complications, an entirely new body was created, the Canadian Universities Foundation, to act as the executive arm of the organization and to attend to all financial matters. The conference itself was to be left with its long-standing mandate as a sounding board for discussion of common problems related to higher education. The only change here was that it would now be entitled the National Conference of Canadian Universities and Colleges, the NCCUC.

While all of these developments were greeted with a great deal of enthusiasm by the academic community they created almost as many problems for the NCCUC as they were designed to solve. However, they would be dealt with as they arose over the next decades. The 1956 Special Conference has always been credited with being the main spring which brought about change of government policy of support for higher education. However, as Gwendoline Pilkington has pointed out, this is an oversimplification:

> Although a great deal has always been made of the role played by this special conference in securing special support for higher education in Canada, in reality it simply represented the dénouement of the lengthy and complex campaign directed by the NCCU Finance Committee. The presentations consisted mainly of re-statements of facts and figures used in speeches given in the course of the long-drawn out case for federal aid which had been pleaded before the judge (Government) and the jury (the Canadian people) over the past few years and for which a final verdict had already been rendered prior to the holding of this conference. All that remained was for the decision to be announced by the Prime Minister in his banquet address, and its content was known beforehand at least to the Executive Committee of the NCCU.[24]

Nevertheless, although it is true that the conference was merely the culmination of the diligent efforts of the NCCU Finance Committee, as is noted in the introduction to the published proceedings, it was an important educational event. With respect to the effects of the new government grants on the individual institutions, except for those in Quebec which were denied access to them at least until Duplessis left the scene, there can be no doubt that the massive infusion of money touched off an unparalleled spurt of progress on all fronts. However, not all institutions were satisfied with the compromise arrangements made necessary by the restrictions imposed on the government by the Canadian Constitution. The main bone of contention was that the grant scheme did not take into account the fact that many smaller colleges and universities, especially those located in the Maritime provinces, catered to large numbers of out-of-province students for whom they received no grants – the money being apportioned according to the provincial population rather than the institutional enrolment. There were a great many other serious limitations to the whole scheme, and finally the NCCUC laid plans to call another special conference in order to re-emphasize the problems and to renew their plea to the federal government and the people for more support for higher education. The decision was made to hold the conference in November 1961, and again it was planned to ensure strong representation from both government and industry. The catchword title for this conference was 'Canada's Universities in a New Age.'

In his keynote address to the 1961 special conference, Claude Bissell referred to the fact that the main characteristics of its predecessor had been 'essentially quantitative.' This one would lay more stress on the quality of higher education being offered in Canadian universities, and it would also highlight their international responsibilities. As Bissell observed in his presentation: 'The university campus now expands to take in the whole world and the international community of scholars, about which we spoke so glibly in commencement addresses, has now become a reality. Political and administrative revolutions have followed the intellectual revolution, and universities have become indispensable to the work of closing the gap between the less well-developed countries and the affluent societies.'[25]

For obvious reasons, the thrust of the 1961 conference was very different from that of 1956. The four main subjects were: Graduate Studies and Research in the Humanities; Science, Medical and Dental Education in Canadian Universities; Scholarships, Bursaries and Fellowships; and International Activities and Opportunities for Canadian Universities. The emphasis in each case was on the need for the development of graduate work and the expansion into new areas of facilities for carrying on research.

Despite the optimism implicit in the title of the published proceedings of the 1961 conference, it is a less impressive document than its 1956 counterpart. The intended emphasis on quality notwithstanding, the papers were more prosaic in tone, and despite the intention of the planning committee, they were heavily laced with statistics - in fact far more so than those given at the supposedly more quantitatively oriented 1956 conference. This time there were no photographs included in the volume, which may be as well since they might have recorded for posterity the dismay and chagrin of the delegates as they listened to the message delivered by a different prime minister, John Diefenbaker, who announced that his government had more pressing problems to occupy them just then, mainly related to the world-wide threat from Russian communism.

The whole disappointing tenor of the 1961 special conference proved to be a precursor of the gradual unwelcome withdrawal of the federal government from direct involvement with the universities, and of the inevitable but equally unwelcome encroachment of the provincial governments into this territory.

1   The National Conference of Canadian Universities (NCCU) was renamed the National Conference of Canadian Universities and Colleges (NCCUC) in 1959.
2   *NCCU Proc.* (1961), 96-7
3   C.T. Bissell, ed., *Canada's Crisis in Higher Education* (1957)
4   The figures in this and the following paragraph are from Dominion Bureau of Statistics, *Survey of Higher Education, 1959-1961* (1962), 34 (table 10).
5   For a detailed account of the DVA program, see G. Pilkington, 'A History of the National Conference of Canadian Universities, 1911-1961' (1974), chap. 5, 305-84.
6   E.F. Sheffield, 'Canadian University and College Enrolment Projected to 1965,' *NCCU Proc.* (1955), 44 (table 3)
7   Sheffield, 'Canadian University Enrolment,' 39-46
8   D.A.A. Stager, 'The Evolution of Federal Government Financing of Canadian Universities,' *Stoa: Can. J. Higher Education*, II, 1 (1973), 23-9
9   Royal Commission on National Development in the Arts, Letters and Sciences, *Report* (1951). The other members of the commission were G.H. Lévesque, dean of the faculty of social sciences, Université Laval; Hilda Neatby, professor of history, University of Saskatchewan; N.A.M. Mackenzie, president, University of British Columbia; and Arthur Surveyer, a Montreal engineer.
10 Ibid., 132
11 Ibid.
12 Ibid., 138-9
13 Ibid., 140-1
14 Ibid., 355
15 Ibid., 358-377, 381
16 Dominion Bureau of Statistics, *Biennial Survey of Education in Canada 1952-54*, part II (1956), 10
17 Letter from M. Duplessis to L. St Laurent of 30 November 1951 in reference to St Laurent's letter to Duplessis of 6 November 1951
18 Stager, 'Evolution of Federal Government Financing,' 27-8
19 *NCCU Proc.* (1949), 76
20 Ibid. (1955), 39-46. See note 7 above.
21 Bissell, *Canada's Crisis*, v
22 The provinces represented were British Columbia, Manitoba, New Brunswick, Ontario, Saskatchewan.
23 Bissell, *Canada's Crisis*, 255
24 Pilkington, 'History of NCCU,' 579-80
25 Bissell, *Canada's Crisis*, 8

26
Institutional Development

By the end of hostilities in the second world war the NCCU had established itself as the recognized spokesman for the Canadian universities. Periodically it had considered expanding its membership beyond institutions in order to include associations of professors and administrators concerned with problems affecting specific areas of professional interest at the national level, and in 1950, after a full afternoon of debate it had rejected an application for membership from one such group, the Council of University Schools of Nursing. In 1949, however, it had granted the privilege of reporting to the annual meetings to the University Advisory Services, an organization which in 1953 became the University Counselling and Placement Association, and in 1955 the same privilege was extended to the Canadian Association of Directors of Extension and Summer Schools.[1] Nevertheless, the formal involvement of such groups in the organization of the conference did not occur until 1965. There were by the 1950s two rivals for the title of spokesman for the universities - the National Federation of Canadian University Students, NFCUS, and the Canadian Association of University Teachers, CAUT, both of which were to establish offices in Ottawa with full-time secretariats.

The NFCUS had been in existence since 1927 but had been dormant during World War II.[2] It was revived in 1944 at a meeting of what was called 'an executive' held at the University of Western Ontario, but only one university paid its fees in 1945 and the organization was not fully reactivated until 1946. In that year representatives from 16 universities attended the tenth congress at the University of Toronto. At that time it was decided that if nothing was accomplished during the coming year the federation should be dissolved. During the ensuing months, the newly elected president, Maurice Sauvé of the Université de Montréal, personally visited almost every campus from coast to coast, and, as a consequence, the next congress held in 1947 was attended by delegates representing close to 60,000 students from 21 universities or colleges.

Among the accomplishments of this eleventh congress were the drawing up of a constitution for a Canadian University Debating Association, the submission of a brief to the NCCU on the need to establish an intercollegiate athletic association, and the setting up of commissions on student income and expenditure, the administration of student councils, university radio, student railway fares, and student loan funds. But much of the delegates' time was devoted to discussing the relationship of the NFCUS to the International Union of Students, IUS, a European-based organization which many believed to be dominated by communists and which certainly held the view that student unions should adopt a syndicalist stance. It was decided to apply for affiliation on a provisional two-year basis but this proved to be unacceptable to the IUS. At the 1948 congress a number of NFCUS members complained that the national program was receiving insufficient attention because of the preoccupation of the executive with international matters, and in 1949 two major universities, Queen's and St Francis Xavier, withdrew and the congress itself resolved not to affiliate with IUS.

Nonetheless, measurable progress was made during this decade and in 1951 an office was set up in Ottawa with a full-time secretariat. By 1956 there were 32 members (including Queen's and St Francis Xavier), a full-time director of a travel department established in 1952 had been appointed, and both a general magazine and a weekly news bulletin were in circulation. The body was not represented at the special conference held by the NCCU in 1956, but a delegate did attend its regular meeting in 1957. In 1958, the NFCUS submitted a brief to the federal government arguing for the need of greatly increased support of higher education and against the inequities of an existing 'system' which denied access to higher education to Canadians from low income families.

In conclusion, then, it needs to be pointed out that we as students are not concerned to lower the academic qualifications for university entrance. This must be avoided at all costs. Indeed increased aid to students will raise the student potential and permit the raising of standards. However, to-day in Canada there are two separate sets of qualifications for university entrance of equal importance. The one is academic; the other is financial. We submit this brief to you, in the hope that you may be able to recommend such steps as will help to lower, even to abolish once and for all, this unjust financial barrier, so that the principle of equality of opportunity may be fully implemented in Canadian university education.[3]

Despite being in a relatively strong position at this time, the future course of the student organization was to be somewhat mercurial. Conversely, faculty efforts to form an association did not begin until the late 1940s, but when the moment arrived the results were more solid. In 1947 the NCCU referred a request that it affiliate with the International Association of University Professors and Lecturers to the member institutions on the grounds that there was no association of university professors and 'that the Conference could not appropriately speak for them.'[4] In 1948 a group of faculty members of the University of Alberta sought information about salaries from other Canadian universities, and one year later what by then had become the University of Alberta Association of the Teaching Staff decided to find out whether there was general interest in forming a national association. This led to the holding of three special meetings arranged by faculty members of Queen's University during the period when the learned society meetings were in session in Kingston in June 1950. It was decided to establish a provisional committee to draw up a constitution for discussion in 1951 when the learned societies were next scheduled to meet at McGill. At this point there were staff associations only at Alberta, British Columbia, Laval, McGill, Queen's, Toronto, and Saskatchewan; they were agreed that any national body should become an association of individuals rather than 'a federation of locals.'[5] The NCCU meetings were also being held at McGill in 1951, and at the opening session on May 30 Professor F.M. Salter of the University of Alberta complained that the conference was dominated by presidents and deans and that teaching staff were inadequately represented. The delegates who responded to these charges made it clear that they believed that 'this was an exaggeration, and it was agreed that the system of representation should not be changed.'[6] One week later, on 6 June 1951, the Canadian Association of University Teachers was born in order 'to promote the interests of teachers and researchers in Canadian universities and colleges and advance the standards of the profession.' It is possible that the less than sympathetic reaction to Professor Salter's remarks gave some impetus to the founding of this body.

In any event, CAUT now existed officially with Professor F.A. Knox of Queen's as president. By 1952 the constitution was amended to permit local associations to become members, and in January 1953 the first edition of a four page mimeographed publication was issued; by 1956 the *Bulletin* had become a well-established quarterly. In the preceding year, 1955, at the annual meeting of the NCCU, one of three papers in a symposium devoted to the economic problems of the university dealt with the topic 'The Development and Aims of the Canadian Association of University Teachers.' A second paper was addressed to 'The Economic Status of University Teachers,' and it was a repeat of one delivered to the 1954 annual CAUT meeting. It was agreed at this same meeting that the NCCU and the CAUT would co-operate in a study of pension plans.[7] In 1956 the CAUT presented briefs to both the Royal Commission on Canada's Economic Prospects and to the Royal Commission on Broadcasting and Television.

During these early years the association's efforts to promote the interests of teachers and researchers and to advance the standards of the profession were largely directed towards financial matters, but the related aspects of academic freedom and tenure had from the outset been considered questions of central concern. In 1958 these issues became of practical as well as theoretical interest as the result of the dismissal of Professor Harry Crowe by United College, a constituent arm of the University of Manitoba. The Crowe case, or the United College affair as it was variously called, brought the CAUT into national prominence and was partially responsible for the decision to establish a national office at Ottawa in September 1959, with J.H.S. Reid as executive director.

The developments thus far described, particularly those pertaining to the NCCU, were the inevitable consequence of the enormously increased dimensions of higher education in Canada – more students, more professors, more programs, and accompanying costs. The latter steadily exceeded the capacity of the provincial governments and the private sector to support the universities which even as early as 1950 were clearly recognized as institutions crucial to the national well-being.

In general terms, enrolment in the Canadian universities tripled between 1940 and 1960.[9] This is true of total full-time enrolment which increased from 37,269 to 114,000 and of undergraduate enrolment which increased from 35,538 to 107,482. At the undergraduate level enrolment in arts and science and in professional programs was almost identical, 51,291 in arts and science, 54,620 in professional programs. It should be remembered, however, that a number of 'professional programs,' notably commerce (6323), secretarial science (221), and journalism (107) were normally offered in a faculty of arts and science, and consequently that this faculty remained the most important one. Enrolment in the school of graduate studies increased from 1402 to 6518.

Initially, the burdens imposed by sudden growth fell upon the existing institutions, both large and small. The most striking increases were at Sir George Williams which had 192 day students in 1940-41, and 1768 in 1960-61, and at the University of British Columbia which increased from 2473 to 11,250. In general, the larger universities tripled, for example Alberta rose from 1861 to 6639; McGill from 2529 to 7708. The smaller ones doubled: Acadia from 399 to 884, and Western Ontario from 1327 to 3279. By 1960, both the universities of Alberta and Saskatchewan had instituted second campuses at Calgary and Regina respectively which would eventually become chartered universities.

In order to cope with the phenomenal growth in student numbers it was necessary to create new institutions and this is reflected in the membership of the NCCU which rose from 29 in 1940 to 38 in 1960. Of the new members, Mount St Vincent, St Mary's, and Sir George Williams already had degree-granting powers in 1940, and Collège Jean de Brébeuf, Loyola, and United College were associated with institutions already members of the NCCU – the first two being linked with Université de Montréal and the third with the University of Manitoba. Assumption, Sherbrooke and

468

Carleton had only recently achieved full university status, in 1952, 1954, and 1957 respectively; Carleton had been operating since 1942, mainly as an evening college; Sherbrooke emerged from a classical college established in the nineteenth century; and Assumption had enjoyed a 34 year association with the University of Western Ontario. The NCCU membership of 1960 did not include all the institutions which had degree-granting powers; Collège Ste-Anne, for example, had been giving degrees since 1903 but was never a member; and the University of Waterloo, Waterloo Lutheran University, York University, and Laurentian University had been chartered too recently to qualify for admission - the first three in 1959 and the latter in 1960.

Two developments of the late 1950s deserve comment before con-cluding this general review of higher education from 1940 to 1960. One is a sharp increase in part-time students, most marked in uni-versities located in the larger metropolitan areas. Sir George Williams in Montreal and Carleton in Ottawa, of course, had been largely evening universities dedicated to providing working adults with an opportunity to obtain academic degrees. But it was a relatively new phenomenon for most institutions. For the 1955-56 session the Dominion Bureau of Statistics reported a part-time enrolment of 29,200 for university level credit courses and an additional 52,104 taking 'other courses.'[10] There were 10,098 taking credit courses in the winter sessions, 14,723 in summer, and 4379 following correspondent courses. In 1960-61, part-time registration had risen to 75,176 for credit courses and 119,255 for 'other courses,' with very large increases in the winter ses-sion, 31,236, and 37,676 in summer. This trend would continue throughout the 1960s placing a tremendous burden on university facilities during the regular sessions and effectively transfor-ming them into year-round operations.

The second phenomenon was the rise in numbers of foreign stu-dents. In 1950, the total full-time student body was 68,306 of whom 3188 or 4.7% were from outside Canada; of these 1758 were from the United States.[11] By 1955, with a very similar total enrolment, 72,737, and almost an identical number of Americans, 1773, the number of foreign students was 4385 or 6%. By 1960 this figure had risen slightly to 6.4% and 4307 of the 7251 out-siders were from countries other than the United States or Britain. There was a particularly noticeable increase in students from the West Indies, 252 in 1950-51 and 1210 in 1960-61. Sir George Williams and McGill had always attracted many students from abroad, the former partly because of its attachment to the world oriented YMCA, and the latter because of its long-established international reputation, especially of the medical school. According to H.J. Somers and J.F. Leddy, both of whom addressed the Special NCCU Conference of 1961, this was a healthy development for Canadian universities.[12] The presence of these students from all over the world did much to broaden the outlook of both staff and students, making the institutions less parochial or provincial. However, their presence did eventually raise the issue as to how generous

469

the Canadian taxpayer should be in providing funds to expand universities in order to accommodate foreign students. This was to become a particularly acute issue in the province of Quebec where McGill came under fire from the government for its reputedly high ratio of foreign students.

The problem quite naturally focused on funding of higher education. Money had been pried out of the federal government during the veterans' period of abnormally swelled enrolments, and more grants had been forthcoming after the 1956 Special NCCU Conference; but obviously, in the face of long years of neglect, it was not enough and the universities were feeling acutely the pressures of increasing enrolments, whether they stemmed from demands for part-time studies, from foreign students, or from the growing feeling abroad in the world that higher education was a good in itself and also a guarantee of instant success and economic stability. Although from 1945 on many of the provincial governments gave increasing monetary support to higher education, there was no systematic policy adopted. Each province tended to deal with the institutions within its jurisdiction on a piecemeal basis. The development of provincial departments, committees, and commissions charged with advising the provincial government on the establishment of a provincial system of higher education dates from the early 1960s.[13] Generally speaking, throughout the 1940s and 1950s, although the provinces were very much aware that the federal government had no constitutional jurisdiction over higher education, with the exception of the legislature in Quebec they were content to let much of the burden of financing the universities fall on the central government and on private benefactors. This entire picture would change, at first gradually and then with gathering momentum, throughout the sixties.

THE MARITIMES

Among the resolutions adopted by the Special NCCUC Conference of 1961 was the following:

> that, since much attention will inevitably be given to the crisis in higher education as it is illustrated in some of our larger universities located in metropolitan areas, it is particularly desirable to re-affirm the value of the contribution of the smaller universities and colleges, many of them of long establishment, to the welfare of the nation, and to recommend to local, provincial and federal governments and to private donors, both individual and corporate, the necessity of maintaining our smaller universities with adequate staff and financial support.[14]

While there were many small universities and colleges in central and western Canada, this resolution was primarily directed to the needs of the institutions in the Maritime provinces, not excluding

470

Dalhousie and the University of New Brunswick, neither of which had an enrolment as large as 2000, nor could be said to be located in a metropolitan area. The argument in support of this resolution was given by H.J. Somers, the president of St Francis Xavier University, at the closing session. He began by noting that a great deal of attention had been given at the conference to graduate and professional education and consequently to the problems of the larger universities where the bulk of this work was being done, and he made it clear that in his view it was essential that they be provided with the means to carry out these tasks. But it was also in the national interest that adequate support be provided for institutions like his own which offered undergraduate courses in the humanities, social sciences, sciences, commerce, education, and nursing, with master's work in selected departments. Despite the fact that their enrolments ranged from 100 to 1800 they served a large number of students seeking higher education in Canada. The focus of their educational offerings was the liberal arts and they were particularly well fitted to provide the broad general education so desperately needed in a world increasingly dominated by science, technology, and specialization:

These smaller universities are largely residential. Even the largest is small enough to maintain an intimate relationship between faculty and students, with a degree of personal contact that assures individual assistance and guidance to the undergraduate. Their students are, generally speaking, not confined to one province or one region, for the majority of our smaller universities are quite cosmopolitan. In this residential atmosphere, students come to know not only their fellow students of their own province, but those of the other Canadian provinces, the United States and abroad. Almost unconsciously they learn to understand and appreciate the point of view and cultures of many lands and in doing so they emerge from the smaller universities better men and women.[15]

Dr Somers suspected that in the course of the next decade some of these institutions would develop professional schools and become large universities, but in doing so they would lose their present character. 'The task of the great majority will be to hold their present aims and purposes in the face of growing numbers. This would seem to indicate that they should not increase to more than 2,000 or 2,500 students.'[16] Colleges of this type had always been feeders of the larger graduate schools, and they would continue to be so if they could continue to maintain a faculty that was properly prepared academically. The great danger was that their best faculty members would be attracted to the larger institutions; and in order to forestall this there must be provided not only adequate salaries but opportunities for research. This in turn meant a continuation and expansion of work at the master's level in selected departments and 'it should also mean that the most qualified faculty members ... be given the oppor-

tunity by the larger universities to participate in doctoral programs.'17

Memorial University College in Newfoundland became Memorial
University in 1949, at the same time that the colony became the
tenth Canadian province. It granted its first degrees in 1950.
At the beginning of this period, in 1940-41, about half of the
students were enrolled in a one year training course for elementary school teachers; in 1946 this program was transformed into
a fusion of liberal arts and professional training, and the liberal arts sector itself was enriched. By 1960 the faculties of
arts and science, education, and applied science were operating
in the former Normal School building as well as in a university
annex which contained classrooms, a chemistry laboratory, an
assembly hall, and a bowling alley. The university was offering
the B.A., the B.Sc., and B.Com. at both general and honours levels,
the M.A. and the M.Sc., and a graduate diploma in education. In
1961 it occupied the first four buildings of a new campus. Its
registration by this time was 1238, a marked increase from the
1940-41 figure of 254.

Numbers had increased at the two post-secondary institutions in
Prince Edward Island; Prince of Wales College had 201 students at
the end of the period as compared to 36 in 1940-41; St Dunstan's
had risen from 36 to 356 and its affiliation with Laval had terminated in 1941. Since that time it had granted its own degrees.
It also had become co-educational and had introduced programs in
business administration in 1947, pre-engineering in 1951, and
teacher training in 1957. However, the situation in this province
remained relatively static.

The position of the Nova Scotia institutions also was basically
unchanged despite a doubling or tripling of enrolment. This is
illustrated in Table A which provides enrolment figures by degree
programs for the three largest institutions at the beginning and
end of the period and in the years that marked the arrival and
departure of the World War II veterans. It will be noted that
the academic program offered at Acadia was the same in 1960 as in
1940 except for the introduction of commerce in 1957. At Dalhousie
music was dropped in 1956 (one student enrolled in 1955-56) and
pharmacy and nursing were introduced in 1954 and 1956 respectively.
The graduate enrolment at Dalhousie increased substantially in the
late 1950s, in part owing to the introduction of a Ph.D. program
in the biological sciences in 1955. In contrast, graduate enrolment had dwindled to practically nothing at Acadia by 1960. The
major development at St Francis Xavier was the establishment of
Xavier Junior College at Sydney in 1951, offering the first two
years of most programs; this explains the failure of the enrolment
at St Francis Xavier to drop off with the departure of the veterans.

In addition to Acadia, Dalhousie, and St Francis Xavier, there
were ten other institutions eligible to receive federal grants in
1960-61; two of these were theological colleges, Holy Heart
Seminary and Pine Hill Divinity Hall. Three institutions were

TABLE A
Enrolment in three Maritime Universities in selected years

Acadia

Year	A&S	Comm.	Soc.Sci.	Ed.	H.Sci.	Engin.	Music	Theol.	Grad.	Total
1940–41	224	–	45	10	60	47	4	18	9	399
1946–47	505	–	54	7	89	185	20	14	17	877
1952–53	291	–	21	26	45	55	10	9	15	463
1960–61	485	55	63	45	36	128	26	44	2	840

St Francis Xavier

Year	A&S	Comm.	Ed.	Engin.	H.Ec.	Nurs.	Grad.	Total
1940–41	247	–	–	30	18	–	17	312
1946–47	603	–	–	188	43	5	31	870
1952–53	504	143	21	154	40	7	13	882
1960–61	819	248	72	246	51	8	3	1,440

Dalhousie

Year	A&S	Comm.	Nurs.	Ed.	Law	Eng.	Dent.	Music	Med.	Pharm.	Grad.	Total
1940–41	321	30	–	10	49	52	31	4	219	–	26	678
1946–47	689	146	–	12	173	232	38	14	217	–	48	1,569
1952–53	498	140	23	17	133	126	50	8	284	–	45	1,324
1960–61	980	138	21	47	103	223	53	–	270	48	136	1,919

The Dalhousie Arts and Science figures for 1940–41 include 46 students enrolled at the University of King's College and the 1960–61 A & S figures include 153 King's students registered in arts, science, and journalism. In the same years King's had 8 and 20 students respectively in theology.

without degree-granting powers: Nova Scotia Agricultural College, the Convent of the Sacred Heart (a junior college for girls whose graduates had been accepted since 1905 by Dalhousie as admissible to the third year of the general course), and the Maritime School of Social Work, a joint enterprise involving Acadia, University of King's College, Mount Allison, St Francis Xavier, and St Mary's. Of the degree-granting institutions, King's continued its relationship with Dalhousie, Nova Scotia Technical College continued to give the final two years of the engineering program for which a half-dozen other Maritime universities provided the first three, and Collège Ste Anne, Mount St Vincent, and St Mary's, despite difficulties, had managed to survive. Despite a disastrous fire in 1951, Mount St Vincent had doubled its enrolment over 1940, from 150 to 375, had introduced programs in nursing and library science, and had strengthened its program in teacher training. St Mary's, which had been taken over by the Jesuits in 1941, moved to a new campus close to Dalhousie in 1951, but the expenses incurred in establishing the new campus prevented much expansion of the academic program during the next ten years. It continued to be a secondary school as well as a university and to cater only to men; its enrolment in degree programs in 1960-61 was 574. Collège Ste Anne had an enrolment of 97 in 1960-61.

At first glance the situation in New Brunswick resembled that of Nova Scotia. The development of Mount Allison paralleled that at Acadia, St Francis Xavier, and Dalhousie. Like the latter two, its enrolment trebled, from 340 to 1160, and there was notable expansion of its physical plant, especially between 1958 and 1960. Its major academic development was in the strengthening of the school of fine arts which continued to offer the only degree course available in Canada to pay significant attention to the practical as well as the theoretical aspects of art. New Brunswick boasted an additional university, that of Université St-Louis at Edmundston chartered in 1947, which brought the total number of institutions up to six. Four of these, including St Louis, were classical colleges with very small enrolments: St Joseph's, 563; St Louis 206; Sacré Coeur, 182; and St Thomas, 115. All four also had high schools, with appreciably larger enrolments than the colleges, and all except St Thomas were French-language institutions. In the early 1960s, as a result of recommendations of a royal commission chaired by John Deutsch, the French-language colleges were merged into the Université de Moncton and St Joseph's was relocated in Moncton; St Thomas was moved from Chatham to Fredericton and entered into federation with the University of New Brunswick.[18]

The most noteworthy advance in the Maritime region between 1940 and 1960 occurred at the University of New Brunswick. Its registration went up from 364 to 1387 and the academic program was expanded both through the strengthening of existing faculties of engineering and forestry, and by the introduction of courses in commerce, nursing, physical and health education, and graduate studies. The physical plant was also greatly improved and expanded, the result of generous donations from Lord Beaverbrook

474

as well as a long overdue infusion of funds from the provincial
government, tangible support which was to continue.

QUEBEC

The most significant event in the history of higher education in
Quebec during the period under review took place at the very end
of the second decade - on 30 December 1960. This was the moment
when the government announced its intention to appoint a Royal
Commission of Inquiry on Education in the Province of Quebec
under the chairmanship of Msgr A.-M. Parent, who had been rector
of Laval for the previous six years. The first of the five volumes
of the *Parent Report* did not appear until 1963 and the revolutionary changes in Quebec's system of education which resulted
from the adoption by the government of many of its recommendations
did not begin to take place until the mid-1960s. But reference
to the *Parent Report* is appropriate in the present chapter, which
is devoted to outlining the general development of the individual
universities and colleges between 1941 and 1960, since in the
case of the French-language institutions the record reveals a
basic weakness in one part of the total system which was rendering
ineffective all the other parts. The problem centred on the
classical colleges. In 1960, these institutions continued to be
the main source of recruits for the professional schools and graduate faculties of the French-language universiites, as had been
the case in varying degrees between 1920 and 1940.[19]
During the 1940s and 1950s, efforts were made by the universities of Laval and Montréal, the classical colleges, and the authorities responsible for public secondary education to widen the
base of recruitment. Matriculation programs were included in
some public schools and the classical college course was revised
in order to prepare a larger corps of graduates for university
studies in the pure and applied sciences and in the social sciences,
these being the areas on which the universities were concentrating
in order to expand and modernize the province's economic base.
But the effort was made too late. By 1960 it was clear that a
more radical change must come about in the total provincial educational system, one which ultimately would affect not just the
classical colleges and the French-language sector in general, but
the English-speaking institutions at all levels as well. This
did not take place until well on into the 1960s, so that the
Quebec educational system was in essence similar in 1960 to that
of 20 years earlier. However, some definite progress had been
made within all institutions, and a number of new ones had been
created - at least 20 classical colleges as well as the Université
de Sherbrooke. The latter was granted a charter in 1954 and by
1960 registered 2167 students in faculties of arts, commerce,
law, and science, an institut de pédagogie, and an affiliated
école de sciences domestiques. The degrees offered in the faculty
of science were a B.Sc. and a B.Sc.App. in three branches of

engineering. While the majority of students in arts were housed
in 11 affiliated classical colleges, 47 students were following
graduate courses, and the associated Grand Séminaire de Sherbrooke
had an enrolment of 148. Plans for a medical school were already
well advanced.

Laval, although still a private university, was now in receipt
of regular financial support from the provincial government,[20]
which aided greatly in its expansion of facilities. In 1960, it
was a divided institution in the sense that it was in the process
of moving from downtown Quebec to its new campus, the Cité universitaire, located in the suburb of Ste-Foy. This decision had been
made in 1947 after being initially proposed in 1944. In 1948,
with the help of money raised in a public campaign and with a $4
million grant from the provincial government, the plan began to
be implemented. The first building, intended for the faculté
d'arpentage et de génie forestier, was occupied in 1950 and by
1960 buildings for commerce, medicine, and theology (the Grand
Séminaire) had been added, as well as the first student residences
and a student centre.

Its greatly improved financial position enabled Laval to expand
its physical and academic facilities. Although the faculty of
canon law was eliminated, three schools were elevated to faculty
status: science sociales in 1944, arpentage et génie forestier
in 1945, and commerce in 1952. The medical faculty set up an
institut de physiologie in 1946, and an école de technologie
médicale in 1951, the latter offering a two year diploma course
for laboratory technicians and more advanced two year courses in
such areas as haematology and microbiology. In the faculté des
lettres an institut d'histoire et de géographie was set up in
1946, the volume of work being reflected by the separation of the
two into separate institutions in 1958. In the area of professional studies, there was an increase in registration in all sec-
tors, most notably in engineering (faculté des sciences), where
the student body increased from 47 in 1940 to 1142 in 1960. By
1960 courses had been introduced in library science and physical
and occupational therapy.

There was also a heavy increase in enrolment in the faculté
des arts, in part explained by the addition of 22 affiliated
classical colleges, bringing the total to 44. In addition, the
faculty's affiliates included nine institutions offering the
first four years of the eight year classical course (4 in 1940)
and seven institutions which offered the equivalent program in
the public schools. The faculty had also been providing in its
own collège universitaire a special one year course designed to
provide a more comprehensive program for classical college students who were planning to enter one of the professional faculties. The faculty's concern with secondary education, both with
respect to the supply of teachers and the coordination of secondary and university programs, was also reflected in its establishment of an Ecole de pédagogie et d'orientation in 1945.[21]

In general terms, the development of Université de Montréal paralleled that of Laval. It too remained a private institution, and it also was, by 1960, receiving firm government support. It was by then adequately housed on its new site. The massive building which had been in the planning and construction stage since 1924 had been completed in 1943 and a number of other buildings, including one to accommodate Ecole polytechnique (in 1957) had been added. The faculté de théologie remained at the Grand Séminaire site on Sherbrooke Street and with the exception of Ecole polytechnique and Ecole d'optométrie, the university's affiliates were either located elsewhere on the island of Montreal or not too far distant, as in the case of the institutes of agriculture and veterinary medicine both situated at Oka. Many of the classical colleges were in other parts of the province.

Since by 1940 Montréal had almost the full range of faculties and schools, there is less to report by way of organizational development during the next 20 years than at Laval. However, the Ecole de pharmacie obtained faculty status in 1943, a faculty of music was established in 1950, and an école d'hygiène in 1945, the latter offering programs in health education, physical education and recreation as well as in hygiene. In 1954 the faculty of medicine established an école de réhabilitation. On the other hand, the period was marked by the creation of a number of institutes, some concerned exclusively with research but most offering graduate work: in the faculty of theology, Institut supérieur de sciences religieuses in 1954 (to provide advanced theological training for laymen); in the faculty of philosophy, Institut de psychologie in 1942, a year which saw the faculty assume full responsibility for the Institut d'études mediévales which had been established by the Dominicans in Ottawa in 1930; in the Ecole d'hygiene, Institut supérieur d'administration hospitalière in 1956; and in medicine, Institut diététique et de nutrition in 1942 and Institut de médecine et de chirurgie expérimentale in 1945. Since 1941 the faculty of medicine had also been providing space for the Institut du cancer de Montréal. As at Laval there were noteworthy increases in enrolment in engineering, pharmacy, and social work, as well as in law (416 compared with 106 in 1940) and medicine (573 compared with 257). Full-time enrolment in graduate studies increased over the period from 263 to 968.

Developments in the faculty of arts at Université de Montréal also resembled those at Laval. The number of affiliated classical colleges increased by 9, a B.A. program for adults was developed on the main campus by the division of extension, and the faculty made arrangements with a number of normal schools whereby their graduates could obtain B.Ed. and B.A. degrees.

In the English-language sector, the largest university, McGill, suffered throughout the 1930s from lack of strong continuous leadership, its much beloved and highly effective principal, Sir Arthur Currie, having died in December 1933. However, on 1 January 1940, F. Cyril James assumed command of the university

and for the next two decades gave it the guidance it required to
maintain and extend its reputation throughout the 1940s and 1950s.

McGill received some government funding during the 1950s, but
the thrust of its progress resulted more from systematic efforts
to increase its endowments, which by 1960 exceeded $60 million.
In 1943 a campaign to acquire funds for the purpose of raising
staff salaries had produced $7 million and campaigns waged in
1948 and 1956, aimed principally at enlarging the physical facilities, realized $8 million and $9 million respectively. With other
generous gifts from individuals, this provided the necessary
accommodation for commerce, engineering, law, music, and medical
research, a large extension of the library, a physical science
centre, the Eaton electronics building, and a radiation laboratory
and cyclotron. In addition, there was physical growth at Macdonald
College and new residences were provided on the main campus.

McGill's enrolment in 1960 was 7668, including 836 in the faculty
of graduate studies and just over 1000 at Macdonald College which
offered the programs in agriculture, home economics, physical and
health education, and teacher training. However, students enrolled
in education spent a large part of their time on the main campuses
since with the establishment of an Institute of Education under
the faculty of arts in 1955, the liberal arts component in the
B.Ed. program had been increased considerably. A degree program
in physical and health education was introduced in 1945, and in
the same year McGill assumed partial and in 1950 full responsibility for the Montreal School of Social Work, which had been established in 1933, following the withdrawal of the McGill social work
program in 1932. A school of physical and occupational therapy
offering a five year course to the B.Sc. as well as a three year
diploma course was established within the faculty of medicine in
1944; in 1948 the cooperation between the affiliated theological
schools which had begun in 1912 was taken to a logical conclusion
with the establishment of a faculty of divinity. In the area of
undergraduate education the chief development of the 1950s was
the introduction of a five year course leading to the B.Sc. in
what was still in 1960 called the School for Graduate Nurses.

However, it was in the area of research and scholarship that
McGill's progress was most marked during these years. The increase in graduate enrolment from 201 to 836 was one indication
of this, particularly when it is noted that the doctoral work was
now no longer almost exclusively confined to physical, natural,
medical, and agricultural sciences. A second indication was the
establishment of new institutes: the Allan Memorial Institute of
Psychiatry (in association with the Royal Victoria Hospital) in
1944, the Institute of Islamic Studies in 1952, and the Institute
of Air and Space Law also in 1952. Along with the Arctic Institute
of North America, an international organization established in
1945 with headquarters on the McGill campus, and the Montreal
Neurological Institute and the Institute of Parasitology at
Macdonald College which had been established in 1929 and 1934
respectively, these new institutes reinforced McGill's world-wide

reputation as a centre for research. During these decades, McGill's fame was spread throughout both the United States and Europe by the humourous publications and lecture tours of its political economy professor, Stephen Leacock, and by the pioneering work in neurosurgery carried out by Dr Wilder Penfield in the Montreal Neurological Institute.

At Bishop's University, between 1940 and 1960, the admissions tripled, but it retained its flavour as a small liberal arts college, 418 of its 426 students being in the faculty of arts and science. It had, nevertheless, made progress since 1940, particularly following the amendment of its charter in 1947 which transferred control of the university from the Anglican Church of Canada into the hands of a corporation. There was a strengthening, too, of the academic staff and some expansion in physical plant; in 1959, for example, a library was erected with a capacity of 100,000 volumes, as well as a dining hall, and a women's residence. The opening of the latter increased student accommodation to 295. It continued to offer teacher training, M.A.s in education, and to train clergy for the Anglican church.

Sir George Williams University described itself in the 1960 edition of *Canadian Universities and Colleges*, the biennial handbook which the NCCU had begun to issue in 1948, as 'a university without a campus.' As the result of a public campaign launched in 1952 which raised $3,300,000, it had constructed in 1956 a five-storey building immediately adjacent to the YMCA building in which it had been born, and in 1960 with the release of the Quebec portion of the federal grants it was able to add a sixth-storey to provide accommodation for a library of 100,000 volumes. It also continued to occupy several floors of the YMCA building, as well as portions of several other buildings in the downtown sector of Montreal. The increased facilities permitted the introduction of a two year engineering course in 1957. In 1960, the full-time enrolment was 1768 (192 in 1940-41), with 1267 in arts and science, 443 in commerce, and 58 in engineering. Though still inadequately housed (this problem would not be resolved until 1966 with the opening of a twelve-storey building (two blocks away) its prospects were good since legislation of March 1960 guaranteed it a statutory operating grant from the province (approximately $400,000 in 1960) in lieu of the federal grant. However, the fact that in keeping with its original purpose it continued to cater primarily to the needs of part-time students through its extensive evening degree and diploma programs meant that it was faced with continuing financial problems since the provincial grant was based on full-time enrolment only. Its right to confer degrees had been confirmed by a provincial charter establishing Sir George Williams College in 1948 and in 1959 a new charter was issued in the name of Sir George Williams University.

Ontario, the largest English-speaking province in Canada, and by
far the wealthiest, by 1960 was providing higher education for
almost as many students as had been registered in all the Canadian
universities in 1940-41. There were some 30,000 students, not
including those following the grade 13 or senior matriculation
course in the high schools throughout the province. Two of the
consequences of this growth were the provision of degree-granting
charters to more than a dozen institutions and the steadily increasing involvement of the provincial government in the financing
of higher education. It was not, however, until after 1960 that
the government became more than tangentially involved in the process of post-secondary education or showed much interest in developing a provincial university system.
   Disregarding the institutions which, under the terms of the
Federation Act of 1887, had placed in abeyance their powers to
grant degrees except in theology, there were only five degree-
granting universities in Ontario in 1940 - McMaster, Ottawa,
Queen's, Toronto, and Western Ontario. By 1960 there were 12,
and here too we must disregard degree-granting institutions whose
relation to another was akin to that of Toronto's federated colleges - St Michael's, Trinity, and Victoria. For example, Huron
College was so related to Western Ontario, Huntington and Sudbury
to Laurentian, and St Jerome's to Waterloo. St Michael's, it
should be noted, did not have degree-granting powers in 1940,
but in 1958 it was recognized by the provincial legislature as a
university in federation with the University of Toronto.
   One of Ontario's new universities was a professional school of
long standing and it was granted limited rather than degree-
granting powers. Osgoode Hall Law School, after being in continuous operation since 1889, was granted a charter in 1957 permitting it to grant degrees in law, following the inauguration
of a three year L.L.B. program.
   Three of the new universities arose out of colleges affiliated
with the University of Western Ontario. Assumption College, which
had been conducted at Windsor by the Basilian fathers since 1870,
obtained degree-granting powers in 1953 and a year later was admitted to membership in the NCCU. As a denominationally controlled institution it was not, however, eligible for provincial
grants. Adopting a procedure that had already been successfully
implemented at Queen's in the 1890s (with the establishment of
the Kingston School of Mines) and at McMaster in 1948 (with the
establishment of Hamilton College) whereby a non-denominationally
controlled institution was established to provide instruction in
certain subjects and which then entered into affiliation with the
denominationally controlled university, Assumption in 1956 accepted
as an affiliate Essex College, established that year to provide
a program in engineering and nursing as well as in mathematics
and the pure sciences. The remaining courses offered at Assumption,
other than theology which continued to be offered by the faculty

of theology, were grouped together in a newly created University
College, for which Assumption also had financial responsibility.
But Essex College being non-denominational was now eligible to
receive financial assistance from the province. In this same year
Assumption College became Assumption University of Windsor and
Holy Redeemer College, a seminary of the Redemptorist fathers,
became a second affiliate authorized to give some instruction
leading to the B.A. degree. A similar arrangement was made in
1957 with Canterbury College, an Anglican institution, probably
the first instance in Canada or indeed in North America where a
Protestant institution has been accepted as an affiliate by a
Roman Catholic university. Despite all these developments
Assumption remained a small university in 1960 with an enrolment
of fewer than 1000 students.

Waterloo College, a Lutheran institution and therefore denominationally controlled, as a University of Western Ontario affiliate, faced identical problems with respect to provincial grants
as Assumption. In 1956 it sought the same solution by arranging
for the establishment of a separate institution, which could then
become an affiliate. The Waterloo College Associated Faculties
was duly incorporated under the Company's Act, and in September
1956 began to offer programs in science and engineering, the
latter using the cooperative approach developed by Antioch College
in the United States whereby the students spent alternate periods
on campus taking academic courses and off campus working under
supervision in industries and commercial firms. For the next
several years Waterloo College's affiliation with Western Ontario
remained in effect, but in 1959 the Ontario Legislature granted
charters to three institutions in the Kitchener-Waterloo area:
Waterloo Lutheran University (the old Waterloo College), the
University of Waterloo (the old Associated Faculties), and the
University of St Jerome's College, a Roman Catholic institution
run by the Resurrectionist fathers, whose history dates back to
1864. Since 1947 it had been offering some instruction in arts
in affiliation with the University of Ottawa. The intention was
to provide for a federated university, a non-denominational
University of Waterloo being the centrepiece with the denominationally controlled institutions occupying a position similar to
that of St Michael's, Trinity, and Victoria with the University
of Toronto. However, differences of opinion developed between
the Associated Faculties group and Waterloo College over control
of the Faculty of Arts:

> Attached to the bill setting up the University of Waterloo were
> schedules, one of which mentioned the agreement by which
> Waterloo College would have the right to appoint the chairman
> for all courses taught in the college, who would also be the
> chairman for the university unless there was mutual agreement
> to the contrary; it also stated that the university would not
> duplicate instruction in arts, humanities and social sciences
> offered by the federated colleges unless the latters' boards

agreed. The leaders of Waterloo College assumed that this meant
that they would control the Faculty of Arts at both undergraduate
and graduate levels and would be represented on the Senate accordingly. Representatives of the University of Waterloo would not
accept their interpretation, and, although the College Board yielded
the point, the Lutheran Synod would not accept the arrangement.[22]

The consequence was that the two institutions went their separate
ways even though the two campuses literally adjoined each other.
St Jerome's, however, did enter into federation with the University
of Waterloo.

The other new establishments of the late 1950s were York University
at Toronto and Laurentian University of Sudbury, incorporated respectively in 1959 and 1960. York was expected to be a very large university within ten years, but the arrangement was that it would begin
as an affiliate of the University of Toronto, offering for a minimum
of four and a maximum of eight years courses authorized by the
University of Toronto Senate, with the students receiving University
of Toronto degrees. In September 1960 York opened in a building on
the University of Toronto campus with an enrolment of 72.

The basis for Laurentian University was the Collège de Sudbury,
a Jesuit classical college which had opened in 1913. This institution was granted degree-granting powers in 1957 but in 1960
entered into federation with Laurentian University, an undenominational institution chartered in that year. In 1960 the legislature
also granted a charter to Huntington University, a United Church
institution established as the result of the efforts of the Northern
Ontario University Association formed in 1958.

The oldest of the new universities was Carleton which, as the
Ottawa Association for the Advancement of Learning, began to
offer instruction at the Grade 13 and first year university levels
to part-time students in September 1942. The institution was
incorporated as Carleton College in 1943, and in the same year
opened an institute of public administration. It had no full-
time students until March 1945 when the first of a series of four
to six month matriculation courses for veterans was provided.
The academic year 1945-46 saw the transfer of the operation from
two Ottawa high schools to the building which had previously been
occupied by the Ontario Ladies College, the establishment of
faculties of arts and science and of public administration, the
introduction of a one-year pre-engineering course and a two-year
course in journalism for which two years of arts and science was
prerequisite, and the granting of three degrees in journalism
and three in public administration to students who had entered
Carleton with substantial credits from other universities.

The college suffered a heavy loss in February 1947 with the
death of its founder and first president, H.M. Tory, but it continued to develop rapidly. Full-time appointments to the teaching
staff were introduced in 1947, the full third and fourth year
programs in arts and science became available in 1947 and 1948
respectively and the first degrees in arts, science, and commerce

were awarded in 1949. The institutions right to grant degrees was confirmed by the Carleton College Act of 1952 and in 1957 a new act transformed it into Carleton University. It was not however until 1959 that the University began to occupy its permanent site and could be said to begin to be properly housed. Its full-time enrolment in 1960-61 was just under 1000 (998 to be precise), but in keeping with the tradition under which it had begun it continued to cater to the needs of large numbers of part-time students.

With respect to the funding of higher education in Ontario, only three of the five universities received provincial grants in 1940, the Universities of Ottawa and McMaster being excluded because of their church affiliation. The provincial grants to Queen's, Toronto, and Western Ontario were steadily increased from 1945 on and by 1960 were close to ten times the 1940 figure: Queen's $2,550,000 ($255,000 in 1940), Western Ontario $2,175,000 ($270,000), Toronto $13,757,000 (just under $2,000,000). The Toronto figures do *not* include grants of close to $1 million to the Ontario College of Education (financed by the Department of Education) and of close to $2 million to the Ontario Agricultural College and the Ontario Veterinary College (financed by the Department of Agriculture). At all three universities enrolment approximately doubled. In the case of Queen's and Western this brought them over the 3000 figure and into the medium size university category with a high proportion of graduate students, 209 at Queen's (29 in 1940), 345 at Western (36 in 1940). At Toronto, graduate enrolment increased from 390 to 1343.

The expansion at Western Ontario was particularly notable in terms of numbers of programs and physical plant, a phenomenon which would continue throughout the 1960s. In 1940 its undergraduate offerings were limited to arts and science (including business administration), medicine, and nursing; by 1960 journalism, secretarial science, physical and health education, household science, music, engineering, and law had been added. Queen's added fewer programs (nursing, physical and health education, law) but in addition to the development of graduate studies over a wide range of disciplines it expanded its medical school substantially (330 students from 266) and greatly improved its physical plant. At Toronto, which in 1940 was already offering programs in almost all fields, the main developments were the re-establishment of a faculty of law[23] and the integration of the Ontario College of Pharmacy within the university as its faculty of pharmacy, offering a four year program in place of the two year one which had been offered by the Ontario College. During this period Toronto also established a number of centres and institutes; industrial relations (1947) which became the School of Business in 1959, aerophysics (1949), the computation centre (1951) which became the Institute of Computer Science in 1962, the Great Lakes Institute (1960), and the Institute of Earth Sciences (1960).

One of the more significant developments of this period, 1940 to 1960, was the working out of arrangements whereby both McMaster and Ottawa Universities could qualify for provincial grants. At McMaster the initial approach was by way of the establishment of an independently controlled Hamilton College in 1948, which entered into affiliation with McMaster and assumed responsibility for the teaching of science and nursing, and of engineering after its introduction in 1952. The first government grant in 1948 was $100,000 for operating purposes; by 1956 a total of $1,650,000 for capital expenditures and $1,550,000 for operating costs had been granted. In 1957 McMaster finally shed its denominational ties. The faculty of theology was then rechristened McMaster Divinity College and it became independently chartered but affiliated with McMaster. In 1960-61 McMaster received $2,150,000 from the province, with another $75,000 being given for its tasks in connection with the adjacent Botanical Gardens.

Provincial assistance transformed McMaster from a small liberal college (474 arts and science and 30 theological students in 1940-41) into a small university which in the 1960s would become a much larger one. In 1960-61 enrolment was 1578, with undergraduate programs in commerce and physical and health education as well as in nursing, engineering, arts, and science. Its 1961-62 enrolment included 172 graduate students, more than 10% of the total enrolment. At the graduate level, McMaster's concern at this time was principally with the sciences, its excellence in this area being symbolized by its acquisition of a nuclear reactor which was fully operational by 1959.

In the case of University of Ottawa the solution to rationalizing provincial funding began with the government's decision to support the establishment of a fifth medical school in the province, a move which led to a grant of $250,000 to Ottawa in 1947. By 1960 the province was providing support for the university's work in pure and applied science in all fields. By 1960-61, the total amounts of government grants to the university were $5,545,000 for capital expenditures and $3,325,000 for operating purposes; the combined 1960 figure was $1,350,000.

This funding enabled enrolment to be increased by a factor of five between 1940 and 1960 to a total of just over 2500, of whom 276 were in graduate studies, the majority in theology or philosophy. Ottawa too had become a multiversity, with the addition of professional programs in medicine (1945), engineering (1946), physical and health education (1950), law (1953), and household science (1956). In addition it retained its somewhat nominal connection with the University of Ottawa Normal School (renamed University of Ottawa Teachers College in 1951), and through its faculty of psychology and education established in 1943, offered courses leading to the B.Ed., M.Ed., M.A., and Ph.D. degrees.

THE WEST

By Canadian or British, if not by American, standards each of the western provincial universities had become a large institution by 1960, offering the full range of professional courses in addition to comprehensive arts and science and graduate programs. British Columbia had become a large university by any standard, being exceeded in Canada only by Toronto and Montréal. This arose in part from the policy of having a single degree-granting university within the province, as opposed to the situation in Ontario where there were twelve such institutions and in the Maritimes where there were many more than could be legitimately supported. The western provinces had decided not to repeat this pattern, and while initially it was a wise decision, by 1960 there were a number of evident disadvantages. Increasing numbers of students were applying for admission, placing a great strain on existing accommodation, and the great distances which students had to travel to attend the universities in Edmonton or Saskatoon, for example, were inhibiting. Thus, early in the 1960s the single university policy was amended in three of the four western provinces; Saskatchewan held out until the 1970s.

However, the situation was not as monolithic as it would seem, the Canadian genius for federation and affiliation providing for considerable diversification within the unitary provincial system. The University of Manitoba, for example, had four affiliated colleges, one of which, United, had close to 1000 students, and a second, Brandon, was located in the city of that name. Saskatchewan, in addition to a number of affiliated theological colleges, had three affiliates which provided instruction in arts and science, and it was developing in the provincial capital of Regina a college that would eventually become a second campus of the University of Saskatchewan and then a university in its own right.

Alberta had two affiliated colleges on its own campus, as well as affiliated junior colleges at Camrose, Calgary (Mount Royal College), and Lethbridge, and at Calgary it was developing a branch which in 1966 would become the University of Calgary. The University of British Columbia's affiliate, the Victoria College, which now offered full programs in arts, science, commerce, and education, had an enrolment of 1368. In addition, two colleges in Saskatchewan, Notre Dame at Wilcox with an enrolment of 47 and Collège classique de Gravelbourg with an enrolment of 60, were affiliated with the University of Ottawa, while in British Columbia Notre Dame University College at Nelson, with an enrolment of 187, was affiliated with Gonzaga University in Spokane, Washington, and the federal government had located one of its tri-services colleges at Esquimault. Nonetheless there was general concern in the West about the development of post-secondary education, both with respect to the size of the universities and the lack of technical institutes. This concern led to the appointment of royal commissions on education in Alberta in 1959 and in both British Columbia and Manitoba in 1960.

Manitoba, which, including its affiliates, had an enrolment of just over 6000 in 1960, continued to have problems arising from the location of its buildings in different parts of Winnipeg. In 1950 the first two years of the university's work in arts and science were moved to the Fort Garry campus, but the affiliated arts colleges remained at their original locations in the centre

of Winnipeg, as did the faculties of law and medicine. The offer
to provide the colleges with sites on the Fort Garry campus was
renewed in the early 1950s and in 1958 St John's and St Paul's
did move to the main campus. But St Boniface and United decided
to remain permanently in downtown Winnipeg. During this period,
degree programs were introduced in social work (1943), nursing
(1948), the fine arts (1950), and dentistry (1958), and in 1960
a diploma course was introduced in physical and occupational
therapy. There was considerable development of the program in
pharmacy, but a marked decline in the numbers of students enrolled
in medicine - 158 in 1960-61 as opposed to 280 in 1940-41. In
architecture the enrolment increased from 25 to 226 despite the
lengthening of the course from four to five years, in part the
result of the introduction of a degree program in interior design
in 1948. Enrolment in graduate studies at Manitoba rose from 68
to 251.

At Saskatchewan, where the enrolment in 1960 was just under
5000, the most significant developments were in education, graduate studies, and medicine, though there were also very large
increases in the enrolment in commerce and pharmacy, and in 1950
a degree program in physical and health education was introduced.
In the school of graduate studies enrolment increased from 23
to 210. In 1947 the one year course for graduates leading to a
certificate for high school teaching, taken by 35 students in
1940-41, was replaced by a four year B.Ed. course which qualified the graduate to teach in the elementary as well as the
secondary schools. In 1960 the enrolment was 900, including a
substantial number at Regina College. In 1955 the University
Hospital was completed on the campus and the full four year
medical course became available.

The University of Alberta was in difficulties at the beginning
of the period partly as a result of the senate's failure to approve the granting of an honorary degree to the premier of the
province, William Aberhart. This widely publicized event, in
conjunction with a number of other criticisms of the university's
administration, led to the appointment by the government of a
University of Alberta Survey Committee, which reported in 1942.[25]
Its recommendations led to a reorganization of the administration
over the course of the next several years and placed Alberta in
a position to make rapid progress from 1945 on. Here, too,
there was a healthy development in commerce, pharmacy, and graduate studies, the enrolment in the latter increasing from 61
to 350. In education, the introduction of a four year B.Ed.
degree in 1946 had the same results as at Saskatchewan, with
the 1960 enrolment close to 2000. New programs were introduced
in physical and occupational therapy (1954), physical and health
education (1956), and music (1959).

In 1946 the Normal School at Calgary was renamed the Faculty
of Education of the University of Alberta at Calgary and for the
next several years it offered courses leading to the University
of Alberta B.Ed. degree. Commencing in 1951, other University

486

of Alberta courses became available at the Calgary campus, initially arts and science and nursing, but by 1957 engineering as
well, and by 1960 it was possible to obtain the B.Sc.N. degree
through work at the Calgary General Hospital at what was beginning to be called the Calgary branch of the University of Alberta.
The branch moved to a new site in 1960 and thereafter more rapid
steps began to be taken towards the development of what in 1966
would become the University of Calgary.

Partly because its efforts to expand its offerings had been
so consistently frustrated during the 1920s and the 1930s, the
development of the University of British Columbia during this
period was even more noteworthy. A program in household economics was introduced in 1943, in law in 1945, in architecture,
physical and health education, and pharmacy in 1946, in medicine
in 1950 (with the full program available by 1953), and in music
in 1959. A B.Ed. degree had been authorized in 1942 and the
department responsible for the program was constituted a school
within the faculty of arts and science in 1950, at which point
enrolment was over 200. Two years later the minister of education proposed that the university assume responsibility for all
teacher training in the province. This led to negotiations
between the university and the Department of Education which
culminated in the establishment of a college and faculty of
education, to be supervised by a special joint board consisting
of representatives of both the university and the department
under a single dean. The 1960-61 enrolment in the college and
faculty of education was 1935, with an additional 554 students
registered in education at U.B.C.s affiliate, Victoria College.
There were 849 students registered for graduate studies at
British Columbia in 1960 as opposed to 129 in 1940.

THE FEDERAL GOVERNMENT

It is already apparent that the federal government became a major
factor in the development of Canadian universities in the 1940s
and 1950s in contrast to the situation that obtained prior to
World War II when its involvement was limited to its direction
of the Royal Military College and to its support of research
through such agencies as the National Research Council and such
departments as Agriculture and Lands and Forests. This important
change in the government's role resulted in part from the financial support it provided first through the DVA program and from
1951 on through the distribution of annual grants to the individual universities and colleges as recommended by the Royal
Commission on National Development in the Arts, Letters and
Sciences. It is important to recognize that this expansion of
the federal role was general rather than specific and that what
the federal government was providing was financial support, not
direction. How the individual university used the funds it received under the federal grant formula was its affair, and this

had equally been true of the $150 it received for each registered veteran student under the DVA program. This was a case where the piper paid for the tune but did not call it. It would have been a very different matter if the amount of the DVA or the federal grant varied with the type of program taken by the individual student, since this would have enabled the government indirectly to encourage or discourage particular programs.

The direct involvement of the federal government in higher education during this period was closely related to the rehabilitation of veterans, its operation of military colleges, and its sponsoring of a second Khaki College or University at the close of World War II modelled on the first such institution initiated after World War I.

The Royal Military College at Kingston had been closed in 1942 after the accelerated graduation of the last pre-war class. It reopened in 1948 as the senior of two Canadian Services colleges, the other being Royal Roads College at Esquimault B.C., a naval cadet college established in 1942 which in 1947 began to enrol Royal Canadian Air Force cadets. A third Canadian Service college was established in 1952 in the Province of Quebec, Collège Militaire Royal de St Jean. The arrangement was that all three colleges would offer a common first and second year program (St Jean also provided for a preliminary or senior matriculation year), with the students from Royal Roads and St Jean then proceeding to the Royal Military College for the final two years.

The curriculum, particularly in the final two years, was a far cry from the program offered at military colleges in Canada or elsewhere before World War II, placing as it did a heavy emphasis on liberal arts subjects such as English and French literature, history, and philosophy. In some of these subjects it became possible to take honour courses at the third and fourth year level. By 1959 there was every justification for authorizing the Royal Military College to grant degrees in arts, science, and engineering. Arrangements were made for students who had completed the program before 1959 to be awarded the degree if qualified, and by the end of 1960 a total of 155 degrees had been granted by the RMC. Its enrolment in 1960 was 430 and there were 211 students at St Jean and 172 at Royal Roads.

The life of the second Khaki University was a short but productive one. 'Within two months from the time when it was merely a partly formed idea, devoid of planning for physical plant, library, staff and students, it became an operating reality. Less than nine months later, its purpose fulfilled, it had ceased to exist.'[26] The institution was established at Leavesden in Hertfordshire in the summer of 1945. It was basically a junior college, offering work at the first and second year levels in arts and science subjects, but it also had a department of extension which made arrangements for close to 200 servicemen to take refresher courses at British universities and technical colleges, and for close to 300 others to obtain temporary employment on British farms or in British industries. A

total of 850 servicemen attended Khaki University during its two
14 week terms; the student normally took two subjects per term
which were the equivalent of a full year course at a Canadian
university. Both the president (G.E. Beament) and the dean of
the faculty (G.M. Churchill) were army officers, but the remainder
of the 45 faculty members who served for one or other or both of
two terms were 'academics' seconded from their military units.
Appropriately enough the president emeritus of Khaki University
was H.M. Tory, who at this time was busily engaged in organizing
Carleton College in Ottawa.

It is appropriate here to make brief reference to the special
relationship that developed throughout the years of World War II
between the federal government and the universities.[27] From the
start the federal government did concern itself very seriously
with both the present and future deployment of students who were
either already in university or were on the verge of matriculation from high school. The executive committee of the NCCU was
in continual discussion with the federal authorities concerning
matters bearing on the role of the universities in the war effort,
and particularly with the questions whether some programs, such
as medicine, dentistry, and engineering, should be accelerated and
whether the liberal arts program should be curtailed. The serious
ramifications of the latter problem are discussed in chapter 27.[28]
The solution to the acceleration policy was of a different order,
and to solve such problems the government created several new
bodies to act as liaison between its representatives and those
from industry and the universities.

Being fully aware of mistakes made in World War I where there
was no attempt to control manpower requirements, especially of
the highly technical types to be found in the universities, the
government, immediately in September 1939, advised all students
of military age to stay in school or university until the moment
when it was clear how they could be used to best advantage in
the war effort. By August of 1940 the National War Service
Regulations were promulgated designating certain groups of students as eligible for call-up and others to remain in college
or university as long as they agreed to join one of the on-campus
military training units. In February 1941, the Wartime Bureau
of Technical Personnel was created by order-in-council and its
mandate was clear. In the words of President J.S. Thomson, then
president of the University of Saskatchewan, 'No member of staff
or student under the control of this body could leave the university and no professional scientist or technician could accept
any appointment or change his employment without the permission
of the Bureau. Thus the entire scientific and technical resources
of the country were mobilized and the detailed operation of the
plan required continual judgment between competitive claims of
what were the most essential services.'[29]

Soon after the creation of the Wartime Bureau of Technical
Personnel an advisory board was appointed, upon the recommendation of the minister of labour. It consisted of representatives

from three key industries, engineering, mining and metallurgy, and chemistry, all of which had been instrumental in convincing the government of the need for such a body, from the Canadian Manufacturers' Association, the provincial professional engineering associations, and the universities. This board met four times a year and kept both industry and the universities informed as to the government's needs and plans for deployment of war personnel. In March of 1942 a second body was created, the National Selective Service (NSS) which collaborated with the Wartime Bureau by way of the Bureau's board.

March 1942 also saw the coming into effect of the Technical Personnel Regulations which 'provided that scientific and techni- cal personnel could not be employed otherwise than through or with the approval of the Bureau or on behalf of the Minister of Labour.' In May 1942, the plans for acceleration of courses in the facul- ties of medicine, dentistry, and engineering were announced, and money was provided by the government to the universities to enable them to implement these plans and loans were provided for students to enable them to attend. These students had to guarantee that they would, immediately upon graduation, join either one of the services or a key war industry, or go into some area of war-related research, such as was being carried on in the National Research Council of Canada laboratories. In September 1942, the government, after consultation with the universities, instituted a plan for offering financial assistance to qualified engineering and science students who could not otherwise afford to obtain technical training at university level, and in December 1942 the University Science Students Regulations took effect, their implementation being placed directly in the hands of the Wartime Bureau of Technical Personnel in cooperation with the universities, i.e., the NCCU.

The universities further cooperated with the government in ac- cepting specific research projects to be carried out in their laboratories and encouraging faculty members to take leave of absence in order to work for government laboratories or for such government agencies as the Foreign Exchange Board and the Wartime Information Board. They guaranteed as well that any students who could not stay in the top half of their class would be reported and made eligible for call-up.

In December 1943, another body was created by the federal govern- ment, the University Advisory Board. At first it concerned itself with the fairness and effectiveness of mobilization regulations as they affected university students, but as the war neared its end the board's main concern turned to the effectiveness and fair- ness of demobilization plans, for example, to ensure that key uni- versity personnel were released from the services as quickly as possible in order to shore up the lamentable shortages of faculty in all universities across the nation. This was especially urgent in the light of the anticipated deluge of veterans who, immedia- tely upon demobilization, would be pouring into the universities at government expense.

490

Thanks to the efforts of this University Advisory Board and to the tireless activities of the various NCCU committees, all the veterans were accommodated and the government was persuaded to provide additional funds and war surplus materials and equipment to the universities to help them meet their respective challenges. The NCCU Committee on Post-War Problems deserves special mention for its work on planning for as smooth as possible a shift from wartime to peacetime conditions. There is no doubt that the NCCU emerged from the war years with a clear mandate to speak for the Canadian universities, and its executive continued to be in constant touch with the federal authorities over the following five years in connection with implementing the DVA program.

The involvement of the federal government with research between 1940 and 1960 will be referred to in chapter 30.

NON DEGREE-GRANTING INSTITUTIONS

The junior college movement, which appeared to be making headway particularly in western Canada in 1920 to 1930,[31] failed to move forward in the post-war period. Alma College in Ontario, one of the nine Canadian institutions which could be described as a junior college in 1940 had, by 1960, reverted to the status of the secondary school; a second had become Memorial University of Newfoundland; and a third, Victoria College in Victoria, B.C., was offering courses at the third and fourth year level and on its way to becoming the University of Victoria in 1963. There was little change in the position of five of the remaining six, Mount Royal College in Calgary, an affiliate of the University of Alberta, Prince of Wales College in Charlottetown, P.E.I., and three of the four affiliates of the University of Saskatchewan, Campion, Luther, and St Peter's colleges. But the other University of Saskatchewan affiliate, Regina College, had extended its program and would in 1961 become a self-contained campus of the University of Saskatchewan.

If one includes Royal Roads and Collège Militaire Royal de Saint Jean, which offered the first two years of the Canadian Services College program, there were eight additional junior colleges by 1960, the most important of which were Xavier Junior College, established by St Francis Xavier at Sydney, Nova Scotia in 1951, and Lethbridge Junior College in Alberta established in 1957. Camrose Lutheran College was established in 1959 and immediately became an affiliate of the University of Alberta. The remaining three were small Bible colleges which offered some work in arts: Mennonite Brethren Bible College in Winnipeg, which had an association with Waterloo College from the time of its founding in 1944 and in 1961 became an affiliate of Waterloo Lutheran University on Waterloo College's attainment of independence; Canadian Union College at College Heights, Alberta, a Seventh Day Adventist foundation; and Hillcrest Christian College, established by the Evangelical United Brethren Church at Regina in 1942, but which moved to Medicine Hat, Alberta, in 1947. Some graduates of the latter two institutions were admissible to the third year of certain American colleges.

Teachers colleges or normal schools were eliminated in Alberta in 1945, Newfoundland in 1945, and British Columbia in 1956, following the decision of the province to place responsibility for the training of elementary school teachers with the universities.[32] The two other western provinces were moving in the same direction, but in 1960 Saskatchewan still had two teachers colleges, one at Regina and another at Saskatoon; and there was also one in Winnipeg, Manitoba. In Prince Edward Island, Prince of Wales College continued to offer a normal school course, in Nova Scotia there was a normal school at Truro, and in New Brunswick one at Fredericton. In Quebec, where education was strictly divided along denominational lines, responsibility for the training of Protestant school teachers lay with McGill's Macdonald College, while training for teachers for both English-language and French-language Roman Catholic schools was provided by a large number of institutions affiliated with one or other of the French-language universities. In 1951, Ontario changed the name of its normal schools to teachers colleges and by 1960 there were 10 such institutions, including one opened in 1959 and another in 1960.

In 1940 one of the most striking features of the Canadian post-secondary education scene was the very few institutions devoted to technical and vocational training.[33] There were a number of agricultural schools across the country, a forest ranger school in Quebec, and an institute of technology in Calgary, Alberta. Over the next 20 years considerable development of such institutions took place, although it was not until 1960 that any Canadian province could claim to have made adequate provision for technical and technological training as opposed to professional education. The universities were very much aware of this and were anxious to have the situation remedied. For example, an important resolution adopted by the 1956 special NCCU conference was 'that the Conference commends to the attention of provincial governments the desirability of establishing more institutes of technology comparable to the Ryerson Institute of Technology in Ontario and other institutions for vocational and technical training at a non-university level.'[34]

In at least three instances the stimulus for establishing institutes of technology came from efforts to rehabilitate returning veterans: the New Brunswick Institute of Technology at Moncton, established in 1949 as an outgrowth of the Canadian Vocational Training Centre which was opened in 1946; the Manitoba Institute of Technology at Winnipeg, established in 1948 when the Provincial Department of Education took over the facilities organized in 1942 by the federal government for War Emergency Training classes and subsequently used for the training of veterans; and Ryerson Polytechnic Institute, established in 1948 from the Training Rehabilitation Institute which had opened in 1945. In New Brunswick, a Maritime forest ranger school was also established at Fredericton

in 1946. No institutes of technology had been established in
Newfoundland, Prince Edward Island, or Nova Scotia by 1960, but
in the latter province there were two vocational schools, the
Nova Scotia Marine Navigation School established in Halifax in
1951 and the Nova Scotia Land Survey Institute at Lawrencetown in
1958, the latter an outgrowth of a land survey school which opened
in 1937. The only new developments in the three most westerly
provinces during these two decades were the opening of a third
school of agriculture in Alberta (at Fairview), and the establishment in 1960 at Moose Jaw of the Saskatchewan Technical Institute.
In 1960, aside from a forest ranger school established in 1946,
British Columbia provided no opportunities for technological
training other than in its university and high schools.

The only province which could be said to have made a systematic
attempt to provide for technical and technological training was
Ontario.[35] Though the real development stems from the establishment of Ryerson Polytechnic in 1948, the effort began in 1945 with
the opening of a Provincial Institute of Mining at Haileybury
offering a two year program in mining technology. A second professional school was established in 1946 at Hamilton, the Provincial Institute of Textiles. In 1948, the Lakehead Institute of
Technology was established and by this time the program at Hamilton
had been expanded to include engineering technology and business
administration; in 1956 it was renamed the Hamilton Institute of
Technology. Two other institutes were set up towards the end of
the period, the Eastern Ontario Institute of Technology at Ottawa
in 1957, and the Western Ontario Institute of Technology at Windsor
in 1958. In 1960, these seven institutes had a full-time enrolment of 3049 and a part-time enrolment of 3481. At Ryerson, the
program had been expanded to include at least a dozen fields but
at all the others it was confined to engineering and business
administration and one or two specialties - textiles at Hamilton,
forestry at Lakehead. The Ontario 'system' also included in 1960
the Ontario College of Art and a forest ranger school established
at Dorset in 1945.

NOTES TO CHAPTER 26

1 Beginning in 1950 the conference also received an annual report
   from the Canadian Committee of International Student Service
   which in 1953 was reorganized as World University Service of
   Canada.
2 A fairly detailed chronicle of the development of NFCUS to
   1948 is provided in a seven-page mimeographed paper entitled
   'History of the National Federation of Canadian University
   Students 1926-1948,' edited by M.J. Diakowsky and distributed
   to all NFCUS chairmen. See also Maurice Sauvé's presidential
   address in *Report of the 11th Conference of the National
   Federation of Canadian University Students held at the University
   of Manitoba, Winnipeg, December 29-31, 1947* (1948), 5-13. For

developments between 1948 and 1956 see the section on Canada in NFCUS, *A History of National Unions* (1957).

3   NFCUS, *A Brief on Government Aid to Higher Education* (1958), 18

4   *NCCU Proc.* (1947), 72

5   V.C. Fowke, 'Professional Association: a History of the C.A.U.T.' in G. Whalley, ed., *A Place of Liberty* (1964), 200

6   *NCCU Proc.* (1951), 58

7   This proposal ultimately resulted in the commissioning of a study by Mark H. Ingraham of the University of Wisconsin sponsored by the Canadian Association of University Business Officers as well as by the NCCUC's successor, AUCC, and CAUT; it was published in English and French in 1966: *Faculty Retirement Systems in Canadian Universities/Régimes de retraite pour le corps professoral dans les universités canadiennes.*

8   For details of the Crowe case see *CAUT Bulletin* 7, 3 (January 1959), an issue devoted entirely to this case and its implications.

9   The figures in the paragraph are from Dominion Bureau of Statistics, *Higher Education in Canada 1940-42* (1944) and *Fall Enrolment in Universities and Colleges 1960* (1961). In the case of 1960-61, some students in agriculture, household science, optometry, and physical and health education were in diploma courses. Some in education (at Ontario College of Education, for example) were also in diploma courses but held a first degree.

10 Dominion Bureau of Statistics, *Survey of Higher Education, 1954-61*, 21

11 *Survey of Higher Education*, 21. See also 40-2.

12 J.F. Leddy, 'The International Opportunites of Canadian Universities,' in A.D. Dunton and D. Patterson, eds., *Canada's Universities in a New Age* (1962), 113-21; H.G. Somers, 'Summation of the Conference,' ibid., 150-3

13 The only province that had begun to develop a systematic approach to the financing of the universities was Ontario. See R.S. Harris, 'The Evolution of a Provincial System of Higher Education,' in D. Dadson, ed., *On Higher Education: Five Lectures* (1966), 55-6.

14 Dunton and Patterson, eds., *Canada's Universities*, 155

15 Somers, 'Summation,' ibid., 151

16 Ibid., 153

17 Ibid.

18 Royal Commission on Education in New Brunswick, *Report* (1962).

19 The problem of the secondary school curriculum as it affected the universities, together with the reforms which were being introduced in the 1950s, is fully outlined in A. Tremblay, *Les Collèges et les écoles publiques: Conflit ou coordination* (1954). See also below, chapter 27, 508-11.

20 In 1960-61 Laval received just over $4 million from the provincial government: $155,000 for its faculté d'arpentage et génie forestier; $200,000 for l'école des mines and other

schools in its faculté des sciences; $50,000 for its institut biologique; $500,000 of the total grant of $2,475,000 to be provided over a number of years for its Pavillon des Sciences; a 'regular' grant of $317,000 for operating purposes, a 'special' grant of $1,100,000 for operating purposes; $1,054,000 as a special grant to meet deficits accumulated in 1958-59; and $766,000 for the expected deficit of 1959-60.

21 An école de pédagogie was established in 1941, an école d'orientation in 1943. The two were merged in 1945 as L'Ecole de pédagogie et d'orientation.

22 W.G. Fleming, *Ontario's Educative Society*, IV: *Post-Secondary and Adult Education*, 22-3

23 Law courses were taught at the faculty of arts prior to 1941, but in that year were transferred to a school of law, which however did not offer a full program until 1949 when it was completely reorganized. In 1955 the school became a faculty.

24 In 1905 the Ontario government made a special grant to the University of Ottawa of $10,000 to assist it to rebuild its Science Hall which had been destroyed by fire. It also made a special grant of $10,000 to the denominationally controlled Université de Montréal at the time of its establishment in 1919.

25 University of Alberta Survey Committee, *Interim Report to the Lieutenant Governor in Council Province of Alberta*, sessional paper no. 50, Alberta Legislative Assembly, 1942

26 T.F. Gelley, 'Khaki University,' *Food for Thought*, (1949), 29

27 For a detailed account of these relationships, see Gwendoline Pilkington, 'A History of the National Conference of Canadian Universities, 1911-61,' 305-84.

28 See below, chapter 27, 498-9.

29 J.S. Thomson, *Yesteryears at the University of Saskatchewan 1937-1949* (1969), 45

30 Canada, Wartime Bureau of Technical Personnel, *Annual Report* (1942), 44

31 See above, chapter 20, 371-2.

32 On developments in the normal schools, see F.H. Johnson, *A Brief History of Canadian Education* (1968), 161-4.

33 See above, chapter 20, 372.

34 C.T. Bissell, ed., *Canada's Crisis in Higher Education* (1957), 245

35 Fleming, *Educative Society*, IV, 448-90

27

Arts and Science

The first meeting of the National Conference of Canadian Universities to take place after the outbreak of war was held in June 1942, and as would be expected, much of the program was devoted to matters related to the involvement of the universities in the war effort. However, there were two major items on the agenda which referred not to the immediate emergency, but rather to what could only be described at that point as the very uncertain future. One of these was a paper delivered by Brigadier H.F. McDonald of the Federal Government Pension Commission, who reported on the details of an October 1941 order-in-council which made provision for a variety of benefits for veterans who would be discharged from the services.[1] McDonald noted that this policy on the part of the federal government was in striking contrast to the attitude taken towards support of veterans of World War I. This time, he said,

> soon after the outbreak of war ... the Dominion Government unostentatiously but nevertheless thoroughly initiated studies of post-war policies, first in relation to the re-establishment in civil life of demobilized members of the fighting forces. Little publicity was permitted in regard to these studies until they had reached a definite degree of fruition. On October 1, 1941 they were crystalized by the passage of Order-in-Council P.C. 7633 which provides the first group of post-war benefits for discharged ... [veterans].[2]

General McDonald said that these measures were not simply aimed at 'individual rehabilitation' but rather they were 'a very definite phase of National Reconstruction.' He also revealed that the government had taken into its confidence several heads of universities and had consulted with them before establishing a policy; indeed as the following statement makes clear, some of these executive heads were key figures in the development of the veteran rehabilitation scheme: 'it would be very ungrateful indeed on my part ... if I did not take this opportunity of expressing the deep gratitude of my Committee and my Minister to those gentlemen who on the subcommittee, which recommended this scheme, gave so generously of their knowledge and experience, and may I in this connection express particularly these sentiments to President Cody, Principal James, and Principal Wallace.'[3] The second long-range item on the 1942 agenda was a symposium on the Future of the Faculty of Arts, which featured papers by Abbé Arthur Maheux of Laval, Principal R.C. Wallace of Queen's, and President N.A.M. Mackenzie of New Brunswick.

Maheux's paper reported on certain changes which had been made in the classical college course since 1920,[4] but his main emphasis was on the timeless value of the study of the humanities, particularly the ancient languages of Latin and Greek, and of the practical value of the former as an aid to the mastery of Canada's two official languages. In his view, Latin should be a compulsory subject in every high school in Canada: 'Unity is impossible without understanding. Understanding is hardly possible without the knowledge of both languages. The knowledge of both languages is difficult without Latin, and easy with Latin.'[5] These views were not challenged in the subsequent discussion but, as we shall see in the section of this chapter devoted to the classical college course, the position of the humanities in French-speaking Quebec in 1942 was not as satisfactory as Maheux suggested.[6]

In contrast to the classicist Maheux, Wallace, whose discipline was geology, was very much concerned about the future of the faculty of arts and particularly about the future of the humanities. In his view, a vocational emphasis was increasingly pervading the universities: this had been accentuated as a consequence of war-time conditions, but it was not basically attributable to the outbreak of war. Throughout the 1930s the proportion of matriculants registering in professional faculties and, within the faculty of arts, in professionally oriented courses such as commerce, had steadily increased, as had the proportion of courses in the professional faculties which were technically rather than theoretically oriented: 'we have gone too far in the purely technical aspect of professional training.'[7] So far as the faculty of arts and science was concerned, the pure sciences were not in danger since they were fundamental to a wide range of professional programs. The established social sciences - history, economics, political science, psychology - were also reasonably safe; they, too, were 'in demand for certain callings' and in addition were 'current in popular thinking.' 'But the whole field of language, ancient and modern, including the study of our own language, is in eclipse, while philosophy is reserved for theological students and for such as wish to probe into the soundness or otherwise of their early religious education.'[8] As a solution Wallace proposed that all students prior to undertaking their professional studies be required to devote a full year to the study of English, a foreign language, history, economics, and philosophy. 'The program may seem ambitious but it would not require more than a year of concentrated work and there is a growing belief that a year could be spared from the purely professional studies by relieving them of those phases of the work which the practice of the profession can best teach.'[9] This liberal or general education year should, in Wallace's opinion, follow senior matriculation and be 'crowned' by an associate of arts certificate. Students wishing to take further work in subjects like philosophy, economics, and physics should do so at an honours level.

The third speaker in this symposium, President N.A.M. Mackenzie, a specialist in law and international relations, was in general agreement with Principal Wallace that there was a vocational bias in Canadian higher education, but he found this consistent with the tradition of universities since the middle ages. He agreed, too, that in the twentieth century 'the arts course should be the core or centre of every university and should have some place in every university course.'[10] He then proceeded to list the subjects which for him constituted 'the irreducible minima of any education that makes any pretence to be real education': language and literature, history, anthropology, philosophy, history of human thought, economics, political science, natural sciences, physical sciences. However, other than indicating that he believed every student should take at least two years of arts and science, Mackenzie did not suggest how this 'irreducible minima' was to be organized. As a matter of fact he had little faith that proposals like Wallace's would appreciably alter the situation: 'My opinion is that the Arts course in the future will occupy very much the place in our curriculum that it does today. It will be taken by the teacher, the preacher, the young man and woman of means and leisure, by some of the professional students because of their own interest in it and some of them because they are "required" to take it. The others will continue to pursue their vocational studies as quickly and in as limited fields as calendars, deans and registrars permit.'[11]

This realistic if somewhat cynical prediction proved to be an accurate one. Six months after Mackenzie made it, a potentially serious crisis arose which could have radically altered the familiar or traditional direction of higher education in Canada. In the fall of 1942, two university heads, F.C. James of McGill and R.C. Wallace of Queen's, are reported to have suggested recommending to the federal government that an order be relayed to the universities to discontinue for the duration of hostilities the faculties of arts and science, commerce, education, and law; in short, all areas of study not directly related to furthering the war effort.[12] To this end, a special meeting of the NCCU was convened on 9 January 1943 and the director of the National Selective Service, A. Macnamara, was invited to attend, his 'address taking the form of a concise review of the manpower situation in Canada and of the Government's policy towards the problem with particular reference to those phases that affect the universities.[13] Present at this meeting were an undisclosed number of the heads of NCCU member-institutions, including President Patterson of Acadia who was spokesman for 45 professors from departments of humanities in universities across the country,[14] and Professor R.A. MacKay of Dalhousie who presented a memorandum on behalf of the Canadian Social Science Research Council.

Although the reporting of the minutes of this meeting are scant, there being no mention of which presidents, principals, and rectors were present, nor any explanation of why the meeting was called, nor any résumé of Macnamara's address, it is known that very strong opposition was brought to bear on the James-Wallace proposal. The outcome was a resolution, couched in terms true to the traditional Canadian spirit of compromise, which recommended that there be no immediate change in the government's manpower policy as it affected university students, but that appropriate changes be made should circumstances require more drastic action.

The resolution, which received unanimous approval, also expressed the conference's appreciation of the 'enlightened policy' of the government with regard to the lack of interference in higher education, its determination to cooperate with the government in the prosecution of the war in every possible way, and the willingness of the universities to make 'any future adjustments in their work that the exigencies of the war effort may demand.'[15] Reference was made to the fact that all physically fit students were required to take military training while attending university and that for many months there had been a general weeding out of incompetent students; both of these policies, it was emphasized, would be continued. There was also mention of 'the value for the war effort and national welfare of those creative forces which flow from sound education and to the importance of there being adequately trained teachers, especially in the secondary schools. 'The Conference ... would urge that students in liberal arts who wish to enter the teaching profession be encouraged to do so, and that those doing so be not called for military service.'[16]

As events transpired, there was no deterioration in the manpower situation until the closing months of the war and the question of abandoning the humanities for the duration was laid to rest with the following government proclamation in February 1944:

On the recommendation of the Universities Conference, National Selective Service provided that if a prospective student had attained an educational standing recognized by the Department of Education of his province as equal to that which should have been attained by one of his age, he should be considered eligible for postponement. This took care of the first year students. After this year of university work was completed, the student again became subject to call unless enrolled in a course defined by the Director of National Selective Service on the recommendation of a University Advisory Board as essential to the national interest or contributing to the prosecution of the war. These courses were defined as medicine, dentistry, engineering, architecture, agriculture, pharmacy, forestry, education, commerce,

veterinary science and specialized courses in mathematics, physics, chemistry, biology or geology ... Law and the arts course
were not, however, abolished but were covered in a general provision that a student in any university course not included in
the above would be considered as pursuing a course essential to
the national interests if he were in the upper half of all the
students enrolled in his course.[17]

Nonetheless, the threat had been a very real one and for the
balance of the war the incident provided an additional reason to
pursue the perennial question of what should be done about the
liberal arts. An immediate outcome was the decision taken in May
1943 to proceed with the establishment of a humanities research
council of Canada, a body designed like the Canadian Social Science
Research Council, to promote research and to defend the interests
of the academic disciplines and the traditions which they represented.[18]

Another significant event which took place in the fall of 1942
was the establishment of an NCCU Committee on Post-War Problems,
a body which shouldered the full responsibility for the post-war
planning of Canadian higher education. The committee was chaired
by N.A.M. Mackenzie, and its report was presented to and with only
minor amendments adopted by the NCCU at its regular meeting in
June 1944.[19] Of its 14 recommendations only two bore directly on
the faculty of arts and science, and neither of these was concerned
with organization of the course of study; one urged that there be
curricular offerings in Chinese, Russian, and Latin American studies, the other that governments be asked to provide funds for
adult education in order that work in this field could be extended.
However, a sub-section of the report was devoted to 'The Liberal
Arts Course,' and a paper on The Arts Faculty and Humane Studies,
prepared by R.C. Wallace at the committee's request, was included
in the published report as Appendix G. The Wallace paper, which
simply repeated the argument he had presented at the 1942 conference and offered the same solution, was used by the committee as
the basis for discussion of the subject. In conjunction with
other statements, it convinced the committee that 'there is a
liberal arts problem' but neither it nor any of the other papers
which the committee members had consulted convinced them that
Wallace or any one else had found the solution. In the committee's
view there was no single solution and consequently they were not
prepared to recommend that all Canadian universities should adopt
any of the formulae that were being widely advertised as panaceas.
Rather, every university that was convinced of the reality of the
problem should study it carefully and make some definite effort
towards finding a solution. The sub-section ended on a wistful
note: 'out of many attempts along varying lines surely some useful general solution should emerge.'[20]
Delegates to the 1944 conference had the opportunity almost immediately to consider two such attempts, one which the University
of Saskatchewan had introduced in September 1941 and one which the

500

University of Manitoba proposed to introduce as soon as the war ended.[21] Papers on these 'experiments' were presented in a 90 minute session on The Future of the Arts Course, the only session of this conference not devoted to the presentation and discussion of reports. It was also the last session until the 1960s which the conference devoted to the question of liberal or general education in the English-language universities. The subject did receive some attention with respect to the French-language universities in 1947 and 1956 when symposia were held on the classical college course; and in 1955 there was a symposia on the fine arts and in 1959 one on Near and Far Eastern studies. It is also true that occasionally in the formal addresses which it had become customary for the president of the NCCU to give at the annual meeting there were indications that the problem of the liberal arts had not been solved. In general, however, it would appear that from 1945 to 1960 the delegates to the conference and certainly the planners of its annual program agreed with the members of the committee on post-war problems that each institution had to work out its own solution.

There are at least three additional reasons for the low priority apparently given between 1945 and 1960 to the matter of liberal education both as a program in a faculty of arts and science and as an ingredient in the course of study of a professional faculty. The first is that, partly because so much attention was paid to these problems between 1939 and 1945, most institutions made curricular changes which reduced if they did not entirely remove the causes for complaint. At Saskatchewan, for example, the plan introduced in 1941 appears to have produced general satisfaction among both staff and students. A second reason is symbolized by the failure of the Manitoba experiment – the second of the two 'solutions' offered at the 1944 NCCU conference. Though described in the calendar each year from 1944-45 to 1947-48 as a program about to be implemented, the four general education courses on Western Civilization which were to be required of all arts and science students were never offered. The scheme required additional staff and this in turn required additional funds; and these the university was not able to obtain. All Canadian universities operated under severe financial constraints throughout the 1940s and 1950s, and this partially explains the lack of innovation in the courses of study.

The third reason for the apparent decline of interest in the undergraduate course in arts and science was the increasing preoccupation of members of the teaching staff with graduate work and with scholarship and research. Undergraduate instruction remained the focus of attention between 1945 and 1950, the period when the campuses were crowded by the dramatic in-flow of veterans, but during these years staff members were fully extended in fulfilling their obligations to the much larger number of students in their classes and had little time or energy to devote to experimentation. In the early 1950s enrolment declined sharply as the veteran students completed their courses, but even by 1954 it was rising steadily and most staff members found themselves carrying heavy teaching loads. By 1955, as a consequence of the publication of the Sheffield projections,[22] it was known that dramatic increases in student enrolment could be expected in the 1960s and therefore that there would soon be a pressing need for much larger numbers of qualified staff. Hence the increasing preoccupation during the middle and late 1950s with the development of graduate studies, a characteristic of Canadian higher education during these years which is clearly reflected in the programs arranged for the two special conferences organized by the NCCU, the one in 1956 on Canada's Crisis in Higher Education, and the one in 1961 on Canada's Universities in a New Age. In contrast, very little attention was paid at these conferences to the problems of undergraduate instruction and almost none at all to the curriculum in arts and science.[23]

GENERAL B.A. AND B.Sc.

When dealing with the curriculum in arts and science in the English-language universities between 1940 and 1960, there is little reason to deal separately with the B.A. and B.Sc. programs. In a few institutions the B.A. continued to be awarded to students who majored or concentrated in the pure sciences, but even in the much larger number which offered both degrees the only real distinction between the B.A. and the B.Sc. derived from the student's choice of subjects in which to major or concentrate during his senior years. Except at Mount Allison, New Brunswick, and Ottawa,[24] responsibility for undergraduate degrees in arts and the pure sciences rested with a single faculty, normally a faculty of arts and science but occasionally still a faculty of arts. The courses of study in those institutions which had separate faculties of arts and of science differed in no significant way from those in institutions which did not.

The chief feature distinguishing the B.A. general programs of 1960 from those of 1940 was the reduction in the number of exceptions to the general rules. The same basic pattern continued to be adopted in almost every institution: a first (or senior matriculation) year which was largely prescribed (four or five subjects); a second year in which English and a language taken in the first year were prescribed and in which the student was required to take a course in the social sciences; and two upper years in which the only requirement was to major or concentrate in either one or two subjects. The first year prescription invariably included English and a language, usually included either mathematics or a science, and often included history. In the Ontario universities, the student was required to take Latin or mathematics as a senior matriculation subject and had to include at least one other language in his program. Latin (or Greek) was also required at McGill, and at Dalhousie either Latin or Greek or classics in translation. Latin was prescribed in both the first and second years in the Roman Catholic colleges of the

502

Maritimes. In many cases the social science prescription of the second year was arrived at by requiring the student to select his electives from specified groups. Religion and philosophy continued to be required subjects in the Roman Catholic institutions, though in the case of philosophy not in all four years. Both McMaster and Western Ontario had withdrawn the requirement of a sequence of courses in history and in philosophy. Carleton did prescribe a course in philosophy in the second year (described in the calendar as 'introduction to problems of thought and conduct'), while both Acadia and McMaster required the equivalent of a one-hour-a-week course in religion in one of the upper years. Saskatchewan and Sir George Williams, as we shall see, prescribed specially designed general education courses in the first and second years.

The most fully prescribed B.A. program in 1960-61 was that offered at St Francis Xavier, and it was also one of the relatively few which departed at a great number of points from what has just been described as the norm. At St Francis Xavier, the first year was entirely prescribed: Latin, English, another language, either mathematics or history, religion, and a course called Orientation, which was designed to introduce the student to his university studies. English (one of the two languages taken in the first year) and religion were continued in the second year and philosophy was introduced, the balance of the year's work consisting of a course in public speaking and an elective. The elective would probably be either economics or political science, since both of these were required to be taken at some point during the four year course. Courses in religion and philosophy continued to be required in the remaining two years. Also prescribed in the third year was a full course in history and a two-hour-a-week course in music appreciation. These were paralleled in the fourth year by a full course in physical science and a one-hour-a-week course in art appreciation. This left the student with seven additional courses to complete the requirements for the degree, but even here there was what could be called either prescription or guidance: either he must take two of these seven courses in each of three subjects or he must take five of them in one subject, in which case after also having prepared a senior seminar and produced a graduating essay he was eligible to graduate with a B.A. with major.

The course in physical science prescribed in the graduating year at St Francis Xavier was especially designed for students who were not specializing in science - 'a general education course' to use the terminology made popular in 1945 by the publication of *General Education in a Free Society*, the widely publicized report of a Harvard College committee. It was the utilization of such courses rather than the reorganizing of the curriculum as a whole which characterized such efforts as the Canadian universities did make during these two decades to improve the B.A. program. It is to be noted that Canadian experimentation in this field antedated by some years the appearance of the Harvard report, which has in some quarters been given credit for stimulating Canadian interest in courses of this type.[25] Pandemic courses, it will be recalled,

503

had been introduced at Sir George Williams in 1936,[26] while the NCCU symposium at which the Saskatchewan and Manitoba programs were described was held a year before the report was published.

Sir George Williams continued to prescribe its three pandemic courses (humanities 210, natural sciences 210, social sciences 210) for all degree students until 1958-59, but it is symptomatic of changing attitudes towards such courses and towards prescribed courses in general which began to reveal themselves in the late 1950s and which became dominant in the mid 1960s that in 1960-61 all three of these long established courses became electives. Henceforth students could take either the pandemic (for example natural science 210) or a departmental course (in this instance, in biology, chemistry, or physics). The change was made partly to accommodate students who, intending to major in, for example, science, preferred to take a course that was basic to their science program rather than one primarily designed for non-scientists, but the chief pressure came from professors who wanted to prescribe additional departmental courses.[27] The other prescriptions in the Sir George Williams program of 1940 also survived the 1950s: four courses in English, including one in composition, three in the social sciences, two in the natural sciences. But - also a sign of the times - in 1960-61 they were reduced to two courses in English and one (additional) course in each of the humanities, social sciences, and sciences.

The general education courses introduced at Saskatchewan in 1941-42 must also be regarded as unusually successful since, in conjunction with a course in English, they remained for over 20 years the core of the arts and science program.[28] The decision to introduce them was based on a recognition of the limitations of the distribution principle as a method of ensuring that the student had some awareness of the full spectrum of human knowledge. At Saskatchewan at least, requiring the student to take one course in the sciences or one course in the social sciences had provided no guarantee that he would graduate with any understanding of the principles or the basic ideas of science or of social science:

> when the original curriculum was drawn up in 1909 a set of regulations had been adopted which were designed to ensure both breadth of study and some degree of concentration, but in any real sense the regulations had proved largely ineffective. Many students had graduated without having made acquaintance with large areas of knowledge. For example, the only scientific education which 50 per cent had acquired was a single class in chemical analysis. They had no biology, geology, physics, or mathematics. As far as the university was aware they knew nothing about the essential principles or generalizations of either the physical or the biological sciences. Similarly, 35 per cent had studied only one of the five social subjects: history, economics, political science, philosophy and psychology.[29]

The Saskatchewan solution was to develop specially designed courses
for students not specializing in four of the major areas of knowledge and to require students not specializing in these areas to
take these courses. Thus students specializing in the sciences
would be required to take history and philosophy 200 and political
economy 100; students specializing in the 'social subjects' would
take biological sciences 100 and physical sciences 100; and students specializing in languages and literature or in the fine arts
would take political science 100 and either biological sciences 100
or physical sciences 100.

These latter two courses, and equally Sir George Williams's
natural science 210, involved the cooperation of one or more science departments. Similar cooperation between departments at a
number of other Canadian universities, for example McMaster and
McGill, resulted in the development of other courses designed to
provide perspective on science for non-scientists. But none of
these was prescribed for such students. The 1940s and 1950s also
saw the emergence at various institutions of courses designed
like the other two Saskatchewan courses or the other two Sir George
Williams pandemics to provide perspective on the world of the
humanities and the social sciences for the scientist, but again
the element of prescription was missing. Such courses tended to
be developed by a single department rather than emerging as a
joint effort by several, and almost invariably they were offered
at the third or fourth year level.

At the very end of the period, ironically just as its neighbour
Sir George Williams was turning its prescribed courses into electives, McGill revised its B.A. program and made what it called
the Faculty Course a requirement in the final two years. Offered
in two parts (full courses in both years) and described in the
calendar as a synoptic course 'which will enlarge and synthesize
the various more specialized studies which the candidate will have
made in his departmental studies,' the Faculty Course was an attempt to achieve integration in the last two years of the course
rather than in the first two (as at Saskatchewan or Sir George
Williams) or throughout (as at St Francis Xavier). Though formally announced in 1960, the Faculty Course, being a third and
fourth year offering, was not introduced until September 1962 and
its six year history falls outside the period covered by this
chapter. It was, however, approved in the late 1950s, and reflects
a renewed interest in the problem of the liberal arts on the part
of the Canadian universities as they entered the 1960s.

HONOUR COURSES

By 1940 the honour course offered in a faculty of arts and science
was a well-known and generally admired characteristic of Canadian
higher education. It was not, however, a characteristic that
applied to all Canadian institutions, and in those where it did

apply its importance ranged from the highly significant to the nominal. The honour course was not offered at all in the French-language institutions since in them the classical college course remained the only route to the B.A., and it also was not offered in a number of English-language institutions which had small enrolments, for example Mount Saint Vincent and St Dunstan's. The honour course was most firmly entrenched in Ontario where it was recognized by the provincial Department of Education as a requirement for the Type A specialist certificate, a secondary school teaching qualification which not only called for a salary bonus but was the key to promotion to headship of a department or to a principalship; but even in Ontario the honour courses attracted a high proportion of arts and science students at only one institution, the University of Toronto, where the numbers enrolled in the four year honour courses approximately equalled those enrolled in the three year general course.[30] At the other Ontario universities and also at Bishop's, McGill, the four western universities, and the older universities of the Maritimes, the proportion of honour students in the faculty of arts and science tended to vary from 5% to 20%. But though at many universities the enrolment in honour courses was small, their importance was considerable, both because many faculty enjoyed teaching classes of able students who were particularly interested in the professor's subject and because the graduate with an honour degree was more likely to be admitted without conditions to a one year M.A. program in a graduate school than was the graduate with a general degree.

Between 1940 and 1960 two developments occurred which further strengthened the position of honour courses in the English-speaking universities. The first was the publication in 1947 of *The Humanities in Canada*, the report prepared by Watson Kirkconnell and A.S.P. Woodhouse for the recently established Humanities Research Council of Canada. Chapter IV of this volume is a detailed analysis of the honour courses offered in all the Canadian universities and a persuasive explanation of their educational value. In the course of the previous 50 years a number of articles arguing the merits of the Canadian honour course system or of particular courses had been published and also one small book, *Honours Classics at the University of Toronto* in 1927. As we have seen,[31] the subject of honour courses frequently appeared on the agenda of the meetings of the National Conference of Canadian Universities and consequently was reported on in the published proceedings. However, relatively few people other than the delegates themselves read the NCCU *Proceedings* with either regularity or care; relatively few people other than classicists or graduates of the course in question read the 1927 volume; and none of the journal articles appears to have attracted wide attention. In contrast, *The Humanitie in Canada* was widely read in academic circles and attracted almost as much attention from social scientists and scientists as from humanists. This was because the authors, though concentrating on the humanities, dealt with the undergraduate courses as a whole and because they documented the pressing need for the development

of graduate studies and for the provision of the facilities, for
example well equipped libraries, which were needed if Canadian
scholarship was to mature. Since social scientists and to a lesser
extent scientists were equally interested in furthering the development of graduate studies and of scholarship (or research),
they responded enthusiastically to the Kirkconnell-Woodhouse report.
In doing so they would inevitably find themselves reading the
chapter on honour courses.

The second development which strengthened the position of honour
courses was the need to develop graduate studies in order to provide adequate numbers of qualified staff for the much larger number of students who would be enrolling in the universities in the
1960s. If there were to be more M.A.s and Ph.D.s, there would
have to be more honour B.A.s, since the normal requirement for
admission to the one year M.A. was an honour degree or its equivalent.[32] This point was made by the physicist H.G. Thode, president of McMaster University, at the Special NCCU Conference of
1961: 'Although the overall enrolment in the universities is increasing rapidly, the enrolment in honour courses is not increasing
proportionately and, of course, it is from these courses that our
graduate students must be drawn. The basic question [with respect
to graduate studies and research] is how are we going to attract
more and better students into our honour courses.'[33]

While the numbers of students in honour courses was not increasing in proportion to enrolment in the faculties of arts and science, it was increasing in absolute numbers. At Toronto the proportion of graduates in honour courses declined between 1941 and
1961 from 50% to 40%, but the actual numbers increased from 275
to 436.[34] At universities where the enrolment had increased
dramatically during these two decades, the number of honour course
graduates had in many cases become significant, for example British
Columbia with 108 and Western Ontario with 123.[35] Furthermore,
honour courses were being offered at seven additional institutions,
St Mary's in Halifax and at all six of the institutions that obtained charters authorizing the granting of the B.A. and the B.Sc.
during these years: Assumption, Carleton, Memorial, Royal Military
College, Waterloo, Waterloo Lutheran. The only English-language
universities not offering an honours B.A. or B.Sc. in 1960-61 were
Mount Saint Vincent, St Dunstan's, St Thomas, and Sir George
Williams.

There had also been a widening of the range of subjects in which
a student could take an honour course; by 1960 it was possible at
one or more institutions to take such a course in anthropology,
East Asian studies (Chinese and Japanese), Islamic studies, and
Slavic studies.[36] What had not changed was the structure of the
honour courses themselves, or rather the several structures.
There continued to be considerable variety in the number of years
required to complete the program and in the point at which the
student was identified as a candidate for honours. At all the
Ontario universities, at three of the four western universities,
and at Acadia and St Francis Xavier, the student was required to

spend four years beyond senior matriculation, i.e., a year more
than was required to obtain a general degree. No additional time
was required at Bishop's, British Columbia, Dalhousie, Memorial,
McGill, Mount Allison, New Brunswick, Royal Military College, or
St Mary's, but five of these (British Columbia, Dalhousie, Mount
Allison, RMC, St Mary's) required the student to take two additional courses. Only at Toronto was the student identified as an
honour course student in his first year; in most cases the program
began at the beginning of the second year, but at Memorial,
Saskatchewan, and RMC it was postponed until the third. Bishop's
no longer permitted the student to take either a general or an
honour degree in three years from junior matriculation.

THE CLASSICAL COLLEGE COURSE

In the four earlier chapters of this book devoted to Arts and
Science, the section entitled 'The Classical College Course' en-
compassed with only minor exceptions all the activities of the
facultés des arts of the French-language universities, the principal exception being the offering of public lectures to which
reference had been made in the sections of these same chapters
entitled Extension.[37] There was a simple explanation for this;
the classical college course, taught in the classical colleges
affiliated with Université Laval or, from 1920 on, Université de
Montréal, was the only degree program offered by the faculties of
arts of these universities, and the teaching staffs of the classical colleges constituted the teaching staff of these faculties.
However, the fact that the role of the two universities with respect to the classical college course was confined to supervision,
examining, and the formal granting of degrees did not lessen the
importance of the course or of the colleges in the eyes of the
universities or of the general public and the government. The
only means of obtaining the B.A. was to complete the classical
college course, and it was taught only in the classical colleges.[38]
Furthermore, the B.A. was, in theory, a requirement for admission
to the other faculties and professional schools of the two universities, and while increasingly from 1920 on students were admitted to certain faculties (for example, sciences at Montréal) and
schools (for example, Ecole des hautes études commerciales) the
regulation was rigorously applied in the older and most presti-
gious faculties, law, medicine, and theology. The classical colleges were thus the only means of entering the liberal professions, and since the élite of French Canadian society tended to
be recruited from these professions, the B.A. was a document of
considerable importance.
   Until 1929 the classical colleges enjoyed not only an effective
monopoly on preparation for admission to the French language universities but also a monopoly on secondary education as a whole.
In that year, however, there was added to the eight year elementary school program, which had been offered in the French-language

public schools since the 1880s, a three year cours primaire, supérieur with, initially, commercial and industrial sections for boys in the final year.[39] By 1939 the sectioning ran through all three years, the industrial section had been designated the scientific section, and three sections had been introduced for girls. This produced an eleven year primary-secondary program which paralleled that of the English-language public schools of the province, in which seven years of elementary schooling, followed by a four year high school course, prepared the student for junior matriculation and admission to university. However, in comparison with the English-language high schools, the emphasis in the école primaire supérieure was on the practical or vocational rather than the academic or the general; the intention from the outset had been to prepare students for entry into business and industry rather than for the professions. Largely to compensate for this, a twelfth year was added to the scientific course in the early 1940s, and graduates of this extended course began to be admitted to the newer faculties and schools of the universities.

However, it was not until the 1950s that the effective monopoly of the classical colleges on qualification for admission to the French-language universities was broken; that this had occurred by 1960 is evidenced by the fact that in the 1960-61 session slightly less than 50% of the students enrolled at Laval, Montréal, and the recently established Université de Sherbrooke had a B.A.[40] With the breaking down of this monopoly the position of the classical colleges in the educational system of Quebec was fundamentally changed.

The breakdown was the result of two decisions affecting the classical college course which were made in 1952 and 1954. The first was the decision of Laval and Montréal to remove Greek from the list of required subjects for the B.A. degree. The second was the decision of the Comité catholique du Conseil de l'Instruction publique to permit Latin to be taught in the public schools of the province.

The removal of Greek from the list of prescribed subjects in the classical college course was the culmination of a thirty year campaign to revise the course in such a way as to enable some of its graduates to be adequately qualified to do advanced work in pure science in a faculté des sciences or to undertake the regular programs in such science-based faculties as dentistry, engineering, medicine, and pharmacy. The Abbé Arthur Maheux had noted in his paper presented at the 1942 NCCU symposium on 'The Future of the Faculty of Arts' that efforts along these lines extended back to the 1920s.[41] Five years later Léon Lortie in a paper entitled 'The New Classical Curriculum and Its Impact on University Courses' reported to the NCCU that both Laval and Montréal had recently authorized sectioning in the final years of the course to permit students who wished to do so to specialize in science and mathematics.[42] In the colleges affiliated with Montréal, he pointed out, the student on entering his final two years was required to choose either Section A or Section B, the

509

latter providing a program which reduced the percentage of marks assigned to philosophy from 55% to 40%, increased the weighting of mathematics by 5% and added biology (10%). However, in terms of classroom work, this 'reform' was a very modest one; the students of Section B continued to take 18 hours of instruction each week in both years in common with students in Section A, and only three as a specializing group.[43]

But with the removal of Greek, which occupied a total of about 14 hours spread over the middle four years of the eight year course, it was possible to introduce a substantial amount of additional science and mathematics and, as well, to give more attention to the social sciences and to art. The outcome was the establishment of two sections (or options): Latin-Grec, a continuance of the traditional course with its heavy emphasis on languages and philosophy; and Latin-Sciences, with emphasis on mathematics and science. But, though permitting specialization in either the humanities or the sciences where before it had permitted it only in the former, the revision represented no radical departure from the traditional bias of the classical college course towards general (or liberal) education as opposed to specialized (or professional) education. The student opting for Latin-Grec continued to take the wide range of elementary science courses that had been included in the course for over a century, while the student opting for Latin-sciences continued to take as much English, French, and Latin as his non-scientist classmate.

Since all classical colleges charged fees, attendance at any one of them was an additional expense to the parents of the students concerned unless they were completely supported by scholarships and/or bursaries; and the expense would be a considerable one if it were necessary to live in residence. By the 1940s every city, most towns, and many villages had a classical college, but there were many communities which were not so served. Among these were a number in the Chicoutimi region and here parents and public school commissioners took illegal but effective action.[44] Between 1944 and 1949, eight communities made arrangements for the religious order which was already providing the teaching staff for the local elementary school to offer the first four years of the classical college course, which included the teaching of Latin, a subject not included on the list of subjects approved by the Comité catholique du Conseil de l'Instruction publique. By 1953 the same procedure had been adopted in nine other communities in five other regions of the province. In all cases, including those in the Chicoutimi region, the step had been taken only after the consent of the Roman Catholic bishop of the diocese had been given. The decision of the Comité catholique to permit the teaching of Latin in the public schools in 1954, three years after it had appointed a committee to report on the coordination of instruction at the various grade levels, was thus a legitimatizing of existing practice.[45]

The importance of the move lay more in the long-range implications than in the immediate consequences. By 1960, relatively

510

few of the hundreds of public schools had introduced what was
called the Latin-Sciences option as one of the several programs
available to their students; setting up such a course was an
added expense since additional teachers were almost invariably
required and it was difficult to guarantee that such expense was
justified since it was impossible to predict how many students
would take this option; the change, after all, guaranteed only
that the first half of the cours classique could be completed
without additional cost to the parents. In order to complete the
program they would have to attend a classical college for four
more years. Parents looking this far forward might well discourage their children from enrolling in the new stream.

The authorizing of the Latin-Sciences stream in the écoles
secondaires, as the écoles primaires supérieures were called after
1954, also posed problems for the classical colleges. Their already increasing enrolments could be notably swelled in the final
four years of the eight year course, since they would be expected
to accommodate the 'classical' graduates of the public secondary
schools. This would inevitably add to their financial problems.
These, of course, would be solved if the government assumed responsibility for the fees, including the residential fees, of all
the classical college students, but if this were to be done was
there any reason why the government should not take over control
of the classical colleges?

In 1960, then, the future of both the classical colleges and
the classical college course was anything but clear. The colleges
themselves had banded together in 1953 as La Fédération des
Collèges Classiques to protect their interests, and an active
secretariat was busily gathering data and marshalling arguments
that would bolster the defence of what Etienne Parent had called
so many years ago 'nos citadelles nationales.' The founding of
this fédération was an indication that relations between the colleges and the universities with which they were affiliated was no
longer as intimate and as congenial as had generally been the
case prior to the outbreak of World War II. Whereas the interests
of the classical colleges had remained basically unchanged from
1940 to 1960, as had also been the case from 1860 to 1940, the
interests of the French-language universities had altered markedly
during these two decades - away from a basic preoccupation with
the humanities, with the liberal professions, and with what,
theology and philosophy perhaps excepted, was essentially teaching
at the first degree level, towards research in all fields, the
applied and the social sciences, and instruction at the graduate
level.

These shifts in interest are reflected in the fact that by 1960
the classical colleges were no longer solely responsible for the
provision of instruction for the B.A., that it was possible to
obtain a B.A. not only without Greek but also without Latin, and
that one's program could include such subjects as economics, political science, and Russian. At Montréal, the department of extension established in 1950 was authorized two years later to

organize a B.A. degree program for adults; by 1960 the course of
study leading to this degree had all the characteristics of a
typical general arts degree program in an English-language institution: neither Latin nor Greek required, a wide range of options
particularly in the social sciences, reliance on the distribution
principle to achieve breadth of study, reliance on the requirement
of including a certain number of courses in one subject as the
means of achieving depth of study. A very similar program leading
to the B.A. was offered for adults by the faculty of arts of the
Université de Sherbrooke from the time of its opening in 1957,
though it should also be noted that the B.A. could also be earned
at Sherbrooke by taking the classical college course at one of
the half-dozen classical colleges in the Sherbrooke area which
transferred their affiliation from Montréal following the establishment of the new university. In 1949, Université Laval established a Collège universitaire, which offered a two year program
principally in the sciences to students who had completed six
years of the classical college course. Completion of this course
was recognized by the granting of the B.A. and reduced by one year
the time required to obtain a second degree in the faculté des
sciences and in the professional faculties.

COMMERCE AND FINANCE, BUSINESS ADMINISTRATION, SECRETARIAL
SCIENCE, JOURNALISM

In chapter 21 it was noted that considerable attention was given
by the National Conference of Canadian Universities during the
1920s and 1930s to the legitimacy of commerce and finance or of
business administration as subjects to be taught at the universities and particularly in a faculty of arts and science, but it
was pointed out that enrolment in these subjects rose steadily
over these years. In the 1940s and the 1950s, this trend continued, with the result that by 1960 students in these degree programs constituted over 6% of total undergraduate enrolment in the
Canadian universities.[46] In contrast to the earlier period, there
was little if any discussion on the merits or dangers of such
programs after 1940. They were not, for example, a subject that
received any attention at the annual meetings of the NCCU or at
the two special NCCU conferences in 1956 and 1961; this despite
the fact that by 1960 virtually every Canadian university was
offering the B.Com. or an equivalent degree, for example, a B.A.
in business administration at Assumption, Bishop's, and Western
Ontario, a Bachelor of Business Administration at Acadia and New
Brunswick, and a B.Sc.Com. at Montréal and St Joseph's.
    So far as the courses themselves were concerned, there had been
little change in either the content or the auspices under which
the course was conducted. Almost all of them were offered at what
was regarded as the honours level and required as many years to
complete as an honour course at the parent institution. The programs continued to emphasize either commerce and finance or busi-

ness administration, but the great majority concentrated on the former. Those which placed more emphasis on business subjects than on accounting were the French-language institutions (with the exception of St Joseph's), British Columbia, New Brunswick, Sir George Williams, and Western Ontario. Furthermore, whether the program emphasized commerce and finance or business administration, it continued in most cases to remain within the jurisdiction of the faculty of arts and science. This was not the case in any of the French-language institutions, but in English Canada only at British Columbia, Saskatchewan, and Queen's had these courses attained faculty status by 1960, and only Alberta, Manitoba, and Western Ontario had followed the example of McGill in establishing semi-independent schools within the faculty of arts and science.

The major development in these closely related fields was the introduction of graduate work. Prior to World War II, a diploma course in business administration, designed principally for university graduates, had been introduced at Western Ontario and the M.Com. had been authorized at McGill and Toronto. However, only three students had qualified for the latter degree by the end of the 1940-41 session. By 1960, Queen's and Sherbrooke were also offering the M.Com.; the M.B.A. had been introduced at British Columbia, Queen's, and Western Ontario; and a program leading to the doctorate had been approved at Western Ontario. Both Laval and Montréal were now awarding a number of licences and doctorats. In addition, since 1952 Saskatchewan had been offering a diploma course similar to that introduced at Western Ontario in 1932, while the latter since 1949 had been conducting a five week summer course in management training, designed for middle-level executives - one that proved enormously successful. A similar summer course had been available at King's College in Halifax since 1956.

The development of these various forms of training for business at the graduate level explains, in large measure, the stability of the undergraduate course during the 1940s and 1950s. Most Canadian academics, including a majority of professors of economics, accounting, and business administration, felt that a course devoted largely if not exclusively to theoretical studies was a much more effective preparation for a career in business than one emphasizing the practical aspects. Having attained his degree, the student, preferably after some experience in business, could then go on to the practically oriented diploma courses or to the M.B.A. programs which by the 1950s were available in all regions of the country. Most B.Com. programs, it should be added, were offered at honours degree level and required an additional year of study beyond the general B.A. The emphasis on mathematics, economic theory, and economic history remained strong.

Of the 1110 students who were reported by the Dominion Bureau of Statistics in 1960-61 as receiving a degree in commerce and finance, business administration, or secretarial science, 60 were women, and of these approximately 30 had graduated in secretarial science.[47] The figures are very similar to those of 1940-41. A

degree program in secretarial science continued to be offered at
Acadia, Mount Saint Vincent, and Western Ontario; Mount Allison
had expanded its two-year diploma course to a four year degree
program, and Waterloo Lutheran, having attained degree granting
powers in 1960, continued to provide the secretarial science course
which, as an affiliate of Western Ontario it had been offering
for years. The degree received was a B.A., except at Mount Saint
Vincent where it was a B.Sc. In all cases, responsibility for
the program rested with the faculty of arts and science.

Two of the English-language universities introduced degree programs in journalism during these years, Carleton in 1945 and
Western Ontario in 1947. The Carleton program was four years
beyond senior matriculation and led to a Bachelor of Journalism
degree. At Western Ontario, the student could take either a four
year course leading to an honour B.A. or a three year course
leading to a general B.A. In the Maritimes, King's College, Mount
Saint Vincent, and St Mary's combined to form the Halifax School
of Journalism, an institution with its own board of governors,
which awarded a diploma to the students who had completed its
three year course. In 1960-61, the total enrolment in these programs was 106 at Carleton, 20 at Western, 24 at Halifax.[48] The
Dominion Bureau of Statistics reported no students in journalism
at Université de Montréal in this year.

THE HUMANITIES

The period 1945 to 1960 saw a considerable extension of curricular offerings in the humanities despite the fact that, with the
exception of English, French, and Spanish, there was a marked
decline in the proportion of undergraduates enrolling in languages
and such long-established subjects as philosophy and religion.
The extension resulted from the introduction or for the first
time the serious expansion of courses in the fine arts (including
drama and film) and in non-European languages and literature,
notably Russian and other slavic languages, Chinese and Japanese,
Arabic, Persian, and Turkish. But it was even more the result
of the greatly increased registration during the veterans' period,
the unexpected failure of enrolments to return to pre-war level
in the 1950s, and – the most significant factor – the realisation
that the number of undergraduates in the 1960s would increase
dramatically. Obviously, to accommodate the students of the
1960s there must be a sizable increase in the teaching staff in
all departments, including those with relatively small enrolments,
and consequently there must be an immediate development of graduate
studies.

Prior to World War II, graduate studies in the English language
universities had been carried on almost as a sideline by professors in the faculty of arts and science and in a few professional
faculties such as engineering and medicine. This tradition was
maintained in the post-war period; graduate studies in classics

or economics or chemistry were continued, though now no longer as a sideline, by professors in the faculties of arts and science. In 1960 there were no independent graduate departments in any of the academic disciplines, and all professors who taught graduate courses and supervised theses also taught undergraduates. In the French-language universities a different situation obtained; there were no departments in the facultés des arts, and in the academic subjects graduate studies was the responsibility of the 'higher' faculties - lettres, philosophie, sciences, sciences sociales. But, as we have seen, there had veen very little development of graduate studies at Laval and Montréal by 1940.[49] One of the more striking features of Canadian higher education during the 1940s and 1950s was the development of strong departments in these faculties. In 1960-61, for example, there were 50 full-time or part-time staff members in the faculté des lettres at Université de Montréal whereas in 1940-41 there had been 6.[50]

Despite the introduction of a science option in the classical college course, there had been little change in the relative importance of classics, English, French, philosophy, and religion in the traditional B.A. program offered in the French-language universities; Greek was no longer a requirement for students electing the Latin-Sciences option, but the lure of the liberal professions remained strong and the majority of students continued to take the Latin-Grec option. In the English-language institutions, on the other hand, classics, philosophy, and religion, which had already experienced decreases in the 1920s and 1930s, though tending to increase modestly in absolute numbers, continued to decline in proportional enrolment. Nonetheless, an examination of the numbers of full-time professors of the rank of assistant professor, associate professor, and professor in the departments of classics and philosophy in the 16 English-language universities listed in the *Commonwealth Universities Yearbook* for both 1940 and 1961 reveals an increase over the twenty years from 56 to 72 in the case of classics and from 44 to 82 in the case of philosophy.[51] The basic explanation is the addition of graduate work.

The analysis of the programs for the B.A. and the B.Sc. in the English-language universities reveals that English was the one subject universally prescribed.

It was also the one non-scientific subject universally prescribed in the first degree programs of almost all professional faculties. Therefore English can be said to have maintained the position it occupied in 1920 and in 1940 as the only subject which could claim to be a core subject for a university degree. Its pre-eminence as well as the fact that it was usually the largest department in the faculty of arts and science continued[52] to be based on practical rather than theoretical considerations; the fact that the staff in English devoted serious attention to the problems of written expression was considered by the majority of their colleagues as of more significance than the intrinsic values of the study of English literature.

Enrolments in French and in Spanish increased steadily over the period while German and Italian had difficulty in holding their own. An increasing interest in Latin American studies proved a stimulus to Spanish and led to the introduction of Portuguese as well at Toronto and Laval.

One of the 15 recommendations in the 1944 report of the NCCU's Committee on Post-War Problems was 'that Faculties of Arts and Science should afford a better understanding of other countries, for example, China, Russia and the South American Republic.'[53] The extent to which the Canadian universities responded to this challenge was systematically examined 20 years later by D.L.B. Hamlin and G. Lalande in two complementary reports commissioned by the NCCU and published jointly in 1964.[54] Their terms of reference were to survey programs in international relations, Russian and East European studies, Asian studies, African studies, and Latin American studies.

The most immediate and the most wide-spread response was in the area of slavic studies. Prior to Russia's entry into the war in 1941, no Canadian university offered instruction in Russian language or literature, and relatively few departments devoted attention either to Russian history, geography, economics, or art. Between 1942 and 1946 no fewer than 14 universities instituted non-credit courses in the Russian language through their extension departments, and by 1960 the same number, though not necessarily the same institutions, were offering courses for credit in Russian language and literature, in most cases in sufficient numbers to enable the student to major or concentrate in this subject. In addition, Polish and Ukrainian had become available at four universities. The major programs were at British Columbia, Montréal, and Toronto, which had established departments in 1946, 1948, and 1949 respectively. The British Columbia and Toronto programs began as undergraduate offerings leading to an honour degree or a major in the general course, but in the late 1950s both were extended upwards into the graduate school. At Montréal, the program began at the graduate level (M.A. and Ph.D.), but an undergraduate program was added in 1956. None of these major programs concentrated solely on language and literature.

There were attempts to establish Chinese studies at McGill, Montréal, and Toronto between 1920 and 1940, but in the latter year the only instruction being offered was in certificate courses at Toronto.[55] In 1943 a School of Chinese Studies was formally established at the Royal Ontario Museum, an affiliate of the University of Toronto, but the work continued at the certificate level until 1948, when a department of East Asiatic Studies was established in the faculty of arts and an honour degree authorized, from which a half-dozen students had graduated by 1960. A degree program in Asian studies was established at British Columbia in 1947, but until instruction in Chinese language and literature was introduced in 1957, rather than being attached to the humanities, it was a course in the social sciences, drawing on the resources of history, economics and political science, anthropology and sociology. In 1959, three-year sequences in Chinese and

Japanese were introduced, and this led two years later to the establishment of a Department of Asian Studies.

Courses in the ancient languages of the near east, Aramaic, classical Arabic, Hebrew, Syriac, had been taught in departments of oriental languages and theological colleges in the nineteenth century, and they continue to be taught under these auspices to this day. What was not being taught in any Canadian institution until the 1950s were the modern languages of the near-east, modern Arabic, Persian, Turkish, Urdu; nor was attention being directed to the culture of the Mohammedan world. The first move to rectify this lacuna in Canadian higher education was the establishment at McGill in 1952 of an Institute of Islamic Studies, offering graduate programs at the M.A. and Ph.D. levels. An undergraduate program in Islamic studies was introduced at Toronto in 1957.

These various responses to the 1944 plea to develop programs in the cultures of the world which lie outside the Western European tradition demonstrated that in order to be successful they must involve the cooperation of humanists and social scientists. The Asian studies program at British Columbia began as a combination of courses in the social sciences, but its full-scale development did not occur until linguistic and literary courses were added. The failure of the early attempts to develop Chinese studies at Toronto resulted from the exclusive concentration on language and literature; success followed the organization of a program which directed attention to all aspects of the culture.

The successful launching of these interdisciplinary courses was facilitated by the experience Canadian universities had gained over many years in developing honour courses, programs which consisted of a sequence of course, the majority of them prescribed and involving study over several years, which drew upon the resources of a number of departments and which in combination could be expected to produce an integrated view of an important area of knowledge.

The second important extension of the curricular offerings in arts and science during these two decades was in the area of the fine arts. More detailed reference to the expansion of programs in fine art and in music will be made in the sections of chapter 28 which deal with these subjects in the context of professional education.[56] Here it is sufficient to note that during the 1950s in particular the opportunities for students to study painting, sculpture, architecture, or music as a liberal arts subject were considerably increased. Five universities (Alberta, British Columbia, McGill, Manitoba) established departments of fine arts in the faculty of arts which, in the first instance at least, were designed to meet the needs of undergraduates who had no intention of becoming artists, architects, or musicians. Furthermore, attention was directed to two other hitherto neglected arts. At Sir George Williams, the department of fine arts included both drama and film within its terms of reference, while at Queen's and Saskatchewan small but effective departments of drama had by 1960 been in operation for over 10 years.[57]

By 1940, history was both a well-established and a well-organized discipline. It continued to be regarded as a social science in the context of university administration (for example, in terms of the grouping of subjects for the purpose of distribution requirements) but its connections with the humanities remained strong and it is significant that it was formally represented on the Humanities Research Council of Canada as well as on the Canadian Social Science Research Council, of which the Canadian Historical Association was a founding member.[58] In the CHA it had a national professional organization which was a recognized learned society, and in the *Canadian Historical Review* it had a scholarly journal in which historians could expect to publish their scholarly articles. It also had the advantage of enjoying a sense of unity. True, its members now tended to identify themselves as medieval historians or modern European historians or American historians or, in increasing numbers, as Canadian historians, but they saw themselves first and foremost as historians. At the level of the individual department, there was opportunity for close personal contact, but at the same time, of access to a range of views. Most departments had from two to seven full-time staff members, and even the largest, Toronto, had not yet reached two figures.

During the next two decades, the total number of full-time historians more than doubled, as did the membership of most individual departments.[59] There was some striking exceptions: New Brunswick rose from 1 to 5, British Columbia from 3 to 10, Alberta from 3 to 13, Montréal (in the faculté des lettres) from 2 to 10. As in the case of the humanities subjects, these increases resulted partly from larger undergraduate enrolments but mainly from the development of graduate work. However, these numbers, which include only professors, associate professors, and assistant professors, are to some extent misleading, particularly in the departments which were active in graduate work. In 1960-61, the department at Toronto had 20 'professors' but it also had 7 full-time lecturers, 3 instructors (normally teaching half-time), and a dozen teaching assistants (graduate students receiving a modest stipend in return for conducting tutorials and marking essays). Since at this time Toronto enrolled a much larger proportion of graduate students in history than any other university, the example is not typical: British Columbia had only two full-time lecturers, one instructor, and three cross appointments from the faculty of education. Nonetheless, the Toronto situation, which represented a change from the cozy atmosphere of 1940, was an indication of the consequences for a department of a serious commitment to graduate studies. It was also a preview of what would happen to many departments within a very few years.

The expansion of staff made it possible to offer a wider range of courses at both graduate and undergraduate levels, not only in British, West-European, and North American history, but in such areas as Eastern Europe and the Far East. Indeed, it was this

518

increased range which made possible the launching of the new programs in slavic studies, asian studies, etc., to which we referred
in the previous section.

To the extent that it, too, had a national organization, the
Canadian Association of Political Science, and a highly regarded
scholarly journal, *The Canadian Journal of Economics and Political
Science*, political economy could also be said in 1940 to be a
well-organized discipline, but it lacked history's sense of unity
since it was a combination of two subjects, economics and political science, which many of its practitioners regarded as independent disciplines. Furthermore, at most English-language institutions it had responsibility for still another potentially independent discipline, sociology, and also for practically oriented
programs such as accounting, commerce, and business administration.
Nonetheless, by 1960 only three universities had established independent departments of economics and of political science:
Dalhousie, Manitoba, and Saskatchewan. The situation was eased
by the fact that at the only three institutions where the
commerce-accounting-business administration wing increased markedly
in size (at British Columbia, Western Ontario, and Queen's the
separation had taken place before the war) responsibility for
these subjects had been transferred to an independent faculty or
school. Consequently, though the total number of staff had increased by a factor of between three and four by 1960, the departments remained reasonably small, the largest being at Toronto,
which embraced sociology, with 34, and only 5 others exceeded 10.
There were, of course, a number of economists and political scientists who argued that both parties benefited from daily contact
with each other. In any event, neither economists nor political
scientists appear to have suffered from the arrangement. In the
French-language universities, the problem did not arise since
economics, political science, and sociology were departmentalized
within facultés des sciences sociales, while commerce was an independent faculty at Laval and Sherbrooke and the responsibility
of Ecole des hautes études commerciales at Montréal.

Three universities had independent departments of sociology by
1960, Carleton, Saskatchewan, and McMaster, though none had more
than three full-time staff members. Both British Columbia and
McGill had departments of sociology and anthropology, with six
and seven staff members respectively. At Dalhousie, Manitoba,
New Brunswick, St Francis Xavier, and Toronto, sociology was
associated with political economy. Only at Toronto was there an
independent department of anthropology. Sociologists had always
been eligible to become members of the Canadian Political Science
Association, and in 1956 an Anthropology-Sociology Chapter was
formed within the larger organization. It was not until the
middle 1960s that anthropologists and sociologists combined to
launch a learned journal.

During the 1930s, geography had been established as an independent department at Toronto, and as a sub-department of geology at
British Columbia and Western Ontario; except at McMaster which

appointed a full-time lecturer in 1939, it received little sustained attention elsewhere in English Canada. It had long received attention at Montréal in both Ecole des hautes études commercial and in the faculté des sciences sociales, and in the late 1930s had been introduced at Laval. But during the war its importance was clearly recognized and there was a rapid development in the field as soon as the war ended. By 1950, McMaster and McGill had also established departments, and Montréal and Laval had established institutes; in Laval's case, l'Institut d'histoire et de géographie.[60] This expansion continued throughout the 1950s, stimulated by the formation of the Canadian Association of Geographers in 1951, the publication in the same year of *Geography in the Canadian Universities*, the outcome of a survey which the Canadian Social Science Research Council commissioned Sir Dudley Stamp to undertake, and the launching of *Canadian Geographer* in 1952.[61] By 1960, virtually every university in Canada was providing undergraduate instruction in the subject and 11 were offering graduate work. The majority of specializing and graduate students were at British Columbia, McGill, Montréal, and Toronto.

The discipline in the social sciences which experienced the greatest development in the post-war period was psychology, which, except at certain Roman Catholic institutions, had become completely independent of philosophy and which at all the larger universities had become one of the largest departments in the faculty of arts and had one of the largest enrolments in the graduate schools. In 1940, 22 staff members were listed under psychology; the comparable figure in 1960 was in excess of 100, including 20 at Toronto, 12 at McGill, 11 at Ottawa (which had a school of education and psychology), and 8 at British Columbia and Queen's. The Canadian Psychological Association had been founded in 1939, and it is symbolic of the demands made upon this discipline that the association found it necessary to establish two journals, *Canadian Journal of Psychology* in 1947 and *Canadian Psychologist* in 1951.[62] Among the reasons for the expansion of psychology at both undergraduate and graduate levels was the realization of its capacity for practical application and the consequent development of specializations within the field - clinical, developmental, educational, physiological, social. These of course had to be based on theory, and in the 1950s in particular experimental psychology became the dominant emphasis. One consequence of this was the identification of psychology with the sciences as well as with the social sciences, a development recognized by the establishment by the National Research Council of Canada in 1948 of an Associate Committee on Applied Psychology.

Like history, however, psychology remained a constituent member of the Canadian Social Science Research Council, a body which had a great deal to do with the advances made in all the social sciences between 1940 and 1960. The activities of this organization are described in chapter 30, where among other things it is noted that the council sponsored surveys of the position of geography, political science, and psychology in the Canadian universities,

which included analyses of the strengths and weaknesses of undergraduate programs.[63] There were no comparable surveys of anthropology, economics, or sociology, and consequently the review of
the state of the social sciences was less all-embracing than that
provided by the Humanities Research Council through its commissioning and publication of the Kirkconnell-Woodhouse study, *The
Humanities in Canada*. However, the attention given by these two
councils to the problems facing the disciplines they represented,
along with the report of the Royal Commission on National Development in the Arts, Letters and Sciences and the implementation in
1957 of its recommendation to establish a Canada Council designed
to provide support for each of these major areas of knowledge,
greatly increased a sense of self-awareness on the part of both
humanists and social scientists. In 1940, Arts and Science was
an appropriate term to apply to a faculty which provided instruction in all these fields; the interests of professors of English
and philosophy, of economics and sociology, were sufficiently
similar to justify their being coupled under the general term
arts in contradistinction to science, the general term applied to
the other departments in the faculty. By 1960, a case could be
made that either the title should be faculty of humanities, social
sciences, and sciences, or that faculty status should be assigned
to each of the three divisions.[64]

This latter step had been taken by the French-language universities, with their facultés des lettres and de philosophie (humanities), sciences sociales, and sciences.

THE SCIENCES

The course of studies in the humanities and the social sciences
underwent considerable change during the 1940s and 1950s but almost entirely through an extension of the subject matter covered.
New subjects were introduced, such as Russian language and literature and film, the number of courses in hitherto neglected subjects such as anthropology and fine art expanded dramatically,
and there was a broadening of the subject matter covered in the
well-established disciplines such as English, which by 1960 was
giving considerable attention to Canadian literature and to linguistics, or history, which now concerned itself with the Far
East, the Middle East, and Latin America. But there was no change
in the basic approach to the subject matter. The invention of
the computer had by the late 1950s given humanists and social
scientists as well as scientists a new method of processing data,
but the implications of this were at this stage almost exclusively
limited to scholarship and research.

In the sciences, including mathematics, there was, however, a
veritable revolution in the approach to subject matter, the general
consequence of which was a shift of attention from the classical
physical or descriptive approach to one that centred on analysis and
structure. This revolution was the consequence of such discoveries

as quantum mechanics and chemical bond theory, and the development of group theory in mathematics, and while its effects were first evident in physics and chemistry the implications soon became apparent in biology and geology as well. One result was an increasing interdependence of the individual sciences symbolized by courses in chemical physics and physical chemistry.

While much of the theory which lay behind this revolution had been developed before World War II, the movement was rapidly accelerated by the crucial importance of the practical applications of scientific activity in the prosecution of the war effort, the invention of radar being perhaps the most dramatic. This in turn stimulated interest in science on the part of many servicemen, and there was a notable demand for graduate work in science by returning veterans. But the 'new science' could not be based on the old undergraduate curriculum, with the result that even in the late 1940s the new theories were being introduced into the undergraduate curriculum. By 1960 the revolution in the undergraduate curriculum was completed in chemistry and physics and it would be completed in biology and geology within a few years. In the meantime, the invention of the computer had downgraded the importance of the classical mathematics training in such fields as actuarial science, but this was more than compensated for by the relevance of group theory to basic science and by the increasing importance of statistics.

These developments were accompanied by a rapid expansion of graduate studies in the sciences and also by the demand for 'service courses' in the professional faculties such as engineering, medicine (in the form of pre-medicine), and forestry. The consequence was at least a doubling and in the case of chemistry and physics a tripling of the full-time professorial staff. There was, however, little change in the organizational structure of the science departments; in the larger universities botany and zoology tended to separate, and as geography departments were established geology became free to concentrate on its traditional concerns. On the other hand, there was a considerable development of research institutes involving scientists from various departments both in the faculty of arts and science and in professional faculties.[65]

In the French-language universities, graduate work in science had been fully developed by 1960, and the equivalent of honour courses in the sciences established in the facultés des sciences.

EXTENSION

Were this section entitled Adult Education, it would be a very large one since by 1960 all Canadian universities had departments of extension or adult education and were engaged in an ever-increasing round of activities, including those designed in conjunction with particular professional faculties to update graduates; for example, continuing education courses in medicine

522

aimed at bringing doctors abreast of recent developments in the
theory and practice of their profession. However, this is a chapter devoted to arts and science, and we are concerned only with
the work of extension departments in the context of faculties of
arts and science.

The role of departments of extension in the provision of B.A.
and B.Sc. degrees for part-time students and the relation of this
role to the other responsibilities of the departments were outlined in symposia included in the programs of the National Conference of Canadian universities in 1953 and 1956.[66] The former
prompted the NCCU, with financial support from the Carnegie Corporation, to commission J. Roby Kidd, the director of the Canadian
Association for Adult Education, to conduct a study of adult education in the Canadian universities, a task which was carried out
during 1954 and 1955. His report[67] was the subject of the symposium held in 1956 and it included a brief history of the development of adult education in the Canadian universities and a detailed
account of the activities being carried on by the extension
departments in the middle 1950s. It was also a strong argument
that the universities had an obligation to provide adequately for
the extramural degree and an analysis of the difficulties departments of extension were experiencing in attempting to meet this
obligation. It was clear from both the report and the papers
commenting on it which were presented at the symposium that faculties of arts and science were not cooperating as energetically
and as imaginatively as possible in resolving these difficulties.
Few universities permitted part-time students to take day-time
courses in the regular session, and many courses were not offered
in the evenings and in the summer sessions. Unfortunately, the
Proceedings did not include a résumé of the general discussion
which followed the presentations and no resolutions bearing on
the report were adopted.

What was not realized in 1956 was that the demand for part-time
degree work was about to increase dramatically. In 1954-55, 10,791
students were registered as part-time students in the winter session and 13,460 were enrolled in the summer session of 1954. There
was a slight decrease in the figures for the following winter
session (10,098) and a modest increase in the summer of 1955
(14,723). During the next five years the numbers tripled:[68]

Year	Winter Session	Summer Session
1956-57	13,000	15,500
1957-58	17,620	16,836
1958-59	27,097	23,583
1959-60	28,938	28,924
1960-61	30,691	34,880

It was thus obvious by 1960 that the problem of the part-time
student would be a major one for the faculties of arts and sciences
and that action to find means of resolving it was sorely needed.

1 H.F. McDonald, 'The Re-Establishment of Ex-Service Men,' *NCCU Proc.* (1942), 77–82
2 Ibid., 77
3 Ibid., 82
4 See above, chapter 21, 379–80.
5 A. Maheux, 'The Future of the Faculty of Arts,' *NCCU Proc.* (1942), 127
6 See below, 508–9.
7 R.C. Wallace, 'The Arts Faculty,' *NCCU Proc.* (1942), 119
8 Ibid., 120
9 Ibid., 119
10 N.A.M. Mackenzie, 'The Future of the Arts Course,' *NCCU Proc.* (1942), 136
11 Ibid., 137
12 Watson Kirkconnell is the source for the statement that the proposal emanated from Principals James and Wallace; on this point, as on so many others connected with this curious incident in the history of Canadian higher education, the *NCCU Proc.* throw no light. Of the persons chiefly involved, Kirkconnell is the only one who has commented on it publicly; see his *A Slice of Canada: Memoirs* (1967), 235–9. The incident is fully described by G. Pilkington in her 'A History of the National Conference of Canadian Universities, 1911–1961,' doctoral dissertation, University of Toronto (1974), 322–35.
13 Canada, Wartime Bureau of Technical Personnel, 'Historical Record of Wartime Activities' (n.d.), 34, quoted by Pilkington, 'History of NCCU,' 323. The minutes of the special meeting of the NCCU held on 9 January 1942 appear as appendix G of the *Proc.* for 1944.
14 The memorandum presented by President Patterson is reprinted by Kirkconnell (*Slice of Canada*, 237–9) under the title 'Memorial on Studies in the Humanities in Canada.' It is described by Kirkconnell as 'the Royal Society Memorial.' All the members of the committee which drafted it were members of Section II of the Royal Society of Canada.
15 *NCCU Proc.* (1944), 65
16 Ibid. (1944), 65
17 L. Thomas, *The University of Alberta in the War of 1939–45* (1948), 14–15
18 For the organization of the Humanities Research Council of Canada, see below, 570–2.
19 NCCU, *Report ... on Post-War Problems* (1944); simultaneously printed as *Rapport de l'Association nationale des Universités canadiennes sur les problèmes d'après-guerre*
20 Ibid., 24
21 J.S. Thomson, 'The Arts and Science Course at the University of Saskatchewan,' and H.M. Fieldhouse, 'The Liberal Arts Course – the Manitoba Experiment,' *NCCU Proc.* (1944), 54–60. For additional comments on these courses, see below, 504.

22 E.F. Sheffield, 'Canadian University and College Enrolment Projected to 1965,' *NCCU Proc.* (1955), 39-46. See above, chapter 25, 457.

23 The only significant reference to the curriculum in arts and science consisted of a plea for the introduction of courses in international studies and in the languages, history, and philosophy of countries outside the western European tradition, made by J.F. Leddy of the University of Saskatchewan at the 1961 conference: 'International Opportunities for Canadian Universities' in D. Dunton and D. Patterson, eds., *Canada's Universities in a New Age* (1962), 113-21.

24 It could be argued that Ottawa is not an exception since as a bilingual university it can be categorized equally well as a French-language institution. All French-language universities have separate faculties of arts and of science.

25 In the United States interest in general education courses began shortly before World War I, some 30 years before the publication in August 1945 of *General Education in a Free Society* by Harvard University Press. American experience undoubtedly influenced those responsible for the development of the courses at Manitoba, Saskatchewan, and Sir George Williams.

26 See above, chapter 21, 377-8.

27 Commencing with the 1958-59 session students were permitted to substitute certain departmental courses for humanities 210 and social sciences 210. Natural sciences 210 continued to be a requirement for all students until 1960-61. When introduced the courses were numbered 101 (e.g., natural sciences 101).

28 The history and philosophy course was withdrawn at the end of the 1960-61 session and students who previously were required to take it did not have to take any specific course in its place. The other three courses continued to be prescribed until the 1968-69 session when a major revision of the arts and science program came into effect.

29 W.P. Thompson, *The University of Saskatchewan: a Personal History* (1970), 157

30 To be strictly accurate the sentence should read ... in the three year Pass Course.' For the previous 20 years the general course at Toronto was a four-year program from senior matriculation, during the last two of which the student selected courses from both the three-year pass course and the four-year honour courses. This program was withdrawn at the end of the 1951-52 session and at the same time the title 'general course' was applied to the revised three year program.

31 See above, chapter 21, 376.

32 For a student with a general B.A. or B.Sc., the equivalent of an honours B.A. would normally be achieved by taking, during what was called a 'make-up year,' a specified number of courses in the subject of concentration and obtaining an average of second-class standing or better.

33 H.G. Thode, in Dunton and Paterson, eds., *Canada's Universities*, 55

34 The numbers refer to students who obtained degrees in the calendar year 1961, i.e., at either the spring or fall convocations.

35 The numbers are taken from the entries for the universities concerned in *The Commonwealth Universities Yearbook 1963*, which is based on 1960-61 data. Not all universities distinguish between honour and general degrees when reporting for this publication.

36 In 1961, the Humanities Research Council of Canada requested F.E.L. Priestly to undertake a new survey of the humanities in Canada. This he did during the 1962-63 session. His report, like its predecessor, was entitled *The Humanities in Canada* and it was published in 1964. It provides detailed information about the honours courses in all universities as they were offered in 1962-63. Few changes had occurred since 1960-61.

37 At both Laval and Montréal the faculty of arts also had responsibility for the supervision of a number of programs, notably in music and pedagogy, for which the instruction was provided by affiliated institutions.

38 Prior to 1931, graduates of the cours classique were awarded the B.A., the B.L., or the B.Sc. depending upon the marks they obtained at the examinations conducted at the end of the sixth and eighth years. See above, chapter 9, 126.

39 For the development of public education in the Roman Catholic schools of Quebec, see L.-P. Audet, *Histoire de l'enseignement au Québec, 1608-1971* (1971), II, 282-91.

40 Fédération des Collèges Classiques, *Notre Reforme scolaire* (1963), II, 50

41 See above, chapter 21, 379.

42 L. Lortie, 'The New Classical Curriculum and its Impact on University Courses,' *NCCU Proc.* (1947), 22-6

43 Fédération, *Notre Reforme*, 20

44 P. Gérin-Lajoie, 'Changing Patterns of Classical Education in Quebec,' *NCCU Proc.* (1956), 76-8. A more thorough account of the background to, and the implications of, the introduction of the Latin-sciences option is provided by A. Tremblay, *Les Collèges et les écoles publiques: conflit ou coordination?* (1954), 21-41.

45 *Rapport du Sous-Comité de coordination de l'enseignement à ses divers grades au Comité catholique du Conseil de l'Instruction publique* (1954)

46 M. Von Zur-Muehlen, *Business Education and Faculty at Canadian Universities* (1971), xix

47 Dominion Bureau of Statistics, *Survey of Higher Education, 1954-1961* (1963), 45

48 Ibid., 30

49 See above, chapter 23, 431-3.

50 The numbers are taken from the *Annuaires* for 1940-41 and 1960-61.

51 The data in the 1940 *Yearbook* were based on information supplied by the institutions in 1939, that in the 1961 *Yearbook* on information supplied in 1960. No *Yearbook* was published in 1941.

52 Several departments of English experienced spectacular staff growth between 1940 and 1960: Alberta from 3 to 23, British Columbia from 8 to 23, Toronto from 16 to 33, Western Ontario from 4 to 15.

53 NCCU, *Report*, 31

54 D.L.B. Hamlin, *International Studies in Canadian Universities;* G. Lalande, *L'Etude des relations internationales et de certaines civilisations étrangères au Canada* (1964)

55 See above, chapter 21, 385.

56 See below, chapter 28, 548-50.

57 Two courses in dramatic production had been offered at Sir George Williams in 1940. Saskatchewan's department of drama was established in 1946, Queen's in 1947. The need for still further expansion of liberal arts offerings in art and music was argued by R.H. Hubbard and H. Adaskin during a symposium on 'The University and the Fine Arts' at the annual meeting of the NCCU in 1955.

58 See above, chapter 24, 443.

59 As in the previous and following sections of this chapter, the staff numbers have been taken from the *Commonwealth Universities Yearbooks* for 1940 and 1961.

60 Separate institutes of history and of geography were established at Laval in 1955.

61 *Canadian Geographer* was initially the proceedings of the annual meeting of the Canadian Association of Geographers.

62 *The Canadian Journal of Psychology*, a scholarly journal from the outset, was preceeded by *Bulletin of the Canadian Psychological Association* (1940-47). *Canadian Psychologist* began as a mimeographed news bulletin but became a printed quarterly in 1955.

63 L.D. Stamp, *Geography in Canadian Universities* (1951); R.M. Dawson, *Political Science Teaching in Canada* (1950); R.B. MacLeod, *Psychology in Canadian Universities* (1955).

64 Sir George Williams had in effect adapted this arrangement by organizing its instruction in divisions of humanities, social sciences, natural sciences, commerce.

65 See below, chapter 30, 581-2.

66 *NCCU Proc.* (1953), 17-35 (the principal speakers were M.M. Coady, St Francis Xavier; Donald Cameron, Alberta; C.H. Stearn, McMaster. *NCCU Proc.* (1956), 51-72 (the principal speakers were J.R. Kidd; J.R. Coulter, Toronto; J.K. Friesen, British Columbia; N. Leblanc, Laval.

67 J.R. Kidd, 'Report of the Special Survey Conducted in Canada during the Last Two Years,' *NCCU Proc.* (1956), 54-60. The full report was published later in the year as *Adult Education in the Canadian University*.

68 *Survey of Higher Education*, 20 (table 6)

28

Professional Education

The only professional programs which did not experience significant
growth during the 1940s and 1950s were agriculture and theology.
Theology remained at approximately the 3000 figure while agriculture increased marginally from 1762 to 1800. However, all the
agriculture students reported in 1960 were in degree programs,
whereas 389 of the 1940 students were in the two-year diploma
courses. The period saw doubled enrolment in veterinary medicine
(to 466), dentistry (to 1055 - still below the 1920 figure of 1276),
and household science (to 1598); enrolments tripled in engineering
to nearly 15,000, in nursing to nearly 1700, in pharmacy to nearly
1500, and in occupational and physical therapy to 476. The increase in medicine was only 50%, but, granted the particularly
heavy costs of medical education, an increase from 2940 to 4244
was a major effort. Numbers in architecture, law, library science,
and social work increased by a factor of four; however, the most
striking development was in education where full-time enrolment
increased from 677 to over 10,000. The only new degree program
was in physical and health education where the enrolment had
passed 1500. The number of students in commerce or business
administration had increased from 1190 to 6554, and if these students were categorized as being professionals rather than belonging
to arts and science, the professional education component at the
undergraduate level would be over 50%.
These figures from Dominion Bureau of Statistics publications[1]
refer to undergraduates, but in fact in some cases they include
students taking a second degree. This applies largely to library
science and social work, and very frequently to education, law,
and theology. The increase in full-time registration in graduate
studies over the period was from 1741 to 6518, a trend that was
to continue during the 1960s, thus providing eloquent evidence of
the professionalization of the Canadian university in the post-
World War II era.

There was little change in either the nature or the extent of
theological education in the universities between 1940 and 1960.
Total numbers of full-time students, both undergraduate and graduate, increased by about 1000 in the university-related institutions, and to these should be added several hundred students
studying in seminaries conducted by Roman Catholic religious orders
and at Protestant Bible institutes. However, this was a token
increase relative to that of the total full-time enrolment in all
universities over these years. It indicates, nonetheless, no unusual falling off of candidates for the ministry, a phenomenon
which would occur in the 1960s and which by the early 1970s had
become a matter of grave concern for the churches.

Of the 3306 full-time theological students reported for 1960-61,
there were 2441 in Roman Catholic colleges and 865 in Protestant;
77 members of the latter group were women. In 1940 there had
been scarcely any women in theology. The only large schools were
the faculties of theology at the three long-established Roman
Catholic universities, where much of the work was at licence or
doctoral level; Montreal had 472 students, Laval 353, and Ottawa
414. Two other institutions had more than 100 theology students:
Sherbrooke with 143, and Emmanuel College, federated with Toronto,
with 114. English-speaking Canada was served by an additional 8
Roman Catholic schools: Holy Heart Seminary at Halifax; St
Michael's, also federated with Toronto; Holy Redeemer College,
since 1956 an affiliate of Assumption, Windsor; Regis College
in Toronto, a Jesuit College operating since 1930 but without
degree-granting powers until 1956; St Peter's Seminary at London,
an affiliate since 1956 of the University of Western Ontario;
three very small seminaries in the West - Thomas College[2] in
Saskatchewan, St Joseph's in Alberta; and Christ the King Seminary
in British Columbia. The 1960-61 DBS figures report no students
at St Mark's College, Vancouver, an affiliate of British Columbia
since 1960 when it had been incorporated with degree-granting
powers in theology. The largest theological college west of
Ontario was the Grand Séminaire de St Boniface, a French-language
institution affiliated with the University of Manitoba, which had
74 students.

There were nine Anglican theological schools: King's College,
affiliated with Dalhousie; Bishop's; Trinity and Wycliffe, both
federated with the University of Toronto; Huron, affiliated with
Western Ontario; Emmanuel and Saint Chad's, affiliated with the
University of Saskatchewan; Anglican Theological College, affiliated with British Columbia; and the Diocesan College of Montreal,
now an integrated part of McGill's faculty of divinity. St John's
College, affiliated with University of Manitoba, had ceased to
offer a theological course. The largest Protestant denomination
in Canada, the United Church had five theological colleges:
Emmanuel College, federated with the University of Toronto; Pine

Hill Divinity Hall at Halifax; Union College of British Columbia, affiliated with British Columbia; St Andrew's College, affiliated with Saskatchewan; and the United Theological College at Montreal, also an integrated part of McGill's faculty of divinity. The Presbyterian schools numbered three: Knox, federated with Toronto; the Divinity College at Queen's; and the Presbyterian College at Montreal which worked closely with McGill's faculty of divinity but which was technically independent. The Baptists were served by Acadia and McMaster, the Lutherans by Waterloo Lutheran and Lutheran Theological College, an affiliate of the University of Saskatchewan at Regina, which in 1958 had been merged with another University of Saskatchewan affiliate, Lutheran Seminary at Saskatoon.

On the Protestant side, then, the picture remained in the main one of a plethora of tiny institutions with correspondingly small staffs, whose impact on the universities with which they were affiliated was minimal. There were two exceptions: those at McGill where the faculty of divinity was under the direct control of the university, an arrangement entered into by the affiliated schools on a five year trial basis in 1948 and confirmed in 1953; and in a less formal way the Toronto group, where from 1944 on, Emmanuel, Knox, Trinity, and Wycliffe began to cooperate in the teaching of theology at the graduate level. They were joined by St Michael's in 1961 in what was called the Toronto Graduate School of Theology.

LAW

It has been demonstrated that there was no basic change in legal education in Canada between 1890 and 1940.[3] During the next 20 years the picture was largely transformed. This was a period which saw the establishment of six additional university law schools, the transformation of the department at Toronto into a faculty, the development of the Osgoode Hall Law School into a degree-granting institution supported by public funds, a beginning of serious work in the area of graduate studies, and the establishment of a half dozen research institutes on university campuses in close association with faculties of law. For the first time in their history, the older law schools were provided with adequate accommodation and, equally important, with reasonably adequate libraries. The number of full-time staff increased to well over 100. In general, while certification of lawyers remained with the provincial law societies, responsibility for legal education had been transferred to the universities.

The basic cause of this dramatic change which took place between 1949 and 1957 was the realization by both the law societies and government that it was in the public interest that lawyers be *educated* in the law as well as *trained* for its practice. However, the immediate cause can be explained in quantitative rather than qualitative terms. Enrolment in the law schools declined drasti-

cally during World War II but increased enormously with the return
of the veterans in 1945. The numbers at Osgoode Law School are
typical: 273 in 1940-41, 109 in 1943-44, 445 in 1945-46. The
problems of schools like Osgoode were compounded by the practical
necessity, and the moral obligation to provide refresher courses
for the large number of qualified lawyers who had served in the
war. In the law schools, the veteran enrolment continued until
1950 and beyond, since, in addition to the three year law course,
some students needed either to complete or to acquire a bachelor's
degree. In 1950-51 full-time enrolment was 2421 in contrast to
697 in 1940-41. Nor did the situation ease off with the departure
of the veterans; in 1955-56 the enrolment was 2624 and in 1960-61
it was 2480.

The arrival of the veterans was directly responsible for the
establishment of the first of the new law schools. In the summer
of 1945 the British Columbia Law Society suggested to the government and the university that a program be introduced for veterans.
In July a government grant of $10,000 was authorized, and in
September a faculty of law was opened with 86 students. By 1949
the enrolment was over 400 and in 1952 the faculty was housed in
its own building. In this same year the faculty of law at Dalhousie
obtained possession of the building which had been constructed for
it in 1923. A faculty of law was opened at Université de Sherbrooke
when it was established in 1954. In 1959 the University of New
Brunswick law school, which had obtained a full-time dean for the
first time in 1957, was moved from Saint John to the main campus
at Fredericton. By 1960, the only law school in Canada which continued to combine articling with full-time attendance at lectures
was the Manitoba Law School, still technically an affiliate of
the University of Manitoba. This practice terminated in 1964
when the school became an integrated part of the university as
its faculty of law.

In the Province of Quebec the older universities continued to
offer the basic three year degree program, but the course of study
had been modernized and the law faculties were now directly involved in the supervision of the students' work during the year
of articling which followed graduation. This latter arrangement,
as well as a number of the other developments which we have just
described, were undoubtedly affected by the dramatic changes
which had occurred in legal education in Ontario between 1949 and
1957.

In March 1948, Cecil A. Wright, who had been a full-time member
of the staff since 1925 and who for years had been arguing in
print that legal education should have an academic rather than a
practical orientation and that both staff and students should be
on a full-time basis, was appointed dean of the Osgoode Hall Law
School in succession to J.D. Falconbridge who had served since
1923. Since his views were well known it can safely be assumed
that Wright understood that, in being offered the appointment,
the Law Society was prepared to reform the School basically along
the lines which Wright had been advocating.[4] At the time of his

appointment a Special Committee on Legal Education had been sitting for some time and at their request he had reiterated his views shortly after his appointment. However, when the committee produced its report in January 1949 it recommended in effect that no changes be made. Wright immediately submitted his resignation as did three of the other five full-time members of his staff two days later, in all cases with effect at the end of the current academic year. In March it was announced that Wright had been appointed dean and two of his resigning colleagues, Bora Laskin and John Willis, had accepted professorships at the School of Law which the University of Toronto had established in 1940 as an expansion of the department in the faculty of arts which had been organized in 1930. There had been a reorganization of the teaching program in 1944 but a more fundamental one in 1949, a new three year L.L.B. program being established as well as the four year honours arts course and the combined B.A. and the L.L.B. program being withdrawn. One of the immediate problems facing the Law Society was what recognition should be given to this new University of Toronto program, and this curiously enough was very quickly resolved. In September it was announced that graduates of the University of Toronto's Law School would be granted standing for the first two years of the three year Osgoode Hall Law Course.

The existence of a second law school in the province, particularly one whose students had to proceed to Osgoode for their final year, did not solve the problem of increasing numbers at the original school. The number of applicants was not noticeably affected by the raising of the admission standard to the B.A. degree. Indeed, enrolment continued to increase and even the construction of an addition to the Law School building, scheduled for completion in 1957, would not solve the problem. As a consequence, in February 1957, the Law Society adopted as the requirement for admission to practice (a) a law degree from any recognized university, (b) one year of articling, and (c) successful completion of a six month bar admission course which the Society itself would offer. By September 1957, the University of Ottawa and Queen's University had established faculties of law, and the University of Western Ontario followed suit in 1959. Osgoode Hall Law School itself obtained a degree-granting charter in 1957, since otherwise its students would not be technically qualified under clause (a) above. It should be added that in 1953 the University of Ottawa had established a faculty of civil law, whose graduates were recognized as fulfilling the requirements other than articling for practice in the Province of Quebec. In 1955, the school at Toronto was elevated to faculty status. By 1960, then, there were six faculties of law in Ontario where there had been none in 1940.

MEDICINE

Commencing in 1945, with the arrival of the war veterans, the number of applicants for admission to medical school began to

increase steadily, and by 1960 it had reached dramatic proportions.
Standards of admission in terms of grade averages, whether at
matriculation or at the completion of a pre-medical course or at
the completion of an arts and science degree program, were raised,
and by 1960 the personal interview had become a part of the normal
admission procedure. In addition, a year of internship following
completion of the four-year medical course had become a requirement for the licence to practice in all provinces. Nor was there
any diminution in the number or the proportion of qualified doctors
who proceeded to postgraduate training with a view to becoming
certified specialists. Indeed, by 1960 one of the most serious
problems facing the Canadian medical profession was the scarcity
of doctors who proposed to become general practitioners. This
was reflected in the establishment in 1954 of the College of
General Practice, with the basic objective of 'establishing and
maintaining high standards in general practice,' but it also
reflected, paradoxically, the need for specialized training for
general practice.[5] The truth of the matter was that developments
in the art and science of medicine had rendered the traditional
four year course inadequate as a preparation not only for a lifetime of practice in any area, but even for as short a period as
a decade.

By 1960, implications for the universities having medical faculties were far-reaching, complex, and costly. Quite aside from
the problems posed by attempting to provide a reasonably reliable
undergraduate program, there were now in full force the difficulties associated with meeting the needs of full-time graduate students whether as potential specialists or, even more important,
as full-time faculty members. A program of continuing education
which would enable all doctors to keep abreast of new developments
in their fields was also needed. In both the areas of graduate
education and continuing education considerable progress was made
during the 1950s, but, despite recognition that the traditional
undergraduate course was rapidly becoming a hodge-podge of increasingly unrelated subjects, there was little basic change in the
curriculum. It is true that new subjects were introduced, particularly in the clinical years, but, as in the period 1920-40,
they tended to be specialized manifestations of aspects of older
subjects. To make room for these, less time was devoted to traditional subjects such as anatomy and physiology. At none of the
schools had an attempt been made to introduce, for example, the
kind of integrated approach to medical education that characterized
the experimental program introduced at Western Reserve University
in Cleveland, Ohio in 1946, which among other things took into
account the relevance of the social sciences to the education of
the doctor.[6] However, change was in the air in 1960, when major
reforms were made in the curriculum at McGill which now permitted
selected students to devote a portion of their third year to study
in depth in a department outside the faculty of medicine; and
this trend continued throughout the 1960s.

At the 1961 Special NCCUC Conference, the two professional fields
that received particular attention were dentistry and medicine.[7]

By this time something close to a crisis had developed in these fields in terms of the discrepancy between supply and demand. In the case of medicine, with the exception of Manitoba where enrolment had gone down from 243 to 185, and McGill which had remained at 419, admissions to the nine schools of 1940 had increased either modestly - as, for example, at Queen's where they had risen from 282 to 330 - or dramatically, as at Montréal and Laval where they rose from 255 to 542 and 312 to 554, respectively. Three new faculties were established: at Ottawa in 1947; at British Columbia in 1950; and at Saskatchewan in 1956. There had been a two-year program at the latter for 30 years.

These developments increased the total undergraduate registration from 2877 in 1940 to 4244 in 1960, but, as was strongly stated at the NCCUC Special Conference in 1961, this did not fill the gap. It was estimated that four more faculties were required to be fully operative by 1976, i.e., producing graduates, and this would necessitate that the plans for such institutions would have to be fully laid during the 1960s. These recommendations were in fact implemented on schedule with the establishment of medical schools at McMaster whose first class graduated in 1972, Sherbrooke in 1973, Calgary in 1973, and Memorial in 1973.

ENGINEERING

Enrolment in engineering tripled between 1940 and 1960 to over 15,000, a development that required the creation of eight new schools of engineering and the introduction of pre-engineering at nine other institutions. In fact, the only institutions with general degree-granting powers which did not provide engineering by 1960 were Bishop's, Mount Saint Vincent, and Waterloo Lutheran. Seven of the faculties had more than 1000 students, including Laval which had had only 46 in 1940. Four had over 600 students, whereas in 1940 only five schools had even 400 students, the largest being Toronto with 954. Seven faculties now offered the doctorate, including Ottawa which had revived its engineering course in 1946 after a half-century interruption; six others offered a master's degree. At the undergraduate level, nearly all schools provided for specialization in civil, chemical, electrical, and mechanical engineering, and several provided for specialization in mining, metallurgy, geology, and engineering physics. Alberta and British Columbia had petroleum engineering options while Toronto offered aeronautical and industrial engineering.

The most interesting innovation in engineering education appeared at Waterloo whose school began in 1956 with a combined work-study program modelled with some modifications on that provided for liberal arts students at Antioch College in the United States since the 1920s. The course at Waterloo lasted five years from senior matriculation in contrast to the normal four, with students alternating periods of academic study on campus with supervised practical experience in industrial and engineering firms.

534

ARCHITECTURE

With the addition of a department of architecture at the University
of British Columbia in 1945, four degree programs were available
in the Canadian universities by 1960. The previous 20 years had
seen a significant growth in the status of architecture, not only
with respect to the numbers of students and the variety of courses
offered, but also in its position within the university hierarchy.
Construction and design elements remained fairly evenly balanced
in the programs constituting the core curriculum, but there was
a growing interest in the field of town planning at British
Columbia, Manitoba, and Toronto, with the latter offering a graduate program in community and town planning.
  At Toronto in 1948 architecture's fifty year association with
the faculty of applied science and engineering ended, and an independent faculty of architecture was established. In the same
year the department at Manitoba was reorganized as a school of
architecture. It immediately revised and lengthened its course
and in addition introduced a degree course in interior design,
the first course of this type in Canada.
  All schools had lengthened the course between 1940 and 1950;
at British Columbia and Manitoba to five years beyond senior matriculation, at McGill and Toronto to six. Total full-time enrolment was 753 in 1960-61, with 248 at McGill, 226 at Manitoba, 196
at Toronto, and 83 at British Columbia.

FORESTRY

By 1960, all four Canadian schools of forestry had attained faculty
status and British Columbia and Laval had authorized doctoral programs. But enrolments remained relatively small: 183 undergraduates at both British Columbia and New Brunswick, 215 at Laval,
which continued also to provide for surveying; 97 at Toronto.
Instruction was concentrated primarily at the undergraduate level
and the curricula had again been revised principally to provide
for additional options in the upper years and to enable students
to specialize in the non-engineering aspects of forestry. At New
Brunswick, which in 1947 had extended its course from four to five
years, there were now two streams in the B.Sc.F. program, Forestry
A (engineering) and Forestry B (entomology and other biological
areas). British Columbia now offered two degrees, the 'old'
B.A.Sc. in forest engineering (through the faculty of applied
science) and the new B.Sc.F., begun in 1947 and providing for
specialization in technical forestry, forestry business administration, and chemical and wood products, and offered in the faculty
of forestry established in 1951. Graduate work to the master's
level was now an important concern at all four institutions, and
the staff members were much more active in research. The establishment in 1953 of a Forest Research Foundation in connection
with Laval, with financial support from the Quebec Department of

535

Lands and Forests and the pulp and paper industry, was a sign of the times.

An unusual and successful experiment occurred at U.B.C. in the late 1950s when, following the Hungarian Revolution the university made provision for the continuance of the work of the staff and students of the Forestry Faculty of the University at Sopron, who, in many cases with their families, had crossed the Austrian border in November 1956. The Sopron School of Forestry was constituted a division of U.B.C.'s Faculty of Forestry, instruction continued to be provided by its staff in Hungarian, and U.B.C. degrees were conferred - the first 28 in June 1958.[8]

In 1956 Memorial University began to offer a two year preprofessional course in forestry in its faculty of applied science, with students proceeding to the University of New Brunswick for the third year of its B.Sc. course. The period 1940-60 also saw the establishment of one or two year technical programs in Ontario (Ontario Forest Ranger School, 1945; Lakehead Technical Institute, 1948), British Columbia (B.C. Forest Ranger School, 1946), New Brunswick (Maritimes Forest Ranger School, 1946), and Alberta (Forest Technical School, Hinton, 1951). L'Ecole Forestière at Duchesnay in the Province of Quebec continued.[9]

AGRICULTURE

The importance of agriculture as a field of study declined between 1940 and 1960 in direct relation to the decline of its importance to the national economy. Over these decades Canada had moved rapidly into the technological age. Therefore, only modest absolute increases took place in admissions to degree programs in agriculture in contrast to giant leaps in engineering. Enrolment rose from 1373 to 1886, but this represented a proportionate decreased from 3.9% to 1.8%. No new schools were established. In the four western universities, where the students were located on the main campus and where agriculture was still a major industry, the faculty retained an important and respected place; but at Laval, Montréal, McGill, and Toronto it was undermined to some extent because the facilities were at some distance from the main campus of the university. Standards at the undergraduate level undoubtedly had been raised since 1940, and there had been a healthy development in graduate programs. At British Columbia, Laval, McGill, Manitoba, and Toronto (Ontario Agricultural College) courses were offered leading to the doctorate.

VETERINARY MEDICINE

Efforts to establish a veterinary school in western Canada date back to at least 1944. During the early and mid-1950s some money was included for this purpose in the University of Saskatchewan budget.[10] The adoption by the Alberta Veterinary Medicine

Association at its 1957 annual meeting of a resolution in favour
of establishing a college led to a meeting of university and
government officials from all four western provinces at the
University of Alberta in April 1958; in January 1959 a further
resolution was adopted that steps should be taken immediately to
establish a college either at Edmonton or Saskatoon. However,
nothing was done until the early 1960s, so that in 1960 there
were still only two schools of veterinary medicine in Canada.

In 1952 the Ontario Veterinary College had extended its program
to five years from senior matriculation, and by this time there
had been considerable development in graduate work and research.

In Quebec, by 1945 the Trappist fathers, who were in charge of
the Institut agricole d'Oka with which the Ecole de médecine
vétérinaire had been associated since 1927, had become convinced
that their limited physical and financial resources should be
concentrated on agriculture and they requested the government to
make other arrangements for veterinary medicine. Thus, in October
1947 an Ecole de médecine vétérinaire de la Province de Québec
was set up at St Hyacinthe. It opened with a student body of 90,
approximately double that enrolled at Oka the previous year. The
new school was affiliated with Montréal in May 1948, with the same
course being offered, although now it was upgraded to justify the
granting of the degree of docteur en médecine vétérinaire.

HOUSEHOLD SCIENCE

Enrolment in household science almost exactly doubled between 1940
and 1960 (from 790 to 1580) despite the fact that almost all the
schools which were well established in 1940 either remained at
essentially the same figure (Alberta increased from 87 to 93,
McGill from 81 to 95) or experienced a considerable decrease
(Manitoba from 288 to 206, Saskatchewan from 145 to 70). The
overall increase resulted from substantially increased enrolment
at Montréal and the Macdonald Institute and the establishment of
new schools at Assumption, British Columbia, Laval, Ottawa, St
Joseph's (at the Collège Notre-Dame d'Acadia established at Moncton
in 1948) and Sherbrooke. Of the new schools, those at British
Columbia, Laval, and Sherbrooke were particularly significant.
British Columbia, which had finally succeeded in establishing the
school in 1944 after a quarter century of effort, had an enrolment
in 1960 of 196; Laval, which had not authorized a degree program
until 1941, 117; and Sherbrooke which had not been established
as a university until 1954, 61. Since 1948 all years of the
Toronto B.H.Sc. program had been offered by the Macdonald Institute
at Guelph. The most impressive development, however, had occurred
at Université de Montréal where, in addition to l'Ecole des sciences
ménagères which continued on a modest scale to provide for the
preparation of elementary and secondary school teachers, an Institut
de diététique et de nutrition had been established within the
faculté de médecine in 1942 for the purpose of providing degree

programs in nutrition at both the bachelor's and master's level.
By 1960 master's programs in nutrition had also been established
at Alberta, Manitoba, and McGill. At Toronto a doctoral program
in food chemistry had been available since 1950.

DENTISTRY

Full-time enrolment in dentistry moved from 468 to 1084 in the
decades 1940 to 1960, despite upgrading of entrance requirements.
A four year course following 2 years of arts and science beyond
junior matriculation was universally required for the D.D.S. degree
by 1960. A sixth Canadian school of dentistry was set up at
Manitoba and 65 students were enrolled in September 1958. The
large increase in registration arose in part from expansion within
the five existing schools, each of which obtained enough money
over the two decades to offer adequate physical accommodation and
full-time staff, not only for the numbers enrolled in 1940, but
also for additional students.

At Montréal, the faculty was housed in the University's permanent building opened in 1942, and by 1947 a postgraduate course
in orthodontics was initiated. However, at the other four schools,
expansion did not occur until the end of the period: at McGill
in 1955; at Dalhousie in 1958; at Toronto in 1959; and at Alberta
in 1960. The McGill faculty moved into the Montreal General
Hospital, whereas new and specially designed buildings were provided at the other three institutions. The staffing problem had
been attended to earlier, particularly at Toronto where a fellowship program supported by funds from the Kellogg Foundation and
the National Research Council was initiated. This permitted
existing and future staff to devote full attention to upgrading
their qualifications and to engage in research projects. Consequently, in 1952 a division of dental research within the faculty
was established which was supported for the next five years by
funds totalling $250,000 raised by the profession and through
appeals to business.

The problem of dental education received considerable attention
at the 1961 Special NCCUC Conference. In one of the presentations
it was demonstrated that the supply of well-trained dentists had
to be greatly expanded if the needs of the population were to be
met over the next two decades.[11] It was noted that the average
number of graduates of which there were only 189 between 1955 and
1960, would have to rise to 550 by 1980 if Canada were to attain
the generally accepted ratio of one dentist for every 2500 persons.
The University of British Columbia had begun planning for an
additional school as early as 1954[12] but the school was not opened
until 1965, by which time three other schools were in the planning
stage at Laval, Saskatchewan, and Western Ontario.

PHARMACY

In 1944 at the founding meeting of the Canadian Conference of
Pharmaceutical Faculties (renamed in 1969 the Association of
Faculties of Pharmacy of Canada) it was resolved that by 1950 a
three year B.Sc. in pharmacy based on senior matriculation should
be the minimum requirement for the right to practise in all
Canadian provinces. Subsequently the conference resolved to increase the minimum requirement, which would be mandatory for all
member faculties, to a four year degree by 1961. On the whole,
these successive objectives were met on or close to schedule
through the joint action of the universities and the provincial
statutory bodies responsible for pharmacy. Manitoba and Quebec
had already adopted the four year degree requirement by 1940.
Alberta achieved the first ojbective in 1945, the second in 1965;
British Columbia the first in 1946, the second in 1957; Saskatchewan
and Ontario both at one step in 1948 and 1954 respectively; New
Brunswick and Nova Scotia the first in 1954, the second in 1957.
Only in Newfoundland and Prince Edward Island where there were no
degree-granting schools did the situation differ from the pattern
established in the other provinces.
   In the process of these general developments, the Ontario College
of Pharmacy became an integrated faculty of Toronto in 1953. A
new school was established at U.B.C., initially as a department
in arts and science in 1946, and as a faculty in 1950. Faculty
status was also achieved at Montréal and Alberta, and there were
noteworthy gains with respect to physical facilities and the number of full-time staff members in all schools. By 1960, undergraduate work in pharmacy was firmly based, but courses at the
graduate level, for which a sound baccalaureate degree program
was a prerequisite, were not fully developed. However, master's
and doctoral degrees were available at Alberta and Montréal, and
master's degrees at U.B.C., Manitoba, Saskatchewan, and Toronto.
The first Canadian Ph.D. in pharmacy was granted by Alberta in 1961.

OPTOMETRY

The two schools of optometry which had been established by 1940
continued to operate throughout the period. In 1945 the Ecole
d'Optométrie transferred its lectures and laboratories to the
main building of the Université de Montréal in the area occupied
by the faculté des sciences, only its clinics remaining at the
school's original location on the Rue Saint André. In 1950 both
its organization (it obtained a new charter) and its curriculum
were substantially revised, its academic offerings henceforth
consisting of a three year course leading to the licence en
sciences optométriques for which a B.A. was the admission require-

ent. At the Ontario College of Optometry in Toronto the course was extended to four years from senior matriculation in 1954, at which point the degree of doctor of optometry was authorized - it was first granted in 1956.[13] The question of affiliation with the University of Toronto, whose departments continued to offer some of the instruction, was raised periodically but for reasons which remain obscure continued to come to nothing. In 1958 discussions began to take place between the College of Optometry and the newly established University of Waterloo, and these culminated in 1967 in the transferral of the college to the Waterloo campus and its establishment as the university's School of Optometry.

NURSING

During World War II demand for nursing in the armed forces provided the Canadian universities with the opportunity to expand their work in the nursing education field. In September 1941, eight of the nine directors of university schools of nursing met with the executive of the Canadian Nurses Association to consider the possibility of introducing a special wartime course. This proposal was rejected but the meeting led to the establishment in 1942 of a Provincial Council of University Schools of Nursing which became in 1950 the Canadian Conference of University Schools of Nursing. By 1960, six more university schools of nursing had been established and full-time enrolment had risen to 1659. In contrast the enrolment in 1941 was 588.

Expansion was made possible by generous financial support from the federal government, which in 1942 granted $150,000 to the Canadian Nurses Association for the development of nursing education; the grant was increased to $250,000 for 1943 and was maintained at this level for another year. In 1942, the Kellogg Foundation began to provide funds for bursary and loan assistance to nursing students, and in 1943 the Victorian Order of Nurses revived the scholarship program which it had supported in the 1920s but had withdrawn in 1933. While not all of this money was available to the universities, they did receive a large portion, and among other things it led to the establishment of schools of nursing at McMaster and Queen's in 1942 and at Manitoba in 1943.

Equally important was the effect of the infusion of funds into the existing schools of nursing, a fact which can be illustrated by McGill's experience. Its share of the 1942 federal grant was $2100, an amount that was increased to $6000 in 1943, and which by 1945 totalled $27,750. This made possible additional appointments to the full-time staff, the introduction of programs in public health and in clinical supervision, and, indirectly at least, to the establishment of a degree program in 1944.

In the immediate post-war period, McGill's position was further strengthened by a Kellogg Foundation grant of $60,000, which was used to increase the full-time staff in obstetrical, paediatric, and psychiatric nursing and to enable staff members to take sabbaticals in order to raise their academic qualifications. Also in the post-war period, degree programs were introduced at Mount Saint Vincent in 1947, Dalhousie in 1949, and New Brunswick in 1959. The Kellogg Foundation granted $50,000 to the Western Ontario school of nursing, and it is certainly not merely coincidence that McGill and Western Ontario were the two English-language schools which by 1960 were able to introduce nursing programs at the graduate level.[14]

Of the schools established between 1940 and 1960, McMaster adopted the concept of an integrated school on the Toronto model, i.e., a course in which hospital training was controlled by the school itself. British Columbia adopted the integrated approach in 1951 after nursing was elevated from a department in the faculty of arts to a school, and McGill followed suit in 1957. In consequence, by 1960 there were four integrated schools, and this was to become more or less universal throughout Canada by 1970.

PHYSICAL THERAPY, OCCUPATIONAL THERAPY, AND MEDICAL TECHNOLOGY

Just as World War I had demonstrated the need for courses in physical and occupational therapy, so World War II highlighted the need for expansion of such programs. Over 100 therapists served as officers in the Canadian Armed Forces, and from 1944 on there was a particularly heavy demand for such people in the veterans' hospitals.

At the University of Toronto, the two year diploma courses in physical and in occupational therapy introduced in the late 1920s were extended in 1946 to three years and in 1950 were merged as a single course. In 1950, too, responsibility for the program was transferred from the division of university extension to the faculty of medicine where it became the nucleus for a division of rehabilitation medicine. By 1960, the division was also offering postgraduate courses in the teaching of physical and occupational thereapy and in speech pathology and audiology. By 1960 some men were enrolling in the basic course.

Four other universities had established programs in physical therapy and occupational therapy by 1960. In 1942, McGill introduced a two year diploma course in physiotherapy. In 1950 occupational therapy was included and a four year combined course offered, still leading to a diploma. In 1954, the two branches were again separated at the diploma level, with parallel three year courses being offered, but at the same time a combined five year program leading to a degree was introduced. Since junior matriculation was required for admission to all three courses, the graduate of the diploma course was in a position to go on to obtain the degree after two further years of study. At Alberta, a two year diploma course in physical therapy established in 1954 was extended by one year in 1960 when a three year diploma program in occupational therapy was also initiated. Efforts dating back to 1951 by the Manitoba branch of the Canadian Physiotherapy

Association and by the Canadian Association of Occupational
Therapists to persuade the University of Manitoba to offer courses
in both fields finally met with success in 1960 with the establishment within the faculty of medicine of two and one year diploma courses for which the admission requirement was senior matriculation. In 1964, these courses were extended to three years,
and in 1966 an optional fourth year was added, leading to a degree
in physical therapy or occupational therapy. A similar course
was established at Dalhousie in 1963 with financial support being
provided by the four Atlantic provinces. In 1959 a special course
in occupational therapy was established in Kingston by the Canadian
Association of Occupational Therapists for students with special
academic qualifications; this course was the forerunner of the
three year diploma program in occupational therapy established by
Queen's University in 1967. British Columbia was offering a
combined course by 1961 and this was extended to a degree program
within three years.
    In 1954, Université de Montréal established two schools within
its faculty of medicine, l'Ecole de réhabilitation and l'Ecole de
technologie médicale. L'Ecole de réhabilitation had two sections,
one offering a three year combined diploma course in physical and
occupational therapy and one offering master's level courses in
speech therapy and audiology. In 1962, separate occupational and
physical therapy courses replaced the combined course and subsequently were extended to three year degree courses. L'Ecole de
technologie médicale offered a nine month course in laboratory
technology leading, after twelve months of hospital internship,
to a certificate. A similar program had been given by Laval since
its Ecole de technologie médicale was set up in 1952. In 1957, Mount
Saint Vincent began offering a B.Sc. in radiological technology.

SOCIAL WORK

Considerable development occurred in the area of social work
between 1940 and 1960. At Toronto, the department of social
science had become a school of social work in 1941 offering degree
programs at the bachelor's, the master's, and (from 1952) the
doctoral levels; the Montreal School of Social Work had again become an integrated part of McGill University (partially in 1945,
fully in 1950); a number of universities in the Atlantic provinces
had combined to establish the Maritime School of Social Work at
Halifax in 1941; and schools of social work had been established
at Manitoba in 1943, at Ottawa (at St Patrick's College) in 1949,
and at British Columbia (within the faculty of arts and science)
in 1951. The basic program offered at all these schools was a
two year course from a B.A. or B.Sc. leading to the master of
social work degree, though British Columbia, Manitoba, and Toronto
granted a B.S.W. degree on completion of the first year of the
course. Montréal offered a three-year course to the master's
degree to graduates of the classical colleges, Laval a three year

542

bachelor's course and a four year master's course to similarly qualified students, and the newly established Université de Sherbrooke a certificate course for social work assistants in its Ecole d'initiation au service social.

All these programs provided for a number of new specializations. Except at Ottawa, where the St Patrick's College program was organized in what was called the block plan, whereby the students spent three academic terms at the university and two in the field, the programs were similarly designed with about two days a week during the first year and the bulk of the second being spent in the field. In all cases a thesis was required for the degree.

LIBRARY SCIENCE

By 1960 both McGill and Toronto had replaced their one year B.L.S. program by a two year M.L.S. program, and the diploma course had been withdrawn. Ottawa, which had finally been able to replace its evening courses by a full year program in 1952, also established the M.L.S. as its basic program in 1954. At Université de Montréal it was still possible in 1960 to obtain a diploma by two years attendance at Saturday classes, but the basic program was a B.L.S. introduced in 1946, with a bachelor's degree as an admission requirement. The Ecole de bibliothécaires continued to be housed in the Bibliothèque municipale until 1954 when it was moved to the Ecole normale Jacques Cartier, though summer courses from 1955 on were offered on the main campus. In 1961 a full-time director was appointed and the university became directly involved in its administration and financing.

In the Maritimes in 1960 the only training in library science was at St Francis Xavier where students at Mount Saint Bernard College could take seven library science courses in their B.A. course. Planning for a library school at British Columbia was initiated in 1947 when the new library was being built, but it did not come to fruition until 1961.

TEACHER TRAINING

The growth of full-time enrolment in education in the Canadian universities between 1940 and 1960 is one of the most striking characteristics of the period, an increase from 667 in 1940-41 to 10,473 in 1960-61.[15] The growth is even more significant if one examines the figures for the final years of the period:

1954-55	2,804
1955-56	3,333
1956-57	4,437
1957-58	5,360
1958-59	7,151
1959-60	8,754
1960-61	10,473

In 1961-62 the numbers had risen to 12,916. These figures include students registered for an undergraduate degree in education or for a diploma for which a degree was a prerequisite. In
the Dominion Bureau of Statistics' returns for this year, all
education students are classified as undergraduates, and since
the total full-time enrolment figure for 1960-61 was 114,000,
education students constituted close to 10%. In contrast, the
677 education students registered in 1940-41 represented less
than 2% of total enrolment. There were almost as many students
in education at Memorial University in 1960-61 (667) as in all
the Canadian universities 20 years earlier, and there were three
times as many (1935) at the University of British Columbia.

Quite obviously, the period demonstrates a remarkable increase
in the involvement of the Canadian universities in teacher training,
and the explanation lies primarily in their belated recognition
of a responsibility for the training of elementary school teachers,
which prior to 1945 was left largely to the normal schools. Of
the 677 education students of 1940, those studying in English-
language institutions were graduates taking the equivalent of a
one year diploma course which qualified them for either elementary
or secondary school teaching positions, but the great majority
were preparing for the latter. The comparable students enrolled
in 1960 were also likely to be qualified to teach at either level
but considerably more than half of them intended to teach in the
elementary schools.

In 1944, in an address to the National Conference of Canadian
Universities, President Carleton Stanley of Dalhousie chastized
the universities for not taking seriously their responsibility
for the training of teachers at all levels.[16] As it happened,
response to this challenge was about to take place in the western
provinces and initially in Alberta, where in 1945, the normal
schools were closed and the responsibility for all teacher training
was assigned to the university. A branch of the university was
established in the same year at Calgary to replace the normal
school which had been located there, a move that laid the foundation for an independent University of Calgary 20 years later. In
1952, Saskatchewan recognized a four year university course as
the basic requirement for the permanent teaching certificate in
either the elementary or the secondary schools, but the normal
schools were retained under the title of teachers colleges until
1964 when, as a supplement to the College of Education at Saskatoon,
a faculty of education was established at the university's branch
at Regina.[17] In 1956 the normal schools were closed at Vancouver
and Victoria, and the faculty of education at the University of
British Columbia became responsible for all teacher training,
with much of the work being carried on at its affiliate, Victoria
College on Vancouver Island. With the establishment of Simon
Fraser University in 1963, a faculty of education was also authorized there. No change occurred in Manitoba until 1959 when a
royal commission recommended the transfer of all teacher training
to the university, a step that was implemented in 1965 at the

University of Manitoba and its affiliate, Brandon College. The
other province which had decided by 1960 to concentrate teacher
training in the university was Newfoundland, which in 1946 established a B.A. in Education program at Memorial University College,
in which all prospective teachers were required to enrol. However,
for many years the majority of students enrolled in this course
completed only one year before taking positions in Newfoundland
elementary schools.

In the other three Maritime provinces there were no new developments by 1960; normal schools, also renamed teachers colleges,
continued to prepare teachers for the elementary schools and universities continued to offer a one year postgraduate diploma course
for secondary school teachers. The teachers college course was
extended to two years in 1962, and by this time, too, elementary
school candidates were being encouraged to take a B.Ed. degree at
one of the universities.

In Ontario, a Royal Commission on Education, which was appointed
in 1945 and reported after five years of study in 1950 recommended
that the requirement for elementary school teachers be completion
of a two year course beyond senior matriculation to be taken at
junior colleges of education, a number of which were to be established throughout the province;[18] but the only result of this
proposal was the renaming of the normal schools as teachers colleges in 1953. These colleges, which had increased from 8 to 10
by 1960, and to 13 by 1965, offered a two-year course from Grade
XII (junior matriculation) or a one year course from Grade XIII
(senior matriculation), but in the latter case the requirements
were less rigorous (eight subjects rather than nine and a lower
overall average) than for admission to university. The professional training of secondary school teachers continued to be the
monopoly of the Ontario College of Education at Toronto, whose
basic program was an eight month course for which a degree was a
prerequisite. However, the demand for teachers became so heavy
in the 1950s, a development which explains the establishment of
additional teachers colleges, that commencing in 1955 it became
possible for a graduate to qualify for a secondary school certificate by attending two summer sessions at the Ontario College
of Education. It was not until the mid 1960s, when faculties of
education were established at Western Ontario (Althouse College,
1965) and Queen's (MacArthur College, 1967) that Ontario followed
the lead of the West in assigning responsibility for teacher
training to the universities that any progress was made in this
area.

In English-speaking Quebec, by 1960 teacher training for both
elementary and secondary schools was concentrated at McGill, which
in 1955 had replaced its teacher training college with an institute of education offering a four year course to the B.Ed. The
new body was able to draw on the resources of McGill's faculty
of arts and science, and it was sufficiently large to be able to
provide for specialization in various fields and for its well-
qualified staff to engage in research. However, a number of its

students left at the end of the second year, at which time they had qualified for a Class II Certificate entitling them to teach in elementary schools. A Class I Certificate and the B.Ed. were awarded to those who completed the four year course. The main problem faced by the McGill Institute was its separation from the main campus, which hampered the extent to which the work in arts and science and in education could be integrated. Bishop's University continued to provide a course for a handful of students, only six in 1960-61 contrasted with McGill's 596; and at St Joseph's Teachers' College a course equivalent to senior matriculation and leading to the Brevet B was offered for teachers wishing to go into the elementary schools.

In French-speaking Quebec responsibility for teacher training was evenly divided between the universities and the écoles normales; at the former, the baccalaureate, the licence, and the doctorat in education were available, and at the latter the course led to the Brevet A&B, the former being equivalent to a bachelier en pédagogie.

In 1960 there were over 100 écoles normales, approximately 10 for men and 70 for women; candidates were required to have obtained junior matriculation to be eligible for the course. There were also 25 studying to be teachers in scolasticates directed either by male or female religious orders. A one year course in any of these institutions led to a Brevet C, permitting the holder to teach in elementary grades; this option was withdrawn in 1962.

In the 1964 report of the Royal Commission of Inquiry on Education in Quebec (the Parent Report) it was stated that the quality of instruction in most of the écoles normales was inadequate and upon the commission's recommendations they were eliminated. The standards were somewhat better in the universities. In 1942 Montréal had established an Ecole normale supérieure in the faculté des arts which for many years had functioned on an evening, week-end, and extension basis. By 1959 it was offering most of its instruction on the main campus during the day. In 1960, its administrative connection with the faculté des arts was severed. At Laval, an Ecole de pédagogie et d'orientation was set up in 1943 to provide for specialization in subjects such as psychology, guidance, and the pedagogy of secondary school subjects; and in 1960 Laval also reorganized its Ecole normale supérieure. Université de Sherbrooke initiated a faculty of education shortly after it began operations in 1954, and by 1960, like Laval and Montréal, it was in a position to offer programs at the doctoral as well as the master's (licence) and bachelor's level. Its full-time enrolment in education in 1960-61 was 835. Laval had 412 students, and Montréal 1557.

PHYSICAL AND HEALTH EDUCATION

Part of the stimulus for the remarkable proliferation of degree courses in this subject area between 1945 and 1965 was provided by the National Fitness Act adopted by the Federal government in 1943. Originally proposed by the Canadian Association for Physical Education in 1939, the act provided funds in the amount of $250,000 a year to be available to participating provinces on a matching basis in order to (a) extend physical education in all educational institutions, (b) encourage sports and athletics, and (c) prepare teachers of physical education. In May 1944, at the first meeting of the National Council on Physical Fitness provided for in the act, a resolution was adopted urging 'every university to conduct a physical program for all students and to establish the degree in physical education and health.' This resolution was forwarded to the NCCU which, at its meeting a month later, passed the following motion: 'Resolved that to promote the physical fitness of the people of Canada, to assist in the extension of physical training in all educational and other institutions and to train teachers, lecturers and instructors in the principles of physical education and physical fitness, Universities in which facilities for the teaching of the fundamental medical sciences are available should consider the establishment of a course in Physical and Health Education at the earliest date possible.'[19]

Also in 1944 the first students in Toronto's degree course in physical and health education, which had begun in 1940, were graduated with their B.P.H.E., and McGill sanctioned a B.Ed. (Phys.Ed.), but the first students did not enrol until 1945.

The proliferation of degree courses in physical and health education between 1945 and 1965 is another example of the striking development in Canadian higher education in the post-war period. Programs were introduced at British Columbia and Queen's in 1946, Western Ontario in 1947, Ottawa in 1949, Alberta in 1950, Saskatchewan and Laval in 1954, Montreal in 1955, McMaster in 1956, and New Brunswick in 1957. By 1960 the 12 schools of physical and health education had an enrolment of 1114 full-time students in contrast to the 42 reported by the Dominion Bureau of Statistics in 1940. The expansion continued on into the 1960s with seven additional programs being established by 1965. Almost as remarkable as the number of programs is the variety of designations accorded the degree: B.P.H.E. and B.Ed. (Phys.Ed.), B.P.E., B.A. (Phys. & Health Ed.), B.A. (Phys.Ed.), and B.Sc. (Phys.Ed.). At several institutions the program led to two degrees, at Queen's, for example, to the B.A. and the B.P.H.E.

By 1960-61 the three largest schools were British Columbia with 177 students, Toronto with 175, and Queen's with 134. The fourth largest was New Brunswick with 125: this is surprising since it was not established until 1957. It was, however, the only school of physical and health education in the Maritime provinces and would remain so until Memorial entered the field in 1963. Two of the smallest schools in 1960-61 were Laval with 36 students and Montréal with 13, but these also were new foundations. In 1961-62 their enrolments had jumped to 104 and 105.

The programs offered in the 12 schools were almost entirely at the undergraduate level. Only two offered graduate programs,

British Columbia (master of physical education) and Alberta (M.A. or M.Sc.). One graduate degree (the first in Canada) was awarded in 1959, two in 1960. The programs were, however, almost entirely at the degree level; the only remaining diploma course was a two year program offered at McGill's Institute of Education which led to an elementary teacher's certificate. Its graduates were encouraged to take two additional years at McGill's school of physical education in order to qualify for a degree.

The programs at two universities, Alberta and British Columbia, provided for specialization in recreation, and at two others, McGill and Toronto, the strong initial link with medicine was reflected in a course of study which permitted, though it did not require, its students to specialize in pure science. The majority of students expected to teach physical and health education in the elementary or secondary schools, and in all the schools the curriculum was designed with this in mind.

MUSIC

In January 1948, a number of university presidents and directors of music met at the University of Toronto to discuss music education in Canadian universities and affiliated organizations:

> At this meeting a review was given of the work being done in the institutions represented, and it became apparent that, although much was being done in the field of music, the financial support being given to this aspect of University work was not in general of the same order as had been given to other subjects of University curricula. It was agreed that uniformity of policy and practice would be undesirable, but there was a unanimous feeling that advancement in music education could only come about through co-operation at both regional and national levels.[20]

The consequence of this was the appointment by the NCCU of a standing music committee. This committee vied with the one on uniform matriculation for being among the least successful of all those appointed during the long history of the conference. It experienced difficulty at the outset in obtaining detailed information about the academic and financial position of the music programs in the various schools involved, and questionnaires distributed in 1948 and again in 1950 proved unproductive. It was then decided that a survey of music education in Canada should be conducted, but efforts over the next five years to persuade a foundation to support the project were also unproductive. The end result was the replacement of the committee by a new one in 1956, but no developments had occurred by 1960.

Nonetheless, some progress was made in music education between 1940 and 1960. Three institutions established departments of music in the faculty of arts: Western Ontario in 1944, Alberta in 1945; British Columbia in 1946; and Acadia also made provision for a music major in its B.A. program. Degree courses designed specifically to prepare teachers of music for the schools were introduced at McGill, Toronto, and Western Ontario, the latter through a Music Teachers' College which was affiliated in 1943. There was also an expansion in the area of performance, McGill adding a Mus.B. in performance to its general Mus.B. and Toronto establishing in 1946 the Royal Conservatory Opera School. By 1960, the University of Toronto had also established a Mus.M. degree, with specialization possible in composition, musicology, theory, and music education.

However, it was still possible for Ernest MacMillan to repeat in 1958 much of what he had said concerning the state of music education in Canada in his 1927 address to the NCCU.[21] Only Toronto, he claimed, was adequately providing for the training of professional musicians within the framework of higher education, and he argued that there ought to be at least one comparable program in each of the five major regions of Canada.

FINE ART

By 1960 credit courses in fine arts had become a fairly normal offering in the B.A. programs of most Canadian universities, the striking exception being the small Roman Catholic colleges, but in about half the cases (Acadia, Carleton, Dalhousie, McMaster, Memorial, Ottawa, Queen's) the staff consisted of a single person, sometimes on a part-time basis. At Sir George Williams there was a full-time professor and nine special lecturers. Only at McGill, Saskatchewan, Alberta, British Columbia, and Toronto was instruction provided on a departmental basis, and only at the latter three were there as many as four full-time staff members. At Alberta, which had established its fine arts department in 1946, drama and music were included.

Mount Allison continued to offer its B.F.A. degree on the same basis as in 1940, and Toronto continued to offer a four year honour course, now called Art and Archaeology. A second B.F.A. program had been introduced at Manitoba in 1950, a school of art being established by the absorption of the Winnipeg School of Art. Most of the training of professional artists continued to be given in institutions like the Ecole des Beaux Arts in Montreal and the Ontario College of Art at Toronto.

In reviewing the situation in 1955 at a symposium on 'The University and the Fine Arts' at the annual meeting of the National Conference of Canadian Universities, R.H. Hubbard, chief curator of the National Gallery of Canada, argued that the marriage of the practical and the theoretical as represented in the programs at Manitoba and Mount Allison should be followed in several other universities. The European tradition of providing for the training of art historians in universities and of practicing artists in independent institutions designed for the purpose was appropriate in large metropolitan centres like Montreal and Toronto, but in

the Canadian provinces generally the American tradition, particularly as represented by the state universities, was the only
practical model to follow. A coordination of efforts was necessary in the interests both of providing a better general education
for the artist and of developing an appreciation of art by the
general public. Hubbard was also concerned with the inadequacy
of the facilities available for the training of art historians:

> Our trained art historians in universities can almost be counted
> on the fingers of one hand; the French-language universities
> have, I think, only one among them. In the language of the
> advertisements, every university (like every housewife) 'should
> have one,' and the larger ones a clutch of specialized scholars.
> A more special plea of mine is that one of the French universi-
> ties establish a centre such as Toronto has supplied for English
> Canada, and thus relieve the abnormal situation by which liter-
> ally *no* French speaking art historians are to be found.[22]

NOTES TO CHAPTER 28

1 The figures in this and the preceding paragraph and, with
   respect to enrolment generally, throughout the chapter are
   taken from three Dominion Bureau of Statistics publications:
   Survey of Higher Education 1954-61 (1963); *Higher Education
   in Canada 1940-42*, Part II of the Biennial Survey of Education
   in Canada 1940-42 (1944); *Fall Enrolment in Universities and
   Colleges 1960* (1961).
2 St Thomas College, a scholasticate located at Gravelbourg,
   Sask., should not be confused either with the degree-granting
   institution located (in 1960) at Chatham, New Brunswick, nor
   with St Thomas More College, an affiliate of the University
   of Saskatchewan, located on its main campus at Saskatoon,
   which confined its instruction to certain subjects in the
   liberal arts.
3 See above, 264-6, 400-1.
4 B.D. Bucknall, et al., 'Pedants, Practitioners and Prophets:
   Legal Education at Osgoode Hall to 1957,' *Osgoode Hall Law J.*,
   6 (1968), 207ff
5 H.E. MacDermot, *One Hundred Years of Medicine in Canada* (1967),
   135ff
6 J.A. Macfarlane, *Medical Education in Canada* (1965), 37-45
7 R.F. Farquharson, 'Medical and Dental Education in Canadian
   Universities,' in D. Dunton and D. Patterson, eds., *Canada's
   Universities in a New Age* (1962), 61-83
8 H.A. Logan, *Tuum Est: a History of the University of British
   Columbia* (1958), 226
9 G.A. Garrett, *Forestry Education in Canada* (1971), 142-81
10 C.H. Bigland, 'Western Canadian Veterinary College - History
   and Status,' *Can. Vet. J.*, 3 (1962), 289

11 Farquharson, 'Medical and Dental Education,' 61-6. Dr
   Farquharson stated that the material in his paper on dental
   education had been based on information supplied to him by
   R.G. Ellis, dean of the faculty of dentistry at Toronto.
12 J.B. Macdonald, *A Prospectus on Dental Education for the
   University of British Columbia* (1956). In the same year,
   K.G. Paynter of the University of Toronto prepared a similar
   report, *Concerning the Establishment of a School of Dentistry
   in Manitoba*.
13 Authority to grant degrees was based on the inclusion in the
   Optometry Act of a clause authorizing the college to charge
   a fee for the granting of a degree.
14 M.Sc. programs providing for specialization in nursing supervision and nursing education were introduced at Western
   Ontario in 1959 and at McGill in 1961.
15 Dominion Bureau of Statistics, *Survey of Higher Education,
   1954-1961* (1963), 26
16 *NCCU Proc.* (1944), 29
17 At Saskatchewan the term 'College' has always been used in
   place of 'faculty,' e.g., college of medicine.
18 Royal Commission on Education in Ontario, *Report* (1950), 579-84
19 *NCCU Proc.* (1944), 29
20 *NCCU Proc.* (1950), 67
21 E. MacMillan, 'Music in the Canadian Universities,' *Can.
   Music J.*, 2, No. 3 (1958), 3-11. Cf *NCCU Proc.* (1927), 66-75.
22 *NCCU Proc.* (1955), 67

29

Graduate Studies

The unsatisfactory state of graduate studies in Canada was emphasized at the 1961 NCCUC Special Conference. It was referred to
in the keynote paper entitled 'The Problems and Opportunities of
Canada's Universities.' It was the main topic of the symposium
on Graduate Studies and Research in the Humanities and the Sciences,
and it received a good deal of attention at the session devoted
to Medical and Dental Education in Canadian Universities as well
as at another focused on scholarships, bursaries, and fellowships.
One of the few resolutions adopted by the conference at the final
session was an appeal to the federal government that, in addition
to increasing the per capita grants to universities from $1.50 to
$2.50, a supplementary grant of $500 be provided for every student
registered in graduate studies and in the professional schools of
dentistry and medicine.

However, the case for graduate studies was expressed much more
strongly in the presentation which dealt with deficiences in the
sciences than on that concerned with the humanities and social
sciences. The argument for greatly increased support for graduate
work in the latter two fields was not put forward as forcibly as
the circumstances warranted. It was embodied in a paper entitled
'Why the Humanities at all?', and it consisted of a traditional
exposition of a familiar and widely held view. There were no
statistical data, no reference to the social sciences, and only
indirect reference to the existing state of the humanities in
Canada. It concluded with a wistful hope that scientists would
become infused with the spirit of the humanities, because, as
the physicist Max Born had said, scientists have 'gained prestige
as men of action but they have lost credit as philosophers.'[1]

The presentation on 'Graduate Studies and Research in the
Sciences,' on the other hand, was a well-substantiated report
on the 'spectacular expansion' of graduate studies in the field

of science in the universities since World War II, and the conclusion constituted an aggressive argument for continuing progress.
'It is clear that this will cost money and it is equally clear that
this money must be found. There is no point in skimping on graduate work and research when these form one of the key factors in
our continued existence as an independent nation.'[2]

It was amply documented that the expansion of graduate work in
science had been largely stimulated by the encouragement and
financial support emanating from the National Research Council.
After its quite remarkable development during World War II, when
it had established 21 additional laboratories,[3] it continued to
expand its activities and to maintain its policy of involving the
universities in the development of science in Canada through the
provision of fellowships for graduate work and grants-in-aid for
individual scientists. By 1960-61, NRC financial support for
Canadian universities amounted to $10.5 million, a threefold in-
crease since 1955-56 and a thirtyfold increase since 1939.[4] As
a result, whereas in 1939 McGill and Toronto had graduated fewer
than 50 science doctorates a total of 13 universities graduated
almost six times that number in 1960.[5] Laval and Montréal had
developed broad science programs at the doctoral level, as had
Manitoba and Queen's, and doctorates had been granted in particular fields at Western in 1947, British Columbia in 1950,
Saskatchewan in 1952, Alberta and New Brunswick in 1953, Ottawa
in 1958, and Dalhousie in 1959.

Of the 305 earned doctorates awarded in 1960-61, two-thirds
were in the sciences, 59 were awarded in the humanities, and 45
in the social sciences.[6] However, more than half of the social
science degrees were in psychology, which in some of its branches
could be categorized as a science. There were no doctorates
awarded in anthropology, art and archaeology, or sociology.

At the master's or licence level, the position of the humanities
and social sciences in relation to the sciences was more evenly
balanced. There were 1167 students in the social sciences and
492 in the humanities, compared to a total of 775 in the physical,
biological, engineering, and applied sciences. However, included
in the figures for the social sciences were students in education,
business administration, commerce or industrial relations, and
social work. Students enrolled in law and music were included
in the humanities figure. There would, of course, be dramatic
increases in undergraduate admissions within a few years which
would send the university administrators scurrying to all parts
of the globe to try to find sufficient numbers of qualified staff
to cope with the added numbers.

The need for rapid and continuing support for graduate work,
particularly with reference to the humanities and social sciences,
had been emphasized by the NCCU Committee on Post-War Problems
whose report was adopted by the conference in 1944. At this
stage, the concern was to ensure an adequate supply of adequately
qualified instructors for the undergraduate courses as well as
for graduate programs. One of four resolutions passed by the

conference following the presentation of the report was:

> Resolved that the Conference direct the attention of the Univer-
> sities and the Governments concerned to the generally inadequate
> state of graduate work in the humanities and the social sciences
> in Canadian universities and to the necessity of restoring and
> building it up to the level of the Master's degree and thereby
> giving life to undergraduate instruction and to the teaching
> profession in secondary and other schools.[7]

This report was mainly concerned with ensuring that justice would
be done to the veterans who would upon demobilization be either
returning to or commencing studies and this required a soundly
based liberal arts program. Hence the need to strengthen teaching
staff in the arts and science faculties which had been reduced
significantly as a result of the demands of war. This point was
eloquently voiced in an appendix to the report entitled 'The
Problem of Graduate Work in Canada' which stressed the lamentable
depletion of teaching staff both at the high school and university
level and the resulting poorer preparation of students, especially
in the sphere of the liberal arts, the exigencies of war having
forced the schools and universities to place greater emphasis on
science and professional courses. Thus, 'with demobilization
returned men will be faced with the results of deterioration in
standards of teaching in the universities. Members of the staff
... returning to academic work will require time to adapt themselves to a new routine and to clear out the accumulation of rust,
and men returning as students will find the change even more
difficult.'[8]
However, the problem was seen to involve more than a matter of
providing effectively for an especially deserving group; it was
basic to the whole course of Canadian, indeed of Western culture.
Postgraduate work in the non-science fields was the key to the
preservation of the liberal arts tradition, and the one certain
means of circumventing the threat of professionalism and the
danger of an unthinking dedication to technology and science.

> The first step in reconstruction is to recognize the position
> of the humanities and the social sciences and to place them in
> their proper place of superiority in the university curriculum.
> The plea for a place in the curriculum of the professional
> schools for liberal arts subjects is of first importance, but
> it should be recognized that without steps to build up the Arts
> subjects it may mean spreading knowledge more thinly and with-
> out effective results. The liberal arts course must combat the
> tendencies towards professionalism particularly evident in
> teaching, and attempt to recapture the traditions which have
> been all but lost.[9]

That this assessment was taken seriously by the NCCU delegates is
evident in the following resolution contained in the Report on
Post-War Problems concerning graduate schools:

That the Conference direct the attention of the universities and
the Governments to the even more serious state of advanced graduate work in the field of the humanities and the social sciences,
and to the necessity of restoring and building it up to the
Doctorate level in at least a small number of Canadian universities, without prejudice, however, to the free future development
of any Canadian university. To maintain existing post-graduate
work in certain fields and extend it to other fields so that
training may be offered comparable to that given in the leading
universities of Great Britain, France, and the United States,
would tend to check the drain of some of the ablest of our graduates to universities outside Canada and to make more secure
our cultural contribution to western civilization.[10]

This was one of four resolutions on the subject adopted by the
conference. One called for special attention to be paid to postgraduate training in medicine, and another directed the NCCU
executive to establish a committee to study the facilities for
postgraduate education 'now available in Canada' and, in conjunction with the Social Science Research Council and the Humanities
Research Council, to appraise the quality of these facilities and
to make recommendations for the improvement of postgraduate education in Canada.[11]

The reference to consultation with the two research councils
arose first from the fact that the Social Science Research Council
had recently published a report on graduate training in arts in
Canadian universities and had subsequently commissioned a more
detailed and evaluative study of graduate work, and second from
the decision of the Humanities Research Council to commission a
detailed survey of the position of the humanities in Canada in
all areas. The Social Science Research Council Report entitled
Scholarship in Canada: The Function of Graduate Studies was
published in 1945 and was discussed by the NCCU at the 1945 annual
meeting. The Humanities Research Council study was not published
until 1947 but a preview of it and the recommendations it would
make were presented at the 1946 conference.

The NCCU Committee on Graduate Studies informed the delegates
at the 1946 meeting that these several documents provided the
committee with information needed for the two areas in question,
but difficulty was experienced in obtaining comparable information for the sciences. In any case, the situation in graduate
work was described in terms of an emergency; the numbers of veterans at both graduate and undergraduate levels were proving to be
even larger than anticipated and the resulting pressures placed on
senior staff were becoming intolerable. Unfortunately, no let-
up was in sight for at least two and possibly four more years.
The universities would have to pool their resources in order to
alleviate the problem:

Mobilization for graduate work must proceed further by arrangements between Canadian universities. It has been suggested
that contacts should be established between the larger graduate

schools and other universities whereby more advanced work should
be given in the latter for credit in the former. This should be
actively encouraged as it provides the immediate reserves of
teaching capacity for the heavy undergraduate loads of the session 1946-47 and 1947-48 in particular. The demands of returned
men can only be met effectively by resort to every device by
which the intellectual capacities of the nation can be developed.
The demands have never been more urgent or undeniable.[12]

Much of the time of the delegates at the 1947 Conference was
devoted to the idea of cooperation among universities, partly
through the presentation and discussion of the reports of a special committee appointed by the executive in November 1946 'to
consider the exchanges between Canadian universities of undergraduates, graduate students and junior members of faculties,'
and of the existing standing committees on international exchange
of students and on ways and means of cooperation between the universities and government research institutes. The Committee on
Post-Graduate Work and the Committee on Graduate Training were
discharged and in their places there was established a single
Committee on Graduate Studies. It was given a mandate to concentrate on the development of cooperation among the universities
in the area of graduate work. The plan was to proceed on a regional basis and between December 1947 and May 1948 regional conferences on graduate studies were held at Saskatoon on behalf of
the Western region, in Kingston and Toronto for central English-
speaking Canada, at Montreal for central French-speaking Canada,
and in Quebec City for the Maritime region.[13] Two more conferences
were held at Sackville, New Brunswick, one in August 1947 and the
other in May 1948, but there the pursuit of cooperation ended.
The Committee on Graduate Studies did not report in either 1949
or 1950. In 1951 it recommended that henceforth it should consist
of the administrative officers in charge of postgraduate studies
at all member institutions where such studies were 'worth being
pursued,' and to this the conference agreed.[14] For the next five
years the committee's report consisted of the listing of the names
of the administrative officers concerned, after which time it
disappeared.
    This should not be construed as a lack of interest in the sub-
ject on the part of the NCCU over the next decade. What it did
signify was a merging of the graduate school problem with the
general issues facing the universities during the 1950s, a fact
that was made clear in the NCCU representations to such bodies
as the Royal Commission on Arts, Letters and the Sciences and to
the federal government. It further indicated that functional cooperation of the type advocated by many spokesmen throughout the
past three decades was sound in theory but difficult to achieve.
In effect, the development of graduate studies was left to the
individual institutions, and the national organization confined
itself to arguing the need for general expansion in the interests
of the nation's welfare.

As has been suggested, the institutions did respond actively; doctoral programs, principally in the sciences, were introduced at nine additional institutions,[15] and the range of subjects for the master's degree was extended at almost all institutions in the fields of humanities, social science, and science as well as in the professions. In 1960 schools of graduate studies were established at Carleton (which granted its first Ph.D. in 1961), Waterloo, and Assumption, bringing the total number of such divisions to 14. Of the institutions granting the doctorate, only Queen's and Montréal continued to organize graduate studies on a committee basis (usually a committee of the academic senate), but this was the normal procedure in institutions which confined their offerings to the master's level.[16]

Despite the fact that the institutions unilaterally developed and extended their programs, there was little variation across the country in the requirements for either a master's or a doctoral degree in the English-language universities or for the licence and the doctorat in the French-language universities. Nor did the two decades produce much change in the requirements for the various degrees. At a few institutions there was some relaxation of the foreign language requirement, and the substitution of additional course work for a thesis at the master's level was beginning to characterize the offerings of some departments of some universities towards the end of the period. There was no change in the basic admission requirements. An honours degree continued to be the basis for admission to a one-year master's program and a master's degree the basis for admission to the two-year doctorate. It was the rare case, however, where the candidate was able to complete the requirements for either the master's or the doctoral degree in the minimum time specified. At the master's level the writing of the thesis normally occupied the student for at least the summer following the completion of the course work, and at the doctoral level the candidate was normally fully occupied during the two mandatory years of residence in completing the course work requirements, in preparing for the general examinations, and in defining his thesis topic. Particularly in the humanities and social sciences, the basic research and the writing of the thesis more often than not required an additional year of full-time work or weekends and summers for as much as five years while teaching full-time at a university. The term *ABD* (All But Dissertation) came into currency in Canada as in the United States to describe the position of many junior staff members.

The fact that so many doctoral candidates took as many as seven years to obtain their degree was, however, causing concern, and this was clearly evident at the NCCUC Special Conference of 1961. The general view was expressed in a series of comments and questions arising out of the two papers delivered on graduate studies:

1. We ask too much course work, too much unrelated to their subject of research, because we distrust their undergraduate preparation and because we are thinking of the probability

of their being asked to teach these subjects. But surely
we want to turn out students who can learn, rather than
students who have learnt.

2. Do we not over-emphasize training in technique to the detri-
   ment of the development of imagination and judgement - even
   of excitement? Are we not concerned too often to screen
   out the mediocre rather than to develop the excellent?

3. Do we not encourage students to write (or fail to discourage
   from writing) too big theses on too great subjects? Surely
   we want to give them a trial run at research under direction.
   But their big work should be done later by them as independent scholars. I am horrified at the number of really able
   young men with uncompleted Ph.D. thesis. It is not all
   their fault.

4. Should we not identify these students for whom something
   different is appropriate and provide for each of them close
   association from the very beginning with a member of the
   staff, who would direct their early preparation and later
   research and thesis writing.

5. Should we not be careful to limit entrance to this programme
   to the really first class?

6. Should we not make sure that these students have financial
   support that enables them to complete their doctorate in
   three years? This means that they must not be diverted to
   teaching and/or helping with the research of others.[17]

One speaker argued that the graduate school had two functions:
to provide what was in effect a second bachelor's degree for students who discovered on graduation that the honours or general
course they had taken was 'not quite what they wanted'; and to
offer additional opportunity for self-development for graduates
of an honours course 'who want to continue in their field and to
proceed to research in that field.'[18] Concern was expressed primarily for this latter group, those who had clearly demonstrated
their capacity to become scholars rather than with those who
wanted, or needed, 'more of the same - an M.S. degree,' as it was
aptly described. There was general agreement, too, with the argument that the Canadian graduate school program should continue to
be based on the honours degree.

The problem of graduate studies would continue to occupy the
NCCUC throughout the 1960s, during which time a special committee
was appointed to study the related problems.

FELLOWSHIPS

Throughout the period, support for graduate students in the pure
and applied sciences continued to be liberally provided for by
the National Research Council. In 1959-60 its scholarships numbered 543 (in contrast to 68 in 1939-40), at a total cost of
$1,188,196 ($24,850 in 1939-40).[19] These included 112 postdoctoral

fellowships. These had been instituted in 1948 and 89 of them were held by students from abroad enrolled at 15 different Canadian universities. The majority of awards were for science and engineering, but there were 45 for medicine, 4 for dentistry, and 6 for psychology. The 423 predoctoral bursaries and scholarships awarded for 1960-61 were held by students enrolled at 19 institutions, including Assumption, Carleton, Memorial, Nova Scotia Technical College, and the Ontario Agricultural College, which though technically an affiliate of the University of Toronto was regarded for NRC purposes as a separate entity. In addition, a large number of fellowships had become available in medicine and psychology through the institution of the Department of National Health and Welfare's fellowship program in 1948, and towards the end of the period, largely through the efforts of the Industrial Foundation on Education, established in 1957,[20] there was increasing support from business and industry. For 1960-61, 122 such awards were made amounting to $165,000, as well as nearly 300 valued at about $300,000, which were provided by the universities from their own resources.[21]

In the humanities and social sciences the situation was very different, though it had improved in 1958-59 following the establishment of the Canada Council in 1957, six years after the recommendation by the Royal Commission on Arts, Letters and Science in 1951 that it be established. Prior to this, support for graduate studies in the non-science fields had been provided chiefly by the Social Science Research Council, which initiated a program of predoctoral fellowships in 1946-47, and by the Humanities Research Council, which instituted a similar program in 1947-48. The funds in both cases were supplied by the Carnegie Corporation of New York and the Rockefeller Foundation. The Social Science Research Council program, which began with four grants, provided over the period 1946-47 to 1957-58 a total of 135 full fellowships, permitting full-time study for one academic year, and 48 partial fellowships, providing for support during the summer months.[22] The Humanities Research Council program over the same period numbered 90 full fellowships and 67 partial fellowships. With the establishment of the Canada Council, these programs were discontinued although both councils continued to make a few awards from their own resources.

The councils cooperated with the Canada Council in the administration of its fellowship program by supplying the panels of professors required to process the applications. The Canada Council program offered support at both the master's and doctoral levels. In 1958-59 premaster's fellowships in the amount of $1200 were awarded to 70 of 274 applicants and predoctoral fellowships in the amount of $2000 plus travelling expenses to 90 of 337 applicants.[23] In 1960-61 the figures were 85 premaster's fellowships (234 applicants) and 136 predoctoral fellowships (568 applicants) representing a total expenditure of approximately $350,000. By 1960 it should be added, the individual universities were themselves providing much more support for graduate work in the humanities and social sciences from their own resources than was the case in 1940, and some of the funds now being raised by business and industry were available to candidates in these fields. Nonetheless, the contrast between the situation in the humanities and the social sciences in contrast to the pure and applied sciences was striking.

An additional stimulus to graduate work, which affected all areas, occurred at the end of the period with the introduction of the Commonwealth Scholarship and Fellowship Plan agreed upon by the governments of 13 countries at a conference held at Oxford in the summer of 1959. This brought 100 overseas students to Canada in 1960-61, of whom 79 continued their studies for a second year in 1961-62. The number of new Commonwealth Scholars in 1961-62 was 103.[24]

NOTES TO CHAPTER 29

1   C. de Koninck, 'Why the Humanities at all?' in A.D. Dunton and D. Patterson, eds., *Canada's Universities in a New Age* (1962), 33-8
2   J.W.T. Spinks, 'Graduate Studies and Research in the Sciences' in Dunton and Patterson, eds., *Canada's Universities*, 49
3   C.J. Mackenzie, quoted in *A Science Policy for Canada: Report of the Senate Special Committee on Science Policy* I (1970), 61
4   Spinks, 'Graduate Studies,' 43
5   Ibid., 43
6   The figures in this and the following paragraph are taken from Dominion Bureau of Statistics, *Survey of Higher Education, 1954-1961* (1963), 52-7.
7   *NCCU Proc.* (1944), 27
8   H.A. Innis, 'The Problem of Graduate Work in Canada' in *Report of the National Conference of Canadian Universities on Post-War Problems* (1944), 58-9
9   Innis, 'The Problem,' 59
10 *NCCU Proc.* (1944), 27-8
11 Ibid. (1944), 28. For the development of the Canadian Social Science Research Council, see above, chapter 24, 443; for the development of the Humanities Research Council of Canada, see below, chapter 30, 570-2.
12 *NCCU Proc.* (1946), 36
13 Ibid. (1948), 21
14 Ibid. (1951), 35
15 In addition to the institutions noted on page 553, Ph.D. programs were authorized at Carleton and Waterloo in 1960 and at Assumption in 1961.
16 For a detailed account of the development of arrangements for the administration of graduate studies in Ontario universities, see N.L. Nicholson, 'The Evolution of Graduate Studies in Ontario Universities' (1975), Ed.D. dissertation, University of Toronto, 259-305.

17 V.W. Bladen in Dunton and Patterson, *Canada's Universities*, 52-3
18 Ibid., 55
19 W.P. Thompson, *Graduate Education in the Sciences in Canadian Universities* (1963), 82-3
20 The Industrial Foundation on Education was established in 1957 following a conference organized by a number of industrial firms and held at St Andrew's, New Brunswick, in September of that year.
21 Thompson, *Graduate Education*, 85
22 The figures for the Social Science and Humanities Research Councils are taken from their annual reports.
23 Canada Council, *Second* (to 31 March 1959) and *Third* (to 31 March 1960) *Annual Reports*
24 Thompson, *Graduate Education*, 86

30
Scholarship and Research

Quoting from a paper presented by G.S. Brett to the NCCU in 1934,
W.P. Thompson noted in 1963 that 30 years earlier

> there were really few posts for Ph.D.'s in Canada - too few to
> justify a large graduate enterprise ... Toronto and McGill did
> not regard doctoral work as an objective which they should
> strive for, but were rather having it forced upon them. They
> were ... employing a temporizing policy in the sense of encou-
> raging graduate work by accepting suitable candidates and yet
> hoping to evade the liability which every graduate student
> created. While the demand for specialized instruction increased,
> the over-worked teacher became steadily less a specialist.[1]

Thompson went on to say that Brett had expressed doubt that many
of the staff were in any significant sense graduate-minded; 'in
their hearts they felt it was enough to give Canadians a good
education and then to let them go to American or European universities for graduate study.'
This attitude of indifference towards graduate students continued
to have an inhibiting effect on research and scholarship in Canada
for many years, since progress in this area depends to a large
extent on the opportunity for students to engage in graduate work.
In 1939, in another address to NCCU delegates, the Canadian universities were accused of harbouring a 'colonial mentality.'[2]
In 1951 the Royal Commission on National Development in the Arts,
Letters and Sciences assessed Canada's contribution to scholarship
and research in the humanities and social sciences in these terms:

> Apart from the work of a few brilliant persons, there is a
> general impression that Canadian scholarly work in the humanities
> and social sciences is slight in quantity and uneven in quality.
> We have, it seems, some able scholars, but no consistent and
> representative Canadian scholarship emanating from the country

as a whole and capable of making its contribution to Canadian intellectual life and to that of the western world. This is the view of Canadian humanists and social scientists, sharpened by their opinion that in the fields of natural science Canada has been able to make important and worthy contributions.[3]

In a report issued two decades later by a two-member commission appointed by the conference of Canadian universities, which after 1964 was entitled the Association of University and Colleges of Canada (AUCC), it was reiterated that in 1940 the country had remained 'colonial and parasitic in relation to scientific accomplishment, and to the fruits of science and technology ...[4] Some improvement in Canada's status in the world community of research and scholarship had resulted from the activities of its scientists during World War II, but inadequate financing had prevented the universities from transferring theory into practice throughout the 1940s and 1950s. Hence it was not until the 1960s that 'the limitations of the pioneer era – financing on a shoestring' were overcome. 'The universities broke out of their fetters in the 'sixties' when governments responded to the need for more, and better educated, manpower.'[5]

The new recognition of the importance of the 'scientific and scholarly estate' which had developed in Canadian higher education by 1960 was partly attributable to the growth of financial support for graduate students. But there were other factors which also contributed to the development of research and scholarship: greatly increased financial support for professors in all fields, the marked expansion of research activity in the fields of dentistry, engineering, and medicine; a proliferation of learned and professional societies and journals; the creation on many campuses of research centres and institutes; much increased activity at the University of Toronto Press, and the creation of publishing outlets on three other campuses; and the launching at long last of a national library and a national art gallery. In addition there was evidence of growing dismay at the abysmal paucity of library and museum facilities across Canada.

The stimulus for much of this activity came from the National Research Council, the Social Science Research Council, and the Humanities Research Council, and in each instance the impetus for their work arose out of the emergency situations created by World War II. It is curious that virtually no encouragement in this direction emanated from within the Royal Society of Canada. The shortcomings of this body were stressed in 1945 in the Social Science Research Council's published report on Scholarship in Canada.

The Royal Society ... was founded in 1881 as a national academy of learning and culture, but for a number of reasons it has failed of its purpose. Its annual meetings were designed to be a series of symposiums in which the best Canadian minds would fertilize each other, and its massive printed transactions were

to preserve the highest products of Canadian artistry and scholarship. Instead, the meetings have been rather drowsy gatherings of pleasant urbanity, but little distinction, and the
transactions slumber for the most part undisturbed on library
shelves.[6]

Another comment on the negative impact of the Royal Society was
made by Mason Wade in connection with the founding at Montreal of
L'Académie Canadienne-Français modelled on the Académie de France.
As he expressed it, its founding was a landmark in the self-
conscious development of a French-Canadian culture distinct from
that of France, but 'it was also a revolt against the artificial
and somewhat strained yoking of two distinct cultures in the
Royal Society of Canada. Many of the members of the Academy were
nationalists who held that French-Canadian and English-Canadian
cultures were irreconcilable and that the Royal Society was merely
a mutual-admiration organization of *bonne ententistes*.'[7]
    Fortunately, the unimpressive record of the Royal Society in this
area was more than compensated for by the other major Canadian
research bodies, each of which will be dealt with in turn.

THE NATIONAL RESEARCH COUNCIL

In September 1943, at the request of the acting president, C.J.
Mackenzie, the National Research Council established a review
committee to consider the policy which the council should adopt
following the cessation of hostilities.[8] Both the staff and the
budget of the council had been enormously increased within months
of the outbreak of war,[9] and this expansion had continued; by
1943 its budget was five times the pre-war figure. The Review
Committee agreed with Mackenzie that this pattern should be continued in the post-war period. In the process of its deliberations it had identified no less than 53 fields which, in the
national interest, required attention. Included were cold weather
and northern latitude studies, housing and building conditions,
petroleum products, and living conditions on farms. The report
also laid down certain principles with respect to how research
should be conducted. The universities should continue to be the
chief centres for the training of scientific personnel and for
the conducting of pure or fundamental research. NRC, while primarily concentrating on applied research and to a lesser extent
on development, should continue to undertake some fundamental research, largely to ensure that it would continue to attract highly
qualified staff. Because the universities would be the main centres for the training of scientists and for the conducting of
fundamental research, it would be necessary for NRC to provide
them with much more support than had been the case in the past.
    The Review Committee's recommendations were accepted and these
policies were implemented in the period 1945-52. Since it was a
period of national prosperity, funds were readily available. In

contrast to World War I, which had been financed by borrowing and the issuing of tax-free bonds, the government had supported the military effort during World War II by current taxes and increased production, and unlike the Western European nations and Japan Canada had suffered no physical damage and was able to convert its much expanded industrial plant to peace-time purposes without difficulty.

As a result, NRC was able to increase its grants to universities – close to $1,000,000 in 1947-48 in contrast to just over $200,000 in 1937-38. In 1945 it also introduced postdoctoral fellowships which could be held either in Canadian universities or abroad, and in 1950 it began to make what were called consolidated grants to well-established research units which could thereby undertake projects extending over a number of years and involving a number of different scientists. The first recipients were the Banting and Best Institute, the Montreal Neurological Institute, the Collip Medical Research Laboratory at the University of Western Ontario, and the University Clinic of the Royal Victoria Hospital in Montreal.

Despite its withdrawal from the field of research related to military purposes, responsibility for which had been assumed by a new body, the Defence Research Board established in 1947, NRC expanded its own activities during this period. By 1951 it had 13 research divisions (in contrast to four in 1939), including Atlantic and Prairie regional laboratories at Halifax and Saskatoon, and three at Chalk River related to the atomic energy project which had been entered upon in 1943. Laboratories were provided in Ottawa for chemical engineering, building research, and radio and electrical engineering divisions, but the division of medical research, established in 1946 with a budget of $200,000, operated through grants to existing laboratories, mainly in universities. The expansion of the council's own research activities was reflected in the number of scientific journals it was publishing by 1951 of which there were seven covering the fields of biochemistry and physiology, botany, chemistry, microbiology, physics, technology, and zoology.

Under a new president, E.W.C. Steacie, who took office in 1952, the council's general policy with respect to the roles of the universities and NRC in the development of Canadian science remained unchanged. Steacie was a strong advocate of both the relevance of fundamental to applied research and of the desirability of fundamental research being carried out primarily by the universities. The amounts of money for such work were greatly increased and the budget for NRC's own laboratories during the period tripled, $36,000,000 being spent on expanded facilities. The direct grants in aid of university research rose to $9.5 million by 1960-61, almost exactly ten times the 1947-48 amount. This included $2.3 million provided by NRC through its division of medical research, but in 1960 it was decided to replace this body by an independent medical research council, and for 1961-62 the latter was provided with a budget of $3.3 million.

In 1960 the National Research Council was not the only source of federal government funds for the support of university research. The total provided in that year was over $15 million, the largest amounts emanating from the Defence Research Board ($1.7 million – almost exclusively for medical research) and the Department of National Health and Welfare ($3 million). The latter represented an increase from the $100,000 initially allocated in 1948 for research in public and mental health and scheduled to increase by $100,000 a year for the first five years. It provided assistance for research in dentistry and psychology as well as in medicine. The other major sources of federal support for university research in pure and applied science in 1960 were two crown corporations, Central Mortgage and Housing Corporation, established in 1945 ($62,248) and the Atomic Energy Control Board, established in 1952 to assume responsibility for the atomic energy operation ($700,000), and the federal departments of agriculture ($159,780), fisheries ($115,000), forestry ($11,600), mines and technical services ($75,000), and veteran's affairs ($389,000).[10]

In total these were considerable sums and it was with some satisfaction that Dr J.W.T. Spinks in the paper on Graduate Studies and Research in the Sciences which he presented to the 1961 Special Conference of the NCCUC reported on the progress that had been achieved in the previous ten years. However, there were gaps – 'areas of science which for one reason or another have so far been relatively neglected' – and there was a need 'for a few absolutely top-notch centres in those areas where Canada has a special competence or interest.'[11] Certainly the amount both of graduate work and research would have to be increased far more in the next decade and this would necessitate much greater absolute expenditures. In Spinks's view a crisis was looming, the result of the increasing scale of the expenditures and the absence of a clear-cut national policy with respect to both research and graduate work. As can be seen from the above figures, a large number of government departments and agencies were providing financial support for scientific research but they were doing so independently. The original intention was for the National Research Council to act as a coordinating agency, but, particularly after the establishment of its own laboratories, it had been singularly unsuccessful in developing a system of cooperation with the existing departments, many of which had been providing support for research for several decades. This would be one of the most serious issues facing the universities as they entered the 'sixties.'

THE CANADIAN SOCIAL SCIENCE RESEARCH COUNCIL

The Canadian Social Science Research Council was formally established in September 1940 with financial support from both the Rockefeller Foundation and the Carnegie Corporation of New York and with the direct involvement of four national social science organizations, the Canadian Historical Association, the Canadian

Political Science Association, the Canadian Psychological Association and the Canadian Committee of the International Geographical Union, each of which was represented on the council as was the Dominion Bureau of Statistics and the Dominion Archives. The two American foundations continued to provide most of the council's financial support for the next 17 years, the Carnegie Corporation providing $61,130 over the period 1940-50 and the Rockefeller Foundation $499,795 over the period 1940-57. In 1957, the council received the first portion of a $150,000 grant from the Ford Foundation, which was designed to see it over the period of adjustment to the situation in which the Canada Council, recommended by the Royal Commission on National Development in the Arts, Letters and Sciences in 1951 but not established until April of this year, would assume major responsibility for support of fellowship and research in the social sciences as well as in the humanities and the creative arts. The total receipts of the CSSRC prior to its receiving any funds from the Canada Council amounted to $718,850, the balance being provided by Canadian universities and colleges ($35,225) and private individuals or organizations in Canada ($47,300). Its expenditures during this same period amounted to $654,573 of which approximately $80,000 was used for administrative purposes - an average of less than $2000 a year for office expenses including publication of the annual report and of less than $3000 for council and committee meetings.[12]

According to its constitution, the sole purpose of the Social Science Research Council was to promote research in the social sciences in Canada. In fact, however, from the outset its aim had been 'to assist the social sciences in every way.'[13] In its tenth anniversary review, the activities of the Council were summarized under five categories:

1. Direct assistance to social scientists in regard to work already underway, or awaiting publication.
2. Assistance in training promising social scientists, or in helping more mature students.
3. Research investigations, especially where the co-operation of scholars from different disciplines or areas is involved.
4. Investigations and conferences with the aim of aiding teaching or research in special disciplines or in special areas.
5. Endeavouring to bring forward the needs and the significance of the social sciences as a whole.[14]

The last category was a reminder of the council's broader interests in addition to its involvement with support for research. Nonetheless, its objective had been primarily to encourage research undertakings and to support potential scholars, and almost two-thirds of its funds over the initial 17-year period fell under the two categories embracing assistance to individuals. In 1941-42 the money went to established scholars to aid them either in completing a piece of research or in publishing the results. In 1947, however, awards began also to be made to doctoral students. Predoctoral fellowships could be granted for a full academic year (normally $1500), or as a partial fellowship for work done over the summer. Four such awards were made in 1947-48, 9 in 1948-49, 18 in 1949-50, 34 full and 24 partials in 1952-53, and 10 full and 7 partials in 1956-57. In all, over 135 full and 48 partial fellowships were awarded over the ten-year period at the total cost of $163,461.

The relatively insignificant sum of $5214 was expended in providing specific books required for their research to some 30 established scholars in small institutions lacking adequate library resources. Assistance to established scholars principally took the form of direct support while on sabbatical leave, the provision of travel and secretarial expenses during the summer months, or of indirect support in the form of grants in aid of publication.

Equally impressive, granted the limited funds that were available, is the list of books that resulted from the cooperative investigations undertaken under Category 3 of the list of the council's activities: *The New Northland*, a collection of studies of various problems related to the Canadian North edited by C.A. Dawson and published in 1946; the 10 volumes of the Social Credit in Alberta series edited by S.D. Clark, initiated in 1944 and completed in 1959; the 11 volumes of the Canadian Studies in Economics series edited by V.W. Bladen, initiated in 1952 and completed in 1959; and *Canadian Dualism*, a collection of parallel studies by English-speaking and French-speaking scholars on more than a dozen subjects involving the two cultures, edited by Mason Wade and published in 1960.

While an excellent book, the volume symbolized the difficulties under which the council laboured during the 1940s and 1950s in achieving its objectives. The original plan, conceived in 1947, was for a series of at least five monographs dealing with various aspects of Canadian biculturalism, but financial restrictions as well as the difficulty experienced by the scholars involved in finding the time to complete the proposed studies made it necessary to settle for a collection of scholarly articles. A cooperative study on problems related to the Canadian Indian population proposed in the mid-1940s was finally abandoned despite the expenditure of close to $20,000 on it.

On several occasions the council sponsored conferences of social scientists to discuss mutual problems but its main work in the area of improving teaching or research in specific disciplines was the conducting and publishing in pamphlet or mimeographed form of surveys of teaching and research in specific disciplines, particularly those judged to be 'underdeveloped,'[15] and of studies of the general status of scholarship and graduate studies. The first two such studies undertaken were of the latter type, W.N. Sage's *Graduate Training in Arts in Canadian Universities*, 1944 and J.B. Brebner's *Scholarship for Canada*, 1945. The studies of individual disciplines, which in all cases involved personal visits

to all or most campuses by the investigator, were in the fields
of political science (R.M. Dawson, University of Toronto, 'Political Science Training in Canada,' 1950), geography (Sir Dudley
Stamp, University of London, 'Geography in Canadian Universities,'
1952), and psychology (R.B. MacLeod, Cornell University *Psychology
in Canadian Universities and Colleges*, 1955). In addition, F.
Mackinnon, Prince of Wales College, Charlottetown, conducted a
study of the special problems of the social sciences in the
Maritime Provinces in 1950-51. A plan to investigate the field
of law with particular reference to the advancement of studies in
penology and criminology was given up when it was discovered that
a detailed investigation of this subject was to be undertaken by
the Canadian Bar Association, but a representative of the council,
J.A. Corry, served on the investigating committee. One of its
earliest actions, in the fall of 1942, was to submit a brief to
the prime minister protesting against a proposal to suspend activities in the faculties of arts, commerce, education and law in
all the Canadian universities for the duration of the war.[16]
Over the years the CSSRC submitted other briefs, for example to
the Royal Commission on National Development in the Arts, Letters
and Sciences, arguing the need for support of the social sciences
per se and at every level.

With the establishment of the Canada Council and its assumption
of major responsibility for the support of individual graduate
students and established scholars in 1958 with approximately three
times the funds available for such support, the Social Science
Research Council of Canada, as it henceforth was called, believed
that it was now in a position to concentrate on major research
projects of national scope involving groups of scholars. With
this mind, in conjunction with the Humanities Research Council,
it established a permanent secretariat, with John E. Robbins as
paid secretary-treasurer of both councils. By 1960 it had launched
three large-scale projects: The Structure of Power: Decision-
Making in Canada, designed under the general editorship of
Professor John Meisel of Queen's University to be a series of
studies respecting the more significant economic, political and
social developments in contemporary Canada; The Atlantic Studies
Programme, a comparable undertaking concentrating on the Maritime
Provinces with J.F. Graham of Dalhousie University as editor;
and The Historical Statistics of Canada Project, a single-volume
but very complicated undertaking to be edited by M.C. Urquhart of
Queen's and K.H. Buckley of Saskatchewan. In the 1960-62 annual
report, other major projects were listed, including The Canadian
Centenary History Series, a projected 16 volume series designed
to be 'the definitive history of Canada for this generation.'[17]

In all these activities it was assumed that very generous support would come from the Canada Council, though it was not expected that the grants would be sufficient to carry the whole
enterprise; in the case of the Historical Statistics of Canada
volume, support was sought and obtained from several federal
government departments, while three Canadian banks and the Atlantic

Provinces Research Board were also involved in financing the Atlantic Provinces Program. Unfortunately, by 1960 the Canada Council had adopted the policy of allocating its funds year by year and with an absolute limit of three years for support for any one project. The history of the Social Science Research Council of Canada during the 1960s was to consist largely of attempts to persuade the Canada Council to adopt a more liberal and flexible attitude towards the support of research in the social sciences.[18]

THE HUMANITIES RESEARCH COUNCIL OF CANADA

The existence of the Social Science Research Council made it possible for Canadian social scientists to react firmly and quickly to the threat to liberal education represented by the proposal in late 1942 to suspend operations in the faculties of arts, commerce, education and law, but at that time there was no organization which could speak on behalf of Canadian humanists. In this emergency Section II of the Royal Society of Canada, which embraced English-speaking humanists and social sciences, appointed a five-man committee of Fellows on the humanities side to take appropriate action.[19] The committee drafted a brief and circulated it to 55 department heads across the country and also to certain influential members of Section I, the French-language counterpart of Section II. A revised document, bearing the signatures of 45 humanists, was forwarded to the prime minister on 30 December 1942 with a copy to the president of the NCCU.

This government threat demonstrated how vulnerable the Canadian humanists were, and action was promptly taken to ensure that should such an emergency again arise their interests would be protected. At its meeting in May 1943, Section II of the Royal Society resolved that a committee be appointed to consider the desirability of organizing a Humanities Research Council in Canada. The committee met in September and drafted a constitution which was sent to a list of proposed members, together with an invitation to attend an organizational meeting on 30 December 1943. At this meeting the draft constitution was 'tentatively approved,' and the Humanities Research Council of Canada came into being. In May 1944 its first plenary session was held and the constitution was formally adopted.

At the December meeting it had been agreed that an essential step for the organization was to undertake a detailed survey of the position of the humanities in Canada, and this project occupied much of the agenda of the May meeting. In September the Rockefeller Foundation announced that it would provide $8000 to finance the survey, which would be supervised by a steering committee consisting of Watson Kirkconnell, Maurice Lebel of Laval, G.B. Phelan of the Pontifical Institute of Mediaeval Studies, John Robbins, and A.S.P. Woodhouse of Toronto. The plan was to have teams of three persons examine the situation in the English-

language universities east of Ontario, the French-language universities and colleges, the English-language universities of Ontario,
and the universities of Western Canada, and also to obtain special
reports on the position of music, painting, and drama in the universities. This plan was carried out, most of the work being
undertaken by Kirkconnell and Woodhouse under whose names the
report was published in May 1947. Two hundred copies of the full
report were circulated in the fall of 1946 and it was formally
approved by the council in December.

The Humanities in Canada was a remarkably comprehensive survey
of 'the state of the humanities in Canada' with attention being
paid to the situation in the secondary schools, the collèges
classiques, and the professional faculties as well as to undergraduate and graduate programs in the universities. It also contained an appendix listing the works published and in progress of
over 240 faculty members.

At the organizational meeting in December 1943 the council had
established committees on aid for research and aid for publication,
but lack of funds led to their temporary suspension in May 1944,
and for the next three years the council was almost entirely preoccupied with matters bearing on the survey. However, with the
publication of the report in 1947 and with the indication of additional Rockefeller and Carnegie Corporation support, the council
was in a position to pursue other tasks. As with the Social
Science Research Council, the main thrust was to provide support
for active and potential scholars to complete their work and to
have it published. Unlike the SSRC it had no need to carry out
investigations in particular fields because this had been done
exhaustively by Kirkconnell and Woodhouse. With one exception,
that of a French-Canadian project designed to advance the study
of French culture in North America which resulted in the publication of a number of individual studies, it did not concern itself
with undertakings involving the cooperative participation of
scholars from different institutions. On the other hand, more
than the SSRC it sponsored regional and national conferences on
various matters bearing on the humanities, and it encouraged the
establishment of local societies of persons interested in and
involved with the humanities. These latter ultimately took the
form of branches of the Humanities Association of Canada, a separate but closely related organization established in 1951. The
Humanities Research Council also sponsored visits by lecturers
from abroad who often spoke to the Humanities Association branches.

Like the Social Science Research Council, the HRC was largely
supported by the Carnegie Corporation and the Rockefeller Foundation
prior to the establishment of the Canada Council in 1957, though
in its case there was no substantial Ford Foundation grant to
cushion the transitional period. Its total revenues to 1958
(including $15,645 from the Canada Council in the final year)
amounted to $372,068, of which Rockefeller contributed $150,648
and Carnegie $137,130. Canadian universities and colleges provided
$32,319 (almost the same amount as they contributed to the SSRC),

and $36,110 was received from other Canadian sources.[20] Approximately two-thirds was expended on aid for research and publication: $120,215 for over 150 predoctoral fellowships, $125,093 in grants to full-time faculty members, and $24,571 in support of publication. Conferences required $17,689, the Humanities Association of Canada $14,751, the French-Canadian project $13,736, and the Dominions Project $23,660. This latter was an effort to foster the comparative study of Canadian and Australian culture and letters, which resulted in the publication of an extremely valuable reference work, R.E. Watters's *Check List of Canadian Literature and Background Materials*, published in 1959, and by 1960 to an exchange of scholars between the two countries, two Australians spending extended periods in Canada and three Canadians going to Australia.

With the establishment of the Canada Council, the HRC found itself in the same position as the SSRC of Canada with respect to finances. Both organizations received payment from the Canada Council for their work in assisting in the evaluation and processing of the now much increased funds for fellowships and for grants in aid of research and publication, but with the cessation of grants from American foundations, it had to rely on Canadian sources to support its own projects. In this connection the Canada Council was not as generous as anticipated.

That teaching as well as scholarship should be regarded as the continuing concern of both the Social Science Research Council and the Humanities Research Council should not come as a surprise, granted the fact that the membership in each case had been wholly made up of practitioners in their respective fields. In contrast, the National Research Council, not all of whose members were practising scientists and which was in addition a government agency, had acted neither as spokesman for Canadian scientists, nor as an advocate of Canadian science; this is not to say that some of its presidents had not in their personal capacity acted in one of these roles. But while NRC had limited its concern to the promotion of scientific research, it had regarded the training or education of scientists as embraced therein. Indeed for all three of Canada's research councils, the promotion of graduate studies and the promotion of research were regarded as inseparable.

THE CANADA COUNCIL

The Canada Council was provided at the time of its establishment with $100 million, half of which was to be used for grants to universities for the construction of buildings related to the humanities, social sciences, and the creative arts. The remaining $50 million was in the form of a permanent endowment, the annual income from which would be used for support of the activities of individuals and organizations. Provision was made for the increasing of the endowment fund through gifts by individuals or corporations, but the yield from this source has never been significant.

The council has been dependent upon the federal government for any extension of its funds, and these were not provided in any quantity until the latter half of the 1960s.

Nonetheless, the creation of the council approximately tripled the funds available for the support of scholarship and research in the humanities and the social sciences. The basic program which had been established by the Humanities Research Council and the Social Science Research Council of Canada for the support of Canadian doctoral students and faculty members were, with the assistance of the councils, continued and expanded and in addition awards were made available to professors and graduate students from abroad who wished to pursue their research or study at Canadian universities. Awards, too, now became available to students, whether Canadian or foreign, who were embarking on programs at the master's level.

In the first year of the program (1957-58), premaster's awards ($1200) were made to 70 of 274 Canadian applicants and predoctoral fellowships ($2000 plus travel expenses) to 90 of 337 applicants.[21] In the same year, there were 25 senior research fellowships ($4000 plus travel) for Canadian faculty members on full-time sabbatical leave and 130 short term awards ($300-$700) available to either full-time faculty or graduate students for support during the summer. By 1960, these numbers had increased: 85 premaster's, 136 predoctoral, 30 senior research fellowships, 152 short-term awards. The awards for foreigners were introduced in 1959-60: nine for faculty members (10 applicants), 79 for graduate students (208 applicants). In addition, Canadian faculty members were eligible for the council's Category 10 awards, short or full-term fellowships 'for scholars and workers of special promise or distinction whose application did not fall within one of the other categories or could not be submitted at the normal time.' Ten of the 27 Category 10 awards in 1960-61 were made to Canadian faculty members. The council also made grants to persons attending conferences or giving lectures or doing specific research abroad, and in 1960-61 24 Canadian faculty members obtained such assistance. In the same year, funds were provided to 12 Canadian universities to bring one and in several cases a number of visiting professors from abroad to their campuses.

The council also provided support for research and scholarship in the humanities and social sciences through grants to learned and professional societies, learned journals, university and commercial presses (for the publication of scholarly books), and individual universities, as well as to the two research councils. In each year from 1957-58 to 1960-61 it assigned $5000 to each of the Humanities Research Council and the Social Science Research Council to assist in meeting the expenses of the members of learned societies associated with these councils to attend the annual conference of the society. In 1957-58, the council provided support for the Canadian Historical Association to hold a special summer study session at Queen's University, to the University of Alberta for its summer school in linguistics, and to Memorial University

of Newfoundland for three separate projects. In 1958-59 there
were grants to the Royal Society of Canada, the Canadian Agricul-
tural Economics Society, the Canadian Mathematical Congress, the
Canadian Historical Association (for the continuance of its
Queen's project), the Association of Canadian Law Teachers, the
Classical Association of Canada (for its journal *Phoenix*), to the
Canadian Music Council (for the *Canadian Music Journal*), the
Canadian Association of Slavists (for assistance in the publication of *Canadian Slavonic Papers*). In 1960-61 there were grants
to the Canadian Research Centre for Anthropology (for support of
Anthropologica), to the University of Toronto's Department of
Anthropology (for archaeological excavations), to York University
(for a study of general education programs), to the Centre de
recherches sociales at Université Laval (for a survey of problems
experienced by rural families when moving to urban centres), to
the University of Toronto Press (for preliminary research on an
illustrated history of Canadian painting, sculpture, folk arts,
and architecture), and to staff members from all Canadian schools
of architecture to attend a seminar on the teaching of architecture at Bloomfield, Michigan. These are selected examples from
the 1960-61 grants, chosen to indicate the range of the council's
interests. They equally represent the range of scholarly subjects
which were in need of financial support.

Since its establishment the Canada Council had consisted of 21
members. As initially constituted, it included two university
presidents. Other academics were added, and it could be said
that not only were universities well represented on the council
in both a qualitative and quantitative sense, but that there was
a reasonable balance of representatives from the humanities, the
social sciences, and the physical sciences. By 1963, however,
this situation had changed and the social sciences were no longer
represented. In view of the importance and complexity of research
in this area, it was not a desirable trend.

LEARNED SOCIETIES, SCHOLARLY JOURNALS, UNIVERSITY PRESSES

A work of scholarship or research is, in the final analysis, the
achievement of an individual or in certain circumstances of a
number of individuals working in direct collaboration with one
another. But a work of scholarship or research is also invariably
a group effort in the sense that the individual or individuals
who produce it have been able to build upon the ideas and discoveries of other persons both living and dead. Banting and Best,
Charles Cochrane, Harold Innis, to take the example of the outstanding Canadian scholars of the 1920-1940 period, were able to
achieve the results they did only because they were in a position
to build upon the efforts of scholars who had preceded them and
whose work they were able to read, mark, learn, and inwardly digest. Their work in turn is now at our disposal to build upon
further because it is available in written form. Unless a piece

of research or scholarship is communicable to others, it cannot truly be said to exist, though the experience of Solzenhitsyn is a recent reminder that the work need not be published in the technical sense. Hence for the healthy development of scholarship and research, the crucial importance of scholarly journals and of publishing houses that give priority to the publishing of scholarly books. But there is also the case of Socrates, whose ideas appear to have had a very influential effect long before they were committed to written form by Plato. Hence, too, especially in a country like Canada where scholars working in the same field are frequently located at great distances from one another, the very great importance of learned societies, which provide not only an opportunity for the presentation and discussion of scholarly work which has not as yet been published but also the opportunity for scholars to discuss the problems and the possibilities in their field. The presence or absence of learned societies, scholarly journals, and university presses is a rough but reasonably accurate index to both the quantity and the quality of the scholarship and research that is produced in a given country at a given time.

If this argument is accepted, it can be said that the position of scholarship and research in Canada improved remarkably between 1945 and 1960. During these fifteen years learned societies with a national membership proliferated, the number of scholarly journals increased substantially, one university press developed to a position of international stature and several others were firmly established. So far as opportunities for productive work in scholarship and research are concerned, the Canadian universities, in contrast with the situation in 1940, had by 1960 quite literally entered upon a new age.

In the humanities the opportunities for productive scholarship were particularly weak in 1940; there were no learned societies of national scope based on a single discipline and, except in the area of mediaeval studies, there was no journal of either national or international reputation. There was, of course, the Royal Society of Canada, Sections I and II of which embraced the humanities and which, through the Society's *Proceedings*, offered the humanists who were Fellows a well-recognized medium for publication. But as Watson Kirkconnell and A.S.P. Woodhouse, two humanists who were in this position, argued in 1947, the Royal Society did not fill the place left vacant by the absence of organizations devoted to a single discipline:

> The sections cover too wide a range of subjects; the division between French and English has some marked disadvantages; and above all the Royal Society is 'a ranking body,' conferring the designation F.R.S.C., with the result that the average age of its fellows is probably well over fifty and a good many of them are (as is elsewhere remarked) extinct volcanoes, while young and vigorous scholars must await election to its strictly limited ranks.[22]

Kirkconnell and Woodhouse admitted that there were very real difficulties in organizing either a single association devoted to the humanities as a whole ('the range of disciplines would still be very great') or associations concerned with a single discipline ('the number of those willing and able to participate would be in most cases too small'). They proposed an organization similar to the American Modern Languages Association, to be under the auspices of the Humanities Research Council and with the cooperation, at least at the outset, of Section II of the Royal Society. The latter, hopefully, would provide time and space during its annual meetings. It would operate in four sections: English, Modern Languages, Philosophy, and Classics and Orientals. The possibility of the Humanities Research Council acquiring a half-share in one of the existing university quarterlies as a medium for the publication of scholarly articles in the humanities was also proposed.

Neither of these suggestions was among the recommendations of their report which received serious consideration following its publication. Nonetheless emphasis on the need probably had the effect of stimulating alternative solutions. In the very year their report was published (1947) the Classical Association of Canada was established and assumed responsibility for *Phoenix*, a journal begun a year earlier. By 1960 there were five other national associations in the humanities field, two of which had successfully launched journals: The Association of Canadian University Teachers of English in 1951; The Canadian Association of Slavists in 1954 (*Etudes Slavs et Est-Européenes*, 1956); Canadian Linguistic Association in 1954 (*Canadian Linguistics Journal*, 1955); Canadian Philosophical Association in 1958, Canadian Association of Teachers of French (1958). These would be followed in the early 1960s by Canadian Associations of Teachers of German (1962) and of Hispanists (1964), and in 1967 by the Universities Art Association of Canada, whose purpose is 'to promote and facilitate the study and practice of the visual arts at the university level.'

The situation in 1940 in the social sciences was much more satisfactory, with well-established national societies in history (Canadian Historical Association, Canadian Catholic Historical Association) and political economy – (Canadian Political Science Association), and recently established organizations in psychology (Canadian Psychological Association) and geography (Canadian Committee of the International Geographical Union), though neither of the latter had established a journal. The Canadian Psychological Association did establish a scholarly journal, the *Canadian Journal of Psychology* in 1947, and in 1950 launched a second journal, the *Canadian Psychologist*, as a vehicle for the discussion of professional matters. The geographers became an independent national group with the establishment of the Canadian Association of Geographers in 1951; a journal, *Canadian Geographer*, commenced publication in the following year. Still unorganized were the anthropologists and the sociologists, but in 1958 an Anthropology-

Sociology Chapter (or section) of the Canadian Political Science Association was instituted, which in 1965 broke away from the parent body as the Canadian Sociology and Anthropology Association. A notable addition to the roster of scholarly journals devoted to history was the appearance in 1947 of *Revue d'Histoire de l'Amerique Française*, a publication sponsored by l'Institut d'histoire established by Université Laval the previous year.

The number of national scientific societies established during this period is too extensive to list in its entirety. During the 1940s the major development was in the basic science disciplines: the Canadian Mathematical Congress in 1945 (which began to publish the *Canadian Journal of Mathematics* in 1949), the Canadian Association of Physicists in 1946 (*Physics in Canada*, 1949), the Geological Association of Canada in 1947, and a reorganization of the Chemical Institute of Canada (dating back to 1920) in 1945, which among other things issued in the publishing of *Chemistry in Canada* from 1949.[23] The year 1949 also saw the establishment of the Canadian Society of Experimental Geophysicists.

One of the basic science disciplines, astronomy, had had a national organization since 1902 - the Royal Astronomical Society of Canada. Another, biology, has so many subdivisions (beginning with botany and zoology) and so many interconnections with applied sciences such as agriculture and medicine that it is not surprising that it has not to this day developed a single national organization but rather has created a large number of national societies devoted to a recognized subdivision of the field. The desirability of interaction between such groups was recognized in 1957 with the establishment of the Canadian Federation of Biological Societies, initially embracing four organizations, the Canadian Physiological Society (1936), the Canadian Society of Anatomists (1956), the Canadian Biochemical Society (1957), and the Pharmacological Society of Canada (1957). The last two of these, it should be noted, were spin-offs from the Canadian Physiological Society whose membership since the late 1930s had included many biochemists and pharmacologists. Not all the societies in the biological field joined the federation; for example, the Canadian Society of Microbiologists and the Canadian Society of Wildlife and Fisheries Biologies, established in 1951 and 1958, respectively, did not become members, nor did any of the five societies in the field of agriculture which were established in the 1950s: the Canadian Associations of Animal Science (1951), of Agronomy (1954), of Soil Science (1954), of Horticultural Science (1956), and of Plant Pathologists (1958).

In the field of medical science at least 15 national societies were established, with the result that almost every scientific and clinical specialty (or subspecialty) had its own organization by 1960. Examples are the Canadian Anaesthetists' Society (1943), the Canadian Association of Pathologists (1944), the Canadian Society of Allergy and Clinical Immunology (1947), the Canadian Psychiatric Association (1951), and the Canadian Psychoanalytic Association (1952).

Among the other societies originating in the 1950s were the Genetics Society of Canada, 1953, the Spectroscopy Society of Canada, 1957, the Canadian Aeronautical Research Society and the Astronomical Society of Canada, both in 1958, the latter a more exclusively scientific body than the Royal Astronomical Society of Canada whose interest had always leaned towards the popularization of the science. Each of these organizations holds annual meetings at which scholarly or research papers are presented, and some of them publish journals; for example, the Canadian Society of Microbiologists brings out the *Canadian Journal of Microbiology*, and the Genetic Society, the *Canadian Journal of Genetics and Cytology*. Most of them, however, rely on existing journals for publication of papers, including the seven now sponsored by NRC.[24] Almost all the learned societies in the humanities and social sciences schedule two to three day annual meetings during a three-week period in late May and early June located on one of the university campuses. This has the advantage of reducing expenses for many who belong to more than one society, and it also brings together on an informal basis professors from a variety of fields. The practice began in the early 1950s, the initial impetus being the annual meetings of the Royal Society of Canada and the National Conference of Canadian Universities, two bodies which for many years met simultaneously on one location. While the former continues to meet in the early summer and provides the nucleus around which the so-called Learned Societies involving over 30 organizations gather, the latter under its new title, the Association of Universities and Colleges of Canada, now meets in early November. It is host to a large number of professional and educational bodies sharing mutual concern for an interest in the state of higher education in Canada.

Since the concerns of the AUCC are professional rather than scholarly, it is perhaps appropriate that it should not meet during a Conference of Learned Societies, but the same argument could be made for other groups, for instance, the Canadian Association of University Teachers, which continues to meet with the Learned Societies as well as with the AUCC. Most learned societies, however, are concerned with professional as well as scholarly matters - with the problems of teaching in their discipline, for example, or with prospects of employment in the 'profession.' By no means can all of the thousands of papers presented during this annual three-week gathering be described as scholarly, and all societies, including the Royal Society, have business sessions. On the other hand, some papers presented at the annual meetings of the AUCC can be properly described as scholarly and certainly its professional concerns include the state of scholarship and research. The same can be said of most professional societies, the Canadian Society of Home Economics, for example. By 1940, professional societies had been established in almost all the professions that are included in the roster of university faculties; therefore, there was little need for further development in this area. The only two new organizations were the Canadian

Association of Optometrists (1946) and the Canadian Veterinary Medicine Association (1949). Both have subsequently sponsored journals which do include scholarly articles, the *Canadian Journal of Optometry* (1939) and the *Canadian Veterinary Journal* (1960).

The organizations mentioned to date are national in nature and as such their membership is open to all qualified Canadians and to foreigners as well. Each, it can be assumed, includes among its membership Canadians whose first language is French. French Canada has, however, special problems related to scholarship and research and not all of these can be dealt with appropriately in the context of a national organization with a membership largely consisting of English-Canadians. There are, as well, problems related to scholarship and research which are of primary interest to English-speaking Canadians in particular provinces or regions; these are the concern of provincial or local societies, the number of which also increased during the 1940s and 1950s. In the Province of Quebec, however, such problems are more serious and more complex, and this explains the particular significance for the history of higher education in Canada of the Association Canadienne pour l'avancement des sciences (ACFAS).

The establishment of ACFAS in 1924 has already been described.[25] In 1960 its 28th Congress was held at Université Laval with 700 persons in attendance and with 304 papers presented in the course of three days. ACFAS has always been supported by the Quebec government and, like the Royal Society of Canada, it provides for the affiliation of local societies. There were 27 such affiliates in 1960, of which 21 made a report to the congress. ACFAS further resembles the Royal Society by being organized in sections, which meet separately and in plenary session. It also embraces the arts and the sciences. In 1960 there were 27 sections, of which 13 were concerned with pure science, 3 with applied science (agriculture, industrial chemistry, applied physics), 5 with the social sciences (economics, geography, history, psychology, and anthropology, sociology and social psychology combined), 4 with the humanities (classics, linguistics, philosophy, slavic studies) and 2 with pedagogy - pedagogy in general and the teaching of science. This was a very wide ranging program, the most surprising omissions being English and French. In addition to the annual congress, the association continued to provide lectures in the classical colleges principally by professors from Montréal and Laval, and to award prizes for academic achievement to secondary school students. It also issued a newsletter or bulletin ten times a year.

With regard to publishing activities, the University of Toronto Press had a creditable record in 1940 but its transformation into a scholarly publishing house of international renown took place after a reorganizaton in 1953. In 1960-61 it published 53 books exclusive of reprints, more than any other publishing house in Canada, and more than all but three of the university presses in North America.[26] In addition, it printed and provided editorial assistance for 10 scholarly journals. Its 1960 catalogue listed over 500 books in print. The press continued to be a self-supporting division of the university and independently financed a new building, opened in 1958, to house its administrative and editorial offices and a bookstore. It was also in a position to provide from its own resources substantial sums each year for the subsidization of scholarly books - $70,000 in 1960-61 - and to attract support for its program not only from the Canada Council but also from the Ford Foundation.

By 1960 the activities of the press included two long-range projects of enormous scope and significance, a collected edition of the works of John Stuart Mill which was expected to run to over 20 volumes (the first appeared in 1965), and the Dictionary of Canadian Biography, in theory an endless undertaking which was made possible by a $1 million bequest from a Toronto businessman, James A. Nicholson.

The DCB project, of which the first volume covering the years 1000 to 1700 appeared in 1966, was a joint undertaking with Les Presses de l'Université Laval, parallel offices and editorial staff being established in the two institutions. The two presses also combined in the publishing of particular books. Les Presses de l'Université Laval had been formally established in 1950 though a number of titles had been published by the university prior to this date. The first book under the new imprint appeared in 1951, and by 1960 the catalogue ran to 146 titles, a number of which were co-editions with European publishing houses. In 1960, it was also publishing six scholarly journals, *Revue de l'Université Laval*, *l'Enseignement Secondaire au Canada*, *Relations Industrielles*, *Recherches Sociographiques*, *Service Social*, and *Laval Théologique et Philosophique*. Les Presses de l'Université Laval was supported partly by a subvention from the university but principally from the operation of a bookstore and from the sales of textbooks published by it and used in the classical colleges of the province.

In 1945 Les Editions de l'Université d'Ottawa, established in 1936, began to publish works in English as well as in French and added University of Ottawa Press to its title. By June 1961 it had published 144 monographs, five of which were produced in the academic year 1960-61, and was responsible for five periodicals: *Revue de l'Université d'Ottawa*, *Histoire sociale/Social History*, *Revue générale de Droit*, *Co-incidences*, and *Inscape*. Les Editions, which did not operate a bookstore or undertake commercial printing, had been financed since its establishment by the university.

In 1957, Dalhousie University announced that it was setting up a press, and in the course of the next several years two titles appeared under this imprint, *A Bibliographical Catalogue of the Works of Rudyard Kipling*, issued in collaboration with the University of Toronto Press, and a pamphlet, *George Munro, the Publisher*. However, the project was basically a committee affair, and with the publishing of the Munro pamphlet the enterprise ceased. A second English-language university press was established in 1960 at McGill, although until it became a joint undertaking of McGill and Queen's in 1968 it was always on the brink of foundering.

CENTRES AND INSTITUTES

The establishment between 1920 and 1940 of seven research institutes or centres by universities was noted in chapter 24 and also
the locating on university campuses of several federal or provincial laboratories. Between 1940 and 1960 there was a significant
development of institutions of this type, notably at McGill,
Montréal, and Toronto.

McGill, which had earlier founded the Montreal Neurological
Institute and the Institute of Parasitology at Macdonald College,
established the Allan Memorial Institute of Psychiatry in 1944,
an institute of air and space law, and an institute of Islamic
studies in 1951, the Bellairs Research Institute for research in
marine biology, geology, geography, and tropical climatology,
located in the Barbados, and a sub-Arctic research laboratory at
Knob Hill, Quebec, in 1953, as well as an industrial relations
centre within its school of commerce in 1960. In addition, it
provided space for and cooperated with the Arctic Institute of
North America, an international organization established at
Montreal in 1945. At Montréal, the activities of Institut de
Radium founded in 1922 and renamed the Institut de cancer de
Montréal in 1941 were considerably expanded, and there were added
l'Institut de psychologie within the faculté de philosophie (in
1942), l'Institut de médecine et de chirurgie expérimentale (under
the directorship of Hans Selye), and l'Institut supérieur des
sciences religieuses in 1954. Also within the faculté de philosophie at Montréal was an institute of mediaeval studies, basically the Dominican centre which had been established at Ottawa
in 1930 and had moved to Montreal and affiliated with the university in 1942. Still another Université de Montréal development,
this time in association with the department of slavic studies,
was a research centre for Central and East Europe, combining the
resources of two institutions established in 1948, L'Institut est
et sud Européene de l'Université d'Ottawa and the Centre d'études
slaves de l'Université de Montréal. The new additions at Toronto
were the Institute for Aerospace Study in 1949, a computer centre
in 1951 which was subsequently expanded into an institute of computer science, the Great Lakes Institute in 1957, and the Institute
of Earth Sciences in 1960.

Both Laval and British Columbia had established three institutes
or centres by 1960; the former an Institut d'histoire et de géographie in 1946, and centres de recherche ethnologique and de
recherche en sociologie religieuse in 1958; the latter an institute of oceanography in 1949, an institute of fisheries in 1953,
and a computer centre in 1957. The Institute of Oceanography
received financial support from the National Research Council,
as did a parallel institute established at Dalhousie in 1959.
Queen's established an institute of local government in 1944 and
an industrial relations centre in 1960. At Saskatchewan, institutes of northern studies and of upper atmospheric physics were
established in the late 1950s; the university was also the site

of NRC's Prairie Research Laboratory, one of the federal Department
of Agriculture's research laboratories, and the Saskatchewan
Research Council. The Alberta Research Council was also located
on the provincial university campus and the university itself, by
1960, had established its Boreal Institute for Northern Studies.
One of the new universities, Carleton launched an institute of
Canadian Studies in 1957. At St Francis Xavier, the teaching and
research programs in cooperative adult education, which dated back
at least to 1929, were institutionalized in 1960 as the Coady
International Institute.

It is questionable whether all the subdivisions of Canadian
universities have been identified which, in 1960, could be classified as institutes or centres. In the French Language institutions,
the term *institut* was also used to denote a teaching division in
certain areas, for example, education, music, and nursing, and
some teaching and research programs offered in particular departments at particular universities were in fact if not in name as
'semi-autonomous' as some of those listed. What we are concerned
with here are programs of an interdisciplinary or highly specialized nature which have been established as a means of undertaking
research and providing advance graduate instruction in specific
areas. The number of such programs proliferated dramatically in
the 1960s and in many cases the basis for the new program had been
effectively laid by 1960.

What was particularly significant about this development in
Canadian higher education, both before 1960 and after, is that,
in contrast to the situation which frequently applied in the
United States, the establishment of institutes, centres, and
specialized teaching-research programs was in almost all instances
organized by the university in question and financed basically
from university funds. The impetus came not from the federal
government, nor from foundations such as Carnegie, Ford, and
Rockefeller; and when institutes, centres, or programs were established, they remained under the direct control of the university.
Robert Nisbet in *The Degradation of the Academic Dogma* argues that
the development of research institutes and centres in the American
universities between 1945 and 1960 was (a) made possible by federal
government and foundation support and (b) led to the breakdown
of the American university as a coordinated organization:

> I firmly believe that direct grants from government and founda-
> tion to individual members of university faculties, or to small
> company-like groups of faculty members, for the purposes of
> creating institutes, centres, bureaus, and other essentially
> capitalistic enterprises within the academic community to be
> the single most powerful agent of change that we can find in
> the university's long history. For the first time in Western
> history, professors and scholars were thrust into the unwonted
> position of entrepreneurs in incessant search for new sources
> of capital, of new revenue, and taking the word in its largest
> sense, of profits. Whereas for centuries the forces of commerce,

trade and industrialization outside the university had registered little if any impact upon the academic community beyond
perhaps a certain tightening of forces within, the new capitalism, *academic capitalism*, is a force that arose within the university and that has had as its most eager supporters the members of the professoriat.[27]

Whether or not Nisbet is correct in his analysis, it is true that
entrepreneurship has not characterized the development of institutes and centres in Canada. The grants from government departments and agencies and from foundations have been modest rather
than substantial, and in organizational terms the directors of
institutes and centres have remained within the university hierarchy in positions either parallel or more frequently subordinate
to that of deans of faculties or schools. Furthermore, Canadian
institutes and centres have almost always combined teaching and
research and have not concentrated upon the latter, with the result that they have had a continuing relation with the academic
senate as well as with the president and the board of governors.

LIBRARIES, MUSEUMS, ART GALLERIES

From the standpoint of scholars, no genuine change occurred with
respect to art galleries and museums during the 1940s and 1950s.
The existing collections were strengthened, particularly those
of the National Gallery of Canada[28] and the Royal Ontario Museum.
Access to materials was made easier in various ways, including
the provision of additional and better qualified staff. However,
the general inadequacy of Canada's galleries and museums was emphasized by the Royal Commission on National Development in the
Arts, Letters and Sciences in 1951, and little had been done by
1960 in the way of implementing its specific recommendations,
for example the provision of appropriate buildings for the National
Gallery and the National Museum (which it was recommended be
called the Canadian Museum of Natural History[29] and the establishment of a Canadian Historical Museum, a Canadian Museum of Science
(to be directed initially by the National Research Council), a
National Zoological Garden, and one or more national acquaria.[30]
Surprisingly enough, the inadequate base for research which required ready access to collections of arts and natural history
was not one of the problems that concerned the universities as a
group during these years; the only reference to this problem at
the annual meetings of the National Conference of Canadian Universities was a glancing one in a paper presented by R.H. Hubbard,
chief curator of the National Gallery of Canada, during a symposium on the universities and the fine arts at the 1956 meeting.[31]
  More surprising still is the lack of sustaining interest in the
NCCU in the adequacy of library facilities for scholarship and
research. It was a topic of discussion or the substance of a
resolution upon occasion, but there was no concerted attack on

the problem as there was on other issues such as adult education.

However, in 1956 a proposal, originating from British Columbia, was put to the delegates that the conference sponsor a survey of Canadian university libraries, to be undertaken by a distinguished American librarian and financed by a grant of approximately $3000 from one of the foundations, but rejected by the Executive Committee: 'It was the general opinion of the executive that whatever the merits of the suggestion - and these were judged debatable - it was not a matter of great urgency, particularly in view of the more pressing problems [which the Canadian universities were facing] ...'[32]

The matter was revived in 1958 and the Executive Committee was directed by the conference to appoint a committee 'to survey (or to draw up a project and seek funds to survey) the needs of university and college libraries in Canada, and to recommend ways and means of meeting such needs on a national scale and in a systematic manner.'[33] Such a committee was appointed under the chairmanship of W. Kaye Lamb, the dominion archivist and national librarian, and in 1960 it reported to the conference that while there was no serious problem with respect to undergraduate collections or in the field of science where the main demand of researchers was for current periodicals, there was a very serious one in the humanities and social sciences where collections could only be brought up to a research level by a systematic building up of library resources in carefully chosen and limited subject fields at particular universities.[34] This led to the appointment of Edwin E. Williams of Harvard University to undertake the survey and to the publication in 1962 of his report, one of the main conclusions of which was that 'except in Canadian subjects and in mediaeval studies there are no collections in major fields that are outstanding as a whole - assuming that an outstanding collection is one strong enough to attract scholars from other countries.'[35] On the other hand Williams noted that considerable progress had been made during the previous half-dozen years. 'Until very recently Toronto [because of its library's relative strength in twenty named fields other than those dependent on Canadian materials] was the only Canadian university engaged in research in the humanities and social sciences on a relatively broad front,' but there were now eight other universities which had the resources to undertake advance graduate work (and scholarship in general) in one or more fields: British Columbia (10), McGill (9), Ottawa (4), Montreal (4), Queen's (2), Western Ontario, Laval, Manitoba (1 each). Other special collections were being developed at these and other universities and Williams expected that the next few years would bring many of them up to the level of those he had identified as adequate. His expectation was fulfilled.

The best excuse for the NCCU's failure to concern itself about the inadequacies of library resources, other than the serious problems it faced in financial matters in general, was the fact that during the 1950s definite progress was at long last made towards the development of a national library in Ottawa with branches stretching out to the ten provinces and to the individual universities. It is true that in 1960 there was still no national library in the physical sense; it occupied the third floor of what its historian, Professor Dolores Donnelly, had described as 'a warehouse type of structure,' which had the added disadvantage of being situated in an Ottawa suburb at considerable distance both from the centre of the city and from the Public Archives building in which the national librarian (who was also the dominion archivist) had his office. It was not until 1967 that the National Library moved to the centre of Ottawa; since that time it has occupied space in a new building erected to provide adequate accommodation for the Public Archives of Canada. The post-war period, had, however, seen a very healthy development of the Public Archives with respect to both holdings and staff. This had markedly improved the national position with respect to scholarship in Canadian subjects, but it also meant that the physical requirements of the Public Archives were continually expanding. By 1975 both the Public Archives and the National Library could legitimately claim that they needed all the available space in the building which they continued to occupy jointly.

The development of the National Library of Canada can be said to date in practical terms either from 1941, when the Canadian Library Council was formed, with representatives from all the provinces; or from 1946 when the Canadian Library Association was established. So far as personnel, motivation, and objectives were concerned, there was little to distinguish between these two organizations; the chief difference was that the CLA was a legally incorporated entity and that existing ties with the American Library Association were reduced. In any event the CLA was able to build immediately on the earlier efforts of the CLC to persuade the federal government to take action on the national library issue. Within six months of its establishment, the CLA in conjunction with the Royal Society of Canada, the Canadian Historical Association, the Canadian Political Science Association, and the Social Science Research Council of Canada presented a brief to the government, which, in a more systematic and persuasive way than had ever been done before, outlined the functions of a national library and, more important, the steps whereby it could effectively and economically be launched. The new approach was to proceed by way of providing services rather than by concentrating on the provision of a building. As a result, in 1948 the government approved a proposal to establish a bibliographical centre and the appointment of W. Kaye Lamb, chief librarian of the University of British Columbia, as dominion archivist 'with the special assignment of preparing the way for the establishment of a National Library in Ottawa.'[36] A National Library Advisory Council was appointed in the same year to assist the dominion archivist in planning the Canadian Bibliographical Centre established in 1950. It commenced work on a national union catalogue, which by September 1951 contained a half million catalogue cards representing the holdings of eleven of the federal government libraries in Ottawa and four other major libraries including the Toronto Public Library's Reference Division and Le Bibliothèque St-Sulpice in Montreal. The centre also assumed responsibility for the *Canadian Catalogue of Books Published in Canada, about Canada, as Well as Those Written by Canadians*, which since 1923 had been published annually by the Toronto Public Library, converting it in 1951 into a fortnightly publication, *Canadiana*.

On 1 January 1953, proclamation of the National Library Act brought the National Library into formal existence, Kaye Lamb being now designated national librarian as well as dominion archivist, and a National Library Advisory Council replaced the Advisory Committee. At this stage, the National Library had virtually no books, but by 1960 its holdings exceeded 250,000, and legislation had been passed requiring the deposit of copies of all works published in Canada. During 1960-61 some 5000 titles were acquired under this authority. The National Union Catalogue by this time had 4,600,000 entries representing the holdings of 164 Canadian libraries, including most of the approximately 40 government libraries in Ottawa and many of the major universities. Though concentrating on the provision of service, the Advisory Council had turned its attention to the planning of a national library building as early as 1954, and by 1960 a plan for a building to be begun in 1962 and completed in 1965 was fully developed. However, as has been previously noted, this project aborted, and it was not until 1967 that its holdings became readily available to interested scholars.

A NATIONAL POLICY

By 1960 the combination of the increasing recognition of the need for more and more research in all areas of scholarship and the mounting costs of the support of individual and group research projects brought into focus the fact that Canada lacked a national policy with respect to scholarship and research in general. So long as relatively small sums of money were involved, the problem of duplication of effort was not a serious one, but with the advent of the cyclotron and the computer, to cite only two examples, coordination of effort became mandatory.

The solution to the problem and all of its ramifications was a long time in coming but the first step, the recognition that a problem did indeed exist, was taken with the appointment of two royal commissions in 1955 and 1960. The first one, the Royal Commission on Canada's Economic Prospects, was chaired by Walter Gordon and it reported in 1958; the second, the Royal Commission on Government Organization, chaired by J. Grant Glassco, reported in 1963.

The Gordon Commission had been asked to study the likely development of Canada's economy during the 1960s and 1970s and to make recommendations as to how this development could be most effectively stimulated and directed. In general, its conclusions resembled those of the Rowell-Sirois Commission of 1937-1940 in emphasizing the need for a redefining of the roles and the financial powers of the federal and provincial governments. Much heavier emphasis, however, was placed on the need for research and consequently on the need for adequate support for the universities which were both the nation's chief source of highly trained manpower and the key centres of fundamental research. Like the Rowell-Sirois Commission, the Gordon Commission acknowledged that technically the problems of the universities lay outside its terms of reference, but the importance of the universities to the nation's well-being made it impossible to ignore them:

> We do not judge it to be the responsibility of this Commission to recommend how public funds should be provided in support of universities. We do, however, feel it our bounden duty to call attention as forcefully as we can to the vital part which the universities must play in our expanding and increasingly complex economy, and to the necessity of maintaining them in a healthy and vigorous condition. The functions of the universities touch every facet of our society. Through the preservation of our heritage they maintain our way of life, and through the interest they generate in the arts, they enrich it. They enliven the perception of social processes and contribute to the orderly development of social institutions and relations. It is incredible that we would allow their services to society in these ways to lapse or to lag. But these contributions are not our direct concern. We are concerned with the contribution made by the universities to the increase in the national productivity and wealth of the country. In relation to this aspect of the national welfare Canadian universities occupy a key position. They are the source of the most highly skilled workers whose knowledge is essential in all branches of industry. In addition they make a substantial contribution to research and in the training of research scientists.[37]

The report clearly stated that the basic problem of the universities was the meagre earnings of faculty members, and it recommended that, in the interests both of retaining existing staff and of encouraging young people to prepare themselves for an academic career, the total amount provided for salaries should be approximately doubled. More and better qualified staff had to be acquired if graduate work was to be properly developed and if the research that needed to be done was to be undertaken. The report stated:

> In the first place, we believe that the rate of technical advance in Canada must accelerate if we are to maintain our position in relation to other countries and to achieve the growth of the economy which we have predicted. This means a continuously expanding research effort. Secondly, the levels at which research will be conducted and technical progress achieved will

be more demanding in terms of skills and facilities than has
been the case in the past. This means generally more elaborate
provision for research. Third, in many areas the scale on which
research must be conducted and the elaborate facilities required
will necessitate industry co-operation and substantial government participation. Finally, while the results of well directed
research effort will yield substantial returns, it is important
that the total research effort should be continuously under review in order to avoid duplication and to detect gaps; and that
research information when available should be rapidly and effectively communicated to those who can use it.[38]

Consequently 'it seems to us that the time is opportune to make
a careful appraisal of the total national research effort, and in
this way to prepare ourselves for the increasing activities in
this vitally important field that will be required.'
The final chapter of the Gordon Commission Report dealt with
the Role of Government, and the Glassco Commission, appointed just
two years later, was largely concerned with government organization in all areas; but it is significant that much of its fourth
and final volume was devoted to scientific research and development. Its detailed analysis of the sums of money being assigned
for research purposes by the various government departments and
agencies revealed instances of overlap and duplication, but its
chief complaint was that there was no government department or
agency held solely responsible for recommending to Parliament and
the government general strategy with respect to the allocation of
such funds. 'A careful appraisal of the total national research
effort' had in fact revealed that there was no national policy,
specifically with respect to science but equally, indeed even
more so, with respect to the social sciences and the humanities.
It could be argued that as originally envisaged the role of the
National Research Council was to develop such a policy with respect to science, but with its preoccupation with both its own research programs and carrying on those in other government departments, NRC became only one of a number of bodies competing for
available funds. It was true that in the late 1940s the NRC Act
was amended to provide that, in its capacity as a privy council
committee, NRC should scrutinize all proposals of a scientific
nature before final authorization by the cabinet; the act also
set up an advisory panel for scientific policy, consisting of the
deputy ministers of the appropriate government departments, the
clerk of the Privy Council, the secretary of the Treasury Board,
and the president of NRC who was chairman, the purpose of this
advisory panel being to advise the NRC on such matters. But these
mechanisms had proved unworkable:

The foregoing pattern would appear to provide a reasonably
workman-like approach, although it is subject to objection on
the grounds of the poverty of provision for advice from non-
government sources, apart from the universities. In practice,

however, the system has failed to function as intended. The Privy Council Committee has met infrequently and between 1950 and 1958 was not called together at all. The N.R.C. has turned aside from its original duty of advising on broad national policy and has concentrated its efforts, albeit with conspicuous success, on the support of research and scholarship in the universities and, in a general way, on its own behalf. The Advisory Panel met formally fourteen times in its first ten years of existence but has since been convened only infrequently. Proposals for new scientific programmes have usually reached Cabinet on the recommendation of individual Ministers, via the Treasury Board, with support provided in some cases by interdepartmental committees or recommendations from scientific and industrial groups outside the government. The Treasury Board has itself provided the principle review.[39]

The Glassco Commission report recommended that responsibility for a national policy be assigned to a specific minister and that a secretariat be established to assist in developing such a policy. The second of these two recommendations was implemented in 1964, but a decade was to pass before a recognizable national policy with respect to scholarship and research could be said to have been established.[40]

Throughout the 1960s, the search for a means of establishing and maintaining a national policy with respect to research was a major preoccupation of the federal government, and, by extension, of the provincial governments and the universities. Among other things, it brought about the creation of the Economic Council of Canada in 1962, the Science Council of Canada in 1966, and an education branch within the Department of the Secretary of State in 1967. Indeed, it has continued to be just as challenging a pursuit in the 1970s. In 1971 a Federal Ministry of State for Science and Technology was set up, and a Senate Committee on National Science Policy appointed in 1968 was still sitting in 1975. But national cooperation has always been an elusive goal of Canadians in their unceasing quest for unity within diversity.

NOTES TO CHAPTER 30

1 G.S. Brett, 'The Graduate Study in Canada - The Arts and Sciences,' *NCCU Proc.* (1934), 29-33, quoted by W.P. Thompson, *Graduate Studies in the Sciences* (1963), 15
2 See above, chapter 24, 347-9. The speaker was R.W. Boyle.
3 Royal Commission on National Development in the Arts, Letters and Sciences, *Report* (1951), 161
4 L.-P. Bonneau and J.A. Corry, *Quest for the Optimum: Research Policy in the Universities of Canada* I (1972), 7
5 Ibid., I, 8
6 J.B. Brebner, *Scholarship in Canada: the Function of Graduate Studies* (1954), 65

7 M. Wade, 'The Culture of French Canada' in J. Park, ed., *The Culture of Contemporary Canada* (1957), 389

8 W. Eggleston, 'A History of the National Research Council,' unpublished manuscript

9 In September 1939 the NRC had a total staff of 300 employees and was operating on an annual budget of $900,000. 'Within months ... [its] staff had expanded to almost 2000 and its yearly budget was close to $7,000,000': *A Science Policy for Canada: Report of the Senate Special Committee on Science Policy* I (1970), 61

10 Royal Commission on Government Organization, *Report* IV (1963), 141-3

11 J.W.T. Spinks, 'Graduate Studies and Research in the Sciences' in A.D. Dunton and D. Patterson, eds., *Canada's Universities in a New Age* (1962), 49

12 The statistics in this section are taken from the *Annual Reports* of the council. A summary of receipts and expenditures, 1946-1958, is given in M. Timlin and A. Faucher, *The Social Sciences in Canada* (1968), 64.

13 *CSSRC Annual Report 1949-50*, 3

14 Ibid., 8

15 Ibid., 1950-51, 8

16 See above, chapter 27, 499.

17 *SSRC of Canada Annual Report 1960-62*, 17

18 Timlin and Faucher, *Social Sciences*, 66ff

19 The establishment of the Humanities Research Council of Canada is outlined in its *First Annual Report* (1943-47). See also W. Kirkconnell, *A Slice of Canada: Memoirs* (1967), 236-9, which reprints the memorial submitted to the prime minister.

20 The statistics in this section are taken from the council's *Reports*, 1943-47 to 1956-58.

21 The statistics in this section are taken from the council's *Annual Reports*, 1957-58 to 1960-61.

22 W. Kirkconnell and A.S.P. Woodhouse, *The Humanities in Canada* (1947), 194

23 For the development of the Chemical Institute of Canada, see C.J. Warrington and B.T. Newbold, *Chemical Canada* (1970), 247-71.

24 See above, 565.

25 See above, chapter 24, 440.

26 University of Toronto, *President's Report* (1960-61), 132

27 R. Nisbet, *The Degradation of the Academic Dogma* (New York: Basic Books, 1971), 72-3

28 J.S. Boggs, *The National Gallery of Canada* (1971). Chapter 6, covering the period 1939 to 1955, is entitled 'Great Years of Collecting.' Note that chapter 8 (1960-65) is entitled 'The Search for Stability.'

29 The commission also recommended that the collection of the Geological Survey of Canada, the original basis of the National Museum of Canada, be separated and provided with its own building.

30 See chapters 7 (Galleries) and 8 (Museums). The commission's recommendations are given in chapter 20 (other Federal Institutions), 314-26.
31 R. Hubbard, 'The Visual Arts,' *NCCU Proc.* (1955), 64-8
32 *NCCU Proc.* (1956), 89
33 Ibid. (1959), 99
34 Ibid. (1960), 95
35 E.E. Williams, *Resources of Canadian Libraries for Research in the Humanities and Social Sciences* (1962), 48
36 F.D. Donnelly, *The National Library of Canada* (1973), 137. Professor Donnelly's book is the source for much of the information in the following paragraphs.
37 Royal Commission on Canada's Economic Prospects, *Report* (1958), 452
38 Ibid., 454-5
39 Royal Commission on Government Organization, *Report* (1963), 220-1
40 The Senate Committee, under the chairmanship of the Hon. Maurice Lamontagne, had by 1974 published the first three volumes of its report. Volume I, *A Critical View: Past and Present* (1970), provides a useful summary of the attempts to establish a science policy up to 1970 and defines the issues.

31
Conclusion

In the Preface I stated that my intention in undertaking this
study was to discover whether there were characteristics of
Canadian higher education which justified the assertion that the
Canadian university was a type of institution that differed in
significant ways from the type of university that has evolved in
other countries. I was not, of course, implying that all Canadian
universities resembled each other; obviously universities in Canada
as elsewhere differ as a consequence of such factors as age, location, size, financial support, and language of instruction. But
were there characteristics which Canadian universities had in
common which set them apart as a group from comparable groups in
other countries? Everything that I have discovered during the
course of my research leads me to the conclusion that this is in
fact the case.

I also stated in the Preface that the study would be confined
to an examination of the curricula offered in degree-granting
institutions and of the conditions pertaining to the carrying on
of scholarship and research by university professors; and I justified this on the grounds that the two essential and interrelated
functions of the university as it has been generally defined are
the dissemination and the advancement of knowledge, and consequently that the only way of defining types of universities was
through a description of their approach to instruction and research. My conclusion that Canadian higher education is *sui
generis* is therefore based on the evidence presented in the central
chapters of this study, those devoted to Arts and Science,
Professional Education, Graduate Studies, and Scholarship and
Research. In this final chapter I shall briefly summarize the
main evidence that has emerged.

Before doing so, it is appropriate to refer to four characteristics
of Canadian higher education which stand out as determining factors
in the eleven chapters of the book included as introductions to

the five sets of central chapters. These introductory chapters, one set centring on an event symbolizing the stage Canadian higher education had reached at the five focal points selected for detailed analysis, and a second dealing with the development of the institutions as corporate bodies, were designed to provide a framework within which the detailed analysis of instruction and research could be seen in historical perspective. The characteristics I am about to mention serve the same purpose with respect to the basic conclusions which follow. They too are introductory and are designed to provide perspective. The first two offer clues as to why Canadian higher education is as diversified as it is; the second two as to why it is so unified.

The first of the diversifying characteristics is the fact that seven elements have combined to form the compound that constitutes Canadian higher education. Six of these elements are the influences represented by the institutions drawn upon as models by the founders of the universities established by 1860: the American liberal arts college; the Jesuit classical college; the Catholic universities as represented initially by the University of Louvain and as subsequently more specifically defined with respect to the faculties of canon law, philosophy, and theology by the authorities at the Vatican; the Scottish university; the combination of Oxford *and* Cambridge; and the University of London. The seventh element, the American state university, entered the compound at the beginning of the twentieth century. It is the blending of these various influences which has given Canadian higher education its particular style.

A second diversifying characteristic is the combined consequence of the factors of time, space, and language. Canada is an immense country and it has been settled gradually over more than three centuries. It is also a country with two major languages, and behind each language lies a culture both rich and complex. One must expect diversity in a higher education system which embraces universities offering instruction in English, in French, and in both languages, in many cases located at great distances from each other, and established under very different political, social, and economic conditions. The roots of the French language universities were planted in the seventeenth century, those of the earliest English language universities at a time when Canada was a cluster of colonies, independent of each other though not of the British Colonial Office, those of the three most westerly provinces in the early twentieth century when Canada had been a dominion for over forty years, and a half-dozen in the 1950s. Inevitably growth has been determined by the conditions existing at the time the individual institution was established. The differing economies of the Maritime provinces, Quebec, Ontario, the Prairie provinces, and British Columbia have also been determining factors in the development of their universities. It is natural, therefore, to think of the Canadian universities in regional terms; this is reflected in the organization of the chapters of this book which deal with institutional development.

But the record shows that there have been unifying factors as
well as divisive ones. The first of the two to be mentioned is
the mechanism of federation or affiliation, two basically similar
methods of arranging for cooperation between institutions that
are legally independent. Neither mechanism is a Canadian invention, but in no other country has either arrangement been adopted
by such a high proportion of institutions. In 1975, over 40 of
the 50 degree-granting institutions either were involved in a
federal arrangement, had affiliates, or had been affiliated with
another university earlier in their history.

The second unifying characteristic to be mentioned has been
the existence since early in the twentieth century of an organization including within its membership virtually every degree-
granting institution in the country, the National Conference of
Canadian Universities, now called the Association of Universities
and Colleges of Canada. Normally meeting annually for a two or
three day conference, it has for over half a century drawn the
universities together on a regular basis for the discussion of
mutual problems, and particularly since 1939 it has served as an
effective lobby for calling to the attention of the Canadian people
and their governments the special problems of Canadian higher education. The fact that there has been such a body embracing the
great variety of institutions that comprise the Canadian higher
education system, whether large or small, old or new, state-
supported or denominational, multi-faculty or professional school,
English language, French language or bilingual, has produced a
situation in direct contrast to that which applied when the Prince
of Wales visited the Canadian colonies in 1860. At that time the
institutions operated in complete isolation from each other; they
were rivals rather than partners in a common enterprise. By 1960,
as the special conferences convened by the NCCU in 1956 and 1961
bear witness, they could speak with a common and authoritative
voice.

The outstanding characteristic of Canadian higher education so
far as the arts and science program is concerned has been the co-
existence from the outset of three different courses leading to
the B.A. or B.Sc., the classical college course, the general course,
and the honour course, each differing in significant ways from
the comparable course offered in, respectively, France, the United
States, and the United Kingdom. The emphasis upon English has
always distinguished the classical college course as offered not
only in the Province of Quebec but in other provinces (for example at St Dunstan's in Prince Edward Island or the Collège
Classique de Gravelbourg in Saskatchewan) from that offered at a
French lycée, while the reforms introduced in the French baccalaureate in 1902, which permitted specialization in science, were
not imitated in Canada. The general course offered in the English
language universities has always borne a close resemblance to the
B.A. course offered in the American universities and colleges,
but it has since at least 1890 contained more elements of pres-

594

cription and less opportunity for specialization. The Canadian honour course does not closely resemble that leading to a British honours degree, particularly as offered at Oxford and Cambridge; it has never been as specialized, particularly in the first two years, and it has often been based on completion of one or two years of a general course, this in the interests of ensuring that the student has had some experience in the disciplines outside his specialty.

These distinctions are important and in themselves justify the claim that in this curriculum area Canadian practice is unique. But the fact of their co-existence is also significant, for each has affected the others. The classical college course has always been a reminder of the importance of the humanities as the basic ingredient of a liberal education, and the inclusion of a broad spectrum of elementary science and mathematics in the final years of the course has had the effect of calling to the attention of English-speaking Canadians the fact that a B.A. program which fails to show the relationship of the arts and the sciences leaves something to be desired. On the other hand, the existence of the two English-language programs has been a constant reminder to at least some French Canadians that in the interests of both certain individual students and the community as a whole specialization at the undergraduate level in subjects other than literature and philosophy is not only possible within the context of liberal education but intellectually and economically desirable.

The co-existence of the two English-language programs, almost invariably in the same institution, has been to the advantage of both. Though it would be difficult to document, the offering of an honours course has tended to raise the standard of the general course, particularly in those institutions where instruction in some courses in both programs is offered to students in the same class. That both courses have been simultaneously offered has made it relatively simple for a student who has initially opted for one to transfer to the other, and in this way has enabled students to escape from a blind alley or to discover where their real intellectual or even vocational interests lie. Finally the presence of the general course has been a continual reminder that a too heavy concentration on one or two subjects can lead to an unbalanced outlook. Without the general course, the Canadian honours course is likely to have led to a duplication of an Oxford degree.

A second characteristic of the Canadian arts and science curriculum has been the inclusion in its offerings of programs of a professional character - commerce and finance, business administration, journalism, secretarial science. A consequence of this has been that such courses have had a more academic character than might otherwise have been the case. Many programs in professional fields, for example, education, music, nursing, pharmacy, and physical and health education, began as offerings in the faculty of arts. In Nova Scotia, the first three years of engineering remained in 1960 a responsibility of this faculty.

The tendency of professional programs, including graduate work in arts and science subjects, to be initiated in faculties of arts and science is partly explained by the small size of most institutions at the time the program was introduced. It is also a reminder of the central position occupied until 1920 by the faculty of arts and science in all Canadian universities other than those like the Nova Scotia Technical College and the Royal Military College which did not offer the B.A. This ceased to be the case in the French-language universities with the establishment of facultés des lettres, sciences, sciences sociales, etc. and the effective assumption of work at the graduate level, but in the English-language universities the faculty of arts and science continued to occupy the central position for the next 40 years. In English-speaking Canada it has been the faculty of arts and science which has dominated the academic body, normally a senate, with responsibility for curricular affairs. This has had the effect of standardizing admission requirements throughout the university, the standard being that adopted by the faculty of arts and science.

Admission to a university in Canada was initially based on ex-aminations conducted by the individual institution, but by 1900 the usual method except at Laval, where since the 1860s the course of study, which embraced secondary and university level work, had been determined by the university in collaboration with the classi-cal colleges, was for the student to write a number of matricula-tion examinations set and marked by the several universities of the province in conjunction with the provincial department of edu-cation. Here, too, professors from the faculty of arts and science occupied a dominant position since they tended to be the univer-sity representatives on the matriculation boards, and the require-ments for admission to this faculty became the matter of prime concern to these boards. But there was another factor in English-speaking Canada which increased the influence of the faculty of arts and science on the matriculation examinations and consequently on the course of study in the secondary schools. This was the introduction of the senior matriculation year, in effect the offering of the first year of a B.A. degree program in the secon-dary schools. By 1900, it was possible to enter the first year of a B.A. program in most English-speaking universities after passing junior matriculation examinations or the second year after passing senior matriculation examinations. One consequence was that junior matriculants in any province entered with similar qualifications; a second was the standardization of the first year of the course offered by the universities since this had to be identical with that offered by the high schools in the senior matriculation year. While these arrangements applied specifically to the universities of the individual provinces, there was a ten-dency for the standard of matriculation at both levels to be essentially equivalent in all provinces. This in turn explains the high degree of similarity in the requirements for the first two years of the B.A. program in the English-speaking universities from coast to coast.

The final point to be made about the arts and science program is one that distinguishes Canadian practice from American: the relative failure of the movement, initiated in the United States at the turn of century, well established by 1920, and of great significance by 1960, to provide the first two years of a B.A. or a B.Sc. program in independent universities called junior colleges, whose graduates received the diploma of associate in arts. A few such colleges were established in Canada in the 1920s, but the need for them was slight, largely because the senior matriculation arrangement achieved the same result for the first of the two years.

With respect to professional education, the most interesting characteristic of the Canadian higher education system is the involvement of almost all the small universities and colleges. The classical colleges excepted, there has never been in Canada an institution which, like Amherst College in the United States, has restricted its activities to the provision of liberal education. It is true that the bulk of responsibility for the provision of professional education has always been borne either by the larger universities, many of which by 1960 would qualify as multiversities, to use Clark Kerr's phrase, or by professional schools. But what has also emerged in Canada is what might be called the *mini-university*, an institution with an enrolment ranging from 200 or 300 to 2000, which offers in addition to an undergraduate program in arts and science, degree programs in such fields as education, fine art, household science, library science, and nursing. This tradition was established at the outset since most of the institutions in operation by 1860, including those established by the state, were denominationally oriented, and particularly interested in providing for the training of ministers or priests. Hence the prominence of theology in chapter 5, which deals with professional education in 1860.

The charters of the universities of 1860 were based on those of the European universities which served as their models, not on those of the American liberal arts colleges; and at this time the American state university had hardly emerged. Normally, such charters called for faculties of arts, law, medicine, and theology, and this, as well as the need for doctors and lawyers, led the fledgling Canadian institutions to make provision for degrees in law and medicine. However, their resources were so limited that they were unable to provide instruction in these subjects as well as in arts and science and theology, which were their main concern. The solution was to draw up courses of study, to conduct examinations, and to grant successful candidates the appropriate degree, but to leave instruction in the case of medicine to schools established by members of the profession and in the case of law to the candidate himself. The arrangement for medicine stimulated the adoption of the mechanism of affiliation as a means of providing for professional education since most of the medical schools were granted the status of affiliates.

Even in the 1860s, there was an awareness that provision for

professional training in agriculture and engineering was needed
in Canada, and attempts were made at McGill and Toronto to establish courses in these subjects. These attempts failed partly because of inadequate resources but mainly because of the lack of
demand for such courses by would-be engineers or agriculturists.
By the 1870s, the candidates for such programs were available,
but the resources of the universities remained inadequate. The
consequence was the decision of the provincial governments in
Ontario and Quebec to establish independent schools to provide
training in these fields. About the same time, the professions
of dentistry and pharmacy became convinced that professional
training in these fields was also necessary; since neither the
universities nor the government could be persuaded to take action,
schools were established by the professions themselves. In one
other field, veterinary medicine, the initiative for establishing
a professional school was assumed by an individual, though in one
case he was able to convince a university (McGill) to assume responsibility for the undertaking.

The other veterinary college, established in Toronto in 1864,
became an affiliate of the University of Toronto in 1897. The
same procedure had already been instituted at the other professional schools established in Ontario by either the provincial
government or the professions and also with respect to l'école
polytechnique, established by the Quebec government, which had
become an affiliate of Laval. Consequently by 1900 the *indirect*
involvement of the universities had been extended to include
agriculture, dentistry, engineering, architecture (as a brand of
engineering), pharmacy, and veterinary medicine. But at this
stage the *direct* involvement of the universities in professional
education, including assumption of responsibility for financing,
was limited to law at Dalhousie, to medicine at McGill and Toronto,
to engineering at New Brunswick, and to theology at a number of
denominationally controlled institutions.

By 1920, however, the situation had changed radically and professional education was recognized as primarily the responsibility
of the universities. This responsibility had been accepted at
the time of their establishment by the provincial universities
of Alberta, British Columbia, and Saskatchewan, and also, with
the adoption of a 1906 Act, by the University of Toronto. It had
also been adopted at Queen's and Western Ontario following their
transformation from denominationally to publicly controlled institutions, by Dalhousie and McGill, indeed by almost all institutions, since by this time the smaller universities were expanding
into such new fields as household economics and education. Among
the consequences was the integration within the university of a
number of the schools established independently by the professions
or the government, the previously affiliated institutions becoming
faculties or schools. In Québec the provincial role continued to
take the form of establishing independent institutions which then
became affiliated with Laval; schools of commerce, forestry, and
surveying were created on this basis early in the twentieth century.

In Nova Scotia the provincial role was limited to the establishing of the degree-granting Nova Scotia Technical College to provide the final two years of an engineering course.

The most significant of these developments was a by-product of the decision of the provincial governments in six of the nine provinces to assign responsibility for the provision of professional education to the university - the decision to provide financial support for all the activities of publicly controlled universities, including arts and science. This had not been the case at Toronto, for example, until the passing of a legislative act in 1906. It is difficult not to conclude that the obvious need to provide support for professional education (including graduate studies) was a factor of crucial importance in persuading provincial governments to provide substantial support for higher education as a whole.

There was no change in the basic pattern of professional education in Canada during the next 40 years. The remaining affiliates became integrated faculties or schools, the range of fields included was extended, the role of the professions was increasingly restricted to that of certifying the graduate to practise, and the federal government's involvement continued to be restricted to its direction of the Royal Military College and to provision of sums of money to the provinces (but not to individual universities) for the general support of vocational training. Most of these federal funds were used by the provinces to provide facilities for technical training at the secondary school level. This, in conjunction with the concentration of the universities on instruction at the degree level, explains why there was so little provision for the training of technicians in Canada in 1960.

By 1960, the chief characteristic of graduate studies in Canada was that it closely resembled the approach adopted in the United States; the only important difference was that the normal requirement for admission to a one year M.A. program was an honours degree, which usually required an additional year of study. The requirements for degrees at both the masters and doctoral levels - number of courses, knowledge of foreign languages, years of residence, general examinations, the thesis (including whether or not one was required at the master's level) were almost identical with those of the American universities, though substantially different from those which had been adopted in the United Kingdom and continental Europe.

In retrospect, one sees that this was not a surprising outcome, granted the way in which graduate studies had developed in Canada since their beginnings in the 1890s. The pace and range of the development were similar, though here one must recognize an approximate 20 year time gap between American and Canadian practice and also a much slower development in Canada of programs leading to the Ph.D. in the humanities and the social sciences, the explanation in both cases being lack of financial resources. But one must also note that a higher proportion of Canadian institutions

became involved in graduate work at the master's level. It is
surprising that by 1960 the same patterns had been adopted by
the French-language institutions, which in 1940 appeared to be
moving along a different route, one that followed the Catholic
universities of Europe as defined by the authorities in Rome.
However, there is a simple explanation for the change that subsequently occurred. In 1920, graduate studies at Université
Laval and the recently established Université de Montréal were
to all intents and purposes confined to theology, philosophy,
and canon law, areas in which Rome had laid down specific regulations as to how the licence and the doctorat were to be conducted. These directions were very different from the guidelines
outlined by the Association of American Universities, which had
been established in 1900 by the leading American universities
for the purpose of ensuring comparable procedures in graduate
work throughout the United States. The AAU 'program' was the
one adopted by the only two Canadian universities, McGill and
Toronto, which by 1920 had been able to develop graduate studies
to the doctoral level. But as in the course of the next 40 years
Laval and Montréal developed programs to this level in the sciences and social sciences, in subjects within the humanities
other than philosophy, and in professional fields other than
theology, the model they followed, as did a number of English-
language universities, was that of McGill and Toronto. Furthermore, since the programs at the master's and licence levels had
been coordinated with those for the Ph.D. by the AAU and by
McGill and Toronto (which became members of that rather exclusive
organization in 1927), the American pattern was generally adopted
by all Canadian institutions.

As described in chapter 23, there was serious discussion at the
National Conference of Canadian Universities in the early 1920s
of proposals to adopt other methods of conducting graduate studies, including that adopted in Australia in 1946 when the
Australian National University was established by the Commonwealth
government as an institution designed solely to undertake graduate
work and to pursue research. Though these discussions led to no
conclusion, they do reflect the uneasiness of the Canadian universities with a situation in which responsibility for advanced graduate
studies rested with only two institutions, one of which (McGill)
was active only in the area of the sciences. Lack of financial
resources cannot excuse the failure of the Canadian universities
at that time to find some means whereby such resources as were
available in universities other than McGill and Toronto could
be used effectively through some form of inter-university cooperation. It does, however, explain in large measure why only
the two richest universities in the country until the late 1940s
entered seriously into this field. It also explains why the
offerings at these two institutions were so limited. It was not
until additional resources became available in the 1950s that
the McGill and Toronto offerings were broadened to include almost
every subject and field and that other major universities became
active.

There is one other explanation for the slow development of graduate studies in Canada: the existence of the honour course. In the view of many professors prior to World War II, an honours degree was comparable to an American M.A., a view shared, it may be added, by a number of American professors, who were familiar with the quality of Canadian honour graduates who enrolled in American graduate schools. Furthermore, the British background of many of the most influential Canadian professors during the first four decades of the twentieth century led them to regard the possession of a Ph.D. as unnecessary for effective university teaching. In their view the primary function of the university was to provide a solid undergraduate course, and for this a first-class Canadian honour degree or a first-class Oxbridge B.A. or its equivalent was sufficient. Finally the stimulation provided these professors by the students in the honour courses offered them as individual teachers the kind of intellectual experience which their colleagues in American universities encountered when dealing with graduate students.

Lack of financial resources has also proved to be a limiting factor in Canadian higher education with respect to scholarship and research. That the role of the university professor was to advance knowledge as well as to disseminate it was a conviction of a substantial number of presidents and professors from at least 1850 on, and, as chapter 6 reveals, the importance of the publication of scholarly investigation was recognized by academic and laymen alike. But chapter 6 also provides evidence of the difficulties under which Canadian scholars laboured in their efforts to complete and to publish their investigations. The parallel chapters in the 1890, 1920, 1940, and 1960 divisions of this book record the relatively slow pace of the development of proper facilities for scholarly activity - well-stocked libraries, research laboratories, learned societies, professional journals, university presses - as well as the provision of the funds needed to carry on certain kinds of research and the allotment of time needed to free the professor from normal teaching responsibilities.

Nonetheless, the record of scholarship and research produced in Canada is at the very least a respectable one, and much of the credit for this has derived from the activities of the federal government in this area. Until World War I, the bulk of research, both pure and applied, was produced by departments and agencies of the federal government, but they frequently drew upon university professors, particularly in the summer months, to carry out some of their investigations. It was the federal government which provided the funds that enabled the Royal Society of Canada to publish its *Transactions*. The government's active involvement in research continued with the establishment of the National Research Council of Canada during World War I, but the policy of this agency was from the beginning to assign a portion of its funds to the support of basic research in the universities. Unfortunately, such assistance was restricted to the sciences, and no comparable agency was established to provide for the humanities and social sciences until the late 1950s. By 1960, however, the Canada Council had been established, and as the universities entered the 1960s the prospects for adequate support of scholarship in these early years appeared to be bright.

The 1950s also saw the establishment of learned societies and scholarly journals in most academic disciplines, as well as evidence that shortly the inadequacies resulting from the failure to establish a national library, an adequate national art gallery, and an adequate natural history museum would soon be removed. There was also by 1960 an awareness of the scarcity of adequate research collections in the university libraries, and evidence that at long last a concerted effort would be made to remedy this situation. Nonetheless, the position in 1960 was, in relative terms, almost as unsatisfactory as it had been a century earlier. The achievements of men like J.W. Dawson, John Watson, Léon Gérin, Frederick Banting, Charles Best, Charles Cochrane, and Harold Innis had been achieved through their own efforts rather than as a consequence of the tangible support of the universities or the provincial and federal governments. The inclusion of Innis in this list is a reminder that the willingness of American foundations, particularly Carnegie and Rockefeller, to disregard the Canadian-United States border in their efforts to promote scholarship and research has in the twentieth century been a factor of great importance.

The establishment of the Royal Society of Canada in 1882 set what might be called the seal of approval on scholarship and research at a relatively early stage, but of more significance are the long-range consequences of the particular form in which the society was organized: a single body embracing the arts and sciences, including English-speaking and French-speaking members, and not confined to university professors. This had a unifying effect; it brought together classicists, historians, and physicists, professors from Laval, McGill, Dalhousie, and (in due course) British Columbia, as well as academics, government employees and independent scholars; and in so doing it encouraged a broad rather than a narrow approach to scholarly activity. On the other hand, the decision to function on a sectional basis had the effect of segregating English-speaking and French-speaking classicists or historians, while the methods of admitting new fellows tended to restrict membership to the disciplines which were well established in the nineteenth century. The aims of the society included the encouragement of learned societies throughout Canada and the promotion of scholarship and research on a national scale; but lack of financial resources prevented the society from achieving very much in either of these areas. At the same time, the fact that the Royal Society of Canada existed inhibited the establishment of other national societies based on a single discipline. A half century was to elapse before such a society would be organized (the Canadian Historical Association in 1923), and until the 1950s the number of such bodies could be counted on the fingers of one hand.

By 1960, Canadian higher education was a well-organized system with all the facilities needed to fulfil its national, regional, provincial, and community roles, a statement that could not have been made 10 years earlier. During the 1960s it faced a series of crises: dramatic increases of enrolment; the need to expand into new areas of instruction and research; a radical change in the mood of professors and students with respect not only to the details of courses of study and the relative importance of instruction and research but also to the whole question of how universities should be governed internally; the creation of literally dozens of non-degree-granting institutions resulting in the establishment at the post-secondary level of an alternative system to that represented by the universities; and the consequences of the decision of the provincial governments to assume financial responsibility for all forms of post-secondary education. In 1975 it can be said that the Canadian higher education system of 1960 proved to be capable of adjusting itself to this series of crises. How it did so, and how in the process it drew upon the particular characteristics it had developed over the previous century will be the subject of a second volume of this history covering the period 1961 to 1980.

Appendices

APPENDIX 1

Degrees Granted
by Canadian Universities
1807–1920

FIRST DEGREES GRANTED BY CANADIAN UNIVERSITIES 1807 TO 1920

Notes

1 The degrees are listed by institution for three time periods
 1807 to 1860 (Pages 607–8)
 1861 to 1890 (Pages 609–11)
 1891 to 1920 (Pages 612–21)

2 Commencing with the year 1921, statistics on degrees granted
 by Canadian universities are readily available in Statistics
 Canada (formerly Dominion Bureau of Statistics) publications.

3 The data has been taken either from official records of the
 universities (annual reports, calendars, etc.) or from statements supplied by the registrars of the institutions concerned.

4 First degrees in Theology have not been included.

B.A.

Year	1807	08	09	10	11	12	13	14	15	16	17	18	19	20	21	22	23	24	25	26	27	Total
King's, Windsor	2	–	3	1	3	–	2	2	2	4	–	4	4	2	4	4	3	4	10	4	7	65

B.A.

Year	1807 to 1827	28	29	30	31	32	33	34	35	36	37	38	39	40	41	42	43	44	45	46	47	48	49	50	51	52	53	54	55	56	57	58	59	60	Total
King's, Windsor	65	3	2	2	4	–	8	4	5	4	1	2	–	8	–	2	7	1	3	5	8	3	5	6	2	10	5	3	4	4	6	4	4	1	196
King's, Fredericton		2	–	4	–	6	2	–	–	3	3	3	1	6	–	–	7	4	4	5	–	5	2	8	2	3	10	1	6	3	2	1	4	11	106
Acadia																																			56
King's, Toronto																		1	14	3	6	7	9												40
Toronto																								7	8	8	5	–	9	14	11	13	10	15	100
Queen's																															9	5	10	8	96
Victoria																															3	6	4	13	34
McGill																															3	6	1	4	29
Bishop's																															2	5	1	5	24
Laval																															2	7	4	1	24
Trinity																												7	12	8	10	13	11	7	68
																																			773

B. ès L.

	56	57	58	59	60	Total
Laval	3	1	–	1	–	5

B.Sc.

	56	57	58	59	60	Total
Laval	2	1	–	4	–	7

Canadian Universities: First Degrees, Professional, To 1860

Year	27	28	29	30	31	32	33	34	35	36	37	38	39	40	41	42	43	44	45	46	47	48	49	50	51	52	53	54	55	56	57	58	59	60	Total
LAW																																			
King's, Windsor		1								1	1				1											1				1	1	6	–	–	13
King's, Fredericton				1			1								1																				3
King's, Toronto																					7	–	1												8
Toronto																								1	2		1					6	4	14	28
McGill																								5	1	1		2		3	1	4	8	7	32
Trinity																													4	1	1		1		7
Laval																														3	1	5	2	5	16
																																			107
MEDICINE																																			
McGill							1	3	3	4	–	–			3	7	13	7	1	4	14	17	10	11	12	15	6	15	10	10	15	11	22	24	238
King's, Toronto																			1	–	–														1
Toronto																							3	2		6	1	3		4	1		6		26
Trinity																													1	3	1	3	2	2	12
Laval																												5	–	1	2	4	1	3	16
Queen's																													9	5	10	11	12	11	58
Victoria																													18	19	23	16	20	25	121
																																			479
ENGINEERING																																			
McGill																															1		3	5	9
MUSIC																																			
King's, Toronto																				1	–	–													1

Canadian Universities: First Degrees, Arts and Science, 1861–1890

Year	61	62	63	64	65	66	67	68	69	70	71	72	73	74	75	76	77	78	79	80	81	82	83	84	85	86	87	88	89	90	Total
B.A.																															
King's, Windsor	3	5	6	10	9	6	8	3	1	5	4	5	2	1	2	3	3	2	3	7	5	3	5	9	6	2	6	4	4	5	137
New Brunswick	4	6	8	5	6	7	6	12	10	11	7	5	17	9	13	8	10	9	14	16	17	14	12	17	9	5	10	18	16	3	308
Acadia	1	10	2	10	10	6	6	4	10	7	2	12	12	4	6	7	2	7	13	13	11	9	11	6	7	15	18	14	16	19	261
Toronto	13	18	16	22	22	28	27	21	29	26	23	23	33	25	29	27	42	30	43	54	57	67	78	65	76	68	77	85	78	88	1290
Queen's	15	16	10	11	10	10	7	3	3	7	4	4	4	6	12	9	14	21	7	6	23	17	24	25	22	28	33	16	34	20	438
Victoria	9	9	19	12	9	8	11	15	9	5	21	17	16	12	17	16	16	19	13	32	28	19	26	20	20	18	28	38	18	31	521
McGill	7	4	13	10	6	18	6	9	13	8	10	13	9	16	5	12	13	13	22	23	22	19	24	20	25	27	33	16	22	18	483
Bishop's	1	5	2	2	3	5	5	4	2	4	1	6	2	2	1	5	2	2	3	3	4	8	8	7	2	8	6	2	5	12	123
Laval	1	1	1	3	5	3	4	6	2	7	6	5	4	8	3	5	14	7	15	17	4	8	21	16	20	13	8	14	19	19	321
Trinity	18	7	10	9	9	12	10	1	1	15	1	12	11	2	10	3	11	5	6	10	7	11	7	3	5	5	13	8	14	8	253
Mount Allison			2	5		6	6	4	3	4	2	3	6	3	7	2	6	5	5	3	7	11	3	3	5	5	13	8	12	17	146
Dalhousie						2	9	6	5	4	3	10	6	7	5	8	14	8	5	5	5	12	6	8	13	14	14	15	16	17	223
Albert							4	4	1	1	1	7	4	4	4	5	4	4	8	6	4	3									64
Ottawa							1					2	1	1	1				5	5	5	2	4	4	4	7	2	6	8	5	65
Manitoba																			1	1	5	9	5	11	8	17	18	18	21	23	136
Western																				1											1
St Joseph's																												2	5	2	9
St Francis Xavier																													2	5	7
																															4786
B. ès L.																															
Laval	5			1	1	2		6	7	4	5	3		1	6	7	7	2	2	5	4	6	3	5	2	11	4	2	5	16	127
B.Lit.																															
Ottawa																			1	6	4	4		4	3		2	1			15
Dalhousie																									3						3
St Joseph's																							1								1
																															19
B.Sc.																															
Laval	3	2	3	1	3	6	4	2	1	8	5	5	8	7	4	6		4	4	6	4	10	8	2	3	3	2	9	11	7	155
Mount Allison		1		1										1				1		3			1	2				1			6
Victoria				1										1		1			3	3		2	1	2	3		3	1	1		16

609

Canadian Universities: First Degrees, Arts and Science, 1861-1890

B.Sc.

Year	61	62	63	64	65	66	67	68	69	70	71	72	73	74	75	76	77	78	79	80	81	82	83	84	85	86	87	88	89	90	Total
Queen's	–	–	–	–	–	–	–	–	–	–	–	–	–	–	–	1	2	–	–	–	–	–	–	–	–	–	–	–	–	–	3
Dalhousie	–	–	–	–	–	–	–	–	–	–	–	–	–	–	–	–	–	–	1	1	2	–	–	–	–	–	–	–	–	–	7
New Brunswick	–	–	–	–	–	–	–	–	–	–	–	–	–	–	–	–	–	–	–	–	–	–	–	–	–	–	–	2	–	–	3
Ottawa	–	–	–	–	–	–	–	–	–	–	–	–	–	–	–	–	–	–	–	–	1	–	–	–	–	–	–	–	–	–	1
Halifax	–	–	–	–	–	–	–	–	–	–	–	–	–	–	–	–	–	1	–	–	–	–	–	–	–	–	–	–	–	–	1
																															__192__

Ph.B.

	61	62	63	64	65	66	67	68	69	70	71	72	73	74	75	76	77	78	79	80	81	82	83	84	85	86	87	88	89	90	Total
Mount Allison	–	–	–	–	–	–	–	–	–	–	–	–	–	–	–	–	–	–	–	–	1	–	–	–	–	–	1	–	–	–	2

Canadian Universities: First Degrees, Professional, 1861-1890

LAW

	61	62	63	64	65	66	67	68	69	70	71	72	73	74	75	76	77	78	79	80	81	82	83	84	85	86	87	88	89	90	Total
King's, Windsor	1	–	–	2	1	–	–	–	–	–	–	–	1	1	1	–	–	–	1	–	–	1	–	1	1	1	1	–	2	2	14
New Brunswick	1	–	–	–	–	–	–	–	–	–	–	–	–	–	–	–	–	–	–	–	–	–	–	–	1	1	–	–	2	2	8
Toronto	12	12	6	8	3	3	2	4	5	1	5	9	3	–	2	4	1	4	2	12	7	5	12	1	8	3	6	12	20	–	172
McGill	13	10	17	12	15	11	14	13	16	8	8	7	11	6	10	12	19	26	21	25	22	20	12	12	9	9	5	5	3	7	378
Trinity	–	–	3	–	3	–	–	–	–	–	–	–	–	–	–	–	–	–	2	2	1	1	1	1	8	6	3	1	–	–	32
Laval	5	5	2	3	1	9	4	7	2	5	3	7	7	5	9	5	5	7	10	18	20	27	35	31	22	27	20	14	6	23	344
Queen's	–	–	5	1	–	–	–	–	–	–	–	–	–	–	–	–	–	–	–	–	1	–	1	–	–	1	–	–	3	3	7
Victoria	1	6	1	6	1	3	2	16	11	9	8	2	5	1	3	1	3	2	1	3	–	1	5	3	3	3	1	2	3	3	103
Albert																															13
Bishop's																															26
Dalhousie																			5	3	–			4	4	2	4	10	12	12	72
Manitoba																						1		1	1	1	2	1	1	1	5
																															__1174__

MEDICINE

	61	62	63	64	65	66	67	68	69	70	71	72	73	74	75	76	77	78	79	80	81	82	83	84	85	86	87	88	89	90	Total
McGill	20	23	31	24	33	33	39	35	40	29	26	31	35	31	31	34	19	27	38	31	38	27	30	36	37	47	45	54	37	56	1017
Toronto	6	3	14	19	19	26	15	13	20	19	18	14	17	17	18	13	24	40	39	34	32	30	10	10	14	16	27	61	51	52	691
Trinity	1	–	1	–	–	1	7	23	21	15	29	21	32	36	31	37	60	65	40	63	52	64	75	69	80						874
Laval	1	4	1	1	4	2	6	3	4	6	7	4	14	19	17	13	11	14	10	15	18	13	8	15	5	29	19	24	17	33	337
Queen's	17	18	30	15	16	10	12	14	18	10	12	5	9	6	12	6	11	10	15	14	16	14	13	15	18	38	29	44	37	37	521

Canadian Universities: First Degrees, Professional, 1861-1890

Year	61	62	63	64	65	66	67	68	69	70	71	72	73	74	75	76	77	78	79	80	81	82	83	84	85	86	87	88	89	90	Total
Victoria	26	31	25	46	21	44	60	30	45	15	15	14	4	7	4	5	5	6	3	27	37	20	19	27	35	45	41	42	40	29	763
Bishop's											1	15	4	6	5	2	1	9	8	4	5	7	4	9	4	4	11	5	3	7	114
Dalhousie											5			3	5	1															14
Halifax																			1	-											1
Western																							1	-	1	7	4	8	6	12	39
Manitoba																										7	4	8	6	6	31
																															4402
ENGINEERING																															
McGill	2	1	3	1									6	5	8	3	5	6	-	4	3	8	4	12	7	9	8	11	11	14	131
King's															1	1						1	1	1	1	1	1	1	2		11
Toronto																										1	1	1			3
Laval																									1	1		1	2	5	10
																															155
AGRICULTURE																															
Toronto																												5	6	5	16
DENTISTRY																															
Toronto																													25	29	54
VETERINARY MEDICINE																															
McGill																													47		47
MUSIC																															
Albert															1																1
Trinity																										4	20	26	18	9	77
																															78

Canadian Universities: First Degrees, Arts and Science 1891-1920

Year	91	92	93	94	95	96	97	98	99	00	01	02	03	04
B.A.														
King's, Windsor	3	–	4	8	3	3	7	8	6	3	3	6	3	8
New Brunswick	10	16	12	13	9	12	6	19	7	10	7	14	21	20
Acadia	43	26	21	23	21	28	30	30	23	28	31	24	38	22
Toronto	111	101	129	125	175	153	159	152	164	147	113	130	149	141
Victoria	29	26												
Trinity	15	15	22	22	17	25	23	21	20	15	19	13	14	32
Queen's	24	22	12	35	42	42	44	66	55	47	58	47	64	55
McGill	31	45	42	40	32	36	47	48	45	46	40	33	30	47
Bishop's	4	3	5	7	7	4	14	13	12	13	6	–	11	8
Laval	24	57	27	40	61	51	55	52	79	31	65	52	14	65
Mount Allison	11	6	14	16	15	14	17	20	22	16	16	14	21	23
Dalhousie	24	19	21	27	26	28	34	30	37	32	26	26	23	31
Ottawa	7	9	12	8	5	6	5	5	5	3	5	5	7	5
Manitoba	32	25	39	45	42	38	54	41	53	50	36	56	22	35
Western	–	–	–	–	–	–	–	3	4	6	4	5	4	4
St Joseph's			4	4	6	4	5	6	6	9	2	8	5	5
St Francis Xavier	3	7	5	13	10	9	7	9	10	4	7	10	9	14
McMaster				16	13	16	25	15	20	34	26	29	27	22
Collège Ste Anne												1	4	2
Sacré Coeur														1
Alberta														
Saskatchewan														
British Columbia														
St Mary's														
B. ès. L.														
Laval	27	23	8	24	45	43	24	46	64	15	124	69	3	39

05	06	07	08	09	10	11	12	13	14	15	16	17	18	19	20	Total
6	4	–	11	8	5	4	8	5	8	–	–	–	–	–	–	124
17	16	17	18	14	15	17	22	17	11	8	13	15	9	5	17	405
32	20	25	21	22	33	29	27	30	31	33	33	18	13	22	32	809
183	174	159	193	224	227	216	264	303	296	314	288	225	201	206	271	5693
																55
																273
57	65	90	85	68	85	93	94	151	146	152	104	94	83	108	109	2197
46	46	53	53	59	61	75	75	69	95	78	59	64	47	59	55	1556
10	11	8	11	12	12	7	10	6	8	14	6	6	7	17	15	267
41	51	73	80	68	51	56	70	79	69	74	26	75	103	129	185	1903
22	19	16	22	18	24	22	23	26	16	22	20	12	14	18	25	544
36	36	26	24	36	41	34	34	35	29	40	30	19	27	25	35	891
4	5	4	5	8	5	9	7	6	11	7	11	10	8	13	9	209
44	43	51	46	59	69	61	74	85	86	93	82	85	47	46	86	1625
3	9	5	2	16	8	7	11	7	7	17	18	7	10	7	22	186
3	4	7	3	4	7	1	7	6	8	9	8	6	5	2	11	155
15	15	14	5	6	17	11	16	9	12	12	16	15	25	9	17	331
31	29	22	38	34	45	39	37	48	35	45	43	27	16	32	39	803
–	–	7	–	9	3	–	2	1	5	3	3	3	1	3	2	49
–	3	–	1	–	–	2	3	6	5	5	–	–	–	–	–	26
						2	17	8	22	33	25	11	21	22	36	197
							7	21	20	32	37	31	34	16	29	227
											40	34	34	47	50	205
													2	1	2	5
																18735
62	37	46	56	32	22	29	20	24	40	36	38	47	9	35	20	1112

Canadian Universities: First Degrees, Arts and Science 1891-1920

Year	91	92	93	94	95	96	97	98	99	00	01	02	03	04
B.L.														
Ottawa	1	–	–	–	–	1	–	–	–	–	–	–	–	–
Dalhousie	2	1	1	1	2	3	1	1	2	1	1	–	–	–
St Joseph's							1	–	–	–	–	–	–	–
Sacré Coeur														
St Francis Xavier														
B.Sc.														
Laval	16	39	11	29	44	21	34	30	57	18	42	14	7	25
Mount Allison														
Victoria		5												
Dalhousie	–	1	2	1	2	2	3	2	1	4	5	4	5	1
New Brunswick	–	–	–	1	–	1	1	–	–	–	1	2	1	–
Ottawa	–	–	–	–	–	–	1	–	–	–	–	–	–	–
King's	2	–	1	–	1	1	–	–	–	1	–	–	–	–
McGill										1	–	–	–	1
St Joseph's														1
St Francis Xavier														
Acadia														
Sacré Coeur														
Alberta														
Saskatchewan														
Manitoba														
B.Comm.														
McGill														
B. ès Sciences Appliques														
Laval														
B. ès Arts Appliquées														
Laval								12	5	1	8	1	5	2

05	06	07	08	09	10	11	12	13	14	15	16	17	18	19	20	Total
–	1	1	–	2	–	–	–	–	3	1	–	–	–	1	–	11
–	–	–	–	–	–	–	–	–	–	–	–	–	–	–	–	16
–	1	–	–	1	–	2	1	2	–	2	8	3	3	1	2	27
			1													1
					1	–	1									2
																57

05	06	07	08	09	10	11	12	13	14	15	16	17	18	19	20	Total
68	25	33	36	48	49	37	53	49	29	34	28	42	57	28	14	1017
													1	1	2	4
																5
5	2	1	2	–	2	2	2	4	1	3	2	–	1	1	1	62
1	–	–	–	–	–	–	–	–	–	–	–	–	–	–	1	9
–	–	–	–	–	–	–	–	–	–	–	–	–	–	1	–	2
–	1	–	1	1	–	–	1	–	–	–	–	–	–	–	–	10
1	4	2	2	3	–	1	–	–	–	3	–	–	1	2	10	31
–	–	–	–	1	–	–	–	–	–	–	–	–	–	–	–	2
3	–	–	–	–	1	–	1	–	–	1	–	–	–	2	1	9
		1	2	5	3	5	6	4	–	–	–	2	1	1	1	31
				1	1	–	–	–	–	–	–	–	–	–	–	2
						1	1	1	–	1	–	1	1	4	5	15
								1	2	1	1	1	3	1	4	14
								1	–	–	1	2	2	5	1	12
																1225

05	06	07	08	09	10	11	12	13	14	15	16	17	18	19	20	Total
										3	4	–	–	1	8	16

05	06	07	08	09	10	11	12	13	14	15	16	17	18	19	20	Total
							6	2	4	2	1	3	5	1	1	25

05	06	07	08	09	10	11	12	13	14	15	16	17	18	19	20	Total
4	2	5	–	10	16	24	9	8	6	21	–	3	8	2	1	153

Year	91	92	93	94	95	96	97	98	99	00	01	02	03	04
LAW														
King's	–	–	–	–	4	–	4	3	3	–	4	4	1	1
New Brunswick	–	1	–	–	–	–	–	–	–	2	–	–	–	–
Toronto	14	15	11	8	18	22	14	3	4	2	6	6	4	12
McGill	4	2	10	9	9	9	18	10	12	18	17	9	13	14
Trinity	3	4	4	2	5	9	4	5	6	4	4	1	–	4
Laval	11	26	12	29	65	19	21	15	46	16	26	31	13	28
Queen's	–	3	1	3	3	4	–	1	–	–	–	–	–	1
Victoria	7	1	–	–	1									
Dalhousie	13	19	21	11	13	13	14	23	23	10	12	12	6	16
Manitoba	2	–	–	2	2	2	2	3	1	3	–	5	3	6
Ottawa					2	–	–	–	–	–	–	1	–	–
Alberta														
Saskatchewan														
Montréal														
MUSIC														
Trinity	12	8	10	3	6	6	5	2	2	3	2	5	–	2
Toronto			2	1	–	5	–	2	3	3	–	3	1	–
Bishop's				1	–	–	1	–	2	–	–	–	–	–
McGill														
Dalhousie														
Mount Allison														
ARCHITECTURE														
Toronto		1	3	1	2	–	3	1	–	–	–	–	1	–
McGill									3	–	–	–	–	–
Alberta														
Manitoba														
Montréal														
PHARMACY														
Toronto		23	50	33	39	68	52	51	62	34	57	51	53	53
Trinity						1	–	–	–	–	–	–	–	–

05	06	07	08	09	10	11	12	13	14	15	16	17	18	19	20	Total
3	3	5	3	6	6	6	4	3	-	-	-	-	-	-	-	63
-	-	-	-	-	-	-	-	-	-	-	-	-	-	-	-	3
19	12	10	10	21	11	13	16	12	9	11	9	7	2	1	2	304
8	11	7	9	7	14	17	16	16	18	13	15	9	13	10	28	365
																55
6	11	16	17	12	17	18	15	32	23	36	3	18	25	29	3	639
-	-	-	-	-	-	-	-	-	-	-	-	-	-	-	-	16
																9
13	13	11	17	13	11	10	12	12	18	20	12	9	5	6	12	400
15	8	12	13	9	8	10	7	16	16	16	12	15	29	17	38	272
-	-	-	-	-	-	-	-	-	-	-	-	-	-	-	-	3
									8	6	10	15	7	2	5	53
										8	8	7	5	7	5	40
														9	31	40
																2262
																66
-	1	-	5	5	6	2	1	3	2	2	2	4	1	2	-	56
-	1	-	-	-	-	-	-	-	-	-	-	1	-	-	-	6
					1	2	-	1	1	-	1	1	2	-	1	10
										4	1	2	4	1	2	14
												1	-	-	-	1
																153
-	3	2	2	-	4	6	-	7	5	7	2	2	-	-	4	56
-	1	2	3	2	4	4	8	-	5	8	9	1	1	1	4	56
												1	-	-	-	1
													1	1		2
															3	3
																118
45	25	28	36	37	33	34	34	39	35	41	36	28	18	19	88	1202
																1

Year	91	92	93	94	95	96	97	98	99	00	01	02	03	04
PHARMACY														
Laval														
Manitoba														
Montréal														
HOUSEHOLD SCIENCE														
Toronto														
Laval														
Manitoba														
Alberta														
Montréal														
FORESTRY														
Toronto														
New Brunswick														
Laval														
MEDICINE														
McGill	50	55	46	56	53	91	76	72	66	76	92	82	100	86
Toronto	55	66	54	59	65	59	39	56	53	55	54	56	83	113
Trinity	72	59	80	68	71	65	74	52	69	71	59	40	58	50
Laval	14	18	22	21	21	17	18	20	20	11	32	37	19	43
Queen's	43	35	24	20	25	24	27	34	25	21	24	31	49	41
Victoria	16													
Bishop's	4	11	5	9	4	4	8	1	6	9	9	7	4	9
Dalhousie	2	6	6	3	7	5	10	9	13	13	11	21	22	15
Western	10	21	4	12	11	6	17	16	20	12	15	17	22	20
Manitoba	6	10	12	17	28	17	25	19	13	18	11	18	18	15
Montréal														
ENGINEERING														
McGill	11	17	18	23	30	33	41	42	41	36	40	30	41	53
King's	–	–	–	1	2	–	1	1	2	1	–	–	–	–
Toronto	–	1	10	12	11	9	5	9	6	10	20	15	16	19
Laval	3	3	7	2	–	5	–	25	14	4	22	7	17	13

05	06	07	08	09	10	11	12	13	14	15	16	17	18	19	20	Total
			3	–	2	2	4	3	–	2	9	8	9	7	–	49
			1	–	–	–	–	–	–	–	–	–	–	3	–	4
														7	13	20
																1276
	2	4	2	–	–	–	–	–	–	–	–	–	–	–	–	8
						8	9	14	5	7	1	–	–	–	–	44
													6	4	5	15
														1		1
															3	3
																71
				1	2	4	9	11	7	7	8	3	3	3	4	62
					4	2	2	3	2	4	5	1	–	5	9	37
							7	11	11	8	3	7	3	6	4	60
																159
79	95	73	68	72	83	35	55	62	68	52	39	63	73	65	49	2032
175	105	116	138	113	149	148	29	67	90	114	95	101	79	57	78	2521
																888
20	18	21	23	28	26	25	19	19	9	21	23	20	18	66	18	687
39	52	32	48	39	35	49	23	11	27	19	34	13	12	14	58	928
																16
11	1															102
12	13	4	11	8	9	16	10	7	15	12	12	14	2	4	4	296
20	27	31	20	34	22	26	42	28	27	13	10	18	15	18	12	566
31	30	30	25	36	3	19	18	28	43	29	18	32	32	30	26	657
															38	38
																8731
43	64	62	89	82	108	100	97	106	115	84	58	42	25	30	79	1640
2	–	–	–	3	2	–	–	–	–	–	–	–	–	–	–	15
24	28	31	50	67	64	99	129	106	151	169	84	52	37	38	97	1368
16	14	28	30	31	33	43	55	63	41	40	23	17	34	19	2	611

Canadian Universities: First Degrees, Professional, 1891-1920

Year	91	92	93	94	95	96	97	98	99	00	01	02	03	04
ENGINEERING														
New Brunswick		1	6	3	–	1	1	1	1	3	1	6	4	6
Queen's							2	3	1	4	3	14	18	14
Dalhousie														
Nova Scotia Tech.														
Manitoba														
Alberta														
Saskatchewan														
British Columbia														
Montréal														
AGRICULTURE														
Toronto	10	7	8	9	8	10	7	11	9	18	1	7	16	21
McGill														
Manitoba														
Laval														
Saskatchewan														
Alberta														
Montréal														
DENTISTRY														
Toronto	19	11	18	27	34	39	35	51	72	72	27	30	53	56
Trinity			1	3	8	1	1	2	1	1	1	10	3	11
Bishop's						9	7	–	5	6	16	3	–	–
McGill														
Laval														
Dalhousie														
Alberta														
Montréal														
VETERINARY MEDICINE														
McGill	22	16	15	20	11	11	11	12	6	4	3	8	3	–
Laval			6	8	3	–	6	–	2	–	–	4	–	7
Queen's								1	–	–	–	–	–	–
Toronto														
Montréal														

05	06	07	08	09	10	11	12	13	14	15	16	17	18	19	20	Total
11	14	13	10	3	16	10	16	20	15	17	6	3	5	1	4	198
21	19	35	34	43	42	42	67	59	52	42	26	28	13	11	31	614
1	1	4	6	7	-	-	1	-	-	-	-	1	-	1	-	22
					9	11	7	13	11	11	10	2	5	-	12	91
						9	9	6	12	5	9	5	-	-	3	58
								5	2	5	8	-	1	-	7	28
											3	-	-	-	-	3
												1	-	1	9	11
															10	10
																4679
30	21	19	33	24	30	41	44	43	43	54	50	33	33	24	59	723
						15	20	19	20	19	17	12	11	2	15	150
						10	6	-	-	-	72	7	8	7	10	120
						3	4	8	12	15	14	30	15	35	8	144
										1	2	5	4	4	3	19
													7	5	6	18
															18	18
																1192
62	51	24	41	57	43	48	43	48	47	51	43	72	67	94	116	1451
																43
																46
		3	-	2	4	3	4	8	9	3	11	5	9	15		76
						22	15	16	4	11	14	19	19	3	1	134
							3	2	4	2	3	2	-	-	2	18
											1	-	-	-		1
															36	36
																1805
-	-	-	-	-	-	-	-	-	-	-	-	-	-	-	-	142
3	-	3	14	7	5	13	10	11	11	11	11	11	24	7	-	177
-	-	-	-	-	-	-	-	-	-	-	-	-	-	-	-	1
				10	67	51	18	10	10	11	9	8	12	9	5	220
															5	5
																545

Enrolment in Canadian Universities in Census Years 1861–1911

Enrolment in Canadian Universities 1861-62[1]

	Arts & Science[2]	Medicine	Law	Pharmacy	Other	Total
Acadia	37					37
Bishop's	16			4		20
King's College, Windsor	39[3]					39
Laval	Part-time only	35	26	6		67
McGill	51	148	42		Engineering 8	249
Mount Allison	10[3]					10
New Brunswick	32					32
Queen's	39	85	7			131
St Mary's	Not known					–
Toronto	260				Engineering 7 Agriculture 2	269
Trinity	39					39
Victoria	97	93				190
	620	361	75	10	17	1083

1 Not included: students in theology; Toronto School of Medicine 93
2 Includes graduate students; no distinction made between matriculated and non-matriculated (special – often – part-time) students
3 Approximate figure

Enrolment in Canadian Universities, 1871-72[1]

	Arts & Science[2]	Medicine	Law	Other	Total
Acadia	37				37
Albert	51[3]				51
Bishop's	18	25 (Montreal)			43
Dalhousie (1870-71)	61	26			87
King's College, Windsor	20[4]				20
Laval	108	71	24		209
McGill	115	150	58	Pharmacy 6	323
Mount Allison	25				25
New Brunswick	51[5]				51
Ottawa	10[5]				10
Queen's	33	6			39
St Francis Xavier	22				22
St Joseph's	Not known				–
St Mary's	44				44
Toronto (University College)	263			Agriculture 3 Engineering 1	267
Trinity	69	57			126
Victoria	85	92 (Montreal) 25 (Toronto)	5		207
	1012	452	87	10	1561

1 Not included: students in theology; Toronto School of Medicine (affiliated with the University of Toronto) not known; Ontario Veterinary College 29
2 Includes graduate students: Acadia 1; Bishop's 13; Toronto 10
3 Some students at Albert may have been registered in law, engineering, or music
4 Includes students with B.A. and students in final 2 years at Petit Séminaire de Québec
5 Approximate figure

Enrolment in Canadian Universities 1881-82[1]

	Arts & Science[2] M	Arts & Science W	Medicine M	Medicine W	Law M	Other M	Totals M	Totals W	Totals T
Acadia	52	6					52	6	58
Albert	113	5					113	5	118
Bishop's	28		53		11		92		92
Dalhousie	114	2					114	2	116
King's College, Windsor	40						40		40
Laval, Montreal			49		80	Pharmacy 49	178		178
Laval, Quebec	83[3]		68		73	Pharmacy 7	231		231
Manitoba	65						65		65
McGill	165		152		62	Engineering 44	423		423
Mount Allison	34	14					34	14	48
New Brunswick	44						44		44
Ottawa	29						29		29
Queen's	176	8	61	1	3		240	9	249
St Francis Xavier	Not known								-
St Joseph's	Not known[4]								-
St Mary's[5]									
Toronto (University College)	355						355		355
Trinity	92		136				228		228
Victoria	138	5	111(Montreal) 32(Toronto)	1	21		302	6	308
Western Ontario	15						15		15
	1543	40	662	2	250	100	2555	42	2597

1 Not included: students in theology; Ecole polytechnique, Montréal; Montréal and Montreal Veterinary College not known; Ontario Agricultural College, Guelph 112; Ontario College of Pharmacy, Toronto 62; Ontario Veterinary College, Toronto 40; Royal College of Dental Surgeons, Toronto 34; Royal Military College 88; School of Practical Science, Toronto 73; Toronto School of Medicine, not known

2 Includes graduate students: Bishop's 3; Toronto 13; Manitoba 5

3 Includes students with B.A. and students in final 2 years at Petit Séminaire de Québec

4 Students at St Joseph's numbered 136 but include students at secondary level

5 Classes were suspended at St Mary's from 1881 to 1903

Enrolment in Canadian Universities 1891-92[1]

Institution	Arts & Science M	Arts & Science W	Medicine M	Medicine W	Law M	Law W	Applied Science & Engineering M	Other M	Graduate Studies[2] M	Graduate Studies[2] W	Totals M	Totals W	Total
Acadia	96	22									96	22	118
Bishop's	23		68	7					2		93	7	100
Dalhousie	139	128	38	3	67		27			1	271	132	403
King's College, Windsor	15										15		15
Laval, Montreal[3]	Not known		Not known	Not known	Not known	Not known	14				14		14
Laval, Quebec	Not known		81		41				14		141		141
Manitoba	177	19	92	2				Pharm. 5			269	21	290
McGill	318	134	288		31		126		8		771	134	905
McMaster	35	4									35	4	39
Mount Allison	77	30									77	30	107
New Brunswick	40	23					12		2		54	23	77
Ottawa	50[4]										50		50
Queen's	206	44	120	16[5]	3				18		347	60	407
St Francis Xavier	136										136		136
St Joseph's[6]													–
St Mary's[7]													–
Toronto[8]	554	123	286		131	2	89	Agric. 159; Dent. 66; Pharm. 97	9		1391	125	1516
Trinity[9]	107	11	208	12	35						350	23	373
Western			58								58		58
	1973	538	1239	40	308	2	268	327	53	1	4168	581	4749

1 Not included: students in theology; Ontario Medical College for Women 11; Ontario Veterinary College 153; Osgoode Hall Law School 197; Royal Military College 56

2 Some of these would have been taking theological degrees. The graduate student at Dalhousie was a woman and a few other graduate students may have been women

3 Includes students at affiliated École polytechnique

4 Approximate figure   5 Students enrolled at affiliated Kingston Medical College for Women

6 Students at St Joseph's numbered 198 but include students at secondary level

7 Classes were suspended at St Mary's from 1881 to 1903

8 Includes students enrolled at affiliated Ontario Agricultural College, Ontario College of Pharmacy, Royal College of Dental Surgeons, School of Practical Science

9 Excludes students registered in music

	Arts & Science		Medicine		Law	Applied Science & Engineering
	M	W	M	W	M	M
Acadia	96	26				
Bishop's	33		56			
Collège Ste Anne	Not known					
Dalhousie	160	55	81	7	42	
King's College, Windsor	26	3				
Laval, Montreal[2]	96[3]		223		114	39
Laval, Quebec	65[3]		97		84	
Manitoba	148	42	99		11	
McGill	176	121	420		47	251
McGill College, B.C.	4	1				
McMaster	109	17				
Mount Allison	74	46				
New Brunswick	86[4]	30				13
Ottawa	60[4]					
Queen's	343	117	185			105 (Kingston School of Mines)
Sacré Coeur	Not known					
St Francis Xavier	82	8				
St Joseph's[5]						
St Mary's[6]						
Toronto[7]	543	254	474			290
Trinity[8]	41	19	69	18	9	
Western	42	1	84			
	2184	740	1788	25	307	698

1 Not included: students in theology; Ontario Medical College for Women; Osgoode Hall Law School 145; Royal Military College 86
2 Includes students at Ecole polytechnique, Ecole de médecine vétérinaire
3 Students at Petit Séminaire de Québec
4 Approximate figure
5 Students at St Joseph's numbered 210 but include students at secondary level
6 Classes were suspended at St Mary's from 1881 to 1903
7 Includes students at affiliated OAC, OCP, OVC, RCDS
8 Excludes 81 students registered in music

Veterinary Medicine	Other		Graduate Studies		Totals		
M	M	W	M	W	M	W	Total
					96	26	122
			4		93		93
							–
					283	62	345
					26	3	29
17					489		489
	Pharm. 7		27		280		280
					258	42	300
15			3	8	912	129	1041
					4	1	5
			9		118	17	135
			4	·	78	46	124
					99	30	129
					60		60
			16	8	649	125	774
							–
					82	8	90
							–
							–
70	Agric. 290						
	Dent. 150						
	Pharm. 116 M						
	3 W		37	14	1970	271	2241
					119	37	156
					126	1	127
102	563	3	100	30	5742	798	6540

Enrolment in Canadian Universities 1911-12[1]

	Arts & Science		Medicine		Law	Applied Science & Engineering	Vet. Med.	Agric.
	M	W	M	W		M	M	M
Acadia	139	50				38		
Alberta	113	28				41		
Bishop's	23							
Brandon College	37	21						
Collège Ste Anne	Not known							
Dalhousie	205	81	69	3	60			
King's College, Windsor	52	5						
Laval, Montreal[2]	14	23	162		145	151	42	82
Laval, Quebec	79		77		83	24 (Ecole d'Arpentage)		
Manitoba	316	98	136	6	47	53		48
McGill[3]	338	135	337		59	453		199
McGill Univ. College, B.C.	96	63				39		
McMaster	127	50						
Mount Allison	78	84				28		
New Brunswick	128	29				80		
Nova Scotia Technical College						32		
Ottawa	103							
Queen's	565	316	256			330 (Kingston School of Mines)		
Sacré Coeur	Not known							
St Francis Xavier	214	6						
St Joseph's[4]	50							
St Mary's	6							
Saskatchewan	122	28						
Toronto[5]	1242	653	455	15		793	74	492
Western	67	12	125					
	4114	1682	1617	24	394	2062	116	821

1 Not included: students in theology; Ecole d'enseignement supérieure pour les jeunes filles 440; Hautes Etudes Commerciales 41; Okanagan College (Arts) 7M, 1W; Osgoode Hall Law School 292; Royal Military College 118
2 Includes students at Ecole polytechnique, Ecole de médecine vétérinaire, Oka (Agriculture)
3 Includes students at Macdonald College (Education and Household Science)
4 Figures are for 1912-13, the first year when separate figures are available for secondary and college level students
5 Includes students at affiliated OAC, OCP, OVC, RCDS

Dentistry		Pharm.	For.	House. Sci.		Education		Graduate Studies	Totals		
M	W			W		M	W	W	M	W	Total
							2		179	50	229
							2	1	156	29	185
							5	1	28	1	29
									37	21	58
											–
17									351	84	435
									52	5	57
114	1	97							807	24	831
		5	40				15		323		323
									600	104	704
				134	6	140	96	14	1488	423	1911
									135	63	198
							37	7	164	57	221
							5	2	111	86	197
			15						223	29	252
									32		32
									103		103
					25	31	27	13	1203	360	1563
											–
									214	6	220
									50		50
									6		6
									122	28	150
199		104	40	236 (OAC)							
				134 (Tor.)							
					126	179	102	13	3627	1230	4857
									192	12	204
330	1	206	95	504	157	350	291	51	10203	2612	12815

Bibliography

CANADIAN UNIVERSITIES

General

Harris, R.S., and Tremblay, A. *A Bibliography of Higher Education in Canada*, Toronto: University of Toronto Press, 1960

Harris, R.S. *Supplement 1965 and Supplement 1971 to A Bibliography of Higher Education in Canada*, Toronto: University of Toronto Press 1965, 1971

Harris, R.S., De Grandpré M. et al., 'Select Bibliography of Higher Education in Canada' in successive issues of *Stoa: The Canadian Journal of Higher Education* I (1971) to V, 1 (May 1975)

Conference of Canadian Universities. *Proceedings.* 1911-16

National Conference of Canadian Universities. *Proceedings.* 1917-58. Hereafter referred to as *NCCU Proceedings*

National Conference of Canadian Universities and Colleges. *Proceedings.* 1959-61. Hereafter referred to as *NCCUC Proceedings*

Association of Universities and Colleges of Canada. *Proceedings.* 1965- . Hereafter referred to as *AUCC Proceedings*

Ashby, E. *Community of Universities: an Informal Portrait of the Association of Universities of the British Commonwealth.* Cambridge: Cambridge University Press, 1963

Bissell, C.T., editor. *Canada's Crisis in Higher Education.* Toronto: University of Toronto Press, 1957

Burpee, L.J. 'Canada's Debt to the Carnegie Corporation,' *Queen's Quarterly*, 45 (1938), 232-7

Commission of Inquiry on Forty Church-Related Colleges and Universities. *Report* ... Ottawa: National Education Office of the Canadian Catholic Conference, 1970

Dawson, J.W. *The Duties of Educated Young Men in British North America.* Montreal: Lovell, 1864

Dawson, J.W. *The Future of McGill.* Montreal, 1881

Dawson, J.W. *The University in Relation to Professional Education.* Montreal: Gazette, 1887

Dunton, A.D., and Patterson, D., editors. *Canada's Universities in a New Age.* Ottawa: National Conference of Canadian Universities and Colleges, 1962

Falconer, R.A. 'American Influence on the Higher Education of Canada,' *Transactions of the Royal Society of Canada.* 1930. Section 2, 23-8

Falconer, R.A. 'English Influence on the Higher Education of Canada,' *Transactions of the Royal Society of Canada.* 1928. Section 2, 33-48

Falconer, R.A. 'Irish Influence on Higher Education in Canada,' *Transactions of the Royal Society of Canada.* 1935. Section 2, 131-43

Falconer, R.A. 'Scottish Influence on the Higher Education of Canada,' *Transactions of the Royal Society of Canada.* 1927. Section 2, 7-20

Harris, R.S. 'The Universities of Canada,' *Commonwealth Universities Yearbook, 1975.* London: Association of Universities of the Commonwealth, 1975. 799-813

Harris, R.S., editor. *Changing Patterns of Higher Education in Canada.* Toronto: University of Toronto Press, 1966

Kirkconnell, W. 'The Universities of Canada,' *Universities Review,* 20 (1948), 153-64

Lord, W.F. 'Degree-Granting Institutions in Canada,' *Nineteenth Century and After,* 61 (1907), 262-71

Lower, A.R.M. 'The Canadian University,' *Transactions of the Royal Society of Canada.* 1953. Section 2, 1-16

Masters, D.C. *Protestant Church Colleges in Canada.* Toronto: University of Toronto Press, 1966

Mitchener, R.D. 'Junior Colleges in Canada,' *Junior College Journal,* 30 (1960), 400-12

Murray, W.C. 'State Support and Control of Universities in Canada,' *Transactions of the Royal Society of Canada.* 1925. Section 2, 19-32

Murray, W.C. 'University Development in Canada,' *Transactions of the Royal Society of Canada.* 1922. Section 2, 77-105

'Official Report of the Allied Colonial Universities Conference ...,' *Empire Review,* 6 (August 1903), 65-128

Ontario, Department of Education. *The Universities of Canada, Their History and Organization, with an Outline of British and American University Systems.* Toronto: Warwick & Rutter, 1896

Pilkington, G. 'A History of the National Conference of Canadian Universities, 1911-1951.' Unpublished Ph.D. thesis, University of Toronto, 1974

Sheffield, E.F. 'Canadian University and College Enrolment Projected to 1965,' *NCCU Proceedings* (1955), 39-46

Sheffield, E.F. 'The Post-War Surge in Post-Secondary Education' in J.D. Wilson, et al., editors. *Canadian Education: a History.* Toronto: Prentice-Hall, 1970

Shook. L.K. *Catholic Post-Secondary Education in English-Speaking Canada.* Toronto: University of Toronto Press, 1971

'The Universities and Higher Educational System of Canada' in J.C. Hopkins, editor. *Canada: an Encyclopaedia of the Country.* Toronto, 1894. IV, 169-344

Wallace, R.C. 'The Universities of Canada' in E. Bradby, editor. *The Universities outside Europe.* London: Oxford University Press, 1939. 115-36

Whalley, G., editor. *A Place of Liberty.* Toronto: Clarke, Irwin, 1964

The Maritime Universities

Bailey, A.G. 'Creative Moments in the Culture of the Maritime Provinces,' *Dalhousie Review,* 29 (1959), 231-44

Crean, J.F., et al. *Higher Education in the Atlantic Provinces for the 1970's.* A Study Prepared under the Auspices of the Association of Atlantic Universities for the Maritime Union Study. Halifax: the Association, 1969

Learned, W.S., and Sills, K.C.M. *Education in the Maritime Provinces of Canada.* New York: Carnegie Foundation for the Advancement of Teaching, 1922

Lester, R.M. *Review of Grants in the Maritime Provinces of Canada and Newfoundland, 1911-1933.* New York: Carnegie Corporation, 1934

MacNutt, W.S. 'The Universities of the Maritimes - a Glance Backwards,' *Dalhousie Review,* 53 (1973), 431-48

Murray, W.C. 'College Union in the Maritime Provinces,' *Dalhousie Review,* 2 (1923), 410-24

Rimmington, G.T. 'The Universities of the Atlantic Provinces,' *Canadian Geographical Journal,* 73 (August 1966), 38-49

The Universities of Quebec

Audet, F.-J. 'Simon Sanguinet et le projet d'université de 1790,' *Mémoirs de la Société Royale de Canada.* 1936. Section 1, 53-60

Audet, L.-P. *Histoire de l'enseignement au Québec, 1608-1971.* 2 volumes. Montréal: Holt, Rinehart et Winston, 1971

Audet, L.-P. *Le Système scolaire de la Province de Québec.* 6 volumes. Québec: Editions de l'Erable (I, III, IV), Les Presses de l'Université Laval (II, V, VI), 1950-6

Audet, L.-P., et Gauthier, A. *Le Système scolaire du Québec: organisation et fonctionment.* 2nd edition. Montréal: Beauchemin, 1969

Beetz, J. et al. *La Crise de l'enseignement au Canada Français: urgence d'une reforme.* Montréal: Editions du Jour, 1961

Chauveau, P.-J.-O. *L'Instruction publique au Canada.* Québec: Augustine Coté, 1876

Gosselin, A.-H. *L'Instruction au Canada sous le régime français, 1635-1760.* Québec: Laflamme et Proulx, 1911

Groulx, L. *L'Enseignement français au Canada I: Dans le Québec.* 2nd edition. Montréal: Granger Frères, 1934

Lavallée, A. *Québec contre Montréal: la querelle universitaire 1876-1891.* Montréal: Les Presses de l'Université de Montréal, 1974

Lebel, M. 'Recent Reforms in Education in Quebec,' *Canadian Education,* 13, 3 (June 1958), 35-47

'Lettre de Monseigneur Hubert en réponse au Président de Comité nommé pour l'execution d'une Université mixte en Canada. 18 Novembre, 1789' in H. Têtu and C.-O. Gagnon, editors. *Mandements lettres pastorales et circulaires des Evêques de Québec.* Québec: A. Coté, 1888. II, 385-96

Lortie, L. 'L'Orientation nouvelle des universités Québécoises de langue française' in G. Stanley and G. Sylvestre, editors. *Canadian Universities Today.* Toronto: University of Toronto Press, 1961, 55-66

Martin, J.-M. 'Quebec' in R.S. Harris, editor. *Changing Patterns in Higher Education in Canada.* Toronto: University of Toronto Press, 1966

Meilleur, J.-B. *Mémorial de l'éducation du Bas-Canada, 1615-1855.* Montréal: J.B. Rolland, 1860

Parent, A.-M. 'L'Enseignement superieur dans la Province de Québec' in J.E. Hodgetts, editor. *Higher Education in a Changing Canada*. Toronto: University of Toronto Press, 1966. 14-24

Pouliot, L. 'L'Enseignement universitaire catholique au Canada Français de 1760 à 1860,' *Revue d'Histoire de l'Amerique Française*, 12 (1958), 155-69

Quebec Legislative Council. *Report of a Committee of the Council on the subject of Promoting the Means of Education/Rapport du Comité du Conseil, sur l'Objet D'Augmenter Les Moiens d'Education*. Québec: Samuel Nelson, 1790

Royal Commission of Inquiry on Education in the Province of Quebec. *Report* ... 5 volumes. Quebec: Queen's Printer, 1963-6

Trudel, M. *Histoire de la Nouvelle France*. Montréal: Fides, 1963

The Universities of Ontario

Bissell, C.T. 'Ontario' in R.S. Harris, editor. *Changing Patterns of Higher Education in Canada*. Toronto: University of Toronto Press, 1966. 87-106

Committee of Presidents of Universities of Ontario. *System Emerging: First Annual Review 1966-67*. Toronto: the Committee, 1967

Harris, R.S. 'The Evolution of a Provincial System of Higher Education in Ontario' in D.F. Dadson, editor. *On Higher Education: Five Lectures*. Toronto: University of Toronto Press, 1966. 36-62

Harris, R.S. 'The Universities of Ontario,' *Canadian Geographical Journal*, 70 (January 1965), 2-19

Hodgins, J.G., editor. *Documentary History of Education in Upper Canada (Ontario) from 1791-1876*. 28 volumes. Toronto: Warwick & Rutter, 1894-1910

Moir, J.S. *Church and State in Canada West: Three Studies in the Relation of Denominationalism and Nationalism*. Toronto: University of Toronto Press, 1959

Ontario, Department of Public Records and Archives. *The College Question: Being the Debate of the Legislative Assembly of Ontario, on December 2, 1868, on the Outlying Colleges and Sectarian Grants*. Reported by J.K. Edwards. Toronto, 1869

Royal Commission on University Finances. *Report* ... 2 volumes. Toronto: King's Printer, 1921

Stewart, E.E. 'The Role of the Provincial Government in the Development of Universities in Ontario.' Unpublished Ed.D. thesis, University of Toronto, 1970

Wright, D. 'Recent Developments in Higher Education in Ontario' in W.R. Niblett and R.F. Butts, editors. *World Yearbook of Education*. London: Evans Bros., 1972, 297-309

The Universities of the West

Craik, W.A. 'University Development in Western Canada,' *Canadian Magazine*, 42 (1913), 421-8

Gordon, J.M. 'The Prairie Universities,' *Canadian Geographical Journal*, 71 (October 1967), 112-25

Johnson, F.H. 'The Universities of British Columbia,' *Canadian Geographical Journal*, 73 (December 1966), 182-93

Macdonald, J.B. *Higher Education in British Columbia and a Plan for the Future*. Vancouver: University of British Columbia, 1962

Macdonald, J.B. 'The West' in R.S. Harris, editor. *Changing Patterns of Higher Education in Canada*. Toronto: University of Toronto Press, 1966. 41-60

Thomas, L.G. 'The Church of England and Higher Education in the Prairie West before 1914,' *Journal of the Canadian Church History Society*, 3 (1956), 1-11

Wesbrook, F.F. 'The Provincial University in Canadian Development,' *Science* (U.S.) 39 (1914), 407-17

The Federal Government and Higher Education

Gelley, T.F. 'Khaki University,' *Food for Thought*, 9, 7 (April 1949), 29-34

MacKenzie, N.A.M. 'Universities, Colleges and Federal Grants,' *Dalhousie Review*, 42 (1962), 5-17

MacKenzie, N.A.M., and Rowat, D.C. 'The Federal Government and Higher Education in Canada,' *Canadian Journal of Economics and Political Science*, 16 (1950), 353-70

Miller, J.C. *National Government and Technical Education in Federated Democracies: Dominion of Canada*. Philadelphia: the author, 1940

Nicholson, N.L. 'The Federal Government and Canadian Universities: a Review,' *Stoa: Canadian Journal of Higher Education*, 3, 1 (1973), 17-28

Royal Commission on National Development in the Arts, Letters and Sciences. *Report*. Ottawa; King's Printer, 1951

Sheffield, E.F. 'Canadian Government Aid to Universities,' *Vestes* (Australia), 3, 2 (June 1960), 20-5

Stager, D.A.A. 'The Evolution of Federal Government Financing of Canadian Universities,' *Stoa: Canadian Journal of Higher Education*, 2, 1 (1972), 23-9

Stager, D.A.A. 'Federal Government Grants to Canadian Universities,' *Canadian Historical Review*, 54 (1973), 287-97

Tory, H.M. 'A Khaki University for Canadian Soldiers,' *University Magazine*, 16 (1917), 600-18

Non-Degree-Granting Institutions

Campbell, G. *Community Colleges in Canada*. Toronto: Ryerson/McGraw Hill, 1971

MacLean, J.S. 'Some Notes Relating to the Place of the Junior Colleges in our Educational System,' *NCCU Proceedings* (1925), 30-3

Mitchener, R.D. 'Junior Colleges in Canada,' *Junior College Journal*, 30 (1960), 400-12

Murray, W.C. 'The Junior College Idea in Canada,' *NCCU Proceedings* (1925), 27-30

Royal Commission on Industrial Training and Technical Education. *Report*. 3 volumes. Ottawa: King's Printer, 1913

Stamp, R.M. 'Technical Education, the National Policy and Federal-Provincial Relations in Canadian Education,' *Canadian Historical Review*, 52 (1971), 404-23

Individual Institutions

Acadia University

Cramp, J.M. *The Inaugural Address ... 1851 and Introductory Lecture to the Theological Course ... with an Appendix Containing a History of the College*. Halifax, 1851

Higgins, W.H. *The Life of John Mockett Cramp, D.D., 1796-1881, Late President of Acadia College*. Montreal: Drysdale, 1887

Kirkconnell, W. *A Slice of Canada: Memoirs*. Toronto: University of Toronto Press, 1967

Kirkconnell, W., editor. *The Acadia Record, 1838-1953*. 4th edition revised and enlarged. Wolfville: Acadia University, 1953

Levy, G.E., *The Baptists in the Maritime Provinces, 1753-1946*. Saint John, N.B.: Barnes Hopkins, 1946

Longley, R.S. *Acadia University, 1838-1938*. Kentville: Kentville Publishing Co., 1939

Memorials of Acadia College and Horton Academy for the First Half-Century, 1825-1878. Montreal: Dawson, 1881

Albert University

McGregor, A. 'Egerton Ryerson, Albert Carman, and the Founding of Albert College,' *Ontario History*, 63 (1971), 205-16

Smith, W.E.L. *Albert College, 1857-1957*. Privately published, 1957

University of Alberta

Alexander, W.H. *The University of Alberta: a Retrospect, 1908-1929*. Edmonton: The University, 1929

Cameron, D. *Campus in the Clouds* [Banff School of Fine Arts]. Toronto: McClelland & Stewart, 1956

Corbett, E.A. *We Have with us Tonight*. Toronto: Ryerson, 1957

MacDonald, J. *The History of the University of Alberta*. Edmonton: The University, 1958

Thomas, L.G. *The University of Alberta in the War of 1939-45*. Edmonton: The University, 1948

University of Alberta Survey Committee. *Interim Report to the Lieutenant Governor in Council, Province of Alberta*. Sessional Paper No. 50, 1942. Edmonton: Queen's Printer, 1942

Wallace, R.C. *The University of Alberta, 1908-1933*. Edmonton: The University, 1933

Assumption University

See University of Windsor

Bishop's University

Bensley, E.H. 'Bishop's Medical College,' *Journal of Canadian Medical Association*, 72 (1955), 463-5
Bishop's University. *A Brief Submitted to the Royal Commission of Inquiry on Education in the Province of Quebec by Bishop's University*. Lennoxville: The University, 1962
Bishop's University. *Historical Sketch of the University of Bishop's College, Established at Lennoxville, C.E., Showing its Origin, Progress and Present Condition*. Montreal, 1857
'The Dental Profession and Bishop's College,' *Canadian Medical Record*, 24 (1896), 241-5
Masters, D.C. *Bishop's University: the First Hundred Years*. Toronto: Clarke, Irwin, 1950
Millman, T.R. *Jacob Mountain, First Lord Bishop of Quebec*. Toronto: University of Toronto Press, 1947

Brandon University

Stone, C.G., and Garnett, F.J. *Brandon College: a History 1899-1967*. Brandon: The University, 1969

University of British Columbia

Gibson, W.C. *Wesbrook and his University*. Vancouver: The University, 1973
Golden Anniversary, Alumni Association of the University of British Columbia. UBC Alumni Chronicle, 20, 3 (autumn 1966)
Logan, H.T. *Tuum Est: a History of the University of British Columbia*. Vancouver: The University, 1958
Shorthouse, T., editor. 'Scrapbook for a Golden Anniversary: the University Library 1915-1965,' *British Columbia Library Quarterly*, 29, 3 (1966), 2-80
Tory, H.M. 'McGill University in British Columbia,' *McGill University Magazine*, 6 (1906), 185-204
The University of British Columbia, Twenty-First Anniversary, 1915-1936. Vancouver: The University, 1936

Brock University

Fleming, W.G. 'Brock University' in *Post-Secondary and Adult Education*, volume IV of *Ontario's Educative Society*. Toronto: University of Toronto Press, 1974. 86-91

University of Calgary

Johns, W.H. 'The Creation of New Universities,' *NCCUC Proceedings* (1960). 33-7

Province of Alberta. *Report of the Royal Commission Appointed to Consider the Granting of Degree-conferring Powers to Calgary College.* Sessional Paper No. 1, 1915

Simon, F.A. 'A Brief History of the Alberta Institute of Technology and Art.' Unpublished M.A. thesis, University of Alberta, 1961

Weston, P.E. 'A University for Calgary,' *Alberta Historical Review*, 11 (1963), 1-11

Carleton University

Bissell, C.T. 'A Retrospective Report, 1942-1956' in Carleton College. *The President's Report* (1955-6). 7-13

Fleming, W.G. 'Carleton University' in *Post-Secondary and Adult Education*, volume IV of *Ontario's Educative Society*. Toronto: University of Toronto Press, 1974. 92-107

Robbins, J.E. *Convocation Address* ... [on the 25th Anniversary of the first Carleton convocation]. Ottawa: The University, 1969

The Classical Colleges

General

Bounadère, R. *Aperçu historique sur les petits séminaires de la province de Québec.* Québec: Les Presses de l'Université Laval, 1945

Chartier, E. 'The Classical Colleges of Quebec,' *NCCU Proceedings* (1923), 24-39

Duval, R. 'The Roman Catholic Colleges of Quebec,' in G.Z.F. Bereday, editor. *The Year Book of Education 1957.* London: Evans Bros., 1957. 270-85

Fédération des Collèges Classiques. *L'Organisation et les besoins de l'enseignement classique dans le Québec.* Montréal: Fides, 1954

Gérin-Lajoie, P. 'Changing Patterns of Classical Education in Quebec,' *NCCU Proceedings* (1956), 73-82

Lévesque, V. 'Les Elèves du Collège Ste-Anne-de-la-Pocatière (1829-1842).' Thése de licence, Université Laval, 1965

Lortie, L. 'The New Classical College Curriculum and its Impact on University Courses,' *NCCU Proceedings* (1947), 22-6

Meilleur, J.-B. *Mémorial de l'éducation du Bas-Canada, 1615-1855.* Montréal: J.B. Rolland, 1860

Tremblay, A. *Les Collèges et les écoles publiques: conflit ou co-ordination?* Québec: Les Presses de l'Université Laval, 1954

Institutions

Campeau, L. *La Première Mission des Jesuits en Nouvelle-France (1611-1613) et les commencements du Collège de Québec (1626-1670).* Montréal: Bellarmin, 1972

Caron, I. 'Collège classique de St. Roch de Québec,' *Bulletin des Recherches Historiques*, 45 (1939), 97-100

Choquette, C.-P. *Histoire du Séminaire de Saint-Hyacinthe depuis sa fondation jusqu'à nos jours, 1811-1911.* Montréal: Institution des Sourds-Muets, 1912

Dansereau, A., and Maurault, O. *Le Collège de Montréal 1767-1967.* Montréal: Le Collège, 1967

Desjardins, P. *Le Collège Ste-Marie de Montréal: la fondation le fondateur.* Montréal: Le Collège, 1942

Douville, J.-A. *Histoire du Collège-Séminaire de Nicolet.* 2 volumes. Montréal: Beauchemin, 1903

Dubois, E. *Le Petit Séminaire de Ste-Thérèse 1825-1925.* Montréal: Editions du Devoir, 1925

Dugas, A.-C. *Gerbes de souvenirs ou mémoires, épisodes, anecdotes et réminiscences du Collège Joliette.* Montréal: Arbour & Dupont, 1914

Forget, A. *Histoire du Collège de l'Assomption 1833-1933.* Montréal: Le Collège, 1933

Lamarche, G. *Le Collège sur la colline.* Rigaud: Editions de l'Echo du Bourget, 1951

Lebon, W. *Histoire du Collège de Ste-Anne-de-la-Pocatière, 1827-1927.* 2 volumes. Québec: Charrier et Dugal, 1948

Morin, L. 'Histoire du Collège de St-Laurent,' *Enseignement Secondaire,* 13 (1934), 210-18

Morisseau, H. 'Un Collège Classique à Saint-Denis-sur-Richelieu dès 1805,' *Revue de l'Université d'Ottawa,* 18 (1948), 356-65

Plante, Sister L. 'La Fondation de l'enseignement classique feminin au Québec, 1908-1926.' Thése de licence en lettres, Université Laval, 1967

Provost, H. 'Le Petit Séminaire de Québec devenu "collège,"' *Revue de l'Université Laval,* 18 (1964), 787-800

Richard, L. *Histoire du Collège des Trois-Rivières, 1860-1874.* Trois Rivières: P.V. Ayotte, 1885

Rivard, A. 'Le Collège de Québec,' *Canada Française,* 23 (1936), 413-21

Roy, J. 'Le Collège de Lévis,' *Enseignement Secondaire,* 9 (1930), 482-8

Collège Ste-Anne

Album souvenir: les cinquantes ans du Collège Sainte-Anne. Church Point: Le Collège, 1940

Munroe, D., et al. *All Eyes Towards the Future: Report of the Tribunal on Bilingual Higher Education/Les Yeux vers l'avenir* ... Halifax: Government of Nova Scotia, 1969

Dalhousie University

Centenary Committee, Dalhousie University. *One Hundred Years of Dalhousie, 1818-1918.* Halifax: The University, 1919

Harvey, D.C. *An Introduction to the History of Dalhousie University* Halifax: McCurdy Printing Co., 1938

Kerr, A.E. *The Post-War Years, 1945-1963* ... Halifax: Dalhousie University, 1963

McCulloch, W. *Life of Thomas McCulloch, D.D.* Truro: Privately
  published, 1920
Patterson, G.G. *The History of Dalhousie College and University.*
  Halifax: Morning Herald, 1887

University of Guelph

Gattinger, F.E. *A Century of Challenge: a History of the Ontario
  Veterinary College.* Toronto: University of Toronto Press, 1962
Ontario Agricultural College. *Half-Century of the College.*
  Guelph: The College, 1924
Ross, A.M. *The College on the Hill: a History of the Ontario
  Agricultural College 1874-1974.* Toronto: Copp Clark, 1974

University of Halifax

Healy, D. 'The University of Halifax 1875-1881,' *Dalhousie Review,*
  53 (1973), 39-56

King's College, Fredericton

See University of New Brunswick

King's College, Toronto

See University of Toronto

University of King's College (Windsor, Nova Scotia)

Akins, T.B. *A Brief Account of the Origin, Endowment and Progress
  of the University of King's College, Windsor, Nova Scotia.*
  Halifax: MacNab & Shaffer, 1865
Harris, R.V. *Charles Inglis: Missionary, Loyalist, Bishop (1734-
  1816).* Toronto: General Board of Religious Education, 1937
Hind, H.Y. *The University of King's College, Windsor, Nova Scotia,
  1790-1890.* New York: Church Review Co., 1890
Thomas, C.E. 'The Early Days of King's College, Windsor, Nova
  Scotia,' *Canadian Church Historical Society Journal,* 6 (1964),
  30-45
Thomas, M.E., editor. 'The Memoirs of William Cochran, Sometime
  Professor of Columbia College, New York, and at King's College,
  Windsor, Nova Scotia,' *New York Historical Quarterly,* 38 (1954),
  55-83
Vroom, F.W. *A Chronicle of King's College, 1789-1939.* Halifax:
  Imperial Publishing Co., 1941

Lakehead University

Ballantyne, P.M. 'A History of Lakehead University: Lakehead
  Technical Institute 1947-1956, Lakehead College of Arts, Science
  and Technology, 1957-1965, Lakehead University 1966.' Mimeographed; only available copies at Lakehead University Library

Fleming, W.G. 'Lakehead University' in *Post-Secondary and Adult Education*, volume IV of *Ontario's Educative Society*. Toronto: University of Toronto Press, 1974. 109-14

Laurentian University

Bouvier, E. 'L'Université Laurentienne de Sudbury,' *Relations*, 20 (1960), 120-3
Fleming, W.G. 'Laurentian University' in *Post-Secondary and Adult Education*, volume IV of *Ontario's Educative Society*. Toronto: University of Toronto Press, 1974. 114-21
Plante, A. *Vingt-cinq Ans de vie française: Le Collège de Sudbury*. Montréal: Imprimerie du Messager, 1938

Université Laval

Chauveau, P.-J.-O. 'The Colleges of Canada: The Laval University,' *Journal of Education for Lower Canada*, 1 (1857), 53-6, 69-72, 85-9, 109-14, 125-8, 141-5
Fauteux, A. *Bibliographie de la question universitaire, Laval-Montréal, 1852-1921*. Montréal: Arbour et Dupont, 1922. Also in Université de Montréal. *Annuaire* (1921-2)
Lebel, M. 'La Faculté des Lettres de Laval,' *Revue de l'Université Laval*, 6 (1952), 449-64
Lussier, D. 'La Faculté des Sciences Sociales,' *Revue de l'Université Laval*, 6 (1951), 272-90
Maheux, A. 'Pourquoi l'Université en 1852?' *Revue de l'Université Laval*, 5 (1951), 381-7
Maheux, A. 'Rétrospectives, de 1852 à 1902,' *Revue de l'Université Laval*, 6 (1951), 266-71
Maheux, A. 'L'Université Laval et la culture française au Canada,' *Culture*, 13 (1952), 117-26
Pouliot, A. 'La Faculté des Sciences,' *Revue de l'Université Laval*, 6 (1952), 378-82
Provost, H. *Historique de la Faculté des Arts à l'Université Laval*. Québec: Enseignement Secondaire, 1952
Provost, H. 'Historique du Séminaire de Québec,' *Revue de l'Université Laval*, 17 (1963), 591-9
Provost, H. 'Les Origines éloignées du Séminaire de Québec,' *Canadian Catholic Historical Association Annual Report* (1955-6), 25-31
Roy, C. *L'Université Laval et les fêtes du cinquantenaire*. Quebec: L'Université, 1902
Sylvain, P. 'Les Difficiles Débuts de l'Université Laval,' *Cahiers des Dix*, 36 (1971), 211-34
Tremblay, A. 'Projét de reform de l'enseignement des humanités à l'Université Laval' in G. Stanley and G. Sylvestre, editors. *Canadian Universities Today*. Toronto: University of Toronto Press, 1961. 67-79
Université Laval. *Mémoire de l'Université Laval à la Commission Royale d'enquête sur l'enseignement*. Québec: Les Presses de l'Université Laval, 1962

Université Laval. *Mémoire sur l'Université Laval avec pièces justicatives.* Québec: L'Université, 1862
Université Laval. *L'Université Laval, 1852-1952.* Québec: Les Presses de l'Université Laval, 1952
Vachon, L.-A. *Mémorial de l'histoire du Séminaire de Québec depuis sa fondation en 1663.* Québec; Les Presses de l'Université Laval, 1963

University of Lethbridge

Holmes, O.G. *Come Hell or High Water.* Lethbridge: Lethbridge Herald, 1974
Lethbridge Junior College. *Past, Present and Future of Lethbridge Junior College.* Lethbridge: The College, 1965
Smith, W.A.S. 'There is no Joy in Mudville,' *AUCC Proceedings* (1969), 97-104

McGill University

Abbott, M.E. *An Historical Sketch of the Medical Faculty of McGill University.* Montreal: Gazette, 1902
Audet, L.-P. 'L'Institution Royale et la Fondation McGill,' *Revue de l'Université Laval*, 7 (1952), 69-83
Collard, E.A. *Oldest McGill.* Toronto: Macmillan, 1946
Collard, E.A., editor. *The McGill You Knew: an Anthology of Memoirs 1920-1960.* Toronto: Longman, 1975
Currie, A.W. *Six Years at McGill: a Review.* Montreal: The University, 1926
Dawson, J.W. *The Recent History of McGill University.* Montreal: The College, 1883
Dawson, J.W. *Thirty Eight Years at McGill.* Montreal: Gazette, 1893
Dawson, R., editor. *Fifty Years of Work in Canada, Scientific and Educational: Being Autobiographical Notes by Sir William Dawson.* London: Ballantyne, Hanson, 1901
Featherstonhaugh, R.D. *McGill University at War, 1914-18, 1939-45.* Montreal: The University, 1947
McGill University, Institute of Education. *A Century of Teacher Education, 1857-1957.* Montreal: The University, 1957
MacLennan, H., editor. *McGill: the Story of a University.* Toronto: Nelson, 1961
MacMillan, C. *McGill and its Story, 1821-1921.* London: John Lane, 1921
McMurray, D. *Four Principals of McGill: a Memoir 1929-1963.* Montreal: Graduate Society of McGill University, 1974

McMaster University

Frost, W.R. *Concerning McMaster: the University's Past and Present in Facts and Figures.* Hamilton: The University, 1948
Hamilton, L. 'The Founding of McMaster University.' Unpublished B.D. thesis, McMaster University, 1938

644

McLag, W.S., et al. *McMaster University, 1890-1940*. Hamilton:
The University, 1940
McMaster University. *A Frank Statement: its Origins, Development,
Present Status and Future Needs*. Hamilton: The University,
1944
Thomson, D.E. 'McMaster University, 1887-1906,' *McMaster University
Monthly*, 16 (1906), 20-8
Vining, C.A.M., editor. *Woodstock College Memorial Book*. Toronto:
Woodstock College Alumni Association, 1951
Wells, J.E. *Life and Labours of Robert Alexander Fyfe, D.D.*
Toronto: the author, 1885

University of Manitoba

Baird, A.G. 'The History of the University of Manitoba' in R.C.
Lodge, editor. *Manitoba Essays*. Toronto: Macmillan, 1937.
10-52
Frazer, W.J. 'A History of St. John's College, Winnipeg.' Un-
published M.A. thesis, University of Manitoba, 1966
Kirkconnell, W. *Golden Jubilee of Wesley College, Winnipeg
1888-1938*. Winnipeg: Columbia Press, 1938
Morton, W.L. *One University: a History of the University of
Manitoba 1877-1952*. Toronto: McClelland & Stewart, 1957
Murray, W.C. 'Manitoba's Place in University History,' *Transactions
of the Royal Society of Canada*. 1928. Section 2, 57-84
Régnier, P.R. 'A History of St. Boniface College.' Unpublished
M.A. thesis, University of Manitoba, 1964
Rumball, W.G., and MacLennan, D.A., editors. *Manitoba College*.
Winnipeg: The College, 1921

Memorial University of Newfoundland

Mansfield, M., editor. *The Official Opening of the New Campus*.
St John's: The University, 1961
Newton, R. *Report ... on His Survey ... Made at the Request of
the Board of Regents*. St John's: The University, 1952
Pitt, D.G. 'Myth, Memorial and Alma Mater: the Story of the
Memorial University of Newfoundland,' *Maritime Advocate and
Busy East*, 43, 4 (1952), 29-36
Rowe, F.W. 'Memorial University of Newfoundland' in *The Develop-
ment of Education in Newfoundland*. Toronto: Ryerson, 1964.
177-82

Université de Moncton

Collège St.-Joseph. *Album souvenir: Collège St.-Joseph, 1864-
1964*. Memramcook, N.B.: Le Collège, 1964
Université St.-Joseph. *Album historique publié à l'occasion des
fêtes du 75e anniversaire, 13-14 Juin, 1939*. Memramcook, N.B.:
Le Collège, 1939

Université de Montréal

Audet, L.-P. 'La Fondation de l'Ecole Polytechnique de Montréal,'
  Cahiers des Dix, 30 (1965), 149-91
Baril, G. 'La Faculté des Sciences: Vingtième anniversaire de
  sa fondation,' *Annales de l'ACFAS*, 7 (1941), 179-220
Fauteux, A. *Bibliographie de la question universitaire Laval-
  Montréal 1852-1921*. Montréal: Arbour et Dupont, 1922. Also
  in *Université de Montréal. Annuaire* (1921-2)
Maurault, O. L'Enseignement supérieure à Montréal, *Revue Trimest-
  rielle Canadienne*, 22 (1936), 113-25
Maurault, O. 'L'Université de Montréal,' *Cahiers des Dix*, 17
  (1952), 11-19
Piette, A.V.J., and Montpetit, E. *Université de Montréal: acti-
  vités et besoins*. Montréal: Arbour et Dupont, 1925
Rumilly, R. *Histoire de l'Ecole des Hautes Etudes Commerciales
  de Montréal*. Montréal: Beauchemin, 1967
Slattery, T.P. *Loyola and Montreal: a History*. Montreal: Palm,
  1962
Université de Montréal. *Mémoire à la Commission Royale d'enquête
  sur l'enseignement*. Montréal: L'Université, 1962
Université de Montréal. *Mémoire à la Commission Royale d'enquête
  sur les problèmes constitutionnels*. Montréal: L'Université,
  1954

Mount Allison University

Argosy Weekly (Mount Allison University), October 1884. Special
  historical issue
Argosy Weekly, 9 March 1940. Special historical issue
'Mount Allison University,' *Municipal Review of Canada*, 28, 8
  (July-August 1932), 8-13
Munro, W.F. 'Mount Allison University: Historical Sketch,'
  Mount Allison University Calendar (1959-60). 23-5

Mount Saint Vincent University

Maura, Sister. 'Mount Saint Vincent College' in *The Sisters of
  Charity*. Toronto: Ryerson, 1956. 252-63
Shook, L.K. 'Mount Saint Vincent' in *Catholic Post-Secondary
  Education in English-Speaking Canada*. Toronto: University
  of Toronto Press, 1971, 96-102

University of New Brunswick

Bailey, A.G., editor. *The University of New Brunswick Memorial
  Volume*. Fredericton: The University, 1950
Bailey, J.W. *Loring Woart Bailey: the Story of a Man of Science*.
  Saint John, N.B.: McMillan, 1925
Fraser, J.A. *By Force of Circumstance: a History of St. Thomas
  University*. Fredericton: Miramichi Press, 1970

Jacob, E. *The Experience, Prospects and Purposes of King's College, Fredericton; Oration Delivered at the Encaenia.* Fredericton: The College, 1851

Keirstead, W.D. 'University of New Brunswick Past and Present,' *Dalhousie Review*, 22 (1943), 344-54

MacNaughton, K.F.C. *The Development of the Theory and Practice of Education - New Brunswick.* Fredericton: The University, 1947

MacNutt, W.S. *The Founders and their Times.* Fredericton: The University, 1958

Raymond, W.O. *The Genesis of the University of New Brunswick with a Sketch of the Life of William Brydone Jack, A.M., D.C.L., President 1861-1885.* Saint John, N.B., 1919

Royal Commission on Higher Education in New Brunswick, J. Deutsch, Chairman. *Report ...* Fredericton, 1962

Shook, L.K. 'St. Thomas University' in *Catholic Post-Secondary Education in English-Speaking Canada.* Toronto: University of Toronto Press, 1971. 113-23

Notre Dame University of Nelson, B.C.

Shook, L.K. 'Notre Dame University of Nelson' in *Catholic Post-Secondary Education in English-Speaking Canada.* Toronto: University of Toronto Press, 1971. 395-405

Nova Scotia College of Art and Design

Kennedy, G. 'Nova Scotia College of Art and Design,' *Arts Canada*, 25, 5 (1968), 30-2

Nova Scotia Technical College

'The Nova Scotia Technical College' in Royal Commission on Industrial Training and Technical Education. *Report ...* Ottawa: King's Printer, 1913. IV, 1669-74

University of Ottawa

Bergevin, J.-L. *L'Université d'Ottawa: vocation sacerdotale et professions liberales 1848-1928.* Ottawa: L'Université, 1929

Carrière, G. *Histoire documentaire de la Congregation des Missionaires Oblats de Marie-Immacultée dans l'Est du Canada.* 9 volumes. Ottawa: Editions Université d'Ottawa, 1957-70. Especially volumes II, VI

Carrière, G. *L'Université d'Ottawa, 1848-1861.* Ottawa: L'Université, 1960

Laframboise, J.C. 'A l'Aube d'un second siècle,' *Revue de l'Université d'Ottawa*, 17 (1947), 19-45

O'Reilly, J.B. 'The College of Bytown, 1848-1856,' *Canadian Catholic Historical Association Annual Report* (1948), 61-9

O'Reilly, J.B. 'The Pontifical University of Ottawa from its
  Origins to the Civil Charter,' *Revue de l'Université d'Ottawa*,
  19 (1949) 119-42
Shook, L.K. 'University of Ottawa' and 'St. Patrick's College'
  in *Catholic Post-Secondary Education in English-Speaking Canada*.
  Toronto: University of Toronto Press, 1971. 242-51, 252-6

University of Prince Edward Island

McKenna, M.A. 'The History of Higher Education in the Province
  of Prince Edward Island,' *Canadian Catholic Historical Associa-
  tion. Study Sessions* (1971), 19-49
Shook, L.K. 'St. Dunstan's University' in *Catholic Post-Secondary
  Education in English-Speaking Canada*. Toronto: University of
  Toronto Press, 1971. 35-56

Prince of Wales College

See University of Prince Edward Island

Université du Québec

Lamarche, S. *L'Université du Québec*. Montréal: Collection du
  C.E.P., 1969

Queen's University

Calvin, D.D. *Queen's University at Kingston, 1841-1941*. Kingston:
  The University, 1941
Clark, A.L. *The First Fifty Years: a History of the Science
  Faculty at Queen's, 1893-1943*. Kingston: The University, 1944
Dewar, D. *Queen's Profiles*. Kingston: The University, 1951
Grant, W.L., and Hamilton, F. *Principal Grant*. Toronto: Morang,
  1904
Gundy, H.P. *Queen's University*. Kingston: The University, 1967
Lower, A.R.M. 'Queen's Yesterday and Today,' *Historic Kingston*,
  No. 20 (1972), 77-89
Neatby, H. 'Queen's College and the Scottish Fact,' *Queen's
  Quarterly*, 80 (1973), 1-12
Queen's University at Kingston: a Centenary Volume. Kingston:
  The University, 1941
Trotter, B. *Queen's University 1963-1968: Some Facts and Figures*.
  Kingston: The University, 1968
Wallace, R.C., editor. *Some Great Men of Queen's* [G.M. Grant,
  J. Watson, N.F. Dupuis, J. Cappon, W.G. Jordan, A. Shortt].
  Toronto: Ryerson, 1941
Watson, J. 'Thirty Years at Queen's,' *Queen's Quarterly*, 10 (1902),
  188-96

Royal Military College

Dixon, F.J. 'Military Education in Canada' in J.C. Hopkins, editor.
   Canada: an Encyclopaedia of the Country. IV. Toronto:
   Linscott Publishing Co., 1898, 444-9
Preston, A. 'The Founding of the Royal Military College,' *Queen's
   Quarterly*, 84 (1967) 398-412
Preston, R.A. *Canada's R.M.C.: the History of the Royal Military
   College*. Toronto: University of Toronto Press, 1969

Ryerson Polytechnical Institute

Fleming, W.G. *Post-Secondary and Adult Education*, volume IV of
   Ontario's Educative Society. Toronto: University of Toronto
   Press, 1974. 452-76

St Dunstan's University

See University of Prince Edward Island

St Francis Xavier University

Edwards, W.X. 'The MacPherson-Tompkins Era of St. Francis Xavier
   University,' *Canadian Catholic Historical Association Annual
   Report* (1953), 49-65
Laidlaw, A.F. *The Campus and the Community: the Global Impact
   of the Antigonish Movement*. Montreal: Harvest House, 1961
MacDonell, M. 'The Early History of St. Francis Xavier University,'
   Canadian Catholic Historical Association Annual Report (1948),
   61-9
Shook, L.K. 'St. Francis Xavier' in *Catholic Post-Secondary
   Education in English-Speaking Canada*. Toronto: University of
   Toronto Press, 1971. 75-95

St Joseph's University

See Université de Moncton

St Mary's University

Shook, L.K. 'St. Mary's University' in *Catholic Post-Secondary
   Education in English-Speaking Canada*. Toronto: University
   of Toronto Press, 1971. 57-74

University of St Michael's College

See University of Toronto

St Thomas University

See University of New Brunswick

University of Saskatchewan

King, C. *Extending the Boundaries*. Saskatoon: The University, 1967

King, C. *The First Fifty: Teaching, Research and Public Service at the University of Saskatchewan, 1909-1959*. Toronto: McClelland & Stewart, 1959

Morton, A.S. *Saskatchewan: the Making of a University*. Toronto: University of Toronto Press, 1959

Murray, J.E. 'The Early History of Emmanuel College,' *Saskatchewan History*, 9 (1956), 81-101

Murray, L.H. 'St. John's College Qu'Appelle, 1885-1904,' *Saskatchewan History*, 11 (1958), 18-29

Murray, W.C. 'The University of Saskatchewan,' *Transactions of the Royal Society of Canada*. 1941. Section 2, 95-117

Spinks, J.W.T. *Decade of Change: the University of Saskatchewan 1959-1970*. Saskatoon: The University, 1972

Thompson, W.P. *The University of Saskatchewan: a Personal History* Toronto: University of Toronto Press, 1970

Thomson, J.S. *Yesteryears at the University of Saskatchewan 1937-1949*. Saskatoon: Modern Press, 1969

Université de Sherbrooke

'Université de Sherbrooke,' *Revue de l'AUPELF*, 7, 1 (Printemps 1969), 70-81

'L'Université de Sherbrooke,' in Université de Sherbrooke. *Annuaire* (1955-6). 11-26

Université de Sherbrooke. *Une Revue Succincte des débuts de l'Université de Sherbrooke*. Sherbrooke: L'Université, 1958

Sir George Willams University

Eber, D. *The Computer Centre Party* ... Montreal: Tundra Books, 1969

Hall, H. *The Georgian Spirit: the Story of Sir George Williams University*. Montreal: The University, 1967

University of Toronto

Alexander, W.J., editor. *The University of Toronto and its Colleges 1827-1906*. Toronto: The University, 1906

Bissell, C.T. *Halfway Up Parnassus: a Personal Account of the University of Toronto, 1932-71*. Toronto: University of Toronto Press, 1974

Bissell, C.T., editor. *University College: a Portrait, 1853-1953*. Toronto: University of Toronto Press, 1953

Burwash, N. 'A Review of the Founding and Development of the University of Toronto as a Provincial University,' *Transactions of the Royal Society of Canada*. 1905. Section 2, 37-98

Dickson, G. and Adam, G.M., editors. *A History of Upper Canada College, 1829-1892*. Toronto: Rowsell & Hutchison, 1893

Hague, D., et al. *The Jubilee Volume of Wycliffe College*. Toronto: The College, 1927

Harris, R.S. 'The Establishment of a Provincial University in Ontario' in D.F. Dadson, editor. *On Higher Education: Five Lectures*. Toronto: University of Toronto Press, 1966. 3-35

Knox College Centenary Committee. *The Centenary of the Granting of the Charter of Knox College, Toronto, 1858-1958*. Toronto: The College, 1958

McCorkell, E.J. *Henry Carr - Revolutionary*. Toronto: Griffin House, 1969

Melville, H. *The Rise and Progress of Trinity College, Toronto with a Sketch of the Life of Bishop Strachan*. Toronto: Henry Rowsell, 1852

Moir, J.S. *Church and State in Canada West: Three Studies in the Relation of Denominationalism and Nationalism, 1841-1867*. Toronto: University of Toronto Press, 1959

Reed, T.A., editor. *A History of the University of Trinity College, Toronto, 1852-1952*. Toronto: University of Toronto Press, 1952

Shook, L.K. 'The University of St. Michael's College' and 'The Pontifical Institute of Mediaeval Studies' in *Catholic Post-Secondary Education in English-Speaking Canada*. Toronto: University of Toronto Press, 1971. 129-209, 210-28

Sissons, C.B. *A History of Victoria University*. Toronto: University of Toronto Press, 1952

University of King's College. *Proceedings at the Ceremony of Laying the Foundation Stone, August 23, 1842; and at the Opening of the University, June 8, 1843*. Toronto, 1843

University of Toronto. *Report of the Royal Commission on the University of Toronto*. Toronto: King's Printer, 1906

Wallace, W.S. *A History of the University of Toronto*. Toronto: University of Toronto Press, 1927

Trent University

Fleming, W.G. 'Trent University' in *Post-Secondary and Adult Education*, volume IV of *Ontario's Educative Society*. Toronto: University of Toronto Press, 1974. 168-71

Symons, T.H.B., in R. Borg, editor. *Peterborough, Land of Shining Waters*. Peterborough: Centennial Committee for the City and County of Peterborough, 1966. 493-509

University of Trinity College

See University of Toronto

Victoria University

See University of Toronto

University of Victoria

Logan, H.S. *Tuum Est: A History of the University of British Columbia*. Vancouver: University of British Columbia, 1958

University of Waterloo

Scott, J. *Of Mud and Dreams: University of Waterloo, 1957-1967*. Toronto: Ryerson, 1967

Wright, D.T. *The First Five Years of the Cooperative Engineering Programme at the University of Waterloo*. Montreal: Engineering Institute of Canada, 1962

Waterloo Lutheran University

Fleming, W.G. 'Waterloo Lutheran University' in *Post-Secondary and Adult Education*, volume IV of *Ontario's Educative Society*. Toronto: University of Toronto Press, 1974. 171-80

Lyon, B. *The First 60 Years: a History of Waterloo Lutheran University from the Opening of Waterloo Lutheran Seminary in 1911 to the Present Day*. Waterloo: The University, 1971

University of Western Ontario

Crowfoot, A.H. *Bishop Cronyn*. London: Synod of the Diocese of Huron, 1957

Crowfoot, A.H. *This Dreamer: Life of Isaac Hellmuth, Second Bishop of Huron*. Toronto: Copp Clark, 1963

Fox, W.S. *Sherwood Fox of Western: Reminiscences*. Toronto: Burns and MacEachern, 1964

Talman, J.J. *Huron College, 1863-1963*. London: Huron College, 1963

Talman, J.J., and Talman, R.D. *Western - 1878-1953*. London: The University, 1953

Tamblyn, W.F. *These Sixty Years*. London: The University, 1938

Wilfrid Laurier University

See Waterloo Lutheran University

University of Windsor

Assumption College, *Golden Jubilee Assumption College 1870-1920*. Windsor: The College, 1920

Ruth, N.J. 'Assumption University and the University of Windsor,' *Basilian Teacher*, 8 (1964), 154-68

Ruth, N.J. 'The University of Windsor: an Example of Ecumenical Cooperation,' *Journal of Higher Education*, 38 (1967), 90-5

Shook, L.K. 'Assumption University' in *Catholic Post-Secondary Education in English-Speaking Canada*. Toronto: University of Toronto Press, 1971. 275-92

University of Winnipeg

See University of Manitoba

York University

Ross, M.G. *The New University*. Toronto: University of Toronto Press, 1961
Ross, M.G. *Those Ten Years 1960-70: The President's Report on the First Decade of York University*. Toronto: The University, 1970
Ross, M.G. 'York University' in M.G. Ross, editor. *New Universities in the Modern World*. Toronto: Macmillan, 1966. 69-86
Verney, D.V. 'The Government and Politics of a Developing University: a Canadian Experience,' *Review of Politics*, 31 (1970), 291-311
York University. *These Five Years ... 1960-65*. Toronto: The University, 1965

ARTS AND SCIENCE

The Faculty of Arts and Science

Fieldhouse, H.N. 'The Liberal Arts Course - the Manitoba Experiment,' *NCCU Proceedings* (1944), 56-60
MacDonnell, J.W. 'The Decline of the Arts Faculty,' *Queen's Quarterly*, 30 (1923), 310-18
MacKenzie, N.A.M. 'The Future of the Arts Course,' *NCCU Proceedings* (1942), 128-40
Nichols, E.W. 'The Arts Course, its Purpose and Essential Elements,' *NCCU Proceedings* (1925), 20-7
Smith, S.E. 'The Liberal Arts: an Experiment,' *Queen's Quarterly*, 51 (1944), 1-12
Stanley, C.W. 'Remarks,' *NCCU Proceedings* (1944), 60-2
Thomson, J.S. 'The Arts and Science Course at the University of Saskatchewan,' *NCCU Proceedings* (1944), 54-6
Underhill, F.H. 'Commerce Courses and the Arts Faculty,' *NCCU Proceedings* (1930), 74-80
Wallace, R.C. 'The Arts Faculty,' *NCCU Proceedings* (1942), 118-22
Wilson, G.E. 'The Problem of the Arts Course,' *Dalhousie Review*, 27 (1948), 75-82

The Humanities

Bernier, J.-A. 'L'Humanisme classique' in R.C. Lodge, editor. *Manitoba Essays*. Toronto: Macmillan, 1938. 151-89

Falconer, R.A. 'A Hundred Years in the Humanities and Social Sciences' in *Queen's University, A Centenary Volume, 1841-1941.* Toronto: Ryerson, 1941. 31-46

Frye, H.N. *By Liberal Things.* Address on his Installation as Principal of Victoria College, University of Toronto. Toronto: Clarke, Irwin, 1959

Kirkconnell, W. 'The Humanities' in J. Katz, editor. *Canadian Education Today.* Toronto: McGraw-Hill, 1956. 200-10

Kirkconnell, W., and Woodhouse, A.S.P. *The Humanities in Canada.* Ottawa: Humanities Research Council, 1947

Lebel, M. *Les Humanités classiques au Québec.* Québec: Editions de l'Acropole et du Forum, 1967

Leddy, J.F. *The Humanities in an Age of Science.* Charlottetown: St Dunstan's University, 1962

Marion, S. 'La Querelle des humanistes canadiennes au XIXe siécle,' *Revue de l'Université d'Ottawa,* 17 (1947), 405-33

Pacey, D. 'The Humanist Tradition' in A.G. Bailey, editor. *The University of New Brunswick Memorial Volume.* Fredericton: The University, 1950. 57-68

Priestley, F.E.L. *The Humanities in Canada: a Report Prepared for the Humanities Research Council of Canada.* Toronto: University of Toronto Press, 1965

Tremblay, A. 'Projet de reforme de l'enseignement des humanités à l'Université Laval' in G. Stanley and G. Sylvestre, editors. *Canadian Universities Today.* Toronto: University of Toronto Press, 1961. 67-79

Vachon, L.-A. *Les Humanités aujourd'hui.* Québec: Les Presses de l'Université Laval, 1966

Woodhouse, A.S.P. 'The Humanities - Sixty Years,' *Queen's Quarterly,* 60 (1953), 538-50

Woodhouse, A.S.P. 'The Nature and Function of the Humanities,' *Transactions of the Royal Society of Canada.* 1954. Section 2, 1-17.

Classics (Greek and Latin)

Alexander, W.H. *The Amiable Tyranny of Pisistratus, or the Future of Classical Studies.* Edmonton: The University, 1931

Alexander, W.H. 'The Classical Discipline in Education 1899-1939,' *Transactions of the Royal Society of Canada.* 1939. Section 2, 9-21

A Group of Classical Graduates. *Honours Classics in the University of Toronto.* Toronto: University of Toronto Press, 1929

Lebel, M. *L'Enseignement et l'étude du Grèc.* Montréal: Fides, 1944

MacDougall, A.J. 'Classical Studies in Seventeenth Century Quebec,' *Phoenix,* 6 (1952), 6-21

English

Alexander, W.J. *The Study of Literature*. Toronto: Rowsell &
Hutchison, 1889
Broadus, E.K. 'The Weakness in English of Large Numbers of Gra-
duates and Undergraduates,' *NCCU Proceedings* (1927), 79-97
Frye, H.N. 'The Study of English in Canada,' *Dalhousie Review*,
38 (1958), 1-7
Harrison, G.B. 'Department of English,' *Queen's Quarterly*, 51
(1944), 378-89
McNeill, W.E. 'James Cappon' in R.C. Wallace, editor. *Some
Great Men of Queen's*. Toronto: Ryerson, 1941. 71-93
Sedgewick, G.G. 'A.M.' [Archibald MacMechan], *Dalhousie Review*,
13 (1934), 451-8
Wallace, M.W. and Woodhouse, A.S.P. 'In Memoriam: William John
Alexander,' *University of Toronto Quarterly*, 14 (1945), 1-33

French

Arès, R. 'Situation de l'enseignment français au Canada,' *Revue
Scolaire*, 14 (1964), 262-8
Association Canadienne des Educateurs de Langue français.
L'Enseignement français au Canada. Montréal: Centre de
Psychologie et de pédagogie, 1952
Goldstick, I., editor. *Modern Language Instruction in Canada*.
2 volumes. Toronto: University of Toronto Press, 1928
Hayne, D.M., et al. 'L'Enseignement de la litterature canadienne-
français au Canada,' *Culture*, 24 (1963), 325-42
Joliat, E. 'Scylla or Charybdis,' *Canadian Modern Language Review*,
17 (1961), 15-23
Lane, D. *Les Objectives du français au cours classique*. Montréal:
Editions pédagogiques de l'Ecole normale secondaire, 1954
Squair, J. *The Autobiography of a Teacher of French*. Toronto:
University of Toronto Press, 1928
Walter, F.W. 'Modern Language Teaching in Universities,' *NCCU
Proceedings* (1932), 44-9

History

Adair, E.R. 'The Study of History at McGill University,' *Culture*,
1 (1941), 51-62
Bruchesi, J. 'L'Enseignement de l'histoire du Canada,' *Canadian
Historical Association Annual Report* (1952), 1-13
Farnham, W.D. 'The Study of American History in Canadian Univer-
sities,' *Canadian Historical Association Annual Report* (1958),
63-76
Grenier, F. 'L'Enseignement de l'histoire dans nos collèges
classiques,' *Enseignement Secondaire*, 32 (1942), 33-43
Trotter, R.G. 'Aims in the Study and Teaching of History in
Canadian Universities,' *Canadian Historical Review*, 24 (1943),
50-62

Wallace, W.S. 'The Life and Work of George Wrong,' *Canadian Historical Review*, 29 (1948), 229-39

Languages Other than Classics, English, and French

Adams, C.J. 'The Institute of Islamic Studies [at McGill University],' *Canadian Geographical Journal*, 65 (1962), 34-6
Buyniak, V.O. 'Slavic Studies in Canada: an Historical Survey,' *Canadian Slavonic Papers*, 9 (1967), 3-23
Garrard, J.G. 'Russian Studies in Canada: an Educational Gap,' *Queen's Quarterly*, 70 (1963), 12-21
Goggio, E. 'One Hundred Years of Italian and Spanish at the University of Toronto,' *Modern Language Journal*, 38 (1954), 129-32
Goldstick, I., editor. *Modern Language Instruction in Canada*. 2 volumes. Toronto: University of Toronto Press, 1928
Hamlin, D.L.B. *International Studies in Canadian Universities*. Ottawa: Canadian Universities Foundation, 1964. Includes 'Russian and East European Studies,' 24-35; 'Asian Studies,' 36-50; 'African Studies,' 52-7; 'Latin-American Studies,' 58-64
Jurkszus, J. 'L'Institut sud et est-européen d'Ottawa,' *Revue de l'Université d'Ottawa*, 19 (1949), 484-7
Lalande, G. *L'Etude des relations internationales et de certaines civilisations étrangères au Canada*. Ottawa: Canadian Universities Foundation, 1964. Includes 'L'Etude des civilisations afro-asiatiques, ibero-américaines et slaves,' 39-87
Lindal, W.J. 'The Department of Icelandic in the University of Manitoba' in *The Icelanders in Canada*. Winnipeg: Canada Ethnic Press Federation, 1967. 330-65
MacGillivray, J. 'German in the Schools and Colleges,' *Queen's Quarterly*, 15 (1908), 211-15
Needler, G.H. *The Secondary School and the University*. Toronto: Ontario Education Association, 1936
Parker, J.H. 'Hispanic Studies in Canada, 1917-1967,' *Hispanics*, 50 (1967), 836-40
Walmsley, L.C. *Bishop in Honan: The Life and Works of Bishop William C. White*. Toronto: University of Toronto Press, 1974
Wickens, G.M. 'Islamic Studies at the University of Toronto,' *Modern Languages Journal*, 49 (1965), 312-13

Philosophy

Bastien, H. L'Enseignement de la philosophie au Canada francais. Montréal: Lévesque, 1935
Gauchy, V. 'Philosophy in French Canada: its Past and Future,' *Dalhousie Review*, 48 (1968), 384-401
Gaudron, E. 'French Canadian Philosophers' in J. Park, editor. *The Culture of Contemporary Canada*. Toronto: Ryerson, 1957. 274-92
Goudge, T.A. 'A Century of Philosophy in English-Speaking Canada,' *Dalhousie Review*, 47 (1967), 537-49

Irving, J.A. 'The Achievement of George Sidney Brett,' *University of Toronto Quarterly*, 14 (1945), 329-65

Irving, J.A. 'The Development of Philosophy in Central Canada from 1850-1900,' *Canadian Historical Review*, 31 (1950), 252-87

Lamonde, Y. 'L'Enseignement de la philosophie au Collège de Montréal, 1790-1876,' *Culture*, 31 (1970), 109-23, 213-24, 312-26

Lebel, Marc. 'L'Enseignement de la philosophie au Petit Séminaire de Québec (1765-1880),' *Revue Historique de l'Amérique français*, 18 (1964-5), 405-24, 852-93; 19 (1965-6), 106-25, 238-53

MacEachran, J.M. 'John Watson, 1847-1939' in R.C. Wallace, editor. *Some Great Men of Queen's*. Toronto: Ryerson, 1941. 22-50

Paquet, L.-A. 'Histoire de l'enseignement de la philosophie,' *Mémoires de la Société Royale de Canada*. 1917. Section 1, 32-60

Villeneuve, J.-M.-R. 'Le Rôle de la philosophie dans l'oeuvre des universités catholiques,' *Revue de l'Universite d'Ottawa*, 1 (1931), 7-31

The Social Sciences

Boucher, J. 'Les Sciences sociales, preparatifs de collège,' *Mémoirs de la Société Royale de Canada*. 1968. Section 1, 9-20

Corbett, D. 'The Social Sciences in Canada,' *Queen's Quarterly*, 66 (1959), 56-73

Falardeau, J.C. *L'Essor des sciences sociales au Canada français*. Québec: Ministère des Affaires Culturelles, 1964. *The Rise of Social Sciences in French Canada*. 1967

Falconer, R.A. 'A Hundred Years in the Humanities and Social Sciences' in *Queen's University: a Centenary Volume, 1841-1941*. Toronto: Ryerson, 1941. 31-46

Garigue, P. *Les Sciences sociales dans le monde contemporain*. Montréal: Université de Montréal, Faculté des Sciences Sociales, 1958

Gérin, L. 'La Vulgarisation de la science sociale chez les Canadiens français,' *Mémoirs de la Société Royale de Canada*. 1905. Section 1, 67-87

Johnson, H.G. 'The Social Sciences in the Age of Affluence,' *Canadian Journal of Economics and Political Science*, 32 (1966), 423-42

Keirstead, B.S., and Clark, S.D. 'Social Sciences' in *Royal Commission Studies*. Ottawa: King's Printer, 1951. 170-90

Lower, A.R.M. 'The Social Sciences in Canada,' *Culture*, 3 (1942), 434-44

Macpherson, C.B. 'The Social Sciences' in J. Park, editor. *The Culture of Contemporary Canada*. Toronto: Ryerson, 1957. 181-221

Montpetit, E. 'Les Universités et l'enseignement des sciences politiques et sociales,' *Revue Trimestrielle Canadienne*, 7 (1921), 390-409

Poulin, G. 'L'Enseignement des sciences sociales dans les universités canadiennes,' *Culture*, 2 (1941), 338-49
Tremblay, M., et Faucher, A. 'L'Enseignement des sciences sociales
au Canada' in *Royal Commission Studies*. Ottawa: King's Printer,
1957. 191-203

Anthropology

Cole, D. 'The Origins of Canadian Anthropology,' *Journal of
Canadian Studies*, 8, 1 (February 1973), 34-45
Connor, D.M., and Curtis, J.E. *Sociology and Anthropology in
Canada*. Montreal: Canadian Sociology and Anthropology Associa-
tion, 1970
McIlwraith, T.F. 'Anthropology' in W.S. Wallace, editor. *Royal
Canadian Institute Centenary Volume*. Toronto, the Institute,
1949. 3-12

Business Administration: Commerce and Finance

Bisson, A. 'L'Evolution de l'enseignement dans nos écoles univer-
sitaires de sciences commerciales,' *Culture*, 22 (1961), 93-8
Bladen, V.W. 'The University and Business,' *University of Toronto
Quarterly*, 26 (1957), 483-95
Cochrane, C.N. 'The Question of Commerce Courses in Universities,'
NCCU Proceedings (1932), 61-9
Macdonnell, J.J., and Clark, W.C. 'The Faculty of Arts and Business
Training,' *Bulletin of the Departments of History, Political
and Economic Science, Queen's University*, 44 (February 1923),
15-22
Macphie, E.D. *The Evolution of the Faculty of Commerce and
Business Administration*. Vancouver: University of British
Columbia, 1957
Rumilly, R. *Histoire de l'Ecole des Hautes Etudes Commerciales*.
Montréal: Beauchemin, 1967
Sipherd, L.W. 'University Training for Careers in Business,'
Business Quarterly, 15 (Summer 1950), 69-75
Skelton, O.D. 'University Preparation for Business,' *NCCU Pro-
ceedings* (1923), 69-77
Underhill, F.H. 'Commerce Courses and the Arts Faculty,' *NCCU
Proceedings* (1930), 74-80
Von Zur-Muehlen, M. *Business Education and Faculty at Canadian
Universities*. Ottawa: Economic Council of Canada, 1971

Economics and Political Science

Bourinot, J.G. 'The Study of Political Science in Canadian Uni-
versities,' *Transactions of the Royal Society of Canada*. 1889.
Section 2, 3-16
Dawson, R.M. *Political Science Teaching in Canada: Report to the
Canadian Social Science Research Council*. Ottawa: The Council,
1950

Hodgetts, J.E. 'Canadian Political Science: a Hybrid with a
Future' in R.H. Hubbard, editor. *Scholarship in Canada, 1967.*
Toronto: University of Toronto Press, 1967. 94–104
Macpherson, C.B. 'On the Study of Politics in Canada' in H.A.
Innis, editor. *Essays in Political Economy in Honour of E.J.
Urwick.* Toronto: University of Toronto Press, 1938. 147–65
Montpetit, E. 'Les Universités et l'enseignement des sciences
politiques et sociales,' *Revue Trimestrielle Canadienne,* 7
(1921), 390–409
Murray, J.C. *The Study of Political Philosophy: the Annual
University Lecture in McGill College.* Montreal: The College,
1877
Shortt, A. 'The Nature and Sphere of Political Economy,' *Queen's
Quarterly,* 1 (1893), 93–101
Skelton, O.D. 'Fifty Years of Political and Economic Science in
Canada' in Royal Society of Canada. *Fifty Years Retrospect.*
Ottawa: The Society, 1932. 85–90
Smiley, D.V. 'Contributions to Canadian Political Science since
the Second World War,' *Canadian Journal of Economics and
Political Science,* 33 (1967), 569–80
Taylor, K.W. 'The Founding of the Canadian Political Science
Association,' *Canadian Journal of Economics and Political
Science,* 33 (1967), 581–5

Geography

Dobson, M.R. *Geography in Canadian Universities.* Ottawa:
Department of Mines and Resources, Geographical Branch, 1950
Grenier, F. 'La Géographie au Canada Français,' *Académie
Canadienne-Française Cahiers,* 6 (1961), 121–31
Kimble, G.H.T. 'Geography in Canadian Universities,' *Geographical
Journal,* 108 (1946), 114–16
Robinson, J.L. 'Growth and Trends in Geography in Canadian Uni-
versities,' *Canadian Geographer,* 11 (1967), 216–30
Stamp, L.D. *Geography in Canadian Universities: Report of a
Survey under the Auspices of the Social Science Research
Council.* Ottawa: The Council, 1951
Watson, J.W. 'The Progress of Geography,' *Canadian Journal of
Economics and Political Science,* 19 (1953), 253–61

Psychology

Appley, M.H., and Rickwood, J. *Psychology in Canada.* Ottawa:
Science Council of Canada, 1967
Bernhardt, K.S. 'Canadian Psychology – Past, Present and Future,'
Canadian Journal of Psychology, 1 (1947), 61–6
Line, W. 'Psychology' in *Royal Commission Studies.* Ottawa:
King's Printer, 1951. 145–64
MacLeod, R.B. *Psychology in Canadian Universities and Colleges:
A Report to the Social Sciences Research Council.* Ottawa:
The Council, 1955

Maillot, N. 'La Psychologie' in *Royal Commission Studies*.
  Ottawa: King's Printer, 1951. 165-78
Myers, C.R. 'Notes on the History of Psychology in Canada,'
  Canadian Psychologist, 6A (1965), 4-17

Sociology

Carrier, H. *La Sociologue Canadien: Léon Gérin, 1863-1951*.
  Montréal: Bellarmin, 1960
Elkin, F. 'Canada' in J.S. Roucek, editor. *Contemporary Sociology*.
  New York: Philosophical Library, 1958. 1101-23
Falardeau, J.-C. 'Léon Gérin: His Life and Work' in L. LaPierre,
  editor. *Four O'Clock Lectures: French Canadian Thinkers of
  the Nineteenth and Twentieth Centuries*. Montreal: McGill
  University Press, 1966. 59-75
Falardeau, J.-C., and Jones, F.E. 'La Sociologie au Canada,' in
  Transactions of the Third World Congress of Sociology. London:
  International Sociological Association, 1956. 14-22
Garigue, P. 'French Canada: a Case History in Sociological
  Analysis,' *Canadian Review of Sociology and Anthropology*, 1
  (1964), 186-92
Gérin, L. 'La Sociologie: le mot et la chose,' *Mémoires de la
  Société Royale de Canada*. 1914. Section 1, 321-56
Hall, O. 'Carl A. Dawson, 1887-1964,' *Canadian Review of Sociology
  and Anthropology*, 1 (1964), 115-17
Hart, C.W.M., editor. *Essays in Sociology*. Toronto: University
  of Toronto Press, 1940
Houston, W. 'The Scientific and Pedagogic Claims of Sociology,'
  Proceedings of the Royal Canadian Institute (1887), 25-6
Keyfitz, N., et al. 'Sociology and Canadian Society' in T.M.
  Guinsberg and G.L. Reuber, editors. *Perspectives on the Social
  Sciences in Canada*. Toronto: University of Toronto Press,
  1974. 10-51
Urwick, E.J. 'Is There a Scientific Sociology,' *Canadian Journal
  of Economics and Political Science*, 2 (1936), 231-40. See
  also 549-51.

The Sciences

Babbitt, J.D., editor. *Science in Canada: Selections from the
  Speeches of E.W.R. Steacie*. Toronto: University of Toronto
  Press, 1965
Un Groupe de professeurs de l'Université Laval. *Cri d'alarme ...
  la civilisation et les Canadiens français*. Québec: Les
  Presses de l'Université Laval, 1963
Lortie, L. 'Les Débuts de l'ère scientifique' in L. Lortie and
  A. Plouffe, editors. *Aux Sources du présent*. Toronto:
  University of Toronto Press, 1960. 90-104
Macdonald, J.B. 'Science Education: Problems and Prospects' in
  J.E. Hodgetts, editor. *Higher Education in a Changing Canada*.
  Toronto: University of Toronto Press, 1966. 66-75

Ouellet, C. *La Vie Scientifique au Canada français*. Québec: Ministère des Affaires culturelles, 1964

Tory, H.M. *A History of Science in Canada*. Toronto: Ryerson, 1939

Astronomy

Chant, C.A. *Astronomy in the University of Toronto: The David Dunlap Observatory*. Toronto: University of Toronto Press, 1954

Douglas, A.V. 'Astronomy at Queen's University,' *Royal Astronomical Society of Canada Journal*, 52 (1958), 82-6

Harper, W.E. 'The History of Astronomy in Canada' in H.M. Tory, editor. *The History of Science in Canada*. Toronto: Ryerson, 1939. 87-99

Hogg, F.S. 'Astronomy' in W.S. Wallace, editor. *Royal Canadian Institute Centennial Volume*. Toronto: The Institute, 1949. 13-24

Kennedy, J.E. 'The Brydone Jack Observatory [at the University of New Brunswick],' *Royal Astronomical Society of Canada Journal*, 49 (1957), 151-5, 181-8; 50 (1958) 152-7

Northcott, R.J. 'The Growth of the R.A.S.C. and its Guiding Mentor, C.A. Chant,' *Royal Astronomical Society of Canada Journal*, 61 (1967), 218-25

Wright, K.O. 'Astronomy in Canada,' *Royal Astronomical Society of Canada Journal*, 61 (1967), 211-17

Botany and Zoology

Bailey, D.L. 'Botany' in W.S. Wallace, editor. *Royal Canadian Institute Centenary Volume*. Toronto: The Institute, 1949. 25-35

Canada Department of Agriculture. *Fifty Years of Progress on Dominion Experimental Farms, 1886-1936*. Ottawa: King's Printer, 1939

Craigie, E.H. *A History of the Department of Zoology at the University of Toronto up to 1962*. Toronto: University of Toronto Press, 1966

Dymond, J.R. 'Zoology in Canada' in H.M. Tory, editor. *The History of Science in Canada*. Toronto: Ryerson, 1939. 41-57

Hachey, H.B. 'History of the Fisheries Research Board of Canada.' Manuscript Report Series (Biological), No. 843. Ottawa: The Board, 1966

Lamb, W.K., and Cameron, T.W.M. 'Biologists and Biological Research since 1864' in G.F.G. Stanley, editor. *Pioneers of Canadian Science*. Toronto: University of Toronto Press, 1966. 36-43

Marie Victorin, Frère. 'Canada's Contribution to the Science of Botany' in H.M. Tory, editor. *The History of Science in Canada*. Toronto: Ryerson, 1939. 35-40

Smith, E.C. *Department of Biology, Acadia University 1910-1960*. Kentville: Kentville Publishing Co., 1961

Thomson, R.B. 'A Sketch of the Past Fifty Years in Canadian Botany'
in Royal Society of Canada. *Fifty Years Retrospect 1882-1932*.
Ottawa: The Society, 1932. 173-9
Willey, A. 'The Development of Zoology in Canada, 1882-1932' in
Royal Society of Canada. *Fifty Years Retrospect, 1882-1932*.
Ottawa: The Society, 1932. 155-8

Chemistry

Faculté des Sciences, Université Laval. 'Twenty-five Years of
Chemistry at Laval,' *Canadian Chemistry & Process Industries*,
29 (1945), 357-64
Johnson, F.M.G. 'Chemistry and the Royal Society of Canada' in
Royal Society of Canada. *Fifty Years Retrospect, 1882-1932*.
Ottawa: The Society, 1932. 113-16
King, J. 'Henry Holmes Croft' in *McCaul, Croft, Forneri: Per-
sonalities of Early University Days*. Toronto: Macmillan,
1914, 103-58
Lortie, L. *Le Traité de chimie de J.-B. Meilleur*. Montréal:
Université de Montréal, 1937
Miller, W.L. 'The Beginnings of Chemistry in Canada' in H.M.
Tory, editor. *The History of Science in Canada*. Toronto:
Ryerson, 1939. 21-34
Nicholls, R.V.V. 'A Century and a Quarter of Chemistry at McGill
University,' *Canadian Chemistry & Process Industries*, 28 (1944),
599-66
Warrington, C.J., and Newbold, B.T. *Chemical Canada: Past and
Present*. Ottawa: Chemical Institute of Canada, 1970
Warrington, C.J., and Nicholls, R.V.V. *A History of Chemistry in
Canada*. Toronto: Pitman, 1949

Geology and Mineralogy

Adams, F.D. 'The History of Geology in Canada' in H.M. Tory,
editor. *A History of Science in Canada*. Toronto: Ryerson,
1939. 7-20
Alcock, F.J. 'Geology' in W.S. Wallace, editor. *Royal Canadian
Institute Centennial Volume*. Toronto: The Institute, 1949.
61-70
Clark, T.H. 'Sir John William Dawson, 1820-1899' in G.F.G.
Stanley, editor. *Pioneers of Canadian Science*. Toronto:
University of Toronto Press, 1966. 101-13
Harrington, B. *Life of Sir William Logan*. Montreal: Dawson
Brothers, 1883
Langford, G.B. 'Teaching the Geological Sciences,' *Transactions
of the Royal Society of Canada*. 1958. Section 4, 39-43
Stearn, C.W. 'Geological Education in Canada' in E.R.W. Neale,
editor. *The Earth Sciences in Canada: a Centennial Appraisal and
Forecast*. Toronto: University of Toronto Press, 1968. 52-74
Wallace, R.C. 'The Educational Function of the Geological Sciences,'
Transactions of the Royal Society of Canada. 1929. Section 4,
1-3

Warren, H.V. 'The Problem of Finding More Geologists,' *Transactions of the Royal Society of Canada*. 1956. Section 4, 83-9

Mathematics

Beatty, S. 'An Outline of the Progress of Mathematics in Canada' in H.M. Tory, editor. *A History of Science in Canada*. Toronto: Ryerson, 1939. 100-19

Beatty, S. 'The Role of Mathematics in a Mathematics and Physics Course,' *Proceedings of the First Canadian Mathematical Congress*. Toronto: University of Toronto Press, 1945. 132-8

Coleman, A.J. 'Mathematics in the Second Half of the Twentieth Century,' *Ontario Mathematics Gazette*, 8 (1970), 75-88

DeLury, A.T. 'Mathematics and its Relation to Other University Studies,' *NCCU Proceedings* (1929), 21-2, 44-5

Eve, A.S. 'Decline in the Study of Classics and Mathematics and the Consequences,' *NCCU Proceedings* (1927), 104-8

Gaultier, A. 'Les Mathématiques' in *Royal Commission Studies*. Ottawa: King's Printer, 1951. 301-16

Gray, W.B. 'The Teaching of Mathematics in Ontario, 1800-1941.' Unpublished D.Paed. dissertation, University of Toronto, 1948

Jeffery, R.L. 'The Future of Mathematics in Canada,' *Queen's Quarterly*, 53 (1946), 304-12

Keeping, E.S. *Twenty-One Years of the Canadian Mathematical Congress*. Montreal: The Congress, 1968

Lortie, L. 'Les Mathématiques de nos ancêtres,' *Mémoires de la Société Royale de Canada*. 1955. Section 1, 31-45

Matheson, J. 'Nathan Fellowes Dupuis (1836-1907)' in R.C. Wallace, editor. *Some Great Men of Queen's*. Toronto: Ryerson, 1941. 51-70

Pillow, A.F. 'The Teaching of Applied Mathematics in Canada' in *Proceedings of the Fifth Canadian Mathematical Congress*. Toronto: University of Toronto Press, 1963. 88-93

Schiff, H.I., et al. 'Report on Mathematical Instruction in Canadian Universities,' *Canadian Mathematical Bulletin*, 7 (1964), 173-6

Physics

Burton, E.F. 'Physics' in W.S. Wallace, editor. *Royal Canadian Institute Centenary Volume*. Toronto: The Institute, 1949. 96-107

Eve, A.S. *Rutherford* ... Cambridge: Cambridge University Press, 1939. Especially 59-162

'Physics at the University: a Review,' *Physics in Canada*, 9 (1958), 13-27

Rose, D.C., et al. *Physics in Canada*. Special Study No. 2. Ottawa: Science Council of Canada, 1967

Shaw, A.N. 'The Advance of Physics in Canada' in H.M. Tory, editor. *The History of Science in Canada*. Toronto: Ryerson, 1939. 120-52

Armstrong, D.P. 'Corbett's House: the Origins of the Canadian Association for Adult Education and its Development under the Directorship of E.A. Corbett, 1936-1951.' Unpublished M.A. thesis, University of Toronto, 1968

Canadian Association for Adult Education. *Report of the Conference on Adult Education in Community Colleges.* Toronto: The Association, 1965

Coady, M.M., Cameron, D., and Stearn, H.W. 'The University Department of Extension ... a Symposium,' *NCCU Proceedings* (1953), 17-35

Corbett, E.A. *University Extension in Canada.* Toronto: Canadian Association for Adult Education, 1952

Daoust, G., et Belanger, P. *L'Université dans un société educative: de l'education des adultes à l'education permanente.* Montréal: Les Presses de l'Université de Montréal, 1974

Draper, J.A., and Yadao, F. 'Adult Education as a Field of Study in Canada,' *Continuous Learning,* 9 (1970), 65-82

Gunn, C.R. 'The Role of the Atlantic Provincial Governments in Adult Education.' Unpublished Ed.D. dissertation, University of Toronto, 1967

Kidd, J.R. *Adult Education in the Canadian University.* Toronto: Canadian Association for Adult Education, 1956

Kidd, J.R., editor. *Learning and Society: Readings in Canadian Adult Education.* Toronto: Canadian Association for Adult Education, 1963

Kidd, J.R., et al. 'Adult Education in the Canadian University,' *NCCU Proceedings* (1956), 51-72

Laidlaw, A.F. *The Campus and the Community: The Global Impact of the Antigonish Movement.* Montreal: Harvest House, 1961

Miller, L. 'Canada' in B. Groombridge, editor. *Adult Education and Television.* London: National Institute of Adult Education, 1966. 19-54

Rouillard, H., editor. *Pioneers in Adult Education in Canada.* Toronto: Canadian Association for Adult Education, 1952

Sandiford, P., et al. *Adult Education in Canada: a Survey.* Toronto: University of Toronto Press, 1935

Selman, G. *A History of Fifty Years of Extension Service by the University of British Columbia, 1915-1965.* Toronto: Canadian Association for Adult Education, 1966

Touchette, C.R. 'Evolution des objectifs et des programmes en education des adultes à l'Université de Montréal, 1876-1950.' Unpublished Ph.D. dissertation, University of Toronto, 1974

Tough, A.M. 'The Development of Adult Education at the University of Toronto before 1920.' Unpublished M.A. thesis, University of Toronto, 1962

Vernon, F. 'The Development of Adult Education in Ontario, 1790-1900.' Unpublished Ed.D. dissertation, University of Toronto, 1969

PROFESSIONAL EDUCATION

Agriculture

General

Chapais, J.-C. 'Notes historiques sur les écoles d'agriculture dans Québec,' *Revue Canadien* (1916), 17, 337-67

Dominion of Canada. *Report of Royal Commission on Industrial Training and Technical Education*. 3 volumes. Ottawa: King's Printer, 1912

Hopkins, L.S. 'Agricultural Research in Canada: its Origin and Development,' *Annals of American Academy of Political and Social Science*, 107 (May 1923), 82-7

Létourneau, F. *Histoire de l'Agriculture (Canada français)*. Montréal: Imprimerie Populaire, 1968

Reaman, G.E. *A History of Agriculture in Ontario*. 2 volumes. Toronto: Saunders, 1970

Reynolds, J.B. 'Matriculation for Agriculture,' *NCCU Proceedings* (1925), 43-9

Shutt, F.T. 'Agricultural Education and Research in Canada,' *Transactions of the Royal Society of Canada*. 1916. Section 3, 1-17

Individual Institutions

(University of Alberta)

Bowser, W.E., editor. *The Faculty of Agriculture, University of Alberta 1915-1965*. Edmonton: The University, 1965

(University of British Columbia)

Logan, H.T. *Tuum Est: a History of the University of British Columbia*. Vancouver: The University, 1958

(University of Guelph) (Ontario Agricultural College)

Ross, A.M. *The College on the Hill*. Guelph: University of Guelph, 1974

(Université Laval) (Ecole d'agriculture de Ste-Anne-de-la-Pocatière)

Fortin, L. de G. 'La Faculté d'Agriculture,' *Revue de l'Université Laval*, 7 (1952), 49-55, 129-44

(McGill University)

Snell, J.F. *Macdonald College of McGill University: a History from 1904-1955*. Montreal: McGill University Press, 1963

(University of Manitoba)

Morton, W.L. *One University: a History of the University of Manitoba*. Toronto: McClelland & Stewart, 1957

University of Manitoba, Faculty of Agriculture & Home Economics. *Golden Jubilee 1906-1956: a Record of the Years*. Winnipeg: The University, 1956

(Université de Montréal) (Institut Agricole d'Oka)

Louis-Marie, Père, *L'Institut d'Oka: cinquantenaire, 1893-1943*. Oka: L'Institut, 1943

(Nova Scotia Agricultural College)

Shuh, J.E. 'A College with a Difference,' *Atlantic Advocate*, 59, 9 (1969), 45-9

(University of Saskatchewan)

King, C. *The First Fifty: Teaching, Research and Public Service at the University of Saskatchewan, 1909-1959*. Toronto: McClelland and Stewart, 1959
Kirk, L.E. 'Recollections and Reminiscences - Early Years in the Faculty of Agriculture,' *Saskatchewan History*, 12 (1959), 23-30
Thompson, W.P. *The University of Saskatchewan: a Personal History*. Toronto: University of Toronto Press, 1970
Turner, A.R. 'W.R. Motherwell and Agricultural Education,' *Saskatchewan History*, 12 (1959), 81-96

Architecture

General

American Institute of Architects, Commission for the Study of Education and Registration. *The Architect at Mid-Century*. 2 volumes. New York: Reinhold, 1954
Bosworth, F.H., and Jones, R.C. *A Study of Architectural Schools*. New York: Scribners, 1933
Morency, P. 'L'Enseignement de l'architecture au Canada français,' *Action Universitaire*, 23 (1957), 16-19
Raymore, W.G. *Survey of the Profession*. Ottawa: Royal Architectural Institute of Canada, 1966
Russell, J.A. 'The University and Architecture,' *NCCU Proceedings* (1955), 74-80

Individual Institutions

'The Architectural Schools - U.B.C., Manitoba, Toronto, Ecole des Beaux Arts de Montréal, McGill,' *Journal of the Royal Architectural Institute of Canada*, 24 (1947), 144-62
Howarth, T. 'School of Architecture, University of Toronto,' *Journal of the Royal Architectural Institute of Canada*, 40 (1963), 56-68
Russell, J.A. 'Architectural Education at the University of Manitoba, 1913-1953,' *Journal of the Royal Architectural Institute of Canada*, 31 (1954), 63-86

Dentistry

General

Farquharson, R.F., et al. 'Medical and Dental Education in Cana-
  dian Universities' in D. Dunton and D. Patterson, editors.
  Canada's Universities in a New Age. Ottawa: National Confer-
  ence of Canadian Universities and Colleges, 1962. 61-83
Gies, W.J. *Dental Education in the United States and Canada*.
  New York: Carnegie Foundation for the Advancement of Teaching,
  1926
Gullett, D.W. *A History of Dentistry in Canada*. Toronto:
  University of Toronto Press, 1971
House, R.K. *Dentistry in Ontario: a Study for the Committee on
  the Healing Arts*. Toronto: Queen's Printer, 1970
Johnson, J.H. 'The History of Dental Research in Canada,' *Journal
  of the Canadian Dental Association*, 18 (1952), 315-20
Macdonald, J.B. *A Prospective on Dental Education for the Uni-
  versity of British Columbia*. Vancouver: University of British
  Columbia, 1956
Paynter, K.J. *Concerning the Establishment of a School of Dentistry
  in Manitoba*. Winnipeg: Queen's Printer, 1956
Paynter, K.J. *Dental Education in Canada*. Ottawa: Queen's
  Printer, 1965

Individual Institutions

The May 1965 issue of *Canadian Dental Association Journal* (31, 5)
  contains articles on the history of the seven faculties of
  dentistry existing at that time:
  H.R. MacLean, 'University of Alberta,' 289-92
  S.W. Leung, 'University of British Columbia,' 293-7
  J.D. McLean, 'Dalhousie University,' 298-302
  J.W. Neilson, 'University of Manitoba,' 303-10
  M.A. Rogers, 'McGill University, ' 311-16
  J.-P. Lussier, 'Université de Montréal,' 312-29
  R.G. Ellis, 'University of Toronto,' 330-57

Engineering

General

Bain, J.W. 'Where Engineers are Educated,' *Canadian Magazine*,
  16 (1901), 497-504
Dawson, J.W. *Plea for the Extension of University Education in
  Canada and Especially in Connection with McGill University*.
  Montreal: The University, 1870
Gaudefroy, H. 'Engineering Education in Canada' *Revue Trimestrielle
  Canadienne*, 37 (1951), 227-36
Lapp, P.A., Hodgins, J.W., and MacKay, C.B. *Ring of Iron: a
  Study of Engineering Education in Ontario*. Toronto: Committee
  of Presidents of Universities of Ontario, 1970

McKiel, H.W. 'Problems of Engineering Education,' *NCCU Proceedings*
(1946), 73-80
Tupper, K.F. 'The Teaching of Applied Science,' in *Royal Commission
Studies*. Ottawa: King's Printer, 1951. 337-52
Wendling, A.-V. 'L'Ingenieur et l'enseignement technique française,'
Revue Trimestrielle Canadienne, 24 (1938), 124-43

Individual Institutions

(Université de Montréal)

Audet, L.-P. 'La Fondation de l'Ecole Polytechnique de Montréal,'
Cahiers des Dix, 30 (1966), 147-91
Maurault, O. *L'Ecole Polytechnique de Montréal, 1873-1948.*
Montréal: L'Ecole, 1948
Maurault, O. 'L'Ecole Polytechnique 1948-1958,' *Ingenieur*, 44
(1958), 20-7

(University of New Brunswick)

Baird, A.F. 'The History of Engineering at the University of
New Brunswick' in A.G. Bailey, editor. *The University of New
Brunswick Memorial Volume*. Fredericton: The University, 1950.
75-86

(Queen's University)

Clark, A.L. *The First Fifty Years: a History of the Science
Faculty at Queen's 1893-1943*. Kingston: The University, 1943

(University of Toronto)

Harris, R.S., and Montagnes, I., editors. *Cold Steel and Lady
Godiva*. Toronto: University of Toronto Press, 1974
Young, C.R. *Early Engineering Education at Toronto 1851-1919.*
Toronto: University of Toronto Press, 1958

(University of Waterloo)

Scott, J.M. *Of Mud and Dreams: University of Waterloo 1957-1967.*
Toronto: Ryerson, 1967

Fine Art

Ayre, R. 'Fine Arts in Canadian Higher Education' in W. Kirkconnell
and A.S.P. Woodhouse. *The Humanities in Canada*. Ottawa:
Humanities Research Council, 1947. 220-8
Boggs, J.S. 'The History of Art in Canada' in R.H. Hubbard, editor.
Scholarship in Canada. Toronto: University of Toronto Press,
1968. 40-50
Cameron, D. *Campus in the Clouds*. Toronto: Ryerson, 1956
Cutler, M.I. 'Crisis in Canadian Art Schools,' *Canadian Art*, 22,
5 (1965), 14-26
Hubbard, R.H. 'The Visual Arts in the University,' *NCCU Proceedings*
(1955), 64-8
Moss, K. 'Arts Schools in Canada,' *Canadian Art*, 4 (1947), 156,
178-82

Forestry

General

Canadian Institute of Forestry. *Forestry Education in Canada: Proceedings of the Joint Forestry Convention.* Quebec: The Institute, 1960
Fernow, B.E. 'Report of the Committee of the Conference of Forest Schools on the Standardisation of Instruction in Forestry,' *Forest Quarterly*, 10 (1912), 341–94
Garratt, G.A. *Forestry Education in Canada.* Macdonald College, Quebec: Canadian Institute of Forestry, 1971
Goodwin, W.L. 'A School of Forestry for Ontario,' *Queen's Quarterly*, 10 (1902), 77–80
Loudon, J. 'Forestry and the University Question,' *University of Toronto Monthly*, 3 (1903), 177–84
Rogers, A.D. *Bernhard Edouard Fernow: A Story of American Forestry.* Princeton: Princeton University Press, 1951

Individual Institutions

(University of British Columbia)

Liersch, J.E. 'Forestry Education in British Columbia,' *Forestry Chronicle*, 22 (1946), 253–60

(Université Laval)

Cinquantenaire de l'enseignement des sciences forestières à l'Université Laval, 1910–1960. Québec: Les Presses de l'Université Laval, 1960

(University of New Brunswick)

Videto, H.E. 'The Growth of Forestry at the University of New Brunswick' in A.G. Bailey, editor. *The University of New Brunswick Memorial Volume.* Fredericton: The University, 1950. 87–97

(University of Toronto)

Sisam, J.W.B. *Forestry Education at Toronto.* Toronto: University of Toronto Press, 1961

Household Science

Duggan, G.L. *A Study of Some Aspects of Home Economics in Canadian Universities.* Edmonton: Canadian Home Economics Association, 1950
Howes, R. 'Adelaide Hoodless' in M.Q. Innis, editor. *The Clear Spirit: Twenty Canadian Women and Their Times.* Toronto: University of Toronto Press, 1966. 103–19
Lloyd, L.E. 'The Direction of Home Economics in Canada,' *Canadian Home Economics Journal*, 19, 3 (1969), 15–18, 31

Moxon, M.C. 'The Training of Teachers of Home Economics in Canada
and in the States of the American Union Adjacent to the Canadian
Provinces.' Unpublished M.A. thesis, University of Manitoba,
1933
Ritchie, E.M. 'Some Historical Aspects in the Growth of Home
Economics in the Province of Alberta.' Unpublished M.Ed. thesis,
University of Alberta, 1954
Rowles, E.C. *Home Economics in Canada: the Early History of Six
College Programs* ... Saskatoon: University of Saskatchewan
Bookstore, 1964. [The institutions dealt with are Acadia,
Guelph (Macdonald Institute), McGill, Mount Allison, Saskatchewan,
Toronto.]
Wilson, J.H. 'A History of Home Economics in Manitoba, 1826-1966.'
Unpublished M.Ed. thesis, University of Manitoba, 1967

Law

General

Audet, F.-J. 'Les Débuts du Barreau dans la Province de Québec,'
Cahiers des Dix, 2 (1937), 207-35
Baudoin, L. 'Les Cadres juridiques' in G. Sylvestre, editor.
Structures sociales du Canada français. Toronto: University
of Toronto Press, 1966. 84-97
Canadian Bar Association. 'Legal Education in Canada,' *Canadian
Bar Review*, 1 (1923), 671-84; 2 (1924), 376-89
Cohen, M. 'The Condition of Legal Education in Canada,' *Canadian
Bar Review*, 28 (1950), 267-314. Also other articles in this
issue.
Cohen, M. 'Legal Education in Canada - Fifteen Years Later, 1949-
1964,' *Canadian Bar Association Papers* (1964), 116-31
Curtis, G.F. 'Trends in Legal Education,' *Canadian Bar Journal*,
4 (1961), 21-9
Falconbridge, J.D. 'Legal Education in Canada,' *Journal of the
Society of Public Teachers of Law*, 9 (1932), 32-9
Giffen, P.J. 'Social Control and Professional Self-Government:
a Study of the Legal Profession in Canada' in S.D. Clark,
editor. *Urbanism and the Changing Canadian Society*. Toronto:
University of Toronto Press, 1961. 117-34
Goldenberg, J.M., et al. 'Practical Training in Legal Education:
Report of a Special Committee of the Conference of Governing
Bodies of the Legal Profession in Canada,' *Canadian Bar Journal*,
2 (1958), 121-31. Also other articles in this issue.
Hoyles, N.W. 'Legal Education in Canada' in J.C. Hopkins, editor.
Canada and its Provinces: an Encyclopedia of the Country.
Toronto: Linscott Publishing Co., 1900. VI, 374-8
Laskin, B. *The British Tradition in Canadian Law*. The Hamlyn Lec-
tures, Twenty-First Series. London: Stevens, 1969
Laskin, B. 'Law Teachers and Law Teaching in Canada,' *Journal of
the Society of Public Teachers of Law*, 30 (1953), 115-21

Law Society of Upper Canada. 'Legal Education ...,' *Canadian Bar Review*, 12 (1934-5), 347-58. Also other articles in this volume.

Rand, I.C. 'Legal Education in Canada,' *Canadian Bar Review*, 32 (1954), 387-414

Reed, A.Z. *Present Day Law Schools in the United States and Canada*. New York: Carnegie Foundation for the Advancement of Teaching, 1928

Reed, A.Z. *Some Contrasts between American and Canadian Legal Education*. New York: Carnegie Foundation for the Advancement of Teaching, 1921

Riddell, W.R. *The Legal Profession in Upper Canada in its Early Days*. Toronto: Law Society of Upper Canada, 1916

Surveyer, E.-F. 'Un Ecole de droit à Montréal avant le code civil,' *Revue Trimestrielle Canadienne*, 6 (1920), 140-50

Vachon, A. *Histoire du notariat canadien 1621-1960*. Québec: Les Presses de l'Université Laval, 1962

Wright, C.A. 'Law and the Law Schools,' *Canadian Bar Review*, 13 (1938), 579-601

Individual Institutions

(University of Manitoba)

Williams, E.K. 'Legal Education in Manitoba 1913-1950,' *Canadian Bar Review*, 28 (1950), 759-79, 880-92

(University of New Brunswick)

McInerney, H.E. 'The Development of the Law School' in A.G. Bailey, editor. *The University of New Brunswick Memorial Volume*. Fredericton: The University, 1950. 98-101

(University of Ottawa)

Caron, G. 'The Faculty of Law at the University of Ottawa,' *University of Toronto Law Journal*, 12 (1957), 292-5

(Queen's University)

Corry, J.A. 'The Queen's University Faculty of Law,' *University of Toronto Law Journal*, 12 (1957), 290-2

(University of Toronto)

Young, J.M. 'The Faculty of Law' in W.J. Alexander, editor. *The University of Toronto and its Colleges*. Toronto: The University, 1906. 149-67

(York University) (Osgoode Hall Law School)

Bucknall, B.D., Baldwin, T.C.H., and Lakin, J.D. 'Pedants, Practitioners and Prophets: Legal Education at Osgoode Hall to 1957,' *Osgoode Hall Law Journal*, 6 (1968), 142-229

Library Science

General

Canadian Library Association. 'Library Education in Canada,'
  Feliciter, 6 (1960), 8-22
Peel, B., editor. *Librarianship in Canada, 1946-1967. Essays
  in Honour of Elizabeth Homer Morton*. Victoria, B.C.: Canadian
  Library Association, 1968

Individual Institutions

(University of British Columbia)

Rothstein, S. 'Historical Notes: University of British Columbia
  School of Librarianship,' *Canadian Library*, 22 (1966), 226-8

(McGill University)

Ross, V. 'The McGill University Library School,' *Canadian Library
  Assocation Bulletin*, 14 (1958), 206-11

(Université de Montréal)

Tanghe, R. *L'Ecole de bibliothécaires de l'Université de Montréal
  1937-1962*. Montréal: Fides, 1962

(Mount Saint Vincent University)

Sister Francis Dolores, 'Mount Saint Vincent Library School,'
  Canadian Library Association Bulletin, 14 (1958), 217-19

(Université d'Ottawa)

Morisset, A.-M. 'Les Vingt-cinq Ans de l'Ecole de Bibliothéconomie
  d'Ottawa,' *Association Canadienne des Bibliothécaires de Langue
  Française Bulletin*, 10 (1964), 112-15

(University of Toronto)

Bassam, B. 'University of Toronto Library School and its Predecessors,' *Canadian Library Association Bulletin*, 14 (1958) 211-15

Medicine

General

Blishen, B.R. *Doctors and Doctrines: the Ideology of Medical
  Care in Canada*. Toronto: University of Toronto Press, 1969
Caniff, W. *The Medical Profession in Upper Canada, 1783-1850*.
  Toronto: Briggs, 1894
Farquharson, R.F. 'Medical and Dental Education in Canadian
  Universities' in D. Dunton and D. Patterson, editors. *Canada's
  Universities in a New Age*. Ottawa: National Conference of
  Canadian Universities and Colleges, 1962, 61-83
Flexner, A. *Medical Education: a Comparative Study*. New York:
  Macmillan, 1925

Heagerty, J.J. *Four Centuries of Medical History in Canada.* 2 volumes. Toronto: Macmillan, 1928

Herald, J. 'A Five Year Course in Medicine,' *Queen's Quarterly*, 1 (1893), 56-8

Leblond, S., et al. *Trois Siècles de Médecine Québécois.* Québec: Société historique de Québec, 1970

Lewis, D.S. *The Royal College of Physicians and Surgeons of Canada.* Montreal: McGill University Press, 1962

Macallum, A.B. *Retrospect, Aspect and Prospect in Medical Science: The Inaugural Lecture of the Faculty of Medicine for 1893.* Toronto: Bryant, 1893

MacDermot, H.E. *One Hundred Years of Medicine in Canada 1867-1967.* Toronto: McClelland & Stewart, 1967

Macfarlane, J.A., et al. *Medical Education in Canada.* Ottawa: Queen's Printer, 1964

McLeod, J.J.R. 'Medical Education,' *Journal of the Canadian Medical Association*, 10 (1920), 638-51

Morin, V. 'L'Evolution de la Médecine au Canada Français,' *Cahiers des Dix*, 25 (1960), 65-83

Ontario. *Report of the Commission on Medical Education in Ontario and Statements on Medical Education in Ontario* (J. Hodgins, Commissioner). Toronto: King's Printer, 1918

Patterson, M.A. 'The Life and Times of the Hon. John Rolph, M.D. (1793-1870),' *Medical History*, 5 (1961), 15-33

Royal Commission on Health Services. *Report ...* 2 volumes. Ottawa: Queen's Printer, 1964

Wilson, D. *Medical Education in Ontario: Letter to the Hon. G.W. Ross.* Toronto: Rowsell and Hutchison, 1892

Individual Institutions

(University of Alberta)

Scott, J.W. *The History of the Faculty of Medicine of the University of Alberta, 1913-1963.* Edmonton: The University, 1963

(Bishop's University)

Bensley, E.H. 'Bishop's Medical College,' *Journal of the Canadian Medical Association*, 72 (1955), 463-5

(University of British Columbia)

'Canada's Eleventh Medical School Graduates First Student Doctors,' *Canadian Doctor*, 20, 7 (1954), 35-9

(Dalhousie University)

Stewart, C.B. 'One Hundred Years of Medical Education at Dalhousie, *Nova Scotia Medical Bulletin*, 47, 5 (1968), 149-52

(Kingston Medical College for Women)

Hacker, C. *The Indomitable Lady Doctors.* Toronto: Clarke, Irwin, 1974

(Université Laval)

Boissonault, C.M. *Histoire de la Faculté de Médecine de Laval*.
  Québec: Les Presses de l'Université Laval, 1953

(McGill University)

Abbott, M.E. *An Historical Sketch of the Medical Faculty of
  McGill University*. Montreal: Gazette, 1902
Cushing, H. *The Life of Sir William Osler*. 2 volumes. Oxford:
  Clarendon, 1925
Howell, W.B. *F.J. Shepherd - Surgeon: His Life and Times*.
  Toronto: Dent, 1934
MacCallum, D.C. 'Reminiscences of the Medical Faculty of McGill
  University,' *McGill University Magazine*, 3 (1903), 125-35

(University of Manitoba)

Mitchell, R. *Medicine in Manitoba: the Story of its Beginnings*.
  Winnipeg: Stoval Advocate Press, 1955

(Université de Montréal)

Auclair, E.-J. 'L'Ecole Victoria de Montréal,' *Transactions of
  the Royal Society of Canada*. 1938. Section 1, 1-20
Dufresne, G. 'L'Ecole de Médecine et de Chirurgie de Montréal
  1843-1891,' *Union Médicale*, 74 (1946), 314-25
Mignault, L.-D. 'Histoire de l'Ecole de Médecine et de Chirurgie
  de Montréal,' *Union Médicale*, 55 (1926), 444-50, 511-14, 536-42
  557-64

(Ontario Medical College for Women)
Gullen, A.S. *A Brief History of the Ontario Medical College for
  Women*. Toronto, 1906

(Queen's University)

Gundy, H.P. 'Growing Pains: the Early History of the Queen's
  Medical Faculty,' *Historic Kingston*, 4 (1955), 14-25

(University of Toronto)

Godfrey, C.M. 'King's College: Upper Canada's First Medical
  School,' *Ontario Medical Review*, 34 (1967), 19-22, 26
Primrose, A. 'The Faculty of Medicine' in W.J. Alexander, editor.
  The University of Toronto and its Colleges. Toronto: The
  University, 1906. 168-79

(University of Trinity College)

Spragge, G.P. 'Trinity Medical College,' *Ontario History*, 58, 2
  (1966), 63-98

(University of Western Ontario

Seaborn, E. *The March of Medicine in Western Ontario*. Toronto:
  Ryerson, 1944

Music

Adaskin, H. 'Music in the University,' *NCCU Proceedings* (1955),
69-73
Brown, A.M. *A Study of Music Curriculum in Degree and Diploma
Programs Offered at Canadian Institutions of Higher Learning,
1968-1969.* Calgary: Canadian Association of University Schools
of Music, 1969
Kallman, H. *A History of Music in Canada, 1534-1914.* Toronto:
University of Toronto Press, 1960
Lasalle-Leduc, A. *La Vie musicale au Canada.* Québec: Ministère
des Affaires Culturelles, 1964
MacMillan, E. 'The Place of Music in a University Curriculum,'
NCCU Proceedings (1927), 66-75
Marcoux, J.C. *L'Enseignement de la musique dans la province de
Québec.* Québec, 1924
Procter, G.A. 'The Bachelor of Music Degree in Canada and the
United States,' *Canadian Music Educator*, 7, 2 (1966), 27-33
Walter, A. 'Education in Music' in E. MacMillan, editor. *Music
in Canada.* Toronto: University of Toronto Press, 1955. 133-45

Nursing

General

DeFries, R.D., editor. *The Development of Public Health in
Canada* ... Toronto: Canadian Public Health Association, 1940
Duncanson, B. 'The Development of Nursing Education at the Diploma
Level' in M.Q. Innis, editor. *Nursing Education in a Changing
Society.* Toronto: University of Toronto Press, 1970. 109-29
Gibbon, J.M., and Mathewson, M.S. *Three Centuries of Canadian
Nursing.* Toronto: Macmillan, 1947
King, M.K. 'The Development of University Nursing Education' in
M.Q. Innis, editor. *Nursing Education in a Changing Society.*
Toronto: University of Toronto Press, 1970. 67-85
Mussallem, H.K. *Nursing Education in Canada.* Ottawa: Queen's
Printer, 1965
Ross, A. *Becoming a Nurse.* Toronto: Macmillan, 1961
Russell, E.K. 'Public Health Nursing Courses in Canadian Univer-
sities,' *Journal of the International Council of Nurses*, 2
(1927), 191-6
Shaw, F.M. 'Nursing Education in Universities in Canada,' *Journal
of the International Council of Nurses*, 2 (1927), 181-6
'University Schools of Nursing in Canada,' *Canadian Nurse*, 46,
4 (April 1970), 41-51
Weir, G.M. *Survey of Nursing Education in Canada.* Toronto:
University of Toronto Press, 1932

Individual Institutions

(McGill University)

Tunis, B.L. *In Cap and Gowns: the Story of the School for Graduate Nurses, McGill University, 1920-1964*. Montreal: McGill University Press, 1966

(Université de Montréal)

Beaudoin, J.A. 'L'Ecole d'hygiene sociale appliquée,' *Revue Trimestrielle Canadienne*, 25 (1939), 198-217
Charbonneau, M.L.G. 'The History of the School of Public Health Nursing at the University of Montreal, Canada, 1925-1950.' Unpublished M.A. thesis, Catholic University of America, 1956

(University of New Brunswick)

MacLaggan, K. 'U.N.B.'s School of Nursing,' *Canadian Nurse*, 56 (1960), 424-6

(University of Toronto)

Carpenter, H.M. 'The University of Toronto School of Nursing: an Agent of Change' in M.Q. Innis, editor. *Nursing Education in a Changing Society*. Toronto: University of Toronto Press. 86-108

Optometry

Fisher, E.J. 'Optometrical Education in Canada,' *Canadian Journal of Optometry*, 29 (1967), 107-36
Messier, J.A. 'Ecole d'optometrie, Université de Montréal,' *Canadian Journal of Optometry*, 29 (1967), 99-105

Pharmacy

General

Commission on Pharmaceutical Services. *Pharmacy in a New Age*. Toronto: Canadian Pharmaceutical Association, 1971
Frewin, M. 'A History of the Pharmaceutical Association, Inc.,' *Canadian Pharmaceutical Journal*, 90 (1957), 72-98
Hughes, F.N. 'The Changing Picture of Canadian Pharmacy,' *Medical Library Association Bulletin*, 48 (1960), 162-7
Matthews, A.W., et al. 'Facilities and Curricula for Pharmacy Education in Canada,' *Canadian Pharmaceutical Journal*, 95 (1963), 215-36
Paterson, G.R. 'The Canadian Conference of Pharmaceutical Faculties,' *American Journal of Pharmaceutical Education*, 22 (1958), 201-8
Sonnedecker, G., Stieb, E.W., and Kennedy, D.R. *One Hundred Years of Pharmacy in Canada*. Toronto: Canadian Academy of the History of Pharmacy, 1969

Institutions

Volume 100 of the *Canadian Pharmaceutical Journal* (1967) contains
articles on the history of pharmacy in each province; these
outline the developments at each institution.

Physical and Health Education

General

Belanger, Y. 'Physical Education in Quebec,' *Canadian Educational
Research Digest*, 2 (1962), 29-36
Consentino, F., and Howell, M.L. *A History of Physical Education
in Canada*. Toronto: General Publishing Co., 1971
Day, J. 'Robert Tait MacKenzie: Physical Education's Man of the
Century,' *Canadian Association of Health, Physical Education
and Recreation Journal*, 33, 4 (April/May 1967), 4-17
Errington, J. 'An Evaluation of Undergraduate Professional Pre-
paration in Physical Education for Men in Canada.' Unpublished
doctoral thesis, Indiana University, 1958
Lamb, A.S. 'Tait MacKenzie in Canada,' *Journal of Health and
Recreation*, 15 (1944), 69-85
Kennedy, W.F.R. 'Health, Physical Education and Recreation in
Canada, a History of Professional Preparation.' Unpublished
doctoral thesis, Columbia University, 1955
Meagher, J.W. 'A Projected Plan for the Reorganization of the
Physical Education Teacher-Training Program.' Unpublished
doctoral thesis, Pennsylvania State University, 1958
Mercier, A. *Le Problème de l'éducation physique dans les
universités canadiennes-françaises*. Montréal: Université de
Montréal, 1948
Pelletier, R. 'A Summary of Physical Education and Athletic Ad-
ministration in Canadian Universities and Colleges.' Unpub-
lished M.S. thesis, Springfield College, 1958
Van Vleet, M.L., editor. *Physical Education in Canada*. Scarborough:
Prentice-Hall of Canada, 1965. Includes J.W. Meagher, 'Pro-
fessional Preparation,' 64-81; M.L. Howell, 'Physical Education
Research in Canada,' 249-75; C.R. Blackstock, 'The Canadian
Association for Health, Physical Education and Recreation, 276-90

Individual Institutions

(McGill University)

Eaton, J.D. 'The Life and Professional Contributions of Arthur
Stanley Lamb, M.D. to Physical Education in Canada.' Unpub-
lished doctoral thesis, Ohio State University, 1964
Slack, Z. 'The Development of Physical Education for Women at
McGill.' Unpublished M.A. thesis, McGill University, 1934
Webb, B.L. *The Basketball Man James Naismith*. Wichita: University
of Kansas Press, 1972

(University of Toronto)

Jackson, D.N.R. *A Brief History of Three Schools: The School of Expression, the Margaret Eaton School of Literature and Expression, the Margaret Eaton School, 1901-1941.* Toronto: privately published, 1953

Wipper, K.A.W. *Retrospect and Perspect: a Record of the School of Physical and Health Education, 1940-1965.* Toronto: privately published, 1966

Physical and Occupational Therapy

General

Azima, H., and Wittkower, E.D. 'A Partial Field Survey of Psychiatric Occupational Therapy,' *Canadian Journal of Occupational Therapy,* 24 (1957), 69-80

Bagnall, A.W., et al. 'A Panel Discussion of Constructive Criticism of Occupational and Physical Therapy,' *Canadian Journal of Occupational Therapy,* 22 (1955), 81-91

Driver, M.F. 'A Philosophic View of the History of Occupational Therapy in Canada,' *Canadian Journal of Occupational Therapy,* 35 (1968), 53-60

Dunlop, W.J. 'A Brief History of Occupational Therapy,' *Canadian Journal of Occupational Therapy,* 1 (1933), 6-10

Ferland, M. 'Physiotherapy in Canada,' *Canadian Physiotherapy Association Journal,* 17 (1965), 154-63

Individual Institutions

(University of Alberta)

Fowler, J.R., et al. 'The School of Physical and Occupational Therapy,' *Canadian Physiotherapy Association Journal,* 13 (1961), 21-4

(University of Toronto)

Le Vesconte, H. 'University of Toronto,' *American Journal of Occupational Therapy,* 1 (1947), 49-51

Social Work

General

De Jongh, J.F. 'Regard rétrospectif sur l'enseignement du service social,' *Service Social,* 21 (1972), 22-44

Falk, J.H.T. 'The Future of Social Work in Canada,' *Dalhousie Review,* 1 (1920), 182-7

King, D. 'Professional Training for Social Work in Canada.' Unpublished M.A. thesis, New York University, 1944

Proceedings of the Canadian Conference on Social Work. 1930. 238-41

Individual Institutions

(Dalhousie University)

MacLean, F. 'The Maritime School of Social Work,' *Atlantic Advocate*, 51 (1961), 9, 74-6

(Université Laval)

Denault, H. 'Les Débuts de l'expérience d'enseignement du service social à l'école de Laval,' *Service Social*, 10 (1962), 102-9

(Université de Montréal)

Paré, S. 'Revue Rétrospective de l'Ecole de Service Social depuis sa fondation,' *Service Social*, 4 (1954), 85-92

(University of Toronto)

Hendry, C.E. *Fiftieth Anniversary 1914-1964, School of Social Work, University of Toronto.* Toronto: The School, 1964
Urwick, E.J., et al. *Training for Social Work in the Department of Social Science, University of Toronto.* Toronto: University of Toronto Press, 1940

Teacher Training

Audet, L.-P. 'Les Cadres scolaires' in G. Sylvestre, editor. *Structures sociales du Canada français.* Toronto: University of Toronto Press, 1966. 29-66
Bailey, A.W. 'The Professional Preparation of Teachers for the Schools of the Province of New Brunswick, 1784-1964.' Unpublished Ph.D. thesis, University of Toronto, 1964
Channon, G. 'Trends in Teacher Preparation Curricula in Canada,' *McGill Journal of Education*, 6 (1971), 144-59
Coutts, H.T., and Walker, B.E. 'The Faculty of Education at the University of Alberta,' *School Progress*, 33, 9 (September 1964), 31-7, 50
Davis, F.M. 'The History of the Growth of the Faculty of Education within the University of Manitoba.' Unpublished M.A. thesis, University of Manitoba, 1957
Harris, R.S. *Quiet Evolution: a Study of the Ontario Educational System.* Toronto: University of Toronto Press, 1967
Hume, J.G. 'Pedagogics as a University Subject,' *Dominion Education Association Proceedings* (1898), 33-47
Lazerte, M.E. *Teacher Education in Canada.* Toronto: Gage, 1951
MacDougall, J.I. 'Recent Developments in Teacher Education in Western Canada.' Unpublished D.Paed. thesis, University of Toronto, 1953
Munroe, D. 'Teacher Education at McGill,' *McGill Journal of Education*, 6 (1971), 29-40
Munroe, D., Scarfe, N.V., and Stewart, A. 'The Role of the University in Teacher Training: a Symposium,' *NCCU Proceedings* (1954), 47-59
Nova Scotia Normal College. *One Hundred Years of Teacher Education.* Halifax: The College, 1955
Ontario Department of Education. *Report of the Minister's Com-*

mittee on the *Training of Elementary School Teachers.* Toronto:
The Department, 1966
Ontario Department of Education. *Report of the Minister's Committee
on the Training of Secondary School Teachers.* Toronto: The
Department, 1962
Pakenham, W. 'The University and the Training of Teachers for
Secondary Schools,' *NCCU Proceedings* (1922), 36-44
Pouliot, A. 'Les Sciences dans notre enseignement classique: la
formation des professeurs de science,' *Enseignement secondaire,*
10 (1931), 446-64
Toronto Normal School. *Toronto Normal School 1847-1947.* Toronto:
The School, 1945
Tremblay, A. 'L'Université Laval, la pédagogie et l'orientation,'
Pédagogie-Orientation, 2 (1948), 227-33
Weir, G.M. 'The College of Education as an Agency for Training
Teachers for Secondary Schools,' *NCCU Proceedings* (1927), 34-47

Theology

General

Blais, H. 'L'Enseignement de la théologie au Canada,' *Culture,*
2 (1941), 206-20
Boone, H.W. 'The Development of the Bible College or Institute in
the United States and Canada since 1880 and its Relationship
to the Field of Theological Education in America.' Unpublished
doctoral thesis, New York University, 1950
Cronyn, B. *The Bishop of Huron's Objections to the Theological
Teaching of Trinity College, with the Provost's Reply.* Toronto:
Rowsell, 1860
Elliot, J. 'The Education of the Clergy,' *Queen's Quarterly,* 2
(1895), 224-34
Feilding, C. 'Twenty-Three Theological Schools: Aspects of
Canadian Theological Education,' *Canadian Journal of Theology,*
12 (1966), 229-37
Garant, C.-O. 'Le Cinquantenaire de l'encyclique "Aeterni Patris"
à Laval,' *Revue Dominicaine,* 35 (1929), 419-37
Hughes, N.L. 'A History of the Development of Ministerial Educa-
tion in Canada from its Inception until 1925 in Those Churches
which were Tributary to the United Church in Ontario, Quebec
and the Maritime Provinces.' Unpublished doctoral dissertation,
University of Chicago, 1945
Jordan, W.G. 'The Standard of Ministerial Education,' *Queen's
Quarterly,* 19 (1912), 202-13
Kelly, R.L. *Theological Education in America.* New York: Institute
of Social and Religious Research, 1924
Langevin, G. 'L'Evolution recente et l'état actual de l'enseigne-
ment de la théologie au Canada français,' *Canadian Journal of
Theology,* 14 (1963), 149-59
Masters, D.C. *Protestant Church Colleges in Canada.* Toronto:
University of Toronto Press, 1966
Peake, F.A. 'Theological Education in British Columbia,' *Canadian
Journal of Theology,* 5 (1959), 251-63

Shook, L.K. *Catholic Post-Secondary Education in English-Speaking Canada*. Toronto: University of Toronto Press, 1971

Thomas, L.G. 'The Church of England and Higher Education in the Prairie West before 1914,' *Journal of the Canadian Church History Society*, 3 (1956), 1-11

Whitaker, G. *Two Letters to the Lord Bishop of Toronto: in Reply to Charges Brought by the Lord Bishop of Huron against the Theological Teaching of Trinity College*. Toronto: Rowsell, 1863

Individual Institutions

(Baptist)

Cochran, O.D. 'The Development of Theological Education at Acadia University.' Unpublished B.D. thesis, Acadia University, 1954

(Church of England)

Frazer, W.J. 'A History of St. John's College, Winnipeg.' Unpublished M.A. thesis, University of Manitoba, 1966

Hague, D., et al. *The Jubilee Volume of Wycliffe College*. Toronto: The College, 1927

Howard, O. *The Montreal Diocesan Theological College: a History from 1873 to 1963*. Montreal: McGill University Press, 1963

Masters, D.C. *Bishop's University: The First Hundred Years*. Toronto; Clarke, Irwin, 1950

Purdy, J.D. 'John Strachan and the Diocesan Theological Institute at Cobourg, 1842-1852,' *Ontario History*, 45 (1973), 113-23

Reed, T.A., editor. *A History of the University of Trinity College, 1852-1952*. Toronto: University of Toronto Press, 1952

Talman, J.J. *Huron College, 1863-1963*. London: The College, 1963

(Congregationalist)

Congregational College of Canada. *A Short History and a Plea*. Montreal: The College, 1921

Marling, F.H. *Congregational College of British North America: the Story of the 50 Years, 1839-1889*. Montreal: The College, 1889

(Lutheran)

Lyon, B. *The First 60 Years: a History of Waterloo Lutheran University from the Opening of Waterloo Lutheran Seminary in 1911 to the Present Year*. Waterloo: The University, 1971

(Methodist)

Falconer, J.W., and Watson, W.G. *A Brief History of Pinehill Divinity Hall and the Theological Department of Mount Allison University*. Halifax: privately published, 1946

Kirkconnell, W. *Golden Jubilee, Wesley College, 1888-1938*. Winnipeg: Columbia Press, 1938

Patton, W.M. 'The Wesleyan Theological College of Montreal' in J.G. Hopkins, editor. *Canada: an Encyclopaedia of the Country*. Toronto: Linscott Publishing Co., 1898. IV, 301-2

Sissons, C.B. *A History of Victoria University*. Toronto: University of Toronto Press, 1952

(Presbyterian)

Calvin, D.D. *Queen's University at Kingston, 1841-1941*. Kingston: The University, 1941

Falconer, J.W., and Watson, W.G. *A Brief History of Pinehill Divinity Hall and the Theological Department of Mount Allison University*. Halifax: privately published, 1946

Knox College Centenary Committee. *The Centenary of the Granting of the Charter of Knox College, Toronto, 1858-1958*. Toronto: The College, 1958

MacRae, D. 'Morrin College, Quebec' in J.G. Hopkins, editor. *Canada: an Encyclopaedia of the Country*. Toronto: Linscott Publishing Co., IV, 1898. 298-9

MacVicar, D.H. 'The Presbyterian College, Montreal' in J.G. Hopkins, editor. *Canada: an Encyclopaedia of the Country*. Toronto: Linscott Publishing Co., IV, 1898. 297-8

MacVicar, J.H. *Life and Work of Donald Harvey MacVicar*. Toronto: Westminster Co., 1904

Rumball, W.G., and MacLennan, D.A., editors. *Manitoba College* ... Winnipeg: The College, 1921

(Roman Catholic)

Université Laval (Grand Séminaire de Québec)
Provost, H. 'Les Origines éloignées du Séminaire de Québec,' *Canadian Catholic Historical Association Annual Report* (1955-6), 25-31

Provost, H. 'Propos sur l'histoire du Séminaire de Québec,' *Revue de l'Université Laval*, 18 (1964), 591-9
Université de Montréal (Grand Séminaire de Montréal)
Grand Séminaire de Montréal. *Centenaire 1840-1940*. Montréal: Le Séminaire, 1941

Pouliot, L. 'Le Premier Ecole de Théologie à Montréal: Le Séminaire St.-Jacques (1825-1840),' *Sciences ecclésiastiques*, 6 (1954), 237-47
Université d'Ottawa
Carrière, G. *Histoire documentaire de la Congrégation des Missionnaires Oblats de Marie-Immacutée dans l'est du Canada*. Ottawa: Editions de l'Université d'Ottawa, volume II 1959; volume VI 1967

Veterinary Medicine

General

Cameron, T.W.M. 'Veterinary Education in Canada,' *Canadian Journal of Comparative Medicine*, 21 (1957), 289-93

Campbell, D.M. 'Development of Veterinary Medicine in North America,' *Veterinary Medicine*, 29 (1934), 48-52, 182-5, 226-8, 268-70, 310-12, 352-4, 458-92

Daubigny, F.T. 'Les Ecoles vétérinaires en Canada,' *Union Médicale*,
    25 (1896), 666-70
Gattinger, F.E. 'Veterinary Instruction at Queen's and O.A.C.,'
    Canadian Veterinary Journal, 3 (1962), 174-80
Mitchell, C.A. 'A Note on the History of Veterinary Sciences in
    Canada,' *Canadian Journal of Comparative Medicine*, 1 (1937-8),
    91-5
'Queen's School of Veterinary Science 1895-1899,' *Queen's Review*
    (December 1928), 256-8

Individual Institutions

(University of Guelph) (Ontario Veterinary College)

Gattinger, F.E. *A Century of Challenge*. Toronto: University of
    Toronto Press, 1962

(Université de Montréal)

St. Georges, J. '75th Anniversary of the School for Veterinary
    Medicine of the Province of Quebec,' *Canadian Journal of
    Comparative Medicine*, 25 (1961), 239-42

GRADUATE STUDIES

Brebner, J.B. *Scholarship for Canada: the Function of Graduate
    Studies*. Ottawa: Social Science Research Council, 1945
De Koninck, C., Spinks, J.W.T., et al. 'Graduate Studies and
    Research in the Humanities and Social Sciences' in D. Dunton
    and D. Patterson, editors. *Canada's Universities in a New Age*.
    Ottawa: National Conference of Canadian Universities and
    Colleges, 1962. 33-57
Falconer, R.A. 'The Gilchrist Scholarship: an Episode in the
    Higher Education of Canada,' *Transactions of the Royal Society
    of Canada*. 1933. Section 2, 5-13
Nicholson, N.L. 'The Evolution of Graduate Studies in the Univer-
    sities of Ontario, 1841-1971.' Unpublished Ed.D. thesis,
    University of Toronto, 1975
Ontario Commission to Study the Development of Graduate Program-
    mes in Ontario Universities, J.W.T. Spinks, chairman. *Report*.
    Toronto: Committee on University Affairs / Committee of
    Presidents of Provincially Assisted Universities, 1966
Ross, P.N. 'The Origins and Development of the Ph.D. at the
    University of Toronto, 1871-1932.' Unpublished Ed.D. thesis,
    University of Toronto, 1973
Sage, W.N. *Graduate Training in Arts in Canadian Universities
    with Special Reference to Requirements for the M.A. and Ph.D.
    Degrees*. Ottawa: Social Science Research Council, 1944
Thompson, W.P. *Graduate Education in the Sciences in Canadian
    Universities*. Toronto: University of Toronto Press, 1963
University of Toronto, President's Committee on the School of
    Graduate Studies, B. Laskin, chairman. *Graduate Studies in
    the University of Toronto*. Toronto: University of Toronto
    Press, 1965

Bailey, J.W. *Loring Woart Bailey: the Story of a Man of Science.*
Saint John: McMillan, 1925
Berger, C.C. *The Sense of Power: Studies in the Ideas of Canadian
Imperialism, 1867-1914.* Toronto: University of Toronto Press,
1970
Boggs, J.S. *The National Gallery of Canada.* London: Thames and
Hudson, 1971
Bonneau, L.P., and Corry, J.A. *Quest for the Optimum: the Report
of a Commission to Study the Rationalization of University
Research.* 2 volumes. Ottawa: Association of Universities
and Colleges of Canada, 1972-73
Bourinot, J.G. 'Our Intellectual Strength and Weakness: a Short
Review of Literature, Education and Art in Canada,' *Transactions
of the Royal Society of Canada.* 1893. Section 2, 3-36
Bourinot, J.G. *The Intellectual Development of the Canadian
People.* Toronto: Hunter, Rose, 1881
Bourinot, J.G., editor. *Bibliography of the Members of the Royal
Society of Canada.* Ottawa: The Society, 1894
Brebner, J.B. *Scholarship in Canada: the Function of Graduate
Studies.* Ottawa: Canadian Social Science Research Council, 1945
Brown, F.M. *Breaking Barriers: Eric Brown and the National Gallery.*
Toronto: Society for Art Publications, 1964
Burpee, L.J. 'A Plea for a National Library,' *University Magazine,*
10 (1911), 152-63
Calvin, D.D. 'Queen's Quarterly, 1893-1943,' *Queen's Quarterly,*
50 (1943), 117-29
Canada, Department of Agriculture. *Fifty Years of Progress on
Dominion Experimental Farms, 1886-1936.* Ottawa: King's
Printer, 1939
Canada, Royal Commission on Canada's Economic Prospects, W.L.
Gordon, chairman. *Report.* Ottawa: Queen's Printer, 1958
Canada, Royal Commission on Dominion-Provincial Relations, N.
Rowell and J. Sirois, chairmen. *Report.* Ottawa: King's
Printer, 1940
Canada, Royal Commission on Government Organization, J.G. Glassco,
chairman. *Report.* 5 volumes. Ottawa: Queen's Printer, 1962
Canada, Royal Commission on National Development in the Arts,
Letters and Sciences, V. Massey, chairman. *Report.* Ottawa:
King's Printer, 1951
Canada, Senate Special Committee on Science Policy, L. Lamontagne,
chairman. *A Science Policy for Canada* I: *a Critical Review,
Past and Present.* Ottawa: Queen's Printer, 1971
Canada Council. *Annual Reports.* 1957/8-1960/1
Cartwright, M.J. 'Survey of the History of Academic Libraries in
Canada,' *Canadian Library,* 25 (1968), 98-102
Creighton, D.G. *Harold Adams Innis: Portrait of a Scholar.*
Toronto: University of Toronto Press, 1957
Currelly, C.T. *I Brought the Ages Home.* Toronto: University of
Toronto Press, 1957

Dales, J.H. 'Canadian Scholarship in Economics' in R.H. Hubbard, editor. *Scholarship in Canada 1967*. Toronto: University of Toronto Press, 1967. 82-93

Dawson, G.M. 'The Progress and Trend of Scientific Investigations in Canada,' *Proceedings of the Royal Society of Canada*. 1894. lii-lxvi

Dawson, R., editor. *Fifty Years of Work in Canada ... Being Autographical Notes by Sir William Dawson ...* London: Ballantyne Hanson, 1901

Defries, R.D. *The First Forty Years, 1914-1955: Connaught Medical Research Laboratories, University of Toronto*. Toronto: University of Toronto Press, 1969

Désilets, A. *Les Cents Ans de l'Institut Canadien*. Québec: l'Institut, 1949

Donnelly, F.D. *The National Library of Canada*. Ottawa: Canadian Library Association, 1973

Drolet, A. *Les Bibliothèques canadiennes 1604-1960*. Ottawa: Cercle du Livre de France, 1965

Eggleston, Wilfrid. 'A History of the National Research Council of Canada.' Unpublished manuscript

Eve, A.S. *Rutherford: Being the Life and Letters of Rt. Hon. Lord Rutherford ...* Cambridge: Cambridge University Press, 1939

Galarneau, C. *La France devant l'opinion canadienne (1760-1815)*. Québec: Les Presses de l'Université Laval, 1970

Goldstick, I., editor. *Modern Language Instruction in Canada*. 2 volumes. Toronto: University of Toronto Press, 1928

Goodwin, C.D.W. *Canadian Economic Thought: the Political Economy of a Developing Nation, 1814-1914*. Durham, N.C.: Duke University Press, 1961

Graham, J.F. 'The Social Sciences: Specific Needs' in R.H. Hubbard, editor. *Scholarship in Canada 1967*. Toronto: University of Toronto Press, 1967. 17-25

Hachey, H.B. 'History of the Fisheries Research Board of Canada.' Manuscript Report Series (Biological) No. 843. Ottawa: The Board, 1965

Hamlin, D.L.B. *International Studies in Canadian Universities*. Ottawa: Canadian Universities Foundation, 1964

Harman, E., editor. *The University as Publisher*. Toronto: University of Toronto Press, 1962

Harrington, B. *Life of Sir William Logan ...* Montreal: Dawson Bros., 1863

Hettick, W. 'Federal Science Policy and Social Science Research in Canadian Universities,' *Canadian Public Administrator*, 14 (Spring 1971), 112-8

Hind, H.L. *Eighty Years' Progress of British North America ...* Toronto: L. Stebbins, 1864

Hopkins, E.S. 'Agricultural Research in Canada: its Origin and Development,' *Annals of the American Academy of Political and Social Science*, 107 (1923), 82-7

Hubbard, R.H. 'The Early Years of the National Gallery of Canada,' *Transactions of the Royal Society of Canada*. 1965. Section 2, 121-9

Hubbard, R.H., editor. *Scholarship in Canada 1967*. Toronto: University of Toronto Press, 1967

Humanities Research Council of Canada. *Annual Reports*. 1943/7-1959/62

Johnson, H.G. 'Canadian Contributions to the Discipline of Economics,' *Canadian Journal of Economics*, 1 (1968), 129-46

Kirkconnell, W. 'Organizing the Humanities' in *A Slice of Canada: Memoirs*. Toronto: University of Toronto Press, 1967. 233-48

Kirkconnell, W., and Woodhouse, A.S.P. *The Humanities in Canada*. Ottawa: Humanities Research Council of Canada, 1947

Klinck, C.F., editor. *Literary History of Canada: Canadian Literature in English*. Toronto: University of Toronto Press, 1965. Includes: H.P. Gundy, 'Literary Publishing,' 174-88; K.N. Windsor, 'Historical Writing in English (to 1920),' 208-50; A.V. Douglas, 'Scientific Writing,' 445-56; W.M. Kilbourn, 'The Writing of Canadian History,' 496-519; H.B. Mayo, 'Writing in the Social Sciences,' 519-28; M. MacLure, 'Literary Scholarship,' 529-50; J.S. Thomson, 'Literature of Religion and Theology,' 551-75; J.A. Irving and A.H. Johnson, 'Philosophical Writings 1910-1964,' 576-97

Langton, H.H. *Sir John Cunningham McLennan: a Memoir with a Chapter on his Scientific Work by E.F. Burton*. Toronto: University of Toronto Press, 1939

Lower, A.R.M. *My First Seventy-Five Years*. Toronto: Macmillan, 1967

MacDermot, H.E. 'Medical Journals' in *One Hundred Years of Medicine in Canada*. Toronto: McClelland & Stewart, 1967. 155-6

Macdonald, J.B., et al. *The Role of the Federal Government in Support of Research in Canadian Universities*. Ottawa: Queen's Printer, 1969

McDougall, R.L. 'The University Quarterlies,' *Canadian Forum*, 38 (1959), 253-8

MacGibbon, D.A. 'The Meeting of the Canadian Economists in Ottawa' in *Contributions to Canadian Economics*. Toronto: University of Toronto Press, 1929. II, 7-10

Medical Research Council of Canada. *Canadian Medical Research: Survey and Outlook*. Ottawa: Queen's Printer, 1968

Merrill, F.J.H. *Natural History Museums of the United States and Canada*. New York State Museum Bulletin No. 62. Albany: University of the State of New York, 1903

Miers, H.A., and Markham, S.F. *A Report on the Museums of Canada ... to the Carnegie Corporation of New York*. London: Museums Association, 1932

Miers, H.A., and Markham, S.F. *Directory of Museums and Art Galleries*, Pt. I The Museums of Canada. London: Museums Association, 1933

Miller, J.C. *National Government and Technical Education in Federated Democracies: Dominion of Canada*. Philadelphia: privately printed, 1940

Morin, V. 'Les Dix,' *Cahiers des Dix*, 1 (1936), 7-36

Morin, V. 'L'Odyssée d'une société historique,' *Cahiers des Dix*, 8 (1947), 13-54

National Research Council of Canada. *Annual Reports*. 1916/17-
1960/1

Neale, E.R.W., editor. *The Earth Sciences in Canada: a Centennial Appraisal and Forecast*. Toronto: University of Toronto
Press, 1968

Neill, R.F. 'The World of Harold Adams Innis: Content and Context.' Unpublished doctoral disseration, Duke University, 1967

Oliver, M. 'Research in the Social Sciences,' *AUCC Proceedings*
(1967), II, 113-22. See also 123-32

Ontario, Royal Commission on University Finances, H.J. Cody,
chairman. *Report*. 2 volumes. Toronto: King's Printer, 1921

Park, J., editor. *The Culture of Contemporary Canada*. Toronto:
Ryerson, 1957. Includes R.O. Earl, 'Science,' 327-66; J.A.
Irving, 'Philosophy,' 243-73; C.B. Macpherson, 'The Social
Sciences,' 181-221; M. MacLure, 'Literary Scholarship,' 222-41;
M. Wade, 'The Culture of French Canada,' 367-95

Porter, J. 'The Ideological System: the Higher Learning and the
Clergy' in *The Vertical Mosaic: an Analysis of Social Class
and Power in Canada*. Toronto: University of Toronto Press,
1965. 491-591

Quebec Literary and Historical Society. *The Centenary Volume
1824-1924*. Quebec: L'Evénement, 1924

Ridington, J., et al. *Libraries in Canada: a Study of Conditions
and Needs*. Toronto: Ryerson, 1933

Rousseau, J. 'Les Débuts de l'ACFAS: notice historique,' *Annales
de l'ACFAS*, 1 (1935), 19-24

Rousseau, J. 'L'Oeuvre de l'ACFAS,' *Annales de l'ACFAS*, 3 (1937),
23-7

Speakman, H.B., et al. *Research in Canada - Planning for the
Coming Years: Papers Given at the Symposium of the Chemical
Institute of Canada*. Quebec: Imperial Oil Ltd., 1946

Shook, L.K. 'The Pontifical Institute of Mediaeval Studies' in
Catholic Post-Secondary Education in English-Speaking Canada.
Toronto: University of Toronto Press, 1971. 210-28

Shutt, F.T. 'Agricultural Education and Research in Canada,'
Transactions of the Royal Society of Canada. 1916. Section
3, 1-17

Spinks, J.W.T. 'Graduate Studies and Research in the Sciences'
in A.D. Dunton and D. Patterson, editors. *Canada's Universities
in a New Age*. Ottawa: National Conference of Canadian Universities and Colleges, 1962. 39-50

Spinks, J.W.T. 'Trends in University Research' in G. Stanley and
G. Sylvestre, editors. *Canadian Universities Today*. Toronto:
University of Toronto Press, 1961. 38-44

Stevenson, L.G. *Sir Frederick Banting*. Toronto: Ryerson, 1946

Story, N. *The Oxford Companion to Canadian History and Literature*.
Toronto: Oxford University Press, 1967; W. Toye, ed. *Supplement to ...* Toronto: Oxford University Press, 1973. Especially entries on 'History Studies in English,' 'History Studies

in French,' 'Literary Magazines in English,' 'Literary Magazines
  in French,' 'Political Writing'
Taylor, K.W. 'Economic Scholarship in Canada,' *Canadian Journal
  of Economics and Political Science*, 26 (1960), 6-18
Taylor, K.W. 'The Founding of the Canadian Political Science
  Association,' *Canadian Journal of Economics and Political
  Science*, 33 (1967), 581-5
Thistle, M. *The Inner Ring: the Early History of the National
  Research Council of Canada*. Toronto: University of Toronto
  Press, 1966
Thistle, M., editor. *The Mackenzie-McNaughton Letters*, with
  Introduction and Epilogue by C.J. Mackenzie. Toronto: Uni-
  versity of Toronto Press, 1975
Timlin, M., and Faucher, A. *The Social Sciences in Canada: Two
  Studies / Les Sciences sociales au Canada: deux etudes*.
  Ottawa: The Council, 1968
Toole, F.J. 'The Scientific Tradition' in A.G. Bailey, editor.
  The University of New Brunswick Memorial Volume. Fredericton:
  The University, 1950. 69-74
Tory, H.M., editor. *A History of Science in Canada*. Toronto:
  Ryerson, 1939
Wade, M. *The French Canadians, 1760-1945*. Toronto: Macmillan, 1955
Wallace, W.S., editor. *Royal Canadian Institute Centennial
  Volume, 1849-1949*. Toronto: The Institute, 1949
West, A.S. *National Engineering, Scientific and Technological
  Societies of Canada*. Ottawa: Science Council of Canada, 1972
Williams, E.E. *Resources of Canadian University Libraries for
  Research in the Humanities and Social Sciences*. Ottawa:
  National Conference of Canadian Universities and Colleges, 1962
Williams, M.Y. 'The Earth Sciences and the Royal Society of Canada,'
  Proceedings of the Royal Society of Canada, 1961, 65-79
Wrenshall, G.A., Hetenyi, G., and Feasby, W.R. *The Story of
  Insulin: Forty Years of Success against Diabetes*. London:
  Bodley Head, 1962
Wrong, G.M. 'The Beginning of Historical Criticism in Canada: a
  Retrospect 1896-1936,' *Canadian Historical Review*, 17 (1936),
  1-8

Index

366, 417, 423; Calgary Branch 485-6; commerce 366, 513; dentistry 290, 538; education 366, 417, 486, 544; household science 285, 366, 537-8; law 264, 401; medicine 268, 366; music 548; nursing 366, 412; pharmacy 410, 539; physical & health education 301, 486, 548; physical and occupational therapy 541
Alexander, William J. 105, 132, 189-90
Allied Colonial Universities Conference (1903) 205-6
Allison, Charles 11
Alma College, St Thomas, Ont. 371, 491
American Library Association 585
Anglican Theological College, Vancouver, B.C. 261, 400, 529
Andrews, W.W. 284
Angus, Henry F. 437
Anthropology 51, 141, 249, 251-2, 387-8, 519, 521, 553
Archambault, Papin 252
Architecture 39, 72-3, 166, 168-9, 271-2, 404, 535
Arctic Institute of North America, Montreal, Quebec 581
Art galleries 333-4, 448, 585
Ashley, William J. 134, 142-3
Association Canadienne Française pour l'avancement des sciences 390-1, 440, 579
Association of American Universities 431, 600
Association of Canadian University Teachers of English 576
Association of Universities & Colleges of Canada. See National Conference of Canadian Universities
Assumption University, Windsor, Ont. 9-10, 12, 109, 155, 224, 363, 468-9, 480-81, 537, 557
Atomic Energy Control Board 566
Audet, Louis-Phillipe 14, 17-18, 380

Bachelor of Arts (B.A.) degree. See Classical College Course, General Course, Honour Course
Bachelor of Commerce (B.Comm.) degree 242-3, 245
Bachelor of Letters (B.L.) degree 126, 239
Bachelor of Paedogogy (B.Paed.) degree 310-11
Bachelor of Philosophy (Ph.B.) degree 126, 239
Bachelor of Science (B.Sc.) degree 126-9, 238-9, 378, 502. See also Classical College Course, General Course, Honour Course
Bailey, Loring, W. 79, 86, 94, 201, 327
Bailly de Messein, Charles-François 18
Baldwin, James M. 250
Banting, Frederick G. 320, 343, 401, 436, 444, 574, 602
Banting and Best Institute 565
Barr, P.M. 405
Barreau de la Province de Québec 67-8
Barton, John W. 300
Basilian Fathers (Congregation of St Basil) 9-10, 21, 111, 366, 480
Beament, G. Edward 489
Beaverbrook, Lord 474

Bedard, Avila 275
Beers, George 289
Belleville Seminary. *See* Albert University
Best, Charles H. 320, 436, 444, 574, 602
Bethune, Alexander N. 61, 153
Bibaud, F.M. 68, 159
Bible colleges 262, 491-2
Bieler, André 423
Billings, E.W. 85
Biological Board of Canada. *See* Fisheries Research Board
Biological stations 322
Bishop Latimer College, Vancouver, B.C. *See* Anglican Theological College
Bishop's College, University of, Lennoxville, Que. 5-6, 11, 28-9, 106, 130, 218, 357, 479, 508
- dentistry 218, 289; education 218, 297, 418, 546; divinity 62, 151; law 106, 159, 218; medicine 106, 160-2, 218; music 178
Bissell, Claude T. 460, 463
Bladen, Vincent W. 341, 557-8, 568
Blake, Edward 143
Blake, William Hume 71
Blanchard, Raoul 389
Blatz, William 449
Botanical Society of Canada 81
Bott, Edward A. 251
Bouchette, Errol 252
Bourget, Ignace 22
Bourgeois, Louis 326
Bourgeois, Marguerite 286
Bourinot, John G. 87, 98-9, 133, 142, 193-4, 200
Bovell, James 84-5
Box, Harold K. 286, 305
Boyle, Robert W. 316, 335, 428, 437-9, 442
Bracken, John 280
Brandon College, Brandon, Man. 114-15, 209, 230, 262, 369, 399, 485, 545
Brebner, J. Bartlett 339, 429, 448-9, 568
Brescia College, London, Ont. 224, 363
Brett, George S. 251, 335, 428, 562
British Columbia, University of, Vancouver, B.C. 114, 226-8, 322, 267-8, 468, 487, 538, 581
- agriculture 277, 281-3, 536; applied science & engineering 269; architecture 535; commerce 513; education 367, 417-18, 487, 544; forestry 272, 275, 404, 535; home economics 285, 407, 537; law 487, 531; medicine 487, 534; music 548; nursing 293-4, 412, 541; pharmacy 487, 539; physical education & recreation 420, 487, 547-8; physical & occupational therapy 541; social work 415, 542
Broadus, Edward K. 384, 395
Brock, R.W. 251, 426-8

Bruneau, O. 173
Bryce, James 205-6
Brymner, Douglas 322
Buckland, George 172
Buckley, Kenneth C. 569
Burpee, Lawrence J. 96, 446
Burwash, Nathaniel 53, 285-7
Business Administration. *See* Commerce

Caldwell, William (McGill, Medicine) 64
Caldwell, William (McGill, Psychology) 251
Calgary College, Calgary, Alta. 225
Calgary Institute of Technology & Art 225, 372, 492
Calgary, University of 534
Cambridge, University of 8, 32-3, 40, 46, 59, 120, 147-8
Campbell, F.W. 162
Campbell, W.R. 444
Campion College, Regina, Sask. 360, 367, 371, 491
Camrose Lutheran College, Camrose, Sask. 491
Canada Council 459, 461, 521, 559, 567-74
Canada Français 199-200
Canadian Association for Adult Education 349, 391, 394
Can. Assoc. for the Extension of University Teaching 255
Can. Assoc. of Directors of Extension & Summer Schools 465
Can. Assoc. of Geographers 520, 576
Can. Assoc. of Hispanists 576
Can. Assoc. of Occupational Therapists 415, 440, 542
Can. Assoc. of Optometrists 579
Can. Assoc. of Physicists 577
Can. Assoc. of Slavists 576
Can. Assoc. of Social Workers 440
Can. Assoc. of University Teachers 375, 465-8, 578
Can. Assoc. of University Teachers of French 576
Can. Assoc. of University Teachers of German 576
Can. Bar Association 265-6, 329, 569
Can. Catholic Historical Association 576
Canadian Committee, International Geographical Union 387, 442-3, 567, 576
Can. Conference of University Schools of Nursing 540
Can. Dental Association 329-30, 409
Can. Dietetic Association 408
Can. Federation of Biological Societies 577
Can. Federation of University Women 434
Can. Forestry Association 273-4, 328-30
Can. Geographical Society 442
Can. Historical Association 387-8, 440-1, 443, 518, 566, 573, 576, 585, 602
Canadian Historical Review 331, 518
Can. Home Economics Association 408, 440
Can. Institute of Forestry 273
Can. Library Association 329, 446, 585

Can. Linguistic Association 576
Can. Literary Institute, Woodstock, Ont. 9, 63, 109-10, 152
Can. Manufacturers' Association 242, 260, 490
Can. Mathematical Congress 577
Can. Medical Association 330, 403, 414
Can. Nurses Association 329-30, 414, 540
Can. Pharmaceutical Association 177, 329
Can. Philosophical Association 576
Can. Physical Education Association 420
Can. Physiotherapy Association 415, 440, 541
Can. Political Science Association 330, 387-8, 442-3, 519, 567,
  576-7, 585
Can. Psychological Association 387-8, 442-3, 520, 567, 576
Can. Public Health Association 329-30
Can. Red Cross Society 293
Can. Social Science Research Council. *See* Social Science Research
  Council of Canada
Can. Society of Agricultural Economists 442
Can. Society of Experimental Geophysicists 597
Can. Society of Forest Engineers 329
Can. Society of Technical Agriculturalists 320
Can. Sociology & Anthropology Association 577
Can. Union College, College Height, Alta. 491
Can. Universities Foundation 462
Can. Veterinary Medicine Association 579
Canterbury College, Windsor, Ont. 481
Cappon, James 111, 207
Carleton University, Ottawa, Ont. 364, 469, 482-3, 514, 557, 582
Carling, John 170
Carnegie Corporation of New York 212, 214, 339, 343-9, 353-6,
  366, 385, 409, 416-17, 421-3, 433, 439, 441, 443, 446, 448,
  460, 559, 566-7, 571, 602
Carnegie Endowment for International Peace 339-40
Carnegie Foundation for the Advancement of Teaching 212, 266,
  343, 354, 397
Carpmael, Albert 194
Cartwright, Ethelmary 298-9, 420
Casault, Louis-J. 22
Casgrain, Henri Raymond 99, 199
Central Mortgage & Housing Corporation 566
Centres. *See* Institutes & Centres
Chapais, Thomas 250
Chapman, Edward J. 85, 93, 164
Charbonnel, Armand François Marie 9
Chartered accountancy. *See* Accounting
Chartier, Emile 380
Chauchetière, Père 15
Chauveau, Pierre-Joseph-Olivier 21, 38, 40, 98-9, 167
Chemical Institute of Canada 330, 577
Cherriman, J.B. 83, 85-6
Chinese 385, 500, 516-17

Federal government, relations of Canadian universities with
    209-10, 470, 489-91, 599-601
Ferguson, George 140
Ferland, Jean-Baptiste A. 50, 55
Fernow, Bernhard E. 273-4
Fields, John Charles 190, 319
Fine Art 345, 422-3, 517, 549-50
Fisher, Katherine 285-6
Fisheries Research Board of Canada 195, 321-2, 355
Fleming, Sandford 72, 94
Fletcher, Andrew A. 44
Fletcher, Lt. Col. H.C. 173
Fletcher, John A. 331
Flexner, Abraham 266-8, 303
Ford Foundation 567, 571
Foreign students 469-70
Forest Produets Laboratories, Montreal and Vancouver 321-2
Forest ranger schools 372, 405, 492-3, 536
Forestry 272-5, 404-5, 535-6
Forneri, James 48
Forrest, John 105, 134
Fox, W. Sherwood 391
French. *See* Modern Languages
Frères Charon 16
Frontier College 392

Gaelic 248, 385
Galbraith, John 164
Garneau, Francois-Xavier 78, 82, 88
Gauthier, Georges 416
General course 38, 40-6, 120-26, 146-7, 235-8, 309-10, 377-8,
    502-5, 595
General education courses 237-8, 377, 501, 503-4
Geography 50-1, 141, 251, 287-9, 519-20
Geological Association of Canada 577
Geological Survey of Canada 82, 96, 194, 196, 321, 334
Gérin, Léon 252, 450, 602
Gilchrist scholarships 188-90
Girard College, Philadelphia, Penn. 9
Girdwood, G.T. 195
Glassco, J. Grant 586
Goldenberg, Carl 342
Goodwin, William L. 189-90, 200, 273
Gordon, Walter 586
Gosselin, Amédée-E. 14, 16
Gosselin, Auguste-H. 199
Gouin, Jean Lomer 275
Gouin, Lomer M. 342
Gould, C.H. 295
Graham, John F. 569
Graduate Studies 75, 185-91, 307-16, 325, 351, 426-35, 501-2,
    514-15, 552-61, 599-600

Grand Séminaire de Montréal 61, 107, 154. *See also* Montréal,
   Université de, théologie
Grand Séminaire de Québec 5, 14-15, 20, 22, 24, 59, 98, 107, 154,
   358, 476. *See also* Université Laval, théologie
Grange, Edward A.A. 171, 283
Grant, George M. 33, 35-6, 94, 99, 110-11, 129-30, 222
Grauer, A.E. 342
Groulx, Lionel 16, 22, 250
Guelph, University of. *See* Ontario Agricultural College
Guiges, Joseph 24
Gymnastics 133, 180-1, 298

Halifax Conservatory of Music 214
Halifax Medical College. *See* Dalhousie University, medicine
Halifax School of Journalism 514
Halifax, University of 13, 103, 105, 117, 160, 163
Hamel, Thomas-Etienne 55, 94, 99
Hamilton, Clare 301
Hamilton, Richard J. 331
Hamlin, D.L.B. 516
Harrison, F.C. 428
Harrison, Thomas 134
Harvard University 9, 190
Harvey, D.C. 105
Harvey, F.W. 299
Haultain, Frederick W.J. 224
Head, Edmund 31-2, 73
Hebrew. *See* Near Eastern languages
Hillcrest Christian College, Regina, Sask. 491
Hind, Henry Y. 83, 85
Historic Landmarks Association of Canada 328
History 50-1, 140-42, 246, 248-50, 387, 518-19
Hodgins, J. George 62, 84, 165
Holmes, Andrew 64
Holmes, John 20, 22
Holstrom, V.M. 298
Holy Heart Seminary, Halifax, N.S. 155, 263, 472, 529
Holy Redeemer College, Windsor, Ont. 481
Home Economics. *See* Household Science
Honour Courses 8, 42-5, 129-32, 146-7, 180, 309-10, 381-2, 428,
   505-8, 517, 595, 601
Horton Collegiate Academy, Wolfville, N.S. 34
Hospital schools of nursing 181, 293, 359, 411, 414
Household Science 284-7, 407-8, 537-8
Howe, Clifton D. 274
Howell, Maxwell H. 418
Hubbard, Robert H. 549-50, 583
Hubert, Jean-François 18-19
Hughes, A.L. 320
Humanities 47-52, 134-40, 246-8, 334-5, 384-6, 497, 514-17
Humanities' Association of Canada 571

Humanities Research Council of Canada   429, 518, 555, 559, 563, 570-3
Hunt, T. Sterry   55, 85-6, 99
Huntington University, Sudbury, Ont.   480
Huron College, London, Ont.   10, 112, 150-2, 480, 529
Hutton, Maurice   132

Icelandic   235, 248, 386
Inch, James R.   134
Industrial Foundation on Education   559, 561
Inglis, Charles   28
Innis, Harold A.   250, 341, 388, 437, 443, 446, 554, 574, 602
Institut agricole d'Oka.   See Montréal, Université de, agriculture
Institut de cancer de Montréal   449, 477, 581
Institut Marguerite d'Youville, Montreal, Que.   413
Institut pédagogique Saint-Georges, Montreal, Que.   418
Institutes & Centres   449, 476-8, 483, 581-3
Institutes of public health   269
Institutes of technology   271, 372, 403, 492-3
Interior design   486, 535
International Association of University Professors & Lecturers   467
International Geographical Union, Canadian Committee   387, 442-3, 567, 576
International Union of Students   466

Jack, W. Brydone   11, 35, 53, 73, 79-80
Jacob, Edwin   31
James, F. Cyril   460, 477, 497-9
Jefferson, Thomas   17
Jeffreys, Charles W.   52
Jesuits (Society of Jesus)   14, 17, 20-1, 51, 252, 356, 369, 474, 482
Johns Hopkins University   190, 312
Johnson, Franklin   294
Journalism   133, 514
Journals
- agricultural   81, 442, 577
- dental   198, 330, 440
- educational   81, 198
- law   198, 444
- literary-political-cultural   81, 198-9, 330-2, 442, 444-5, 580
- medical   81, 197-8, 330, 440, 577-8
- professional   197-8, 330, 440, 579
- scholarly-scientific   82-6, 196-200, 326-8, 330-2, 437-42, 444-5, 574-80
Junior colleges   6, 365, 371-2, 491, 597

Keirstead, W.D. 249
Kellogg Foundation 538, 540-1
Kerr, Clark 597
Khaki University of Canada, 1918-19 230-1
Khaki University, 1945-46 488-9
Kidd, J. Roby 523
King's College, New Brunswick. *See* New Brunswick, University of
King's College, Toronto. *See* Toronto, University of
King's College, Windsor, University of Windsor, N.S. 4-5, 11, 27-9,
  34, 36, 40-1, 103, 127, 130, 212-16, 264, 354-5, 473-4, 513-14
- engineering 168, 270; theology 62, 151, 529
Kingston, G.T. 194
Kingston Women's Medical College, Kingston, Ont. 116, 163
Kingston School of Mines. *See* Queen's University, applied science
  and engineering
Kirkconnell, Watson 251, 429, 441, 447-8, 506, 524, 570-1, 575
Kirschmann, August 251
Klinck, Leonard S. 281
Knox College, Toronto, Ont. 7-8, 12, 59, 63, 109-10, 151, 400, 530
Knox, Frank A. 342, 467

Laboratories 144-5, 253
La Flamme, J.-C.-K. 94, 99, 199, 201
La Galissonière, Comte de 81
Lakehead Institute of Technology, Thunder Bay, Ont. 493
Lalande, G. 516
Lamb, Arthur S. 299, 419
Lamb, W. Kaye 584-5
Langton, John 80
Lansdowne College, Portage la Prairie, Man. 114
Laskin, Bora 532
Latin-American studies 500, 516
Laurentian University, Sudbury, Ont. 224, 469, 480, 482
Laval, François de 14-15
Law 16, 19, 21, 23, 59, 66-72, 156-60, 264-6, 400-1, 530-2
Law Society of Upper Canada 69, 71, 156-8, 174, 401, 531-2
Lawson, George 55, 94, 99, 104, 145, 163
Leacock, Stephen 219, 249-50, 327, 479
Learned, William S. 212, 319, 353, 382
Learned and professional societies 81-6, 196-7, 326-30, 437-42, 574-9
Lebel, Maurice 570
Leddy, J. Francis 469, 525
Lee, R.W. 265-6
Lethbridge Junior College, Lethbridge, Alta. 485, 491
Lévesque, Georges Henri 464
Libraries 80, 308, 333-4, 446-7, 583-6
Library Science 237, 257, 295, 416-17, 543
Licence 313-15, 432-3
Lillian Massey School of Household Science and Art, Toronto, Ont. 285
Literary and Historical Society of Quebec 81-3, 97, 196, 329
Lockhart, Grace 11, 116

Logan, Harold A. 364-5, 367
Logan, William E. 72, 78, 81, 84-5, 88
Lomer, G.R. 295
London, University of 8, 188-9
Lortie, Léon 509-10
Loudon, James 93, 200, 222-3, 274, 300, 312
Lower, Arthur R.M. 340-1, 446
Loyola College, Montreal, Que. 219-20, 232, 468
Lutheran College, Regina, Sask. 365, 491
Lutheran Theological College, Regina, Sask. 365, 530
Lutheran Theological Seminary, Saskatoon, Sask. 262, 399, 530
Lyall, William 99, 104, 135

Maass, Otto 316
Macallum, Archibald Byron 190, 324, 326
McCaul, John 49-50, 52, 86
McCrimmon, A.L. 249
McCulloch, Thomas 33, 55
McDonagh, A.J. 288
McDonald, Brigadier H.F. 496-7
Macdonald College. See McGill University
Macdonald Institute of Home Economics, Guelph, Ont. 276, 285,
    407-8, 537
Macdonald, William 106, 277
McEachran, D.N. 172
MacEachran, John 251
McEvoy, Fergus P. 263
McGill-Queen's University Press 580
McGill University, Montreal, Que. 6, 11, 20, 28-9, 32-3, 55, 93,
    116, 146, 218-19, 319-20, 325, 330-2, 357, 469-70, 477-79, 550-1
- agriculture 74, 275, 277, 283, 478, 536; architecture & engi-
    neering 73, 107, 164, 167-8, 257, 269-72, 404, 535; arts &
    science 42-3, 130-1, 133-4 (Donalda Special Course), 505;
    commerce 243-4, 383, 513, 581; dentistry 289, 538; divinity
    263, 400, 478, 529-30; education 6, 74-5, 140, 179, 285, 296-7,
    418, 478, 545-6, 548; graduate studies 186, 308-10, 312, 315-16,
    428, 430-1, 478; law 68-9, 156, 158-9, 264-6, 401; library
    science 295, 416-17, 543; medicine 64-6, 160, 267-9, 402, 478,
    533-4; music 301-2, 540; nursing 293-4, 412-13, 418, 540-1;
    pharmacy 117, 177, 291, 410; physical & health education 298-9,
    419-20, 478, 547-8; physical & occupational therapy 541; social
    work 294-5, 415, 478, 542; veterinary medicine 172
- Institute of Islamic Studies 517, 581
- Macdonald College, Ste Anne de Bellevue, Que. 285-6, 405-6,
    478, 492, 581
- McGill University College of British Columbia, Vancouver, B.C.
    226-7
McGilvray, Charles D. 283
McGregor, Donald C. 342
McGregor, James Gordon 94, 99, 105, 145, 189-90, 200
Machattie, Alexander 165

702

Machray, John A. 368
McIlwraith, Thomas F. 388
Mackay, Robert 437, 499
MacKenzie, A.E. 369
MacKenzie, C. Jack 564
Mackenzie, Norman A.M. 341, 464, 497-8, 500
McKenzie, Robert Tait 181, 298
MacKinnon, Frank 569
Mackintosh, William A. 341-2
McLean, J.D. 368
MacLennan, John C. 320
McLeod, Alexander 105
MacLeod, Robert B. 251, 569
MacLure, Millar 78
McMaster University, Toronto and Hamilton, Ont. 9, 12, 110, 129,
   221, 224, 230, 363-4, 480, 483-4, 534
- fine art 442, 549; graduate studies 186, 484; nursing 540-1;
   divinity 152, 262, 484, 530
MacMillan, Ernest 420-1, 549
McMurrich, J. Playfair 190, 192
Macnamara, A. 498-9
Macphail, Andrew 322
MacPherson, Hugh 216
MacRae, D.F. 301
MacVicar, Donald H. 154
Maheux, Arthur 238, 297, 313-14, 379, 497, 509
Manitoba Agricultural College. See Manitoba, University of
Manitoba College, Winnipeg 114, 151, 263
Manitoba College of Pharmacy. See Manitoba, University of, phar-
   macy
Manitoba Institute of Technology, Winnipeg 491
Manitoba Law School. See Manitoba University of, law
Manitoba Medical College. See Manitoba, University of, medicine
Manitoba, University of 10, 12, 101, 114-16, 228-9, 367-9, 485-6,
   537-8
- agriculture 229, 276, 278-80, 283, 368, 405, 536; architecture
   & engineering 269, 271, 369, 404, 486, 535; arts & science
   115, 130-1, 368, 485-6, 501; commerce 513; dentistry 290, 486,
   538; education 368, 417, 544-5; fine art 549; graduate studies
   431, 486; household science 285; law 114, 158, 229, 264-6,
   368, 401, 531; medicine 114-15, 160, 163, 267-8, 368, 486,
   534; music 368; nursing 486, 540; pharmacy 178, 292, 410,
   486, 539; physical & occupational therapy 542; social work
   416, 486, 542
Margaret Eaton School of Literature & Expression, Toronto, Ont.
   300, 419
Marie-Victorin, Frère 380
Marion, Seraphin 340
Maritime College of Pharmacy. See Dalhousie University, pharmacy
Maritime Dental College. See Dalhousie University, dentistry
Maritime School of Social Work 416, 474, 542

National Selective Service 490, 497-8
Natural History Society of Montreal 81-3, 97, 195-7, 329
Near-Eastern Languages 62, 132, 138, 514, 517
Nelles, Samuel 53, 100
New Brunswick Institute of Technology, Saint John, N.B. 492
New Brunswick, University of, Fredericton, N.B. 10-11, 27-8, 31-2,
    58, 74, 104, 116, 127, 148, 187, 212-13, 216, 355, 471, 474
- arts & science 43-4, 130-1; education 297; engineering and
    forestry 73, 164, 168, 269-70, 272-4, 403-5, 535; law 355,
    401, 531; nursing 540; physical & health education 542
New York, University of 9
Newton, Robert 428
Nicholson, James A. 580
Nightingale, Florence 181
Nisbet, Robert 582-3
Normal School of Domestic Science & Art, Hamilton, Ont. 285
Normal schools 20-1, 75-7, 179, 217, 285, 296, 371, 419, 492,
    544-6
Norwegian 386
Notre Dame College, Wilcox, Sask. 485
Notre Dame University College, Nelson, B.C. 485
Nova Scotia Agricultural College, Truro, N.S. 168, 208, 278, 372,
    474
Nova Scotia College of Art, Halifax, N.S. 422
Nova Scotia College of Pharmacy. See Dalhousie University,
    pharmacy
Nova Scotia Historical Society 197, 328
Nova Scotia Land Survey Institute, Lawrencetown, N.S. 493
Nova Scotia Marine Navigation School, Halifax, N.S. 493
Nova Scotia Technical College, Halifax, N.S. 213-14, 217, 270,
    403, 474
Nursey, Walter R. 295
Nursing 181, 293-4, 399, 411-14, 540-1

Oblates of Mary Immaculate 21, 24, 369
O'Brien, Cornelius 263
Observatories 195, 321
Okanagan College, Summerland, B.C. 230
O'Keefe, Eugene 263
Ontario Agricultural College, Guelph, Ont. 117, 169-71, 209, 255,
    274, 275-81, 283, 406, 483, 536
Ontario College of Art, Toronto, Ont. 422, 493, 549
Ontario College of Education. See Toronto, University of,
    education
Ontario College of Optometry, Toronto, Ont. 411, 540
Ontario College of Pharmacy. See Toronto, University of, pharmacy
Ontario Historical Association 328-9
Ontario Library Training School, Toronto, Ont. 295
Ontario Medical College for Women, Toronto, Ont. 116, 161, 163
Ontario Normal College, Hamilton, Ont. 297
Ontario School of Pedagogy, Toronto, Ont. 297

Ontario Veterinary Association 283
Ontario Veterinary College, Toronto and Guelph, Ont. 117, 166,
  171-2, 282-3, 406, 483, 537
Optometry 259, 261, 399, 410-11, 539-40
Osgoode Hall Law School, Toronto, Ont. 156-8, 209, 264-6, 400,
  480, 530-2
Osler, William 94, 99, 172, 181, 190-1, 198, 200
Ottawa, University of, Ottawa, Ont. 12, 24, 109, 112-13, 126,
  130, 221, 224, 364, 480-1, 484
- canon law 364, 531; commerce 133; engineering 112-13, 168,
  484, 534; household science 484, 537; law 156, 158, 264, 484,
  532; library science 364, 417, 543; medicine 484, 534; nursing
  364, 413; philosophy 364; physical & health education 484;
  political and social sciences 389; theology 61, 154-5, 264,
  364, 529
Ouellet, Cyrias 254
Oxford University 8, 32-3, 38, 40, 45-6, 59, 120, 147-8

Paquet, Louis-Adolphe 51, 155, 314, 335
Parent, Alphonse-Marie 475
Parent, Etienne 25, 475, 511
Parent, Madeleine 393
Pariseau, Leo 380
Parker, Gilbert 205-6
Part-time students 469
Patterson, Frederick William 498, 524
Pelletier, François 314
Pelletier, J.R. 302
Penfield, Wilder 449, 479
Perkins, James A. 460
Peterson, William 206-7, 218, 286
Pharmacy 176-8, 291-2, 409-10, 539
Phelan, Gerald B. 570
Philosophy 39, 41, 51, 60, 135, 143-4, 246-51, 386, 515
Physical & health education 180, 298-301, 418-20, 546-8
Physical & occupational therapy 299, 399, 415, 541-2
Piché, G.-C. 275, 397
Pictou Academy, Pictou, N.S. 33
Pilkington, Gwendoline 462
Pine Hill Divinity Hall, Halifax, N.S. 11, 63, 151, 354, 400,
  472, 529-30
Pinkham, William 113
Plamondon, Louis 68
Political economy 51-2, 141-4, 248-50, 387-8, 519-21
Political science. See Political economy
Pontifical Institute of Medieval Studies, Toronto, Ont. 445, 449
Porter, A.A. 326
Post-doctoral fellowships 434, 558-9, 565
Pouliot, Adrien 380
Prairie College, Rapid City, Man. 114
Presbyterian College, Halifax. See Pine Hill Divinity Hall

708

Roberts, R.D. 207
Robertson, James W. 276-7
Robertson, William 64
Robertson College, Edmonton, Alta. *See* St Stephen's College
Rockefeller Foundation 214, 269, 344, 402, 413-14, 443, 559,
  566-7, 571, 602
Rolph, John 64-5, 161
Ross, A.H.D. 274
Ross, George W. 142
Ross, James 105
Roy, Camille 296, 314
Royal Architectural Institute of Canada 329
Royal Astronomical Society of Canada 328-30, 577
Royal Canadian Institute 72, 81-3, 97, 195-7, 318, 326-9, 349
Royal College of Dental Surgeons of Ontario. *See* Toronto,
  University of, dentistry
Royal College of Physicians, Kingston, Ont. *See* Queen's University,
  medicine
Royal College of Physicians & Surgeons of Canada 402-3
Royal Commission of Inquiry on Education in the Province of
  Quebec 475, 546
Royal Commission on Canada's Economic Prospects 467, 586-9
Royal Commission on Dominion-Provincial Relations 342, 388-9,
  437, 446-7, 587
Royal Commission on Education, Ontario 545
Royal Commission on Government Organization 586, 588-9
Royal Commission on Industrial Training and Technical Education
  270, 372
Royal Commission on King's College, New Brunswick 58, 73-4
Royal Commission on National Development in the Arts, Letters and
  Sciences 458, 464, 487, 521, 556, 559, 562-3, 583
Royal Commission on University Finances, Ontario 222-3, 318-19,
  361
Royal Commission on the University of Toronto (1905-6) 260, 274,
  283, 287, 297
Royal Conservatory of Music, Toronto, Ont. 301
Royal George College 16
Royal Institution for the Advancement of Learning 20
Royal Military College, Kingston, Ont. 100, 117, 168, 173-4,
  230, 369-70, 487-8
Royal Ontario Museum, Toronto, Ont. 334, 385, 516, 563, 583
Royal Roads Triservice College, Esquimault, B.C. 485, 488
Royal Society of Canada 93-101, 188, 190, 196, 200, 326-30,
  349, 433, 438-41, 563-5, 575, 578, 585, 601-2
Royal Victoria Hospital, Montreal, Que. 565
Russell, Benjamin 160
Russell, Kathleen 413
Rutherford, Ernest 219, 320, 335
Rutherford, W.J. 226, 280
Ruttan, Robert F. 427
Ryerson College, Vancouver, B.C. *See* Union College of British
  Columbia

407, 537; law 264, 266, 401; medicine 268, 365, 486, 534; music 366; nursing 366, 413, 487; pharmacy 292, 410, 539; physical education 301, 366, 420, 486

Saunders, Charles 190, 192

Saunders, William E. 195, 197, 200

Sauvé, Maurice 465, 493

Sawyer, Artemas Wyman 103

Schools of art 422

School of Practical Science, Toronto, Ont. *See* Toronto, University of, engineering

Schurman, Jacob G. 105, 189

Science Council of Canada 589

Sciences 31, 33, 42-3, 53-4, 144-7, 253-4, 379-80, 390-1, 497, 521-2

Scott, Frank R. 341

Scottish universities, influence of 8, 32, 41, 59, 64, 124

Seath, John 270

Seccombe, Wallace 286

Secondary School specialist teaching certificate 129-30, 240

Secretarial Science 382-3, 513-14

Selye, Hans 581

Séminaires sociales du Canada 252

Sheffield, Edward F. 457, 460, 502

Sheraton, James P. 153

Sherbrooke, Université de, Sherbrooke, Que. 10, 475-6, 512, 529, 531, 534, 546

Shortt, Adam 111, 134, 143, 249, 446

Shotwell, James T. 339-40, 342

Shuttleworth, Edward B. 177

Sills, Kenneth C.M. 212, 319, 353, 382

Simcoe, John Graves 28-9

Simon Fraser University, Burnaby, B.C. 544

Sir George Williams University, Montreal, Que. 139, 353, 357-8, 377-8, 392-3, 468-9, 479, 503-5

Sisam, J.W. Bernard 272-3

Skelton, Oscar Douglas 242, 244, 249-50, 330

Slavic Studies 386, 500, 514, 516, 581

Smith, Andrew 171-2, 282-3

Smith, Donald. *See* Strathcona, Lord

Smith, Goldwin 99

Smith, Sidney E. 368

Smith, William 17

Snodgrass, William 109

Social Science Research Council of Canada 349, 388, 429, 437, 443, 499, 518, 520, 555, 559, 563, 566-70, 573, 585

Social Sciences 47-52, 134, 140-4, 248-52, 334-5, 386-9, 497, 518-21

Social Work 244, 294-5, 399, 415-6, 542-3

Société d'économie social et politique 252

Sociology 51, 141, 251-2, 262, 387-8, 519, 521, 553

Soddy, Frederick J. 320, 335

Wilfrid Laurier University. *See* Waterloo Lutheran University
Williams, Edwin E. 584
Williamson, C.C. 416
Willis, John 532
Wilson, Daniel 45-6, 50, 83-6, 93, 99, 134, 144, 147-8
Windle, Bertram 249
Winnipeg School of Art, Winnipeg, Man. 549
Women 351, 398-9
Women, admission to higher education of 116
Wood, F.W. 300
Wood, Georgina 299
Woodhouse, Arthur S.P. 381-2, 429, 445, 447-8, 506, 570-1, 575
Workers Educational Association 256, 318, 349, 394
World War I veterans 209
World War II veterans 456-7
Wright, Cecil A. 531-2
Wrong, George M. 249
Wycliffe College, Toronto, Ont. 109-10, 151, 153, 529-30

Xavier Junior College, Sydney, N.S. 491

York University, Toronto, Ont. 469, 482
Young, C.R. 164
Young, George Paxton 86, 99, 135
Young, Hester 295
Young Men's Christian Association 357, 364

Zavitz, Edmund 274